DATE DUE

MAR 0 1 2004		
APR 0 6 2004		
JUL 7 2004		
AUG 2 2005		
MAR 0 8 2006		
JUN 2 0 2008		
JUL 0 8 2011		

Demco

DISORDERS OF LEARNING IN CHILDHOOD

SECOND EDITION

DISORDERS OF LEARNING IN CHILDHOOD

SECOND EDITION

Archie A. Silver
Rosa A. Hagin

John Wiley & Sons, Inc.

Copyright © 2002 by John Wiley & Sons, Inc., New York. All rights reserved.

Published simultaneously in Canada.

This publication is designed to provide accurate and authoritative information in regard to the subject matter covered. It is sold with the understanding that the publisher is not engaged in rendering professional services. If legal, accounting, medical, psychological or any other expert assistance is required, the services of a competent professional person should be sought.

Designations used by companies to distinguish their products are often claimed as trademarks. In all instances where John Wiley & Sons, Inc. is aware of a claim, the product names appear in initial capital or all capital letters. Readers, however, should contact the appropriate companies for more complete information regarding trademarks and registration.

Library of Congress Cataloging-in-Publication Data:

Silver, Archie A.
    Disorders of learning in childhood / Archie A. Silver, Rosa A. Hagin.—2nd ed.
        p.   cm.
    Includes bibliographical references and index.
    ISBN 0-471-39259-6 (cloth : alk. paper)
    1. Learning disabilities—United States.   2. Learning disabled
children—Education—United States.   3. Learning disabilities—Treatment—United States.
I. Hagin, Rosa A.   II. Title.
LC4705 .S59 2002
371.92—dc21

                                                                        2001024903

Printed in the United States of America.

10 9 8 7 6 5 4 3 2 1

To Rob and Keith, whose trials and triumphs over their own learning problems, we have intimately shared.

AAS
RAH

Foreword ───────────────────────────────────

The history of the helping professions has long been marked by an uneasy alliance among administrators, scientists, and practitioners. Administrators typically determine how professions are organized, what types of rules and regulations govern them, the extent to which they are funded and their members compensated, and the manner in which persons are educated and trained to enter them. Scientists produce conceptual formulations and research designs that expand knowledge and enhance our understanding of people and events. Practitioners influence the methods that are used by appropriately qualified persons to assist those who seek or need their services. In a perfect world, these perspectives would be closely intertwined: practitioners would base their methods as much as possible on the findings and guidelines generated by scientists, scientists would ferret out kinds of information critical to improving practice, and administrators would be dedicated primarily to promoting the goals of science and practice. In the world as it is, however, among the helping professions and elsewhere as well, administrators, scientists, and practitioners frequently give short shrift to each other's purposes and overlook valuable opportunities to communicate.

In this second edition of *Disorders in Learning and Childhood,* Archie A. Silver and Rosa A. Hagin make a strong commitment to bridging such gaps in communication among professionals concerned with helping young people handicapped by learning disabilities. Their text addresses the nature and recent history of administrative regulations and requirements that influence how learning disabled children are likely to be identified, placed, and taught in the school system.

They present extensive information gleaned from scientific study concerning the nature and origin of various types of learning difficulty. And they translate the implications of contemporary research findings into practical recommendations for identifying and working with young people whose biological, psychological, and social circumstances have combined in some way to impair their ability to learn. As they do so, their message is clear: Persons with learning disorders can best be helped by the coordinated efforts of administrators, scientists, and practitioners, and it behooves professionals in the area to be broadly informed from all three perspectives.

The authors themselves bring extraordinary professional breadth to the volume they have produced. By virtue of their training and experience, they are able to draw on scientific and applied perspectives from the fields of education, psychology, psychiatry, and neurology. The result is an exemplary compilation and synthesis of information concerning various types of learning disorders, the broad range of etiologies that cause them, and multidisciplinary strategies for working with learning disabled people and their families in clinical and school settings. In presenting this information, the authors have done a great service for helping professionals and their students, who will learn much from it, and for children with learning disorders, who will be its eventual beneficiaries.

IRVING B. WEINER
University of South Florida

Preface ————————————————————————————————

Textbooks, by their very nature, are ephemeral. A comprehensive textbook presents a cross-section of its field; drawing on the past, even looking into the future, but essentially describing its field as it is at the moment the book is published. Time, however, does not stay; but, faster or slower, sooner or later, time overtakes a book, leaving it a static image of the past. So it is with the first edition of *Disorders of Learning in Childhood*.

In this second edition, we have infused the events of the past 10 years: the literally thousands of papers that have been published, the laws passed, the administrative dicta issued, all of which affect how and where children, particularly those with special learning needs, are placed and taught in the classroom. The events have not flowed evenly or even continuously in time. In some areas, such as the neurosciences and genetics, advances have been continuous and remarkably rapid; in others—even identification of the best ways to teach reading, have been painfully slow, filled with polemic and anguish over problems that appeared to have been resolved years ago. What is apparent is that, with certain exceptions, the multivaried individual differences of children with learning disorders do not, as yet, influence teaching of children with learning problems and that the ultimate, and perhaps defining variable in the outcome of these children is still the teachers who work with the child, what they do and how they do it. Some verities, although not necessarily eternal, are still valid. What is most disturbing is that with all our new knowledge, the academic, emotional, social, and educational outcomes of most children in the lowest quartile of the learning curve have not significantly changed since the first edition of this book was published. There is still a dearth of communication among disciplines resulting in the relative isolation of the educational system as it tries to manage children with learning disorders while coping with powerful political and social forces, each attempting to bend educators its own way.

The second edition of *Disorders of Learning in Childhood* breaches the public schools' relative isolation from the biological, psychological, and social sciences by integrating the new knowledge in these fields toward the goal of effective education in this democratic society.

In Part I, the changes in administrative and teaching strategies that have occurred in the past 10 years are discussed as well as the effects of political and social forces. All of these factors have had profound effects on where and how children, particularly those with learning disabilities, are taught. In a less polemic fashion, the discussion covers advances in the neurosciences and the reports of research emanating from Reading Research Centers supported by the National Institute of Child Health and

Human Development. All of this research affects understanding of the processes involved in reading and by extension the management of reading-disabled children.

Part II first reviews the historical concepts of reading disability and how advances in research have attempted to operationalize the definition of learning disabilities. Second, it brings to bear advances in the neurosciences to a classification of learning disability based on presumed etiologies, the base of a hypothetical iceberg. This discussion leads to the aberrant neuroimaging, and electrophysiological findings that have been identified in learning disabilities, and then to the spectrum of neuropsychological deficits and the academic domains of inadequate function in learning disabilities.

Part III is a practical discussion of the identification and management of children, adolescents, and adults with learning disabilities resulting from the varied presumed etiological factors derived from educational, psychological, and neuropsychiatric perspectives.

Developmental learning disabilities occupy a major section of Part IV. The origins of developmental learning disabilities are described from the precursors of language emanating from hemisphere specialization and laterality, and practical application of theory is provided, based on the educational management of children examined and treated by the authors. Part IV also describes the educational problems and educational management of children with Attention-Deficit/Hyperactivity Disorder, those with organic injury to the central nervous system, including in this edition, sections on children with HIV infection, fetal alcohol syndromes, cocaine babies, seizure disorders and, most important, children with prematurity and hypoxia. There is an important chapter on the effects of poverty, inadequate language stimulation, and diverse cultures on learning and a chapter on a group of children appearing with increasing prevalence—those with Gilles de la Tourette's syndrome.

This is not a book written by multiple authors and put together by editor or editors; rather, it is a synthesis of the opinions arising from the experience of the two authors as they have worked in schools, clinics, and private practice with children who suffer from disorders of learning, as well as with their parents and their teachers. Although the authors have been trained in different disciplines, they have shared the special knowledge of each and have emerged with a comprehensive amalgam of psychology, education, psychiatry, and neurology. It is this comprehensive view of the multiple causes of learning problems, the idiosyncratic academic, social, emotional, and biological problems presented by each child, and the resulting individual intervention needed for each child, that we hope to convey in this book.

ARCHIE A. SILVER, M.D.
ROSA A. HAGIN, PH.D.

Acknowledgments ————————————————————

When Jennifer Simon, associate publisher at John Wiley & Sons, called to ask us to write the second edition of *Disorders of Learning in Childhood,* we hesitated because we knew full well that reviewing the literature of the past 10 years, related to academic learning problems, would be an enormous task—and it was. Fortunately, we had able assistance, not only in compiling references but also in the magical appearance of reprints and books, so that we could devote precious time to productive reading, thinking, and writing. For this invaluable help, we are indebted to Berney Wilkinson, MA, a graduate student in school psychology, to Erin Penny, RN, whose computer responds willingly to her every command, and to Irene Serrano, secretary, who has become adept at searching the library as well as the Internet. We are indebted also to Sandra Gubar for compiling lists of references. Translating the written manuscript into legible type was the unenviable responsibility of Sarah Daadi, MA, whose transcription was done with understanding and competence. When Sarah had to move to another state with her family, Claudia Clark struggled valiantly and successfully with calligraphy. The references were collated and endlessly typed by Irene Serrano. Susan Killacky of the Franklin, New Jersey, School District contributed her positive insights on the inclusion of children with learning disabilities in regular classrooms, and Justine McCarthy supplied current information on Parent Advocacy and the Learning Disabilities Association of America. Without the generous and intelligent effort by these people, the manuscript would never have met its deadline.

Each step in the completion of the manuscript was tactfully guided and encouraged by Ms. Simon and her assistant, Isabel Pratt. Deborah DeBlasi, an assistant managing editor at John Wiley & Sons, was responsible for the very thorough copyediting including: clarifying ambiguities, eliminating inconsistencies, and generally making this a scholarly and practical book for its readers.

We are much indebted to Dr. Irving B. Weiner who, in the midst of the awesome task of editing a twelve volume psychology series, generously wrote the foreword to this book. We are also indebted to each of the authors and investigators whose papers and books we have read and whose contributions we have summarized in *Disorders of Learning in Childhood,* second edition. Their names appear in the references.

With all of these helpful hands and minds, the final product with its errors of omission and commission is our own.

The acknowledgment of A.A.S. would not be complete without mentioning his gratitude to his wife, Mary Louise, who tolerated months of sequestered weekends with her usual quiet understanding and support.

A.A.S.
R.A.H.

Contents

PART I

CURRENT DEVELOPMENTS INFLUENCING EDUCATION OF CHILDREN, ADOLESCENTS, AND ADULTS WITH DISORDERS OF LEARNING

Chapter 1

DEVELOPMENTS IN EDUCATION

He who ne're learns his ABC,
forever will a blockhead be;
but he who to his books inclin'd,
will soon a golden treasure find.

—New England Primer, 1785

Major changes have occurred in the field of learning disabilities since the original edition of this book appeared in 1990. Some of these changes have come from within the field itself as a part of the evolutionary processes that are to be expected as increased knowledge accumulates and is reflected in the ways services are provided. Changes such as the noncategorical classification of students for special education, increased efforts to provide services to students with learning disabilities in regular classrooms, and greater emphasis on secondary and postsecondary education as the children identified as learning disabled aged beyond elementary school are all examples of attempts by professional educators to improve services within the field.

However, even more striking changes were imposed on the field by outside forces. These legal, economic, social, demographic, and political forces may have had more profound effects on the way students with learning disabilities are educated than the changes coming from within educational systems themselves. Education in the final decade of the twentieth century and, from all prospects, for the beginning of the twenty-first century, is no longer being left to educators. It has become a major issue in political campaigns at all levels of government. It has major budgetary effects as governments strive to meet the costs of what the 1975 law described as "a free appropriate public education for all handicapped children." It has engaged the critical concern of many more parents than in the past as they search for modifications of traditional schools and develop alternatives to meet what they perceive as the educational needs of their children.

The organization and management of schools is also influenced by the changing demographics of our country. Changes in family structure, employment of many mothers outside the home, increased ethnic and cultural diversity, and population mobility have all influenced education. Important legal changes have occurred through the federal laws promising equal educational and vocational opportunities for all people with

3

disabilities as well as through the rapidly expanding case law reflecting the vigilance that parents and other advocates maintain for the rights of the disabled. There has also been an explosion of research on many aspects of learning problems. Facets of learning disabilities have, in recent years, engaged the attention of researchers not only in the field of education, but also in pathology, psychology, psychiatry, neurology, neurophysiology, genetics, and epidemiology. Technological advances in medicine have enabled investigators to examine aspects of brain anatomy and brain functioning that have previously been accessible only to inferences. Developments in computer technology have made vast databases readily available to investigators and practitioners. Indeed, many changes in the past decade have influenced the field of learning disabilities.

The purpose of Part I of this book is to survey the impact of these developments on the education of students with learning disabilities; later parts examine in detail how these forces affect the management of individuals within the spectrum of learning disability.

LEGAL PROVISIONS FOR EDUCATION OF CHILDREN WITH DISABILITIES

In 1975, the federal government acknowledged the responsibility for educating all of the nation's children in Public Law 94-142, the Education for All Handicapped Children Act. By this law, Congress stated that a "free, appropriate, public education" was a right for all children, including those with disabilities, and established processes by which state and local educational agencies may be held accountable for providing these services. The law was renamed the *Individuals with Disabilities Education Act* (IDEA) and reauthorized in 1990 and again in 1997. Current provisions for special education in public schools today exist under the provisions of IDEA and the accompanying regulations issued by the United States Department of Education. Although these legal provisions do not apply directly to nonpublic schools, they have become an important influence on all educational services countrywide.

IDEA (United States Code, Volume 20, sections 1401 to 1407) consists of four parts. Part A, entitled General Provisions, Definitions and other Issues, deals primarily with purposes of the law and definitions of terms used in the statute. Part B, Assistance for Education of All Children with Disabilities, sets forth the processes for direct services by states, including states' plans for services and funding, determining eligibility, evaluations, procedural safeguards for the rights of parents and students, matters of discipline, and delivery of services through individual educational plans. Part C, Infants and Toddlers, sets forth procedures for finding young children at risk for substantial developmental delay and for providing early intervention services. Part D is devoted to National Activities to Improve Education of Children with Disabilities through disseminating information, preparing professional personnel, supporting research, and applying research findings to special education (P. W. D. Wright & Wright, 1999). IDEA reaffirms the six basic principles of the original law as the framework around which educational services are provided to students with disabilities:

1. Free appropriate public education.
2. Appropriate evaluation.
3. Individual Education Program (IEP).
4. Least restrictive environment.
5. Parent and student participation in decision making.
6. Procedural safeguards.

The Twentieth Annual Report to Congress on the Implementation of IDEA (1998) highlights amendments that augment and strengthen the previous laws:

- *Discipline.* More specific language requires that a free appropriate public education must be made available to students who are suspended or expelled from school. It states that the state and local educational agencies are responsible for implementing the goals and objectives contained in the individual education program even though the student may have been removed from school.
- *Personnel Development.* State improvement grants for personnel development were provided to fulfill the need for qualified special education, regular education, and related services personnel. Amendments also permit the use of "appropriately trained and supervised paraprofessionals" to provide services under certain conditions.

Other legal sources have also shaped the educational management of students with learning disabilities since the passage of PL 94-142. A major influence comes from the Code of Federal Regulations, Volume 34, part 300. The purpose of the regulations is to clarify, explain, and instruct the implementation of the law.

There is, in addition, a growing body of case law that evolves in the courts as specific cases are heard. These ongoing decisions, findings, and interpretations result in expansion and clarification as the provisions of the original law are applied in individual cases, in impartial hearings and court findings.

IMPLEMENTATION OF IDEA

Despite criticism of the failure of the federal government to provide adequate financial support for the services mandated by PL 94-142, the two reauthorizations have not embodied major changes in the original law. Advocacy groups have worked hard to preserve the spirit of the law, and most changes have been refinements rather than modifications of the document's original intent.

The Individual Education Program

A unique feature of the special education legislation was the Individual Education Program (IEP) that the Department of Education describes as "the cornerstone of special education." (U.S. Department of Education, [OSERS], 2000, p. 16). A special manual entitled *A Guide to the Individual Education Program* explains the critical elements "to insure effective teaching, learning, and better results" with students with learning disabilities. A flowchart in this document (Figure 6.1) outlines the process and provides procedural details to inform professionals and parents:

1. *Child is identified as possibly needing special education.* Identification may occur through "Child Find" or by referral or request submitted by a parent or a professional. Parental consent is required prior to evaluation, which must be completed within a reasonable time.

2. *Child is evaluated.* Measures and observations of any areas of suspected disability must be conducted by qualified professionals in the student's dominant language. These data are used to determine eligibility for special education services and to plan intervention. If parents disagree with the evaluation, they have the right to take their child for an independent evaluation and ask the school district to pay for this evaluation.

3. *Eligibility is decided.* Qualified professionals and the parents consider the evaluation results and together they decide if the student is a child with a disability as defined by IDEA. Parents have the right to challenge the eligibility decision.

4. *If student is found eligible.* Within 30 days of any student's being found eligible for special education, a team must meet to write an IEP.

5. *IEP meeting is scheduled.* School staff is responsible for contacting team participants, including parents, to schedule a meeting and to inform parents of meeting details, team members attending, and their right to bring to the meeting "people who have knowledge and special expertise about the child."

6. *IEP meeting is held and IEP is negotiated.* Team members discuss student's educational needs with parents (and older students where appropriate) who serve as members of the team. Services may not begin until parents have approved the IEP. If an agreement cannot be negotiated within the team, parents may ask for mediation, or may request a due-process hearing with an impartial hearing officer.

7. *Services are provided.* Copies of IEPs are given to teachers and parents containing details of services, accommodations, modifications, and supports that have been agreed on by the team and parents.

8. *Progress is measured and reported to parents.* Progress toward the annual goals as set forth in the IEP must be reported to parents at least as often as parents are informed of their nondisabled children's progress.

9. *IEP is reviewed.* IEPs are reviewed at least once a year or more often if parents or teacher request review. The same protections for parents available during the original IEP construction continue to be available to parents.

10. *Student is reevaluated.* The reevaluation (often called a triennial) must be done at least every 3 years to determine whether the student continues to have a disability as defined by IDEA and, if so found, the nature of his or her current educational needs.

The manual continues with detailed explanations and references to federal regulations concerning IEPs. It includes Details of Content, Team Membership, Related Services (clinical services needed in order that the student can benefit from the special education program), Transition Plans, Reviews and Revisions, and Negotiations with Parents. The final section contains a sample IEP with the caution that the federal law details what information must be included, but does not require a specific form. It is expected that IEP forms will differ among individual states; what is important is that they be clear and useful in the education of students with disabilities (OSERS, 2000, p. 6).

IEPs, important and useful as these documents were conceived in the federal special education laws and regulations, have not received a positive response from the educators responsible for their implementation in the classrooms. Teachers and other members of the school teams refer to them derisively as "special education paperwork" and seek ways of handling their responsibilities for this task by complying with the letter rather than the spirit in which the IEP process was conceived. Thus many hours are spent reporting data, conferring, and writing goals and objectives that may have little relationship to what actually happens in the teaching-learning transactions. (D'Amato & Dean, 1987). Does this mean that school personnel set out consciously to sabotage this important guide to individualization for students with disabilities? This does not appear to be true. On the other hand, does the IEP process operate as effectively as it is described in the U.S. Office of Education manual? This is also not true. The IEPs are often lengthy, clumsy documents, difficult to implement for two reasons.

First, it is difficult to impose what is essentially a clinical function, that of planning effective interventions for learning disabilities and securing the agreement of the diverse group constituted as the IEP team. This is a matter of education and training, administrative leadership, group dynamics, development of resources, and equitable sharing of meager funding. Some schools districts have persisted and have reached reasonable solutions; others have not.

A second reason lies in the gap between federal mandates in the legislation and implementation at the state and local levels. Wary of litigation and confused by conflicting interpretations of the special education laws and regulations, many state and local officials have overloaded the IEP process with provisions for documentation, legalistic explanations of alternatives, and quasi-legal procedures that frighten and confuse parents while contributing little to the effective education of students—the real purpose of the IEP process. A lead article in the *NEA Today: The Magazine of the National Education Association* (Green, 2000, pp. 8–10) entitled "Taming the Paper Tiger" is a typical statement from classroom teachers. It cites outrageous examples (46-page IEPs) and makes some suggestions of varying quality for action by teachers:

- Sending offensive forms to U.S. Department of Education's Office of Special Education Programs to determine whether the "paperwork is too burdensome."
- Using "standardized IEPs."
- Providing additional compensation for the work.
- Providing clerical assistance by aides.

- Posting paperless IEPs on the Internet with electronic templates to be filled in by teachers.

One teacher is quoted as saying, "The last thing we want to do is shortchange our kids." Possibly, but Green's suggestions do not appear to solve the problem, but just to move the IEP process closer to " the one size fits all" kind of program that failed to educate students with learning disabilities in the public schools before 1975.

Criticism of the Special Education Laws

This legal foundation for services for people with disabilities did not result in a high level of satisfaction either among advocates or critics of the role the federal government began playing in 1975. Opponents of special education services in general have raised issues about the cost to the regular education programs of local schools, appropriateness of placement of students with special needs within the regular school settings, and presumed threats of disciplinary infractions by special education students. Most telling of all has been their criticism of the *educational effectiveness* of special education services.

Advocates for students with special learning needs are also dissatisfied. They are most critical of the failure of the federal government to provide anything close to the funding required to implement the services mandated by the legislation. Despite the rise in funding for Part B Section 611 Grants to States Program from approximately $250 million in 1977 to over $3 billion in 1997 (the last year reported), federal funding accounts for only a small proportion of the actual costs of educating children with disabilities. For example, the average 1997 per child allocation from the federal government is reported at $535, far below actual per pupil costs that may be as high as $12,000 to $20,000 (U.S. Department of Education, 1998, p. III-43). While actual costs vary according to local conditions (e.g., the unique needs of individual children, personnel costs, transportation, and other operating expenses), it is estimated that the overall federal contribution to special education costs in New York State is approximately 7% of the actual costs; in Florida it is approximately 14% of actual costs.

Continuing Needs

IDEA reaffirmed the federal government's recognition of education as an "essential element of our national policy of ensuring equality of educational opportunity, full participation, independent living, and economic self-sufficiency" (20 U.S.C. s1400) for individuals with disabilities. However, the developing legal and legislative processes have produced changes in the way the original law is implemented. In their discussion of the findings of Part A of IDEA, P. W. D. Wright and Wright (1999) highlight these developments and continuing needs.

Low Expectation

The special education legislation has mandated access to public education that would provide equal educational opportunity to the one million children with disabilities who were excluded entirely from the public schools and to the 50% of all children with disabilities who did not receive appropriate services. Low expectations, however, have impeded the implementation of these laws. The original focus of the legislation was to provide *access* to the benefits of education and emphasized the location of the educational services, the fine-tuning on issues of *where* the child was to be taught. Decisions on placement of the services within as instructional system, number of children in the class, teacher/pupil ratios, and frequency of service overshadowed considerations of *how* the child was to be taught. Given the understanding that special education is "specially designed instruction that meets the unique needs of the individual," it has been a great disappointment to find that schools may abdicate responsibility for teaching methods used in the well-considered placements. The amended IDEA emphasizes accountability and results. Problems of access to services having been resolved to a great extent, effective instructional practices are a major concern of the new legislation. IDEA now conceptualizes special education as a *service,* rather than a place where students with disabilities are sent (P. W. D. Wright & Wright, 1999).

The problem of low expectations is especially significant for students with learning disabilities. Of all the developmental disabilities, this is the one that is most likely to improve in response to appropriate instruction. All too often, a low level of achievement is accepted and the disability is reinforced rather than remediated. The low return rates of special education students to a regular education program is an indication of the low expectations in many programs.

Insufficient Application of Results of Research

IDEA emphasizes that special education must draw on the growing body of research available to improve the results of instruction.

Accountability

Although the methods for teaching special education students may vary according to individual needs, they should be involved and included to the maximum extent possible in the regular curriculum of the school. This recommendation is especially significant for students with learning disabilities because they may be expected to compete in mainstream life as adults. To reinforce the need for accountability, IDEA directs that children with disabilities be tested in state and local assessment programs. Heretofore, it was the practice of many school districts to excuse students with learning disabilities from taking these examinations on the assumption that such a testing experience might be destructive to their sense of achievement. It may also be that the pervasive low expectations led school personnel to anticipate negative effects of special education students' scores on assessment results for the school as a whole. With the current emphasis on "high-stakes testing" mandated both locally and nationally, this continues to concern educational administrators. IDEA states unequivocally that including students with disabilities in the general state accountability system extends their franchise in the general system, but at no point "exonerates a state from ensuring individual protections promulgated by IDEA" (U.S. Department of Education, 1998, p. ii). The law also encourages the development of alternate methods of assessment appropriate for students with disabilities.

Strengthening the Role of Parents

IDEA continues the practices initiated in PL 94-142 that required parents to be included in educational planning for their children. The amended law strengthens the role of parents to the extent that they are included as full members of eligibility, IEP, and placement teams.

Services in Regular Classrooms

The revised law and accompanying regulations shifts provisions of special education and related services to regular classrooms whenever possible. Although the original law spoke firmly about the placement of eligible students in the "least restrictive environment," this recommendation was not always complied with. Actual placement data are expected to show gradual improvement in this area since it has become part of the monitoring system of the Department of Education. IDEA moved services into regular classrooms in the belief that such inclusion would result in higher standards for achievement and, concurrently, less expensive instructional and related costs for special education programs.

CHANGES FROM WITHIN THE FIELD OF EDUCATION

Change in education comes slowly. As might be expected, the idealistic programmatic changes mandated in PL 94-142 and IDEA were neither accepted enthusiastically nor implemented easily in the school districts across the country. Practical problems of definition and classification, recruitment of personnel, organization of instructional services, and financing beset school administrators charged with putting the new law into practice. The need for services to students with learning disabilities was recognized by professionals and families of children who experienced the problem. Appropriate services for these students were advocated by an increasingly strong parent group, the Association for Children with Learning Disabilities (later to be renamed Learning Disabilities Association of America in recognition of the lifelong nature of learning disabilities). Underlying all was the very limited knowledge base available to educational administrators. Prior to the passage of the special education law, the diagnosis and remediation of learning disabilities was generally the clinical function of personnel in clinics, hospitals, special schools, some university programs, and tutors engaged by the families of the children. The passage of PL 94-142 and later IDEA meant that what were essentially clinical functions for service to individuals and their families became the responsibilities of public schools, which had to provide diagnostic and intervention services to increasingly larger numbers of students. Clinicians are used to thinking in terms of individual clients or patients, one at a time; school personnel (despite their familiar statements about individual differences) are used to dealing with large numbers of students in groups. The implementation of the laws providing a free appropriate public education to all individuals with disabilities was not an easy fit. Despite the watchful monitoring of compliance in state plans by the Department of Education, the situation required compromises, concessions, substitutions, and adjustments.

Most school districts faced problems in improving personnel to perform the diagnostic and instructional work mandated in the laws. The pool of trained teachers, supervisors, school psychologists, and social workers was not large enough to fill the needs of all the schools. To further complicate the situation, the number of students continued to grow. Over the past few years, school-age students with disabilities served have increased at a higher rate than that of the general school enrollment. A high proportion of this increase results from the identification of students with learning disabilities, accounting for more than 2½ million children, 51.1% of the school-age children served by IDEA in 1996 to 1997 (U.S. Department of Education, 1998, p. iii). When recruiting and retraining efforts failed to meet the ever-increasing needs for trained personnel, attention was focused on modifications of organizational plans. Administrators began to question the need for the intensity of diagnosis that had been transferred along with other clinical procedures to school settings. Was such painstaking assessment really relevant to the instructional program in the classroom? Were classroom strategies really different among students with low levels of academic skills whatever the reason? Did teachers teach children with different clinical diagnoses differently? One result of these concerns was noncategorical placement of students in special education.

Noncategorical Organization of Classes in Special Education

The comprehensive multidisciplinary diagnosis recommended in the regulations of the special education legislation represented an expensive component of the programs. In addition, some theoreticians in the field of learning disabilities raised questions about the utility of such studies. Because of the heterogeneous etiology of learning disability as manifested in individual students, the diagnosis has been called " judgmental" (i.e., based on inferences by clinical personnel who integrate a variety of observations and measures). The variation implicit in the nature of learning disability resulted in inconsistencies in identification that dismayed some theoreticians who needed a concrete value on a single measure to be convinced that learning disabilities are not figments of the imaginations of clinicians. The single measure chosen was educational achievement, an attribute that could be measured directly (Algozzine, Ysseldyke, & McQue, 1995; Deno, 1985; Ysseldyke, 1983). These theoreticians were not concerned about the niceties of diagnosis. Neither the causative factors underlying the learning problems nor the trajectory of individual students' learning outcomes interested them. They concluded that these issues were irrelevant to classroom instruction.

Some investigators questioned the utility of clinical diagnostic procedures. Gresham, MacMillan, and Bocian (1997) investigated the discriminant validity of teacher judgments in such assessments with 240 students in Grades 2, 3, and 4. Three groups of subjects, defined as learning disabled, low IQ, and low achievement were contrasted with a group of normally achieving controls. Results from cross-validated stepwise discriminant function analyses showed that teacher judgments correctly identified 91% of the learning-disabled group, 100% of the low-IQ group, and 95% of the low-achievement group. On the basis of these data, Gresham et al. (1997) criticized what they termed "the time-consuming and expensive practice of differentiating among mild disability and low achievement groups for classification, placement, and intervention" in the light of the validity of teacher judgment. The validity of clinical classifications has also been criticized severely because of the overrepresentation of minority students (MacMillan & Reschley, 1998; Valles, 1998) and the disparities in diagnosis and placement existing among the various states (Lester & Kelmen, 1997). Whether the dissatisfaction with clinical diagnosis resulted from the inferior quality of the clinical services or the diagnostic process itself is not clear from these studies. Whatever the reason, noncategorical classification became widely accepted.

In many states, students are grouped on the basis of educational achievement, irrespective of diagnostic findings. In such formulations, children with learning disabilities may find themselves enrolled in classes with children who have a mild degree of mental retardation and children with emotional problems. Altogether, they are classified in some states as "mildly handicapped." Although noncategorical placements may ease some administrative tasks, such mergers of students with disparate diagnoses multiply the instructional responsibilities of teachers.

These mergers also provided partial relief to the difficulties in recruiting teachers to serve children with learning disabilities. Generic certification in special education became a trend in many teacher training programs and state standards for certification. Thus harried administrators searching for candidates to fill faculty openings did not need to find a learning disabilities specialist; the open slots could be filled with candidates with generic certifications as special educators, whose training ranged across all areas of special needs students and who might or might not be prepared to provide the specially designed instruction so necessary for students with learning disabilities.

The noncategorical organization of classes and the generic certification of teachers as temporary solutions have continued long after the passage of the special education laws. Only 28 states now report data on teachers in funded positions to provide services for children and youth with learning disabilities; the only comment on the other states is, "States were allowed to use their own classification scheme in identifying special education teachers. Thirty states and outlying areas used schemes other than the federal disability categories" (U.S. Department of Education, 1998, p. A-164).

Noncategorical organization of classes has been praised as a forward-looking departure from the much maligned "medical model," a surprising denial in view of the debt special education owes to a number of physicians. The pioneers in management of children with special needs—Itard, Seguin, Montessori, Strauss, and Orton—all came from the field of medicine.

Inclusion

Evolving applications of IDEA have placed increasing emphasis on inclusion, the organizational principle that provides special education and related services, aids, and supports in the regular classroom to students with disabilities whenever it is appropriate. For the past decade, the inclusion of students with disabilities in general education classes and schools has been a preeminent concern of special educators, administrators, parents, advocates, and policy makers (U.S. Department of Education, 1998, p. III-3). Earlier efforts were directed toward the development of a continuum of educational placements. These placements ranged from the least restrictive to the most restrictive environments, as seen in Table 1.1.

Table 1.1   Cascade of special education placements

Regular class with support services to the teacher through consultation
Direct services within a regular class
Resource room services
Self-contained special class
Private day school for students with disabilities
Special public day school for students with disabilities
Public residential facilities
Private residential school facilities
Hospital day school
Homebound instruction

PL 94-142 directed that placements were to be made in the "least restrictive environments," and most IEPs required a rationale justifying the placement decision for the individual. The early forms of special education legislation, however, advised against the isolation of students with handicaps through the policy of "the least restrictive environment." The past decade has interpreted this admonition as a strong positive statement recommending regular class placement through inclusion. This change is reflected in the annual statistical reports by the U.S. Department of Education to Congress of the percentage of children ages 6 to 21 served in various educational environments. The report for the 1985 to 1986 school year showed that 15% of the students identified as learning disabled were served in regular classrooms, 62% received pull-out services in resource rooms, and 21% were in self-contained classes. (Lerner, 1988, p. 21). In contrast, in the 1995 to 1996 school year, services in regular classes were reported for more than 42% of the students, resource room placements were reported for 39%, and 17% of the students with learning disabilities were reported to be in self-contained classes (U.S. Department of Education, 1998, p. A-51).

Many forces led to this change in emphasis. The need for trained special educators and the increaseing number of students identified as learning disabled continued. The costs of special education soared. Critics complained that the services for handicapped students mandated by the federal government (and not adequately funded) were threatening programs in regular education. U.S. Department of Education data indicated that costs for special education have grown about twice the cost of regular education expenditures, an average 4.1% in contrast to 2.1% annually (U.S. Department of Education, 1998, p. III-34).

Furthermore, research on the outcomes of special education programs were equivocal at best and did not produce empirical evidence of their effectiveness. In the opinion of some critics, the results did not justify the enormous expenditure of effort and money at a time when even the existence of the Department of Education was under attack by a conservative administration.

The National Longitudinal Transition Study of Special Education Students (M. Wagner, D'Amico, Merdu, Newman, & Blackorby, 1992) reported trends in employment, wages, postsecondary education, and residential independence of youth with disabilities.

Initial results were not encouraging and led to the conclusion that many youth with disabilities did not leave school with the knowledge and skills necessary to fulfill adult roles. The National Transition Study reported that 3 to 5 years after leaving high school, "fewer than 25% of youth with disabilities had been enrolled in post secondary education, many were engaged in low-wage jobs with few opportunities for advancement, and more than half continued to live in their family homes" (U.S. Department of Education, 1998, p. III-33). Longer term follow-up, however, led the researchers to conclude that strong gains in all four outcome areas occurred over time. Nevertheless, youth with disabilities continued to lag behind their peers in the general population in all areas (Blackorby & Wagner, 1996). In the Chicago Longitudinal Study, A. J. Reynolds and Wolfe (1996) investigated outcomes with 1,234 low-income children who had received special education services or had been retained in grade. They found that children who had received special education had lower scores in reading and mathematics achievement than other children in the study, especially during the upper elementary grades. Although family mobility and grade retention were associated with lower achievement, it is not clear whether selective factors may have operated, so that the children receiving special education were more severely impaired than the members of the retained group. Alarmingly, these investigators found that children with learning disabilities benefited less from special education services than did children with other disabilities. Kavale and Dobbins summarized the findings of meta-analyses investigating the effectiveness of special education. This work pointed out the variability and unpredictability of interventions, particularly because teachers are central characters in the effectiveness of interventions. The success or failure of the intervention is contingent on the individual teacher's skills and abilities that interpose "among the intricate concentration of events involved in the teaching/learning process" (Kavale & Dobbins, 1993, p. 38).

A literature review by Tindal (1985) raises even more questions about methodological flaws in attempts to evaluate the effectiveness of special education programs for mildly handicapped students. Such flaws as ill-defined treatments, lack of clearly identified subjects, weak experimental designs, inadequate tests, and inappropriate statistical measures raise questions about interpretations of findings in such studies. However, the lack of clear-cut research evidence of success, together with the signs of discontent with the rigid structure of the program by those responsible for implementing and funding it, made change inevitable.

Regular Education Initiative

From within the field of special education came innovation approaches directed at bridging the gap between special education and general education for at-risk children: teacher assistance teams (Chalfant, Pysh, & Moultrie, 1979), cooperative learning (D. W. Johnson & Johnson, 1975), collaborative consultation (Huefner, 1988; Idol, Nevin, Paolucci-Whitcomb, 1995), and inclusive neighborhood schools (M. Hardman, McDonnell, & McDonnell, 1989). These innovations earned enthusiastic acceptance in some schools and one, teacher assistance teams, continues to be used under different names as a required prereferral procedure prior to special education referral in many school districts. None, however, had the dramatic effect of the Regular Education Initiative (REI), probably because of its active sponsorship by Madeleine C. Will, assistant secretary for the Office of Special Education and Rehabilitation in the U.S. Department of Education during the Reagan administration.

In a paper entitled "Educating Children with Learning Problems: A Shared Responsibility," Will asserted that the categorical nature of programs for students with learning problems and the pullout approach had failed to meet the needs of these students and cited the mixed results of program reviews to justify this observation. She argued that pullout programs have a stigmatizing effect on students and focus on failure. She proposed alternative models that educated mildly handicapped students entirely within the regular setting (Will, 1986).

The same year Wang, Reynold, and Walberg (1986) published a paper entitled "Rethinking Special Education," a paper highly critical of special education programs for mildly handicapped students. They said that the programs placed the onus for learning problems on deficits in the children, when it should rightly be placed on inadequate learning environments. They argued that students with learning disabilities were not essentially different from other students and that similar instructional methods could be used to teach them in regular classrooms. They advocated class organization based on mixed categories and curriculum-based, rather than clinically based identification methods.

Although few professionals in the field of learning disabilities considered that special education as implemented at that time was without flaws, many individuals questioned the rush to embrace REI with little critical analysis of the assumptions underlying it and only limited practical application and research to assess its effectiveness. Experienced professionals argued that it was premature to launch any large-scale restructuring of special education services for the following reasons:

- Learning-disabled students differ from their achieving peers in information-processing abilities; modifications of classroom structure alone cannot meet the needs of the heterogeneous group of students identified as learning disabled (T. Bryant, Bay, & Donahue, 1998).
- REI theorists failed to take into account the differences between the organization and curricula of elementary and secondary schools and the often wide gap between the skill levels of students and the requirements of secondary school classrooms (Schumaker & Deshler, 1988).
- Information (Haggerty & Abramson, 1987; McKinney & Hocutt, 1988) and research results were inadequate for major restructuring (Hallahan, Keller, McKinney, Lloyd, & Bryan, 1988).
- Methodological limitations were present in the major model proposed by REI proponents, the Adaptive Learning Environments Model (ALEM) (Hallahan et al., 1988; Keoghe, 1988).
- Regular education teachers were not prepared in perceptions, attitudes, and teaching techniques to welcome special education students into their classrooms (Coates, 1989; Gerber, 1988).

- Legal mandates for inclusion cannot ensure that children will be accepted and treated equitably. Attitudinal barriers can continue to prevent the full participation of students with disabilities (Brosnan, 1998; Marks, 1997).

These issues demonstrate the concerns of individuals in the field of learning disabilities about the "wholesale mainstreaming" recommended by the proponents of REI. P. W. D. Wright and Wright (1999) cite questions that might occur to parents of children with learning disabilities: Will regular education teachers receive the training, support, and supervision they need to teach children with disabilities? How will children be taught to read, write, and spell by methods found to be successful with learning-disabled students? Will they be regarded as a burden by regular classroom teachers? Will they receive the intensive one-to-one instruction they need, or will they be shifted to teaching by untrained aides and educational assistants? Will there be backlash from parents of nonhandicapped students who feel their children are being held back by the including of students with disabilities in their classes? A dissertation by K. D. Hubert (1998) appears to support this concern: "Students who previously demonstrated above-grade level achievement skills were negatively affected by inclusionary practices and students with below grade level skills showed primarily positive effects." These findings would lead to caution in the wholesale implementation of inclusionary practices on the total school population.

Despite the warnings of individuals working in the field and misgivings of parents of children with learning disabilities, there has been an inexorable shift to regard inclusion as a "preeminent concern" in the education of students with disabilities. *The Twentieth Annual Report to Congress on the Implementation of the Individuals with Disabilities Education Act* cites these reasons for this change in emphasis:

- Growing recognition that many students with disabilities left school without the knowledge and skills necessary for independent adult life.
- The rapid rise of the number of students eligible for special education.
- The increasing costs of special education services. (U.S. Office of Education, 1998, p. III-33-4)

Only the first of these reasons has any relationship to quality of instruction; the second and third justifications for the change in policy emphasis are directly or indirectly related to money—the high cost of providing the free appropriate public education promised to all handicapped individuals by the special education legislation. However, educational policy is sometimes driven by expediency, and so despite misgivings, the educational community recognized its obligation to find ways of putting the policy of inclusion into practice.

Inclusion in Practice

Elbaum, Vaughn, Hughes, and Moody (1999) studied outcomes in reading achievement in relation to various grouping formats: student pairs, small groups, whole class instruction. Meta-analysis of 20 studies indicated positive effects for grouping methods compared with whole-class teaching, with particular efficacy of students pairing formats. Tralli, Columbo, and Deshler (1996) discussed the implementation of the Strategies Intervention Model (SIM) in general education classrooms. They illustrated three major categories of strategies applied in two schools: (a) learning sequential cognitive strategies for task completion, (b) content enhancement routines, (c) empowerment interventions that motivate students to perform at an optimum level. They also observed that a broad base of faculty and administrative support and commitment was necessary for this approach and concluded that "supported inclusion," not merely inclusion was necessary to produce meaningful results. Several investigations dealt with attitudes of regular education students, parents, and teachers (Gibb et al., 1997; Mamlin, 1999; Vaughn, Elbaum, Schumm, & Hughes, 1998). The need for collaborative consultation between regular and special education teachers was also emphasized by Barnes (1999) and Stone (1998).

The educational effectiveness of inclusionary formats was investigated by two groups. Waldron and McCleskey (1998) used a curriculum-based measure to evaluate effects of an inclusive school program on reading and mathematics achievement of students with learning disabilities in second through sixth grades. They found that included students made significantly more progress in reading and comparable progress in mathematics, when compared with students who received services in resource rooms. In addition, more of the students with mild learning problems made progress in reading that was comparable to that of their general education peers, than did students with mild problems who were in noninclusive settings. In contrast, students with severe learning disabilities "made comparable academic progress regardless of the setting." Klingner, Vaughn, Hughes, Schumm, and Elbaum (1998) examined educational outcomes of students with or without learning disabilities placed in regular education classes. Results show that, although most students with learning disabilities made some gains over the school year, differential effects were seen. Fewer low-and average-achieving students improved than did students with learning disabilities. Virtually all high-achieving students showed improvement, but the students who began the year as very poor readers made little progress. Investigators concluded that full-time placement in inclusionary classrooms (with in-class special education support) did not adequately meet the needs of all students. Comments by Mather and Roberts (1995, p. 248) would seem relevant: "Placement decisions should not be dictated by current political or educational trends, but by the needs of individuals. Most enabling environments are emphasized over least-restrictive ones, where severely learning disabled students will receive appropriate and effective instruction.

Inclusion in One School

An experienced special educator was asked to describe the implementation of the inclusion model in the school where she has worked for 24 years. Her firsthand report follows:

> Inclusion in our building means working with mainstream teachers for different periods
> of the day. For example, my present schedule is:

- Periods 1 and 2 Replacement Language Arts in 7th Grade

These students receive their language arts instruction from me in the Resource Center. Generally between three and six students are in the group. This allows me to individualize instructional techniques as needed.

- Period 3 Science in 5th Grade

I travel to a fifth-grade science class in which there are five classified (special education) students whose reading levels are at least second-grade level. In this class, the regular class teacher and I take turns teaching. Tests, quizzes, and homework may be modified for the classified students. Both teachers take active role with regular and special education students.

- Period 4 Replacement Math in the 8th Grade

Students falling below grade level or those with learning disabilities are instructed in the resource room. At the eighth-grade level, we try to follow the regular eighth-grade curriculum as closely as possible.

- Period 5 Supplemental Instruction

This period is critical for classified students who are included. It is used to review material that was taught in the regular classes, to help them prepare for tests and quizzes, and to assist with homework. Here we also give tests orally, if it is necessary in content subjects and readminister tests when they have been unsuccessful the first time. Classroom teachers provide us with notes, plans, copies of tests, assignments to guide this work.

- Period 6 Lunch Duty
- Period 7 Inclusion Social Studies in 7th Grade
- Period 8 Replacement Math in the 7th Grade
- Period 9 Preparation, Conferences with other teachers and Child Study Team

We feel our program is successful. It was planned by teachers and the principal with the following guidelines:

- No inclusion takes place before third grade. Students with learning disabilities are either in replacement or self-contained classes in lower elementary grades.
- Recommendations for inclusion come from teachers who have taught the students.
- Inclusion teachers are responsible for monitoring the progress of included students; regular education teachers provide us with copies of tests, notes, and lesson plans so that we can do this.
- At Back-to-School Night, parents are made aware of the inclusion program. They are encouraged to tell their children that both of us (regular teacher and inclusion teacher) are their teachers.
- Because regular education students also ask me for help, the classified students don't feel embarrassed to be working with me. It's important for me to get involved with all the students in the classrooms, hallways, sports activities (I coach basketball and soccer); then I am not known as a special education teacher.
- The regular classroom teacher has to be open to the classified students, as well as to input from the inclusion teacher.

- Only students who have mild learning disabilities are included into language arts in the seventh and eighth grades. All of our younger classified elementary students are taught by the special education teacher in a small group setting.
- No more than five classified students are placed in one class or in the resource room. If scheduling makes this impossible, an aide is assigned to the resource room.

To date, we have not had any inclusion in our math classes. Just by including the classified students in science, social studies, and some language arts classes, we believe the gap is lessened between classified and nonclassified students.

As can be seen from this report from the field, a well-managed elementary school can deal with the complexities of inclusion. Several factors have made the transition possible. At the outset, the faculty contained a number of mature, experienced educators who respected each other's professional skills. Administration was in the hands of a principal whose low-key leadership style encouraged the faculty's efforts. The transition to inclusion was gradual; there was no rapid change that discarded insights gained in the past. Placement decisions are based on teacher judgment, not on test scores. Policies have developed gradually as teachers worked together in planning, teaching, and grouping students. Opportunities for team teaching in the content areas of science and social studies have opened new vistas for the special educator and have strengthened her abilities to plan transitions into the mainstream as the students move on to a regional high school. The Supplemental Instruction period is an important bridge to the mainstream for the classified students. This important safety net depends on the close relationships among teachers. Finally, the whole system is powered by an overriding concern for teaching every child well.

FALSE DICHOTOMY: THE READING WARS

Methodological issues in the teaching of reading have been a continuing focus of attention both within the field of education and in the popular press during the past decade. These issues are relevant to a discussion of learning disabilities for three reasons: (a) reading as a skill area presents problems for the greatest proportion of students with learning disability (Lerner, 1988); (b) difficulties in reading soon impact on other curricular areas, so that their effects are inescapable; (c) reading is a complex task, probably the most difficult one our culture asks of the education of young children.

Skilled reading is a complex, multilevel system that requires the reader to deal with letters, graphophonemic patterns, words, and syntactic and semantic units. The differences in theoretical models of the reading task lie in the weight and relationship ascribed to these components by various theoreticians. Inevitably, these theoretical models influence the methods and materials that then find their way into classrooms and reading centers. One theoretical dichotomy is that of the bottom-up versus the top-down models of reading. The *bottom-up models* are based on the idea that the analysis of smaller units (such as graphophonenes and words) is essential to the processing of larger conceptual units. Examples of this model are the "linguistics" and the Orton-Gillingham approaches. In contrast, *top-down models* assume that readers use knowledge of higher-order language structures to anticipate oncoming text. K. S. Goodman (1967) has called this process as "the psycholinguistic guessing game." The language experience and the "whole language" approaches exemplify this theoretical model. An additional formulation, somewhere between the two extremes is a *parallel-interactive model,* which suggests that all sources of information, from signal cues of the perceptual features of words to syntactic and semantic information, are used simultaneously. Basal reader text-book approaches are examples of these methods. Detailed descriptions of the applications of models to the teaching of students with learning disabilities appear in Chapter 8. However, these brief descriptions of models are necessary to the current discussion of the flow of controversy about the teaching of reading in the past decade.

Application of Models in the Classroom

Application of models of reading instruction was not nearly so pure as the model-makers may have assumed. In reality, few classrooms implemented only a single model. Experienced teachers drew on several sources: the language and experiential background of the children, the range and quality of the teaching materials available, the individual teacher's skill and comfort with a given approach, even the persuasiveness of the textbook salesperson who met with the principal or the curriculum committee most recently. In the past, local option prevailed, sometimes even extending to individual classrooms within the same school building. With some few exceptions, the teachers selected from a range of techniques, methodologies, and materials as individual training and skills dictated and blended them into classroom approaches. Jeanne Chall, in conducting the field studies for her significant book *Learning to Read: The Great Debate* (1983) remarked about the variations between the official statement of reading approaches articulated in the principals' offices and what was actually occurring in the classrooms she visited.

Whole Language Approach

When the reading wars heated up during the 1990s, attitudes changed; educators, parents, critics, chose sides. As with many dichotomies, the issues were over-simplified between the alternatives of "whole language" and "phonics." As it turned out, "whole language" swept the country during the early part of the 1990s. K. S. Goodman's (1976) speculations about how children learn to read were revived and quoted widely. Basal readers disappeared. Their disciplined texts and accompanying workbooks with their controlled vocabularies were replaced by what teachers called "literature." Even the major textbook publishers picked up the cues and published as textbooks what look like storybooks and trade books.

The unstructured nature of the whole language approach makes it difficult to describe it succinctly. This instructional strategy has been recommended for use with children with learning disability by Brand (1989), who believes it can alleviate some of their difficulties including problems in memory, cognition, anxiety, self esteem, locus of control, and attention. Such a cure-all is indeed intriguing. G. G. Duffy and Roehler (1989) present a more modest picture of the approach. They portray the teacher of whole language as establishing a literate environment in the classroom, demonstrating how language is used for real communication in recreation and functional activities. There is emphasis on free choice reading of literature and student authorship, so that reading instruction is integrated in natural ways with the other language arts of listening, speaking, and writing. Reading and writing always involve communication that is meaningful to the children. Organized so that the physical, intellectual, and social-affective components of the setting emphasize communication, this environment contrasts with the classroom that provides isolated worksheets, memorized rules, and skill tests.

All of this sounds ideal for children with learning disorders, until one considers how this approach teaches word attack skills, one of the major educational difficulties encountered by students with learning disabilities. Goodman and others criticized methods that "chop language into bits and pieces" and recommended instead "authentic" reading activities, closer to the reading experiences of children. Goodman opposed instruction about phonics and concern for accurate spelling and punctuation. He felt sure that children would learn to read when they had a need to communicate. He said, "Language learning is easy when it's whole, real, and relevant; when it makes sense and is functional; when it's encountered in the context of its use; when the learner chooses to use it" (K. S. Goodman, 1976, p. 37).

Not all proponents of whole language approaches place as much faith in spontaneously developing word attack skills as Goodman does. In their college textbook on methods for teaching reading, G. G. Duffy and Roehler (1989), suggest that teachers instruct children to recognize sight words by having them read words to be learned in phrases from flashcards "until students instantly recognize the word." With otherwise unfamiliar words, the student is encouraged to use context cues (guess on the basis of the words around the unknown word) or structural analysis (using structural units like roots, prefixes, suffixes, and inflectional endings). As a last resort, they suggest that a student might use phonics to " sound out" the word, but they warn, "Phonics is the slowest of the three decoding methods because it requires that each separate letter-sound unit be retrieved from memory and then blended together" (G. G. Duffy & Roehler, 1989, p. 108).

Thus, whole language advocates rejected "negative, elitist, racist views of language purity that would limit children to arbitrary, proper language instead of helping children to expand on the marvelous language they already use." Goodman wrote that if teachers surrounded children with a rich environment in which they had lots of opportunities to read and write, they would learn to read without direct instruction about the sounds and the letters they represent. At the heart of his theory was the belief that "literacy develops in response to person/social needs": When children want to read, they will learn to do so (Ravitch, 2000, p. 444).

Origins of Romantic Pedagogy

These ideas did not appear spontaneously. Historians like Diane Ravitch trace them to the educational philosophy she calls the *romantic pedagogy*. One of the early advocates of this point of view is G. Stanley Hall, whom psychologists will recognize as one of the founders of modern psychology. A prolific writer, speaker, and teacher, he blended his own interpretation of Rousseau with the then developing evolutionary sciences and genetics. An exponent of natural education, he started the Child Study Movement, encouraging the collection of data on the natural development of children unspoiled by the discipline imposed by traditional schooling. He believed that the teacher's real mission was not to impart knowledge, but to learn about the needs of growing children by observing them. These observations would enable teachers to "fit the school to the child, rather than the child to the school" (G. S. Hall, 1948). Hall did not place a high value on literacy. He criticized the academic curriculum with its emphasis on learning to read. Ravitch (2000, p. 72) quotes him as saying, "It would not be a serious loss, if a child never learned to read. Charlemagne could not read, and he had quite an influence upon the world's history and was a fairly brainy man."

The beliefs of romantic pedagogy did not go unchallenged by other educational movements. The defenders of the academic curriculum emphasizing general education for all students, advocates of vocational education to train students early for their roles in the world of work, the measurement psychologists with their preoccupation with IQ and ability testing, the emphasis on science and mathematics in the post-Sputnik era, all had their influences at various times during the last half of the twentieth century. However, a broad view of the history of education in the United States shows that two competing viewpoints can account for the changes—child-centered and curriculum-centered education. While the methodologies of these viewpoints are ephemeral and difficult to document, the content of the readers helps us to understand how children were taught to read as each philosophy was implemented in the classroom. Textbooks of the early half of the century contained fables, poems, stories, and classical literature, all chosen to acquaint all children with their literary heritage. By 1940, W. S. Gray, major author of the "Dick and Jane" textbooks announced proudly that the problem of teaching children to read had been clearly differentiated from the effort to cultivate appreciation for classic literature (Ravitch, 2000, p. 256). How ironic that 50 years later, the advocates of the whole language approach rejected the Dick and Jane readers and their accompanying *Think and Do Books* to return to stories, legends, and poems self-selected by the students as the content of their reading lessons!

Other Viewpoints

These pendulum-like swings in orientation have occurred without regard to diatribes (like that of Rudolph Flesch's 1981 book, *Why Johnny Still Can't Read),* policy statements (such as National Academy of Education's 1985 report, *Becoming a Nation of Readers: The Report of the Commission on Reading*), or careful research studies, (e.g., Chall's 1967 and 1983 books, *Learning to Read: The Great Debate*). Chall's research (conducted originally in the 1960s and updated in 1983) was based on an analysis of reading materials and extensive classroom observations. She showed that code-based reading (bottom-up) approaches were more effective than meaning-centered (top-down) approaches not only for children with reading disorders, but for all students in beginning reading. Her work documented the modest statement written many years earlier (1937) by Samuel T. Orton, a pioneering neurologist in the field of specific language disability (which he called strephosymbolia) written in 1937:

> There has been in recent years a striking swing toward the use of the sight or flashcard method of teaching and away from the use of phonetics. The writer is not in a position to offer an opinion as to the efficacy of either of these methods as a general school procedure but their effect on children suffering from varying degrees of strephosymbolia has come under his immediate attention and he feels that there can be no doubt that the use of the popular flash card method of teaching reading is a definite obstacle to children who suffer from any measure of this disability.
>
> (Orton 1937, p. 104)

Despite opposing viewpoints from clinical, research, policymaking, and popular sources, the last years of the twentieth century saw organized education move away from classical conceptions of the mission of schools and move toward romantic pedagogy. Advocates of this viewpoint denied the existence of the clinical entity of learning disability, adopting such terms as "learning differences" and "maturational lag" to describe the learning problems these students encountered. The onus for their failure was assumed to lie within the instructional system because teachers had failed to use the functional language and to draw content from the authentic experiences of the learners. It was believed that literacy would develop in response to individual needs and that parents who criticized this approach were part of the problem—they had not read enough to their children. Professional and political lines were drawn more firmly than ever before between the people espousing the natural development of literacy from the top-down and those who believed that skills needed to be taught directly from the bottom-up. It was a case of whole language versus phonics first, both extreme expressions of the differences of opinion.

These differences were aired largely among educators. Parents grumbled about the journal writing their children did at school using inventive spelling that in many cases bore little resemblance to the alphabetic code of the English language. Parents of children with learning disabilities waited anxiously for the promised breakthrough in reading that did not occur, despite the teachers' reassurances. Their children cooperated in the charade by pretending to "read" the storybooks provided in school, using a blend of picture cues, story sense, and judicious guessing. Few of them discovered for themselves the phonetic generalizations that enable readers to decode unfamiliar words. They continued to practice the often incorrect spelling that they invented for their journals. The effect of whole language approaches for students with learning disabilities was nothing short of disastrous.

Suspicions that this approach had not been as successful as promised with students in general was discovered when in 1996 the U.S. Department of Education announced state-by-state reading scores on the federally funded National Assessment of Educational Progress (NAEP) studies. In 1992 scores, the state of California had been fourth from last in reading (surpassing only Mississippi, District of Columbia, and Guam); two years later in 1994 California slipped behind Mississippi. Educators and legislators tried to account for this decline, particularly distressing because the state superintendent of public instruction was William Honig, a leader among state school administrators. He said his plans to reform education in California were "hijacked" by the ideology of whole language approaches that were inserted without his knowledge, into new guidelines for the teaching of English in California.

A storm of protest by parents, educators, and politicians in meetings, publications, and on the Internet followed. Even the *Atlantic Monthly* joined the fray in an article entitled "The Reading Wars" (Lemann, 1997). In 1997, the California State Board of Education responded with a new curriculum in English and the language arts that required both phonics and literature in the primary grades. According to the *School Reform News* (1998) article entitled "States Embrace Phonics to Combat Illiteracy" many other states followed suit. The Ohio, North Carolina, Texas, Virginia, and Wisconsin state legislatures passed laws requiring instruction in systematic, explicit phonics, and spelling. In several other states (Mississippi, Nebraska, Georgia, Tennessee, and Florida) bills were introduced to require use of specific phonics programs in the schools, essentially taking curriculum decisions out of the hands of educators and placing them in the hands of political leaders. Of this trend Allington and Woodside-Jiron observed sadly (1999, p. 4), "There is a demonstrated pattern of increased legislative activity designed to influence the nature of beginning reading instruction and the language of such legislation is becoming increasingly specific and restrictive."

However, the issues involved in reading instruction in the primary grades have not been resolved to the present time. Advocates for the whole language approach continue to defend the theory. Krashen (2000) defended the approach in a paper entitled "Has Whole Language Failed?" written for circulation on the Internet. Reacting to the bad press being received by the term "whole language," he renamed the approach the *comprehension hypothesis* and defined it as follows:

> The Comprehension Hypothesis claims that we learn to read by reading and that other aspects of literacy competence are the result of meaningful reading. Reading is claimed as the source of much of our vocabulary knowledge, writing style, advance grammatical competence, and spelling. (p. 1)

Krashen cited studies that show that students taught with whole language approaches have greater fluency in written language, more favorable attitudes toward reading, and read more than children taught with skill-based methods. Krashen denies that there has been a decline in reading scores in California explaining the poor results for California students on the NAEP test as results of the state's poor quality of public libraries, number of children living in poverty, and consequent lack of books in homes. All these factors, he believes, point to the conclusion that "California's problem is not whole language, but a lack of reading material" (2000, p. 4).

Krashen also cites work by Constance Weaver, who shows methods by which phonics can be taught in whole language classrooms (Weaver, 1994). Review of these methods shows that many are so tangential that student mastery would be doubtful; others would appear to violate the authentic, natural, realistic reading criteria that the founders of whole language have set for this approach. Finally, Weaver shows some doubts about the invincibility of whole language in her comment, "Children who are exceptionally slow in grasping letter/sound relationships may benefit from tutorial assistance, such as that offered in Marie Clay's Reading Recovery Program" (p. 3).

What has been the overall effect of these confusing, often strident discussions of initial reading instruction for students vulnerable to learning disabilities? While ultimately, bottom-up approaches are most effective with most of these students, there are some positive lessons to be learned from the whole language approach:

- Effective teaching does not isolate reading and the language arts. The important interrelationships between listening, speaking, reading, writing language, spelling, and appreciation of literature should be exploited for the benefit of the learner.

- The student's motivation is an essential element of the teaching-learning transaction. Effective teaching uses content relevant to students' interests as well as their instructional needs.

Unfortunately there have been negative effects of the "reading wars." The polarization of viewpoints has resulted in wider swings of the pendulum between bottom-up and top-down approaches. The reactions have been more extreme, making it less likely that the strengths of the two approaches will be blended in classrooms for more effective instruction.

The broad, uncritical acceptance of the theories of the whole language approach, also have been unfortunate for the training of teachers. Many teacher educators in the colleges and universities, remote from the realities of classroom instruction, viewed these theories as the cutting edge of methodology and advocated strongly for them in training courses. The role for teachers in whole language approaches is a passive one, more that of a facilitator available to respond to the needs of students by enhancing their language development in broad ways, but avoiding direct instruction in skills. Teachers trained in this model would have little understanding of the methods, techniques, and content necessary in bottom-up skill-based approaches. Thus, the whole language approach produced a generation of teachers who were strong on theory, but essentially did not know how to *teach* reading and the language arts. While this does not bode well for most students, it is particularly tragic for children vulnerable to learning disabilities and for those from what S. A. Stahl (1999) has called "low-literacy-press homes" who need to be taught every step of the way on the road to literacy.

The emphasis on reading for enjoyment led to the use of trade books, the literature emphasis of whole language approaches. This led to a neglect of the skills required for reading expository material, such as textbooks in the content subjects, reference books and encyclopedias, and detailed directions for science experiments. The responsibilities for teaching students to adapt their reading strategies to the purposes for reading different kinds of text was postponed to the middle grades of school, if they were to be taught at all.

Finally, students with potential learning disabilities often cannot be recognized in the literary environment of the whole language classroom with its focus on "learning to read by reading." Such students could go through the motions of reading to themselves without demonstrating the decoding problems that ordinarily bring them to the attention of teachers and result in referral for services for their disabilities. It is ironic that this purportedly child-centered approach to early reading instruction assumed that all children arrived in school equally prepared for learning.

THE NATIONAL READING PANEL

Although the professional literature on the teaching of reading is voluminous, it often has little impact on what happens in classrooms. In 1997, the need to make results of research accessible and relevant to teachers and parents was recognized in legislation in which Congress asked the director of the National Institute of Child Health and Human Development in consultation with the Secretary of the Department of Education to create a National Reading Panel. The panel was charged with the task of determining from existing research the most effective approaches for teaching children to read. The panel was not expected to conduct research, but rather to review existing research, identify methods that show the most promise, and translate the research into key findings that would be disseminated to teachers and parents through its final report to the Secretaries of the Department of Health and Human Services and the Department of Education. The panel's critical review, analysis, and synthesis of the research literature focused on the following seven areas:

1. What is known about the basic processes by which children learn to read?
2. What are the most common instructional approaches in use in the United States to teach children to read? What are the scientific underpinnings for each of these methodological approaches and what assessments have been done to validate their underlying scientific rationale? What conclusions about the scientific basis for these approaches does the panel draw from these assessments?
3. What assessments have been made of the effectiveness of each of these methodologies in actual use in helping children develop critical reading skills, and what conclusions does the panel draw from these assessments?
4. Based on answers to the preceding questions, what does the panel conclude about the readiness for implementation in the classroom of these research results?
5. How are teachers trained to teach children to read, and what do studies show about the effectiveness of this training? How can this knowledge be applied to improve this training?
6. What practical findings from the panel can be used immediately by parents, teachers, and other educational audiences to help children learn how to read, and how can conclusions of the panel be disseminated most effectively?
7. What important gaps remain in our knowledge of how children learn to read, the effectiveness of different instructional methods for teaching reading, and improving the preparation of teachers in reading instruction that could be addressed by additional research?

These important questions were raised in the hope that the panel's deliberations would put an end to the rhetoric, lobbying, and impulsive decision making that were characterizing discussions of early reading instruction.

A distinguished panel was appointed. It was chaired by a physicist (now university system administrator) and included individuals from the following occupational groups:

Researchers in the field of reading	4
University professors (urban education, human development, educational technology, pediatrics)	4
Administrators in higher education	2
Teacher/Educators	1
Certified public accountant	1
Reading teacher	1
School principal	1

The panel comprised a broad range of accomplished and distinguished individuals, all with a strong investment in literacy. Although the minority report by one panel member criticized the panel's large number of college professors and its failure to submit findings to review by outside teacher reviewers, one can understand the need for a broad range of professional backgrounds among the panel members. Professional educators have not done an effective job in setting their own house in order during this past decade; assistance from outside the profession may have seemed necessary to the conveners of the panel.

A series of panel meetings resulted in a number of management decisions. To understand the perspectives and gain insights from practitioners that could supplement their own views, they held a series of regional meetings involving 400 people, with presentations by 44 invited speakers and 73 members of the public.

The literature search was divided among five subcommittees: Alphabetics, Fluency, Comprehension, Technology, and Teacher Preparation. The panel decided to seek contributions of specific elements of the reading process from existing research: phonemic awareness, phonics, guided oral reading, vocabulary instruction, independent reading. In each case, they also wished to determine how this specific element could best be taught. They also planned to examine research on technology and the teaching of reading and to study the influence of teacher education on the teaching of reading.

Each subgroup was directed to review 300 to 400 of the most recent research sources dealing with reading instruction in preschool through 12th grade appearing in refereed journals. A common protocol was developed for coding the details to compare the outcomes of teaching methods.

In the course of these reviews, 100,00 studies were identified and analyzed according to rigorous criteria, "standards normally used in psychological and medical research." It was the view of the panel that "the efficacy of materials and methodologies used in the teaching of reading and in the prevention or treatment of reading disabilities should be tested no less rigorously." The panel also commented that such standards had not been universally accepted or used in reading education research, so that only a fraction of the research literature in reading met the panel's standards for use in the topic analysis (National Reading Panel: Addendum, 2000, p. 1).

A minimum of two databases, PsychINFO and ERIC, were searched; other databases were searched where necessary. To be included in the analysis, studies had to measure reading as an outcome. Reading was defined to include reading real words in isolation, reading pseudowords, reading text aloud or silently, and comprehending text that is read silently or orally.

To ensure a unified analysis of the subgroup findings, common procedures and criteria for inclusion of research studies were agreed on. These criteria might well serve as a model for any research on educational interventions:

- Study participants must be carefully described in terms of age, demographic, cognitive, academic, and behavioral characteristics.
- Study interventions must be described in sufficient detail to allow for replicability, including how long interventions lasted and how long the effects lasted.
- Study methods must allow judgments about how fidelity of instruction was ensured.
- Studies must include a full description of outcome measures. (National Reading Panel: Addendum, 2000, p. 3)

The panel also adopted a common coding protocol to identify each piece of research used in the analysis. Thus, careful plans were made by the panel to structure their review of research on reading instruction.

The panel provided public information in a progress report in February 1999 and in summaries of Panel and Regional Meetings during the course of its two-year period of operation. Work was completed in April 2000. Three final reports are available:

1. National Reading Panel Final Report and Materials.
2. Findings and Determinations of the National Reading Panel by Topic Areas.
3. National Reading Panel Releases Report on Research-Based Approaches to Reading Instruction.

The detailed findings and determinations in topic areas are especially relevant to the discussion of methodology in Chapter 8 and will be discussed there. The general implications contained in the public information document are relevant to this account of directions in the teaching of reading.

After a brief description of the purposes of the panel and its work, the public information document states that the panel's review of the literature found that for children to be good readers, they must be taught (a) phonemic awareness skills, (b) phonic skills, (c) the ability to read fluently, (d) comprehension strategies to enhance understanding and enjoyment of what they read. The panel's findings also highlighted the need for further research in three areas: teacher education, the potential of computers in reading instruction, and whether students with learning disabilities have distinct instructional needs and can benefit from instructional techniques that are different from those used with nondisabled students. These general recommendations do not convey the depth of the research reviews and the detailed implications for reading instruction the panel produced in each of the topic areas. It is to be hoped that the panel's sophisticated review of a massive literature will be reflected in future improvements in both research design and classroom applications.

A minority view presented by Joanne Yatvin, a school principal and panel member, pointed out some concerns about the panel's procedures and conceptions of the reading process. Dr. Yatvin's Minority View (2000) stated that the panel did not fulfill its oblig-ation to answer the questions from Congress that would put an end to what she called the "inflamed rhetoric, partisan lobbying, and uninformed decision-making" that have been detrimental to the progress of reading instruction in the schools. This ambitious charge was not fulfilled because the panel did not realize the implications of their work for practice. The minority report stated, "As a body made up mostly of university pro-fessors, its members were not qualified to be the sole judges of the readiness for imple-mentation in the classroom of their findings" (Minority View, 2000, p. 2). It suggests that outside teacher reviewers should have been brought in to critique the panel's con-clusions. In addition to the gap between scientific research and the realities of the class-room, the minority report maintained that the panel failed to look at the field of reading in terms of basic theoretical models: the word identification model, word identification plus skills model, and integration of language and thinking model. (These models can be recognized as the bottom-up, parallel-interactive, top-down models discussed ear-lier.) Yatvin's view proposed an alternative approach for the review in that the research foundation for each model of reading would have formed the structure for the review, rather than the more pragmatic one in which the structure was defined by the quality of research found and the validity of its findings on meta-analysis. Finally, the minority report provided a list of topics, many involving methods related to the whole language approach, that were insufficiently dealt with in the panel's work. Most of these topics are current issues of serious concern to teachers and parents. However, they may have been omitted from the panel's reviews because research on these topics to meet the high standards set at the outset by the panel was just not available.

The differences in the viewpoints embodied in the panel's report and those of the Minority View raised issues about the nature of teaching. Is teaching a process that can be reduced to a series of research variables? If so, it would follow that the efficacy of particular teaching methods could be evaluated most efficiently in experiments uncon-taminated by the natural realities of classrooms. It would also follow that methods then could be rated in terms of efficacy and mandated for use or discarded as ineffective, rather in the way the Food and Drug Administration evaluates medications.

On the other hand, can the experimental variables in even the best designed experi-ments capture *all* the influences involved in the teaching/learning transaction? Are there, in addition to the variables that one can define and measure, other variables that influence the outcomes of instruction? Is teaching, in addition to being a science, also an art? Are there extra-cognitive variables having to do with the nature of the learners and the nature of the teachers, and the match between the two, that cannot be con-trolled in even in the most precise experimental designs? It would appear so.

Finally, the panel's report in recommending that the issues of differences between the learning needs of students with learning disorders and those of other students should be the subject of further research sidesteps the reality that children with learn-ing disorders *are* different from achieving students. The position of the authors of this book is that real differences exist between students with learning disorders and those without. These differences become apparent when careful diagnostic studies are con-ducted, and when characteristics are understood. Of necessity they lead to differences in educational and medical management.

SUMMARY

The Education for All Handicapped Children Act, passed in 1975, reauthorized in 1990 and again in 1997 as the Individuals with Disabilities Education Act (IDEA), re-affirmed six basic principles: free appropriate public education for handicapped children, appropriate evaluation of handicapped children, development of individual education programs (IEP), least restrictive environment, parent and student participation in decision making, and procedural safeguards. Implementation of IDEA has been handicapped by the high cost of funding resources for the handicapped (particularly those with learning disabilities), and by the criticisms of the effectiveness of special educational services, the utility of clinical diagnostic procedures, and the difficulty of recruiting adequately trained teachers. Modifications in the day-to-day operation of IDEA included noncategorical classification, generic certification of teachers, the shift from resource room to the mainstream classes for children with learning problems, and the "inclusion" of children with learning disabilities in the regular classroom. Although this wholesale mainstreaming raised concerns, the gradual implementation to inclusion has been effective in schools that have close teacher relationships and special education skills available in the staff.

The 1990s also saw a controversy in the "best way" to teach children to read; the whole language (top-down) approach versus the phonetic (bottom-up) approach represents extreme positions in this debate. This controversy has appeared in the press as "The Reading Wars." This polarization of viewpoints is nonproductive; the strengths of the two approaches are lost in the controversy. A National Reading Panel to determine the most effective ways to teach children to read, was created in 1997. Their report concluded that the child must be taught phonetic awareness skills, phonic skills, and the ability to read fluently and with comprehension. A minority report points to the gap between scientific research and the realities of the classroom and recommends that the panel look at the field of reading in terms of basic models of reading as it is practiced. The Reading Panel also did not deal with the differences in learning experienced by children with learning disabilities.

Chapter 2

SOCIOECONOMIC, POLITICAL, AND LEGAL DEVELOPMENTS

By the year 2000 every American will be literate and will possess the knowledge and skills necessary to compete in a global economy and exercise the rights and responsibilities of citizenship.

—Governors Educational Summit, 1989

Although some changes during the past decade came from within the field of education itself, socioeconomic, political, and legal developments in the broader society may have had a more striking effect on how American children are taught. During the last years of the twentieth century, the management of education was no longer left to educators. The impact of this change has resonated louder and longer than any of the in-house developments reported in Chapter I. The reasons for these changes are many. Rapid technological advances increased the need for knowledgeable, literate workers; economic prosperity heightened interest in the material things such technology could produce; improvements in communication and transportation made the world smaller and its population more mobile. Parents, students, and political leaders began to question whether schools were meeting these changing conditions, and, unfortunately, the educational community did not consistently rise to the challenges.

Education's response to specific problems was often to convene a committee, task force, or panel to study the situation. The outcome would be a report that made headlines and scholarly reading, but had less than a significant effect on the original issue. The usual response of professional educators was not so much to act, but to react. It is not surprising that in view of this abdication of authority by professionals in the field, leadership shifted to forces far outside professional education.

DEMOGRAPHIC CHANGES

The last years of the twentieth century were a time of growth and prosperity. The United States enjoyed one of the longest periods of economic growth in its history. For three years in a row a surplus in the federal budget was reported. Except for some soft spots in businesses in the technology sector, economic conditions were favorable, with low rates of inflation and unemployment.

The 2000 United States census also reported significant population growth. Since 1990, the total population has increased more than 32 million to a total of 281,421,706 in 2000. Even more important for schooling is the increased ethnic diversity of the U.S. population. The census planners provided for the range of languages by using forms printed in English, Spanish, Korean, Chinese, Vietnamese, and Tagalong. At this writing, details of nativity from the 2000 census were not available, but estimates of ethnicity made in 1999 show increasing diversity in languages and cultural backgrounds in the U.S. population. As can be seen from Table 2.1, growth rates for three ethnic groups, White, Black, and Native American, Eskimo, and Aleut were 8%, 14%, and 16% respectively. In contrast, growth rates for Hispanic and Asian groups, where language differences can be most apparent, were 40% and 46%, respectively.

Educational Programs for Limited English Proficient Students

Schools have responded to these changes in the demographics of school enrollment through several kinds of programs to ensure students with limited English proficiency (LEP) access to the benefits of education:

- *English as a Second Language (ESL).* Specific language skills are taught for specific periods of time in separate classes with emphasis on grammar, vocabulary, and communication.
- *Content-Based ESL/Structured Immersion.* Instruction through English with an emphasis on learning English through study of content subjects but using simplified vocabulary and grammar.
- *Sheltered Instruction.* Teaching of all subjects in English at a level modified to the students' level of language proficiency.

Table 2.1   Resident population: Ethnicity (1980–1999)* (estimates in thousands)

	1980	1990	1999
White	194,713	208,727	224,692
Black	16,683	30,511	34,903
Hispanic	14,609	22,372	31,365
American Indian, Eskimo, Aleut	1,420	2,065	2,396
Asian, Pacific Islanders	3,729	7,482	10,887

*Source of Estimate: Statistical Abstract of the United States (Time Almanac, 2001, p. 122).

- *Transitional Bilingual Education.* Students are instructed one half of the day in English and the other half in their native language, with gradual transition to all-English instruction in approximately three years.
- *Maintenance Bilingual Education.* LEP students from the same language background are instructed in that language. The aim is to develop academic proficiency in both English and the native language (Shokraii & Yousef, 1998, p. 4).

Estimates vary as to the number of LEP students enrolled in the schools; the Department of Education estimate is approximately 2.8 million students, and the TESOL Advocacy Group quotes the Council of Chief State School Officers 1998 estimate at 3.4 million students. Definitions of limited English proficiency vary, and a child can live in a household that is bilingual, but may not necessarily be limited in the ability to speak English. Department of Education sources provide the following distribution of languages among the LEP students they identified: Spanish, 73%; Vietnamese, 3.9%; Hmong, 1.9%; Cantonese, 1.7%; Cambodian, 1.6%; Korean, 1.6%; Laotian, 1.3%; Navaho, 1.3%; Tagalong, 1.3%; other (including Russian, French Creole, Arabic, Japanese, Armenian, Mandarin, Farsi, Hindi, and Polish) 12.5%. Furthermore, the U.S. Bureau of the Census has forecasted that 88% of the increase in the child population between the years 2000 and 2050 will be children of new immigrants (Shokraii & Yousef, 1998, p. 3).

School districts met the needs of LEP students in various ways until 1974 when the Supreme Court ruling in *Lau v. Nichols* barred discrimination on the basis of national origin with the following decision:

Where inability to speak and understand the English language excludes national origin minority children from effective participation in the educational program offered by a school district, the district must take steps to rectify the language deficiency in order to open its instructional program to these students. (*Lau v. Nichols*)

The ruling did not mandate any specific procedure, but a task force appointed by Department of Education's Office of Civil Rights drafted what were called the *Lau Remedies* and circulated the provisions to every school district that received federal funding. The Lau Remedies say in essence that if a school has 15 students who speak a single language, it must offer instruction to those students in their native language (i.e. Transitional Bilingual Education). English as a Second Language programs were defined by this document as an inappropriate method because "an ESL program does not consider the affective or cognitive development of the students" (Shokraii & Yousef, 1998, p. 5). Except for a brief time during the Reagan Administration, the Office of Civil Rights and the Office of Bilingual Education and Minority Language Affairs (OBEMLA) have guided the development of programs for LEP students up to the present time. To a more limited extent, support has been available (e.g., through the Elementary and Secondary Education Act) for other approaches than Transitional Bilingual Education.

Through financial incentives for program development and the compliance review role of the Office of Civil Rights, the Department of Education has had considerable control of the school districts' efforts to provide services for children with limited English proficiency. OCR's reviews have frequently addressed procedural issues, such as methods of identification, availability of programs, provision of information to parents in their native languages, inadequate procedures for existing programs, and placement of students in special education programs. Apparently OCR believed that limited English proficiency conferred some kind of immunity to learning disability!

LEARNING DISABILITY IN EITHER LANGUAGE

TESOL reported that 23% of children with limited English proficiency in their program have limited skills in their native languages. Work with the public schools of New York City with the preventive program, *Search & Teach,* (Silver & Hagin, 1990) has led to a similar conclusion. Details of the preventive aspects of *Search & Teach* appear in greater detail in Chapter 10; what is relevant to this discussion of English learners are the findings with *Busqueda,* the Spanish adaptation of the scanning test *Search* that is used to identify children who are vulnerable to learning problems.

There are several reasons for the construction of a scanning instrument for Hispanic children. For one thing, teachers with only a limited knowledge of Spanish themselves may conclude that being bilingual explains lack of progress in reading. Second, such a scanning instrument is a necessary step in understanding the differences among the children with limited English proficiency enrolled in the schools. Third, it was our purpose to differentiate among these children and locate those who were vulnerable to learning problems so that preventive approaches could be implemented. Moreover, there is a legal recognition of the need for testing in the child's primary language. Finally, common sense and sound test practices both indicate the usefulness of local norms, particularly for a test that predicts academic achievement.

Busqueda, like its predecessor Search, assesses 10 neuropsychological subskills basic to reading and the language arts. Clinical and educational follow-up of children receiving this test as kindergartners has shown that children earning adequate scores in 8 to 10 test components made adequate progress in learning to read in first grade. Children earning scores of 6 and 7 have about a 50% chance of success with beginning reading. Scores of 5 or below indicate vulnerability to learning problems.

A sample of approximately 200 children was identified by their teachers as having limitations in English proficiency. *The Bilingual Syntax Test* (Burt, Dulay, & Hernandez, 1973) was used as a criterion measure. The bilingual syntax measure uses samples of the child's discourse as a measure of language proficiency. Syntax has been shown to be a more stable measure of language proficiency than either vocabulary or judgments of functional use of language. This test elicits natural speech in English and Spanish. From a comparison of the samples, the test administrator is able to infer language dominance and level of second language acquisition.

After appropriate explanations of the purposes of the research, permission was obtained from parents (this was easy) and from the New York City Board of Education (this was somewhat harder), and the two tests were administered by native speakers of Spanish, students specializing in a program for training bilingual school psychologists at Fordham University-Lincoln Center, New York. The Bilingual Syntax Test showed that about a dozen children who had been nominated by their teachers were clearly English-dominant and had only fragmentary knowledge of Spanish. They were eliminated from the sample, since it was pointless to test them on Busqueda. Absences during the time that examiners were at the schools accounted for the loss of another dozen of the original group. Complete test results were obtained for a sample of 176 kindergartners. Results of Busqueda were related to language proficiency through analysis of subsamples using the cross-tabs program. Results of this analysis appear in Table 2.2.

Three subgroups of children were identified:

- *Spanish Dominant Children.* This group of 81 children, comprising 46% of the sample, earned scores showing high Spanish proficiency and limited English proficiency on the bilingual syntax measure. Although some of them earned vulnerable scores on Busqueda, the majority (69%) showed a considerable degree of readiness for academic learning. These do not appear to be children with learning disorders, but rather youngsters who can profit from programs teaching English as a second language in the schools.
- *Stars.* This group of 58 children, 33% of the sample, showed a high degree of proficiency in both English and Spanish on the Bilingual Syntax Test. Very few of them show difficulties with the subskills underlying reading, for only 12% earned vulnerable scores on Busqueda. In contrast, 88% earned scores of 8 or above. For these children, good progress in both languages is anticipated. For them, the educator's task is to provide a rich educational program appropriate to their superior language proficiency.
- *Children with Limited Proficiency in Both English and Spanish.* Thirty-seven children (21% of the sample) composed the group who lacked proficiency in both English and Spanish. The majority of this group earned scores within the vulnerable ranges on Busqueda: 71% earned scores of 5 or below and 90% earned scores of 7 or below. Very few gave indications of readiness for reading instruction. This is a group of children who need more careful diagnosis to understand the reasons for their limitations in both languages. It would seem that language

Table 2.2   Language subgroups: Busqueda and language proficiency

	Spanish Dominant	Stars	Limited in Both Languages
	Se	SE	ee
N	81	58	37
Percent	46%	33%	21%
Busqueda Score Group	Percent of Subgroup		
0 to 5	31%	12%	71%
6 to 10	69	88	29

stimulation activities would be appropriate, but might be inadequate for meeting all the needs represented here. Individual diagnostic studies would be important in planning intervention programs for them, otherwise they run the risk of being the children who remain in bilingual programs year after year with little apparent progress in language development or school achievement.

Considering Program Outcomes

Research and evaluation of programs for second language learning have been inconclusive. A National Research Council committee concluded in 1997 that nearly $100 million and 10 years of research and evaluation yielded few clear-cut results to guide school programs. The committee was critical of OBEMLA's failure to disseminate and use the results of projects it had funded. In a 1992 audit of OBEMLA research, a U.S. Department of Education analyst found that of 91 studies funded by that agency, 40 final reports were discarded or lost, 29 were relevant for policy information, and only 12 were considered to be significant enough for policy-relevant decisions (Shokraii & Yousef, 1998, p. 6).

If research on program effectiveness was inconclusive, there were also signs of parental discontent with existing programs. A 1988 Department of Education survey found that 80% of Cuban and Mexican parents were opposed to having their children receive instruction in their native language if it meant less time devoted to studying English (Chavez, 1991, p. 29). A 1996 survey of Hispanic parents found that 63% of the parents surveyed indicated that Hispanic students should be taught English as soon as possible and only 17% indicated that they should learn Spanish first (LaVelle, 1997). A major complaint from parents is that, once enrolled in bilingual programs, many children never rejoin their agemates in regular classes because they have missed so much of the work in the content subjects that they cannot keep up.

The 1997 passage of Proposition 227 in California, which imposed severe limitations on the role of bilingual education in the schools, was another indication of the dissatisfaction with outcomes of these programs. The assumptions on which this legislation was based are broad and may be open to question and qualification. One assumption states, "The public schools of California do a poor job of educating immigrant children, wasting financial resources on costly experimental language programs whose failure over the past two decades is demonstrated by the current high drop-out rates and low English literacy levels of many immigrant children" (Office of the California Attorney General 1997, Chapter 3 Article 1 s 300 (d)). However, as of the present writing, these rulings are part of the Educational Code of California. They acknowledge the obligation of the government and the schools to provide "all of California's children, regardless of ethnicity or national origin with the skills necessary to become productive members of our society" [ibid., 1 s (c)]. This law provides that all public school children shall "be taught English by being taught in English" in English language classrooms. Children who are "English learners" shall be educated through sheltered English immersion during a temporary transition period, not to exceed one year, after which they would be transferred to English language mainstream classrooms. Waivers for bilingual class placement are available for children whose parents request them and for children with special needs on the basis of clinical evaluations. The law also recognizes the need for community-based tutoring in English and makes provision for financial support for it. Overall, the provisions of the law are not so draconian as reports have suggested, but the degree of implementation in the school districts and long-term outcomes of the ruling remain to be seen.

Relationship to Learning Disabilities

It is recognized that schools have a moral obligation and constitutional duty to educate all children well regardless of national origin or ethnicity. A range of educational approaches has been developed, although research has generally failed to define an optimal program. It seems prudent to abandon the search for the one best way, and defer instead to local option to select those programs that most effectively meet the needs of a given community. Government agencies should respect the wisdom of local school districts to select among the range of existing models those that meet local needs as determined by local evaluations and local outcome studies. When students do not succeed, it is the school district's responsibility to investigate why well-intentioned, well-funded programs have failed.

One hypothesis suggested by the studies with Busqueda is that some of the students who remain year after year in bilingual programs are learning disabled in *any* language. This notion is further supported by the finding of the U.S. Department of Education study cited in the TESOL Advocacy Statement (1999) that 23% of the LEP students have limited skills in their native languages as well. This percentage, as well as the percentage of children who showed prereading deficiencies on Busqueda, is suspiciously close to the estimated incidence of learning disability. It seems reasonable to expect that such students need psychodiagnostic studies to help teachers understand the reasons for their problems. If they are found to have learning disabilities, they need approaches to language learning that take into account basic neuropsychological problems, as well as their limited English proficiency.

Changes in Family Constellations

Census Bureau statistics show changes in family constellations that can affect children with learning disabilities. Data from 1998 show that, for the first time in a majority of American families, the number of families in which both parents are employed exceeds the number in which only one parent is employed. In 1998, both parents were employed in 57% of the families, in contrast to 33% in 1976. When data are divided in terms of the age of children, the trend continued, with mothers of children under one year of age employed (usually part time) in 59% of the families, in contrast to 31% in 1976. With older children, the numbers increased to 73% in 1998, with 52% of these mothers in full-time jobs. Reasons for employment were in part economic, for 55% of dual-employed parents earned incomes above the $50,000 level. The increase may also reflect higher educational levels for women and broader employment opportunities. Of the college-educated mothers, 68% were employed, in contrast to 38% of the women who had not graduated from high school.

The implications of these data for students with learning disabilities lie in the crucial role parents, and particularly mothers, have played in educational support and advocacy for their children. Parents with both work and homemaking responsibilities often do not have the time required for assisting the learning-disabled student with school assignments, reviewing for tests, or collaborating on projects. Their limited time makes them less of a presence at parent-teacher functions, for conferences with teachers, for joining the class for trips, for monitoring their children's school progress. Finally, they have less time for advocacy in organizations for people with learning disabilities. The legislative gains on behalf of students with learning disabilities passed in the 1970s were accomplished largely because of the informing, advocating, lobbying efforts of parent organizations, like the Learning Disabilities Association of America.

Expansion of Early Childhood Services

The increasing employment of women outside the home, in addition to other forces, had a strong influence in the expansion of services for young children. The positive climate for such services was set by the popularity of Head Start, a strong survivor of the War on Poverty of the 1960s. Long-term research on the positive effects of early intervention was accumulating. It showed that money invested in preventive programs for at-risk children was well-spent in terms of health, educational, vocational, and motivational outcomes. These findings appear in greater detail in Chapters 10 and 12. There is strong evidence that prevention of disabilities is not only possible, but it is cheaper and better for the mental health of the children and their families.

The studies of early intervention also helped to influence the prevailing philosophy of many early education programs. The strong experimental findings produces a shift in program philosophy away from enrichment and life adjustment to a marked cognitive emphasis. The work of Jean Piaget focused interest on the stages of cognitive development in children. Other innovators developed teaching approaches, such as direct teaching, that translated the findings of cognitive psychology into classroom procedures. The passage of PL 99-457 gave legal support for the growing preschool services for young children at risk for learning disabilities. This law provided:

- Full rights and protections for handicapped children ages 3 through 5 years by the years 1990 to 1991.
- Noncategorical reporting of children, ages 3 through 5; they could be designated as "developmentally delayed" thus avoiding premature labeling with specific diagnoses.
- Increased federal contributions to support services.
- A new state grant program for infants and toddlers.
- Recognition that planning should include family services in an individual family service plan, rather than the IEP.
- Funding for demonstration and outreach projects through early education discretionary programs.

With the reconstitution of IDEA in 1997, these provisions became Part C of that law.

By 1996, 187,348 at-risk infants and toddlers were receiving services in a variety of settings: early intervention classrooms, family child care, outpatient service facilities, regular nursery schools, and residential facilities. By the 1996 to 1997 school year, 548,441 at-risk preschoolers were served under the Preschool Grants Program in public and private settings, including regular class, resource rooms, separate classes, separate schools, residential facilities, and homebound/hospital programs. The majority (51.6%) of the children were served in regular classrooms. With the exceptions of Hawaii and the District of Columbia (for which percentages served were 1.5% and 2.5% respectively), all the agencies reported serving between 3.2% and 7.2% of the young children in the estimated resident population. Thus, the final years of the twentieth century saw the building of foundations for services to children with special needs from birth to adulthood in the United States.

THE ROLE OF PARENTS

The idea of greater parental involvement in the education of children with learning disabilities was formalized in PL 94-142, although the informal activities of both individual parents and parent organizations were significant for many years prior to that time. The current IDEA recognizes the need for parents to have information about special education, so that they can participate actively in planning and decision making. Parents need understanding of the laws, the nature of the handicapping conditions, and skills for effective participation. IDEA provides for grants to fund parent training and information centers to fulfill some of these needs.

Parental advocacy may show up in many forms. There is, first of all, the advocacy on behalf of the students in their own families during diagnosis, intervention planning, schooling, and transitions. Second, there is advocacy in support of other parents in securing appropriate services for their children. This may take place in informal discussions, more formal meetings in connection with local organizations, or accompanying a parent to an IEP meeting, hearing, or other school procedure concerning individual children. Finally, there is the advocacy at policy-making levels that usually is carried on by organizations in contacts with legislators and program administrators at the local, state, and national levels. These activities are ongoing, not only because of the changes in personnel in organizations and governmental agencies, but also because of the appearances of families with newly diagnosed children with learning disabilities.

The Advocacy Committee, a standing committee of the Learning Disabilities Association of America, provides a fact sheet with some realistic advice for parents that is summarized here:

Commonsense Steps to Resolving Disagreements
between Parents and Schools

Before a meeting

- Review your child's record and be sure you understand how your child's disability affects his schoolwork.
- Have a clear vision of what your hopes and expectations are for your child.

- Know the laws that determine the rights your child has to a free public education.
- Prepare a list of your issues, then prioritize them and decide what the most important issues are at this time.
- Believe in yourself, your rights, your knowledge of your child's strengths and needs.

At the meeting—communicate effectively

- Engage in active listening to make sure that you understand accurately what the others are saying.
- Don't get personal or defensive with the other participants.
- Take someone with you to the meeting, a friend, another parent from your local LDA affiliate, or a volunteer who can support you by taking notes so that you can concentrate on listening and communicating.

Good practices and operating procedures

- Follow the chain of command and discuss your concerns and issues with the teacher. If you can't obtain results, find out who has the authority to make the necessary changes.
- Wear your problem-solving hat, be creative, offer solutions.
- Create a paper trail by keeping accurate, written records.

What can you do when you've reached an impasse?

- Call your state department of education special education coordinator for information on requirements, training, technical assistance, consultative services.
- Contact your district Civil Rights Coordinator to find out if your issue is a violation of civil rights laws.
- File a child complaint with your state department of education if you think your disagreement with the school represents a violation of the special education law.
- An impartial mediator might be able to help you and the school reach an agreement.
- When all else fails, you may request an impartial Due Process Hearing for issues that involve a disagreement about evaluation and eligibility for services, IEPs, and educational placements.

This fact sheet serves an excellent advocacy role by instructing parents on the levels of negotiation for the resolution of disagreements concerning schooling.

In addition to organizations such as the Association for Learning Disabilities of America (LDA) and Children with Hyperactive and Attention Deficit Disorder (CHADD) that focus on specific disorders, there are organizations that bring together many groups to work on behalf of people with disabilities. The National Council on Disabilities, whose members are appointed by the president, is charged with advising the president and Congress about disability policies. A January 25, 2000, report of this body focused on lack of compliance with IDEA requirements in many states. Using a multilayered oversight model, this group works within the system to strengthen Department of Education and Department of Justice activities to address these violations. Another organization, the Consortium for Citizens with Disabilities, brings together the combined efforts of 50 organizations representing the disability community on be-half of people with disabilities. Unlike situations in which disabilities compete for limited funds, the cooperative approach of these organizations in securing and main-taining services for all people with special needs is enlightened and effective (Justine Maloney, personal communication, November 2000).

INCREASED EDUCATIONAL CHOICES

Rumbles of discontent with the quality of American education began to be heard in the 1980s. The popular press reported instances where trivial courses replaced solid aca-demic studies. Parents found that their children were spending too much time on nonacademic courses. They were appalled at the low expectations at all instructional levels. There was little consensus about curriculum content; schools seemed to be re-sponding to the quest for relevance of the 1960s and nearly anything was considered worthy of academic credit. The decline in Scholastic Aptitude Test scores was ex-plained by the increase in the number of students who were taking these examinations. The National Assessment of Educational Progress reported embarrassingly low skill levels in reading and arithmetic. Noncredit remedial courses were commonplace at the college level. Ravitch (2000) summarized the situation: "Opening the doors of college to unprepared students was a sham sort of democratization. Real democracy in educa-tion would have required public schools to make sure that every high school graduate gained the literacy, numeracy, and other skills necessary for technical occupations and higher education" (p. 411).

In 1989, President George Bush invited the governors of all the states to a meeting in the hope of redirecting the course of education by establishing national goals and voluntary standards. President Clinton, at that time the Governor of Arkansas, took a leadership role in the movement toward establishing national educational standards. In 1994 as president, he fostered legislation to fund a federal board to certify national and state standards. There was much activity in the states in drafting standards, but no appointments were ever made to the federal board. When conservative legislators gained control of Congress later that year, the board was abolished.

The Department of Education, together with the National Endowment for the Hu-manities and the National Science Foundation encouraged organizations of educators to develop national curricula as a part of the reform movement the national goals gen-erated. Unfortunately, the resulting documents revealed the deep divisions between the academic fields and the day-to-day business of schooling.

Curriculum Revision

The curriculum offered by the National Association of Teachers of Mathematics took an approach that emphasized the students' construction of their own solutions to prob-lems through discovery and hypothesis building. While these are admirable skills for students to develop eventually, the curriculum did not provide for mastery of essential computational operations in a systematic fashion. To the dismay of parents and nonmathematicians, the association acknowledged that achieving an accurate solution was not an important objective.

The history standards, prepared by the National Center for History in the Schools, were intended to strengthen the historical content in the social studies curricula in the schools. In an attempt to broaden the horizon of students and to free them from rote learning of facts, the resulting document minimized the positive contributions of Western civilization and emphasized its failings to such an extent that both historians and parents questioned the value of the document.

The National Council of Teachers of English curriculum fostered an approach to reading and the language arts consonant with whole language practices, the failure of which is described in Chapter 1. Eventually, some modifications made the resulting curricula more acceptable, but this experience demonstrated how far out of touch professional educators were with the goals and aspirations of the country at large. It seemed apparent that leadership in educational reform would have to come from outside the field of professional education.

Searching for Alternatives to Public Education

Parents lost confidence in public schools in general and began to look for alternatives. Some parents decided to try home-schooling of their children as an alternative to local public schools. Although there had always been a few children educated at home because of the mobility of the family or the religious convictions of the families, the movement has grown considerably in recent years. Parents of students with learning disabilities sought services for them in private schools for learning-disabled children, even in cases in which adequate services were available in the local public schools as a result of special education legislation. While special private schools may be necessary for students with serious disabilities or in cases of multiple disabilities, this kind of isolated education violates the basic principle of "least restrictive environment" that is an essential management principle for people with disabilities. Such placements may involve either family sacrifices to pay the high costs of tuition in private settings or extensive litigation to secure payments by the school district. The result leads to situations in which the needs of the individual child often become lost in the struggle.

School Governance

Parents' suspicions that public school administrators do not consistently support special education efforts are confirmed in such research as that of Allington et al. (1999). These investigators interviewed school administrators in six school districts to determine (a) their perspectives of learning disabilities and (b) their districts' responses when such difficulties occurred. They found that the school administrators failed to perceive learning disability as a condition that was remediable through appropriate education, but tended to explain the low achievement of the children with learning disabilities by calling up images of "an unsatisfactory inventory shipped to the school by manufacturers (parents)." Virtually all of the explanations placed the school outside the central sphere of influence, offering few ideas for altering the current general education programs as a potential means of addressing the problems of at-risk children. The solution offered by the majority of these administrators was an administrative one: "ingrade retention" (i.e., staying back).

On the other hand, Larrivee, Semmel, and Gerber (1997) found a very different picture among the schools they studied. To investigate which variations in school organization account for their relative instructional effectiveness, they compared measures of academic performance, self-esteem, and school adjustment of children with learning disabilities with results of overall school environment ratings and teacher interviews. Their findings indicated that no single feature, structure, or organization of the school environment consistently indicated a school's standing or its relative effectiveness, based on student performance. Case studies of schools describe the combinations of variables that operated in individual cases to provide the effective environment for learning in the target samples.

Despite the evidence that intangibles in the total school environment appear to account for effective schools, some other solutions have been offered. A frequent solution is to bring the free market into the public schools. Private, for-profit companies have been engaged by school districts to take over the management of failing schools. One of the largest of these corporations is Edison Schools, which has taken over the management of schools attended by 57,000 students, 70% of whom are regarded as "disadvantaged." Yearly reports from this company indicate that test scores have improved each year in schools that it has taken over at a faster rate than have test scores in schools across the country. Although American Federation of Teachers affiliates in New York and Miami have worked with Edison to manage jointly some school programs, teachers' groups are not generally enthusiastic about for-profit management of schools. As might be expected, teachers' groups have been critical of Edison's enthusiastic reports of students' gains. A report of the American Federation of Teachers examined the publicly available state test data from Edison schools in eight states. In a comparison of Edison-administered schools and traditionally managed public schools serving similar students, the report found that while students in some Edison schools perform better than similar students elsewhere, the Edison students for the most part perform as well as or worse than students in comparable schools. Ultimately, the evaluation results lie with the methods of data analysis (gain scores vs. mean achievement scores). Definite conclusions depend on long-term outcomes that are not yet available.

School Vouchers

School vouchers are a frequently proposed method for introducing competition as a means of forcing public schools to improve in order to remain competitive. They appeal to many different segments of the population. Parents of children already enrolled in private schools see vouchers as a way to lighten the burden of tuition payments. Politicians on both sides of the aisle propose them as an extension of equal opportunity to families of limited incomes and to families of minority children. Administrators of religious schools see vouchers as a help in meeting their increasing school operating costs. Wealthy self-made philanthropists see vouchers as an opportunity to provide children in the inner cities with educational advantages that they, themselves, did not enjoy in their youth.

At present, more than 15,000 children use publicly financed vouchers to attend private schools, most of them in Cleveland, Milwaukee, and Florida. An additional 50,000 children have scholarships financed by philanthropists. The NEA President, Robert Chase, noted that voters in California and Michigan rejected school voucher proposals by 2-to-1 margins in the 2000 elections. Additionally, 28 other states have defeated or delayed voucher-related legislation this year. In court, federal appellate judges have rejected the use of tax money for parochial school education, on the principle of the separation of church and state. The few research results available on the topic are inconclusive at best (R. Rothstein, *New York Times,* 12/13/2000, p. B11).

While the National Education Association (NEA) agrees that parents have the option of sending their children to the nonpublic schools of their choice, it does not support this movement. NEA policy states, "Instead of diverting scarce school resources to vouchers for a select few, we should help public schools work for all students by instituting proven reform efforts to increase student achievement, improve teacher quality, and set high standards" (National Education Association Web site, 1999, p. 2). Consequences of widely adopted vouchers would seriously deplete the money available for public schools because voucher programs would transfer the funds for per pupil costs to the school chosen by the families. Furthermore, having a voucher does not guarantee wider educational opportunities to low-income families. The amount of transferable funds contained in a voucher would seldom meet the tuition costs of the private schools the families may aspire to. Finally, nonpublic schools have their own criteria for admission. It can be expected that the nonpublic schools would skim off high-achieving students and at the same time, reject admission to children with learning problems, who require more extensive (and expensive) educational services. The provisions of federal special education legislation do not apply to nonpublic schools and few, if any, provide these services. For students with learning disabilities, vouchers would appear to have few positive implications.

Vouchers presently are regarded as a lively issue with political and legal, as well as educational implications. Some millionaires are financing public relations campaigns that criticize the "monopoly of the public schools" and advocate replacing the term *voucher* with the more positively sounding word *choice.* It is to be hoped that the opportunity for all children to have a free, appropriate public education will not be diminished and that the unifying influence of public education in the United States will not be endangered by the voucher movement.

Charter Schools

Groups of parents, educators, community leaders, and for-profit companies have joined forces to create independent public schools known as *charter schools.* They are chartered by the state government education agencies, but are deregulated and autonomous in terms of the state education regulations, curriculum requirements, attendance regulations, budget controls, and special education services. Charter schools are established because their organizers believe they are more flexible, innovative, and capable of offering a more stimulating school environment than traditional schools that are bound by regulations and bureaucratic procedures. In return for their charters from the state governments, these schools are expected to show results, or face losing their charters. During the 1999 to 2000 school year, 1,800 charter schools operated countrywide. Some charters are new schools; others are converted from existing public schools. Many have specific curricular or instructional approaches. Some may be very traditional in character, requiring school uniforms and conformity to behavioral patterns reminiscent of the schools of past generations. Others take their orientation from the computer age and emphasize modern technology and science.

The National Education Association has expressed a number of concerns about the charter school movement:

- *Relative Homogeneity of Students.* Studies have shown that because of the small size of enrollments, charter schools tend to be relatively homogeneous with regard to race, socioeconomic status, and academic achievement. Special education requirements do not apply to charter schools. Few schools make provisions for students with learning disabilities, if they manage to be admitted.
- *Systems of Accountability.* Accountability in charter schools has been inconsistent and ill-defined. The NEA states, "Some enthusiastic educational administrators feel frustrated by traditional assessment methods. Researchers are finding that by commonly used measurements, charters have mixed success in increasing student achievement, with some schools showing strong gains, and others struggling or even failing" (NEA; Sund, 2000, p. 2).
- *Quality of Personnel.* The NEA reports that many teachers, particularly those hired by for-profit companies, are new to the field and have little opportunity for supervision by more experienced colleagues. Even experienced teachers who choose to work in charter schools because of the opportunity for educational innovation become frustrated by heavy workloads and lack of resources. Believing that essential services and rights of employees are key factors in successful schools, the NEA is currently working with its members in four states to create charter schools through its Charter Schools Initiative and to inform others of such educational innovations.

Wells, an expert in educational policy who has completed intensive studies of 10 charter schools in California, has raised similar concerns about charter schools. She found that differences in structure and purposes often make it impossible to hold charter schools to accountability. The schools she studied have not been models of innovation; few new curricula or teaching approaches have emerged to be shared with regular public schools. Even more impressive was her finding that the 10 charter schools she studied were not able to do more with less public money, as is often promised by advocates. She found that they relied on private funds to supplement revenues, so that in some California charter schools, 40% of operating costs came from private sources. Finally, she questioned the claim that charter schools broaden educational choices. By their limited recruitment efforts, strict admission standards, and requirements that parents sign contracts mandating active involvement, the California schools she studied actually narrowed the educational choices open to parents (New York University, 2000, p. 7).

What are the implications of charter schools for students with learning disabilities? Their autonomy insulates them from federal regulations to a great extent, but specific on-site observations are necessary for understanding the real issues involved. One such study investigating charter schools in Colorado was reported by McLaughlin and Henderson (1998). These investigators used documented reviews, surveys, interviews, and site visits to assess how students with disabilities access the schools and how special education services are provided in charter schools. They found a general lack of information flowing to charter schools about special education and a disparity in how services are funded and provided. Legal and administrative responsibilities for special education are not clear. However, they concluded that "some charter schools appear to offer individualized educational approaches that are perceived by many parents and teachers as meeting the needs of many students who had experienced learning as well as behavior problems in the public school" (McLaughlin & Henderson, 1998, p. 108).

If the schools in this report can be regarded as typical, enrollment in a charter school would not appear to be the placement of choice for a student with a learning disability. In review of the problems many of these schools face in adequacy of financing, resources, and staff, opportunities for children with learning disabilities to receive the necessary comprehensive diagnoses, targeted intervention, and transition services would appear to be uncertain at best.

A Naturalistic Experiment

Fiske and Ladd (2000), in their description of what are essentially charter schools and vouchers in New Zealand, strike a note of caution for any wholesale acceptance of these innovations. In 1989, New Zealand abolished its "heavy handed central education bureaucracy" and turned the running of each school over to a local board of trustees dominated by parents. A few years later, the reform program gave parents the right to choose which school their child would attend. These changes provided a long-term experiment with a combination of charter schools and vouchers called *Tomorrow's Schools*. The one important differences between this program and the charter schools of the United States is that all schools were included in the reform movement; no choice was offered.

The change to autonomy was welcomed by most educators. Fiske and Ladd report a downside in that administrative tasks once handled by the central education authority became the responsibility of individual schools. This transfer included record keeping associated with accountability, budgeting, hiring, dealing with boards of trustees, and marketing their services in the newly competitive educational marketplace. Another negative consequence was the difficulty, experienced particularly by schools in disadvantaged areas, in assembling trustees with financial, legal, and governing skills necessary for running a school. In these areas, as is not uncommon in the United States, more than half of the parents have had unfortunate school experiences and have found them unwelcoming at best. *Tomorrow's Schools* is asking some of these same people to run the schools.

Another negative consequences of New Zealand's school reform resulted from open school choice. Low-income parents found it hard to compete for their children's admission to the more desirable schools. They lacked information for selection and money to pay for transportation outside their neighborhoods. Furthermore, popular schools tended to turn down students who might be difficult to teach because of the effects of poverty, learning or behavior problems, or limited English proficiency. Despite the good intentions of the reforms to broaden educational opportunities for all children, the total effect was a greater polarization of schools, with some schools emerging as winners and others as losers, overwhelmed by the task of educating children hampered by poverty, language, and learning problems. After extensive analysis of outcomes of these self-governing schools, Fiske and Ladd warn American policy makers about counting on governance changes *alone* to solve the problems of troubled schools (Fiske & Ladd, 2000).

HIGH-STAKES TESTING

High-stakes testing has been defined as the use of standardized group achievement tests to make decisions with important consequences for individual students on matters of promotion and graduation and for schools and for teachers as a means of assessing the effectiveness of school programs. Although most educators and measurement specialists agree that crucial educational decisions should not be made on the basis of a single test, government policy makers have a good deal more confidence that the tests can be used to make decisions about promotion and graduation in the case of individuals and to determine educational effectiveness of a school or a teacher.

At the 1989 Educational Summit, the governors of all states agreed on the importance of establishing national goals for education. These goals, among other things, led to efforts to establish voluntary national standards that were expected to describe what children might be expected to learn in different grades in major academic subjects. The movement was derailed by the controversies between academicians and the general public concerning proposed curricula on which to base the standards and by the lack of any national review panel to oversee the establishment of national standards. However, President Clinton pledged to establish national standards and tests in an effort to improve education. In 1997, his proposal to create national tests in reading and mathematics brought testing to the top of the educational agenda and resulted in contentious debate by educators, parents, policy makers, and social scientists. Congress and President Clinton asked the National Research Council, through its Board on Testing and Assessment, to conduct fast-track studies of issues concerning the use of large-scale achievement tests as instruments of educational policy and in high-stakes decisions involving tracking, promotion, and graduation. These studies were commissioned to ensure that tests "are used properly and fairly." The Board on Testing and Assessment was to make written recommendations on appropriate methods, practices, and safeguards that (a) existing and new tests to assess student performance are not used in a discriminatory manner or inappropriately for student promotion, tracking, or graduation and (b) existing and new tests adequately assess students' reading and mathematics comprehension in the form most likely to yield accurate information regarding student achievement of reading and mathematics skills.

Acknowledging that tests may be seen as a means of raising academic standards, holding educators and students accountable for meeting those standards, and boosting public confidence in the schools, the National Research Council report cautions that the potential benefits of tests should be weighed against unintended negative consequences. It warned that testing policy should be sensitive to the *balance* among individual and collective benefits and costs of various tests and that the value of tests should be considered with the use of other information in making high-stakes decisions about students. Three principal criteria for determining whether a test use is appropriate were cited:

1. *Measurement Validity.* Whether a test is valid for a particular purpose and whether it measures accurately the test taker's knowledge in the content area being tested.
2. *Attribution of Cause.* Whether a student's performance on a test reflects knowledge and skill based on appropriate instruction or is attributable to poor instruction or to such factors as language barriers or disabilities unrelated to the skills being tested.
3. *Effectiveness of Treatment.* Whether test scores lead to placements and consequences that are educationally beneficial (Heubert & Hauser; National Research Council, 1999, p. 12).

The report states some basic principles for the appropriate use of tests for educational decision making. It cautioned that the general validity of a test is not nearly so important as its validity for the specific use that is being made. For example, tests are inappropriate for making decisions about promotion or graduation of individual students unless the content is aligned with existing curriculum of the schools the students attended. Thus for high-stakes decisions about individuals, tests should tap content domains these individuals have had opportunity to learn in the course of their education, rather than content that is believed to be "something that every high school graduate *should* know."

The report also cautions that tests are not perfect. Test items are samples of what might be asked in a given area. A test score is not an exact measure of student's skills or knowledge, but rather can be expected to vary within a margin of error defined by the reliability measures reported by the test's authors. In addition to the nature of the sample of test content and the statistical characteristics of the test, transitory factors, such as the student's health and motivation on the day the test was administered, affect the results for individual students. Thus the report strongly recommends that *no single test score should be regarded as a definitive measure of an individual student's knowledge* (Heubert & Hauser, 1991, p. 13). Other relevant information about a student's knowledge and skills should be taken into account for such decisions.

The report further recommends that test scores should not be used to justify a bad decision, pointing out that simple retention and repetition of a grade in school, without remedial or other instructional support, is damaging to the student. In the absence of effective services for low-performing students, better tests will not lead to better educational outcomes (Heubert & Hauser, 1991, p. 13).

On the other hand, the report points out some positive uses of tests. When relevant test standards are maintained, tests can be used to identify learning differences among students that need to be addressed in the curriculum and services provided. When test scores for ethnic minority students, English language learners, and students from low-income families reflect persistent inequalities in educational opportunity test patterns can assist school faculty in planning remedial measures to modify these inequities.

The report strongly states that accountability for educational outcomes is a shared responsibility of states, school districts, public officials, educators, parents, and students. In the belief that high standards cannot be established and maintained by imposing them on schools, the report recommends dissemination of information about the nature and interpretation of tests to the public and to school personnel and public officials. Only after implementing changes in teaching and curriculum, should tests be used for high-stakes decisions about individual mastery of the curriculum. It suggests that schools plan a gap of several years between the introduction of new tests and the attachment of high-stakes to individual performance, during which "schools may achieve the necessary alignment among tests, curriculum, and instruction." It reports danger in using a test that lacks "instructional validity" (i.e., a close correspondence between test content and instructional content).

This correspondence of instructional and test content does not imply that tests should drive the curriculum. The report specifically cautions against "teaching to the test." Test users are cautioned to respect the differences between genuine remedial education and coaching students to pass a test. Such coaching impoverishes the curriculum and fails to provide the broader academic skills the test is intended to measure.

The report states that students with disabilities and English language learners are particularly vulnerable to the negative consequences of tests and, therefore, require complex technical and policy provisions. Such students' participation in large-scale assessment is recommended so that schools are held accountable for their educational progress. It is recommended that testing for each such student should provide appropriate accommodations for the effect of the disability or the limited English proficiency on the subject matter being tested, while maintaining the validity of the test results among all students.

The report takes no position on whether the voluntary national tests being considered in 1997 (testing of reading in fourth grade and mathematics in eighth grade relative to the standards of the National Assessment of Educational Progress and the Third International Mathematics and Science Study) were practical or appropriate for their purpose, which was to inform students and their parents and teachers about their achievement in these skills. Furthermore, the report expressed a strong need for research on the intended benefits and unintended negative consequences of using high-stakes tests to make decisions about individuals.

What benefits would accrue to the students? Would the tests result in increased academic achievement? Reduced dropout rates? What type of accommodations had assisted disabled or LEP students in demonstrating their true abilities in the assessments? What safeguards for appropriate test use were developed? The report pointed out that compliance with the existing Joint Standards for Educational and Psychological Testing and the Code of Fair Testing Practices in Education is voluntary and dependent on the professional ethics of the test user. Enforcement of these standards is weak and legal action is expensive and so time-consuming that it may occur too late to protect the people affected by the negative consequences of misuse of tests.

The report of the National Research Council is thoughtful, temperate, and judicious. It shows that tests, used properly, can improve teaching, learning, and the quality of educational opportunity and that tests used improperly can result in inaccurate conclusions that may damage school systems, schools, teachers, and individual students. This report represents a balanced view of issues involved in high-stakes testing. However, only by reviewing the actions in the years following its dissemination can one see the limited extent to which the Report's recommendations and cautions were heeded.

First of all, there has been a rush to get tests in place in all the states. Information available as of January 2001 shows that 48 of the 50 states have tests in place or are in the planning stages. The only states that do not report any current testing activity are Iowa and Nebraska. Twenty-five states report a graduation test in effect or planned; seven states (Delaware, Florida, Louisiana, New York, North Carolina, Ohio, and South Carolina) report a promotion test in effect or in the planning stages (Pilotin, 2001, p. 10).

Response of education-oriented organizations has been critical of high-stakes testing. In a letter to the editor of *USA Today* headed "High Stakes Testing Flunks" Monty Neil, the executive Director of the National Center for Fair and Open Testing, deplores the "one-size-fits-all standardized exams (that) assume that every child learns the same day at the same time." Despite claims by proponents that high-stakes exams make students learn more, Neil claims that teachers take time away from the regular curriculum to drill students on how to beat a particular test. As an example of this, Neil cites the situation in Texas, a state that he calls "the poster-boy for high-stakes testing." He claims that, while scores on that state's high-stakes exam have risen, they failed to improve on the independent National Assessment of Educational Progress reading test. He complains that minorities whose parents do not speak standard English and students with disabilities are at particular risk because the fast-paced exams fail to assess their learning accurately (Neil, 1999, p. 1). Part of this criticism is unfair, because the problems of students with disabilities have been addressed.

Bob Chase, President of the National Educational Association, took a temperate approach. In his column in *NEA Today,* he described himself as "an outspoken advocate of standards-based reform" concerned because he feels that reform is being jeopardized by abuses and excesses involving high-stakes tests. He acknowledges that tests should be one facet of a multifaceted approach to assessing children's progress, but he warns that tests should not be allowed to drive curriculum, promotion, and graduation. Chase regards this as a fundamental mistake, noting that "there are important things we should be teaching that cannot be measured by tests." He suggests that school districts now engaged in designing accountability systems remember a quotation from Albert Einstein: "Not everything that counts can be counted, and not everything that can be counted counts" (Chase, 2001).

High-Stakes Testing and Students with Disabilities

The Office of Civil Rights has addressed the effects of high-stakes testing in a letter from Norma V. Cantu, Assistant Secretary. This letter cites principles of good assessment practices and shows how testing can be used to provide a quality education, "a key civil right for the twenty-first century" (Cantu, personal communication, 2000). While such advice is reassuring, there is little concrete evidence of the benefits of this aspect of educational reform.

A memorandum from the Office of Special Education and Rehabilitation (OSERS) of the U.S. Department of Education to State Directors of Special Education, addresses in detail the provisions schools must make in complying with the current regulations that require inclusion of children with special learning needs in high-stakes testing (Heumann & Warlick, 2000). This document emphasizes the need for assessment as a part of educational accountability because the information that is secured benefits students by measuring individual progress against standards and by evaluating programs. It further states, "Because of the benefits that accrue as the result of assessment, exclusion from assessments on the basis of disability, generally would violate Section 504 and ADA" (p. 1). The document points out the need for state and local policies to address individual modifications and accommodations in order that scores will be reported and used appropriately. State and local educational agencies should consider intended and unintended results of policies that may affect student opportunities, such as promotion and graduation (e.g., whether students receive regular diplomas or certificates of attendance on completing high school). The document also recognizes the challenge that assessment programs introduce in maintaining rigorous testing procedures, while at the same time, protecting the rights of students with disabilities to accommodations. One solution suggested is to collect additional portfolio evidence that allows a student to demonstrate competency in lieu of a single test score.

The OSERS memorandum defines the use of *alternate assessments* as mechanisms designed for students who are unable to participate in large-scale assessments, even when accommodations are provided. Alternate assessments need to be aligned with the curriculum so that they do not, in themselves, preclude students from access to the same benefits available to nondisabled students for their participation. Such terms as *out of level testing, aggregation and disaggregation of data, and statistically sound,* are defined in the document, which makes clear that the Department of Education intends to enforce the provisions of IDEA for inclusion of all special needs students in assessments insofar as possible.

Responses from Educators

The view of high-stakes testing from the field is somewhat more pessimistic than that conveyed from the highest levels of government. For example, two special educators with specialization in learning disabilities have written persuasively that the potential negative effects of minimum competency exit examination for secondary school students with disabilities can outweigh the benefits (Manset & Washburn, 2000). Their paper traces the emergence of minimum competency tests for more than 20 years as a means of raising academic standards and "attaching politically acceptable benchmarks to the high school diploma." These authors do not find it surprising that there is lack of information on the impact of these tests on students with learning disabilities because educational reforms, in general, have been designed and implemented with little serious consideration of the impact on students with special learning needs. They suggest that their concerns may be irrelevant now, because reforms may be based on aggregate data, in which the results of students with learning disabilities will not be examined separately. Instructions from OSERS indicate that data for students with special learning needs should be disaggregated in reports, but that data would not be broken down in terms of disability categories (Heumann & Warlick, 2000, p. 10). Although schoolwide implications of the inclusion of test results of special education students in schoolwide data may be unimportant, these concerns will not be irrelevant in terms of individual students seeking high school diplomas. Manset and Washburn believe that these tests make special education students, already vulnerable to dropping out of school, even more so. Department of Education statistics indicate that while 13% of students without disabilities drop out of high school, 25% of students with disabilities do so. They cite data from MacMillan and Reschley (1998) showing that students who failed the minimal competency test were 10 times more likely to drop out than students who passed it. Although they admit the school-leaving decisions result from a complex set of factors, they point out that conditions that encourage students to persist—support and resources, opportunity for vocational training, opportunity for individualized instruction, tutoring, counseling—are less likely to be available in schools with less flexible, test-driven curricula. "By creating inflexible or seemingly irrelevant programming and increase opportunities for academic failure, the new graduation standards can further contribute to the disengagement of students with learning disabilities from school and increase the rate of students dropping out" (Manset & Washburn, 2000, p. 164).

Apart from theoretical considerations, the practical aspects of test quality also are causes for concern in the field. Much of the high-stakes testing has been implemented hurriedly, without the careful program development recommended in the National Research Council report.

After finding enormous failure rates on high-stakes examinations, nearly one-third of the 23 states that have drafted high-stakes examinations have reconsidered the passing grades or the length of the examinations. California, Maryland, Massachusetts, Delaware, Ohio, Wisconsin, and Alaska are scaling back original efforts. New York lowered its passing grade for the Regents Examination in English from 65 to 55. In Arizona, 88% of the sophomores failed the mathematics test and 72% failed the writing test. Ronald Pfeiffer, a state education spokesman said that Arizona had included calculus and trigonometry on the 10th-grade mathematics examination, subjects that most students would not be taught until 12th grade, if ever (Steinberg, 2000). New Jersey, after two years of giving the test to all the state's fourth graders, continued to experiment with how to score it (Moore, 2000, p. 11). Perhaps the most telling effect of the use of a single test score to determine policy and administration is seen in the experience of New York City, with a reading test that identified children required to attend summer school in 1999. Mayor Rudolph Giuliani and the then-School Chancellor, Rudy Crew, required that all students in the third through sixth grades who scored below the 15th percentile on the reading section of the CTB/McGraw Hill Achievement Test must attend summer school. By September, the Board of Education revealed that more than 8,668 were assigned to summer school because of an error, the miscalculation of the percentile scores, by the test publisher. More than five thousand of these children went to summer school, but 3,492 either never appeared or attended school, but failed to pass the retest given at the end of the summer. As it turned out, all of these children were promoted to the next grade unless their parents requested that they repeat the grade. Two district superintendents, identified by the test as leading "failing schools," were relieved of their positions. David Taggert, president of CTB/McGraw Hill, told Dr. Crew and the Board of Education: "Maybe the word apology isn't enough." Board policy, approved the following week, indicated that while next year administrators will continue to rely heavily on standardized tests, they will also take into account a portfolio of a student's classroom work, as well as attendance. This conclusion leads one to wonder how much the New York City Board of Education learned from the entire episode (Archibold, 1999, p. B8).

Disability Rights Advocates and the Oregon Case

Action on high-stakes testing in Oregon through the efforts of Disability Rights Advocates (DRA), an Oakland, California, based law-firm and advocacy organization for the rights of people with disabilities, resulted in a more hopeful outcome. The Oregon State Department of Education initiated high-stakes testing that determined not only high school graduation, but also type of high school diplomas and access to honors programs. A group of Oregon parents charged that Oregon State Department of Education "did not take into account the needs of children with learning disabilities when it devised the tests. And it is now implementing a testing system that will destroy educational attainments and self esteem, violate federal and state rights, and damage educational opportunities." Although the expected outcomes had been litigation in a class action suit, a Blue Ribbon Panel was appointed in 2000 to recommend resolution between the parents and the State Board by reviewing the Oregon Statewide Assessment System to determine the extent to which its provisions and implementation ensure that students with learning disabilities have equal opportunity to participate in and attain all the benefits of the statewide assessment program. The Blue Ribbon Panel reviewed the system and made recommendations to ensure "legally required and educationally sound" opportunities for students with learning disabilities. Details of the Panel's report are available in the DRA monograph, *Do No Harm: High Stakes Testing and Students with Learning Disabilities* (2001), but the underlying principles of the report are summarized here because of their general implications for other states:

- Students with learning disabilities should be provided with an option that leads to the Certificate of Initial Mastery (CIM) with or without accommodations or through alternative assessments.

- Tests should not assess the learning disability, but should provide alternative measures, scoring procedures that will assess in a specific area the extent to which a student is meeting or exceeding the benchmark for obtaining the CIM.
- The CIM should be scored, reported, and awarded separately by subject rather than across all subjects.
- Waivers of assessment should be specifically and narrowly defined and reserved only for students whose parents or guardians request them.
- A three-tiered appeals approach is proposed to include informal problem solving and formal problem solving at the local level and formal appeal at the state level.
- Expansion of information for parents and school personnel is recommended with systematic training in participant options, guidelines for accommodations, alternative assessments, and appeal procedures.
- Ongoing research is recommended on the nature of accommodations and such psychometric characteristics as reliability and validity of measures, and fairness of the testing system for students with disabilities.

Most significant of all was the principle that the Oregon System of Statewide Assessment should not be used for high-stakes consequences for individual students. To avoid unfair consequences for students with learning disabilities, the State Department of Education was advised to track potential misuses and to be proactive in its efforts to discourage inappropriate use of the CIM by any local school districts. These are thoughtful and innovative recommendations; yet to be seen are their outcomes in Oregon and in other parts of the nation.

Position of the American Educational Research Association

A position statement by the American Educational Research Association (AERA) summarizes professional policy on high-stakes testing. The statement is based on the 1999 *Standards for Educational and Psychological Testing,* a consensus on sound and appropriate test use by the three major organizations involved in measurement and test development, AERA, the American Psychological Association, and the National Council on Measurement in Education. This statement summarizes the possible serious consequences of testing programs for individuals, schools, and school districts. Enacted by policy makers to raise standards and encourage greater efforts by students, teachers, and administrators, reporting of test results may be beneficial in directing public attention to achievement disparities in the schools. However, if testing programs are implemented where educational resources are inadequate or where tests lack sufficient reliability and validity for their intended purposes, there is potential for serious harm. Policy makers may be misled by spurious test score increases that are unrelated to any real improvements in education; students may be placed at increased risk of failure and dropping out; teachers may be blamed or punished for inequitable resources; instruction may be distorted if high test scores, rather than broad learning, become the goal (AERA, 2000, p. 2). The AERA Policy Statement sets forth conditions essential to sound implementation of high-stakes educational testing programs:

- Protection against high-stakes decisions based on a single test.
- Validation of each separate intended use.
- Full disclosure of likely negative consequences of high-stakes testing programs to policy makers.
- Careful alignment between the test and the curriculum to avoid narrowing the curriculum to fit the test.
- Valid passing scores and achievement levels (distinguishing among such terms as "minimum competency," "grade level," "world class") and recognition of ranges of scores.
- Appropriate attention to language differences among examinees.
- Appropriate attention to students with disabilities.
- Specific rules and reporting of students exempted from testing.
- Sufficient reliability for each intended test use.
- Ongoing evaluation of intended and unintended effects of high-stakes testing through mandated resources set aside to evaluate consequences of tests.

Although not mentioned in any of the comments on high-stakes testing, the matter of cost also needs to be considered. Careful, continuing cost/benefits analyses should be done as part of any high-stakes testing program.

ADULTS WITH LEARNING DISABILITIES

Experience has shown that learning disability is a lifelong condition. It does not disappear at the end of elementary school or when one has managed to attain grade-level achievement in reading. Although appropriate interdisciplinary diagnosis and educational interventions may help a student to deal with current educational requirements, each new set of symbols encountered (as in dealing with a foreign language) or set of organizational responsibilities may call up again the problems experienced during earlier years. Children with learning disabilities do indeed grow up and bring their basic problems in literacy along with them. The challenges are intensified as the literacy requirements of our economy have increased. As the United States has shifted from an industrial-based manufacturing economy to one that is based in technology, service, and information systems, the demands for literacy from its citizens have increased. Although overall the American population is better educated and more literate than at any time in its history, the rapid growth of technology places higher demands on these skills than ever before. The kinds of written materials are multiplying and citizens are expected to understand and use this wide-ranging information to earn a living and participate in our complex society. A substantial number of citizens have not attained the required levels of literacy to adapt to these changes; for these people, there is an imbalance between the educational demands of adult life and their levels of attainment. This imbalance was recognized by the governors of the states in the Educational Summit in 1989 in one of the six goals they adopted:

By the year 2000, every American will be literate and will possess the knowledge and skills necessary to compete in a global economy and exercise the rights and responsibilities of citizenship.

Although this goal was not realized, there has been discernible progress in some areas. Gradual increases in funding show the recognition of the problems by the federal government. The recommended budget item for grants to states for Adult Education Programs increased from $450 million in the fiscal year 2000 to $540 million for the year 2001. Additional amounts were recommended for leadership activities, prison, literacy services to youthful offenders, Even Start, Reading Excellence Act. Community technology centers also appear in the budget, so that the recommended total increased from $931,500,000 in 2000 to $1,183,500,000 in the 2001 budget.

Accommodations on Licensing Examinations

One might believe that, with legal provisions for educating individuals with disabilities entering their third decade and with the Americans with Disabilities Act (ADA) entering its second decade, adults with learning disabilities would be able to realize their professional goals to the full extent of their abilities. This is not always the case. Indeed, some adults complete their education and training only to find their entry into professions for which they are otherwise qualified beyond their grasp because of the examinations that govern licensing.

Learning disability is recognized as a developmental disability that has lifelong influences on the individuals who experience it. Unlike some other developmental disabilities, it does not remain as a static condition. It is remediable with appropriate education, but may manifest itself differently in terms of the stage of the person's development and the requirements of his or her lifestyle. The individual with learning disability, even with the benefits of appropriate educational intervention, continues to deal with academic tasks by methods that are different from those of nondisabled persons. These methods are observable clinically in their use of cues to deal with reading and writing tasks. Such cues may include verbalizing the syllables aloud or rereading text to use contextual cues in dealing with difficult words, visual motor cues to avoid errors in orientation or sequencing of letters in spelling, slow writing as they search their vocabularies to find words they know how to spell and to avoid words they can't. Such maneuvers take more time than required by the average person, who by adulthood has mastered these basic literacy components and handles them automatically. Bright, ambitious people with a history of learning disabilities are willing to expend the extra time and effort required. Enlightened schools, colleges, and professional schools encourage them by providing extended time accommodations with examinations when students request them and offer credible and timely documentation of their disabilities.

Unfortunately this is not a consistent practice with the licensing examinations in the professional fields of law and medicine. Decisions in these professional fields have resulted in much frustration, controversy, and litigation. The result is that some of the most promising young adults with learning disabilities are delayed or shut out of the practices of professions for which they have trained and are otherwise qualified.

Licensing Requirements

Admission to practice law is governed by rules and regulations established by courts, legislatures, and bar associations of the individual states. The regulations must not violate the requirements of due process and equal protection and must be related to the candidate's ability to practice law. Although there are slight differences in procedures in the various states, some general themes are discernible. An applicant must have good moral character, reside in (or be employed in) the state, be a graduate of an accredited law school, and pass the bar examination. State bar examinations, administered by bar examination commissions within each state, usually consist of two parts: a multistate examination of general legal content; and specific knowledge of the laws of the state. In addition, some states require a Multistate Professional Responsibility Examination, which tests professional ethics.

Examinations for physicians are administered by the National Board of Medical Examiners in three stages: Step 1, after the first two years of medical school; Step 2, on completion of didactic training; Step 3, on completion of training and as a prerequisite for licensing in the state in which the candidate expects to practice. In addition, examinations (often both written and practical) are given in the various medical specialties after residency. Thus individuals with learning disabilities face many challenging examinations before entering these professions.

Legal Provisions in Current Laws

The Americans with Disabilities Act (ADA) and Section 504 of the Rehabilitation Act of 1973 place an affirmative legal obligation on those who administer examinations to ensure that individuals with disabilities taking the exams have a full and equal opportunity to demonstrate their knowledge, skills, and competency (Konecky & Wolinsky, 2000). When these laws were passed, Congress authorized the U.S. Department of Justice and the U.S. Department of Education to establish regulations for defining and enforcing the basic requirements of the laws. The regulations provide that the test administrators must ensure that the tests accurately reflect the applicants' abilities in the area being tested and *not* their disabilities. The entity providing the examinations must make reasonable accommodations to individuals with learning disabilities as necessary to ensure that the examination measures only the skills and knowledge it is designed to measure and not the limitations imposed by the applicants' disabilities.

The Definition of Disability

The right to have reasonable accommodations as provided by ADA and Section 504 is only available if the impairment rises to the level of a disability. A disability as defined in the statutes is "a physical or mental impairment that substantially limits one or more of the major life activities of the individual." These activities include reading, learning, writing, studying, test-taking, working, or any other basic activities that the average person in the general population can perform with little or no difficulty (Konecky & Wolinsky, 2000, p. 75). This definition is the center of many of the disputes concerning accommodations for law or medical school graduates. The testing entities question whether the law or medical school graduate with a learning disability can be considered substantially limited in the major life activity of reading if the individual performs better than the average person in the general population. The regulations further define the "most people" standard as applying to the individual who is restricted in the activity when compared with the "condition, manner, and duration" in which the average person in the general population performs that activity.

Although the "most people" criterion can be applied easily to medical judgment of physical or sensory disabilities, its application to people with learning disabilities has been problematic because of the complexities in the diagnosis of learning disability. The testing entities frequently reject the considered judgment of doctoral-level clinicians based on extended examinations that are submitted as part of the documentation by applicants. Instead, they search the reports for the few average scores that may be a small part of a clinical picture and then base their denial of accommodations on these specific test scores. It is not uncommon for the entities to deny a request for extended time accommodations for *reading comprehension* on the basis of an average score on a test of *oral reading* of single words. Another is to attack the clinician's choice of a specific test, as in the following quotation from a rejection letter to a medical student's request for extended time:

> Your evaluation was very thorough. However, though your score on the Woodcock Word Identification Test is in the average range, Word Attack is above average and consistent with verbal IQ. In addition it is the very superior score on the vocabulary that allows the verbal IQ to be in the high average range. It is noted that according to the Nelson-Denny Reading Test you have a slow rate of reading. However, it should be noted that the Nelson-Denny, as stated by its manufacturers is not intended as a diagnostic instrument for the identification of learning disabilities.

Thus the representative of the testing entity rationalized the rejection of the extended time accommodation by scouring the report for average or above scores on the tests that were irrelevant to the extended time accommodations requested. The letter further attempts to recalculate the IQ earned on the Wechsler Adult Intelligence Scale, and dismisses out of hand the Nelson-Denny Reading Test, one of the few measures of reading speed and comprehension currently available at the college level.

Apart from the presumptuous manner in which the reasons for the denial of accommodations is frequently made, the very concrete interpretation of the definition of learning disability (as defined by ADA and Section 504) leaves students in a difficult position. After having improved their literacy skills and met the demands of undergraduate education and professional schools, their hard work is rewarded by the decision that they read too well to be learning disabled. They have improved so much that they are no longer entitled to the protection of the laws. The actions of the testing agencies, in effect, shuts the gates leading to independent functioning in the professions for some of the most promising students with learning disabilities.

Testing entities justify these decisions in the belief that they are protecting the public from incompetent professionals. Although this is an admirable goal, it suggests that the testing entities may have more faith in written examinations as valid determinants of professional competence than is warranted. Common sense would dictate that decisions on professional competence might be better placed in the hands of the faculties of law schools and medical schools, where faculty members are professionals in their own field. They have the opportunity to observe students in academic settings, laboratories, and in clinics as they apply their knowledge over their years of training. As it stands today, the situation is unfair to the students and discouraging to their professors. It stands in opposition to the spirit in which professionals in the field of learning disabilities operate. Professionals working in the field of learning disabilities are not attempting to lower the standards in law and medicine, but are asking that the protection provided by the laws be extended to students who by their perseverance through law school and medical school demonstrate their potential contributions to society. The Americans with Disabilities Act and Section 504 do not guarantee that every person with a disability will pass the bar examination or the medical boards, but only that reasonable accommodations will permit them to demonstrate the full extent of their knowledge and skills in the professional field, in which they have completed their training.

The situation is, as yet, unresolved. Readers who would want greater detail concerning current litigation, the growing body of case law, and discussions of documentation are directed to the Spring 2000 issue of *Learning Disabilities: A Multidisciplinary Journal* published by the Learning Disabilities Association of America.

SUMMARY

The management of education is no longer left to educators. Socioeconomic, political, and legal forces have had a striking effect on how American children are taught during the past decade. Economic prosperity and population growth have brought reconsideration of school organization. The wider ethnic composition of American society has required that schools meet the changing ethnic and cultural backgrounds of the student body. Changes in family constellations, particularly the rise in the number of women employed outside their homes, have produced changes in the organization and the content of early childhood education. The role of parents of children with special needs has been strengthened by the special education laws. Parents, in general, have taken a more active role in decision making about school curricula and teaching methods. They have joined with innovative educators in broadening school choices through homeschooling, vouchers, and charter schools. Greater concern about accountability is expressed by both parents and politicians. This concern is reflected in high-stakes testing, a movement fostered by political forces despite cautions expressed by professionals in educational measurement and special education. Lagging behind are adequate provisions for adults with learning disabilities, both those who are marginally employable because of inadequate literacy skills and those whose entry into licensed professions is delayed by narrow interpretation of the Americans with Disabilities Act and Section 504 of the 1973 Rehabilitation Act. It is to be hoped that the attention focused on education by these developments will result in progress toward solutions of the many problems facing American education.

Chapter 3 ──────────────────────────────────────

DEVELOPMENTS IN
THE NEUROSCIENCES

> *The new advances in neuro-imaging technologies make possible the creation of data bases of the anatomical structure of human brain development in addition to cognitive and perceptual development over the entire human life span.*
>
> —Robert W. Thatcher, 1996

Over the past 10 years, discoveries in the neurosciences have drastically increased our understanding of the genetics, the brain morphology, and even the brain function of children and adults with developmental learning disabilities, particularly developmental reading disabilities. This chapter summarizes these discoveries and reviews specific contributions of the program projects and the learning disability research centers funded by the National Institute of Child Health and Human Development.

NEUROIMAGING TECHNIQUES

Advances in brain morphology and brain function in dyslexia have been driven by technological advances in neuroimaging, new techniques to obtain high-resolution images of the brain at rest and as it performs relevant cognitive tasks. These new methods "provide a window through which to capture a glimpse of brain activity" (Rumsey & Eden, 1998). They include positron emission tomography (PET), single photon emission computerized tomography (SPECT), structural nuclear magnetic resonance imaging (MRI), functional magnetic resonance imaging (fMRI), and magnetic resonance spectroscopy (MRS). Computerized tomography (CT)—with its use of X-rays, its problem with artifacts, its poor resolution and contrast compared to MRI—has been superseded by MRI in dyslexia research. A brief review of the physics of these new technologies follows (for a detailed description, see Krasuski, Horwitz, & Rumsey, 1996).

Positron Emission Tomography (PET)

PET scan is based on the measurement of radioactivity produced by radioactive isotopes that are attached to tracer molecules and injected into the subject intravenously. As the isotype decays within the body and in the specific areas of interest in the brain, it emits gamma rays and positrons. The positron, as it is emitted, collides with an electron, annihilating both. In the process, it releases a pair of high-energy gamma rays. The gamma rays are counted by detectors positioned around the subject's head. The gamma ray counts are then mathematically transformed into quantitative measures of the physiological process of interest. The radioactive isotopes used are those of elements ubiquitous in the body (^{15}O, ^{11}C, ^{13}N) or those which can replace common elements (^{18}F, which can replace an H atom of deoxyglucose). All of these isotopes are proton emitters that, to minimize risk to the subject, have very short biological half-lives. The tracer to which the isotope is attached (and the molecule whose concentration PET indirectly measures) is one whose metabolism, as with deoxyglucose, or whose concentration, as with water (blood), we are interested in understanding. As a measure of glucose metabolism, deoxyglucose is used because it accumulates in the brain after its first metabolic step, phosphlorylation, permitting its measurement over the length of time ^{18}F remains radioactive. Thus, it provides a measurement of regional cerebral metabolic rates of glucose (rCMRglu). ^{15}O H_2O affords a measure of regional cerebral blood flow (rCBF). The presumption is that an increase in neuronal activity in a particular region of the brain will be accompanied by an increase in rCMRglu utilization and in rCBF, increased blood flow to the area. Neuronal activity, however, may be activation or inhibition. Each process may be energy demanding and regions of inhibition thus may be hypermetabolic or hypometabolic. While a PET scan can yield quantitative measures of regional blood flow, and has good spatial resolution (ability to discern two objects as separate), the radiation, even at low doses, makes it questionable for use in children. Further, the use of radio isotopes with short half-lives (minutes) requires a cyclotron to be within half-life of the scanner and makes the procedure costly.

Single Photon Emission Computerized Tomography (SPECT)

In contrast to PET, SPECT radioisotopes, xenon (^{133}Xe), technesium (^{99}Tc), and iodine (^{123}I) decay by emitting a single gamma ray, have long half-lives obviating the need for an on-site cyclotron, and are attached to tracers that have slow washout from the brain. This combination of low intensity radiation and long half-life permits multiple observations useful for quantification of regional cerebral blood flow. The principal isotopes used by SPECT allow for measurements of rCBF. Procedures however, are not well standardized and normative states are not as robust as in PET. A modification in SPECT technique gives promise of functional SPECT in which density, distribution, and receptor binding characteristics of neuroreceptors may be studied (Holman & Devous, 1992).

Nuclear Magnetic Resonance Imaging (MRI)

Nuclear magnetic resonance imaging (MRI) has become the preferred modality for anatomical studies of the brain, and functional MRI the preferred modality for study of blood flow and, indirectly, brain activity. The lack of ionizing radiation in MRI makes it safe for repeated scanning of single individuals including children. The principle behind the MRI is the magnetic movement of the protons and neutrons of atomic nuclei, which are in constant movement called spin. The single proton of the hydrogen nucleus has the largest magnetic movement of any atom. Without the application of external magnetic fields, the direction of each proton's magnetic field is random, causing the individual magnetic movements to cancel each other out. Such is the normal state of the brain. However, with application of the magnetic field strength of the MRI scanner (typically 0.5 to 2.5 teslas, equal to 10,000 to 50,000 times the earth's magnetic field), the protons will align parallel to the field, a low energy state, or antiparallel to the field, a high energy state. When the magnetic field emitted by the scanner is turned off, the protons return to a lower energy state and in doing so emit a radio frequency (RF) signal, called the free induction decay signal. This signal is detected by the receiver coil of the MRI scanner. The time for return of the proton to its original state, following discontinuing the MRI pulse, is called the relaxation time. This is divided into two phases: T2 an arresting of the alignment of the proton occurring in response to the MRI pulse, and T1, the return of the proton to its original orientation. T1 and T2 relaxations and proton densities are the physical properties of tissue being studied; tissues with short T1 relaxation times emit higher radio frequency signals. Structural MRI is used in the measurement of volume of selected brain areas, as found in groups of subjects, or across time in a single group. The outline of the brain or brain region on consecutive image slices can be traced and volume generated by adding the areas across slices. To control for differences in individual total volume of the brain, the volume of the region of interest is divided by the total brain volume; and so can yield comparable percentages among groups of the volume of the region of interest. In the corpus collosum where total volume is difficult to measure, cross-sectional size through the midsagittal slice may be done.

Functional Nuclear Magnetic Imaging (fMRI)

Functional MRI (fMRI) uses conventional MRI scanners to detect alterations in blood flow and blood volume in areas of the brain in response to tasks designed to study activation (function) of those areas. In contrast to anatomical MRI where group data are needed, in fMRI single individuals may be studied. The ability of fMRI to detect differences in blood flow stems from the finding that, contrary to the intuitive belief that neuronal activation reduces the oxygen level of venous blood from that region, the oxygenation of such blood is paradoxically greater. The reason is that in activated brain regions, the blood flow increases more than the oxygen utilized by activation. Hence the oxyhemoglobin to deoxyhemoglobin ratio actually increases in the capillary blood emanating from the activated areas (Ogawa, Lee, Kay, & Tank, 1990). Oxy and deoxyhemoglobin differ in susceptibility to the magnetic field induced by MRI; oxyhemoglobin is weakly responsive; deoxyhemoglobin is more strongly responsive to the applied magnetic field. Greater susceptibility causes a weaker signal. Signal strength thus depends on the ratio of oxyhemoglobin to deoxyhemoglobin in the blood vessels emanating from the area of interest. In practice, the lower the deoxyhemoglobin concentration and the greater the oxyhemoglobin concentration, the stronger the emitted RF signal from the surrounding brain tissue. This is the signal that is detected by the scanners. Like MRI, fMRI is not dependent on radiation and the time limits it imposes; the fMRI can generate hundreds of sequential images to analyze change across time; it can evaluate change in single subjects; it has better spatial resolution than PET or SPECT.

Nuclear Resonance Spectroscopy (NRS)

Nuclear resonance spectroscopy (NRS) (Minshew & Pettegrew, 1996a, 1996b) is an emerging technology with the capacity for investigating neural organization and its disorders. It does so because of its ability to measure localized changes in phosphate concentrations and membrane phospholipid metabolism by utilizing the naturally occurring isotopes of the phosphate nucleus (^{31}P) as it responds to the influence of an externally applied magnetic field and returns to its original state once the applied pulse is terminated. In doing so, it emits its excited state energy, as a resonance frequency. The receiving coil of the spectrometer records this signal as a continuous wave, called a free inductive decay. Fourier transformation produces a spectrum, with resonance peaks recorded quantitatively in time. A spectrum of molecules containing different energy levels may thus be obtained in producing *in vivo* and *in vitro* spectra of mammalian brain. With *in vivo* NRS, the phosphorus nuclear magnetic spectrum (^{31}PMRS) of the human brain at 11.7 teslas provides spectral peaks for phosphomonesters (PME), inorganic orthophosphates (Pi), phosphodiesters (PDE), phosphocreatine (PCr), the α, β, and γ phosphates of nucleotide triphosphates, and the α and β phosphate of nucleotide diphosphate. Thus NRS directly measures brain levels of adenosine diphosphate (ADP), adenosine triphosphate (ATP), phosphocreatine (PCr), and orthophosphate (P_1), molecules vitally important to metabolism of the cell. It measures steady state levels, whereas PET and SPECT measure rate of utilization of glucose or of oxygen. Changes in phospholipid metabolism in the development of the rat brain from newborn to senescence (Pettegrew, Panchalingam, Withers, McKeag, & Strychor, 1990) in aging and normal humans (Pettegrew, Panchalingam, Klunk, McClure, & Muenz, 1994), and in autism (Minshew, 1996) have been studied. Because growth spurts and growth changes involve parallel periodic and anatomical changes in phosphate concentrations, the naturally occurring P^{31} phosphate nucleus uniquely provides a method to assay developmental changes in membrane and synaptosomal structure. It is only a question of time until this technique is applied to developmental disorders.

NEUROIMAGING STUDIES

The Anatomical Background

Although gross morphological asymmetries of the mammalian brain have been known for many years, the relationship between these asymmetries and specific language disability has only recently been unfolding. As early as 1968, Geschwind and Levitsky found, in routine autopsies of unselected brains, that in approximately 65% to 70% of the brains examined, the left planum temporale was larger than the right, whereas in approximately 10% it was larger on the right, and in 20% to 25% there was no difference in planum size. Broca's area, too, has been found to be asymmetrical in routine autopsies of nondyslexic individuals, with the posterior third of Broca's region on the left containing greater surface area than the right. Also those areas of the angular gyrus related to language show the left brain larger than the right in most cases. The gross anatomical findings of asymmetry in areas related to language in these unselected brains are reflected in cytological differences as well. Microscopic evidence of a greater number of cells was found in the left Wernicke's area (area designated as Tpt) and in that portion of the left angular gyrus (designated as Pg) than the right (Eidelberg & Galaburda, 1982, 1984; Galaburda, Sanides, & Geschwind, 1978; N. Geschwind & Levitsky, 1968). Many of the gross and microscopic anatomical asymmetries described in the brains of adults and children are present, too, in the fetal human brain (Witelson & Pallie, 1973). Witelson (1985; Witelson & Kigar, 1988) found that the midsagittal area of the human corpus callosum obtained from postmortem measurement varied with tested hand preference. It was larger by 11% in left-handed and ambidextrous people than in those with consistently right-handed preferences. The relationship of these findings to dyslexia has not yet been documented.

The first anatomical study in dyslexia was done by Drake (1968) on the brain of a 12-year-old boy who died of a cerebellar hemorrhage. Although this child had defects in reading, writing, and calculation, there were complicating problems with the diagnosis. Hyperactivity, "dizzy spells," and blackouts were reported in the history. These reports raise questions about the purity of the dyslexia and thus render the relationship of the anatomical findings to dyslexia questionable. Galaburda (1989) approached the problem of the anatomical substrate for dyslexia on the basis of several questions:

- What is the evidence of an unusual brain underlying dyslexia?
- Could anatomical studies produce a description of the brain that would explain the observed behaviors in dyslexia?
- If a different architecture of the brain is demonstrated, what might be the cause of the change? At what level of development was this change initiated?

Observations were based on autopsies of eight people (six males and two females) diagnosed as dyslexic by experts in the field. Ages ranged from 12 to 88 years and included right-handers and left-handers and ambidextrous individuals. All earned IQs within the 100 to 130 range; all had had opportunities to learn to read. None had a significant psychiatric history. Galaburda acknowledged that this group may not represent the full spectrum of the disorder, but he was confident that they were all dyslexic individuals.

The first two major phenomena Galaburda observed relates to symmetry in language areas. He regards symmetry as an anatomical characteristic rather than an abnormality. Among unselected brains, only 20% to 25% are symmetrical; in *every one* of the eight dyslexic brains, however, the planum temporale is symmetrical. Galaburda (1989) concluded that this is a strong association statistically and that symmetry, a variation from the expected structure, is significant in the dyslexic brain. Further studies were directed toward describing the nerve-cell networks that underlie processing in these brains. Galaburda hypothesized that in unselected brains naturally occurring regressive events in neurogensis cause a decrease in the number of neurons in the right hemisphere, although the number of neurons in the left side does not change significantly. In other words, a differentiating characteristic of the dyslexic brains is that they have "too much language in the right." The normal asymmetries are observable early in human development, as early as 4 to 5 prenatal months. They can also be observed in studies of the development of the sensory cortex of animals in the laboratory (Galaburda, 1989, p. 74). Galaburda speculated on the functional effects of hemisphere specialization. He believes that the elimination of neurons is a physiological process observable in Type I neurons in response to environmental requirements. When too few are eliminated (as in the case of the dyslexic brains he examined), there is a less precise match with environmental requirements, as well as differences in connections that determine functional properties. Galaburda and others in his laboratory inferred from animal studies of the development of asymmetries, that the dyslexic brain may be excessively connected *between* the two hemispheres and not well enough connected *within* each hemisphere. The significance for language development, as Galaburda sees it, is that the dyslexic lacks the connectivity of structures within the left hemisphere to deal with the various subprocesses involved in language (Galaburda, 1989).

The second phenomenon Galaburda observed in the eight dyslexic brains he studied is evidence of ectopias, collections of neurons appearing outside expected locations and associated with distortion of the architecture of the brain. These evidences of *microdysgenesis* are focal and multiple, and they vary in the brains in both number and distribution. What is least variable about these foci is that all the brains have involvement in the anterior language area. In addition, two of the male brains and both female brains contain a cluster of abnormalities that are dramatically different from the microdysgenesis previously described. These findings are small scars that first were thought to be the results of minor strokes that occurred during the life of the person. However, staining of the scars indicate that they contained myelin, a finding that placed the scars early in the development of these individuals. The significance of these scars to language development is not clear from present observations. However, the presence of such scars in a strain of autoimmune laboratory mice (New Zealand Black mice) has led Galaburda to consider the contribution of autoimmune disorders to these anatomical findings. Galaburda's findings, if the eight brains in his laboratory are at all representative of the population of people with dyslexia, have special significance for the field of learning disorders. As with any new research, these formulations need to be considered in relation to what has already been learned about dyslexia in previous behavioral research and clinical observations, and in relation to more recent neuroimaging studies.

The findings that the brains of the dyslexic sample were consistently more anatomically symmetrical than those in an unselected sample is consistent with the results of investigations demonstrating that people with dyslexia are not well lateralized. Studies of dichotic digits, visual half fields, and tactile discrimination have all reached this general conclusion (see Chapter 11). Studies of cerebral blood flow suggest inefficient processing within the language hemisphere; this, too, would be consistent with the implications of disturbances in connectivity. The suggestion that these differences in brain architecture are pervasive and manifested early in life is also not inconsistent with the results of genetic studies. Galaburda points out, however, that symmetries of the cerebral cortex and focal areas of cortical malformations "sometimes—but not always affect the classical language areas . . ." and:

> . . . it also suggests that optimal functional capacity may be related to an optimal match between the numbers of neurons and connection in a neural net involved in a particular behavior, so that too little or too much is deleterious. Excess being the common factor on both the symmetry and the anomaly found in the dyslexic brains raises the possibility that in these individuals there may be generalized difficulty with developmental processing of some neural substrates both in normal development and in the elimination of developmental errors. (1991, p. 129)

Imaging Studies of Morphology

In the past few years, morphological data have been viewed through the techniques of neuroimaging. Imaging studies are not immune from the problems encountered in any other research on learning disability and on reading disabilities; namely, problems of heterogeneity of samples, conflicting definition, disparate demographic characteristics of samples and difference in imaging techniques. In current studies, the characteristics of the sample are in general well defined, but age, sex, intelligence, handedness—variables that influence the relative size of brain regions—were not always controlled, so that results across studies are not always comparable. Despite many contradictory findings, the "most recent studies of individuals with reading disabilities point to structural and functional abnormalities in bilateral perisylvian regions" (Filipek, Pennington, Simon, Filley, & DeFries, 1999, p. 43). As an example of contradictory findings, Hynd, Semrud-Clikeman, Lorys, Novey, and Eliopulus (1990) reported normal posterior widths (temporal-parietal-occipital areas) but smaller anterior widths (frontal) while Duara et al. (1991) using a different measurement technique found right larger than left posterior asymmetry and normal (right larger than left) frontal asymmetry. The findings of Duara et al. (1991) are replicated by other studies. Rumsey et al. (1996) found, on MRI, a "high incidence" of symmetry of temporal lobe volume in an uncontrolled study of adult males with severe dyslexia. Seven years later, Kushch et al. (1993) found symmetrical posterior and total superior lobe surface area in 9 male and 8 female dyslexics adults compared with 21 control subjects, matched for handedness. The findings are consistent with the anatomical findings of Galaburda.

The morphological findings of Galaburda (1989) and of Humphreys, Kaufmann, and Galaburda (1990) focused attention on the language areas of the brain, particularly the planum temporale. It is pointed out (Filipek, 1996) that the planum temporale is not a discrete structure with clearly defined borders. For example, R. L. Green et al. (1999) view the planum temporale as part of the caudal infrasylvian surface because of the similar cellular structure of the entire area. With this extended area measured, it was found to be slightly larger in 8 right-handed male dyslexic Dartmouth students than that in 8 control subjects with no left or right asymmetry. MRI studies of this area as reviewed by Filipek (1996) and Filipek et al. (1999) report varying methods for its measurement. Based on PET and MRI scans, there is variability in volume of the planum temporale, but there is currently insufficient evidence to confirm anomalous asymmetry in all dyslexic subjects based on neuroimaging studies. More concordant results have been in measures of insula size with significantly smaller bilateral insula size found in 75 twins with reading disability than in 22 control twins (Pennington, Filipek, et al., 1999).

The corpus callosum has also been investigated with neuroimaging techniques. The underlying reason for obtaining anatomical measures of the corpus calossum is that the reversal of the normal asymmetry of the brain in dyslexia may be related to anomalies in neural pathways connecting the hemispheres via the corpus calossum. The midsagittal area of the corpus calossum is reported to vary normally with handedness; with right-handed individuals having smaller area than nonconsistent right-handers or left-handers. The splenium (posterior fifth) receives fibers from the occipital cortex; fibers from superior temporal and posterior parietal cortex cross via the isthmus. Duara et al. (1991) found that in right-handed dyslexics the splenium was larger than in controls, whereas Larsen et al. (1992) found no difference in total callosal area or in area of the splenium in adolescents, mostly male with dyslexia. Hynd et al. (1995) found no difference in splenium size in a sample of children with dyslexia, but they found a reduction in size of the anterior fifth (genu) of the corpus callosum and correlation of smaller areas with poorer reading scores. Rumsey et al. (1996) found no differences in the anterior middle third, but the posterior third was larger in adult male dyslexics. This finding received confirmation by Nijiokiktjien, de Sonneville, and Vaal (1994) who found total callosal size increased in children with "familial" dyslexia. However, comorbid attention deficit disorder is a confounding factor, since there are reports of reductions in area of the posterior portion of the corpus callosum in attention deficit disorder.

Functional Imaging

Functional imaging studies, examining blood flow or glucose metabolism in selected areas of the brain, have—more clearly than anatomical studies—implicated the language area of the brain in dyslexic individuals as different from that in nondyslexic controls. Early studies, such as Rumsey et al. (1987) examined blood flow (Xenon inhalation) in right-handed dyslexic adults with three tasks all of which were initiated by visual inputs and responses indicated by pressing one of four buttons. These tasks were semantic classification involving reading a series of concrete nouns and classifying each in one of four categories, a judgment of line orientation requiring matching of the angle of the stimulus lines with one of four sample lines, and a number-matching task as an attentional baseline. During semantic classification, control subjects showed increased blood flow on the left side of the brain and during the line orientation task had increased blood flow on the right side of the brain. Contrary to expectation, the reading impaired group had a greater increase in blood flow than did controls; the impaired group "showed an exaggerated leftward asymmetry of blood flow during semantic classification and a trend toward an exaggerated rightward asymmetry during line orientation." The authors interpret this finding as a difficulty with hemispheric integration or inefficient allocation of cognitive resources (more effort had to be expended by dyslexic individuals to perform the same task as controls). In another early Xenon study, Flowers, Wood, and Naylor (1991) found that accuracy on a task of listening to concrete nouns and identifying those with four letters, was correlated with increased blood flow only at Wernicke's area. However, poor readers had greater blood flow at the temporo-parietal region. The interpretations of these findings may reflect different cognitive strategies or the authors suggest that axons normally targeted for Wernicke's area, instead synapse in the temporo-parietal area.

A series of studies by Rumsey and her associates (Rumsey, Nace, & Andreason, 1995; Rumsey et al., 1992, 1994) used ^{15}O PET scan to measure cerebral blood flow in "severely dyslexic" men and matched controls in a series of tasks involving auditory stimuli and button-press response: (a) rhyme detection (listening to paired words and indicating which pairs rhymed) designated to probe the posterior language cortex, (b) auditory syntax task (listening to paired sentences that differed in grammatical structure and indicating which pairs had the same meaning) to probe anterior language cortex, (c) a tonal memory task (indicating which of paired sequences of 3 to 4 were identical) to probe right hemologous regions. With normal readers, the rhyme task activated the left temporo-parietal area near the angular gyrus and a left posterior temporal region near Wernicke's area, with lesser activation on right temporal and parietal cortices; the syntactic tasks activated left middle to anterior temporal as well as left temporal cortex. In subjects identified as dyslexic, the rhyme task in general failed to activate left temporo-parietal cortex and the left posterior temporal as in controls; the syntactic task showed normal patterns of activation of middle to anterior temporal and inferior frontal cortex despite mild performance deficits; the tonal memory task elicited activation of fewer right frontal temporal regions than it did in controls. Rumsey concludes (1996, p. 72):

> These findings suggest that neuropsychological deficits in severe cases of dyslexia are unlikely to be limited to phonological deficits. . . . severe uncompensated dyslexia is associated with involvement of widely distributed neural circuits, affecting bilateral temporal and other brain regions [and] cortical anomalies may be variably distributed and additional subcortical structures (i.e: thalamus) may be affected.

Hierarchical sequential tasks to study the progression of language functions in normal subjects were used by S. E. Petersen, Fox, Posner, Mintun, and Raichle (1988) via ^{15}O PET scans. The hierarchical tasks included (a) fixating vision on a blank screen, (b) viewing nouns, (c) reading nouns aloud, (d) viewing nouns when generating a semantic association. The extrastriate cortex was involved in processing visual words; the left temporo-parietal in phonological processing; the left prefrontal cortex in semantic association. Subsequent studies demonstrated activation of the left posterior temporal cortex in reading aloud. In 1998, S. E. Shaywitz et al. utilized a similar hierarchical series of five tasks to make progressively increasing phonological demands on subjects with reading disability and on controls. This study is discussed later in this chapter. In reviewing the brain activation patterns of dyslexic and control subjects in that study, dyslexics showed underactivation in the posterior language areas (left Wernicke, angular gyrus, and striate cortex) and relative overactivation in the inferior frontal gyrus and the right posterior persylvian region. Functional imaging studies using different paradigms have been reported by each of the Program Project and Research Centers supported by the NICHD. These studies are reviewed in this chapter following this general discussion of neuroimaging and electrophysiology.

ELECTROENCEPHALOGRAPHY, DIGITAL EEG, QUANTITATIVE EEG, EEG BRAIN MAPPING, AND EVENT-RELATED POTENTIALS

In the past 10 years, digital EEG technology has begun to replace the standard, most frequently used for clinical evaluations, analog paper-recorded EEG for electroencephalographic research in learning and memory. Digital EEG is the paperless acquisition and recording of the EEG via computer-based instrumentation with wave form storage in a digital format on electronic media and wave form display on an electronic monitor or other computer output device. Digital EEG has many advantages: It is flexible in the way EEG data may be displayed. It may be quantified. Quantitative EEG (QEEG) may include topographic display (EEG brain maps) of the frequency of each wave form, their voltage (power), the temporal relationships of frequency components at different recording sites (coherence). Statistical analysis may be asked to compare variables derived from digitally recorded EEGs between groups or between a subject and a group (i.e., comparison to normative values) and to perform discriminate function analysis. Also, it is admirably suited to record dynamic changes in EEG as the brain is challenged by tasks requiring the active processing of information.

All is not clear sailing, however. Studies on learning disabilities are plagued with the same generic research problems mentioned throughout this book: problems related to definition and classification of learning disability; the imprecise boundaries of samples under study; and the heterogeneity of learning disabilities, with differences in etiology, symptoms, treatment, and prognosis. Added to these generic problems are those inherent in the EEG technique itself. Traditional EEG artifacts can appear in unusual ways and new artifacts can be caused by data processing algorithms (e.g., eye movement may produce significant QEEG abnormalities; epileptiform spikes may be overlooked or misinterpreted; transient slowing may be missed). False positives with an average of 5% of the number of statistical tests run, can reach 15% to 20% in some individual control subjects. Changes seen statistically (e.g., decreased delta) may be clinically meaningless; others are controversial (changes in coherence). And as in all studies, individual demographics, use of medication, and state of alertness must be considered (F. H. Duffy, Hughes, Miranda, Bernard, & Cook, 1994).

In a report of the American Academy of Neurology and the American Clinical Neurophysiology Society, Newer (1997) concludes, "Despite such potential advantage,

QEEG clinical usefulness is now quite limited, although it has potential for future applications." Nevertheless, QEEG along with fMRI and MRS is in active exploration.

Two of the pioneers in the use of QEEG in reading disabilities are Frank Duffy at the Children's Hospital Medical Center in Boston and E. Roy John at New York University College of Medicine. The Duffy technique reduces the complex wave forms obtained in the EEG in response to different testing conditions into their frequency components (spectra) and the quantity of the forms with that frequency (power). The result is a power spectrum plot for each frequency at each electrode. This technique reduces the complex data of the EEG into a set of four single numbers (a power for each spectral band) for each electrode. Topographical maps of the head, representing the power of each spectrum band, may now be drawn and displayed on a computer-driven color video screen. This technique, called brain electrical activity mapping (BEAM), has been widely adopted and is now available at many centers. The effect of sensory stimuli and of tasks requiring active processing of information on the topographical maps may be studied over time in a sequential display of images. Duffy has developed statistical methods (statistical probability mapping) to delineate regions in which brain electrical activity from an individual subject differs from that of a referenced population. In addition, differences between groups—such as those between dyslexics and controls—may be studied by comparing each point on the topographical maps evoked for each test in the control and dyslexic groups. The significance of differences between values for each point is determined by the standard two-sample statistic, which is then transformed into a "percentile index" that is, in turn, converted into a topographical image.

Two papers report the findings of these techniques for dyslexic boys. In the first (F. H. Duffy, Denckla, Bartels, & Sandini, 1980), with 8 dyslexic boys and 10 "normal" boys, ages 9 to 11, topographic mapping revealed four discrete regions of differences between the two groups, involving both hemispheres, the left more than the right. The eight dyslexics fulfilled the criteria for "dyslexia-pure," and full scale IQ scores (WISC-R) ranged from 94 to 114. Two of the children were left-handed, two were ambidextrous, and four were right-handed. The controls came from a socioeconomic group similar to that of the dyslexic children. Two controls were left-handed, one was ambidextrous, and seven were right-handed. The EEG was recorded during 10 different tasks, 2 of which involved "simple resting brain activity" with eyes opened and eyes closed and 8 of which were designed to activate either the left (speech and reading) or the right hemisphere (music and geometric figures) and both hemispheres together (paired visual-verbal associations). In addition, 2 evoked potential tasks (visual and auditory) and 1 requiring a difficult phonological discrimination were given. Significant percentile index differences between the two groups were found in four regions: bilateral medial frontal (supplementary motor); left antero-lateral-frontal (Broca's area); left mid-temporal (auditory associative); and left postero-lateral quadrant (Wernicke's areas, parietal associative areas, visual associative areas). The authors concluded that "dyslexia-pure may represent dysfunction within a complex and widely distributed brain system, not a discrete brain lesion" (F. H. Duffy et al. 1980, p. 417). In addition, there was greater mean alpha in response to event-related tasks in the dyslexic group, a finding in agreement with that of Fuller (1978), and which may signify underactivation of frontal systems in dyslexic boys. Of the test challenges, a sound-symbol association test and a phonetic discrimination test produced the greatest differences between groups. In the evoked-potential challenges, positive waves at 282 msec after visual stimulus (flashes from a strobe light) were found in the dyslexics, but negative waves at 282 msec were found in the controls; for the auditory evoked-potential differences, usually positive waves were found in the dyslexic children, whereas negative waves in the controls appeared at 114, 198, and 342 msec.

The BEAM data obtained in this study of 18 boys were used to identify diagnostic rules for dyslexia and were tested against similar data gathered from an additional group of six boys (three normal and three dyslexic). The 183 measures obtained in F. H. Duffy et al. (1980), were statistically reduced to the 55 that differentiated between control and dyslexic groups, and these, in turn were reduced to the 24 best discriminating features. Multivariate analysis, in which each subject was represented by the 10 highest ranking features, separated the dyslexic and normal groups. The combined analysis of EEG and evoked-potential features was superior to analysis of either alone. Ultimately, two features, the auditory evoked-potential task involving a difficult phonological discrimination and the auditory evoked-potential task involving clicks, were used to correctly identify five of the six test groups (all three normal and two of the three dyslexics), a diagnostic success of 80%. When all 24 subjects are considered (the 18 previously tested boys plus the 6 additional), a correct classification was obtained in about 90%. These diagnostic rules have yet to be applied to a larger number of children. Denckla (1985) reports preliminary results of 44 "dyslexic-pure" boys involving brain maps obtained with the BEAM technique. While differences in bilateral frontal regions characterized all dyslexic groups when compared with controls, the extent and magnitude of differences also are found in three dyslexic subgroups: the global language-disordered group had the greatest difference, followed by the anomic subgroup; fewer differences were found in the dysphonemic-sequencing disordered group.

In a 1990 paper, F. H. Duffy and McAnulty confirm the electrophysiological differences between subtypes of children with learning disability, the anomic, the dysphonemic, and the global subtypes and state that regions of difference may represent compensatory mechanisms rather than pathological changes.

The group at New York University Medical School (John, Prichep, Fridman, & Easton, 1988) derived a set of equations that transform data obtained from the resting EEG and from waves resulting from 58 tasks that challenge sensory, perceptual, and cognitive functions into standardized (Z statistics) form so that they may be compared with data obtained from a normative group. The technique is called *neurometrics*. The normative data from subjects, ages 6 to 16, include univariate and multivariate descriptions of absolute power, relative power (power for each frequency band divided by total power across the frequency bands), mean frequency, and coherence and asymmetry between homologous leads for both monopolar and bipolar derivations, all for delta, theta, alpha, and beta frequency bands. Evoked potentials and event-related potentials are recorded within 10 msec latency intervals for 500 msec after stimulus onset. "With these data an individual neurometric profile may be constructed for each patient, describing the statistically deviant measures and the regions in which they deviate from normal values" (Hughes, 1985, p. 81).

The normative data for children are based on 600 "normally" functioning children, ages 6 to 16. Approximately half of these are Swedish subjects, ages 1 to 21, whose normative data for 16 EEG features were described by Matousek and Petersen in 1973. To this group, John et al. (1980) added the same EEG features they found in 306 "healthy, normally functioning" American children, ages 6 to 16. The resulting 32 absolute power features were normalized as a relative power for each derivation, transformed so that the features could be expressed as Z scores. The range of values is reported to correspond well with that obtained from normal children in other countries.

The neurometrics technique was able to identify abnormality in approximately half of three different diagnostic groups: those at risk for neurological disorder, learning-disordered children with generalized disabilities, and learning-disordered children with specific learning disorders. Studying more specific learning disabilities, comparing normal children with verbal underachievers, with arithmetic underachievers, and with a group of "mixed" underachievement, John et al. (1988) found children with different patterns of underachievement to have different neurometric profiles.

The verbal underachievers had visually evoked potential amplitude differences in the left parietal and central areas, occurring at 200 to 350 msec after stimulus; the arithmetic underachievers had excess theta at the parieto-occipital locations; the mixed group had excessive delta and theta at the posterior regions. Differences in amplitude of visual evoked potential were seen in two domains presumably related to perceptual (at 100 to 200 msec) and cognitive processes (at 200 to 300 msec). This report of the New York University group is supported by the finding that, using visually presented discrete word stimuli, reading-disabled children appeared to have two peaks between 200 to 300 msec in the ensuing wave form, in contrast to one peak for normal readers.

Conversely, when the different neurometric profiles were examined, the theta-excess group showed poor performance on tasks requiring sustained attention, including reaction times and Digit Span; the delta-excess group had deficits in Digit Span and the Trail-Making test; the auditory evoked potential asymmetry group had more errors on Color Naming and Trail Making and longer delays on the Digit Span test. As John et al. (1988) pointed out, however, most of their reading-disordered children came from a special education facility and did not meet the criteria for "dyslexia pure." One other report (Yingling, Galin, Fein, Peltzman, & Davenport, 1986) described a low incidence of abnormal neurometric findings on a sample of pure dyslexics, with most subjects in both the normal readers and the poor readers groups neurometrically classified as normal. However, the same investigators (Galin et al., 1986) found EEG spectra difference in slow waves when dyslexics and normal controls were recorded while they read easy and difficult tasks, silently and orally. They suggested that the groups differ in reading strategies in these tasks. Support for these findings was found by Harmony et al. (1995), Rumsey, Coppola, Denckla, Hamburger, and Kruesi (1989), Byring, Salmi, Sainio, and Orn (1991), and Chabot, Merkin, Wood, Davenport, and

Serfontein (1996). Although there are variations in samples and in methodology in these studies, the Harmony group (1995) study is representative, finding that children with severe reading and writing difficulties had a greater number of slow waves (delta) in frontal-temporal regions than control children. Repeating the EEG records of 49 children in 2½ to 3¼ years, those with severe and even those with minor reading and writing difficulties, did not mature as did control children, retaining their stamp of immaturity, more diffuse theta absolute and relative power, and less alpha relative power. In a recent paper, D. L. Molfese, and Molfese (2000) suggested that reading problems can be identified by auditory event-related potentials recorded at birth. Recording speech and nonspeech syllables from 6 scalp electrodes discriminated between newborn babies who 8 years later would be characterized as dyslexic, poor, or normal readers.

Event-related potentials have also been recorded as wave forms appearing in defined miliseconds from the time the stimulus (event) is applied. With these techniques, disabled readers may be differentiated from controls by reduced amplitude of a positive wave appearing 500 msec (P300) after stimulation in tasks requiring discrimination or detection of unexpected or significant semantic elements. These findings are not robust. Stelmack, Saxe, Noldy-Cullum, Campbell, and Armitage (1988) explored the recognition memory for words in 7 reading-disabled boys and 10 control subjects at 7 to 12 years of age. The task was to read, silently, words visually presented on slides and to try to remember as many as possible in a subsequent memory test. There was an enhanced amplitude of the P200 component but a decreased amplitude of the N400 wave in both the acquisition and the memory tasks in reading-disabled children compared with the controls. These findings suggest differences in the early sensory stage of encoding and retrieval (P200) and semantic or memory search (N400). The N400 wave appears to be a sensitive indicator of the semantic relationship between a word and the context in which it occurs (Kutas & Hillyard, 1980).

A different approach using an event-related potential probe technique was taken by Shucard, Cummins, Gray, Larismith, and Welanka (1985). This study, part of the Colorado Reading Project, actively engaged subjects in an ongoing information-processing task, and while subjects performed these tasks, pairs of task-irrelevant tone pips were presented to them binaurally over headphones. Two experimental conditions, letter sounds and letter shapes, are described. The former required a visual-phonemic transfer; the latter visual-shape processing. In both conditions, the pattern of auditory event-related potential amplitude asymmetry found for disabled readers was opposite to that for normal readers, with reduced right-hemisphere responses for disabled readers, suggesting that these tasks involved "different cerebral processes" in the two groups studied (Shucard et al., 1985). This study is important because it is part of the Colorado Reading Project, whose electrophysiological findings may be integrated with neuropsychological and genetic ones.

Despite the methodological problems, the electrophysiology of event-related potentials and the quantitative study of neurometrics and of BEAM offer an additional parameter in which to study the brain as it is challenged with tasks that require the processing of information. When electrophysiology is correlated with neuropsychological and clinical data, the results will add another dimension to our understanding of learning disorders.

THE INFLUENCE OF THE NATIONAL INSTITUTE OF CHILD HEALTH AND HUMAN DEVELOPMENT (NICHD)

Although the NICHD, a part of the National Institute of Health (NIH), had funded research in disorders of language and cognition since 1963, the available funds were then mostly provided to individual investigators, who for the most part, were studying single aspects of the problem of learning disabilities consistent with their interest and training. By the middle to late 1970s, the continuing lack of agreement, even on a definition of learning disorders, emphasized the need for more systematic multidisciplinary, longitudinal, theory-based studies. In 1976, Public Law 94-142, the Education of all Handicapped Children Act, provided an impetus for these studies and NICHD initiated support for the multidisciplinary program of research already underway at the University of Colorado. In 1974, a conference on biobehaviorial measures of dyslexia made clear the need to fund studies that included the "biological and behavioral measures of dyslexia to define and sub-type dyslexia" (D. B. Gray & Kavanaugh, 1985, p. 9).

Subsequently, four program projects in addition to that at the University of Colorado were funded: at the Bowman Gray School of Medicine (1986), under the direction of Dr. Frank Wood, to study the relationship between poor reading and its neurological basis; at Yale University School of Medicine (1987), under the direction of Dr. Bennett Shaywitz, to develop a classification scheme for reading, mathematics, and attention disorders of children; at the University of Miami (1987), to Dr. Herbert Lubs, to investigate the role of genetics in dyslexia and, to Dr. Albert Galaburda (1987), to develop animal models of dyslexia and to study the neurological characteristics of individuals with dyslexia. In 1985, the Health Research Extension Act (Public Law 99-158) mandated the establishment of an Interagency Committee on Learning Disabilities to review and assess "federal research priorities, activities, and funding regarding learning disabilities including central nervous system dysfunction in children" and recommended "that NICHD establish multidisciplinary research centers to carry out prospective, longitudinal investigation" to illuminate the causes, developmental course, outcomes, and treatment possibilities for individuals with learning and attention disorders. With this mandate, three Learning Disability Research Centers were funded, two of these three continued the work of the Program Projects: the Yale Center (1989), under the direction of Dr. Bennett Shaywitz, and the Colorado Center (1990), under the direction of Dr. John DeFries. The third Learning Disability Research Center at Johns Hopkins University (The Kennedy-Krieger Center) under the direction of Dr. Martha Denckla, was to study behavioral aspects of genetic anomalies (i.e., Fragile X, Turner's syndrome, and Tourette's syndrome) and find specific domain deficiencies characteristic of learning disabilities. Funding for research related to specific language disability went from $1.75 million in 1975 to $10.42 million in 1990, an aggregate total of $76 million.

By 1993, Moats and Lyon were able to report that as a result of studies from these centers, some basic assumptions concerning learning disabilities had to be modified:

- While male/female ratio found in clinics and in school-identified samples was approximately 4:1, the boys and girls were approximately equally reported in samples studied in the centers.
- Disorders of reading and attention may coexist, but the two disorders are distinct and separable and have different effects on reading and linguistics processing (Felton & Wood, 1989).
- Accurate and fluent reading ability depends on automatic recognition and decoding of words (Felton & Wood, 1989; Rack, Snowling, & Olson, 1992; S. E. Shaywitz, Shaywitz, Fletcher, & Escobar, 1990). The decoding process is related primarily to phonological processing skills (B. A. Shaywitz et al., 1991). Decoding ability and phonological processing are highly heritable (DeFries, Olson, Pennington, & Smith, 1991). Phonological deficits impede reading regardless of IQ. Thus, discrepancies between IQ and achievement do not adequately identify learning disabilities (see Chapter 5).
- Children with dyslexia differ from each other along a continuous distribution (DeFries, Olson, Pennington, & Smith, 1991; S. E. Shaywitz, Escobar, Shaywitz, Fletcher, & Makuch, 1992) and do not clump together in syndromes marked by distinctive diagnostic boundaries.
  (Author's note: This conclusion has been challenged by studies other than from the Yale Group; see Chapter 5.)
- Reading disabilities reflect a persistent deficit rather than a developmental lag. Longitudinal studies show that 74% of third-grade children with reading disabilities continue to read significantly below grade level in ninth grade (S. E. Shaywitz et al., 1999).
  (Author's note: This conclusion implies that a "persistent deficit" is immutable and cannot be modified. Appropriate and sufficient educational treatment can and does modify the deficit and changes a pessimistic prognosis to an optimistic one; see Chapter 8.)
- Deficient word recognition is associated with less than normal blood flow in occipital and prefrontal cortex of the brain.
- Systematic phonics instruction is more effective for disabled readers than a whole language approach.

The University of Colorado Learning Disability Research Center, Directed by John DeFries

The University of Colorado Center's major goal is "a comprehensive research program to use the methodology of behavioral genetics to assess the genetic and environmental etiologies of reading disabilities and their co-variation with measures of reading and language processes, ADHD, mathematics deficit and executive functions" (DeFries, Filpeck, et al., 1997). A common subject pool of 191 pairs of identical twins, 143 pairs of same-sex fraternal twins, and 99 pairs of opposite-sex fraternal twins in which at least one member of each pair has a "substantial" deficit in reading, math, and/or ADHD, along with a control sample of 170 pairs of monozygotic twins, 100 pairs of same-sex dizygotic, and 68 pairs of opposite-sex dizygotic twins, links the subjects of the component research programs. Six programs currently comprise the work of the LD Research Center:

1. Measurement of cognitive abilities and development and application of advanced behavioral-genetic analysis (John C. DeFries and David W. Fulker).
2. Reading and language processes (Richard K. Olson).
3. ADHD and executive function (Bruce F. Pennington).
4. Search for major genes or quantitative trait loci (Shelly D. Smith).
5. Computer-based remediation of reading and related deficits in phonological processing (Richard Olson and Barbara W. Wise).
6. MRI studies of twins' brain morphology and its relation to reading disability (Bruce Pennington and Pauline A. Filipek).

These important studies go back to 1973 when between then and 1996, 133 probands, their parents, and siblings were found to have substantial and highly significant deficits on measures of reading and processing speed when compared with 125 control children and their families for a total of 1,044 subjects, thus demonstrating the familial nature of reading disability (reviewed in DeFries, Knopik, & Wadsworth, 1999, p. 17).

In a 5-year follow up of 69 matched pairs of children in the original study (DeFries, 1985), the contributions of family (parental) influence on the magnitude of longitudinal stability of reading score on control children accounted for less than 1% of the stability over time, whereas for families of children with reading disabilities over 60% could be attributed to parental influences (genetic and/or family environment). Also sons of fathers who have reported problems learning to read have a 40% risk of developing a reading disability (seven times greater than normal assuming a 5% prevalence of reading disability); sons of mothers who report reading problems, have a 35% risk (5 times greater than if mothers do not have a reading problem). For daughters, the risk is lower (17% to 18%), but still 10 to 12 times the risk for daughters whose parents do not report having reading problems.

By 1982, sufficient twin data was available to consider analysis of genetic linkages. The concordance rate for MZ twins was 0.67, whereas that for the same-sex DZ pairs was 0.38 ($p = < 0.001$). Further support for a genetic factor in reading disabilities was obtained by DeFries and Fulker (1985). They hypothesized that the average scores in reading and in specific processing deficits of DZ twins should regress more toward the mean than the scores of MZ twins. This is because the DZ twins share only about one-half the segregating genes, whereas MZ twins are genetically identical. Also using the same hypothesis, the average regression scores toward the normal population mean of the DZ twins who do not have a reading disability will be greater than that of the MZ twins who do not have a reading disability. DeFries and Fulker formulated two multiple regression models; a basic equation in which the partial regression of the cotwins score on the coefficient of relationship provided a test for genetic etiology and a second equation to estimate the degree to which differences were due to shared environmental influences. Using these equations, DeFries and Alarcon (1996) estimate that half of the group deficit in word recognition, reading comprehension, and spelling is due to genetic factors; the heritability factor of word recognition, reading comprehension, and spelling equals 0.56. Deficits in phonological decoding, and problems in accuracy and fluency of word recognition had a hereditary factor of 0.6. These data suggest that these deficit functions have a strong genetic component. These effects appear to be independent of gender. However, the genetic influence appears greater in reading-disabled children with high IQs compared with those with low IQs (Olson, Rack, Conners, DeFries, & Fulker, 1991).

These studies supported and expanded earlier reports of the familial nature and heritability of reading disabilities. At the turn of the nineteenth century, C. J. Thomas (1905) had described "congenital word blindness" in two brothers and in another boy whose sister and mother also had "congenital word blindness." Hallgren (1950) carefully defining his criteria for specific dyslexia, found 81 children belonging to 77 families from the Psychiatric clinic of the Karolinski Institute in Stockholm, 22 additional children from a junior high school in Stockholm, and 9 children from a control population sample to fit his criteria. Ninety of his 112 cases had families with one affected parent and one or more affected siblings, 10 had both parents affected, 12 had no affected relatives. These data, reported Hallgren, were consistent with an autosomal dominant mode of inheritance. The ratio of male proband to female was 3.3:1. Although this study has been criticized because of Hallgren's failure to consider genetic heterogeneity (B. Childs, Finucci, & Preston, 1978), it was the first to provide presumptive evidence of familial transmission of developmental reading disabilities.

During the 1970s, reports from centers, in addition to Colorado, had reinforced the principle of the familial nature of developmental reading disabilities (Finucci, Guthrie, Childs, Abbey, & Childs, 1976; Owen, 1978). Owen (1978), for example, matched 76 sets of children who were 1½ to 2 years below grade level expectancy in reading and spelling (EH, "educationally handicapped") with successful academic (SA) children and found:

- Reading and spelling of *siblings* of EH children were significantly lower than controls.
- The WISC subtest scores of both EH children and their siblings were highly correlated in comprehension and similarities; for SA children the correlation was not significant. On the WISC performance scale, object assembly and coding scores were significantly correlated with reading and spelling for both EH and SA groups, but slightly higher for the EH group.

- The parents of EH children had academic problems in language in their school careers.
- Impairment in auditory tapped patterns, right-left discrimination, extinction in double simultaneous stimulation and difficulty with fast alternating finger and hand movements were found in EH children and their siblings.

By 1978, McClearn wrote, "There are bountiful data attesting to the familial nature of (developmental reading disability) and strong presumptive evidence that this familial distribution is due at least in part to genetic factors, (but) assessment of specific hypothesis concerning modes of inheritance has been confusing and inconclusive" (p. 287).

With these family studies as a background, the Colorado group focused on the identity of specific gene(s) and specific gene loci for developmental reading disabilities and related component skills. As early as 1983, Smith, Kimberling, Pennington, and Lubs, found that reading disability in 84 individuals from 9 extended families had apparently been transmitted in an autosomal dominant manner. Also cotransmission between reading disability and a marker on chromosome 15 occurred with high enough frequency (LOD score 3.2) to be significant. Since 70% of the LOD score, however, was due to one family, and another family yielded a negative score, this linkage analysis indicated that reading disability must be genetically heterogeneous. Linkage data from a larger sample (250 individuals from 21 families) yielded a LOD score of 1.33 for linkage between chromosome 15 and learning disability, a nonsignificant result (Smith, Pennington, Kimberling, & Ing, 1990b). Using markers (located near the HLA region) on chromosome 6 suggested some linkage to chromosome 6 but not to 15 (DeFries & Gillis, 1991). Subsequent linkage analysis used diagnostic data from sibling pairs who had been studied in the Colorado Research Center's extended family study and twin study. Results confirmed evidence for the presence of susceptibility loci for reading-related difficulties on both chromosomes 6 and 15; a possible Quantitative Trait Locus (QTL) for reading disability localized to a region on the short arm of chromosome 6 near the HLA complex and single word reading to a DNA marker on chromosome 15. Markers for phonological awareness and orthographic choice were linked to five DNA markers on chromosome 6p. Confirmation of these findings has been obtained by other independent laboratories.

As DeFries et al. (1999) points out, using the methods of these studies, additional markers may be used to determine more precisely the location of the gene(s). "It may eventually be possible to identify mutations in correlated genes in the regions that have a functional relationship to reading disabilities . . . such findings could be used to identify children at risk for reading disability . . . facilitating pre-school intervention" (p. 36). More than that, however, it may be possible to discover what the gene does to change function of the brain and possibly to correct the defect before learning disabilities even occur.

The Colorado group also has data on gender prevalence of reading disabilities. If children with reading problems are ascertained by referral from clinic populations, there is a male:female ratio of 3 to 4 boys to 1 girl; when drawn from the Colorado Twin study, there is a male:female ratio of 1:1 (DeFries et al., 1999).

The Yale University Learning Disability Research Center

In accordance with the charge of the Interdisciplinary Committee on Learning Disabilities (1987):

> The mission and focal point of the [Yale] Center is the development of a single, comprehensive, classification system for the range of the most common disorders that can influence school performance, that is learning and attention disorders. . . . a critical first step in the effort to describe the nature of cognitive and biological mechanisms in learning and attention disorders. (B. A. Shaywitz, Shaywitz, & Fletcher, 1992, p. 1)

Because reading disabilities encompass approximately 80% of children with learning disorders (Lerner, 1988), the Yale Group directed its attention to dyslexia.

They proposed a dual-level hierarchical classification of disorders of reading and learning (B. A. Shaywitz et al., 1991). At Level I, learning disabilities are classified into areas of academic impairment with 3 major areas proposed: reading, mathematics, and reading and mathematics. Three comparison groups are proposed: ADD children without mathematics disability and without reading disability, a cognitively below average/mentally deficit group, and a normal reading and mathematics group. Children with academic impairment, however, may have their impairment considered as a discrepancy between ability (as measured by comprehension cognitive testing) and achievement (as measured by achievement testing), or as occurring irrespective of a discrepancy. Thus, the Yale group includes 9 a priori groups in their study sample:

1. Discrepancy (ability/achievement) in reading.
2. Discrepancy (ability/achievement) in mathematics.
3. Discrepancy (ability/achievement) in reading and mathematics.
4. Low achievement (irrespective of a discrepancy) in reading.
5. Low achievement (irrespective of a discrepancy) in mathematics.
6. Low achievement (irrespective of a discrepancy) in reading and mathematics.
7. Attention deficit disorders without accompanying achievement deficit.
8. Average (do not meet criteria for groups 1 to 7).
9. Mentally deficient/below average with IQ in 60 to 79 range.

Also at Level I, children in the ADD group are considered as being with and without hyperactivity, each of whom may have behavior problems (oppositional/conduct disorder).

At Level II, the domains of academic achievement are classified by a battery of detailed neurolinguistic and neuropsychological tests reflecting the major dimensions of the reading task, including phonological awareness, short-term memory, and word finding, speech perception, speech production, morphological awareness, syntactic comprehension, and attention. On the basis of these data, reading disabilities and reading and mathematics disabilities are grouped into phonologic, phonologic-short-term memory and general cognitive areas of neuropsychological deficit. The ADD group at Level II is divided into three subtypes, disinhibited, overfocused, and behavioral.

An additional conceptual approach to defining reading disabilities is considered; those learning disciplines that are influenced by cognitive, attentional, and behavioral factors. Problems in these areas lead to the Level I categories. All Level I subtypes (academic domain) may lead to Level II (neuropsychological processes). All subtypes in turn may lead to Level III, a subdivision based on etiologies, with distinct mechanisms, differing causes, and response to different interventions. These are not discussed or spelled out but are a guide for future research. In Chapter 5 of this book, the possible etiological bases for learning disorders are discussed and form the basis for the metaphorical iceberg structure of learning disorders.

Data for testing their hypothetical constructs were derived from 445 children comprising the Yale Connecticut Longitudinal Study (S. E. Shaywitz et al., 1990). The sample was followed from kindergarten to third grade at the time these early papers were written and all children in the sample had comprehensive ability and achievement tests. The prevalence of dyslexia in this sample was 17.5% (Shaywitz, Fletcher, & Shaywitz, 1994b), and, contrary to the repeated observation that dyslexia was more prevalent in boys than girls (Finucci & Childs, 1981), in the Connecticut Longitudinal Sample 8.7% of reading-disabled children were male, 6.9% female; the prevalence of male and female dyslexics was reported as comparable (S. E. Shaywitz, Shaywitz, Fletcher, & Escobar, 1990). Shaywitz et al. (1990) states that the increased prevalence in males found in referrals from clinics and from school may reflect sampling bias inherent in school-identified samples. In contrast, when results are based on studies where all children in a population are individually tested, no sufficient difference in prevalence rates is found.

In a 1994 report of this sample (Francis, Shaywitz, Stuebing, Shaywitz, & Fletcher, 1994), 407 children were included. Screened in kindergarten, all children were assessed for progress in reading achievement every academic year from first through sixth grade using the reading subtests of the Woodcock-Johnson Psychoeducational Tests (Woodcock & Johnson, 1977). Intelligence testing using the Wechsler Intelligence Scale for Children-Revised (Wechsler, 1974) was done in first, third, and fifth grades. Using the Full Scale IQ of the WISC-R (≥ 80) as a measure of expectancy for decoding skills and a score representing an average of Word Identification and Word Attack Skills from the third-grade assessment, Francis et al. identified two groups of children with reading disabilities: (a) those with aptitude-achievement discrepancy RD, ($n = 32$) with WISC-R Full Scale IQ ≥ 80, on a regression-based achievement-FSIQ discrepancy of at least 1.5 standard deviation units; (b) low achievement (LA, $n = 12$) who did not meet criteria for RD but who scored at least 1.5 standard deviation units below average in comparison to their Full Scale IQ on the WISC-R.

Francis et al. (1994) conceptualized change as a continuous rather than an incremental process and developed a mathematical function that had the power to describe the change in learning of any skill, in a learning curve or learning trajectory for individual subjects over time. Thus, individual differences in growth rates, correlates of differences in growth rate, and the individual variations in growth rates as in reading will affect the final level of reading performance (i.e., the height or plateau of the curve) and the age at which the particular child reached that plateau. Application of the Francis formula in children from the Connecticut Longitudinal Sample found that growth curves describing discrepancy-based (RD) reading disabilities and curves of children who are poor readers but who are low in all aspects of performance (a low IQ, general reading backwardness) were qualitatively similar, differing only in severity. These data, according to B. A. Shaywitz and Shaywitz (1994), "lend further support to the notion that reading ability/disability occurs along a continuum and that dyslexia represents the lower tail of this distribution" (p. 63).

The growth curves of the sample in this study also reveal that the level of the plateau of children with reading disability is consistently lower than in children without reading disability and that there is no difference between groups in the age at which these children reach the plateau. These data are interpreted that, over time, children with reading disability continue to achieve below their peers without reading disability and support the hypothesis that reading disability represents a deficit not a lag. Francis et al. (1994) also found that factors that predict the plateau of the curve might also be examined. In this study, measures predicting reading achievement were related to tests of language function (letter identification, Boston Naming Test, Token Test, Horst reversal, naming of letter/sound in a word), consistent with other studies relating disability to abnormalities within the language system. The mathematical trajectories used in these studies may also be used to evaluate the effect of remediation on the growth trajectory and on the level of the ultimate plateau. Francis et al. point out, however, that for the implementation of this mathematical model, the measures of cognitive ability and academic achievement must be based on interval scale properties.

The 1990 to 1992 studies of the Yale center questioned two additional previously accepted concepts of the nature of dyslexia. Rather than consider dyslexia as an aberrant disorder, distinct from the normal distribution of reading abilities, B. A. Shaywitz, Shaywitz, et al. (1992) concluded that dyslexia represents the lower tail of a normal distribution of reading ability, part of the normal continuum not marked by a distinctive diagnostic boundary. The identification of subtypes then would be arbitrary depending on where cutoff points are set. Further, the present thinking that the gap between good and bad readers widens over time (the Matthew effect), a concept used to predict reading ability over time and to describe the developmental course of reading ability, was not verified (B. A. Shaywitz, Holford, et al., 1995). When reading achievement scores are plotted by grade, there is no significant relationship between reading achievement in the early grades and rate of change in reading; children who are reading at the lowest levels in early grades continue to read at a low level in later grades, and those reading at average or above-average levels in early grades continue to read well over time. The influence on intervention on the reading slope is not discussed. What Shaywitz may be saying is that without intervention, the deficit neuropsychological processes do not mature spontaneously.

In the past five years, the Yale Center has extended its work to include functional magnetic resonance imaging (fMRI), particularly observing changes in MRI as the subject is presented tasks that make demands on different brain functions and, by inference, observing activation of neural systems in particular brain regions responding to the different tasks. S. E. Shaywitz et al. (1998) used fMRI to compare brain activation patterns in dyslexic and nondyslexic subjects as they performed tasks that made progressively greater demands on phonological analysis. In this study, subjects viewed two simultaneously presented stimuli displays, one above the other, and were asked to make same/different judgments by pressing a response button if the displays matched on a given cognitive dimension (Pugh et al., 1996). Five tasks, ordered in hierarchical levels of difficulty were presented. At the lowest level was a line orientation judgment task, which tapped visual-spatial processing but made no orthographic demands. Second was a letter case judgment task, matching patterns in upper and lower case letters, adding an orthographic demand but no phonological demand; third, single letter rhyme match required a transcoding of the letters into phonological structure and then a phonological analysis to determine whether they rhymed; fourth, nonword rhyme required more complex phonology; and fifth, a semantic category required activation of the word meaning. Dyslexic subjects differed from normal readers most strikingly on the nonword rhyme task. Brain activation patterns differed markedly between dyslexic and normal readers with dyslexics showing relative underactivation in the posterior regions (Wernicke's area, angular gyrus, and striate cortex) and relative overactiviation in an anterior region (inferior frontal gyrus). "These findings add neurobiological support to cognitive/behavioral data, pointing to the critical role of phonological analysis and its impairment in dyslexia" (S. E. Shaywitz, 1999, p. 123). These findings also have implications for methodology in the remediation of reading disabilities.

The Johns Hopkins Kennedy Krieger Institute for Learning Disorders Research Center, Directed by Martha B. Denckla, M.D.

This Center's central research interest is "Neurodevelopmental Pathways to Learning Disabilities." The work of this center has spanned both biomedical and psychoeducational investigations: Biomedical investigations examine children with clinically defined disorders in which learning problems are a symptom; psychoeducational studies examine children across all projects whether or not a specific medical disorder is present. Significant early reports from this Center were concerned with the concept of "executive function": its definition; the primary constraints within the "executive function" model; the development of measuring instruments; their relation to ADD, ADHD, and learning disorders; and the utilization of imaging methods to correlate neuropsychological and electrophysiological functions with brain morphology (Denckla, 1994, 1996). The concept of executive function is discussed in Chapter 13 of this book.

A Medline search reveals that from 1990 through October 1999, 32 papers from this center with Denckla among the authors were published in refereed journals. These papers reflect a clinical, neuropsychological, genetic, and brain morphology (predominantly MRI) approach to the problem of learning disorders. The disorders studied include not only dyslexia and attention deficit disorder but also medical conditions that have as part of their clinical presentation, a disorder of learning; neurofibromatosis; fragile X syndrome, Turner's syndrome, and Tourette's syndrome.

Neurofibromatosis (Von Recklinghausen's disease) is characterized by benign tumors arising primarily from peripheral nerves, including the optic nerve, but may occur in the brain and spinal cord. It is most often clinically recognized by café au lait patches on the skin, typically seen at birth and by pigmentation of the iris which appears later in life. Approximately 60% of patients with neurofibromatosis have brain lesions that may be seen as bright objects with magnetic imaging resonance. A cognitive phenotype is described by the Kennedy-Krieger group. Hoffman, Harris, Bryan, and Denckla (1994) using neurocognitive testing and MRI, studied 12 families each having one child with Neurofibromatosis-1, an unaffected sibling of the same age range (6 to 16 years) and both biological parents. Children with NF-1 had significant learning problems in written language and reading ($p < 0.05$) and in neuromotor function ($p < 0.005$). A significant difference was found between each child with NF-1 and his sibling on Full Scale and on Verbal IQ of the WISC-III and on a visuospatial test (judgment of line orientation). Further, a significant lowering of the Full Scale IQ and visuospatial judgment was correlated with the number of brain lesions seen on MRI. A subsequent study found 77% of all subjects with NF-1 to have deeply located brain lesions; lesions in the basal ganglia and brain stem were seen in all age groups (children and young adults) "with relatively high frequency" while lesions in cerebellum and dentate nucleus were mainly found in patients younger than 10 years. It is possible that the brain lesions in the younger children are "probably transient" (T. Itoh et al., 1994). Only the number of locations occupied by the MRI identified lesions was correlated with a continuum of lowered IQs (Denckla, Hoffman, & Mazzocco, 1996).

The presence of a fragile X chromosome (fraX) causes the most common form of inherited mental retardation, with a known gene located at the fragile site (Xq21.3-q22) containing a trinucleotide repeat (cytosine-guanine-guanine), the number of which range from 200 to 3,000 in the full mutation (Suzanne, Sundheim, Ryan, et al., 1998). The protein encoded by this gene (FMRP) is related to the presence of fragile X retardation; a decrease or inactivation of the protein induces the fragile X syndrome. The fraX mutation inactivates the FMRP. Reiss, Freund, Baumgardner, Abrams, and Denckla (1995) report that most males with the full mutation function in the mentally retarded range of intelligence; females with the full mutation show a broader range of intelligence from mental retardation to normal IQ. Reiss, Abrams, Greenlaw, Freund, and Denckla (1995) found that subjects with the full mutation have increased volume of the caudate nucleus and in the male increased volume of the lateral ventricle. Both caudate and lateral ventricular volumes are correlated with IQ. In additional MRI studies Mostofsky et al. (1998), reported that in males with fraX, the cross-sectional area of the posterior vermis of the cerebellum was significantly smaller than in subjects with other causes for mental retardation and in normal subjects. Although in female subjects with fraX the posterior vermis was also smaller than in controls, it was larger than that in males with the fraX syndrome. The posterior vermis size predicted 10% to 23% of the variance in Full Scale, verbal, performance scales, Block Design, Wisconsin Card Sorting test, and the Range inventory.

Tourette's syndrome (TS) and Attention-Deficit/Hyperactivity Disorder (ADHD) were studied from clinical, neuropsychological, and brain-imaging perspectives. The morphology of the corpus callosum—its total area, five subregions, centerline length, parameters, and bending angle—was evaluated in 77 subjects ages 6 to 16 years, including 16 subjects with TS, 21 with TS and ADHD, 13 with ADHD, and 27 controls, using MRI (Baumgardner et al., 1996). The total area of the corpus callosum, four of its five subdivisions, and its parameter were greater in TS than in controls and in

ADHD children, while there was a significant decrease in the rostal area in ADHD. These differences were independent of age, handedness, and intracranial area. Among girls, however, there were no significant differences in size of the corpus callosum or any of five individual subregions between those with TS, TS with ADHD, and controls (Mostofsky, 1999). In children with ADHD, measurement of the area of the cerebellar vermis utilizing MIR morphometry (12 males with ADHD, 23 controls matched for age and for Full Scale IQ on the WISC) found that the area of the posterior vermis was significantly decreased in males with ADHD and that the inferior posterior lobe (lobules VIII–X) and not the superior postural lobe (VI–VII) was the area reduced (Mostofsky et al., 1998). An earlier study (Aylward, Reiss, Allan, Reader, & Singer, 1996) of 10 boys with ADHD, 16 with TS and ADHD, and 11 normal controls found that the boys with ADHD and those with TS and ADHD had significantly smaller volume of the left globus pallidus and smaller volume of the total globus pallidus than normal controls. The authors concluded that small globus pallidus volume, particularly on the left side, is associated with ADHD.

Neuropsychological correlates of learning disabilities (LD), ADHD, and TS were examined particularly in relation to measures of executive function. Denckla (1996), reviewing research in these disorders, suggested that neither attention nor long-term memory is a critical correlate of LD and ADHD. Instead, the critical deficits of ADHD and LD are in the encoding processes, particularly working memory. In ADHD, however, intention and inhibition are impaired. In a sample of 65 TS children, ages 6 to 14 years, formed in three groups—TS only, TS + ADHD, TS ± ADHD (the TS ± ADHD group was composed of children whose ADHD status was not strongly confirmed by the three different instruments used for the ADHD diagnosis), and a comparison group of 27 unaffected siblings who had no diagnosis of ADHD—23% of the total sample had LD but LD was not present in the TS only group. The TS only group was significantly poorer in the Letter Word Fluency Test (Schuerholz, Baumgardner, Singer, Reiss, & Denckla, 1996; see Chapter 15 for findings of other groups of investigators).

Neuromotor function was assessed in 3 groups of children of normal intelligence those with TS, TS + ADHD, and ADHD only. Using the Physical and Neurological Examination of Subtle-Signs, 76% of the TS only group, 54% of TS + ADHD, and 65% of ADHD only performed movements within normal limits for age, suggesting that TS is not associated with motor slowing (Schuerholz, 1997). A similar grouping was studied specifically for executive function deficits (E. L. Harris et al., 1995). Children with TS only had fewer executive function impairment and higher perceptual organization scores than those with TS + ADHD and those with ADHD alone. Neuropsychological and neuromotor functions were compared between boys and girls with TS, TS + ADHD, and ADHD only (Schuerholz, Singer, & Denckla, 1998). There were no timed neuromotor differences among the groups (see, however, 1996 report of Schuerholz et al. summarized earlier) but there was a group × gender difference for Letter Word Fluency and Rapid Automatized Naming Test with girls faster than boys on both tests. When data for girls were analyzed separately, those with TS + ADHD had greatest variability on the tests of attention and were slow on Letter Word Fluency. Girls with TS only, however, were slowest on Letter Word Fluency. (There is some inconsistency in the findings in neuropsychological tests among the papers reviewed. These are discussed in Chapters 9 to 11.)

The Dyslexic Program Project at Bowman-Gray School of Medicine, Directed by Frank Wood

This school of medicine was funded in 1986 to study the relationship between poor reading and neurological function. This center had uniquely available to it, the group of adults evaluated in their childhood during the years 1957 and 1972 by June Lyday Orton and whose childhood evaluations, including intelligence and achievement test scores, had been stored in the June Lyday and Samuel T. Orton Collection of the Columbia University Libraries. From the records of these former patients, it was possible to relate their reading ability in childhood to their cognitive skills in adulthood, independent of their adult reading ability. There were 115 subjects in the samples (age range 20.2 to 44.6, mean 33.1), 97 males, 18 females; all but 6 of whom had age-appropriate Wechsler Intelligence Test Scores, scores from reading subtest of the Wide Range Achievement Test (Jastak & Jastak, 1940), from the Gray Oral Reading Paragraphs (W. S. Gray, 1955) or from the Gilmore Oral Reading Test (Gilmore, 1951), and the IOTA Word Test (Monroe, 1935). On the basis of their childhood evaluations, the adults were classified as reading-disabled if their childhood reading quotients [Reading age $\times \frac{100}{CA}$ = Reading quotient (RQ)] were then 82 or less, as non-reading-disabled if their RQ > 91, and as borderline with RQ greater than 82 but less than 91. It is noted that this classification did not include a discrepancy from IQ. The adult cognitive phenotype was determined with a battery of neuropsychological tests including Wechsler Adult Intelligence Scale, revised and specific tests of phonemic awareness, naming, visuospatial skills, and memory. The reading disability group performed consistently worse than the other two groups on tests of memory, visual perceptual processing, visuomotor speed, and "mental flexibility." On the other hand, after differences in IQ and socioeconomic status were accounted for, the only processing tests of significant difference were tests of rapid naming, phonological awareness, and nonword reading tests. These results suggest that central processing effects found in children with reading disabilities will persist into their adulthood. This is so, even though the adults had improved in reading (Felton, Naylor, & Wood, 1990; F. Wood, Felton, Flowers, & Naylor, 1991). "The persistence of these phenotypic cognitive markers of phonemic processing and rapid naming deficits . . . into adulthood . . . (gives) strong impetus to the concept of a persisting constitutional defect" (Wood et al., 1991, p. 13).

The question of whether there are reliable cognitive-neuropsychological correlates of first-grade reading test performance and, if so, whether these correlates are separable from cognitive correlates of ADHD was investigated in a parallel series of studies of 485 randomly selected first graders from the Winston Salem-Forsyth County School system (F. Wood et al., 1991). Children were designated as reading disabled when the discrepancy between their score on the Word Identification Subtest of the Woodcock-Johnston Psychoeducational Battery was significantly (−2 standard deviations) below their score on the Peabody Picture Vocabulary Test. Children whose scores were within the −1 to +1 standard deviations range were considered nondiscrepant readers, those with discrepancies between −2 to −1 were considered borderline. Here, as in other studies, reading disability itself was "strongly related" to tests of rapid naming (Denckla & Rudel, 1976b), confrontation naming (Kaplan, Goodglass, & Weintraub, 1982) and phonemic awareness (Stanovich, Cunningham, & Cramer, 1984). Other language, visuospatial and memory tests were unrelated to reading disability. Further, ADHD and reading had separable cognitive effects, unrelating and noninteracting to each other (Felton et al., 1987; Harten et al., 1988). The authors note that these data do not exclude the possibility that deficits other than linguistic exist, but such subtypes have no measurable impact on group differences between dyslexic and normal readers.

Just as had been reported by the Yale group (S. E. Shaywitz et al., 1990), in this study of a random cross-section of the first-grade population of the Winston-Salem school system, the gender ratio of the children designated as dyslexic was no different from the gender ratio of the sample as a whole (53% male). Further, once vocabulary and age were known, race added no additional power to predict reading scores of first-grade children. However, when 350 of the original 485 children were tested with the Woodcock-Johnson Word Identification Subtest in third grade, race *was* a significant predictor of the 3rd grade reading scores. Other demographic variables involving parents' marital status, education, whether or not they were readers, or socioeconomic status could not account for that result. The question remains as to what factors in "race" are responsible for this finding.

The Bowman-Gray Center explored neuropsychological processing deficits other than phonological processing such as visual sequencing and visuospatial perception in reading-disabled and normal readers. A group of 93 children [$N = 39$, RD = 26, backward readers (no IQ achievement discrepancy) = 12] were compared on a visual competence game consisting of a temporal and an analogous spatial dot counting test. Results suggest that dyslexics performed worse on tasks that require fast, sequential visual processing and "that this impairment may be partially responsible for their reading difficulties" (Eden, 1995a). When the same group was given the Benton Judgment of Line Orientation Test, reading-disabled subjects performed significantly worse than normal readers, but similarly to the backward readers. Reading-disabled children had more difficulty with lines in the left hemifield and tended to scan the task in reverse order from that of the normal readers. The authors concluded that reading-disabled children not only have poor phonological awareness, but also have visuospatial deficits and that reading disability cannot solely be attributed to left-hemisphere dysfunction. There are other neuropsychological defects than phonological impairment, possibly caused by a "common mechanism" (Eden, 1995b; Eden, Stein, Wood, & Wood, 1996).

The neurobiological correlates of dyslexia have been a concern of this Center as they have been at Colorado, Yale, and Johns Hopkins. As the technique of neuroimaging has become increasingly sophisticated and perhaps more complex, the studies at Bowman-Gray have progressed from 133-Xenon regional cerebral blood flow (rCBF) method to integration of positive-emission tomography, magnetic resonance imaging, and evoked electrical potential. The 133-Xenon method with its relative safety and low cost permits observation of a task minutes in duration, with good resolution of blood flow in both gray and white matter, factors well-suited for monitoring macroneural correlates of language. Two separate samples using this method were studied: the first 69 subjects, healthy adults, right-handed with no history of reading problems; the second 83 subjects, 7 left-handed, 6 ambidextrous, a subset of the Orton cohort, subclassified into reading levels by their documented childhood reading scores. Each sample was given an orthographic task during rCBF measurement in which the subject was required to listen to common concrete nouns, occurring one every 2.5 seconds and to signal with a bilateral finger lift response if the word was exactly 4 letters long.

In the "normal" group with no history of reading problems, accuracy on the orthographic task was related to focal activation of the left Wernicke's area (posterior portion of left superior temporal gyrus). This finding was independent of IQ, gender, age, or task order. In the Orton cohort, there was an *inverse* relationship between childhood reading ability and blood flow at Wernicke's area (i.e., the poorer readers had the higher blood flow); and in the angular gyrus also, the RD group had a higher blood flow. The higher blood flow at the angular gyrus was independent of the accuracy of task performance. F. Wood et al. (1991) offer theoretical reasons for this phenomenon: (a) Lifelong dyslexia induces impoverished verbal experience, requiring additional effort and excess activation by subjects who perform poorly (compensatory theory); (b) different strategies are used by normal and dyslexic readers; (c) there is altered connectivity due to congenital lesions in the brain; (d) function is displaced from temporal lobe to angular gyrus as a compensatory measure. The finding of left temporal and angular gyrus activation in dyslexia suggests that dyslexia is not simply an extreme on the normal distribution but has features (e.g., angular gyrus activation) distinct for dyslexia that are not present in the normal population.

In the past 10 years, the Bowman-Gray Center has extended its investigation of neurophysiology and neuroanatomical correlates of behavioral measures of dyslexia (F. B. Wood, 1990; F. B. Wood & Flowers, 1999; F. B. Wood, Garrett, Hart, Flowers, & Absher, 1996), using positron emission tomography (PET), MRI, functional MRI (fMRI), and Event Related Potentials (ERP). In the 1999 PET study, 22 regional areas of the brain were selected for study. These regions were chosen because preliminary data indicated that increases or decreases in glucose utilization could be expected in these areas in relation to reading skill differences, attentional features, task performance, or other variables. The areas ranged from visual receptive areas (area 17) through parietal, temporal, and pretemporal cortex, to deeper areas of the brain (thalamus, striatum, hippocampus). Results are tabulated in terms of the brain areas encompassed by each, by their presumed neurobehavioral and dyslexic relevance and by results of previous neuroimaging studies. F. B. Wood and Flowers (1999) report on the first 100 subjects studied, 50 normal adults reading above the 25th percentile on both Word Identification (single word reading) and Word Attack (nonword reading-phonological decoding) subtests of the Woodcock–Johnson; 50 dyslexic adults, 31 of whom had been below the 25th percentile in their childhood psychometric records; 6 of whom were unselected normals scoring below the 10th percentile on both Word Identification and Word Attack. In addition, there were 13 blood relatives of affected probands. During recording of glucose uptake, an attentional standardization test was done, requiring a right index finger lift response if a letter instead of a nonletter is

flashed on the computer screen. The increase or decrease variation in glucose metabolism may be recorded in each of the regional areas of interest and may be studied between subjects. The glucose values in each of these areas, as they respond to the task,
were subjected to a principal component factor analysis using a verimax rotation. Nine
factors representing nine regions of the brain were identified: (a) bifrontal, (b) left
posterior, (c) rt. Sylvian/posterior, (d) bioccipital, (e) bicaudal/putamen, (f) bipari-
etal, (g) bilingual/hippocampal, (h) bithalamic, and (i) biorbital. To test the behavioral correlates of glucose utilization in these factors, three different phenotypes were
considered: (a) phonemic awareness (tested by auditory-oral test requiring phonemic
segmentation), (b) phonological decoding (nonword reading), and (c) single word reading. There were overlapping types, but phonological awareness was so defined regardless of the presence of any other phenotype; similarly single word reading was so
defined regardless of the presence of other phenotypes.

Phonemic awareness, phonological decoding, and single word reading each utilized glucose differently in three brain regions: inferior temporal-occipital, right
central frontal, and thalamic regions. F. B. Wood and Flowers (1999) suggest that
these clusters of regional brain activation may represent different aspects of reading
disabilities, perhaps different subtypes. For example, phonological "decoding" is reflected in increased glucose utilization in factor c (rt. Sylvian/posterior); phonemic
awareness is reflected in decreased utilization in region c but increased in factor g
(bilingual-hippocampal) single word decoding with increased glucose utilization in
factor h (bithalamic).

A study similar to that of 1999 in that it was a PET scan, measuring glucose utilization in specific regional brain areas in responses of normal adults to a letter recognition task was published in 1996 (F. B. Wood et al., 1996). It differed, however, in three
important ways:

1. It correlated PET scan with event-related electrical potential (ERP) generated
   simultaneously with PET scan glucose utilization during the letter recognition
   task.
2. There were 13 regional areas of interest in contrast to the 22 of the 1999 report.
3. The subjects were normal adult volunteers.

Thus, the focus was to correlate the higher temporal resolution (in terms of miliseconds) of the physiological events seen by ERP with the higher spatial resolution (the
order of millimeters) of PET scan, as the subject responded to a letter recognition task.
The technical details of the methods used in PET scans and in ERP electrode placement are described in the F. B. Wood et al. paper. However, the ERP generates a series
of waves that appear over time in response to the stimulus; the time is measured in
miliseconds, and the waves are described as they appear during the course of 900 ms.
For example, the P1 wave (1st positive wave) appears at 100 ms; N-7 at 700 ms. A correlation matrix between the PET (glucose utilization measured at the 13 areas of the
brain sampled) and ERP is presented. There were 13 significant correlations, 10 of
which were negative correlations; that is, the 10 areas had *inverse* not positive relationships between glucose metabolism and amplitude of ERP components. The extrastriate
visual association cortex (area 37) of the left hemisphere had metabolic activity that is

inversely correlated with the classic P3 component (P3 amplitudes are considered to reflect reaction to novel events), so that area 37 activity is related to reduced P3 amplitude. These results were unexpected. We would expect P3 to have a positive peak rather than a negative one with high glucose metabolism at area 37 or in the angular gyrus. Also unexpected was the finding that the left area 37 was the only brain region measured that showed significant correlation with task accuracy and this correlation is also an inverse one. These data may provisionally offer evidence that inverse correlations between PET and ERP measurements are not only possible, but likely. The authors state, "We cannot feasibly explain them [the results] by chance alone and must seek the beginnings of an explanation that is more complex than the simple notion that glucose metabolism and ERP amplitude both reflect a simple process of neuronal activity" (p. 203). The complexity of these findings evokes speculation as to their meanings in terms of brain function in response to task stimulation. The authors state that interpretation of the findings may "require a consideration of differential activity of separate neuronal populations within a given region" . . . "many correlations will reflect synchronous events occurring in widely different locations" . . . "most correlations will not be interpretable except by reference to task or subject variables" (p. 206).

The integration of data from neuroimaging techniques that can visualize and quantify the millisecond interactions of neural functions as well as the spatial dimensions of that function appears to be a direction of the future. With the application of non-invasive high spatial and temporal resolution imaging methods, "issues concerned with linear versus non-linear synaptic genesis, changes in strength and number of brain connections at different ages or the presence or absence of cyclic reorganization processes may be addressed through the use of these new techniques" (Thatcher, 1996, p. viii).

The University of Miami, Program Project, Directed by Dr. Herbert Lubs

At the University of Miami, a Program Project to study the genetics of dyslexia was funded in 1987, under the direction of Dr. Herbert Lubs. Dr. Lubs, a clinical geneticist previously on the team at the University of Colorado initiated a study of linkage to chromosome 15 in the three-generational families of dyslexics who appeared to transmit the disorder in an autosomal dominant mode (S. D. Smith, Kimberling, Pennington, & Lubs, 1983). By 1990, 20 families had been studied. The data were indeed consistent with an autosomal dominant mode of inheritance, but overall only 18% of the 20 families fit the hypothesis of linkage to chromosome 15, with the linkage near the centromere of 15 (S. D. Smith, Pennington, Kimberling, & Ing, 1990).

At Miami, Lubs continued these investigations to define chromosomal location of the several genes that produce autosomal dominant inherited dyslexia and "to define the effects each of these different genes produce on the form and function of the brains of people." "We start with a gene and then define its clinical expression" (Lubs et al., 1991, p. 89).

Initial study of 5 three-generational families with dyslexia had not confirmed the studies (S. D. Smith, Brower, Cardon, & DeFries, 1998; S. D. Smith et al., 1983, 1990b) linking dyslexia to chromosome 15. However, when the 35 polymorphic protein markers available at that time were used, there were two families with positive LOD scores with glyoxuylase, a marker for a locus on chromosome 6p (6p 21.3-21.11) and two other families had "slightly positive" LOD scores with the Rh blood group, a marker for chromosomes 1p (1p 36.2-p36.13) and for group GC, group-specific component on chromosome 4 (4q12-q13). Possible localization to chromosome 1p was also reported when the number of three-generational families was increased to 9 and when linkage analysis was done on these families with polymorphic protein markers (Rabin et al., 1993). Overall, the Miami studies supported the concept that dyslexia has a polygenetic origin.

The Miami project included, in addition to genetic analysis, immunological, visual physiology, neuropsychological, and neuroimaging studies.

Immunological Findings

Based on the N. Geschwind and Galaburda hypothesis (1985) that there was relationship between dyslexia, immunological abnormalities, and left-handedness, the Miami group found no increased frequency of "non-right handedness" and no increased frequency of autoimmune disease or atopic disorders in their sample. No antinuclear antibodies (ANA) were found. However, there was an interesting and unexplainable finding. In two females with dyslexia, there was an elevated T4/T8 ratio (high ratio of lymphocyte helper cells to lymphocyte suppressor cells). There is as yet no explanation for this finding.

Visual Information Processing

The group did find that some dyslexics had a visual information processing deficit, that dyslexics appeared to have temporal problems, requiring a longer time to perceive detailed visual information such as the letters in a word when compared with the nondyslexics. This is paralleled by findings in the auditory system with dyslexics requiring greater time than nondyslexics to perceive temporal sequences of auditory information. These findings are similar to those of Livingston in the visual system and Tallal in the auditory system. The implication of these findings is discussed later in this section and in Chapter 5.

Neuroimaging Studies

MRI measurements were done on 31 dyslexic and 30 nondyslexic adults. A progression in asymmetry was found in both groups; progression from right greater than left asymmetry anteriorly to left greater than right asymmetry posteriorly. However in the mid-posterior region, encompassing the angular gyrus, the groups differed with the right side larger than the left in the dyslexic group, the left larger than right in nondyslexics. In addition, the dyslexics had a relatively larger splenium of the corpus callosum; while female dyslexics had a significantly larger genu and total corpus callosum volume than male dyslexics and male and female nondyslexics. The reverse asymmetry of the dyslexic population is concordant with Galaburda's anatomical data.

Positron Emission Tomography

PET was done on 25 right-handed adult male volunteers reading aloud a list of simple words. A simple reading task produced widespread variations in metabolic activity in many brain regions. When normal readers were compared with impaired readers on the same task, significant difference in glucose metabolism was found in the prefrontal and the inferior visual (lingual) regions (Duara et al., 1989; Gross-Glen et al., in press). The inferior visual (lingual) area is part of the occipital-temporal pathway felt to be important for the identification of complex visual patterns. Lubs et al. (1991) state, "Taken together PET, MRI, and visual psychophysiological studies suggest a difference in visual system functioning for dyslexics, perhaps localized to extrastriatal regions adjacent to temporal and inferior parietal cortex" (p. 113).

The Miami group thus had converging evidence from two different experimental paradigms (neuropsychological and metabolic) that there is a problem in visual processing in individuals with reading disability. Subsequent work by groups other than Lubs (Livingstone, 1999; J. Stein & Walsh, 1997) suggested that dyslexia differs from controls in fast or phasic visual information processing, in poor contrast sensitivity, and in poor visual localization. These findings are subsumed by the dorsal (magnocellular) division of the visual pathway. This system is fast, has high contrast sensitivity, is color blind, and has slightly lower acuity than the ventral (parvocellular) division of the visual pathway which is slower, responsive to color contrast, and lower in contrast sensitivity. The magnocellular system may be responsible for spatial localization, depth perception, figure/ground perception, the position of objects in space, and movement of objects; the parvocellular with color perception and object recognition, and with analyzing a scene in "greater leisurely detail." The suggestion is made that a subset of individuals with reading disability will have a deficit in the magnocellular visual pathway. Because of this deficit, the image of the words on a paper cannot be spatially ordered fast enough to match the movements of the eyes during reading.

Livingstone (1999) offers a further observation for the deficit in the magnocellular system. Sensory systems in addition to the visual are functionally divided into fast and slow components. It is the rapid processing system that is phylogenetically the older system. An antibody called CAT 31 has been found (McGuire, Hockfield, & Goldman-Rakic, 1989) to selectively stain the magnocellular component of the visual system, selected somatosensory areas, and a subset of motor areas. Therefore, says Livingston, the neurons involved in fast information processing in each modality share specific molecular components. Individuals with dyslexia may have a deficit in many sensory systems with resulting difficulty in tasks requiring varying rapid processing of information. Tallal found a similar fast processing deficit in the auditory system. "This global system deficit may arise from effects on common proteins or damage at common developmental stages" (Livingstone, 1999, p. 89) (see Chapter 5).

SUMMARY

Techniques to visualize brain structure and brain function, particularly in children and adults with developmental dyslexia, have become increasingly available over the past 10 years. While findings across studies are not always comparable and contradictory results are many, the most recent studies comparing individuals with reading disability with control subjects point to structural and functional differences in areas of the brain subserving language. The lack of normal temporal lobe asymmetry suggested by Galaburda's anatomical findings, is consistent with a high incidence of symmetry of temporal lobes found by MRI in dyslexics. However, in portions of the temporal lobe such as the planum temporale, an area with ill defined borders, there is currently insufficient evidence to confirm anomalous asymmetry.

Functional imaging studies examining blood flow or glucose utilization in selected areas of the brain, as the individual responds to specific tasks, have more clearly than anatomical studies, implicated differences between reading disabilities and control subjects. For example, the activation (blood flow) of the left temporo-parietal area near the angular gyrus and a left posterior temporal region near Wernicke's area, seen in normal readers in response to a task that requires rhyming ability, was increased in dyslexic subjects. However, the neural circuits involved in dyslexia have been found to be widely distributed, consistent with the need for dyslexics to find alternate routes to compensate for their dysfunction or to expend more effort to perform the same tasks as controls.

Imaging studies are revealing not only patterns of brain function in response to sensory and cognitive stimuli, but also patterns as the functions mature and as the brain compensates by adjusting to developmental deviations. The trend now is to correlate data obtained from sets of imaging techniques. For example, data from evoked electrical potential (ERP), (electrophysiological) with that of PET scan (glucose metabolism), may be correlated thus obtaining data in high temporal resolution (ERP) and in high spatial resolution, PET.

The past decade has also seen results of research funded by the National Institute of Child Health and Human Development. This chapter details major contributions from each of five centers (the University of Colorado Learning Disability Research Center, Yale University, the Kennedy-Krieger Center at Johns Hopkins University, the Learning Disability Research Center at Bowman-Gray School of Medicine, and the University of Miami). Lyon (1996) has summarized these major findings in relation to the educational management of children with learning disabilities:

Definition of Learning Disabilities

- Definitions that measure the discrepancy between IQ and achievement do not adequately identify learning disabilities, particularly in the area of basic reading skills. (See, however, Chapter 4.)

Reading Processes

- Disabled readers with and without an IQ-achievement discrepancy show similar information processing, genetic, and neurophysiological profiles. This indicates that the existence of a discrepancy may not be a valid indicator of disabilities for all children with reading disabilities.
- Epidemiological studies indicate that as many females as males manifest dyslexia; however, schools identify three to four times more boys than girls.
- Reading disabilities reflect a persistent deficit rather than a developmental lag. Longitudinal studies show that, of those children who are reading disabled in the

third grade, approximately 74% continue to read significantly below grade level in the ninth grade. (*Note:* Educational intervention is not described.)

- Children with reading disability differ from one another and from other readers along a continuous distribution. They do not aggregate together to form a distinct "hump" separate from the normal distribution. (*Note:* Differing findings are reported in Chapter 11.)
- The ability to read and comprehend depends on rapid and automatic recognition and decoding of single words. Slow and inaccurate decoding may be one of the best predictors of deficits in reading comprehension. (*Note:* Individual children with learning disabilities may have a variety of neuropsychological defects. Review this chapter and Chapters 5 and 11.)
- The ability to decode single words accurately and fluently depends on the ability to segment words and syllables into phonemes. Deficits in phonological awareness reflect the core deficit in dyslexia. (See previous note above.)
- The best predictor of reading ability from kindergarten and first-grade performance is phoneme segmentation ability.

Attention

- A precise classification of disorders of attention is not yet available; however, operational definitions are emerging.
- Approximately 15% of students with reading disability also have a disorder of attention. Approximately 35% of students with disorders of attention also have reading disability. However, the two disorders are distinct and separable.
- Disorders of attention exacerbate the severity of reading disability.

Genetics

- There is strong evidence for a genetic basis for developmental reading disabilities, with deficits in phonological awareness reflecting the greatest degree of heritability.

Neurology

- Regional blood studies indicate that deficient word recognition skills are associated with less than normal activation in the occipital and prefrontal regions of the cortex.
- PET studies indicate that dyslexic adults have greater than normal activation in the occipital and prefrontal regions of the cortex.

Intervention

- Disabled readers do not readily acquire the alphabetic code because of deficits in phonological processing. Thus, disabled readers must be provided highly structured programs that explicitly teach application of phonological rules to print.
- Longitudinal data indicate that systematic phonics instruction results in more favorable outcomes for disabled readers than does a context-emphasis (whole language) approach.

PART II

DEFINITIONS AND CLASSIFICATION

Chapter 4

CURRENT DEFINITIONS: A REVIEW AND CRITIQUE

He who ignores history is doomed to repeat it.

—George Santayana

Although the problem of the intelligent child, growing up in an intact home, who is unable to read has been known for over a century (Morgan, 1896), we have not yet reached a consensus on a definition of learning disabilities (Berninger & Abbott, 1994). Yet so important, for practical and theoretical reasons as well as for education, social policy, and research, is such a consensus that in 1985 the United States Congress mandated the formation of an Interagency Committee on Learning Disabilities, one function of which was to develop a reliable and valid classification for a range of learning and attention disorders (PL 99-158). By 1992, a conference on measurement and assessment strategies for diagnosing and assessing individuals with learning disabilities was held (Lyon, 1994).

Diagnosis involves the assignment of exemplars to classes (Keogh, 1994). By its inclusionary and exclusionary provisions, diagnosis decides by fiat who has and who has not a learning disability. More often than not, this also decides who does and who does not get help for academic problems. For particular children, their educational future, as well as their socioeconomic and emotional destiny may hang on this decision. For their parents too, it may portend economic and emotional grief. The effects of definition reach out beyond the individual, however. For the schools, definition determines how many children with learning disabilities they must serve, what trained personnel they must have to work with these children, what physical space is needed, what teaching material—and how much all this will cost and where the money is to come from: whether from the school district, from the state, from federal funding, and ultimately from the taxpayer. The practical importance of definition is clear.

Accurate definitions, moreover, are essential to research. Samples under study must be specifically defined; the variables under investigation need to be relevant to the definition and the definition itself must be based on theory supported by research and clinical data using valid and replicable assessment instruments. To some extent, the inability of one group of investigators to replicate the findings of another may result from differences in definition. What may be true for the sample in one study may not be true for the sample, derived with different criteria, of another study. How then does one operationally define the heterogeneous array of disorders in so many domains of learning, listening, speaking, reading, comprehension, written language, spelling, math? How can one find the "critical constructs" within each domain? What test instruments currently exist to test these constructs, all within a developmental and socially relevant context?

HISTORICAL BACKGROUND

To understand the progress being made in answering these questions, it is helpful to review the evolution of current concepts from the historical definitions that have preceded them. Table 4.1 lists terms to describe learning disabilities that reveal the theoretical orientation behind them.

The early reports (Hinshelwood, 1917; Kerr, 1897; Morgan, 1896) refer to the inability to read despite being "bright and intelligent" (Morgan, 1896) as congenital word blindness. Hinshelwood defined congenital word blindness as a "congenital defect occurring in children with otherwise *normal and undamaged brains (italics ours)*, characterized by a disability in learning to read." Hinshelwood felt that this was presumably due to a congenital agenesis of the dominant angular gyrus. It is remarkable that recent anatomical studies suggest that Hinshelwood was not far from wrong.

The influenza epidemic of 1918, however, with its sequel of encephalitis in children and the resulting irritability, impulsiveness, hyperactivity, emotional lability, and learning problems observed in affected children, led to the thinking that *all* children who displayed behavioral and learning symptoms similar to those found in post-influenza encephalitis suffered from structural brain damage (E. D. Bond & Appel, 1931; Neal, 1942). E. Kahn and Cohen (1934) specifically related a hyperkinetic behavior disorder in children, to brain stem pathology, which they labeled as *organic driveness*. The same symptoms were described in children recovering from head injury (Blau, 1946) obstetrical casualty (Kawi & Pasamanick, 1959; Pasamanick, Rogers, & Liliendfeld, 1956), and prematurity (Shirley, 1939). The Kahn and Cohen paper and Pasamanick's *continuum of reproductive casualty* had great influence in reinforcing an organic stamp on behavior and learning disorders. The thinking in those years is summarized by L. A. Bender (1956) who, in reviewing the history of the Child Psychiatry Service at Bellevue Hospital in New York City, noted: "In the 1930's it was assumed that most of the children in residence at Bellevue Psychiatric Hospital were disturbed because of some form of brain damage."

Strauss and Werner (1943), Strauss and Lehtinen (1947), and Strauss and Kephart (1955) reinforced the *brain-injured theory* by reporting that the diagnosis of brain injury could be presumed on the basis of central processing defects, particularly in figure-ground perception and conceptual thinking. The complex of perceptual and cognitive defects described by the group from the Cove School in Racine, Wisconsin, became known as the Werner-Strauss syndrome.

Table 4.1 Historical definitions of learning disorders

Year	Definition
1887	Dyslexia (Berlin)
1895–1917	Congenital Word Blindness (Hinshelwood; Kerr; Morgan)
1922–1925	Postinfluenzal Behavioral Syndrome (Ebaugh; Hohman; Stryker)
1928	Strephosymbolia (Orton)
1929	Congenital Auditory Imperception (Worchester-Drought & Allen)
1934	Organic Driveness (Kahn & Cohen)
1941	Developmental Lag (L.A. Bender & Yarnell)
1943–1947	Brain-Injured or Damaged Child (Strauss & Lehtinen; Strauss & Werner)
1947	Minimally Brain-Damaged Child (Gesell & Amatruda)
1960	Psychoneurological Learning Disorders (Mykelbust & Boshes)
1962	Learning Disabilities (Kirk)
1962–1963	Minimal Brain Dysfunction (MBD) (Bax & MacKeith)
1963	Developmental Dyslexia (Critchley)
1967–1968	Specific Learning Disabilities (National Advisory Committee on Handicapped Children, USOE)
1969	Specific Learning Disabilities (P.L. 91-230)
1970	Psycholinguistic Learning Disabilities (Kirk & Kirk)
1977	Learning Disabilities (P.L. 94-142)
1980	Specific Developmental Disorders (*Diagnostic and Statistical Manual of Mental Disorders,* Third Edition)
1969	Specific Developmental Disorders (*Diagnostic and Statistical Manual of Mental Disorders,* Third Edition-revised)
1987	National Joint Committee on Learning Disabilities
1994	Learning Disorders (*DSM-IV*)
1994	Dyslexia (Orton Dyslexia Society Research Committee)

There was evidence that organic factors, such as the results of difficulties during pregnancy or labor, infections, or injuries, were implicated in behavior and learning in some children, but the term *brain injured* began to appear as a designation for *all* children with learning and behavior disorders, although in most of these children classical neurological examination and laboratory studies were entirely normal. Attempts were made to mitigate the implications of brain damaged, and the term *minimally brain damaged* was suggested by Gesell and Amatruda (1947). The term *minimal brain dysfunction,* suggested by an International Study Group in Child Neurology (1962) to remove the disturbing connotation of "damage," appeared. Aided by Ciba Pharmaceutical's promotion of Ritalin, the acronym MBD became widely used and was adopted by 1966 by a Task Force on Terminology and Identification sponsored by the National Society for Crippled Children and Adults and the National Institute of Neurological Disease and Blindness. In a resulting monograph, the concept of MBD was described in detail.

The term "minimal brain dysfunction syndrome" refers in this paper to children of near average, average, and above average intelligence with certain learning or behavioral disabilities ranging from mild to severe, which are associated with deviations of function of the central nervous system. These deviations may manifest themselves by various combinations of impairment of perception, conceptualization, language, memory, and control of attention, impulse, or motor function. Similar symptoms may or may not complicate the problems of children with cerebral palsy, epilepsy, mental retardation, blindness or deafness.

These aberrations may arise from genetic variations, biochemical irregularities, prenatal brain insults or other illnesses or injuries sustained during the years which are critical for the development and maturation of the central nervous system, or for unknown causes. The definition also allows for the possibility that early sensory deprivation could result in central nervous system alteration which may be permanent. During the school years a variety of learning disabilities is the most prominent manifestation of the condition which can be designated by this term. (Clements, 1966, pp. 9–10)

This definition encompasses such a heterogeneous group of symptoms, with such diverse etiology, that despite its acceptance, it hindered the search for conceptual clarity and did not meet the needs of educators who were faced with the problems of identification and the impossible task of teaching all the children who were so conveniently placed in the MBD category. By restricting the diagnosis to children of near-average, average, and above-average intelligence, it also excluded all children with less than "near average" intelligence.

The Retreat from MBD

Samuel Orton, a neurologist working first at the University of Iowa, then at Columbia University, presented conclusions he had drawn from almost 1,000 children with learning problems (Salmon Memorial lecture at the New York Academy of Science, 1937). Orton, like Hinshelwood, did not see these problems as stemming from brain damage, but from an aberrant development, possibly genetic, a delay or difficulty in establishing hemisphere specialization for language. Orton stressed the great variety in clinical symptoms, all relating to disorder in the acquisition of language. He described five main symptom complexes: developmental dyslexia, writing disability, developmental word deafness, motor speech delay, and developmental apraxia. Orton reasoned that because hemisphere specialization had not been established, information was received equally by both hemispheres; images from a nondominant side were not suppressed in awareness, so that symbols became mirrored images of each other, resulting in "twisted" symbols or *strephosymbolia*. Although his theoretical assumptions have not met the test of time, his clinical descriptions were superb, and his concept of a developmental, possibly hereditary factor, in nonorganic learning disabilities is valid today.

The retreat from MBD was seen clearly in the 1960s with terms such as *psychoneurological learning disorders* (Myklebust & Boshes, 1969); *psycholinguistic learning disorders* (Kirk, McCarthy, & Kirk, 1968; Myklebust, 1968); *primary reading retardation* (Rabinovitch, 1968); *primary, constitutional reading disability* (Critchley, 1964).

The term *learning disability* was proposed by Kirk (1962):

A learning disability refers to a retardation, disorder, or delayed development in one or more of the processes of speech, language, reading, spelling, writing or arithmetic resulting from possible cerebral dysfunction and/or emotional or behavioral disturbance and not from mental retardation, sensory deprivation, or cultural or instructional factors. (p. 261)

This early definition contributed substantially to the definition presented to Congress by the National Advisory Committee on Handicapped Children in 1967. The National Advisory Committee definition served as the basis for legislation, incorporated into the Education for all Handicapped Children Act (PL 94-142) of 1967 and appearing in the *Federal Register* in 1977:

The term "children with specific learning disabilities" means those children who have a disorder in one or more of the basic psychological processes involved in understanding or in using language, spoken or written, which disorder may manifest itself in imperfect ability to listen, think, speak, read, write, spell, or do mathematical calculations. Such disorders include such conditions as perceptual handicaps, brain injury, minimal brain dysfunction, dyslexia, and developmental aphasia. Such term does not include learning problems which are primarily the result of visual, hearing, or motor handicaps, of mental retardation, of emotional disturbance, or of environmental, cultural, or economic disadvantage. (National Advisory Committee on Handicapped Children, 1967 and U.S. Office of Education (USOE) *Federal Register* 42:250, 1977)

This definition remains as government policy. It attempts to restrict the definition to "children who have a disorder in one or more basic psychological processes"; it attempts to delineate domains in which that disorder is manifest and by its term *specific learning disabilities* removes the stigma of the term *brain dysfunction.*

However, the definition has many problems. It does not define the "basic psychological processes," offers no way of operationizing their characteristics, no ways of measuring them, and is vague about what constitutes a disorder in these processes. It includes "such conditions as perceptual handicaps, brain injury, minimal brain dysfuntion (MBD), dyslexia, and developmental aphasia." These are so heterogeneous a group of symptoms, with such diverse etiology that their inclusion only confuses definitions. Its exclusionary factors also raise questions; it "does not include learning problems which are primarily the result of visual, hearing or motor handicaps, of mental retardation, of emotional disturbance, or environmental, cultural or economic disadvantage." The application of these exclusionary criteria in any individual case, however, is not easy. The problems of real children are complex and multidetermined. Does learning disability occur independently of the exclusionary criteria? Does poverty produce a different kind of learning disability than does affluence? Can we separate emotional consequences of learning disability from the learning disability itself? Is it not possible that the organizational and retrieval problems associated with learning disability will result in intelligence scores that underestimate a child's potential abilities? How can the "primary" influence of the exclusionary factors be determined? These

inclusionary and exclusionary criteria, rather than simplifying the problems of definition, make it more complex. And as Eisenberg stated (1978), "The categories of exclusion will deny service to a significant number of children with learning disabilities,
particularly those who suffer from socioeconomic disadvantage and emotional disturbance" (p. 41).

Dissatisfaction with the 1967 and 1977 definitions has led to attempts at redefini-
tion. In 1981, representatives from six professional organizations concerned with
learning disabilities (American Speech and Hearing Association, Association for Children and Adults with Learning Disabilities, Council for Learning Disabilities, the
Division for Children with Communication Disorders, the International Reading Association, and the Orton Dyslexia Society) agreed on the following definition:

> Learning Disabilities is a generic term that refers to a heterogeneous group of disorders
> manifested by significant difficulties in the acquisition and use of listening, speaking,
> reading, writing, reasoning, or mathematical abilities. These disorders are intrinsic to
> the individual and presumed to be due to central nervous system dysfunction. Even
> though a learning disability may occur concomitantly with other handicapping condi-
> tions (i.e., sensory impairment, mental retardation), social and economic disturbances
> or environmental influences (i.e., cultural differences, insufficient/inappropriate in-
> struction, psychogenic factors), it is not the direct result of those conditions or influence.
> (Hammill, Leigh, McNutt, & Larsen, 1987, p. 109)

The revised definition clarified certain aspects of previous definitions. It emphasized
the heterogeneity of the domains of learning disabilities; it used the term "individual"
rather than "children," recognizing that the problems associated with learning disabilities may continue into adult life; it acknowledged the complexities of clinical diagnosis
by stating that learning disability can occur concurrently with other handicapping conditions and that the disability is related to dysfunction of the central nervous system.

In 1987, The Interagency Committee on Learning Disabilities suggested that "social skills deficit also represent a specific learning disability," but consensus was lacking for this modification and the Department of Education did not endorse the addition
of social skills possibly for legal and economic reasons; legal because it would necessi-
tate changes in existing legislation and increase confusion in criteria for identification;
economic because it would overidentify children as learning disabled.

Each of the definitions, so far discussed, is concerned with the broad spectrum of
academic difficulties (listening, speaking, writing, reading, reasoning, and mathematics) seen in children with learning disabilities. Such definitions says Stanovich, "made
little sense given what we already know about heterogeneity across various learning
domains. Research investigations must define groups specifically in terms of the domain deficit (reading disability, arithmetic disability)" (Stanovich, 1993, quoted in
Lyon, 1994, p. 5).

Two definitions currently used by physicians and psychologists in their own practices, are definitions by domain of academic disability. The American Psychiatric Association's *Diagnostic and Statistical Manual of Mental Disorders (DSM-IV)* and The
World Health Organization's classification of Mental and Behavior Disorders in its *International Classification of Disease (ICD-10)* have codified diagnostic criteria for

specific domains—reading, writing, mathematics. Criteria for each domain are listed separately, each with its own code number. Yet the criteria for each, with exception of the domain, are similar, each stressing a discrepancy criterion: academic achievement below level expected on the basis of the child's chronological age, general intelligence, with educational and cognitive tests standardized for the child's culture and educational opportunities (*ICD-10*). *ICD-10* also requires a discrepancy of two standard deviations for inclusion. These definitions do not delve farther than academic achievement into the characteristics of the deficits in each domain; each reinforces the discrepancy criteria; and each offers no guidance for assessment of the discrepancy or for intervention or for prediction of outcome.

The Orton Dyslexia Society Research Committee proposed a "new research definition" in 1994:

> Dyslexia is one of several distinct learning disabilities. It is a specific language based disorder of constitutional origin characterized by difficulties in single word decoding, usually reflecting insufficient phonological processing. These difficulties in single word decoding are often unexpected in relationship to age and other cognitive and academic abilities; they are not the result of generalized and developmental disability or sensory impairment. Dyslexia is manifested by variable difficulty with different forms of language, often including, in addition to problems with reading, a conspicuous problem in acquiring proficiency in writing and spelling. (Lyon, 1995)

This definition, in contrast to the earlier ones described in this chapter, differs in two important ways. It restricts itself to one domain of academic difficulty (reading), and it includes phonological processes, which current research supports as the key neuropsychological deficit underlying difficulty in learning to read. In this definition, dyslexia is not synonymous with the term learning disabilities; dyslexia is but one of the many domains of disorders of learning. While other domains (i.e., spelling, writing) may occur with dyslexia, they also occur without dyslexia. The neuropsychological deficits of these domains may be different from the specific phonological deficits that in this definition, characterize dyslexia. Also while there is evidence that a deficit in phonological processing characterizes most children with reading difficulty, this may not be the only processing deficit that characterizes dyslexia: Temporal sequencing, rapid automatized naming, short-term memory, comprehension, and syntactic confusion may also be important. Phonological processing itself will change with maturation and intervention, so that in an adult with good cognitive functioning (e.g., medical students, law students), their compensating skills have obscured the basic phonological defect, but slow reading with possible comprehension or memory defect remains. The definition thus creates a condition, that may, in effect, act as an exclusionary factor, excluding by fiat some children and adults with reading problems who do not have specific phonological deficit but who do suffer from reading disability. It is noted, however, that this definition is reported as a working one, capable of being modified as new evidence arises from replicated empirical findings.

The definition also removes some of the exclusionary and inclusionary restrictions of earlier definitions. The USOE definitions specifically exclude learning disabilities that are "primarily the result . . . of mental retardation, of emotional disturbance, or of environmental, cultural, or economic disadvantage." The Orton Society Research Committee does exclude "generalized and developmental disability or sensory impairment" (i.e., cognitive retardation), but, by their omission, presumably includes emotional disturbance or socioeconomical difference. In short, if "emotionally disturbed" children or poor children have specific phonological processing deficits and meet the other criteria of the definition, they may be considered dyslexic and receive the benefits of remedial teaching available to these children.

The implied deletion of inclusionary factors is also significant. USOE states that specific learning disabilities include "perceptual handicaps, brain injury, minimal brain dysfunction, dyslexia, and developmental aphasia." The National Joint Commission on Learning Disabilities states, "These disorders are intrinsic to the individual and presumed to be due to central nervous system dysfunction." The Orton definition, however, states that dyslexia is of "constitutional origin." Presumably, that means a significant genetic factor, that in ways yet unknown directs the perturbation in brain development leading to dyslexia. It does not include brain damage or any of the prenatal, neonatal, or postnatal factors that also may lead to reading difficulty. The Orton definition thus narrows the population, hopefully making it more homogeneous for the drawing of research samples.

The Orton definition also questions the use of discrepancy formulas as a criterion for inclusion. It states, "the difficulties are often unexpected in relation to age and other cognitive and academic abilities." In discussing the "unexpected" criteron, Lyon specifically says, "It does not embrace the idea that basic deficits in decoding and word processing must be significantly lower than IQ as specified in typical discrepancy formulas but discrepancy is assessed by comparing reading age with chronological age and/or comparing reading ability to academic performance in other domains" (1995, p. 15).

From a practical point of view, the definition of learning disability on the basis of IQ-achievement discrepancy, even following a single evaluation, has been helpful in emphasizing that a child who has difficulty in learning to read, or learning to write or do mathematical calculations may not be "mentally slow" (Berninger, Hart, Abbott, & Karovsky, 1992). Indeed, discrepancy formulas are generally accepted, in various forms, by most school districts as their case-finding tool (Mercer, Jordan, Allsop, & Mercer, 1996). Yet discrepancy formulas have been subject to criticism on the basis of their conceptual and statistical assumptions and dissatisfaction with existing measures of intelligence and academic achievement.

The use of the IQ in the discrepancy formula implies that the IQ scores are indices of learning potential, that IQ represents some innate, biologically derived factor that sets the upper limit on ability attainment (Spearman, 1923). The intelligence quotient is a summary of several aspects of cognitive function, which does not measure some skills relating to reading proficiency (Francis, Espy, Rourke, & Fletcher, 1991). The correlation of IQ with reading is approximately 0.70 (Sattler, 1988). Also, as has frequently been stated, a lower IQ may result from, not cause, a reading disability.

In 1983, The United States Department of Education convened a work group to suggest "best practice-state of the art" measurement solutions to the discrepancy problem.

The working group's final report (C. R. Reynolds, 1984), recognizing that a "severe" discrepancy between aptitude and achievement was a critical component of the definitions in use, first surveyed a number of measurement models. The use of constant grade-equivalent discrepancies (e.g., at least one standard deviation between aptitude and achievement when both tests are expressed on a common scale) was criticized as lacking statistical sophistication. The standard deviation of a distribution created by subtracting the scores of one univariate distribution (e.g., IQ test scores) from another (e.g., achievement test scores) could not be expected to be the same as the standard deviations for the two original distributions. Deviation from grade level was rejected because such models may underidentify children with higher IQ scores and overidentify children in the lower IQ groups. The child with high IQ scores who must struggle to achieve grade level academic achievement scores would not be identified as having a learning problem. Standard score comparisons (i.e., the age-corrected or grade-corrected achievement score is subtracted from the standard score deviation in IQ) were also criticized because they, too, do not take into account the regression of IQ score with achievement score. And as in grade-level discrepancy, the cutoff criterion for significant discrepancy is arbitrary.

The Working Group concluded that severe discrepancy required definition from a statistical perspective. A regression model that dealt with reliable differences that were infrequent in the normal population and used standard scores rather than age or grade equivalents, was recommended. The Working Group formula addressed the regression between IQ and achievement and assessed the severity of this discrepancy by comparing it with the base rate in the population from which the correlation of the two measures were derived. A deviation of two standard deviations was suggested. Aside from the formidable statistical work required to implement this regression-discrepancy model in the public schools, it assumes, like previous definitions, that IQ sets the upper limit of expected level of achievement. Practically, however, the calculation of reading disability based on the absolute difference between IQ and reading, and on regression scores that control the correlation between IQ with reading, did not yield significantly different findings (Rispens, van Yperen, & van Dvijn, 1991). The assumptions of the discrepancy formulas raise theoretical questions:

- That a simple global aptitude score is representative of a child's abilities.
- That achievement could be reduced to a single score for comparison with aptitude.
- That regression-based predictions made at the national or state level may be appropriate for crucial decision making for individual children at local levels.
- That the heterogeneous condition we call learning disability is normally distributed in a population and can be regarded as a unified trait for the purpose of statistical analysis.

These conceptual and statistical problems associated with using IQ-reading discrepancy as a marker for the definition of dyslexia are major reasons for not using this criterion in the Orton Research Committee Definition. Another and, more important reason, is that when assessed by decoding, word recognition, and phonological skills, there is evidence that poor readers with average or high IQ do not differ from poor readers whose reading scores are not discrepant from their IQ. Stanovich and Siegel (1994) state:

> The discrepancy assumption survived for decades because there was no good evidence on the neurological, genetic, or phenotypic information-processing differences between children with and without a discrepancy. Our data undercut one component of the discrepancy assumption: children with and without a discrepancy do not differ in the information-processing skills (phonological and orthographic coding) that determine word recognition. (p. 48)

Data from the Connecticut Longitudinal Study suggest that the IQ-reading discrepancy formula be deleted from the definition of dyslexia. In 1992, B. A. Shaywitz, Fletcher, Holahan, and Shaywitz followed good and poor readers from kindergarten through fifth grade. Over the years of the study, there was minimal difference between the discrepant and the nondiscrepant groups of poor readers on measures of linguistic function, manual dexterity, visual perception, and teacher's assessment of learning and behavior. In 1994, B. A. Shaywitz and Shaywitz found that the growth curves were quantitatively similar, differing only in severity. Shaywitz and Shaywitz state that these data lend further support that reading ability/disability occurs along a continuum and that dyslexia represents the lower tail of this distribution. (S. E. Shaywitz et al., 1992).

There are however, studies finding differences between the two groups. For example, in what by now is their classical study of all 8-, 9-, and 10-year-old children—all 3,519 of them—living on the Isle of Wight, Rutter, Graham, and Yule (1970) found 86 of them, 3.68 % of the total, to be suffering from specific reading retardation (SRR). This group was defined as educational achievement in reading below expected level relative to IQ); 155 of the children (6.64% of the total) did not fit the discrepancy criteria and their difficulties were termed *reading backwardness* (nondiscrepant reading disability). The SRR group differed from the backward readers in the greater prevalence of males, 76.7% compared with the backward group (54.4 %). The backward group, however, had a greater incidence of overt neurological dysfunction with 11.4% having evidence of "hard" (classical) neurological signs and 25.3% having "soft" neurological signs, whereas *none* of the SRR children had hard neurological signs and 18.6% had possible soft neurological signs (see Chapter 7 for a discussion of neurological signs). The backward readers were clumsier, had more choreiform movements and more problems with right-left discrimination. When these children were reexamined at age 14, the SRR children were poorer spellers and readers, but better at math than the backward readers. Rutter and Yule (1975) concluded that SRR is a relatively distinct disorder that can be summarized as a deficit that is peculiar to language, whereas backward readers demonstrate multiple difficulties in intellectual, neurological, and language areas.

A significantly greater prevalence of neurological abnormalities—difficulties in motor and language measures—was also found in backward readers compared these with specific reading retardation by Silva, McGee, and Williams (1985) in 7- and

9-year-old children from Dunedin, New Zealand, and by Jorm, Share, Maclean, and Matthews (1986) in Australia, where the SSR group had significantly more difficulty with language skills (name writing, letter copying, syntax, receptive vocabulary, sentence/meaning) than the backward group, which had more global difficulties.

DEFINITIONS IN CURRENT SCHOOL PRACTICE

While there is much to be said on both sides of the question of the use of discrepancy measures to identify learning disability, school administrators do not have the luxury of extended discussion and debate. Decisions concerning eligibility and funding must be made in the everyday process of educating the nation's children; they cannot be deferred until the ultimate research study has been reported and the last rejoinder published. Any discussion of the discrepancy approaches to identification must be viewed within the context of the actual processes in use in the schools at the present time. The real question is "How are learning disabilities defined in the schools today?"

The answer to this question is not a direct one, because in the United States the implementation of educational policy and procedures is the responsibility of the individual state governments. Data are available though the studies of Mercer and his colleagues who have surveyed state departments of education four times since the passage of the special education laws in 1975 (Mercer, Forgnone, & Wolking, 1976; Mercer et al., 1996). The most recent survey found that 94% of the states mentioned the discrepancy factor in their criteria for learning disability, an increase from 88% in the 1990 survey. In contrast, only 27% of the states mentioned it in their official definitions. Yet many authorities consider discrepancy a key factor in the determination of learning disability and an important component of any definition. It is in the operationalizing of this concept that the issue becomes cloudy and procedures vary from state to state.

The survey by Mercer et al. (1996) identified a variety of procedures currently in use for operationalizing discrepancies:

- *The use of standard score comparisons was reported by 42% of the states.* This involves the comparison of ability and achievement measures using scores that have been converted statistically utilizing the same mean and standard deviation. As a result, scores are expressed in terms of the same metric (proportions of the normal curve). Most authorities agree that such score comparisons are more respectable statistically, provided that the difference between the scores is reliable (that it is not due to chance variations) and that the difference is great enough to be considered rare.

- *The use of standard deviations within the achievement test was reported by 42% of the states.* Rather than using grade scores (which have been shown to vary from test to test) some states report using some proportion of the standard deviation of the achievement test score (e.g., one and a half or two standard deviations from the mean) to identify children eligible for services. While this method may be more respectable statistically, it does not take into account the variations in learning potential and, for that reason, may fail to identify high-ability students with learning disabilities.

- *The use of grade-level discrepancies was reported by 6% of the states.* Although easily administered and familiar in popular usage, this method ignores both the variations among different tests and fact that there are no objective grade-level standards. Furthermore, it would tend to overidentify slow learners and under-identify students with high abilities.

- *The use of verbal performance differences on the Wechsler Intelligence Scale for Children was reported by one state (0.2%).* Since Kaufman (1979) has reported the high degree of variability of verbal/performance scale relationship among students with learning disabilities, this method would appear to be ineffective in identifying a significant portion of the children who need services.

- *The use of proportional comparisons on aptitude and achievement tests to define discrepancy was reported by 6% of the states.* These states indicated the use of a discrepancy of 40% to 50% or more between aptitude and achievement to locate children eligible for services.

Perhaps the most significant finding of the Mercer study is that 32% of the states made no statement in either their definitions or their eligibility criteria concerning operationalization. A number of states reported that the operationalization procedures were left to the judgment of the individual school districts. Several states reported that the operationalization issue was left to the judgment of the multidisciplinary teams responsible for the diagnosis and placement of students with special learning problems. This trend toward the use of comprehensive clinical data in the context of the student's educational setting is an enlightened approach. It is in direct contrast to identification by administrative fiat, irrespective of the statistical procedure on which it is based.

Thus, while definitions have become more specific in criteria for identifying individuals with learning disabilities, their use in specific practical and research situations may still raise questions and problems. Different situations may need different criteria for identifying an individual (child or adult) as having a learning disability. Schools need a definition that is practical and useful for them, that not only identifies the child who needs remediation, but that also can guide intervention. Public policy in terms of funding, concern for overidentification, and limitations imposed on special classes, may, in effect, dictate such a definition. Parental demands and legal suits for and against services to these students may be affected by the wording, the inclusionary-exclusionary factors of a definition, the rigidity and narrowness of a definition in providing or denying needed help. Consensus in research definitions also is crucial in the selection of samples and in the validity and replicability of the assessment instruments.

SUMMARY

The definition of learning disability is important. It guides the selection of children who need special education and the resources school and parents must mobilize to provide help; it guides public policy and is essential for selection of homogeneous and comparable samples for research. Yet in the century since "congenital word blindness" was described, we have not reached consensus on the definition of learning disabilities. The reasons for this may be the heterogeneity of the academic domains in which the disability is seen; the variability of neuropsychological processes that underlie the domains; and the multiplicity of etiological factors, acting singly or synergistically, that initiate the events leading to disability. The various terms used to define learning disorders of childhood, reveal the attempts made to bring order out of the diverse factors of domain, processing deficits, and etiology. It was not until 1967 that the National Advisory Committee on Handicapped Children was able to shed the label of minimal brain dysfunction (MBD) and propose a definition that included the domains of impaired function, related these impairments to "basic psychological processes," and provided inclusionary and exclusionary criteria. This definition became the basis for the Education for All Handicapped Children Act (PL 94-142). It remains federal policy. Subsequent definitions such as that of the National Joint Committee on Learning Disabilities (1987) attempted to refine the 1967 definition to be more specific in the functional domains and to state that learning disabilities "are presumed to be due to central nervous system dysfunction." In 1994, the Research Committee of the Orton Society defined one of the domains of learning disabilities (dyslexia), and was specific in declaring that its proximal processing defect is phonological processing, a defect critical to the definition. Further, the Orton definition rejected the discrepancy between academic achievement and intelligence as an essential part of the definition.

While there is some support that the key processing defect in reading disability is phonological processing, there is less agreement for omission of a discrepancy criterion in the definition. Most schools in the United States consider discrepancy between achievement and ability to be a key factor in the identification of the child with a learning disability. The most recent survey found that 94% of the states include a discrepancy factor in their criteria for learning disability. It is the measurement of the discrepancy that, in practice, varies. Standard score comparisons are reported by 42% of the states, and an additional 42% favor standard deviations with achievement tests.

Despite the lack of consensus on all aspects of definitions, there are some generally accepted assumptions in the use of the term learning disabilities:

- The domain of academic difficulty is proximally related to a defect in neuropsychological processing skills of the central nervous system.
- The academic difficulty is determined by a discrepancy estimate.
- The processing defects found are characterized by a disorder in the development of language.

Chapter 5 ————————————————————————————

CLASSIFICATION AND CLINICAL PATTERNS OF LEARNING DISABILITIES

Ultimately dyslexia is a nervous system dysfunction, and as such must be reducible to problems at a level more basic than that at which it is expressed (behavior), that is to the realm of neuronal or synaptic malfunction.

—Rudolfo Llinas, 1993

Classification involves the ordering or organization of concepts according to contiguity or similarity (Bailey, 1973, quoted by Keogh, 1994, p. 16). Classification should evolve from theory, based on a unifying thread that ties together the subgroups of the taxonomy, all of which share the common characteristics that identify the entire class; yet each subgroup possesses singular variations that identify its uniqueness.

What then is the thread binding all individuals with a learning disability? Three major strands of the thread have been described:

1. Unexpected low academic achievement relative to aptitude or ability.
2. Deficits and uneven profiles in specific perceptual or cognitive processes.
3. Evidence for in-child, presumably causal neurological condition (Kavale & Forness, 1985; Keogh, 1988, 1994; Stanovich, 1986a, 1988).

First, all individuals with learning disabilities must have problems with learning, with academic achievement inconsistent with their age and/or intelligence and/or educational experience. This is the first strand of the thread and is accessible to measurement (Lyon, 1994). A better analogy would be that academic achievement below that expected for the individual's age and/or intelligence is only the tip of the proverbial iceberg, that part which can readily be seen above the surface of the water. (Figure 5.1). However, as discussed in Chapter 4, academic difficulty may be seen in various domains and in a combination of domains including listening, speaking, reading,

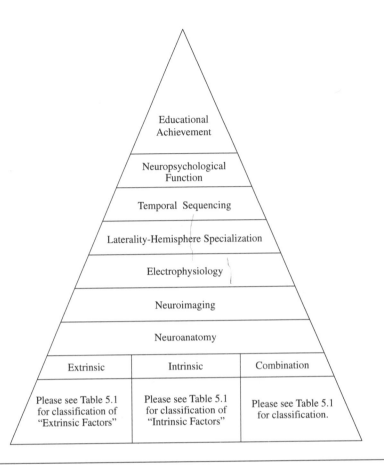

Figure 5.1   The hierarchy of defects in learning disabilities.

spelling, handwriting, composition, and mathematics. Below the surface of the domains of academic disability, each individual with a learning disability has some deficit in the way his or her brain processes information in the auditory, visual, tactile, or body-image modalities, in one or more neuropsychological functions related to language in its broadest sense: the processing of symbols from all modalities including decoding, sequencing, association, comprehension, retention, retrieval, and expression. Subgroups based on the patterns of central processing deficit have been delineated. Phonological processing deficits have been identified as the foremost deficit in individuals with reading disability and indeed as the "proximal cause " (Lyon, 1994) of reading disability. As seen in Figure 5.1, however, processing deficits while most important in subgrouping and in remediation, are themselves the result of more distal functional deficits. Hierarchically, proceeding into deeper depths of the iceberg, hemisphere specialization, particularly in relation to language function is not clearly established in individuals with learning disabilities. The blurring of functions between right and left hemispheres may lead to the processing deficits of learning disability.

During the past 10 years, the findings in neuroelectrophysiology and in neuroimaging suggest that functional differences in the brains of individuals with learning disabilities are accompanied by changes not only in neuropsychological processing and in varying degrees of hemisphere specialization, but also in the computerized electroencephalogram, in evoked potentials responding to specific auditory and visual stimuli, and in coherence in the wave patterns seen in the electroencephalogram. Neuroimaging has discovered differences in metabolic processes and in regional blood flow in areas of the brain relating to processing of information, in the performance of academically related tasks. These differences have not yet been classified into subgroups and are not yet correlated with specific neuropsychological processing deficits. All of these physiological functions, however, may in turn be secondary to or emanating from anatomical changes, as described by Galaburda (1991, 1993a, 1993b, 1993c, 1994).

There is still to be considered the third criterion for identification of a learning disability, the "in-child, presumably causal neurological condition" (Keogh, 1994, p. 16). These are factors intrinsic to the individual that may be the underlying cause of the anatomical deviations. What is the base of the iceberg and how can this be related to classification and subgrouping of learning disabilities? The problem here is that clinically the presumed etiology of learning disabilities is heterogeneous. For example, of all first graders of an average urban school in New York City, 50% boys and 50% girls, coming from low to middle-to-low socioeconomic families with an ethnic mix of 55% White, 25% Hispanic, 10% Black, and 10% Asian, approximately 25% of approximately 100 children, one-fourth would be found to have some difficulty with learning in some academic area, most in reading and spelling but many with difficulties in handwriting and arithmetic. If these 25% with academic performance below that of their peers were examined with an intensive battery including cognitive, neuropsychological, educational, social, psychiatric, and neurological evaluations, approximately 60% of the vulnerable group, approximately 15% of the entire first grade, will include children with low average or higher intelligence, who have neuropsychological deficits in one or more areas of function, educational experience which may or may not be considered adequate for school learning. Many but not all have a family history of learning problems and none of whom have evidence of a structural defect of the central nervous system, nor with defect in the peripheral sensory apparatus. An additional 3 to 5 children of the vulnerable 25 will have evidence for a structural defect of the central nervous system, some with only the soft signs of neurological dysfunction, deviations in one or more areas of neurological examination including muscle tone, power, and synergy; gross and fine motor coordination; cranial nerves; posture and equilibrium; deep, superficial, and pathological reflexes; immaturity in praxis, right-left orientation, and finger gnosis. Others will have focal neurological signs including cerebral or cerebellar palsies, dyskinesies, extinction of tactile stimuli. All of these children with neurological findings will also have central processing deficits. An additional 5 to 7 of the vulnerable 25 children will not have neuropsychological processing defects inconsistent with their age and/or intelligence. This group includes children with attention deficit hyperactivity disorder (approximately 3/100 vulnerable children); those with emotional and behavioral problems in reaction to family psychopathology, and/or cultural differences (again approximately 3/100 children with academic problems); children with peripheral sensory deficit, particularly hearing, and those with cognitive retardation, cause unknown.

Table 5.1   Disorders of learning: Clinical classification based on possible causative factors

I Extrinsic Factors	II Intrinsic Factors	III Combination

1. Social, economic, and cultural deprivation
2. Language differences
3. Inadequate or inappropriate prior education
4. Emotional barriers to learning
5. Drugs including prescription drugs
	1. Genetic
	  (a) Developmental learning disorders
	  (b) Other developmental disorders
	    (i) ADHD
	    (ii) Tourette's syndrome
	  (c) Known genetic abnormalities
	    (i) Metabolic disorders
	    (ii) Down syndrome
	    (iii) Fragile X syndrome
	    (iv) Other genetic neurological disorders
	  (d) Presumed genetic disease
	    (i) Autism
	    (ii) Other
	2. Experientially induced organic disorders
	  (a) Disorders of pregnancy and labor
	    (i) Prematurity
	    (ii) Toxicity
	    (iii) Infections
	    (iv) Trauma
	  (b) Postnatal neurological disorders
	    (i) Infections
	    (ii) Toxicity
	    (iii) Trauma
	    (iv) Neoplasticity
	  (c) Seizure disorders
	3. General cognitive retardation—cause unknown
		Both extrinsic and intrinsic factors

Table 5.1 shows the etiological diversity of children with learning disorders (Disorders of Learning: Clinical Classification Based on Possible Causative Factors). Children with central processing deficits in any of the categories delineated here may have associated problems with attention, distractibility, or impulsivity. In some of these children, ADHD symptoms may be reactive to the neuropsychological deficit of the learning disorder itself, or as part of the syndrome of organic brain damage (Chapter 14). ADHD however, may be seen in children who *do not* have central processing deficits. These children are considered as a group separate from those with neuropsychological processing deficits. Evidence for this may be found in Chapter 13. We do not neglect symptoms of ADHD and we do not minimize them, but ADHD is not synonymous with developmental learning disabilities.

LEARNING DISORDERS RESULTING FROM EXTRINSIC FACTORS

Extrinsic factors act *on* the child, particularly events that offer inappropriate or inadequate stimulation at critical developmental ages in the child's life. This is seen in the culture of poverty when, in the first few years of life, language development is affected. These children may have neuropsychological processing deficits; they are important not only in terms of the sheer numbers of children affected but in the high percentage of them who do not complete high school. These children are often excluded in the definition of learning disabilities and so do not have the advantage of remedial classes, yet they are in dire need of inclusion and remediation. Also included in the extrinsic group are children with emotional barriers to learning, problems of motivation, inhibitions to learning resulting from anxiety, depression, obsession, or from psychologically induced behaviors such as aggression, truancy, or drug and alcohol abuse. These children do not categorically have neuropsychological processing deficits and their management and prognosis requires services other than or in addition to education.

LEARNING DISORDERS RESULTING FROM INTRINSIC FACTORS

Intrinsic factors lie within the biological makeup of the child and are expressed in dysfunction of the central nervous system. Table 5.1 identifies diverse biological factors: Some children have a history of experientially induced injury occurring prenatally, at birth, or postnatally; those who do not have such a history may have a family history of learning problems. A genetic aberration is believed to be responsible for perturbation in the normal process in the development of language, and underlies the central processing defects of learning-disabled children. This entity is classified as developmental learning disability or specific learning disability (SLD). It is the most prevalent group of learning disorders found in the classroom (15% of the total number of children in early elementary grades). It is identical to the diagnoses known as congenital word blindness (Hinshelwood, 1917), congenital auditory imperception (Worcester-Drought & Allen, 1929), primary reading disability (Rabinovitch et al., 1954), psychoneurological learning disabilities (Myklebust & Boshes, 1969), developmental dyslexia (Critchley, 1964), strephosymbolia (Orton, 1937), dyslexia-pure (Denckla, 1993), and specific reading retardation (Rutter, 1978; B. K. Shapiro, Accardo, & Capute, 1998). While these definitions focus on dyslexia and dyslexia is the most prevalent academic domain of difficulty, we include all other domains of academic difficulty and all variations of neuropsychological processing deficits in the term developmental learning disability when postulating a specific genetic etiology for a child's disorder.

Central processing defects, however, are not exclusive to the developmental learning disability. As detailed in the chapters on learning disorders stemming from etiologies other than genetic (e.g., organic, inappropriate or insufficient stimulation at critical age) other developmental disorders, even variations in genetic aberrations, may also have processing defects. They fit the general classification of learning disabilities. Each, however, has unique factors stamped on them by their etiology. If each etiological group forming the base of the iceberg were the same in terms of symptoms, management, prognosis, and prevention, then to distinguish them as separate subgroups would be moot. As seen in Tables 5.2, 5.3, 5.4, and 5.5, however, they are different in clinical presentation and, as they grow from preschool to adult, they require management of their unique features. Both cross-sectional and longitudinal clinical studies of children with learning disorders also support the classification described here. Tables 5.2 to 5.5 contrast the clinical presentation and needs of those with developmental language disability, with structural defects of the central nervous system, with Attention-Deficit/Hyperactivity Disorder, and with overall cognitive functioning in the borderline range, in various academic, social, and emotional parameters as the children grow from preschool age into adulthood. In preschool, the child who will develop a specific language disability frequently has delayed speech with articulation errors, generally good gross motor ability but immature fine motor skills, good mathematical ability except where sequencing is needed, and good conceptual organization, particularly in nonverbal concepts. At this age, he is socially and emotionally normal. The organic child at preschool age may also be delayed in language ability; he may be dysarthric with oral inaccuracies. His gross and fine motor skills are poor; he may be hyper- or hypoactive; he has difficulty matching finger to object in counting in arithmetic; his conceptual organization may be concrete and preservative; and he may have difficulty in social adjustment. The ADHD child is already exhibiting hasty, impulsive behavior, with generally unfocused conceptual organization; she may already be self-centered and feel misunderstood. The cognitive borderline child is immature in all aspects of functioning.

By elementary school, the SLD child will have decoding and encoding difficulty; he is not highly verbal, his body image problems are seen in right-left confusion, his mathematics achievement suffers when verbal problems are introduced, and he may make multiplication and long division errors. His conceptual abilities, particularly nonverbal, are generally good, but he is suffering emotionally from his academic difficulties and may feel that he is stupid. The organic child is more uneven in her academic skills; she may lack systemic decoding and encoding, her written work is difficult, she may

Table 5.2 Etiological subtypes of learning disorders: A longitudinal view of specific language disability

	Reading and Language Arts	Motor Skills	Mathematics	Conceptual Organization	Social Development	Psychological Development
Preschool	Delayed speech Articulation errors	Gross motor—good Fine motor—immature	Good except sequences	Good—especially nonverbal	Within normal limits	Within normal limits
Elementary	Decoding and encoding difficult Not highly verbal	Gross motor—good Left-right errors Fine motor—improving	Good if not too verbal Multiplication and long division errors	Good, nonverbal	Reactive to learning problems	Feels stupid
Secondary	Needs mastery of decoding or bypass methods	Improved Often exceptional artwork	Multiplication and long division errors	Depends on language stimulation Compulsive approaches	Reactive to school success	Worries about competency

Table 5.3 Etiological subtypes of learning disorders: A longitudinal view of classical organic defects

	Reading and Language Arts	Motor Skills	Mathematics	Conceptual Organization	Social Development	Psychological Development
Preschool	May be delayed, accelerated, or dysarthric	Poor—hyperactive or hypoactive	Sequencing errors	Chaotic Concrete	Poor	Depends on environmental support
Elementary	Uneven Lacks systematic decoding and encoding Written work difficult	Poor Impulsive Clumsy	Uneven Rapid Erratic	Rigid Difficulty integrating	Often lonely Sometimes clowning	Sees self as misunderstood Anxious May be ingratiating
Secondary	Uneven	Uneven	Homework problems Sloppy	Disorganized Verbal may be good Nonverbal poor	Not social	Defensive, suspicious Anxious, sometimes an "operator"
Adult	Uneven May take refuge in reading May be overly verbal	Clumsy	Uneven	Disorganized Depends on others	Self-centered	Defensive Anxious Potential unrealized

Table 5.4   Etiological subtypes of learning disorders: A longitudinal view of attention-deficit/hyperactivity disorder

	Reading and Language Arts	Motor Skills	Mathematics	Conceptual Organization	Social Development	Psychological Development
Preschool	Little opportunity to learn	Hasty Primitive	Sequencing difficulties	Poor	Poor	Driven Self-centered Impulsive Feels misunderstood
Elementary	Uneven Difficulty in completing work although often can do it	Sloppy Hasty	Mechanical approach	Superficial	Provocative	Driven Self-centered Impulsive Feels misunderstood
Secondary	Uneven Gaps in background Illogical	Sloppy Impatient	Gaps in background Weak logic	Superficial	Impatient Often unpopular	Feels misunderstood Weak defenses
Adult	Uneven Seeks verbal-type occupations Easily bored	Avoids motor tasks	Avoids details of this field	Superficial	"Own worst enemy"	Dissatisfied, restless Dependent on others Vulnerable to anxiety

Table 5.5 Etiological subtypes of learning disorders: A longitudinal view of borderline cognitive function

	Reading and Language Arts	Motor Skills	Mathematics	Conceptual Organization	Social Development	Psychological Development
Preschool			—Immature for age—			
Elementary	Out of sync with curriculum	Within normal limits	Concrete	Concrete thinking	Immature for age	Within normal limits
Secondary	Difficulties with abstractions	Within normal limits	Difficulties with abstractions	Concrete thinking	Within normal limits	Within normal limits
	—"School day retardates" if schooling is not modified to meet developmental levels of students.—					
Adult	Skills fairly good but does not read much	Within normal limits	Fair	Concrete thinking	Within normal limits Responsible about work done	Within normal limits

be impulsive and clumsy; she may be sloppy, have difficulty organizing her daily activities, and be rigid in her thinking. She is often lonely and anxious. The ADHD child has difficulty completing work although he can do it; he is driven, self-centered, and impulsive; and he has a superficial conceptual organization. The cognitive borderline child is generally weeks behind her peers in academic skills, although her written work may be legible and orderly but her thinking is generally concrete.

At the secondary school level, the SLD child continues to have difficulty. She may still need to master decoding skills or methods to avoid the specific deficits with which she suffers; she has trouble putting her thoughts together for compositions and reports; her fine motor coordination may have improved; and mathematics (particularly problems involving complex verbal mediation or requiring spatial skills or geometry) may be difficult, but on the other hand, she may be proficient with computers. Her school difficulties may be reflected in self-doubts and in social adjustment. The organic child continues to be disorganized and rigid; his achievement is uneven and his anxiety is still present; he may develop compulsive patterns and become socially isolated; the physical coordination needed in writing is still not developed and written work is difficult, although his reading is good. The ADHD child is sloppy and impatient; his academic skills are uneven and his thinking is sometimes superficial and illogical. There are gaps in the knowledge he has acquired; socially he is often unpopular and he tends to project his problems to others. The borderline child now has obvious difficulty understanding abstractions; he may be considered "retarded" if the academic demands are not adjusted to his limitations.

As an adult, the SLD is not an avid reader, although she may have learned to be well organized; she generally enters visual/mechanical, quantitative, or graphic vocational fields; emotionally, however, she may be suffering from the self-doubts engendered by her disability. The organic adult may be a good reader and be overly verbal; his motor clumsiness remains, and his academic achievement is not in keeping with his potential; he may still be disorganized and may have developed compensatory mechanisms of rigidity; his anxiety is still present. The ADHD adult is also uneven in academic achievement; he avoids detailed work requiring sustained attention; he seeks verbal-type occupations and becomes easily bored; he may appear dissatisfied, restless, and dependent on others. The borderline adult may have skills consistent with her abilities and may be conscientious and responsible in routine work.

This cross-sectional and longitudinal observation of children with learning disorders provides additional justification for the separation of children with structural defects of the central nervous system, those with ADHD, and those with generalized cognitive immaturity from children with a specific language disability. Thus, the term *learning disability* should have the qualifying etiological factor attached; for example, learning disability with organic CNS injury (specify the type and location of the injury); inappropriate stimulation at critical ages.

There are children with learning problems who do not have neuropsychological processing deficits (e.g., ADHD without processing problems). For these children, the term learning disorder is suggested and, here again, the classification should have the etiological factor included. The key issue is the presence or absence of central processing defects. Those with academic difficulty inconsistent with age and/or intelligence and/or educational opportunity and with neuropsychological processing deficits that are related to the academic difficulty are termed *learning disabilities,* those who do not have central processing deficits are *learning disorders.* Each of these groups may be subgrouped in accordance with the presumed etiology.

In practice, the term learning disability is applied to all children who have academic difficulty, regardless of etiology. Since 1991, however, children with ADD and ADHD are reported by the Department of Education as "other health impairments," a category different from "specific learning disabilities" (see Table 11.1). We are attempting to retain the basic criteria for inclusion in the term of learning disability as outlined by Keogh (1994)—academic achievement inconsistent with expectancy, specific processing deficits and "in-child" causal neurological disorders. It is the absence of processing deficits that makes those children different from those with processing deficits, and those whom we are classifying as learning disorders.

This book is not alone in attempting to classify learning disorders on the basis of causative factors. Rabinovitch (1968) and Rabinovitch, Drew, DeJong, Ingram, and Withey (1954) proposed classifying learning disorders as either "primary" (those for which we do not know the cause) or "secondary" (those that appear to result from known disturbances such as structural damage to the central nervous system). Quadfasel and Goodglass (1968) also thought of learning disorders as "symptomatic" (resulting from early brain damage), "primary" (without evidence of brain damage but possibly genetic), and "secondary" (resulting from environmental, emotional, or health factors). Bannatyne (1971) classified the universe of "all language and reading disabilities" into six major groupings: low IQ, dyslexia, emotional, asphasia, autism, and other. The dyslexia group, in turn, was divided into four groups of factors: genetic, social or environmental deprivation, minor neurological dysfunction, and primarily emotional. The characteristics of genetic dyslexia were considered to be language delays and deficits; the minor neurological group was thought to encompass a series of disorders in each perceptual avenue. Thus, the classification presented in this book is not unique. It has attempted to classify the population of learning disordered children as they are seen in the classroom and not as preselected from neurological, neuropsychological, and psychiatric clinics. We have stated that subgroups of children who have academic difficulty on the basis of causative factors compose the base of the iceberg, the structure from which the peripheral signs and symptoms emanate.

So far in this chapter, we have presented a classification of learning disabilities beyond that based on academic domain and neuropsychological processing deficits. We have attempted to classify the possible factors that, in hierarchical fashion, lead through levels of anatomical and physiological deviations, to problems in hemisphere specialization and to the neuropsychological deficits and the final emergence into difficulties with academic learning. The more prevalent of these putative causative (etiological?) factors are discussed in Chapters 11 through 15. However, the most prevalent of these putative etiological factors is now believed to be genetic polymorphism in a gene or genes that encode for specific perturbations in development of language in its broadest sense, to emerge as the clinical entity termed developmental learning disabilities.

Recent developments in the identification of these polymorphisms are described in Chapters 3 and 11. The remainder of this chapter will discuss the subgrouping of developmental learning disabilities.

In studying central nervous system dysfunction in developmental learning disabilities, we are faced with the same problems encountered in proposing a definition: the heterogeneity of samples, their disparate demographic characteristics, difference in selection of samples, differences in research methodology. Children in subgroup studies have varied as to sources, age, sex, IQ, definitional boundaries, neurological signs, and socioeconomic status. Most studies have neglected the clinical diagnostic grouping, as outlined in the first section of this chapter, and are not clearly defined. Samples are drawn from medical, neuropsychological clinics and from highly selective or from intact populations in the school. The tests used to identify a child as learning disabled and the probes used to identify central processing deficits may differ; even the same probe may vary among groups of researchers and in the criteria of reliability and validity. Further, the emphasis overall has been to find patterns of deficit and to neglect patterns of assets. Our guiding principles for subgroup analysis should have samples:

- Clearly defined as to the domain of academic dysfunction.
- Based on comprehensive multidimensional and multidisciplinary data involving information from a range of modalities (auditory, visual, visuomotor, body image, social, neurological) singly and integrated; utilizing standardized measures of established reliability and validity; providing for variations within individual subjects, ages of subjects, and sources of samples.
- Providing a taxonomy clinically useful in guiding management.

To paraphrase Rourke (1994, p. 477), the patterns of assets and defects in various domains of academic difficulty and in the underlying various clinical etiologies of persons with learning disabilities differ markedly from one another and need to be considered in subgroup patterns. The problem of heterogeneity in children with learning disabilities is summarized by M. Farmer and Klein (1995):

> Learning to read calls upon many cognitive processes and involves many areas of the brain. A breakdown in any one of the contributing processes or areas may thus lead to an inability to read in the normal way. A difficulty in learning to read or dyslexia should not be viewed as a condition in itself, but as a symptom in a breakdown of one or more of the various processes involved. (p. 460)

SUBGROUPS IN DEVELOPMENTAL READING DISABILITY

Phonological Deficits

Early studies attempted to relate reading failure to single variables or to combinations of variables. As far back as 1928, Nila Blanton Smith found that letter matching in first grade (an orthographic skill) yielded a correlation of .87 with the Detroit Word Recognition Test. Barrett (1965b, 1965c) found that measures of prereading visual discrimination were "valuable" predictors of reading ability. In another paper, however, Barrett (1965a) stressed the importance of auditory discrimination of beginning sounds as a predictor of later reading skills. In contrast, Hammill and Larsen (1974) found that auditory discrimination, auditory memory, sound blending, and audiovisual integration were not useful in predicting reading ability. A review of the Cooperative Research Progress in First Grade Reading Instruction (G. L. Bond & Dykstra, 1967) concluded that auditory *or* visual discrimination, pre-first-grade familiarity with print, and intelligence were all related to success in beginning to read; with knowledge of letter names accounting for 25.3% of the variance in reading ability at the end of first and second grades (Dykstra, 1968). Birch and Belmont (1964, 1965) found auditory-visual and visual-auditory integration distinguished the good from the poor reader. Blank and Bridger (1967) found "symbolic mediation," applying verbal labels to stimuli was needed for reading comprehension.

The need for verbal mediation was stressed by Vellutino (1978), who believed that "apparent perceptual problems in poor readers at both younger (7 to 8 years) and older (9 to 14 years) age levels are a secondary manifestation of verbal mediation deficiencies, possibly associated with basic language problems" (p. 107). Vellutino and Scanlon (1985) reviewed the decade of work they and their associates did at the Child Study Center in Albany, New York. Their work is a systematic exploration of the reasons for the difficulties encountered by poor readers in learning to identify the printed word. Exploring first the hypotheses that deficiencies in visual perception, cross-modality transfer, and temporal order recall are basic problems for the poor reader, Vellutino and his associates concluded that specific reading disability in young children is not caused by these dysfunctions. The visual perception hypothesis as advanced by Orton (1937) and Hermann (1959) was not compatible with Vellutino's finding that poor readers (Grades 2 through 8) could copy tachistoscopically presented scrambled letters, words, numbers, and geometric designs as well as normal readers, but could not name them as well. This finding was reinforced by poor readers (Grades 2 through 6) performing as well as normal readers on immediate visual recall of three-, four-, and five-letter Hebrew words. The intersensory integration problems, which Birch and Belmont (1964, 1965) inferred from the difficulty poor readers had in associating the auditory stimulus of Morse code with the visual representation of that stimulus, were not confirmed when the Vellutino group used paired associative learning tasks with nonverbal as well as verbal associations. They found no appreciable differences between readers and nonreaders on nonverbal tasks, including visual associations, auditory associations, and visual-verbal learning tasks. The Albany group also criticized the temporal order recall dysfunction (Bakker, 1972), suggesting that inaccuracies in serial order may be a function of the specific content of the items used in the testing and that one cannot dissociate serial-order recall from memory. Vellutino concluded that the differences between poor and normal readers on the measures used in the visual perception, cross-modality, and temporal sequencing research are secondary manifestations of reader-group differences in verbal encoding ability.

A series of studies, systematically varying verbal and nonverbal stimuli on measures of short- and long-term memory, found that poor readers were consistently differentiated when verbal factors were introduced, but not when the effects of verbal encoding were minimized. Poor readers in the second grade were found to have significant difficulty encoding the structural properties, especially phonological properties, of spoken and written words. By sixth grade, the reader-group differences were greater on verbal learning and verbal memory tasks that relied more heavily on encoding of word meaning than on encoding of word structures. Vellutino and Scanlon (1985) concluded that "difficulties in learning to read, as measured by deficiencies in word identification, may be caused primarily by limitations in coding structural or purely linguistic attributes of spoken and printed words" (p. 210). The Albany group (Vellutino, Scanlon, & Tanzman, 1994) have advanced additional evidence to support their earlier findings, that "adequate word identification is the central component of the reading process and that adequate facility in word identification is prerequisite to adequate reading comprehension, along with adequate language comprehension" (p. 279). The Albany group have been concerned with the visual and linguistic underpinnings of word identification and the problems in operationalizing phonological and orthographic coding. Using data from a large psychometric battery, administered to young and older, poor and normal readers, they employed both stepwise and hierarchical regression analysis of skills and abilities presumed to underlie word identification as predictor variables. They found that "a composite measure of pseudoword decoding by itself accounted for most of the variance on the word identification composite" (p. 323). Visual abilities did not contribute significant variance on word identification for younger children (Grades 2 and 3). The language measure evaluating phonological skills accounted for greater variance than did measures of semantic and syntactic abilities, whereas in the older group (Grades 6 and 7) semantic abilities accounted for more of the variance than other phonological or semantic abilities. Vellutino et al. (1994) suggest that those who conceptualize word identification in terms of phonological and orthographic coding underemphasize the role of semantic and syntactic skills in the process.

Parallel to the work of the Vellutino and his associates at Albany has been the long-term investigation of Iabelle Liberman and the group at Haskins Laboratories in New Haven, Connecticut. As early as 1967 I. Y. Liberman, Cooper, Shankweiler, and Studdert-Kennedy have theorized that learning to read and to write depends in large part on "special language related skills" that "go beyond primary abilities required in producing and understanding speech" (I. Y. Liberman & Shankweiler, 1985). A series of reports of the Haskins Laboratories spanning over two decades has identified three major problems of the poor reader:

> Difficulty in becoming aware of sublexical structure for the purpose of developing word recognition strategies, unreliable access to the phonological representation in the internal lexicon for naming objects and for performing metalinguistic tasks involving phonological properties of words, and finally the deficient use of phonetic properties as a basis for short-term working memory operations that underlie the processing of connected language in any form. (Liberman, Rubin, Duques, & Carlisle, 1985, p. 15)

The awareness of phoneme segments is a developmentally acquired skill, not present in the average 4-year-old, beginning to be acquired in some (less than 20%) of 5-year-olds and normally acquired in 70% of children at the end of their first year in school (I. Y. Liberman, Shankweiler, Fischer, & Carter, 1974). The failure to achieve proficiency in phonological strategies is a "causal link" to reading and writing abilities. However, phonological strategies needed for lexical access can be learned (Morris et al., 1998; Blechman, 1991; Torgesen et al., 1997) suggesting phonological processing as a technique in remediation of reading disabilities. Adult poor readers also have problems on tasks requiring an understanding of phonemic structure. Errors in word naming tasks in 8 to 10-year-olds as seen in the Boston Naming Test, (Kaplan, Goodglass, & Weintraub, 1982) and short-term memory storage, also depend on knowledge of phonological structure (A. M. Lieberman, Mattingly, & Turvey, 1972). Thus, the contribution of Lieberman and the Haskins group is to describe the primary defect in decoding the written word as phonological processing; this difficulty in phonological processing also underlines the ability to store the word in short-term memory resulting in reading comprehension problems. These findings have had significant support from studies such as those of the Learning Research Center at Yale, the Colorado Learning Project, and at the NICHD-funded Learning Disabilities Center of Bowman-Gray. As seen in Chapter 4, a defect in phonological processing is a central criterion in the Orton Research Group's definition of reading disability. However, as a predictor of future reading scores, phonological awareness in prekindergarten and kindergarten children accounts for less variance (18% to 20%) than does letter identification or traditional reading scores (27% to 31%) (Scarborough, 1998). Given the maturational sequence in the development of phonological skills (I. Y. Lieberman et al., 1974), it is not surprising that 4- and 5-year-olds do not normally require such skills. Those who do, will become good readers.

While agreeing that "awareness of the internal phonological structure of words is of prime importance in success with the alphabetic principle in word recognition" P. Lindamood (1994) (P. C. Lindamood, Bell, & Lindamood, 1992, p. 42), stress a specific aspect of phonological processing that the group have termed *comparator* function, "the ability to compare two phonological structures by holding their phoneme and/or syllable elements in mind, so any variations in the number, identity or order of the segments can be explicitly noted and represented." This skill requires the ability to discriminate sensory and motor attributes of phoneme perception and to store the sensory and motor scheme in memory as stable phonetic percepts. The auditory, oral-motor, and visual attributes of speech sounds are linked together to form that perception. "The processing and awareness of phonological information must be brought to *conscious* attention for its most efficient appreciation to coding with the alphabetic principle in spelling and reading" (I. Y. Liberman, Shankweiler, & Liberman, 1989; P. Lindamood, 1994, p. 355). Thus, in remediation, "Individuals become aware of the mouth actions that produce speech words so that they can feel sounds within words, enabling them to become self-correcting in reading, spelling and speech" (Lindamood & Bell, 2000).

In an assessment of "phonological processing," Lindamood (1994) goes beyond oral discrimination tasks to counting phonemes or syllables in words. The Auditory Conceptualization Test (C. Lindamood & Lindamood, 1984) evaluates a level of metalinguistic processing, the concept of number and order of isolated phonemes, the comparator function of how and where two syllables differ, and conceptualization of that difference in a visual, sensory-motor medium. The LACT requires that two syllables have to be held in mind, compared, and their point of phonemic contrast analyzed, categorized, and represented in the visuomotor field. The authors point out that the central processes involved in these tasks are directly comparable to the cognitive load for self-correction of decoding and spelling errors, "an important aspect of independence in literacy" (P. C. Lindamood et al., 1992, p. 246).

According to the Lindamood group, the ability to conceptualize the number, identity, and order of isolated phonemes appears to emerge "spontaneously" for the "bulk of the population by about 8 to 9 years of age; the ability to compare and conceptualize phonemes spoken in syllables appears not to emerge developmentally for one third of the population, even into adulthood" (P. Lindamood, 1994). These conclusions are not documented in relating scores on the original LACT to reading and spelling in the 1992 and 1994 papers. However, earlier testing with 660 students, K-12, revealed at every grade level mean correlations of .73 on LACT and at or above-grade reading and spelling ability in the WRAT. While testing for reading comprehension in 1,440 third graders, Calfee, Lindamood, and Lindamood (1973) found that those who scored at or above the LACT normative minimally recommended score for their grade had a 78% probability of being at or above grade level in reading comprehension on the California Primary Reading Test.

Temporal Impairment in Auditory and Visual Processing

In a series of reports starting in the early 1970s, Paula Tallal and her associates (see Tallal, Miller, & Fitch, 1993 for a review of these studies) have cumulative evidence that the acquisition of "higher level speech processing and reading development, may be impaired by difficulties in the processing of basic sensory information entering the nervous system in rapid succession, "within milliseconds" (Tallal et al., 1993, p. 27). Thus, there is a basic temporal impairment, a tenth-of-millisecond delay in the time information from the peripheral sensory apparatus is relayed to the central nervous system. The delay in temporal integration causes "a cascade of effects, starting with the normal development of efficient phonological abilities, and in turn resulting in subsequent failure to learn to speak and read normally. Normal temporal sequencing is essential to develop neural representation of phonemes, which must be distinguished from the stream of speech and combined to form words" (Tallal, Merzenich, Miller, & Jenkins, 1998).

In their initial work (Tallal & Piercy, 1973), twelve children, ages 6 to 9 years, language impaired (LI), and matched controls, were first trained to detect and discriminate fundamental varied sequential presentation of two steady-state tones with different fundamental frequencies (100 Hz and 305 Hz) and to respond by pressing appropriate panels on the response box. Subjects were next trained to respond to different sequences of the tones, then tested with these tones and varying interstimulus intervals from 8 ms to 4,062 ms. Serial memory was tested using the same 2 tones in sequences of 3 to 7 elements at 428 ms intervals. While there were no significant differences between performance of language impaired (LI) children and controls in detecting, associating or sequencing when the interstimulus interval (ISI) was 428 ms or over, no LI subject reached a criterion of 75% accuracy at 150 ms ISI or shorter. In contrast, all controls reached 75% correct at ISI of 8 ms or longer. On a three-element memory task at 75 ms tone duration, only 2 of 12 LI children reached criterion whereas all of controls did so. When stimulus duration was lengthened to 250 ms, 10 of the 12 subjects reached criterion on the 3-element task, but when the number of elements for sequencing was increased to more than 3, even increasing the duration resulted in impaired performance in the LI subjects.

Similarly, in tests of the ability of LI children to detect and sequence pairs of speech sounds rather than tones, LI children were impaired when steady-state vowel stimuli were used; when stop consonant-vowel (CV) syllables were used, 10 of the 12 LI subjects were impaired, stating that they could not hear the difference between two CV syllable presentations. When the ISI was 40 ms, even vowel-vowel stimuli were impaired. At 80 ms, processing CV syllables was unimpaired. Tallal et al. (1993) concluded that LI children "were impaired in their ability to interpret brief acoustic components of information occurring within tens of milliseconds in the ongoing speech stream regardless of phonetic classification" (p. 72).

The temporal integration-sequencing defect of auditory stimuli supported in LI and in children with developmental dyslexia suggested that these deficits could be significantly modified through training aimed at reducing temporal integration thresholds (Tallal et al., 1996, 1998). The finding that in primates neural circuitry can be remapped after specific temporal training regimes demonstrated the dynamic plasticity of the brain and its response to training of deficit functions. A system approach to such training in developmental dyslexia has been described by Tallal and associates.

The deficit in temporal sequencing, however, is not limited to the auditory area. The magnocellular visual pathway that integrates rapid reception and rapid processing of visual information has been described as poorly functioning in dyslexia compared with the slower processing component of the visual system, the parvocellular system, the component important for analyzing a scene in greater and more leisurely detail (Galaburda & Livingstone, 1993; Livingstone, 1999). In their morphological studies of dyslexia, Livingstone, Rosen, Drislane, and Galaburda (1991) found that cells in the magnocellular layers of the lateral geniculate bodies of dyslexic subjects were found to be smaller than in control brains, whereas the neurons of the parvocellular system were not significantly different from the controls. Smaller neurons with their thinner axons have slower conduction velocities than the normal cell. Livingstone et al. conclude that these findings were consistent with visual evoked potential responses: In dyslexia, visual evoked potential to slow stimuli were normal, but were decreased when rapid stimuli were presented. Evidence concerning a temporal deficit in the magnocellular system in subsets of developmental dyslexia is reviewed in Chapter 3.

Temporal processing deficits in dyslexia are reviewed by M. Farmer and Klein (1995). They describe as four separate components of temporal information processing: detection or identification of a single stimulus, stimulus individuation (minimum separation threshold determination), temporal order judgment for two stimuli (including same/different discriminations), and discrimination of sequences that have been studied in literature reviews. The authors conclude, "Temporal processing difficulties occur frequently in dyslexics and may be an important consideration for the investigation of the underlying cause of dyslexia." In criticism of the temporal perception theory, Studdert-Kennedy and Mody (1995) argue that errors in temporal order judgment of syllables and tones reflect difficulty in identifying stimuli rapidly and are independent deficits in speech and nonspeech discrimination capacity, not a general defect in rate of auditory perception, as would be found in dyslexia.

The question has been raised, however, Can the problems of temporal sequencing in auditory and in the visual functions in children with developmental dyslexia, "be attributed to a generalized defect in the processing of rapidly changing signals by the central nervous system" (J. Stein, 1993, p. 83). Peter Wolff (1993) has reviewed temporal resolution in motor coordination, on coordinated bimanual action with emphasis on temporal variables of timing, precision, and serial ordering. There are experimental studies in humans and other mammals to suggest that timing and sequencing in speech and in language overlap with neuronal processes for the temporal organization of unimanual and bimanual motor skills, at a neuroanatomical, physiological, and behavioral level. Based on studies of 230 children, adolescents, and adults meeting "accepted" inclusion and exclusion criteria for developmental dyslexia, Wolff summarizes four findings:

1. Dyslexic individuals performed bimanual tasks with significantly greater variability of interresponse intervals than age-matched controls in each of the groups tested; they also deviated more from the prescribed response frequency.
2. Pathological controls did not differ from controls, but like normal controls they differed significantly from dyslexic subjects.
3. The various tasks were not equally discriminating at each age:
   (a) None of the dyslexics differed from controls on analogous unimanual tapping.
   (b) Nine to ten-year-old dyslexics differed from controls on bimanual synchronous tapping tasks that were no longer discriminating at 11 to 13 years.
   (c) Bimanual alternation tasks discriminated dyslexic adolescents and controls until age 17 to 18 years, but not in adults.
   (d) Asymmetrical discriminating tasks were differentiated groups at all age levels.
4. There were no differences between dyslexics with and without motor deficits on conventional academic achievement tests of reading and spelling, standardized intelligence tests, or the extended classical examination for minor neurological signs.

Wolff (1993) concludes, "Temporal resolution in bimanual coordination appears to be a developmentally invariant finding in a substantial proportion of dyslexic subjects" (p. 90). Developmental dyslexia does have a generalized impairment of temporal processing according to J. Stein (1993): "There is probably enough evidence to speculate that there is indeed a generalized neuronal system, transcending sensory and motor boundaries, specialized for processing rapidly changing signals," and involving auditory, visual, motor or somatosensory. Wolff (1993) states:

"One of the general findings from experimental studies is that dyslexic children differ from normal readers in the temporal resolution and serial order perception of linguistically neutral and verbally meaningful auditory and visual events, in their ability to impose serial order on sequences of finger and hand movements, and in their ability to impose rhythmic structure on word strings to establish phrase boundaries in the reception and production of connected text." (p. 88)

Timing may be one of the significant physiological defects in developmental dyslexia.

Llinas (1993) suggests that the controls of a specific intrinsic clock, the normal properties of neuronal circuits responsible for temporal aspects of cognition are, in developmental language and learning disabilities, modified in a particular range slower than that needed to respond to rapid temporal stimuli. While the mechanism for this alteration in intrinsic brain rhythmicity is unknown, Llinas wonders whether there are pharmacological tools to improve the timing properties of CNS circuits in dyslexia.

"Double–Deficit" Hypothesis

Using a strict definition of specific development dyslexia available at that time, Boder (1970), Boder and Jarrico (1982), and Ingram, Mann, and Blackburn (1970) selected 92 boys and 15 girls, ages 8 to 15 years, who were two or more years behind grade placement in reading and spelling. Three types of reading disability were described:

1. A dysphonetic group (67%) that lacked word analysis (i.e., phonetic) skill, had difficulty sounding out and blending component letters and syllables.
2. A dysidetic group (10%) with selective impairment in remembering and discriminating visual gestalten.
3. A mixed dysphonetic and dysidetic group (23%).

Morton (1969) proposed a "dual route" model of developmental dyslexia, two independent pathways for printed word recognition: a phonological sounding-out route, and a direct lexical route read by visual processing of the letters of the word without phonological mediation. A review of the dual route model appears in Barron (1986). A mixed group, as described by Boder, was not mentioned. Similar models termed "surface dyslexia" (with intact phonological skills but poor orthographic reading as seen in difficulty with identification of irregular words) and "phonological dyslexic" with impaired phonological skills (difficulty with nonsense word reading) were described. These groups were identified by Manis et al. (1996) in an examination of 51 children reading below 30th percentile in word recognition, compared with 51 age-matched younger readers and 27 younger normal readers who scored in the same range as dyslexics in word recognition. The surface dyslexics were impaired in orthographic knowledge but not in phonology; phonological dyslexics showed the opposite pattern.

Three major studies from the Colorado Reading Project have supported the componential analysis of word recognition in dyslexia. This is not to diminish the importance of a phonological decoding deficit. When appropriate reading level match procedures were used in difficult nonword recognition trials, a phonological decoding deficit "nearly" always was found (Olson, Forsberg, Wise, & Rack, 1994). Nevertheless, dysidetic readers (surface dyslexics) with poor orthographic skills do exist and differ from those with phonological deficits not only in their approach to reading, but also in the possible heritability of the disorder. Castles, Daha, Geyen, and Olson (1999) and Olson et al. (1994) in their study of twin data from the Colorado Reading Project found a difference in heritability between phonological processing and orthographic skills. There was an equal balance of shared genetic ($h^2g = .41 \pm 17$) and shared environmental ($c^2g = .41 \pm 16$) influence for the orthographic coding deficits in the lexical route, whereas there was a high heritability of the group with phonological deficit ($h^2g = .80 \pm 17$) with no significant influence of shared environment ($c^2g = .06 \pm 15$).

Separate assessment of orthographic and phonological skills in word recognition is supported by the "independent contribution of the two skills to individual differences in word recognition, and by behavioral-genetic evidence for the high heritability of the group deficit in phonological decoding" (Olson et al., 1994, p. 263). In contrast, the orthographic deficits are less heritable than are the deficits in phonological decoding.

Maryanne Wolf (1999) hypothesized two core neuropsychological processing deficits of individuals with developmental reading disabilities: processes underlying phonological deficits and those underlying slow naming speed. The double-deficit hypothesis represents not a reflection of the phonological core deficit, but the realization that there remain children with dyslexia with adequate decoding and phonological skills but with poor fluency-related deficits.

The history of naming-speed deficits goes back to N. Geschwind's paper of 1965 suggesting that a predictor of reading readiness would be color naming. Picking up the thread, Denckla (Denckla & Rudel, 1974, 1976a, 1976b) found that color naming *speed,* rather than color naming *accuracy* differentiated dyslexic children from normal reading controls, that speed for basic symbols (letters, digits, colors, pictured objects) was a reliable and valuable test to differentiate some dyslexic children from normal readers. Wolf (Wolf, Bally, & Morris, 1986) in a 5-year longitudinal study found that differences in naming speed particularly for letters, could be found in early kindergarten and were maintained through Grade 4 (Meyer, Wood, Hart, & Felton, 1998) and into adulthood (Scarborough, 1998; Wolff, 1993).

Further naming-speed performance was found in German, Finnish-speaking, and Spanish-speaking children with reading disabilities, and was a better predictor of later reading than phoneme detection tasks. The difference between children with rapid-naming difficulty appeared to be only for the interstimulus intervals, the gap between one stimulation and the response to the next. (Obregon, 1994). Naming speed (Wolf & Bowers, 1999b) began to be considered as "a window on the brain's ability to inhibit, activate, and interpret discrete constellations of neurons within a small period of time" (Wolf, 1999, p. 10) and could no longer be categorized as a phonological task. Phonological awareness tasks predict significant variance in word-attack; naming speed best predicts word-identification (Bowers & Swanson, 1991); "Deficits in both variables would impede both aspects of reading, leaving no compensatory route easily available" (Wolf, 1999, p. 14).

Classification of subtypes of reading disabilities according to the double-deficit hypothesis includes (a) the rapid naming deficit group with intact phonological awareness, (b) the phonological deficit group with intact naming speed but impaired comprehension, and (c) the double-deficit group with both naming speed and phonological awareness deficit and comprehension deficits.

Bakker and his associates (Bakker, 1979; Bakker, Bouma, & Gardien, 1990; Bakker, Van Leeuwen, & Spyer, 1987), on the basis of reading errors made by children with reading disabilities, distinguish between an L- and P-types of dyslexia. The L-type reads relatively fast while making substantive errors such as omissions, additions, and other "word-mutilating mistakes," have low scores in verbal short-term memory, and on dichotic auditory processing have a right ear advantage (REA) (Masutto, 1994). The P-dyslexics tend to read slowly, to make time-consuming errors such as fragmentations and repetitions and to have short attention span, with low scores on the coding subtest of the WISC-III; they do not have a REA. Bakker hypothesized that initial reading primarily requires the visuoperceptual analysis of the printed word and is thus primarily dependent on right-hemispheric processing. Fluent reading, on the other hand, a characteristic of more advanced reading, requires semantic-syntactic processing of text, a function primarily mediated by the left hemisphere. At some point in the normal development of reading, the primary subservice of reading switches from the right to the left hemisphere. The P-style of slow readers fails to make the "hemisphere shift," whereas the L-type dyslexics skip the initial phase of reading, in which the visual-perceptual features are mastered. Thus although the L-type readers are rapid readers, they are prone to substantive errors. Bakker validated this dichotomous taxonomy by finding that when words to be read are flashed on the central visual field, they are processed differently by the two groups, as evidenced by hemispheric differences in the evoked potentials. Interestingly, Bakker found that hemisphere-specific stimulation (right-hemisphere stimulation in L-dyslexics; left-hemisphere stimulation in P-dyslexics) not only brought about relative changes in the electrophysiological activity of the stimulated hemispheres, but also improved aspects of reading and spelling (Bakker & Vinke, 1985, p. 523). The L- and P-types of dyslexia have been termed hemisphere-specific types (Van Strien, Stolk, & Zuiker, 1995).

Both the Boder and the Bakker sub-groupings of reading disabilities have been subject to criticism. Using quantified EEG, Flynn, Deering, Goldstein, and Rahbar (1992) did not find the predicted regional differences in theta and beta wave amplitudes suggesting "recapitulation of the theoretical base for the Boder subtyping system was needed" (p. 139). Hynd (1992) in a critical review of the Bakker model states that validation of the model and of the treatment effects has not been done.

MULTIVARIATE STUDIES

Parallel to the clinical observations of subgroups in developmental dyslexia, multivariate statistical approaches attempted to find clusters of neuropsychological processes in individuals with developmental dyslexia. These statistical studies are not exempt from the problems described for classical research—heterogeneity of samples, disparate demographics, and differences in research methodology. Early studies with subjects from clinical populations have been studied with batteries of neuropsychological tests and analyzed with multivariable statistics. Mattis, French, and Rapin (1975) isolated three independent "dyslexic syndromes" accounting for 90% of a sample of 82 "dyslexic children." This sample (ages 8 to 18 years) was selected from a larger group of children and referred by pediatric neurologists to a neuropsychological clinic of a large metropolitan hospital that drew its patients from a low socioeconomic population. Fifty-three percent of the 82 subjects were considered "brain damaged." Although the subjects' performance varied on a wide variety of speech, motor, and perceptual tasks, these syndromes were identified:

1. A language disorder (39%) consisting of anomia (20% or greater proportion of errors on a Naming Test) and one of the following:

   (a) Disorder of comprehension (Token Test one sigma below mean).

   (b) Disorder of imitative speech (Sentence Repetition Test).

   (c) Disorder of sound discrimination (10% or greater errors on discrimination of rhythmic letters).

2. Articulatory and graphomotor dyscoordination (37%) consisting of:

   (a) Poor performance on the Illinois Test of Psycholinguistic Ability (ITPA) Sound Blending Test.

   (b) Poor performance on graphomotor tests.

   (c) Acustosensory and receptive language process within normal limits.

3. Visuospatial Perceptual Disorder (16%):

   (a) Verbal IQ more than 10 points above performance.

   (b) Raven's Colored Progressive Matrices less than the equivalent performance IQ.

   (c) Benton's visual retention test at or below borderline level.

Mattis (1978) conducted a cross-validation study of 163 dyslexic children, ages 8 to 14, drawn from a clinic serving a Black and Hispanic population. He found the same three syndromes previously described, but in different proportions. Language disorder accounted for 63%; articulatory-graphomotor, 10%; and visuospatial, 5%; overlapping (two syndromes) was found in 9%. An additional 10% were found to have a "sequencing disorder" in which children did not have stable concepts of "before" or "after" and some could not identify their own left and right hands. Ingram et al. (1970) reviewed 82 children referred to the Department of Child Life and Health in Edinburgh for dyslexia; the majority of them had been examined in the neurological and speech clinics of the Royal Hospital for Sick Children. He was able to identify a group of children with specific reading disabilities, "without evidence of brain disease, and with a positive family history of reading and writing difficulties," among whom were those whose errors were predominantly "visuospatial" and those whose errors were predominantly "audiophonic." A mixed visuospatial and audiophonic group was also found (p. 419). These reports underline the heterogeneity of children included as learning disabled, heterogeneous not only in the patterns of neuropsychological processing defects, but also in the environmental and neurological stressors that accompany their learning difficulties.

Subgroups on the basis of multivariate analysis, cluster analysis, and Q type or inverted factor analysis have had increasing use as a statistical technique in subtype classification of learning disabilities. The use of these methods does not diminish methodological problems in variations in (a) the target sample (same source, age, IQ, definitional boundaries, socioeconomic status, educational experience, presence or absence of neurological signs); (b) clustering variables, their reliability and construct validity; (c) the statistical methodology itself. All of these problems may produce variations in numbers of subgroups identified as well as in the individual characteristics of each subgroup. Fisk, Finnell, and Rourke (1985) review the methodological problems in subgroup analysis: They stress that "one could hardly expect reliable scientific findings to emerge through use of complex, poorly understood measures to some ill-defined set or grouping of learning impaired children" (p. 332). A review of methodological problems in factor analysis and in cluster analysis may be found in Fletcher and Satz (1985), Morris, Blashfield, and Satz (1981, 1986), Morris and Fletcher (1988), and DeLuca (1991).

Early studies in statistical clustering of children with reading disabilities (Doehring, 1968; Doehring & Hoshko, 1977; Doehring, Hoshko, & Bryans, 1979; Myklebust & Boshes, 1969; Petrauskas & Rourke, 1979) are described in detail in A. A. Silver and Hagin (1990). In summary, disabled readers were differentiated from normal readers by a basic impairment of sequential processing ability seen in (a) verbal tasks (oral word rhyming, oral vocabulary, in speed of naming verbal sequences) and (b) nonverbal tasks such as speed of perception of visual forms, immediate memory for visual sequences. The subgroups thus derived were not surprising, reminiscent of the Boder (1970) and the Castles et al. (1999) groupings. There were, however, important variations on the verbal-nonverbal theme. For example, Petrauskas and Rourke (1979) applied a Q-sort technique on data from 160 children, ages 7 to 8-years, of whom 133 were "retarded" readers scoring in the lowest percentile on the WRAT. Twenty seven were "normal" readers. All were drawn from the neuropsychological laboratory at the University of Windsor and the Windsor Western Hospital. All had an IQ greater than 80, came at least from middle socioeconomic families and had intact vision and hearing. Each child was studied with a battery of tests grouped into 6 categories: tactile perceptual, sequencing, motor, visuospatial, auditory-verbal, and abstract-conceptual. Five subtypes were identified, of which 3 were fully described:

1. $N = 40$ (males : females = 3:1) most difficulty on verbal tasks (i.e., verbal fluency and sentence memory; low scores on WISC digit + span; language discrepancy on the verbal and performances scores on WISC, with lower verbal scale scores.

2. $N = 26$ (males : females = 12:1) most difficulty on tests for finger agnosia on both hands and on a measure involving immediate memory for visual sequences; small WISC verbal-performance discrepancy with poor Arithmetic, Coding Information, and Digit Span; verbal and language-related problems less severe than subgroup 1.

3. $N = 13$, of whom 2 were normal readers. Better performance on left than on right side of the body on tactile performance tests and on finger recognition test; difficulty with conceptual flexibility especially when verbal coding was involved, some difficulty in psychomotor skills, lower verbal than performance IQ (WISC); poor Arithmetic, Information, and Digit Span.

4. Group 4, 8 of whom were normal readers, and Group 5 (normal readers) were not fully described.

What this all suggests is that in studying the central processing defects found in children with "learning disabilities" one must look for problems other than in the phonetic or in the orthographic domains.

Doehring, also, continued studies of the classification of disabled readers on the basis of language, neuropsychological, and reading deficits (Doehring, 1985). The 88 subjects of his previous reports were "deficient" on all 31 of the reading measures used, most deficient in oral reading of nonsense syllables, least deficient in visual matching of letters and words. There was, however, a large overlap on reading measures between the reading-disabled sample and normal readers of the same age. Statistical classification of the reading measures revealed the three subtypes previously found: (a) (38% of the sample) poor in oral reading of letters, nonsense syllables, and words; (b) (25% of the sample) slow and inaccurate in associating printed and spoken letters, syllables, and words; (c) (19%) poor oral and silent reading of orthographically regular letter sequences in syllables and words relative to reading single letters; (d) (16%) unclassified, many of whom had relatively mild problems. Doehring (1985) is confident that these subtypes are stable and reliable. However, on Q-type analysis, the subtypes were not homogeneous and independent with 26% of the subjects having high loadings on 2 or more of the 3 factors defining the subtypes, and there was no simple correspondence between reading and neuropsychological measures. Children with sound-letter problems were most impaired in verbal skills and finger tapping, those with letter-sequence problems tend to perform poorly on the Progressive-Matrices Test and on a measure of finger agnosia; those with oral reading problems were least impaired on neuropsychological tests.

Satz and Morris (1981) used cluster analysis to describe subtypes within a sample of 89 White boys, mean age 11 years, tested at the end of their fifth grade in Alachua County, Florida, who were 2 years behind grade in reading. Rather than subgroup on the basis of reading measures as did Doehring (1985), Satz and Morris used four neuropsychological tests based on a high factor loading on (a) language factor (WISC similarities, verbal fluency), and (b) on a perceptual factor (Berry-Buktenica test of visuomotor function, visual recognition, and visual discrimination). The verbal fluency test (Spreen & Benton, 1969) requires children to verbalize words beginning with different letters of the alphabet under timed conditions, the Recognition and Discrimination test (Fletcher & Satz, 1985) is a geometric figure-matching test. Five distinct cluster groups emerged:

1. ($N = 27$) global language impairment; nonlanguage perceptual tests normal.

2. ($N = 14$) specific language impairment with selective impairment on the verbal fluency test.

3. ($N = 10$) mixed global language and perceptual impairment.

4. ($N = 23$) visuomotor perceptual impairment.

5. ($N = 12$) unexpected type: no impairment on any of the neuropsychological tests.

This study is of interest because it is the foundation for a longitudinal study, albeit a retrospective one of the same 89 boys of the 1981 study. Three of the subtypes remained essentially unchanged (general verbal, global language, and visual-perceptual motor, subgroups 1, 3, 4). Specific language impairment (subgroup 2) was found to have persistent deficit in verbal fluency but increasing improvement in cognitive performance.

Spreen (1987), too, has been concerned with statistically defined subgroups. Based on cluster analysis of two groups of children, ages 8 to 12, referred to the University of Victoria Neuropsychology clinic because of learning problems, tested with variables including sentence repetition, right-left orientation, reading, spelling, and arithmetic, subtests on the WRAT, scaled scores for Similarities, Vocabulary, Coding, Block Design, and Arithmetic subtests of the WISC-R. He found 3 subgroups, visual-perceptual, linguistic, and articulate-graphmotor. The visual-perceptual cluster was low in Vocabulary, Block Design, and Coding; the linguistic cluster, low in Similarities, Vocabulary, and Coding; the articulate-graphomotor group, in Sentence Repetition, right-left discrimination, and Coding.

A similar pattern was found by Watson and Willows (1995) in 50 "unsuccessful" readers, ages 6 to 10 years. When compared with controls, both first-grade and older "unsuccessful" readers differed from control on short-term auditory/working memory and decoding/encoding, while the reading-matched older disabled group had weakness in phonological coding and in visual sequential memory. Cluster analysis of the 50 poor readers yielded 3 subtypes: (a) symbolic processing/memory defect, (b) symbolic processing/memory in combination with visual processing deficiencies, and (c) symbolic processing/memory with visual processing and rapid automatized naming.

The spectrum of neuropsychological dysfunction described in this chapter reflects what William James had described in 1890. James stated: "In some individuals the habitual 'thought stuff,' if one may call it, is visual; in others it is auditory, articulatory or motor; in most perhaps it is evenly mixed" (James, 1890/1950). By motor, James referred to those who "make use in memory, reasoning and all their intellectual operations, of images derived from movement" (kinesthetic) (p. 61).

So it is in the studies reported in this chapter. Despite the diversity in samples of children studied—their source, their ages, and their intelligence, and the presence of cultural or neurological complications—the diversity in tests to which these samples were subjected, the diversity of professional bias, and the diversity of methodology, there appears to be a general consensus in the heterogeneous range of subgroup patterns. Many children with reading disorders appear to have difficulty in the "language" functions of the central nervous system, with lower verbal scores than performance scores on the WISC-R; poor performance on the PPVT; disorders of naming, auditory comprehension, imitative speech, and sound discrimination; difficulty in putting sounds together to make words; and problems with the sequential processing abilities. These language dysfunctions may be general or global, or they may involve specific functions such as naming. This group, the language impaired, appears to represent the largest number of children. Some children with learning disorders, however, are deficient in visuospatial-graphomotor skills and in the orientation of the body image in space, but they have intact auditory-sequential-perceptual areas. When the subjects are selected only for their symptoms of poor reading achievement, they present mixed skills and deficits and borderline cognitive functioning. The unanimity of findings in subgroup studies is more apparent than their diversity. As Kavale and Forness (1987) stated, "Statistical methods alone cannot deal with the subtle tasks and nuances of subtype research" (p. 379) and "it is quite possible that clinical-inferential classification might possess more heuristic value for particular outcomes [treatment] than numerical techniques" (p. 38).

The reports of subtypes in the preceding sections of this chapter have been concerned mainly with subtypes of reading disabilities. Rourke and his associates at the University of Windsor, Ontario, have reported studies of differences in neuropsychological function in other domains of academic learning, particularly in arithmetic, and have defined the nonverbal learning disability. (Rourke, 1994; Strang & Rourke, 1985). Rourke views subgroups as based on more than one neuropsychological function and processing measure; he attempts to "integrate dimensions of individual and social development on the one hand, with relevant control processing features on the other"; "the patterns of control processing abilities and deficits may predispose a youngster to predictably different patterns of social as well as academic difficulty" and are "designed to encompass developmental change and outcome in learning and behavioral responsibility" (Rourke, 1994, p. 476).

Thus, to study individuals with learning problems, Rourke uses a broad sampling of tasks involving sensory, perceptual, motor/psychomotor, attentional, mnestic, linguistic, and concept-formation/problem-solving/hypothesis testing abilities. In addition, comprehensive personality and behavioral data are obtained, the developmental demands (behavioral tasks, skills, and abilities) faced by the individual, the cultural milieu in which the individual must function, psychological reaction to these demands, and the support he receives in doing so. These evaluations are not static, but will change with age and the vicissitudes of life experience. The emphasis in these evaluations is on analysis of assets and deficits that hold implications for prognosis, including treatment. We would add to this clinical evaluation, neurological evaluation, both classical and soft signs, and detailed family history.

Two contrasting subgroups of learning disabilities are described. One group with reading and spelling disability (RS) are those who exhibit relatively poor linguistic skills in conjunction with "very well developed" visuospatial-organizational, tactile-perceptual, psychomotor, and nonverbal problem-solving skills. They have very poor reading and spelling skills and better, although still impaired, mechanical arithmetic competence. The other group (A), the nonverbal learning disability, exhibits outstanding problems in visuospatial-organization, tactile-perceptual, psychomotor, and nonverbal problem-solving skills, within the context of clear strengths in psycholinguistic skills such as rote verbal learning, regular phoneme-graphone matching, amount of verbal output, and verbal classification. Their major academic difficulties are in mechanical arithmetic, but they have advanced levels of word recognition and spelling. They have good attention and memory attained through verbal modulation, but do not have attention and memory problems with data from tactile and visual perceptual areas. They have an aversion for novel experience; problems in judgment, problem-solving, and reasoning lead to difficulties in social competence. There is risk for psychopathology especially of the internalized variety. Activity tends to decline to hypoactivity by late childhood. Long-term prognosis for socioemotional development is guarded.

The delineation of the nonverbal disability (NLD) is an important contribution, relating a domain of academic learning disability—arithmetic—to a constellation of central processing deficits, to behavior and emotion and indirectly to management. Whether that nonverbal disability has the genetic loading of the developmental reading disability is as yet obscure. In out own clinical practice, the NLD is frequently associated with some traumatic event during pregnancy or birth.

In his appendix to the 1994 paper, Rourke divides reading and spelling into three subtypes:

1. A basic phonological processing disorder (BPPD) similar to the RS subtype described earlier.

2. Phono-grapheme matching disorder (PGMD) with phoneme-grapheme or grapheme-phoneme matching problems, with assets similar to BPPD, except that phonemic hearing, segmenting, and blending are normal. Academic difficulty is seen in spelling of words not known by sight. Word recognition and word decoding skills are poor. Spelling of words learned by sight may be average or better.

3. Word-finding disorder (WFD) characterized by outstanding problems in word-finding and verbal expressive skills; the only deficit in accessing a normal store of verbal associations. Academically, reading and spelling are very poor during early school years, with improvement by sixth to eighth grade. Arithmetic and mathematics are strengths, writing of words is average to good.

In addition to the nonverbal learning disorder, Rourke adds another subtype: Output Disorder in all modalities, similar to the word-finding subtype, but with the additional difficulty of "organizing, directing" and all aspects of behavior expression. This group has severe problems in oral and written work in early school years, with some improvement in word recognition, word decoding, and reading comprehension in middle school years. Written work remains poor. They are at risk for internalized and/or externalizing psychopathology.

SUMMARY

This chapter views the academic domains of learning disabilities as symptoms, the final common pathways, the metaphysical tip of the iceberg, resulting from a series of hierarchical processes that underlie the symptoms. Some of the hierarchical processes are known, some not yet well understood; all have commanded intensive research. Immediately proximal to the academic difficulty are problems in the neuropsychological processing of information. For reading, there is a general consensus that immaturity in phonological skills is critical. However, there is also a consensus that there is no support to tie dyslexia to one specific modality or type of process. Thus, subgroups of reading disabilities have been described as "phonological or orthographic or mixed," "surface and phonological," dual-deficit (phonological and rapid automatic naming), and L- and P-type—each with an emphasis on different neuropsychological processes important as leading to the academic difficulty. Multivariate statistics have revealed a multitude of subgroups.

Underlying the neuropsychological deficits is a possible abnormality responsible for the processing deficits in the problem of hemisphere specialization. This suggests that children with developmental learning disabilities have not clearly established normal hemisphere specialization, that the normal (for right-handers and most left-handers) specialization of the left brain for language, and the right for spatial functions, is somehow perturbed so that the brain has difficulty processing language functions, body-image, and spatial functions.

A disturbance in temporal processing of auditory, visual, and somato-sensory information is offered as another hypothesis underlying perceptual processing deficits. As we look deeper into the iceberg, newer knowledge of brain imaging and brain functioning has revealed differences in the way the dyslexic brain deals with information compared with that of the normal reader. These data confirm that the activity of the brain in the areas involved in processing information is indeed different from normal. The findings, however, are not consistent. Regions of activity and measures of activity reveal multiple regions involved and activated, so that dyslexia itself appears to be heterogeneous in the way it affects information processing. Further in the depths of the iceberg are anatomical differences in adult dyslexics, suggesting abnormalities in hemisphere specialization.

The base of the iceberg is the motor driving the varied functional processes that cause the learning disability—the presumed etiological factors. Genetic factors have been implicated; organic injury from whatever source may lead to learning disabilities; experiential factors needed for the development of language may be inadequate or inappropriate. Each of these etiological factors produces a different clinical picture of the learning disability.

It is the theme of this book that the clinical understanding of the individual child with a learning disability must include data from each of the postulated levels, not only the academic domain of disability, but the unique neuropsychological processing deficits, the adequacy of hemisphere specialization, and the possible cause of it all. Then the symptoms can be understood and appropriate remediation given.

PART III

PRINCIPLES OF DIAGNOSIS AND TREATMENT

Chapter 6

EDUCATIONAL AND PSYCHOLOGICAL DIAGNOSIS

It is in connection with intelligence and the tests that measure it, that some of the most violent polemics in psychology and all the behavior sciences have raged.

—J. M. Hunt, 1961

Effective intervention is based on a clear understanding of the factors that contribute to a learning disorder. The process by which the understanding is obtained is sometimes described as assessment or evaluation; we use the term *diagnosis* because it is more appropriate to the multiaxial character of our approach.

Diagnosis is necessary because the constellation of contributing factors may differ for individual children, not only in terms of the mix of specific factors involved, but also in the compensations and supports available. Each child is unique within the population of children with learning disorders, and effective remediation of these disorders is more likely to occur when intervention is based on careful definition of the child's strengths and needs. The complex nature of learning disorders implies that diagnostic processes will be broad based, because no single discipline can provide all the skills necessary for comprehensive diagnosis.

Among the disciplines concerned with children with learning disorders, the term diagnosis has come to have various meanings. Among reading specialists, diagnosis implies an analysis of the child's educational skills—the manner in which children deal with written text, the errors they make in word attack, the comprehension of written text, and their understanding of language. For such a survey, educators may use conventional achievement tests, individual diagnostic tests of educational achievement, informal reading inventories, and other curriculum-based assessment tools. They may observe children at work in their classrooms, teach trial lessons to assess responses to various interventions, and assemble information on educational history from interviews with parents and teachers.

School psychologists assess cognitive functioning quantitatively and qualitatively, and analyze the extent to which academic achievement is appropriate to estimates of cognitive functioning obtained from individual tests of intelligence. They study motivation, learning style, and defensive operations. They may also collect data on the child's development and adjustment through interviews with parents and teachers, and through interview and observation of the child.

Neuropsychologists view diagnosis in terms of a series of tests designed to elucidate brain-behavior relationships. Such tests tap the peripheral manifestations of brain functioning, such as visual, auditory, tactile, and kinesthetic perception; motor and psychomotor control; language and conceptual abilities; and executive functioning. From the results of these measures, neuropsychologists make inferences about the intactness of brain processes and localization of brain pathology.

Neuropsychiatrists use the classical neurological examination, as well as the soft signs of neurological dysfunction to assess the integrity and maturation of the central nervous system. They study intrapsychic signs and symptoms through interviews and observations of parent-child interaction. These findings are viewed within the total body of medical knowledge to determine whether these findings relate to groups of disease entities or known syndromes, to understand the idiosyncratic way in which the disorder emerges in the individual child, to determine treatment modalities that have been helpful for the specific condition, and to predict the outlook for the child under study.

While each discipline attempts to diagnose learning disorders within its own frame of reference and through its own unique skills, comprehensive diagnosis depends on the integration of these findings to answer specific questions about a specific child. What questions should diagnosis answer about a child with a learning disorder? To some extent, this question can be answered by considering the purposes for which the diagnosis is being done.

The purpose of diagnosis of learning disorders is (a) to understand the causes for the disorder in an individual child; (b) to delineate the specific abilities and disabilities of the child; (c) to evaluate the environmental supports available; (d) to guide intervention processes; (e) to provide some idea of prognosis; (f) to set timelines for reevaluation. In the final analysis, diagnostic formulations that cover these points will serve the child well. While diagnostic data, well integrated in terms of planning, are considered essential, practical considerations raise the question whether all aspects of diagnostic study can or should be provided to every child who experiences learning problems. In the light of the criticisms of the assessment procedures that have been mandated as part of federal special education legislation (Algozzine & Ysseldyke, 1986; Cruickshank, 1986; J. J. Gallagher, 1986), this question requires serious consideration. From a practical standpoint, all aspects of multidisciplinary examinations may not be available in all settings to which children come for service.

Given that all multidisciplinary services may not be either necessary or available for individual children, the question becomes one of defining services that *are* necessary or available. This does not imply support for the extreme position that would eliminate all diagnosis as unnecessary. For example, the applied behavior analysis approach regards diagnosis as irrelevant to treatment and operates as though learning failure results from the lack of practice or from learning inappropriate responses to instructional stimuli (Koorland, 1986). Wholesale acceptance of this approach would impoverish the field of learning disorders. Information secured in diagnostic study is important not only in targeting interventions with individual children, but also in building a database that can add to the theoretical understanding of the nature and variety of learning disorders.

Too little diagnostic information can have unfortunate results both for individuals and for the overall intervention program. For example, the decision to ignore cognitive differences among children and to offer remedial services to all children whose educational achievement scores fall below a given level can result in disservice to children at both ends of the distribution. Bright children who are "getting by" with low or average achievement may fail to be recognized and served; children with limited academic potential may be deprived of appropriate curricular provisions they may need. The field of learning disorders is faced with the dilemma of preserving the benefits diagnostic data provide while avoiding cumbersome and redundant assessment. This chapter describes a stepwise decision-making process designed to focus testing and to preserve the values of comprehensive clinical assessment. These steps are summarized in Figure 6.1. Each decision point represents a single diagnostic question. The first four steps, which constitute educational and psychological diagnosis, are discussed in this chapter; the fifth step, psychiatric and neuropsychological diagnosis, is discussed in Chapter 7.

In theory, a multiaxial evaluation to answer the diagnostic questions is required for each child. However, in practice, every child may not need *all* aspects of the evaluation. Diagnostic resources are more prudently used in a decision tree that prioritizes levels of diagnosis (Figure 6.1) through a systems approach. This decision tree indicates the decision points necessary for definition of the various disorders of learning. At each point, a decision of adequacy or inadequacy implies consideration of specific program provisions and/or further diagnostic studies necessary for understanding, defining, and meeting the individual's educational needs:

1. *Educational Achievement,* assessed both formally and informally, is the first step in diagnosis. If it is found to be inadequate, further study is necessary to understand the reasons for the problem.

2. *Educational Opportunity* is assessed through reconstruction of the formal and informal educational experiences that the child has enjoyed. The quality and consistency of parenting and early stimulation, preschool education, elementary and secondary schooling (depending on the age of the child), language, and cultural background are assessed at this point. Information secured at this second diagnostic step can be related to gaps in learning suggested by the previous decision point. If educational opportunity is found to be inadequate or inappropriate, programmatic changes to compensate for these inadequacies can be devised. If educational opportunities have been found to be adequate, further steps in diagnosis are required.

3. *Peripheral Sensory Functioning,* the third step in the formulation, involves assessment of visual and auditory acuity. If these sensory functions are found to be inadequate, recommendations for medical treatment and educational modifications

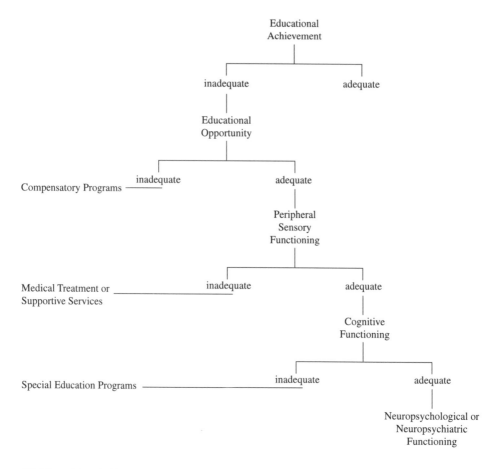

Figure 6.1 Decision tree: Decision making in the diagnosis of learning disorders.

can be devised. If sensory acuity is found to be adequate, further diagnostic steps are required.

4. *Cognitive Functioning,* the fourth step, involved administration of individual measures of cognitive abilities to provide quantitative and qualitative data on the child's cognitive functioning and adaptive behavior. A decision of inadequacy at this step leads to modification of education provisions through special education programs. A decision of adequacy leads to further diagnosis to tease out specific strengths and disorders of learning.

5. *Neuropsychological and Psychiatric Functioning* evaluates the integrity and maturity of the central nervous system. The skills of these disciplines are used to examine brain/behavior relationships with emphasis on sensory, motor, perceptual-integrative, associative, and language processes. If functioning is found to be

unimpaired, further diagnosis defines the effects of motivational and emotional factors essential for learning. Results of these examinations define intervention priorities, delineate assets and needs, and suggest long-range outcomes.

This decision tree indicates the *minimal* amount of information needed for planning broad-based educational programs for students with learning disorders. A decision of inadequacy at any point does not imply that further diagnostic study is unnecessary for appropriate education of the youngster; rather, it seeks to focus diagnosis on those services that will provide information that is *relevant* to decision making in order to select the appropriate educational program for each individual.

At the same time, this decision tree seeks to avoid lengthy diagnostic studies that involve the administration of the same extensive battery to every child irrespective of the problems they present. The decision tree offers a practical approach that is economical in the use of diagnostic services to define the learning disorders of individual children. It is a system that can be used to understand the forces that created the problems, the unique patterns in which the problems are expressed in each child, and the appropriate educational and clinical services needed for their resolution.

HOW ADEQUATE IS THIS CHILD'S EDUCATIONAL ACHIEVEMENT?

At the first decision point, the question to be answered is whether a learning disorder is present. Answering the question calls for information from two data sources: historical information and educational assessment.

Assuming that the usual referral sources of teachers and parents have drawn attention to the child's learning difficulties, much of the historical information will be elicited in interviews with the persons who made the referral. The teacher can provide concrete information about the difficulties seen in the classroom, present samples of current schoolwork, and supply anecdotal information about motivation and adjustment to school. Parents can provide information about the child's developmental history, including opportunities for formal and informal educational experiences and patterns of language development in the family. Descriptions of special abilities demonstrated in both academic and nonacademic work are also useful along with characteristic behavior patterns, reactions to stress, and adjustment in interpersonal relationships.

The first decision point also requires data on current academic skills. A variety of formal and informal methods for collecting data on school achievement is available. The selection of specific examination techniques should depend on the examiner's level of training, available test resources, and personal preferences. Some examiners use informal reading inventories consisting of materials actually in use in the child's classroom. These informal inventories have the advantage of drawing on content similar to that which the child has encountered in school. However, the proximity of the assessment may be outweighed by questions about the representativeness of the content sampled, as well as the unknown validity and reliability of the measure (Klesius & Homan, 1985; Lerner, 1988).

The psychometric characteristics of the formal measures of achievement are more readily available, either in the technical manuals of published tests or in such sources as the *Mental Measurements Yearbooks* (Buros Institute of Mental Measurement, various years). Although there are many achievement tests and test batteries in print, educators would do well to select tests by considering the psychometric characteristics described in the manuals and test critiques. Answers to the following guiding questions should be considered:

- What does this test measure?
- How recently was this test standardized?
- What is the underlying rationale for this test?
- Is the test content aligned with the content taught in the school this child attends?
- What methods were used to ensure the representativeness of the test items in the domain tested?
- How adequate was the sample on which the test was standardized?
- What evidence of reliability is presented?
- What evidences of validity—construct-related, content-related, criterion-related, or predictive—are presented?
- What kinds of units of measurement are used to express test scores? Are these units defensible statistically and useful in practice?

Other considerations that may guide selection are the experience required on the part of the examiner, the time requirements for administration, and the test format (group or individual). Irrespective of the educator's choice of assessment instruments, the significant aspect at this decision point is the interpretation of results to determine whether the child's educational achievement is adequate. This question cannot be answered by numerical test scores alone, but requires a formulation of the process by which the child handles the specific educational tasks. The three major areas of skills assessment—reading, written language, and mathematics—are discussed in the next sections.

Assessment of Reading Achievement

Reading is a complex process that must be analyzed to understand learning difficulties. One way to analyze the reading process is through the *Job Analysis of Reading,* which delineates four main skill areas that children must master if they are to read well: prereading skills, word attack, comprehension, and study skills (Table 6.1).

Prereading Skills

This area includes such visual perceptual skills as the discrimination of likenesses and differences of letters, the recognition of these symbols in their correct orientation in two-dimensional space, and the organization of these symbols into groups as syllables or words. Auditory skills involve discrimination and blending of isolated sounds so that a recognizable word results; accurate temporal sequencing of sounds in words and sentences is also required. To read English, children must know the arbitrary convention

Table 6.1   Job Analysis of Reading

Prereading Skills	Word Attack	Comprehension	Study Skills
Visual	Using	Oral vocabulary	Locating
Discrimination	Sight words	Literal comprehension	Selecting
Chunking	Language cues	Interpretation	Organizing
Perceiving	Picture cues	Appreciation	Retaining
Figure-ground	Context cues		
relationships	Phonics		
	Word structure		
Auditory			
Discrimination			
Sequencing			
Blending			
Laterality			
Orienting symbols			
Left-to-right progression			

of left-to-right progression. They must learn to separate figure from background and to focus on the figure or parts of words on a line and to ignore the surrounding text and to make an accurate return sweep to the succeeding line of text.

Word Attack

This skill involves the versatile use of processes to decode words Some words may be recognized visually on the basis of signal cues such as letter combinations, down-strokes, and tall letters. Other words may be identified by context cues, such as guessing what makes sense in terms of the ideas in the content and the conventions of the language. Some children will also begin to use phonic cues by drawing their own conclusions about the letter correspondences in words they know or by applying rules that have been taught for phonic generalizations. As word attack skills develop, children learn to use word structure (prefixes, suffixes, inflectional endings) to unlock new words. Because in English, word attack principles must be qualified by many exceptions, these skills are used with what Gibson (1969) termed "a set for diversity."

Comprehension

Basic to getting meaning in reading is the development of rich vocabulary. Reading requires children to select from the range of multiple definitions the exact meaning implicit in the content they are reading. Understandings may range from literal comprehension of factual content to inferential reasoning and appreciation of the abstract aspects of the content.

Study Skills

This is the area in which reading becomes a tool for acquiring information. These skills enable children to locate and retrieve elements within a sequence. They learn to select relevant content and to organize for retention and application the content that is appropriate to the reader's purposes.

The following example shows how the Job Analysis of Reading can be used to integrate the results for Michael, a 17-year-old tenth grader.

CASE STUDY: MICHAEL

Michael earned a score at grade 6.8 (21st percentile) on the Reading Cluster of the Woodcock-Johnson Psychoeducational Battery. His oral reading shows that he needs to be taught independent word attack skills. When he meets an unfamiliar word, he tends to guess on the basis of its visual configuration. This results in miscalling (*early* read as "really" and *benign* read as "begin"), omission of syllables (*deteriorate* read as "detorate" or *humiliate* read as "humilate"), or reversal of the order of syllables (*abysmal* read as "absymal"). He read correctly 15 of the 26 phonetically regular nonsense syllables on the Word Attack test. Thus, although some sound-symbol relationships are familiar to him, some key associations are not known: soft *g,* the diphthongs *ai* and *au,* and finally, *qu* and *-igh.* Because these decoding skills are not automatic, Michael tends to read in a word-by-word fashion that interferes with higher level comprehension. With text containing fewer difficult words, he was able to handle both factual and interpretive questions accurately. In addition to his difficulties in word attack, Michael's limited oral vocabulary also contributes to his difficulties with reading. He has a general idea of word meanings, but is not always able to deal with multiple meanings of words and select that meaning relevant to a given context. For example, he knew only one meaning for the word *till:* a place where cash is kept. The phrase, "tiller of the soil," used to describe a farmer, was completely incomprehensible to him. Because reading is not yet developed to the point that it is a tool for Michael, assessment of his progress with study skills must await the acquisition of more automatic word attack skills and more fluent comprehension.

The Job Analysis of Reading can be used to structure diffuse information on ways students handle various aspects of reading. By highlighting *how* the student reads, this analysis provides richer data than numerical estimates of reading levels for use in educational planning.

Assessment of Spelling and Written Language

Because of the relationships of reading and the language arts, it is essential that written language skills be evaluated as a part of the study of any student suspected of having a learning disorder. Formal and informal measures of written language make it possible to answer several diagnostic questions:

- What evidence is there of systematic teaching of the mechanics of written language either in the samples of schoolwork or in the written productions of the student?
- How fluently does the student communicate in writing?

- How familiar is the student with spelling generalizations?
- Have irregular words been mastered?
- How serviceable is the student's handwriting?

The examiner might begin this assessment with a review of the contents of the student's backpack and find answers to these questions in current schoolwork. With elementary school students, it is important also to note the school's approach to spelling. Although most school personnel steadfastly maintain that they teach phonics in reading, application of phonic generalizations in spelling instruction is less well supported. This is unfortunate. Linguistic research has shown that, despite the apparent irregularity of English, there are predictable spelling patterns and morphological regularities that can be useful in spelling. In a corpus of 17,000 words, Hanna, Hodges, and Hanna (1971) reported that correct spelling patterns could be predicted for a phoneme 90% of the time when main phonological facts of position in syllables, stress, and internal constraints in orthography are taken into account. Organizing spelling lessons on the basis of phonic or structural generalizations (and their exceptions) would seem to be both logically and pedagogically sound. However, only a few spelling books use linguistic approaches. Word lists in most spelling books are selected on the basis of frequency counts and seasonal themes (e.g., words such as *Halloween, costume, ghost, pumpkin* are listed in lessons that are expected to be taught in October, although they are totally unrelated linguistically and must be learned by rote). Frequency counts are based on lists and word counts such as those by Fitzgerald (1951) and Rinsland (1945) that fail to take into account recent developments in linguistic studies. Such lists may result in random placement of words, so that they must be learned by rote rather than in the context of generalizations that would draw on logical linguistic relationships.

Examination of the spelling book the child is using at school can indicate whether the child has had an opportunity to learn spelling generalizations. Dictation of a few words from the recent spelling lessons can indicate the extent to which the child has retained the words studied for the weekly school spelling test.

A spontaneous writing sample is an essential part of this evaluation. However, most children need some structure to respond to a request for a writing sample. Some examiners solve this problem by following the request for a human figure drawing with the following instructions:

> Draw a person doing something. I am going to ask you to write a few lines after you have finished the drawing. Please answer these three questions:
>
> Who is the person you drew?
> What is the person doing?
> What will happen next?

The writing sample can then be analyzed in terms of mechanics of written language, accuracy of spelling, verbal fluency, and syntactical maturity. These structuring questions usually elicit at least minimal responses from children beyond the first grade. Sometimes they elicit considerable educational and clinical material, as in this 8-year-old girl whose response to the questions appears in Figure 6.2. From an educational point of view, this third-grade youngster finds it easy to get her thoughts down on paper. She shows awareness of some writing conventions and attempts to organize her thoughts in a numerical sequence. She has some idea of capitalization and punctuation (commas in a series, an apostrophe in one of the two contractions), but she has not learned to use periods at the end of sentences. Endings must be stated verbally and emphatically. She is learning cursive writing at school, but serious communication of ideas results in regression to print. With print, there are occasional doubts about *orientation* ("clud"), but most letters are oriented correctly. Although she has been taught reading and spelling (sight word basal reader approach), sound-symbol associations are generally accurate. Her version of the word *capture* is a phonetically accurate transcription of the pronunciation of it, but it suggests the perils of transcribing unaccented syllables in English. The writing of *thick* as "thic" indicates that she has not mastered the redundancies of spelling. The most serious phonic error is the misspelling of *paper* as "papper." This error shows that she has not mastered the spelling generalization for open syllables. The general picture, however (apart from the interpersonal relationships the essay suggests), is of a youngster who is making good progress in written communication.

A formal test of written spelling appropriate to the child's age and grade completes this section of the evaluation. Such a test represents a contrast with the spontaneous language sample in which children have the opportunity to select words they can spell

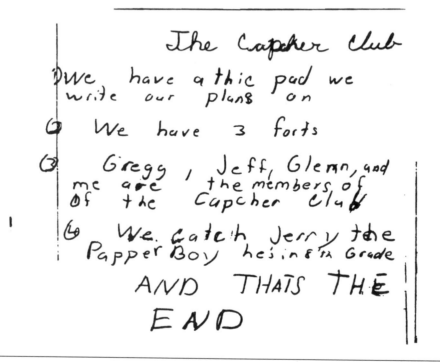

Figure 6.2   Spontaneous writing sample: The Capcher Club, Susan, age 8 years.

and avoid those they can't. The formally dictated spelling test can provide both a normative estimate of spelling achievement and of the extent to which the child has mastered spelling and encoding skills.

Assessment of Mathematics Achievement

Assessing achievement in mathematics presents more difficulties than assessing progress in reading. One reason for that lies in basic differences in the way skills are acquired in the two areas. With reading, once children have mastered a rather limited set of basic word attack and comprehension skills, they can proceed more or less on their own. Mathematics achievement depends to a large extent on direct teaching. Only a very few gifted students are able to discover for themselves the skills and generalizations required in learning mathematics. Thus assessment in mathematics must take into account the content of the curriculum to which the child has been exposed through formal instruction.

To complicate matters further, there is less agreement about the scope and sequences of the curriculum in mathematics than in reading and the language arts. Wide swings in educational philosophy have affected the field of mathematics education for the past 30 years, so that there is no generally accepted content domain on which assessment can be based. Moreover, the field of mathematics encompasses a broad range of skills, abilities, and understandings.

The National Council of Teachers of Mathematics (1980) has recommended 10 content areas for inclusion in curricula: problem solving; application of mathematics in everyday situations; alertness to reasonableness of results; estimation and approximation; appropriate computation skills; geometry; measurement; understanding of charts, tables, and graphs; use of mathematics to predict; and computer literacy. With this breadth of content, it is not surprising that achievement tests may represent only minute samples of the curricular content in mathematics. Furthermore, different educational philosophies (and even different textbooks representing similar educational philosophies) may use different sequences of content, so that the times at which given skills are introduced in the classrooms may vary considerably.

Given the nature of the learning process in mathematics, the breadth of curricular content, and the variation in the scope and sequences in mathematics instruction, assessment of individual achievement must take into account the relationship between the content of the test and what this child has experienced at school. Accurate information from school personnel, parents, and the child's own schoolbooks is essential in the evaluation. Where formal tests are used, careful inquiry to determine *how* the problem was solved is as important as the accuracy of the child's response. Evaluation of both computational skills and applications in solving practical problems is essential. Answers to the following diagnostic questions would help integrate the observations on both formal tests and informal measures in mathematics, all in relationship to previous instructional opportunities:

- Has this child developed basic concepts of time, space, numeration, coin values, and measurement?

- Has this child acquired functioning skills in the fundamental processes with whole numbers? With fractions? With decimals?
- Does this child understand and use mathematical symbols?
- To what extent does this child use simple algebraic concepts?
- Are concepts of geometry understood and applied?
- What computer skills does this student possess?

Educational achievement in reading, language arts, and mathematics should be considered in terms of the child's age, ability, and current grade placement. At this point in the decision process, adequate achievement would indicate that further diagnosis is unnecessary, while inadequate achievement would require the second step on the decision model.

ADEQUACY OF EDUCATIONAL OPPORTUNITY

Educational history may be obtained from all available sources and should be relevant to educational problems under consideration. A detailed educational history should be assembled from caregivers and teachers and, for this reason, may differ considerably from the usual family history that might be taken in a clinical setting. Clinical histories may often gloss over points essential to understanding the schooling a child has received and may focus on details of the parents' marital adjustment or aspects of gestation and delivery. In both cases, this information can hamper, rather than clarify, diagnosis. This is not to minimize the importance of historical data. However, because it is not easy to define one-to-one relationships between later outcomes in school learning and many individual events in gestation and early development, obstetrical and pediatric data are best understood within the total context of the child's physical development. Taken by itself, a single early event may sound pessimistic, but it may have little relationship to the child's later functioning. There is danger of an interviewer's focusing on such an event, so that it becomes an unevaluated artifact, accepted by both parent and educator as unmodifiable. Such assumptions can produce a pessimistic attitude toward the youngster's learning problem. When educational interviewers approach these areas, parents are advised to take the Fifth Amendment (see Chapter 14).

By and large, children from stable, well-managed homes might be expected to achieve more easily at school than those from unstable homes. It might also be expected that good achievement would prevail in homes that are free from marital discord. Yet it is difficult to show a direct relationship between marital disharmony and learning disorders in children; conversely, one sees many children with learning disorders whose homes are tranquil and supportive. Interviews that focus too specifically on marital discord as it might, even by implication, be related to the child's learning problems may leave the parents guilt ridden and defensive. The interviewer who expects to work cooperatively with these parents is advised to avoid such sensitive areas at this decision point.

What are the relevant data for assessing educational opportunity? First of all, the diagnostician is advised to make use of data that have already been accumulated in the first stage of the study. This would mean a careful rereading of notes of conversations with teachers or parents taken during the referral process and the assessment of educational achievement. A second source of data on educational history would be gained in a thoughtful perusal of the school's permanent records. This should include objective information that has been recorded at regular intervals during the child's schooling: attendance records, summaries of grades, results of group achievement tests, notes on health examinations and special health conditions, photographs, work samples, and communications between the school and the family. A few minutes spent in organizing the data chronologically will give the diagnostician clues for further exploration in face-to-face interviews. Records of excessive absences in the early grades or habitual tardiness may hold important clues on the continuity and intensity of educational opportunities available to the child. The chronological record, starting with the nursery years and extending to the time of referral, should be expanded on the basis of information provided by parents and the children themselves. Comparing and contrasting data provided by adults with that provided by the referred child can be useful in obtaining a well-rounded picture of past developments and defining the current problem. The focus should remain on the methods and content of educational experiences. It is especially important to obtain information about the child's initial adjustment to nursery school and/or kindergarten and to get an impression of the prevailing school philosophy and organization (open education? individualized instruction? formal reading groups?). Such conversations usually evoke thumbnail sketches of the personal characteristics of teachers and tutors; these discussions should be kept on track by focusing on the methods and materials used. It is especially important to elicit information about how beginning reading was taught and to secure concrete examples of any assistance that has been provided to the child. What may be described as "years and years of private tutoring" might, on more careful questioning, turn out to have been once-a-week sessions with high school students who helped the child with homework.

This decision point is also a useful time to obtain information about language development. This includes not only the usual information on age of talking, age when sentences were used, persistence of oral inaccuracies, or disfluencies in speech. It is also a time to ascertain the child's first language, the language background of the parents, and the communication patterns in the household. The availability of educational opportunities for a youngster who heard little English before being enrolled in school is quite different from that of a child who heard only English throughout his life, even though both children may have attended school for the same number of years.

It is important to determine the child's first language for use in other aspects of diagnosis. A cardinal principle of psychological testing is that it should be conducted in the child's major language; this principle has become a legal requirement since the enactment of special education legislation. Of additional interest also is the fortunate situation of the child who may be truly bilingual, that is, fluent in at least two languages. It has been shown that, far from impeding learning as the proverbial myths would have us believe, having more than one language enriches a child's language development.

This step in the decision model obtains a record of the educational methods and content to which children under study were exposed, in order to assess the opportunities they have had to learn. This record should be organized in a chronology, so that data from several sources (school records or interviews with children, teachers, and parents) can be integrated to show the temporal sequence of the child's educational development. The final answer to the question raised by this step depends on the judgment of the diagnostic team as they survey the information the chronology had accumulated. They must decide whether the youngster under study has indeed enjoyed formal and informal educational opportunities adequate for learning the skills and content children of his or her age and ability might be expected to have learned. Granted, this is a subjective decision. At this point, a major intervention decision is made: the choice between regular and special education. If educational opportunity is deemed adequate, further study should be directed according to the steps in the decision tree. If educational opportunity is deemed inadequate, the choice is for compensatory teaching within the framework of regular and or compensatory education. It should be emphasized that every child who is underachieving is not a candidate for special education. There can be a variety of reasons for the inadequate educational opportunity:

- Chronic illness such as rheumatic fever or asthma that might interfere with both consistent attendance at school and active participation in the school program even when the child was attending school.
- Mismatch between the child's developmental level and the demands of the school program; the misguided notion that parents want their 5-year-olds to be taught reading has resulted in the extension into kindergarten of formal academic content; this trend may move some youngsters from home or informal nursery or day-care programs to a formal classroom without the readiness activities they need as a basis for formal instruction in reading.
- Differences between the child's dominant language and that used in the classroom that are not provided for by bilingual or English as a Second Language programs.
- Family disorganization and/or mobility that deprives children of educational roots and exposes them often to a conflicting sequence of instructional methods and content.
- Deficient classroom instruction resulting from various conditions of school disorganization: lack of clearly defined instructional goals, curricular content, or educational philosophy; lack of supervision and training of beginning teachers; excessive mobility in the teaching and administrative staffs; and breakdowns in professional relationships between classroom and administrative and/or supervisory personnel.

Although these unfortunate educational circumstances are often cited as causes for the learning difficulties of inner-city children, they can occur with children at any socioeconomic level or geographic location. The quality of educational opportunities that have been available to the child is a major consideration in planning appropriate intervention. In a wider sense, the provision of appropriate educational opportunity is the responsibility of all people concerned with the welfare of children. This responsibility cannot be met by assigning children in need of better quality regular education to special education services. Diagnostic teams may resort to such misclassification in the mistaken belief that it is "for the good of the child," but it represents an unacceptable response to the child's needs. These needs will be better met through effective teaching in the rich atmosphere of a regular classroom. Such misclassification will dissipate the resources of special education without providing constructive and appropriate services to the children thus misclassified. (The education of children with learning disorders of extrinsic origin is discussed at greater length in Chapter 12.)

IS SENSORY ACUITY ADEQUATE FOR LEARNING?

Except for gross clinical evaluation of vision and hearing, evaluation of these functions must be turned over to the specialists in these areas. This section provides general information about sensory evaluations because of concerns often raised by parents and teachers concerning sensory defects as causal factors in learning problems. This section draws on the work of J. B. Smith (1971) and Lobovits (1982) for recommendations on vision examinations. Recommendations for auditory screening are based on the Report of the Interdisciplinary Committee on Reading Problems (A. Hayes & Silver, 1970).

Examination of Vision

Ocular screening procedures that J. B. Smith (1971) recommended as part of regular health care for children include (a) vision testing appropriate for the age of the child (i.e., the E chart with preschoolers and the Snellen chart with school-age children), (b) inspection of the external appearance of the eyes and lids, (c) motility evaluation, (d) fundoscopy to detect retinal pathology, and (e) the cover/uncover test to detect strabismus. The more sophisticated the examination is, as part of regular health care by the pediatrician, the greater the opportunity for earlier detection of conditions that require the diagnostic and treatment services of an ophthalmologist. The most frequent eye problems encountered among preschoolers are strabismus, infections of the conjunctiva and eyelids, refractive errors, and fundus abnormalities; with school-age children there is a shift, with refractive errors and strabismus appearing in greater frequency than retinal pathology and infections (J. B. Smith, 1971). The ophthalmologist's evaluation begins with a detailed history of family eye problems, the child's general health, previous eye conditions and treatment, and the symptoms requiring examination. The examination of preschool and school-age children uses both subjective and objective methods to determine visual acuity, motility, and the anterior structure of the globe. Smith stated that the use of eyedrops to dilate the pupil and relax lens accommodation is indicated in children if the initial evaluation discloses fundus abnormalities or the possibility of refractive error great enough to warrant glasses.

From an etiological point of view, visual defects (disorders of visual acuity, ocular motility, stereopsis, or fusion) are not usually found to be primary causes of learning disorders; they may contribute to learning problems by preventing children from obtaining and maintaining with ease a single clear visual image, by producing fatigue and resistance to reading, and by impairing concentration and making it difficult for them to respond to instruction. People with unsophisticated concepts of learning disorders may attribute them to "something wrong with the child's eyes" and expect that an eye examination and glasses will resolve the problem. Thus the eye specialist may be the first person some parents consult in seeking help for their children. The eye specialist who understands the complexities of the diagnosis of learning disorders can guide the family in obtaining appropriate diagnostic and treatment services for the child.

Examination of Hearing

To discriminate aurally among all the sounds of English uttered in isolation, a child should have good hearing in the frequency range from 100 to 6,000 Hertz. While most audiologists recommend audiometric examination of all children with learning disorders, it is acknowledged that sufficient diagnostic facilities may not be available throughout the country for this. Practical considerations may require the use of screening methods to select those children most likely to require the service. The diagnostician should be alert for indications from history and behavior that might suggest the need for audiometric study. These indications include a history of repeated middle ear infections, particularly in the first 3 years of life, a history of allergies or repeated respiratory tract infections, the presence of articulatory defects (*particularly in high-frequency sounds*), or frequent requests for repetition or misunderstanding of simple directions. Some schools also use group audiometric procedures—recordings simultaneously feeding into as many as 40 sets of earphones. The content consists of pairs of digits spoken by a female voice. While this test offers a gross screening method, it has been criticized by audiologists because it fails to detect losses in hearing that affect the high-frequency portion of the range where most of the "intelligence" of the language is concentrated. Pure-tone audiometric techniques have been adapted for use with groups by modification of the instrumentation. They are valuable in that they avoid the limitations of the fading numbers test while permitting the screening of more than one person at a time. The hearing examination of any child for whom sensory acuity is in doubt should include threshold pure-tone audiometry. By itself this relatively simple test can provide the examiner with almost all the information required to determine the adequacy of the auditory system for normal language development. The test should be conducted in a sound-treated room with absolute minimum ambient noise. The room should be simply furnished so that no distracting influences interfere with the child's attention. Needless to say, the audiometric equipment must be precisely calibrated.

Whisper tests, ticking watches, and calibrated noisemakers are not recommended by audiologists because these techniques fail to control the sound levels and frequencies and, in the case of whisper tests, variations in voice quality. Their use may result in invalid findings because the child responds to the test situation itself or to random percussive elements instead of to the expected stimulus. In using such informal methods, the examiner might be misled into concluding that a major avenue of sensory input is adequate when, in fact, it is not.

Specialized methods, such as play audiometry using operant conditioning techniques, electrodermal audiometry, and evoked response audiometry using computer averaging of records may be utilized as additional sources of data. These methods will probably not be necessary with many school-age children.

All these examinations have but one purpose: to provide the examiner with a reasonably accurate estimate of the child's auditory thresholds to pure tones within the hearing range. Once this information has been obtained, further testing can be employed to add additional data about the child's hearing problem and its possible etiology. These other tests, however, must always be considered as adjuncts to, rather than replacements for, pure-tone audiometry. Speech reception threshold is an excellent indicator of the youngster's ability to hear simple samples of speech. The standardized auditory discrimination test using phonetically balanced word lists provides still more information about a child's ability to perceive speech once it has been made loud enough for the child to hear comfortably.

It is also desirable to obtain bone conduction thresholds. Assessing hearing by means of bone conduction, makes it possible to differentiate between pathologies affecting the conductive portion of the auditory mechanism and those defects of the sensorineural system. Conductive losses, as a rule, do not result in language pathology. That is, those hearing impediments caused by external or middle-ear defects do not usually affect the development of language to a significant degree. One reason for this is that the child with a conductive hearing loss is able to hear his own voice normally and with adequate loudness and clarity. He can also hear the speech of others with normal clarity, although it may be a little soft for him.

Sensorineural losses on the other hand, will almost always be accompanied by some retardation in language development. The child with a sensorineural loss may hear speech with adequate loudness, but may have poor auditory discrimination. Speech to him is loud enough, but often garbled and distorted. The child with a mild sensorineural loss has an especially subtle problem: She hears well enough so that deafness is not suspected, yet her hearing is deficient enough that some of the consonant sounds of English speech cannot be distinguished. Therefore, language development may be affected and learning problems will eventually result.

Traditionally, it has been assumed that a loss of less than 30db in the middle-speech frequencies (500 to 2,000 Hertz) is not handicapping. When one considers all areas of language function, however, this is not true. Hearing may be good in the middle-frequency range and yet poor for frequencies above 2,000 Hertz. This will lead to a distortion in the hearing of high-frequency consonant sounds that will inevitably affect language development. Any deviation from normal, therefore, must be considered significant and taken into account in planning educational programs.

Any problems found in the screening of either vision or hearing need medical attention through referral by the health services of the school or through the family's health provider. If problems are found with the child's hearing, the school will be asked to offer assistance through such measures as preferred seating locations in the classroom and, if necessary, supportive instruction.

WHAT ARE THIS STUDENT'S COGNITIVE STRENGTHS AND WEAKNESSES?

Effective assessment of cognitive factors in diagnosis has a number of hallmarks. It is, first of all, data based. The quantitative foundation on which it rests is one of the unique contributions of the field of psychology. Over the course of nearly a century, psychologists have employed theoretical, statistical, and clinical approaches to improve the quality of these assessment methods. While imperfections remain, the *Standards for Educational and Psychological Testing,* first published in 1954 and updated at regular intervals, are evidence of the efforts to maintain high standards of technical quality for assessment methods (American Psychological Association, 1985). Effective assessment of cognitive functioning requires the judgment of trained personnel. An integral part of training curricula in psychology is theoretical and supervised clinical instruction in test administration. This training goes beyond routine test giving. Training should develop professional judgment in selection of appropriate instruments, critical understanding of their rationale and psychometric characteristics, and ethical use and interpretation of test results.

Effective cognitive assessment is parsimonious. Given the quality of the instruments and the professional training of the psychologists who administer them, effective diagnosis does not need to call on several measures to supply data for answering the diagnostic questions that have been raised. In the final analysis, these answers come from the conceptual integration of the data elicited from well-chosen clinical measures.

In a child with a learning disorder, assessment of cognitive functioning involves using one of the individual tests of intelligence. Group tests of cognitive functioning are to be discouraged in the diagnosis of learning disorders. The obvious reason is that many group tests involve reading or other skills in which deficiencies caused the children to be referred for diagnosis in the first place. Group testing does not permit the observations of qualitative aspects of children's behavior that are essential in understanding the resources and problems in learning,

Defining Intelligence

J. M. Hunt (1961) has wisely observed, "It is in connection with intelligence and the tests that measure it, that some of the most violent polemics in psychology and all the behavior sciences have raged" (p. 3). Although some common themes can be found, definitions of intelligence are almost as varied as the psychologists who provide them. The methods of assessment reflect these variations in conceptualization, as well as the times in which the definitions were framed. The earliest theorists conceptualized intelligence in terms of innate hereditary factors (Galton, 1907) and sought to measure them by methods involving sensory discrimination, motor coordination, attention, and memory (J. M. Cattell, 1890). As studies of intelligence moved outside the laboratory to the solution of practical problems in such settings as schools, the definitions became broader in scope and assessment methods began to draw on more complex mental processes (Binet & Simon, 1916; Terman, 1916). Dissatisfaction with age-scale formats and with the content and standardization of existing scales for use with adult subjects led Wechsler (1944) to develop the first of his series of scales. The rapid adoption of these scales was part of the expansion of clinical services to adults after World War II. As technical resources for statistical analyses became available, definitions of intelligence focused on multifactor theories (E. L. Thorndike, 1927) and hierarchical models of intelligence (R. B. Cattell, 1963b; Guilford, 1967; Thurstone, 1938; Vernon, 1979). More recently, the emphasis on computer technology is reflected in information-processing models that use such terms as capacity, storage, control processes, and knowledge base in the formulation of the model (Campione & Brown, 1978).

Weinberg (1989) emphasized the implicit theories of intelligence that constitute popular definitions. People, in general, view intelligence as it is represented in intelligent behavior: the ability to reason and to solve practical problems, to express one's ideas verbally, and to sense social cues. Weinberg noted further that researchers in the field of human intelligence are in strong agreement with these popular conceptions. For example, Wechsler's (1944) definition states: "Intelligence is the aggregate or global capacity of the individual to act purposefully, to think rationally and to deal effectively with his environment" (p. 3). Not all the explicit definitions agree that intelligence is a global capacity. Some theorists such as Guilford (1967) and H. Gardner (1983) emphasize the multiple nature of intelligence, composed of many separate mental abilities that are independent of each other.

Between these two positions is an intermediate one that may be more meaningful for clinicians. This view holds that intelligence is hierarchically organized with one or two general factors and other more specific skills. These theories have drawn on the psychometric tradition that seeks, through statistical models, to understand the structure of the intellect. Also relevant for clinicians is the contribution of Piaget (Piaget & Inhelder, 1958) who studied cognitive development qualitatively, by probing ways in which children perceive and understand the world around them.

Vernon (1979) described three kinds of intelligence. According to his formulation, Intelligence A represents the innate capacity of the individual, the genetic equipment with which the individual enters the world. Obviously this cannot be measured directly, although there have been attempts (largely unsuccessful) to do so by using various physiological measures. Intelligence B involves more than the individuals' capacities because it includes the total schemata and mental plans built up through an individual's interaction with the environment. Intelligence B can be influenced by such things as constitutional handicaps, physical deprivation, lack of sensory stimulation, lack of language stimulation, environmental disorganization, or inappropriate demands made by teachers or caretakers. Intelligence A and Intelligence B interact. Vernon proposed that Intelligence C represents the results obtained from individual psychological testing. This formulation highlights a major limitation of intelligence tests: that they represent very limited samples of the behaviors that become the basis for the inferences psychologists make about Intelligences A and B when they interpret test results.

A caution was sounded early in the history of intelligence testing by Terman (1916) when he advised psychologists to guard against defining intelligence as the ability to pass tests. His warning that "no existing scale is capable of measuring the ability to deal with all possible kinds of material on all intelligence levels" (p. 130) is no less true today than when it was written. Current theories stress a hierarchical and multi-factorial view of intelligence with a general factor entering into a large variety of cognitive operations and narrower group factors and specialized abilities forming the core of the hierarchy (Sattler, 1988). It is also generally accepted that both innate and developmental influences are reflected in assessments of cognitive functioning.

VALUES AND LIMITATIONS OF INTELLIGENCE TESTS

There have been criticisms both of the uses of intelligence tests and of the tests themselves. Test users are obliged to be aware of these criticisms and to modify testing practices so that tests are used responsibly. It is important to be aware of the extrinsic factors that can influence test behavior. A child's unfamiliarity with the test situation and the requirements of responding to formal cognitive measures can influence test results. Mistrust of the examiner may also affect an individual's performance. Past experience with testing can have both positive and negative effects on test outcomes. Difficulties in communication between examiner and examinee ranging from language differences to a lack of real rapport with the subject, even though the two people may speak a common language may also invalidate test results. Wechsler (1975) also has reminded us that nonintellectual factors must be considered in any assessment of cognitive functioning. Intelligent behavior may call on a host of factors that are more conative than cognitive. They are not so much skills and know-how, but, rather drives, attitudes, and sensitivities to social, moral, or esthetic values. They may also involve effort, persistence, impulse control, and goal-awareness. They are seen as the "enzymes of personality" that affect the capabilities of all individuals. In a larger sense, they may account for the uniqueness in cognitive functioning that can be discovered through individual intelligence tests. Awareness of these influences on test behavior can do much to avoid the unfair educational consequences of invalid or incomplete interpretation of test results.

Bias in Testing

While the validity of test results may to some extent depend on the skill and resourcefulness of the examiner, the tests themselves have been the subject of criticism. A. S. Kaufman (1979) feels that charges of test bias based on single test items or on studies that demonstrate unequal mean scores for various ethnic groups are an oversimplification of the problems related to test bias. Careful psychometric studies of the validity of major instruments do not support systematic or intentional biases in test construction; abuses are more apt to occur in interpretation and the *uses* to which test results are put. Efforts to counteract these abuses have used both ethical and legal measures. The Joint Committee on Testing Practices (1988), a cooperative effort of several professional organizations, has aimed to improve the quality of testing through a *Code of Fair Testing Practices in Education.* The code states the obligations to test takers of professionals who develop or use tests. These obligations are important in matters of admissions, educational assessment, educational diagnosis, and student placement.

Four areas comprise the standards defined in the code: developing and selecting appropriate tests, interpreting scores, striving for fairness, and informing test takers.

Legal Safeguards

Public Law 94-142 (*Federal Register,* 1976) made definite stipulations for testing procedures mandating:

- Tests and other evaluation devices must be administered in the child's primary language.
- Testing and evaluation materials and procedures must be selected and administered so as not to be discriminatory on the basis of racial or cultural differences.
- Tests must be administered by trained personnel.
- No single procedure should be used as the sole criterion for determining an educational placement for a child.
- Evaluation is the responsibility of a multidisciplinary team or group including at least one classroom teacher and a specialist in the area of the suspected disability.
- Periodic reevaluations must be made to assess progress.

Further legal guarantees for the children and their families are contained in procedural safeguards that mandate written parental consent before evaluation, parental opportunity to see all information used in decision making, confidentiality of all reports and records, and opportunity for an impartial hearing conducted by regional or state education authorities if parents disagree with placements planned by the school team.

Despite these guarantees, litigation on the overrepresentation of minority children in special education has influenced diagnostic procedures. In the 1979 *Larry P. v. Riles* decision, the U.S. Federal District Court in California ruled that standardized intelligence tests are culturally biased and cannot be used in the assessment of black children for possible placement in classes for educable mentally retarded children. Since psychologists cannot predict the outcome of a test before giving it, this decision effectively ended the use of conventional individual measures of intelligence in California schools. The decisions were upheld by a 2 to 1 margin in the Ninth Circuit Court of Appeals in 1984. Judge William B. Enright noted in a minority opinion, however, that evidence had not been presented that intelligence tests had resulted in improper placements and that the court was striking down the only objective criterion for placement decisions (Sattler, 1988). In 1986, the California State Department of Education issued a directive forbidding the use of individual intelligence tests with any special education placement decisions. Weinberg (1989) has commented that it is ironic that tests are outlawed in California for the very purpose that Binet and Simon originally designed the first individual intelligence test. More confusion has been added to the issue by a decision (*P.A.S.E. v. Joseph P. Hannon, 1980*) in the U.S. Federal District Court in Illinois that individual intelligence tests comply with federal guidelines established by PL 94-142 when used with other criteria in the assessment process. Judge John Grady's examination of the test items led him to rule that the WISC, WISC-R, and Stanford-Binet tests were not culturally biased. It may be that the court is not the best setting for considering the professional use of tests.

Substantive Criticisms of Tests

Some substantive criticisms have come from professionals in the field of measurement. A. S. Kaufman (1979) argued that test construction has failed to grow conceptually along with advances in psychology. Test materials have been improved and modernized and advances in psychometric theory have been applied to test construction, but the content of tests remains virtually unchanged over the years and fails to reflect advances in learning theory, educational methods, and neuropsychology.

Kaufman also criticized current test instruments for their failure to include direct measures of new learning. Actual measures of learning ability are infrequent on most instruments, even though one of the most frequent uses of intelligence test results is to predict learning ability. In response to this failure, there has been a growth of interest in nontraditional techniques, such as Feuerstein's (1979) *Learning Potential Assessment Device* or Campione's (1989) assisted assessment, both of which use a test-teach-retest model to assess ability for new learning. In defense of existing tests, however, there is agreement on their psychometric excellence, There are relatively small standard errors of measurement of IQs, and the tasks of the tests lend themselves to analyses in keeping with different theoretical approaches. In general, they have been found to predict educational outcomes effectively. McCall (1977) found the IQs for a sample of children aged 3 to 18 were significant predictors of educational success and occupational status at age 26 or older. Coefficients of correlation remained fairly stable at about .50. Sattler (1988) enumerated the many educational applications of tests as measures of accountability, evaluation of program effectiveness, and criteria for admission to enrichment programs. He believes that tests are a standard for evaluating the extent to which children of all ethnic groups have learned the basic cognitive and academic skills necessary for survival in our culture, adding that few "reasonable alternatives" have been proposed by critics.

MAJOR INTELLIGENCE TESTS

Wechsler Intelligence Scale for Children-Third Edition

This scale, first published in 1949, was revised in terms of norms and content in 1974 as the Wechsler Intelligence Scale for Children-Revised (WISC-R) (Wechsler, 1974) and revised again in 1991 (WISC-III). Probably the most frequently used measure in the diagnosis of learning problems, it reflects Wechsler's concept of intelligence as a global but multifaceted entity that can be inferred from a series of tasks. It provides a full-scale deviation IQ and verbal and performance scale IQs. Standardized on a sample of 2,200 children representative of sex, age, parental educational levels, religion, race, and ethnicity, it is linked to an achievement battery, the Wechsler Individual Achievement Test, which was standardized on a sample matched to the WISC-III sample on demographic variables and ability. WISC-III contains the 12 subtests from earlier editions and adds a measure of processing speed. Results of factor analytic and other statistical studies of the scale are presented in tables that assist psychologists in interpreting differences among subtest scores, variability within records, and index scores for the four dimensions of verbal comprehension, perceptual organization, freedom from distractibility, and processing speed.

Stanford-Binet Intelligence Scale

The fourth American edition based on Binet and Simon's original intelligence scale appeared in 1986. The authors of this edition, who are distinguished in the field of measurement, have provided information about the development of the revision (R. L. Thorndike, Hagen, & Sattler, 1986). The fourth edition uses a point scale, rather than the age-scale format of previous editions of the Binet scales. It introduces some entirely new subtests and represents a complete restandardization. The authors of the fourth edition have attempted to meet criticisms of the previous editions of the Stanford-Binet scale regarding its emphasis on verbal content and the unrepresentativeness of its standardization sample. The scale yields scaled scores, and percentile ranks on four areas: Verbal Reasoning, Abstract/Visual Reasoning, Quantitative Reasoning, and Short-Term Memory, as well as a Composite score, based on all four areas and described as the best estimate of general intelligence. The Composite score is actually a deviation IQ, although the authors seem to avoid use of that term. However, it not completely comparable to WISC-III IQs because it has a mean of 100 and a standard deviation of 16 while the WISC-III has a mean of 100 and a standard deviation of 15. The subtests are organized into four areas: Verbal Reasoning, Abstract/Visual Reasoning, Quantitative Reasoning, and Short-Term Memory. However, factor analysis has not supported these areas, so that it is inadvisable to use them for test interpretation. Because all subtests are not used with all age levels, subtests are not continuous throughout the scale. In response to criticisms on the length of time required by the age-scale organization of previous editions of the Binet scales, the authors have advised a routing test (Vocabulary) to be used by the examiner to determine the beginning point for testing. This helps somewhat, but the problem of test length continues, especially at the upper levels. Technical characteristics of the Fourth Edition, as it has come to be known, are excellent.

Kaufman Assessment Battery for Children

This test, known as the K-ABC, was developed in response to recent interest in neuropsychology and recent criticisms of the use of conventional measures with children of diverse ethnic and cultural backgrounds. A. S. Kaufman and N. Kaufman (1983) set out to minimize the role of language and verbal tasks and to include stimuli that were as fair as possible for children of diverse backgrounds. Planned for use with children 2 through 12 years of age, the K-ABC yields scores on four scales: Sequential Processing, Simultaneous Processing, Achievement, and Nonverbal. The Simultaneous and Sequential Processing scales together provide a Mental Processing Composite that is essentially a measure of intelligence. The K-ABC has as its theoretical basis, the information-processing model of Luria (1966) and Das, Kirby, and Jarman (1975) that proposes two primary modes of cognitive processing: *simultaneous processing,* which deals with many stimuli at once through spatial or analogical organization, and *successive processing,* which emphasizes serial organization of stimuli. The Achievement Scale, planned to measure factual knowledge, is not a test of educational achievement in the usual sense. Like the two mental processing scales, acquired skills are assessed through novel gamelike subtests including Expressive Vocabulary, Picture Identification, Recognition of Faces and Places, Solving Riddles, Decoding in Reading, and Reading Understanding, in which the child demonstrates comprehension through gestures. The Nonverbal Scale draws from the Mental Processing Scales, those subtests that do not require words in the instructions or the responses. Not all subtests run throughout the age levels; only three (Hand Movements, Gestalt Closure, and Faces and Places) run through all age levels. The technical quality of the K-ABC is good. The test was standardized on 2,000 children at nine age levels. The standardization sample was stratified to match the 1980 census in terms of age, sex, geographic region, socioeconomic status, ethnicity, and community size. Handicapped children were included in the sample. Factor analysis supports the organization of the K-ABC into three scales. Factor loadings for subtests are higher with the scales they were assigned to than with other scales. The finding that Black/White and Hispanic/White group differences are smaller on the K-ABC than on the WISC-R is seen by the test authors as an indication of its appropriateness for use with children from culturally and linguistically different backgrounds. These data have resulted in criticism of the test content, however. Page (1985) found no new testing principles in the K-ABC that would account for the smaller minority group differences in the data. He concluded that the test:

> . . . has been designed to emphasize skills on which blacks have performed best on traditional tests, have weighted these highly in the intelligence portion, have excluded from this portion all vocabulary and other verbal tests, and have diminished the influence of more complex non-verbal tests which, together with the verbal, have frequently been the (justified) core of intelligence testing. (p. 777)

No matter whether Page's reasoning is accurate, the K-ABC lacks verbal comprehension and verbal reasoning items. Instead, some of the items of the Simultaneous Processing Scale draw so heavily on attention and short-term memory that the test may underestimate the cognitive abilities of children whose learning disorders center around attentional or memory difficulties. Questions have also been raised about the simultaneous/successive information-processing model, which has its basis in hypotheses on hemisphere specialization in adults. The preliminary state of knowledge about such constructs, particularly with children, precludes practical applications in educational remediation. As Page stated, "The question is not where the process is carried out, but how well" (1985, p. 775). Certainly the constructs are ambiguous, and the data show some degree of overlap. Many of the subtests contain elements of more than one processing style. Sattler (1988), in pointing out this and other measurement problems with the K-ABC, has cautioned that it should not be used as the primary instrument for measuring intelligence in clinical assessments of children with learning disabilities.

Woodcock-Johnson III

This recently published battery consists of two parts—Tests of Cognitive Abilities III and Tests of Educational Achievement. According to the authors, both batteries are "appropriate for use for ages 2 years through 90 years, and together, they provide a "comprehensive system for measuring general intellectual ability, specific cognitive abilities, scholastic aptitude, and oral language" (2001, p. 6). The Cognitive battery is based on the Cattell-Horn-Carroll theories of the structure of human cognitive abilities usually referred to as crystallized intelligence/fluid intelligence (Carroll & Horn, 1981; Cattell, 1963b). The battery provides an analysis of general intellectual ability based on the results of the 7 standard tests, each of which represents a different theoretical factor. An extended analysis of general ability can be based on a total of the 14 cognitive tests, each representing a different theoretical factor. According to the authors, this protocol will provide the best analysis of intraindividual variability for diagnosis. Broad cognitive factors include Comprehension Knowledge, Long-Term Retrieval, Visual-Spatial Thinking, Auditory Processing, Fluid Reasoning, Processing Speed, and Short-Term Memory. Because this battery is co-normed with an excellent achievement test battery, it will be useful in work with students with learning disabilities.

ANSWERING THE DIAGNOSTIC QUESTIONS

Whichever measure or measures one chooses for assessment, cognitive functioning is the means by which the fourth diagnostic question of the decision model is answered. If this question is answered negatively (if the child demonstrates general limitations in cognitive functioning), the decision model would indicate that special educational provisions are needed. These provisions would be curricular modification in terms of goals and content and timing of instruction appropriate to the level of cognitive functioning as determined by psychological study. If, on the other hand, psychological study establishes that the child's cognitive functioning is adequate and that the child in question did not learn well despite conventional educational opportunities, the focus should move toward understanding the reasons for the learning disorder. At this point, clinicians should begin to integrate the multidisciplinary data already generated and to define further questions to clarify etiology. The data already generated would describe current levels of cognitive functioning and estimates of educational expectancy. These data could then be used to determine the extent to which educational achievement was appropriate and to define special instructional needs. Results of the cognitive assessment would also be used to build a picture of how the child went about solving cognitive tasks. The examiner would use knowledge of the organization of the cognitive measure that had been administered to set hypotheses about the child's resources for learning and the deficits that must be considered in instructional planning. The examiner would not be led astray in search of "typical patterns" or pathognomonic signs of learning disorders, but would use the behavior samples collected thus far in the decision model to answer the questions, "Why isn't this child learning?" and "What can we do about it?"

SUMMARY

Because every child is unique within the population of children with disorders of learning, systematic diagnosis is necessary to understand the constellation of contributing factors in each case. Furthermore, intervention is more likely to be effective when it is based on a systematic formulation of each child's strengths and needs. The complex nature of learning disorders implies that broad-based, multidisciplinary skills are necessary to provide comprehensive diagnosis. To provide sufficient diagnostic data and yet avoid redundant assessment processes, a five-step decision-making process is recommended to evaluate (a) educational achievement, (b) educational opportunity, (c) sensory acuity, (d) cognitive functioning, and (e) neuropsychiatric functioning. Integration of the diagnostic data at each of these decision points will provide clues for appropriate intervention strategies. Assessment of the adequacy of educational skills may include data from informal observations and well-standardized measures. However, information thus obtained must be formulated so that strengths and needs in the complex skills of reading, handwriting, spelling, written language, and mathematics are readily apparent. Adequacy of educational opportunity is best judged from a thorough history that emphasizes opportunities for informal and formal schooling. Examination of sensory acuity is best left to specialists in the fields; however, a careful observation of the child may provide much useful data. Use and interpretation of one of the well-standardized individual measures of intelligence by a well-trained school or child clinical psychologist can provide both quantitative and qualitative descriptions of the child's cognitive functioning. Rather than combing the data for elusive typical patterns or signs of learning disorders, however, the psychologist might better use the data generated to answer the two questions that have practical significance for intervention: "Why isn't this child learning?" and "What can we do about it?"

Chapter 7 ———————————————————————

PSYCHIATRIC AND NEUROLOGICAL DIAGNOSIS

Insight into the aetiology of psychic events cannot be achieved at all without some knowledge of somatic function, more particularly the physiology of the nervous system . . . the unity of soma and psyche seems indisputable.

—Karl Jaspers, 1963

The previous chapter has taken the reader through educational and psychological steps in evaluating a child who has problems in academic learning. A child who fulfills all of the following criteria is considered to be learning disabled: Educational achievement is found to be significantly less than expected from the child's age, educational opportunities, and cognitive potential; the child has neuropsychological processing deficits related to language considered in its broadest sense, the processing of symbols from all sensory modalities; and the child's sensory acuity (hearing, vision) is adequate so as not to impede learning. The task of the education system is then to provide appropriate and sufficient educational experiences to teach the child to read and spell and write and learn mathematics to his maximum potential.

The neuropsychiatrist is rarely included in this evaluation. With the majority of children whom schools classify as having a learning disability, sufficient data is collected within the school system to evaluate their intellectual function as measured by intelligence tests; the domains and the extent of their academic disability; the patterns, the deficits as well as the adequacies, of their neuropsychological processing; behavioral observations in the classrooms; and even the tensions and the support experienced at home. However, only the first two levels of the metaphorical iceberg, the academic domain and the neuropsychological processes (see Chapter 5, Figure 5.1) are uncovered by the school evaluation. The causes of the learning disability are not. The importance of understanding the cause/causes of learning disability in terms of its influence on clinical presentation, natural history, treatment, and prognosis has been described in Chapter 5. For this level of understanding, the knowledge and skill of the neuropsychiatrist may be needed. In practice, schools refer a learning-disabled student to the neuropsychiatrist when the child:

- Fails to respond to the treatment plan devised and implemented by his school.
- Has or develops behaviors that interfere with his learning and/or the learning of his classmates.
- When a diagnosis is needed to support special-education placement.
- When the teacher suspects there are neurological or psychiatric reasons for his behavior and/or that medication is needed.

It is the task of the neuropsychiatrist to integrate the educational, cognitive, behavioral, and social data obtained by the school with his/her neuropsychiatric-medical findings for a comprehensive understanding of the child and his problems.

Our approach to this evolution involves the gathering and integration of data along a pentaxial scheme (Table 7.1) including information from psychiatric, biological, cognitive-developmental, environmental-social, and educational parameters. The multiaxial scheme approach adapted by the *Diagnostic and Statistical Manual of Mental Disorders* (in *DSM-IV-TR*, 2000), parallels in many respects our pentaxial scheme. Unlike our pentaxial scheme, however, the multiaxial scheme of the DSM is not designed specifically for children.

Psychiatric data reveals the content, dynamics and genesis of the child's thoughts, wishes, and conflicts; it considers the nature and quality of his feelings and moods; the quality and intensity of his interactions with family, friends, teachers, strangers; his reactions to frustration, failure, and success; the stresses and supports of home, school, and society. It evaluates the development and structure of his personality, the strength of its various components, its age and gender appropriateness and the capacity of its "stimulus barrier." Finally, the psychiatric examination, together with the data from the entire pentaxial scheme, presents a diagnosis within the framework of *DSM-IV-TR*.

Biological data investigates the integrity of the central nervous system, particularly its level of maturation and integration; it examines the neurological system, including soft neurological signs; it considers the presence of complicating problems with attention and impulse control and provides evidence for diffuse or focal organic syndromes. Integration of the central nervous system also implies a neuropsychological study; a profile of perceptual assets and deficits; the capacity for sequential information storage and its access for comprehension and expression; the metalinguistic functions of organization, abstraction, analysis, and synthesis; and the capacity for adjustment in time and space. At times, laboratory studies such as electroencephalogram, computerized tomography, nuclear magnetic resonance scan, and genetic and metabolic studies are indicated.

Cognitive-intellectual data looks at the level of a child's overall cognitive function and the patterns of cognitive abilities as determined by individual tests of intelligence (recognizing that the learning disorder itself influences the child's achievement on intelligence testing) and at neuropsychological function.

Environmental-social data involves an understanding of the family, the stresses and strengths, both independent of and dependent on the learning disorder; and evaluation of the emotional, social, and economic life of the parents; and an evaluation of the relationship between the child and her parents, the child and her social group, and the

Table 7.1   Pentaxial scheme for diagnosis in child psychiatry

As Outlined by the Authors	As Outlined in *DSM*

I. Psychiatric
  1. *DSM-IV*-TM diagnosis
  2. Content of thought, feelings, and behavior
  3. Personality structure
  4. Genesis of emotional and behavioral symptoms
  5. Developmental trajectories and levels (Erickson, 1986; A. Freud, 1977; Greenspan, 1981; Piaget, 1954)
	I. Clinical syndrome

II. Biological
  1. Structural nervous system integrity
  2. Level of biological maturation
  3. General medical examination
  4. Possible genetic influences
	II. Personality disorder; specific developmental disorders

III. Cognitive-Intellectual and Neuropsychological
  1. Functioning intelligence
  2. Levels of maturation in perceptual development and CNS processing
	III. Physical disorders

IV. Environmental-Social
  1. Patterns of mothering (Brody & Axelrad, 1978; Greenspan, 1981)
  2. Adequacy and appropriateness of stimuli at critical ages
  3. Reality events
	IV. Severity of psychological stressors

V. Educational
  1. Quality and quantity
  2. Levels of achievement
	V. Highest level of adaptive functioning in past year

child and her siblings. We are also interested in the educational experience of other members of the family, the presence of other family members with a learning disorder, language disorder, or left-handedness, and historical evidence of a possible genetic disorder. Details of the pregnancy and labor with this child are obtained, and the possibility of intrauterine toxemia, trauma, or infection as well as the presence of perinatal problems are considered. Details of the child's growth and development are reviewed.

Educational data includes the levels of academic achievement together with the quality and quantity of educational experience and remedial effort, the child has experienced.

The following case study shows the integration of data from these pentaxial parameters.

CASE STUDY: CHARLES

Charles was 10 years 3 months of age when he was referred from a class for severely emotionally disturbed children because he was making no academic progress and was having daily temper outbursts. Psychological testing revealed a full scale IQ of 90 on the WISC-III (verbal IQ of 94, performance IQ of 88). Academically, his oral reading (WRAT) was at a mid-third-grade level and spelling was at early second-grade level. There was a history of previous diagnosis of hyperactivity and attention deficit disorder for which he received methylphenidate (for the past 3 years) but which Charles said only made him "worse."

Neurological Examination

Neurological examination revealed a sturdy 10-year-old, who came willingly for the examination. There is a tic of both eyes, a press of speech with mild circumstantiality, and gross motor restlessness. At times, he is definitely hyperkinetic, distracted by small items in the examining room. His gross motor coordination is poor; muscle tone appears decreased in the upper extremities, slightly increased in the lower; synkinesis is marked. There is nystagmus on lateral gaze and a mild esophoria. He has difficulty with finger gnosis, where he cannot correctly perceive bilateral asymmetrical stimuli. Extinction phenomena are easily elicited and praxis is definitely immature, at about an 8-year level particularly on the left side. On extension of the arms, there are marked adventitious movements, his right hand is elevated in this right-handed boy, and pencil grip is abnormal. The remainder of the classical neurological examination is within normal limits. The electroencephalogram is abnormal with high-voltage slow waves characteristic of diffuse cerebral dysfunction.

Perceptual Examination

Visual discrimination is accurate by our measures. Visual recall of asymmetric stimuli, however, is no higher than at a 7-year level; and visuomotor function is primitive, no higher than at an 8-year level, with gross angulation difficulty and verticalization (Figure 7.1). His figure drawing is made with wild, impulsive pencil strokes, the head enlarged to be the most prominent feature, the mouth dominant, the body contained in two squares each filled in with a penciled scrawl; the arms and legs were small and puny (Figure 7.2).

Auditory discrimination appeared accurate. Auditory rote sequencing, however, is dramatically immature with confusion of the sequences of before and after. To do any segment of sequencing, he had to run through the entire sequence in his mind.

Emotional Examination

Here Charles shows great difficulty. Extremely anxious, he is afraid to go to sleep, has to take a baseball bat to bed with him, has many "scary" events to the extent of illusions and hallucinations: illusions of his chair "looking like a lady without a

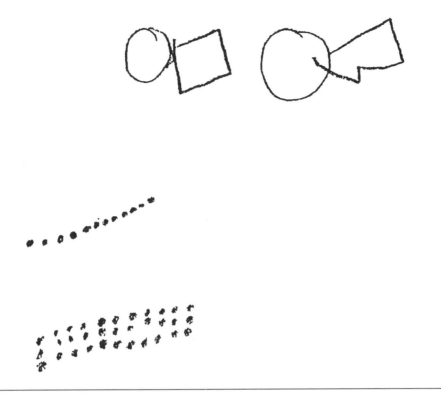

Figure 7.1   Bender-Gestalt drawing, Charles: Age 10 years 3 months.

head"; a snake coming at him; the devil talking to him, telling him to do things. The devil tells him he will "burn forever." He has bizarre thoughts of a ghost coming out of the picture in his bathroom, slicing up his grandmother into bits, hanging the bits on the wall. He feels that he has done some bad things, like killing a puppy by jumping on him by accident, and one time he "almost killed a newborn baby." He feels his classmates pick on him because they know he loses his temper quickly and then he hits himself. He fears to go into a dentist's office because he might "cut all my teeth out." He fears a robot dressed up as a real person and talking like a real person. The relationship with his mother appears distant. A new sibling evokes ambivalent feelings of jealousy, sexual thoughts, affection, and aggression toward the child. He had not had a male figure in his home with whom to identify.

As we review these data, we find that Charles has problems throughout the pentaxial scheme. His neurological examination is replete with nonfocal neurological signs involving primarily motor impulse control, gross motor coordination, muscle tone, and severe immaturity in visual motor function, finger gnosis, and praxis. He has difficulty discriminating bilateral asymmetrical touch, and in sequencing a rote strand of auditory stimuli (auditory temporal sequencing). His arm extension test is normal. His electroencephalogram is reported as abnormal with high voltage slow waves. There is history of hypoxia at birth, and indeed he remained in the newborn

Figure 7.2   Goodenough Draw-a-Person, Charles: Age 10 years 3 months.

intensive care nursery for 5 days after his mother had returned home. The neurological findings are consistent with the effects of trauma and hypoxia at birth.

The eye blink is interpreted as being induced by the methylphenidate, which he had been taking (10 mgm bid) for the past 3 years. Methylphenidate, in our experience, does not have impulse-control effect in children who have evidence of organic (structural) deficit of the central nervous system. In fact, it may have an opposite effect, decreasing, rather than increasing impulse-control

This basic biological problem, setting the stage of increased vulnerability to anxiety is confounded by an emotionally difficult first five years of life. His father set the stage, too, by beating his mother even to the extent, says Charles, of "tying her up" and burning Charles with a cigarette. His mother verifies the truth of these events. His mother's second marriage has only this month produced a boy whose presence adds to Charles's jealousy. These biological and environmental events create a child characterized by marked anxiety and aggressive personality structure, with difficulty controlling his aggression; to which Charles reacts with guilt, fear, and a turning of his aggression onto himself. Despite all this, this child is verbal and appealing, evoking sympathy and interest.

Data from each axis of the pentaxial scheme is essential for understanding and managing children like Charles who are experiencing academic difficulty and behavioral problems. Educationally, Charles needs teaching to build the preacademic skills that form a foundation for reading and the language arts. His teacher, too, recognizing his low threshold for anxiety, should try to protect him from anxiety-producing stimuli and to provide a verbal outlet for his aggression. When a task requires sustained attention, a quiet place with minimal external stimuli is helpful. In addition, however, medication (see Chapter 14) is indicated. Here, methylphenidate was gradually discontinued and clonidine substituted. Individual psychotherapeutic help for Charles to help him deal with his new family and with the sources of his anxiety is indicated. Support for his family also will be helpful.

This brief clinical vignette illustrates how the data from the multiaxial evaluation provide an understanding of the many facets of this child's academic difficulty, an understanding from which appropriate and adequate remedial measures may be derived.

PSYCHIATRIC EXAMINATION

As indicated, the psychiatric examination explores the feelings and thoughts of the child, her goals and desires, her reactions to the stresses and supports of her life, and the abilities and the disabilities with which she confronts the world. It attempts to trace the origins and development of these reactions and views them within the framework of the events of the child's life as they unfold with time. The task of the psychiatrist is to acquire the data to understand each of these parameters, and then to synthesize the data to make a coherent picture of the child in his world. How to acquire that data has been the subject of a vast body of literature, with each successive textbook on child psychiatry providing chapters on the assessment of children.

In the 1930s and 1940s, with the ascendancy of the child guidance movement, data about the child's behavior and development were obtained largely from the child's parents or caretakers. The first edition (1935) of the classic Kanner text in child psychiatry emphasizes such a framework, but the book also points the way to careful, individual examination of children. By 1947, M. B. Hall published one of the earliest texts, *Psychiatric Examination of the School Child;* and by 1957 the Group for the Advancement of Psychiatry (GAP), concerned with the rapidly developing field of child psychiatry, formulated the *Diagnostic Process in Child Psychiatry.* The GAP report, however, was concerned largely with statements of basic assumptions as they relate to the diagnostic process and described the actual diagnostic progress only in general terms. The authors state, for example:

> Diagnosis involved primarily an investigation of the child's relative successes and failures in mastering, in orderly sequence, certain universal anxieties which confront all children as they move through the several stages of personality development. In general, the major task in this growth is directed toward the achievement of a biologically satisfying utilization of life energies (the libidinal or psychosexual and the aggressive drives) through constructive patterns which is socially and ethically satisfying. (p. 317)

However weak on the what and how of psychiatric diagnosis, the 1957 GAP report did provide a standard for the child psychiatrist in examination of an individual child.

More specific descriptions of the *content* of psychiatric examinations of children and adolescents appear in most textbooks of child and adolescent psychiatry. In the first edition of the four-volume *Basic Handbook of Child Psychiatry,* edited by J. Noshpitz in 1979, a chapter on assessment written by R.H. Cohen is prominently included; the second edition, *The Basic Handbook* (Noshpitz, 1979), has grown to seven volumes and an entire volume is devoted to clinical assessment and intervention planning (*Basic Handbook of Child Psychiatry,* Vol. 5, Noshpitz, Harrison, & Spencer, 1998). While sections on assessment appear in most textbooks of child and adolescent psychiatry (Adams & Fras, 1988; Simmons, 1987; J. M. Wiener, 1991), texts concerned specifically, with assessment are available (Kestenbaum & Williams, 1988; Mash & Terdal, 1997). An assessment of young children within the Anne Freud-Hampstead clinic psychoanalytic model is available (Flapan & Neubauer, 1975; Eissler, Freud, Kris, & Solnit, 1977) and evaluation of the preschool child to age 3 years has been developed and described by Greenspan (1981).

The details of assessment procedures and the interpretation of the findings will differ in response to the idiosyncratic orientation of each examiner, the frame of reference in which he or she views the process of development. No matter what the theoretical orientation, however, examiners need a template for the content—the data that all agree are needed for evaluation of the emotional and behavioral problems of children. Simmons, for example, includes in the psychiatric evaluation of a child, 11 areas for investigation: appearance, mood, orientation, and perception; coping mechanisms, neuromuscular integration, thought processes, and verbalization (as seen in dreams, drawings, wishes and play); superego, concept of self-awareness of problems, and estimate of intelligence.

Our approach to the psychiatric component of the pentaxial scheme is outlined in Table 7.2.

Psychiatric Examination Summary

The psychiatric examination may be divided into 11 content areas: (1) general appearance, (2) affect, (3) object relations, (4) impulse control, (5) reality testing, (6) thought processes and cognitive function, (7) speech, (8) identification, (9) defense mechanisms (neurotic type, somatic type, character traits), (10) structural elements of the

Table 7.2   University of South Florida College of Medicine Division of Child and Adolescent Psychiatric Examination—Summary

Name _____   Chronological Age _____

Date _____

1. General appearance:

2. Affect:

3. Object relations:

4. Impulse control:

    A.   Motor

    B.   Emotional

    C.   Affective response

5. Reality testing:

6. Thought processes and cognitive function:

7. Speech:

8. Identification:

9. Defense mechanisms:

    A.   Neurotic type:

    B.   Somatic:

    C.   Character traits:

10. Structural elements of personality:

11. Behavior (description in various settings):

12. Biological factors:

13. Diagnosis:

personality, and (11) behavior. Each of these areas may be further defined, by content and by description. When the data of this evaluation are put together, a picture of the child, his behavior, the areas of his deviation from normal as well as his strengths, his feelings about himself and the people around him, his failures and successes including those at school, his hopes and fears, and the way he deals with all the good and the bad will emerge and the child becomes an individual.

To outline the parameters of the psychiatric examination, however, to identify the content of what is evaluated, is not to describe the *manner* in which each is collected, the questions to be asked, the way the questions must be individualized for each child's age, levels of development, comprehension, levels of anxiety, sensitivity, resistance, and acceptance. Bird and Kestenbaum (1988) provide specific questions that may be asked in a semistructured interview, guiding the examiner to each aspect of the child's life: school, interpersonal relations, self-concept, anxiety, anger, reality testing, depression, and fantasy. Our own preference, however, follows the directions in which the flow of the child's feelings takes us, exploring each new area as it is revealed but always keeping in mind the areas yet to be explored and the depths of those areas capable of being probed during a particular visit. This open-ended, semistructured clinical interview is the type of interview taught in most child psychiatry training programs and is the type done by most child psychiatrists in daily practice. The interrater reliability of this open-ended examination is demonstrated daily in centers for the training of child psychiatrists. Objective evidence is scant, however, with Rutter and Graham (1968) providing one of the few test-retest and interrater reliability studies. Rutter and Graham found a half-hour interview was a valid instrument "to make a provisional judgement on whether or not the child exhibits any psychiatric disorder" (p. 574). In practice, an initial interview most often needs at least a full hour.

A diagnosis, however, usually requires a parent interview along with that of the child. At the University of South Florida, a lengthy questionnaire covering details of pregnancy, birth, and neonatal period; development in multiple parameters; family health; social and economic history; reasons for this visit; the development of present symptoms and previous management; school, medical, and social history of the child and his siblings is sent to the parents as early as possible so that it may be reviewed by the clinician before the visit. The parents are interviewed in a visit following that in which the child is evaluated; the questionnaire is reviewed and the child's history, problems, and management are obtained.

There has been accumulated "dissatisfaction with the reliability and validity of traditional diagnostic procedures" (Edelbrook & Costello, 1984). This dissatisfaction has stemmed from a "lack of reliability often found in office practice diagnostic evaluations" (Greenhill & Malcom, 2000). The lack of reliability is said to arise because office procedures have not been defined or described in a standardized manner; diagnostic criteria are not standardized, training standards vary from training program to training program, professionals in the same program may not make the same diagnosis for the same patient even when given the same material, and there is a tendency to selectively collect information that conforms to initial diagnostic impression while ignoring exclusionary information or seeing a correlation where none exists. Current service delivery system, managed care organizations, research programs particularly those with specific symptom targets in psychopharmacological research, have sought to overcome variability inherent in office evaluations. This trend has been accelerated by the explicit diagnostic criteria that categorize the specific disorders of the *Diagnostic and Statistical Manual of Mental Disorders (DSM)*.

To provide standardization in gathering data for diagnosis and establish rules for the way information is gathered, standardized structured diagnostic and screening interviews have been developed for use with children and adolescents. Although these instruments facilitate a systematic diagnostic assessment in accordance with specific criteria, these criteria are most often those of the *Diagnostic and Statistical Manual.* These criteria are both good and bad: good because they provide uniform diagnostic criteria accessible to the entire mental health community; a diagnosis made in New York will be characterized with the same criteria as the same diagnosis in San Francisco. This is essential in research, in communication among professional mental health workers with schools, with managed care organizations, with government agencies and with patients and parents. The method is bad, because *DSM* criteria are based on a collection of symptoms.

The symptoms themselves may not be specific for the disorders so identified, but may be present in a variety of conditions each with a different etiology. As McHugh (1999) complains about *DSM* diagnosis: "If you can describe it, you can name it; and if you can name it then you can claim it exists as a distinct entity (disorder). Proposals for new psychiatric disorders have multiplied so feverishly that the *DSM* itself has grown from 119 pages in 1968 to 886 in 1998" (p. 34). What the standardized interviews have done is to reinforce the concept that the *DSM* diagnostic clusters are discrete entities; deifying the label has transformed the symptom clusters into discrete disorders with specific etiology and specific treatment. There is an old adage that things equal to the same things are equal to each other. The structured interview is considered reliable if it mirrors the *DSM* diagnosis. This takes us no further in understanding the cause of the collection of symptoms, nor in an awareness of their lack of unifying etiology.

To be fair, however, psychiatry cannot yet identify the etiological mechanism of psychiatric disorder, to understand the changes in the brain that lead to specific disorders. It is also true that we are making progress in understanding the changes and the causes of these changes. The hope is that we will be flexible enough not to be trapped in today's *DSM,* but will discard *symptoms* diagnosis when new knowledge emerges, as most certainly it will.

Nevertheless, the weight of opinion now is heavily in favor of structured interviews, particularly for epidemiological and clinical research projects. Clinical use of these measures has not been included in standards for practice, so that they are not routinely used in clinical assessments.

The development of the structured interview has been and continues to be supported by the National Institute of Mental Health. By 1980, eight such scales suitable for epidemiological and clinical research were described in a report from the Division of Biometry and Epidemiology, NIMH (Orvaschel, Sholomska, & Weissman, 1980) and in

1984, seven of the eight scales of that report, together with the NIMH-supported Diagnostic Interview Schedule for children (DISC), were reviewed by Edelbrook and Costello, in a study paper for the Center for Studies of Child and Adolescent Psychopathology, Clinical Research Branch, NIMH. Each scale is discussed in terms of its item content, response scaling, administration time, degree of structure, informant, age range, training of interviewer, information yield, and psychometric properties (reliability and validity and applications). Data from this review are also seen in Orvaschel, 1985. Since 1985, the number of scales and the fine tuning of scales have proliferated, so that by 2000, an intensive review of general diagnostic instruments and diagnostic-specific symptoms (symptom checklists) for adults as well as for infants, children, and adolescents required a volume in itself (First, 2000).

The general diagnostic measures are "broadband," aimed at classifying children into *DSM* diagnostic categories, while also having some ability to assess changes in presenting symptoms and to evaluate their severity. The broadband symptom diagnostic measures are really checklists of symptoms developed to measure clusters of symptoms on a continuous scale.

The symptom checklist may be "narrowband," concentrating in symptoms of one disorder (i.e., Connor's Rating Scales Revised for ADHD) and structured to identify individuals who statistically deviate from the norm in the specific symptoms quantified in the scale.

Evaluating the validity of a broadband general diagnostic scale is difficult because as yet there is no gold standard to determine whether the diagnosis is valid. Further, revisions of *DSM* over the past 16 years have demanded revisions of the structured interview so that new, current psychometric properties may not be available. To ascertain a diagnosis, Greenhill and Malcom recommend the Schedule for Affective Disorders and Schizophrenia for School-age Children, Present and Lifetime Version (K-SADS-PL) (Chambers et al., 1985; J. Kaufman et al., 1999); the NIMH-Diagnostic Interview Scale for Children, parent version, youth version, teacher's version (NIMH-DISC. 2.3) (D. Shaffer et al., 1996; D. Shaffer et al., 1993); the Diagnostic Interview for Children and Adolescents (DICA), the Child and the Child and Adolescent Psychiatric Assessment (CAPA) (Angold & Costello, 1995, 1996), and the Child Assessment Schedule (CAS).

The characteristics and content of commonly used schedules are shown in Table 7.3, based on data obtained in H. Orvaschel (1985), "Psychiatric Interviews Suitable for Research with Children and Adolescents," *Psychopharmacology Bulletin, 21*(4), pp. 739 to 740 and from Greenhill and Malcom (2000). Detailed review of structured tests may be found in Greenhill and Malcom (2000).

For our everyday clinical use, however, we are left with the open-ended clinical interviews outlined in Table 7.1. The content of the clinical interviews must be complete and covers most of the information of comprehensive structured interviews. In the clinical interview, however, the structure for gathering the information may be individualized and flexible depending on the age, intelligence, verbal ability, level of development, anxiety, and comprehension of the child.

How the data provided on this psychiatric assessment, contributed to the diagnosis of a child with a learning disorder may be seen in the study of Jay, who was 6 years 2 months of age when seen with the parent and school complaint of hyperactivity.

Table 7.3   Characteristics of structured psychiatric interviews

Interview Properties	CAS	DICA	NIMH-DISC	K-SADS-PL
Number of items	>300	267–311	358+	300+
Time period assessed	Current or past 6 months	Current or lifetime	Past year	Current or lifetime
Age assessed	4–18	6–18	6–17	6–17
Completion time	150 min	180–240 min	140 min	90–150 min
Structured Semistructured	X			
Symptom oriented	X		X	
Category oriented		X		X
Severity ratings				X
Precoded	X	X	X	X
Computer scoring		X	X	
Administration				
Lay interviewer		X	X	
Clinician	X	X	X	X
Reliability data	X	X	X	X
Affective disorders				
Adjustment disorders with depressed mood				
Cyclothymia	X		X	X
Dysthymia	X	X	X	X
Hypomania				X
Major depression	X	X	X	X
Mania	X	X	X	X
Minor depression				X
Anxiety Disorders				
Avoidant	X	X	X	
Generalized anxiety	X			X
Obsessive-compulsive	X	X	X	X
Overanxious	X	X	X	X
Panic	X		X	X
Phobic	X	X	X	X
Separation anxiety	X	X	X	X
Behavioral disorders				
Attention deficit	X	X	X	X
Conduct		X	X	X
Oppositional	X	X	X	
Eating disorders				
Anorexia nervosa	X	X	X	X
Bulimia	X	X	X	X

(continued)

Table 7.3   (Continued)

Interview Properties	CAS	DICA	NIMH-DISC	K-SADS-PL
Psychotic disorders				
Psychotic signs (only)	X	X		
Schizoaffective				X
Schizophrenia				X
Schizophreniform			X	X
Substance disorders				
Alcohol	X	X	X	X
Drugs	X	X	X	X
Tobacco		X		
Other disorders				
Encopresis	X	X	X	
Enuresis	X	X	X	
Gender identity		X	X	
Schizoid	X	X		
Sleep terror	X			
Sleepwalking	X			
Somatoform		X		
Axis II disorders				
Borderline				
Compulsive				
Histrionic				
Schizoid				
Schizotypal				X
Other content				
Developmental questions		X		X
Observational items	X	X		X
Stressor		X		
Sexual behavior		X		

Note: From "Psychiatric interviews suitable for use in research with children and adolescents" by H. Orvaschel, 1985, *Psychopharmacology Bulletin, 21* (4), 739 to 740. Material in public domain, and from *Handbook of Psychiatric Measures,* American Psychiatric Association, 2000.

CASE STUDY: JAY

Jay is a handsome, dark-haired, 6-year-old boy. His hands and feet are dirty, his clothes are stained, and in general, he appears unkempt. He leaves his mother with no overt anxiety. However, he immediately says he would like to sit at my desk and begins to tell the examiner that he does not like school, especially when he has to write. He is not hyperkinetic and does not examine objects on the desk or in the room. On questioning, he says he has trouble falling asleep. He sees a man's face in the wall and sometimes sees rattlesnakes, spiders, or tarantulas in his room. He hears the devil talking to him saying "vulgar" words. He says he would rather be "in a crib. I can play baby in there and people play with you more." "I know I'm too old for that now, but they [his parents] don't know I like it." He wishes to be a baby when he is asked to do things he feels he cannot do. When he cannot, he regresses and becomes rebellious, demanding, and repeatedly frustrated. At these times, he may hurt himself or has a fantasy of being hit by a car. He feels guilty about the bad things he does. Sometimes he pretends there are no problems, or that he would like to be invisible so that he could scare people or to be a rocket and look like his father or talk as loud as he does. As Jay felt less anxious in the examination, he was able to leave the examiner's desk and play with the toy cars on the child table.

From this interview, we may conclude that Jay has emotional problems, which, by themselves, could account for his behavior and problems in school adjustment. He is depressed and sometimes discouraged; his object relations vary between being demanding and attention seeking and being clinging and infantile. His motor impulse control in this evaluation is good; his emotional impulse control is poor with a need for immediate gratification; his reality testing is adequate. He is anxious, already feeling that the world is too demanding. He has fears of animals, visual illusions, and even auditory hallucinations. His anxiety makes him restless, even hyperactive. His personality structure is already rife with guilt.

From this interview alone, however, we do not have a complete picture of Jay and his school problems. The pentaxial evaluation adds further dimensions to Jay's picture. He has superior verbal intelligence but average performance ability. Neurologically, he has difficulty with fine-motor coordination, in praxis (where his performance is not higher than age 4) and in visuomotor function. His father is demanding, overbearing, and physically and emotionally abusive to his wife, Jay's mother. She, in turn, is self-effacing, mouselike, and browbeaten. On questioning, Jay's father says that Jay has no problems, that Jay is just as he was, that he also had trouble in school because he could not write clearly and that he still dislikes writing.

With these data, a fuller picture of Jay unfolds. There may be a basic developmental delay that is mild and possibly genetic, involving fine motor coordination and praxis. On this, however, is superimposed the specter of a father whom he cannot please and who actually frightens him, a mother who cannot give Jay the support he needs, and now a school that is making demands on him that physically he cannot meet. He reacts with anxiety, hyperactivity, regression, denial, withdrawal into fantasy, depression, and guilt. Dynamically, he has not resolved the anxieties of the oedipal phase and has remnants of even earlier psychosexual developmental phases. He is already failing in first grade.

In management, he needs the cooperation of his school, not only in understanding his high capabilities as well as his poor motor function, but also in offering intervention so that he can overcome his poor function; help for his parents in resolving their emotional difficulties and their impact on the child; and at the very least supportive psychotherapy for Jay himself. Without the understanding of this child's emotional problems, treating him for inattention would not solve his school or behavioral difficulties. Medication was not used in the successful resolution of Jay's difficulties.

NEUROLOGICAL EXAMINATION

The value of a neurological examination for children with learning disorder has been questioned by some educators and even by psychiatrists. In 1980, G. Weiss stated, "It is known that children with learning disabilities and/or hyperactive impulse disorders may not have abnormal neurological or EEG findings, and even if they had (aside from the rare treatable neurological conditions, such as brain tumors or frank epilepsy), the findings would make no difference whatever to their educational and psychological rehabilitation or their total management" (p. 349). Kinsbourne and Caplan (1979) broadened the criteria for neurological examination to (a) where there is suspicion of organic disease of the central nervous system, (b) where the examiner has elicited signs "which lend themselves to ambiguous interpretation," or (c) where a satisfactory examination of the nervous system has not been done.

Our position is clearly on the side of Kinsbourne. Although children with learning disabilities may not have abnormal neurological or EEG findings, of course, some of them do. In a study of 494 children comprising the entire first grades of seven schools on the East Side of New York City, Hagin, Beecher, and Silver (1982) found approximately 25% of the entire group had signs suggesting vulnerability to learning disorder; 4% of the total sample did have neurological findings. This study was done on an unselected population, a normative group to be found in any first-grade classroom in a typical inner city school in New York City.

When dealing with older children who have already failed in academic achievement and who are in classes for emotionally disturbed children, neurological examination is most important and, in our opinion, an evaluation of such children is not complete if it does not include neurological study. In an examination of the first 60 children placed in self-contained classes for severely emotionally disturbed children in a west Florida county (A. A. Silver, 1984), 18 (30%) of the 60 had evidence of some structural defect of the central nervous system, another 18 (30%) were children with long-standing specific learning disability (dyslexia), and 10 (17%) were suffering from an attention deficit disorder. Tables 7.4 and 7.5 outline the neurological and cognitive findings in these 60 children. In a second study (A. A. Silver et al., 2001), electroencephalograms were done on 28 of 31 children between the ages of 12 and 16 who were consecutively referred to our child psychiatry clinic because of academic and behavior difficulty in classes for emotionally disturbed children (see Table 7.6). Of these, nineteen EEGs were reported as borderline or abnormal and nine as normal. Abnormalities included abnormal focal slowing, multifocal or focal spikes, paroxysmal spikes, or generalized excessive slowing. It was clear that neurological examination and, in selected children, neurological and electroencephalographic examination contributed an important dimension to understanding these children who were having so much difficulty in learning and in behavior.

Even with younger children in the early elementary grades who are beginning to show signs of a learning disorder, neurological examination can be of importance in guiding teachers in their work. Generally children with neurological problems, particularly those with diffuse central nervous system dysfunction, are more vulnerable to

Table 7.4   Diagnosis of children in self-contained classes for the severely emotionally handicapped

Predominant Diagnosis	School S (n)	School M (n)	Total n	Total %
Attention Deficit Disorder	5	5	10	17
Organic Defect of the Central Nervous System	10	8	18	30
Specific Learning Disability	6	12	18	30
Schizophrenia	1	2	3	5
Borderline Mental Retardation	3	8	11	18
TOTAL	25	35	60	100

Note: From "Children in classes for the severely emotionally handicapped" by A.A. Silver, 1984, *Journal of Developmental and Behavioral Pediatrics, 5,* p. 50. Baltimore: Williams & Wilkins. Reprinted by permission.

anxiety. Their stimulus barrier is thin, they have difficulty controlling the impulses that spring from within themselves, and they are more sensitive, overreacting to stimuli that impinge on them. Thus they may be easily distracted and cannot always sustain attention in the midst of the average classroom. Quiet places may be necessary. They are sensitive, however, not only in their responses to physical stimuli (children talking,

Table 7.5   Variety of neurological disorders for children in self-contained classes for the severely emotionally handicapped

Disorder	Total n
Prematurity*	3
Cerebral Palsy	3
Genetic (Chromosome Defect)	3
Seizures, Idiopathic	2
Cerebellar Palsy	2
Rh Incompatibility	1
Tourette's Syndrome	1
Unknown Dyskinesia	1
Pb Toxicity	1
Birth Trauma	1
TOTAL	18

* One with fetal alcohol syndrome.

Note: From "Children in classes for the severely emotionally handicapped" by A. A. Silver, 1984, *Journal of Developmental and Behavioral Pediatrics,* 5, p. 50. Baltimore: Williams and Wilkins. Reprinted by permission.

Table 7.6 Results of electroencephalogram—31 consecutive referrals from SED classes

EEG Report	Number	Percent of Total
Normal	9	29.0
Borderline	2	6.4
Diffuse abnormalities	7	2.3
Focal abnormalities	6	19.0
Paroxysmal	2	6.4
Combinations	2	6.4
Not done	3	9.8
Totals	31	1.00
Total abnormal	19	61

papers rustling, or outside noises), but also to emotional stimuli and are easily emotionally hurt. They may react with aggression or withdrawal. In either event, the teacher's awareness of emotional sensitivity can provide a buffer to emotional stimuli as well as to the more obvious perceptual ones (see Chapter 14).

From a learning point of view, there are additional problems in children with organic defects of the central nervous system. Their perceptual deficits are more resistant to change than are those in children with developmental dyslexia. In a 12-year follow-up study of children with learning disorders, children with an organic diagnosis did not outgrow their perceptual defects (A. A. Silver & Hagin, 1964). The same perceptual problems found at age 8 were found in these people when they were in their 20s. Also these children have difficulty with memory. What they may learn one day is forgotten the next. In children with neurological findings, teaching requires more time, proceeds more slowly, and may have a more guarded prognosis than in children with dyslexia who have similar perceptual defects (see Chapters 8 and 14).

Neurological findings, contrary to the opinion expressed by G. Weiss (1980), have much to contribute to educational and psychological rehabilitation. Part of the problem in referring a child for neuropsychiatric study, is that the classical neurological examination—muscle tone, power and synergy, deep and superficial and pathological reflexes, cranial nerves, and gross sensory evaluation—is essentially normal and must be amplified by the study of soft signs: kinetic patterns in various states; postural responses; the so-called higher cortical functions (Luria, 1966), spatial orientation and temporal organization in visual, auditory, and body image modalities; and the receptive, associative, and emissive aspects of language. Our outline for neurological evaluation is seen in Table 7.7. Findings must then be placed on the background of a normal developmental curve.

Classical neurological examination needs no amplification here. An expanded outline for neurological examination may be found in the Appendix. Soft signs, however, including testing of higher cortical function, do need definition and description.

Table 7.7   University of South Florida College of Medicine Division of Child and Adolescent Psychiatry Neurological Examination (summary)

Name: _____   Birthdate: _____

Address: _____   Present Date: _____

Telephone No.: _____   Age Now: _____

School and Grade: _____

Head Circumference: _____

Ectoderm: _____

Gross Posture and Gait: _____

Hand used for writing: _____

I. Neurological
  1. Extension with counting
    a. adventitious movements
    b. convergence-divergence
    c. elevated extremity
  2. Rotation of head
    a. standing
      1. head to left
      2. head to right
    b. sitting
  3. Muscle tone
    a. increased-decreased-normal
    b. fluctuating
    c. myoclonic activity
    d. synkinesis
  4. Classical
    a. cranial nerves-nystagmus
    b. tendon reflexes
    c. pathological reflexes
    d. superficial reflexes
    e. cerebellar function
  5. Patterned motor behavior
    a. gross patterns
      1. hyper-hypo
      2. antigravity play
      3. relationship to adult
      4. toe walking
        hopping
        tandem walk
      5. other
    b. Fine-motor coordination
      1. F.F.
      2. F.N.
      3. Praxis:
        R 1–3, 1–5, 1–2, 1–4
        L 1–3, 1–5, 1–2, 1–4
      4. Ozeretsky Test
        Rt hand, Left hand
  6. Language
    a. receptive
    b. associative
    c. emissive
    d. Van Alystine (picture vocabulary)
    e. Word recognition (WRAT)
    f. Spelling (WRAT)
    g. Arithmetic (WRAT)

II. Autonomic Nervous System
  1. Pupils
    a. size 1. s. n.
    b. shape
    c. position
    e. convergence
  2. Ptosis
  3. Salivation
  4. Vasomotor and Sudomotor
    a. perioral pallor
    b. skin temperature N. Abn.
    c. sweating of palms
    d. other
  5. Heart rate
  6. Blood pressure

III. Perceptual-Cognitive
  1. Visual
    a. discrimination
    b. recall
    c. figure-ground
    d. visual-motor
    e. block design
  2. Auditory
    a. discrimination
    b. rote sequencing
    c. sentence memory
    d. code sequencing
  3. Tactile
    a. extinction
    b. stereognosis
    c. finger gnosis
      Single   Sym.bilat
      R-1, L-3, L-5, R-4 R2-L2,
      R4-L4
      Asym. bilat
      R3-L5, R2-L4, R4-L3, R3-L4
  4. Body Image
    a. right left discrimination
      1. In self, unX, X'd
      2. In examiner, unX, X'd
    b. draw-a-person
  5. Clock drawing

Testing for Neurological Soft Signs

Soft signs on neurological examination have been defined in two ways.

1. As "non-normative performance on a motor or sensory test identical or akin to a test item of the traditional neurological examination, but which is elicited from an individual who shows none of the features of a fixed or transient localizable neurological disorder" (D. Shaffer, O'Conner, Shafer, & Purpis, 1983). These signs may be elicited in three general areas: (a) movement, including spontaneous tremors, tics, synkinesis and choreiform movement: (b) coordination, including dysmetria, dysdidochokines, and awkwardness, and (c) sensory integration, such as sterognosis, and graphesthesia. Shaffer's concept of soft neurological signs further states that these signs cannot be related to "any serious postnatal neurological insult that might be expected to leave residual neurological signs" nor may "groupings of soft signs have a pathognomic pattern that would indicate localized structural lesions, generalized encephalopathy, or CNS involvement" (p. 144).

2. As representing the persistence of a primitive form of response (Kinsbourne & Caplan, 1979), a failure of the child to have matured in a particular function consistent with that expected for his or her age. Such functions may not only be in the motor area, in coordination, and in sensory integration as described in the D. Shaffer et al. (1983) definition, but may also be found in such perceptual functions as in tests of spatial orientation and temporal sequencing. In the motor area, for example, the choreoathetotic movements of the infant as he grasps for a rattle are perfectly normal. The persistence of such choreiform movement in a 7-year-old or in a 10-year-old, even in the absence of an identified neurological disease, suggests that the function of modulation of motor movement is immature in that child. Similarly, in the concept of the body image in space, as in right-left discrimination, praxis, or finger gnosis, a soft sign means that performance in these functions is less than that expected for the child's age. A soft sign thus suggests that the maturation of a particular function is delayed; it is a sign of neurological or neuropsychological immaturity.

The concept of soft neurological signs as an indication of immaturity in development is a concept broader than that delineated by D. Shaffer et al. (1983). It is more consistent with the concepts proposed by Gesell many years ago (1945/1969) and the more recent ones of Robert Thatcher (1996) derived from the spatial integration of electrophysiological and magnetoencephalographic studies. Gesell described development as proceeding in a hierarchal fashion in a spiral continuum of space and time. Functions and behaviors gradually emerge from the latent biological *anlage* of the trait into behaviors, initially present in dormant fashion, and finally developing into manifest behavior. Thatcher conceives development as a dynamic process involving cyclic cortical organization, with traveling waves, of coherent neural activity. The neural activity, really electromagnetic waves, behaves in an orderly fashion exhibiting specific spatial directions and velocities, most commonly observed along lateral to medial and the rostral to caudel anatomical axes of the cerebral cortex. These occur during prenatal neurogenesis and postnatal cortical development (Thatcher, 1994), in oscillating fashion corresponding to growth spurts and to reorganization of cortical activity. At any point in space and time, factors within and external to the organism may interfere with the maturation of a particular function, thus interfering, not only with neuronal organization but also with the hierarchal functions emerging from that organization (see Chapter 11).

Some of these interfering factors may lie within the organism itself, such as polymorphism inherent in the genes; some may result from toxic interference in embryonic development, such as seen in the fetal alcohol syndrome or in cocaine babies, or from some lesion (i.e., traumatic, anoxic, or infectious acquired at birth or in early life); and some may occur in children in whom the environmental stimulus needed to transform the available biological *anlage* into manifest function is inappropriate or insufficient.

In any one child, of course, combinations of these possible origins of soft signs may be found. A child with a genetic predisposition to a developmental language disability, for example, but with the genetic disposition not great enough to result in language disorder, may per se experience an event during prenatal, natal, or neonatal life that can bring out the latent predisposition. As Zangwill (1960) said of reading disabilities, "the ambilateral constitution provides no more than a setting for the interplay of genetic and acquired tendencies in growth and development" (p. 26). Contrary to D. Shaffer's statement that "soft signs cannot be related to any serious postnatal insult that may be expected to leave residual neurological signs," our experience and the literature suggest that with prenatal or postnatal events such as prenatal distress, postnatal trauma, or infection, classical neurological signs may be obtunded with age or may indeed be entirely absent so that soft signs or a learning disorder may be the only residuals of such events. In this context, soft signs may represent manifestations of definite neurological abnormalities; the behavioral and educational consequences of which may be profound. For example, Tandon et al. (1998) compare a cohort of 54 children who had hypoxia (asphyxia) at birth and were apparently "unimpaired" with 57 matched controls at age 7 years and at age 10 years. A significantly higher proportion of the hypoxic children had low scores on the Bender-Gestalt Test and showed the presence of soft neurological signs. That soft neurological signs may be associated with behavioral consequences is suggested by the Heidleberg Delinquency Study (Krober, Scheurer, & Sass, 1994) when in a study of 129 adult offenders of violent crimes, there was a "high relevance of non-focal neurological signs," associated with "problems in social adjustment and conduct disorders in childhood, cognitive impairment, reduced emotional responses, eternalizing attributional style and a pattern of delinquent relapses."

What happens to soft signs as the child grows older? Are they simply transient phenomena that disappear with maturation? Longitudinal studies suggest that they do not necessarily disappear with maturation but that there is a consistency of soft signs over time. The concept of "developmental lag," as advanced by Gesell and Thompson (1934) and later by L. A. Bender and Yarnell (1941), was applied to children whose classical neurological examination was normal. Structural central nervous system defects could not be identified in these children, and functional defects (soft signs) were not considered fixed but to have a potential for maturation. This potential, however, does not mean that the lagging function will accelerate and spontaneously become age appropriate.

Longitudinal studies (Hertzig, 1982; Minde, Weiss, & Mendelson, 1972; D. Shaffer et al., 1983; A. A. Silver & Hagin, 1964; G. Weiss, 1983; G. Weiss & Hechtman, 1993; G. Weiss, Minde, Werry, Douglas, & Nemeth, 1971) demonstrated the consistency of soft signs over time. S. Q. Shaffer et al. (1986) and Pine, Shaffer, and Schonfeld (1993) followed African American subjects (118 boys, 54 girls) from the first few months after their birth to ages 16 and 18. These subjects were originally studied as part of the Collaborative Prenatal Project, funded during the years 1959 and 1965 to study the relationship between prenatal problems and neurological and cognitive deficits in infancy and childhood. Columbia Presbyterian Medical Center, one of 12 sites participating in the study, collected data on standardized forms at prenatal clinic visits, at admission for delivery, during labor and delivery, and at specific intervals through the age 8 years. The children reported by S. Q. Shaffer et al. (1986) and Pine et al. (1993) were free of gross neurological disease. In addition to classical neurological examination, evaluation for soft signs, including finger to finger opposition, finger to nose, sequential opposition of thumb to same hand, rapid sequential pronation and supination of the same hand (Ozeretsky), alternating toe/heel tapping, tandem gait, hopping, diadochokinesis, and Romberg were evaluated. A child was considered to have soft signs if there were abnormalities in age appropriateness, fluency, rhythm, or speed in these tests. In addition, any child with abnormal involuntary or dystonic movements, awkwardness, or poor coordination in any of these tasks was considered to have soft neurological signs. More than half the children who had dysdiadochokinesis and synkinesis at age 7 years also had these signs at 16 to 18 years. Equally important, however, is the suggested relationship between the presence of soft signs and psychiatric disturbance, particularly anxiety syndrome. Pine et al. (1993) suggests that "an evaluation of motor signs in young children with anxiety or affective symptoms may have prognostic significance for the persistence of the disorder" (p. 1234).

Hertzig (1982) reported two examinations, four years apart, on 53 children who were part of an original study of 198 children comprising a sample of children attending a special school for learning-disabled and neurologically impaired children. The mean number of nonfocal (i.e., soft) signs did decrease in stepwise fashion from 4.8 in the $9\frac{1}{2}$-year-old to 2.5 in the $15\frac{1}{2}$-year-old; however, "the number of children who displayed 2 or more non-focal signs on each examination did not differ significantly on two examinations conducted four years apart" (p. 231). G. Weiss et al. (1971) and Minde et al. (1972) followed the fate of children diagnosed as hyperactive and treated with phenothiazines or dextroamphetamine for 5 years. In general, hyperactive children had significantly higher rates of academic failure and more behavioral problems than the controls. Further, on the Lincoln Ozeretsky Motor Development Scale, the hyperactive children actually dropped in their performance from the 31st to the 15th percentile. The results of the WISC, Goodenough Draw-a-Man, and Bender VMGT tests showed no significant change over time (see also case reports in Chapter 14).

In a 10 to 12-year follow-up study, 24 children with a learning disability (21 boys, 3 girls), who were ages 8 to 10 in their initial examination at the Bellevue Hospital Mental Hygiene Clinic, were reexamined at median age 19 years with the same battery of tests used earlier (A. A. Silver & Hagin, 1964). A control group of 11 children, also referred to the Bellevue Hospital Mental Hygiene Clinic, matched with the reading disability children in age, sex, IQ, socioeconomic status, and psychiatric diagnosis, were also followed. It was specifically noted that some of the tests were modified for use with the older group but were designed to measure the same function that had been studied earlier. In studying visual figure-ground perception, for example, the Marble Board test (Strauss & Werner, 1943) was used for the younger children; to this was added the Gottschaldt visual figure-ground test for the young adults. Findings indicated that despite maturation in some areas, specific reading disability is a long-term problem, the signs of which may be detected in young adult life. The ability to distinguish right and left was improved, but evidence of immaturity in visuomotor function; in figure-ground perception in the tactile, auditory, and visual area; and in finger gnosis remained. Also, subjects who, as children, had neurological evidence suggesting a structural defect of the central nervous system tended to retain in young adulthood, the same signs they had as children, while those designated as having developmental learning disabilities recovered partially or developed cues to help cope with spatial or temporal problems.

It appears, then, that there is a consistency of soft signs over time, although they need not be static. The important issue is that although some maturation may be found, the developmental immaturity still persists relative to normal age-appropriated levels of the same function as the child grows older. Tests must be adapted to the age of the child. The ceiling of a test suitable for a younger child will not reveal the defect in an older child. An example of adapting figure-ground tests to age is seen in the previous paragraph. Another example may be seen in tests for right-left discrimination. A 6-year-old with a learning problem may not be able to identify his own right hand. An adolescent with a learning problem may be able to identify her own right hand but cannot identify the right hand of the examiner in front of her, a task that the intact adolescent has no difficulty performing.

Not only must tests for the same function be adapted to age, but also tests for new functions that normally emerge over time must be done. Satz, Taylor, Friel, and Fletcher (1978), for example, postulate that in kindergarten children in whom learning disabilities will develop later, there is a lag in the development of skills of perceptual discrimination and analysis. These skills are subsumed under the term "sensory-perceptual-motor-mnemonic" ability. By the fifth grade (age 10), these skills, said Satz, will eventually catch up, but there will be a subsequent lag in the conceptual-linguistic skills, which have a slower and later ontogenetic development. The emergence of hierarchal function lags in time, is certainly to be expected. However, if the perceptual skills of a 10-year-old with a learning disability are tested in a framework suitable to that age, they may not "catch up" at all, but will reveal telltale evidence of the immaturity foretold by their earlier testing.

Protocol for Examination of Soft Signs

A standardized procedure for comprehensive testing for soft signs has not been generally accepted. L. A. Bender has generally been credited with viewing soft signs as evidence of immaturity of the central nervous system. Her techniques for eliciting soft signs are included in her extensive publications, but these techniques have lacked systematic studies of reliability and validity. Nevertheless, students who have worked with her have evidence of their clinical reliability in their daily work.

Attempts have been made to structure the neurological examination for soft signs by the Collaborative Perinatal Study (P. L. Nichols & Chen, 1981), by the Psychiatric and Neurological Examination for Soft Signs (PANESS, Close, 1973, revised by Denckla, 1985), by Rutter, Graham, and Yule (1970), by Hertzig (1982), Peters (1987), and by A. A. Silver and Hagin (1972). A timed motor coordination battery, along with sample norms, is included in the Denckla (1985) revision. Nevertheless, procedures for comprehensive testing for soft signs generally vary among investigators. Not only may different investigators examine different functions, but also, even when different investigators study the same functions, the method for studying that function may vary. Table 7.7 compares methods that have appeared in the literature for testing soft signs.

In testing for stereognosis, the CPP study uses a bottle cap, nickel, and button, which the child must, with eyes closed, identify by touch. Those who fail are given a "more gross" test using a key, marble, and ¾–inch block. The directions as given in P. L. Nichols and Chen (1981) are not clear, but it is presumed that each hand is tested separately and the children's responses are verbal identifications. In the scored neurological examination (Close, 1973; Denckla, 1985), a coin, ring, safety pin, and key are used; in the Rutter, Graham, et al. (1970) protocol a rubber (eraser), matchbox, key, and penny are used; Hertzig (1982) uses a comb, key, quarter, and penny. These subtle differences make comparisons uncertain. Tests for finger gnosis are even more variable. The CPP examination uses "abnormal tactile finger recognition." Children were asked to identify fingers that were lightly touched when the fingers were out of their sight.

Each of the 10 fingers was tested with a single stimulus and results were quantitatively coded by number of errors. It is not clear whether the identification was verbal, by number, or by name of the finger, or simply by indicating by gesture which finger is touched. Rutter, Graham, et al. (1970), PANESS (Close, 1973; Denckla, 1985) and Hertzig (1982) do not test for finger gnosis. A. A. Silver and Hagin (1972), however, make finger gnosis an important part of their study for spatial orientation of the body image. They use a sequence of developmental skills: first single stimuli, then bilateral simultaneous symmetrical stimuli, and finally bilateral simultaneous asymmetrical stimuli. As far back as 1959, Benton stated that "the methods employed to assess right-left discrimination and finger localization in patients have been so diverse that the findings of various clinical investigators are not comparable" (p. 162). Diversity among methods in examinations for soft signs, which renders comparisons difficult, is still true.

Equally important for most of the functions studied, age norms are sadly lacking. How many Prechtl movements of the outstretched hands, for example, are normal and at what age? At what age do synkinetic (mirror) movements tend to diminish? Quantitative data for this type of soft signs is generally lacking, and the examiner is left to rely on clinical experience and judgment. For sensory-perceptual tests, however, norms may be established. The problem here is that except where standardized neuropsychological batteries are used (e.g., Reitan), idiosyncratic examination techniques make norms useless for general application. In addition to the idiosyncratic manner in which different protocols perform the various test items, the interpretation of test results may also suffer. For example, five of the protocols on Table 7.7 describe an arm extension test. For Hertzig, the arm extension that reveals the frequency and severity of Prechtl movements is important; for Denckla, it is coordination and posture. For us, the arm extension test is important not only in Prechtl movements, in coordination and posture, but as an indication of the establishment of hemisphere specialization of language. In evaluating a child with learning disability, this is most important. In Chapter 11, we describe the reason for this interpretation. Further we suspect, but have not subjected to research evaluation, that convergence of the outstretched hands to overlap in the midline, strongly suggests the learning disability of that child is more than developmental, but is evidence of a complicating organic factor in etiology. Dystonic movements other than Prechtl movements are also brought out in the arm extension test. A part of the arm extension maneuver, too, primitive postural reflexes (tonic, neck, and neck righting) may be evoked by gentle turning of the head to the right side, then the left. The so-called whirling response (a persistence of the neck, righting reflex) may be elicited. Table 7.8 outlines various schemes for the evaluation of soft signs. The Collaborative Perinatal Project (Nichols & Chen, 1981) bases its evaluation on the classical neurological examination but in addition stresses motor coordination and synergy, the presence of abnormal movements, sensory-perceptual evaluation of position sense, stereognosis, and finger gnosis. PANESS (Close, 1973) consists of 43 items to be scored, involving tasks of motor coordination and synergy: finger to nose (items 1 to 4); heel to shin (items 5 to 8); walking tiptoe (item 21); heel walking (item 22); hopping (items 23 to 24); tandem walking (items 25 to 26); tongue extrusion (time able to extend) (item 30); arms extended, eyes open (item 31); arms extended, eyes closed (item 32); standing on one foot (items 33 to 34); Romberg (items 35 to 36); finger tapping (items 37 to 38); foot tapping (items 39 to 40); synchronous finger and foot tapping (items 41 to 42); sensory perceptual (graphesthesia, items 9 to 16); stereognosis (items 17 to 20); two-point discrimination (item 29); face-hand test (item 27); face-nose test (item 28); and opticokinetic nystagmus (item 43). The revision of the 1973 PANESS (Denckla, 1985) deletes items that were reported to be cumbersome, ambiguous, or unreliable or to be scored abnormal in less than 4% of the subjects: these items included eye tracking (item 43), stereognosis (items 17 to 20), extinction (items 27 to 28), and synergy (items 1 to 8). Other items were added to amplify the 1973 items involving station, gait, and rapid coordinated movement. A timed motor coordination battery replaces the more static examination involving hopping, balancing, and alternating movement. Rutter, Graham, et al. (1970) add an evaluation of language and speech, involving comprehension, phonics and rhythm, and production of language. They also evaluate muscle tone in several ways—flapping hands by holding the lower forearm, flexing the wrist, supinating and pronating the arm, bending fingers back, and flexing and extending the elbow.

Inclusion and exclusion of items in these schemes depend not only on the interest of the examiner, but also on the purpose for which soft signs were studied. P. L. Nichols and Chen's (1981) protocol was to understand the place of soft signs along with learning disability and hyperkinesis in the syndrome of minimal brain dysfunction. The

Table 7.8   Protocol for examination of neurological soft signs

Domain	CPP[a] 1981	PANESS[b] Denckla 1985	Hertzig 1982	Rutter 1970	Peters 1987	Silver 1972
Arm extension	No	Yes	Yes	Yes	Yes	Yes
Primitive reflexes	No	No	No	No	Yes	Yes
Finger to finger	No	Yes	No	No	No	Yes
Finger to thumb	No	Yes	No	No	Yes	No
Finger to nose	Yes	No	No	Yes	No	Yes
Coordinated movements	Yes	Yes	Yes	Yes	Yes	Yes
Timed coordinated movements	No	Yes	No	No	Yes	Yes
Synkinesis	Yes	Yes	Yes	Yes	Yes	Yes
Muscle tone	No	No	Yes	Yes	No	Yes
Visual discrimination	No	No	No	No	No	Yes
Visual recall	No	No	No	No	No	Yes
Visual motor	Yes	No	No	No	No	Yes
Praxis	Yes	No	No	Yes	No	Yes
Stereognosis	Yes	Yes	Yes	Yes	No	No
Finger gnosis	Yes	No	No	No	No	Yes
Extinction	No	No	No	No	No	Yes
Temporal sequencing	No	No	No	No	No	Yes
Phonics	No	No	No	No	Yes	Yes
Auditory comprehension	No	No	No	Yes	Yes	Yes
Right/left discrimination	No	No	No	No	Yes	Yes
Writing	No	No	No	No	Yes	Yes

[a] Collaborative Perinatal Project.
[b] Psychiatric and Neurological Examination for Soft Signs.

scored neurological examination was formulated to provide a standard for the study of psychopharmacological effects; the Isle of Wight study (Rutter, Tizard, & Whitemore, 1970) was "to detect the presence of neurological disorder rather than to diagnose the nature of pathogenesis or to form part of an assessment for treatment purposes" (p. 27). The Cambridge Neurological Inventory was designed by Chen et al. (1995) for the assessment of soft neurological signs in adult psychiatric patients. In addition to the classical neurological examination, the Cambridge inventory included two additional broad groups of "non-focal," "subtle" soft signs of dysfunction, each encompassing many of the tests we use for children, a motor group and a sensory integration group. The motor group consisted of finger-to-nose testing, dysdiadochokinesis, fist-edge-palm, and supination and pronation of the hand (Ozeretsky). The sensory integration group includes tests for extinction, finger gnosis, stereognosis, graphesthesia, and left-right disorientation. Specific directions for administering and scoring these tests are described (Chen et al., 1995). Significant interrater reliability was obtained for each of these tests. As the authors indicate, the inventory was designed for adult psychiatric patients and, as reported in their 1995 paper, was tested on 62 patients with schizophrenia, all of whom were receiving neuroleptics at a mean daily chlorpromazine dose of 1224 mgm ($SD = 1,540$ mgm). The concepts embodied in Cambridge Neurological Inventory may be modified for children.

Our examination was formulated to aid understanding children with disorders of learning. It is formulated with two principles in mind: (a) a neurological examination including that for soft signs is an essential part of the pentaxial evaluation; (b) a study of soft signs must include an evaluation of the neuropsychological processes involved in the reception, memory, comprehension, organization, and expression of symbols from all sensory modalities, skills that experimental and clinical evidence leads us to believe are basic for the learning of academic skills of reading, spelling, and arithmetic. (Table 7.7 outlines the neurological evaluation used in our clinics. The Appendix details this examination.) The evaluation stems from the work of Schilder (1935), which was applied to children by L. A. Bender (1956) and modified by one of us (A. A. Silver). The examination has been quantified for use with children ages 5 years 3 months to 6 years 7 months (A. A. Silver & Hagin, 1981) and has been used in its qualitative form since 1960 (A. A. Silver & Hagin, 1964) in a study of children with learning disabilities referred to Bellevue Hospital Mental Hygiene Clinic. Its reliability has been assessed by examination of children by generations of child psychiatry fellows supervised by one of us (A. A. Silver).

The examination for soft signs is thus part of our routine neurological evaluation. For convenience, our neurological examination (Table 7.8) is divided into three general parts: (a) the classical neurological evaluation, including motor coordination, muscle tone, power, and synergy, cranial nerves, deep and superficial and pathological reflexes, and gross sensory evaluation; (b) autonomic nervous system stability; and (c) perceptual-cognitive functions. Soft signs include evaluation of overall motility, adventitious movements, synergistic movements, synkinesis, primitive postural responses, right-left discrimination, praxis, finger gnosis, double simultaneous stimulation, testing for extinction phenomena, displacement of sensory stimuli; and visual and auditory perceptual tests relating to visual spatial orientation and auditory temporal organization.

While the classical neurological examination needs no expansion here, unique features of this evaluation require description.

Arm Extension Test

The arm extension test has been described in Chapter 11, and the data suggesting its uses as an indication of hemisphere specialization for language are reported in that chapter. These data will not be repeated here. This test has had a long history.

The arm extension test stemmed from two sources: (a) the early work of Gesell (1938) and Gesell and Thompson (1934), in which the direction of the tonic neck reflex (TNR) successfully predicted handedness in later life; the TNR is one of the earliest manifestations of hemisphere asymmetry and may offer clues to the establishment of hemisphere asymmetry and later lateralization of function; (b) the observation of

L. A. Bender and Freedman (1952) that motility in schizophrenic children is based on tonic neck and neck-righting responses; the neck-righting response is referred to in the literature as the "whirling test." In our own work, the arm extension test followed by rotation of the head was at first used to detect the remnants of primitive postural responses such as the TNR and the neck-righting responses. However, the test has come to yield other important information. Adventitious movements, myoconic movement, and choreiform and athetotic motility are dramatically visible on extension of the arms. Tremors are readily visible and tics tend to emerge. Use of this test with children with learning disabilities is helpful as a noninvasive clinically performed, rapid evaluation of hemisphere specialization for language (see Chapter 11).

Spatial Concept of the Body Image

As seen in Table 7.8, the skills of right-left discrimination, finger gnosis (including the extinction phenomenon), and praxis are not stressed in examinations for soft signs in learning disorders other than in our routine protocol. Historically, disorders of the body schema were described by the early twentieth-century neurologists (Pick, 1908; Schilder, 1931, 1935), particularly in adult patients with aphasic disorders and disorders of "symbolic formulation and expression" (Head, 1926/1963) and by Gerstmann (1924, 1927, 1930), who related right-left disorganization to focal disease in the parietal-occipital region of the dominant hemisphere. Associated with this spatial disorganization, Gerstmann described a syndrome including difficulty with right-left discrimination, finger agnosia, acalculia, and agraphia. Head postulated the existence of a mental schematic "model of the surface of the body," the integrity of which was a prerequisite for correct localization of body parts. The Gerstmann syndrome was descriptively also a disturbance of the body image. Benton reviewed (1959) the early history of the body image concept as it relates to right-left discrimination and finger localization, and Schilder (1935) described the importance of body image in relation to psychiatric integrity and to psychopathology. As indicated in Chapter 5, the development of an age-appropriate concept of the body image in space is a necessary function on which to build skills in reading, writing, and arithmetic.

Right-left discrimination attempts to tap the stability of body image in space. Right-left discrimination was part of the original Binet-Simon test (done in 1908): 75% of Parisian schoolchildren of that time were able to identify their right hand and left ear by age 7; all 8-year-olds passed both items (Binet & Simon, 1916) In 1916, Terman placed the identification of right hand, left ear, and right eye at a 6-year-old level. It was dropped from the 1937 revision probably, said Benton, because it did not discriminate between mental age levels as well as other tests. Piaget noted that a 6- or 7-year-old can identify right and left in his own body but not in a person facing him (Piaget & Inhelder, 1958). Benton (1959) studied right-left discrimination with a protocol of 32 items involving verbal commands (20 with the subject's eyes open and 12 with eyes closed): pointing to lateral body parts on a schematic, front view representation of a person (obviously eyes open), and execution of double-crossed and uncrossed commands involving lateral body parts of both subject and schematic representation. Benton did not require immediate response and spontaneous corrections were permitted, but noted that in 158 children, 6 to 9 years of age, representing IQs between 85 and

115, and of average socioeconomic level, "right-left discrimination showed a progressive development . . . the growth of this skill begins at about age 5 years; the 9-year-old has . . . a level of performance somewhat below that . . . [of] the average adult. The performance of the average 12-year-old child is virtually the same as that of the average adult" (p. 27). However, the representation of a person facing a child is more difficult than identification of own body parts, and performance is not significantly greater with eyes open than with eyes closed (Benton, 1959).

In 6-year-olds, there was a tendency to make an ipsilateral response to crossed commands, Benton stated that where the age factor (and mental age) is controlled, there is no significant difference between boys and girls in the development of right-left discrimination.

Our examination (Table 7.9) uses eyes-open verbal commands to identify the child's own right and left hands (4 items), double simultaneous ipsilateral commands (i.e., right hand on right eye) (4 items), double crossed, contralateral commands, (i.e., right hand on left ear) (4 items), and the identification of right and left examiner facing the child, uncrossed (2 items) and crossed (1 item), for a total of 15 items. This examination uses a portion of the protocol of Benton's form A of his right-left discrimination battery, using 15 of his 32 items and eliminating the items done with the subject's eyes closed. Benton's form V, which requires the child to name lateral body parts, is not used in our evaluation.

Table 7.9   Protocol for right-left orientation

I.   Single commands

    A. Show me your left hand.

    B. Show me your right eye.

    C. Show me your left ear.

    D. Show me your right hand.

II. Double simultaneous ipsilateral commands

    A. Put your left hand on your left ear.

    B. Put your right hand on your right knee.

    C. Put your left hand on your left knee.

    D. Put your right hand on your right ear.

III. Double simultaneous, contralateral commands

    A. Put your left hand on your right ear.

    B. Put your right hand on your left knee.

    C. Put your left hand on your right knee.

    D. Put your right hand on your left ear.

IV. Examiner facing child

    A. Which is my left hand?

    B. Which is my right ear?

    C. (Examiner's arms crossed) Now which is my right hand?

For the 5- and 6-year-olds, our protocol has been modified into a 10-item test for which norms are available for inner city, suburban, and private schools. Quantification of results in this 10-item test, and its use on a battery in kindergarten to detect potential learning disabilities, is discussed in Chapter 10.

Our experience shows that average 5-year-olds in kindergarten can identify their own right and left hands; 6-year-old first graders have ipsilateral double simultaneous skills; and 7-year-olds have contralateral double simultaneous recognition. It takes 8 years to correctly identify right and left in the examiner facing the child. Some children with learning disabilities (see Chapter 5) have not developed skills in right-left orientation, and it is not infrequent to find adolescents with reading problems still hesitant in correct identification of their own right and left hands. Systematic reversals—consistently identifying right for left and left for right—and hesitations in response are considered as immaturity in the development of spatial orientation. While Benton did not classify systematic reversals as failure in his testing, and while children with systematic reversal did not show defects in finger localization or in arithmetic skills, they did have "impressive" impairment in the development of language functions (Benton, 1959). Children with systematic reversals in a right-left discrimination task for normal 5- to 6.4-year-olds were also found to have lower scores on a variety of cognitive tasks exploring verbal fluency, syntactical comprehension, working memory, visuospatial ability and number processing (Dellatolas, Viguier, Deloche, & De Agostini, 1998).

We have pointed out that right-left discrimination along with finger gnosis and praxis forms skills necessary for the spatial concept of the body image and as such is important in writing and in mathematics ability. There is evidence also that visuospatial discrimination (of which right-left discrimination is a part) plays a role in efficient reading. McMonnies (1992), states that "arguments used to reject visuospatial theories in mirror image letter reversals are flawed" (p. 261) and that discrimination of letters is based on right-left awareness. Confusion in right-left body awareness is found in association with reversal problems. Chapter 5 of this book has reviewed the importance of phonological mechanisms in efficient reading. McMonnies concludes that both linguistic and visuospatial processes both play a role in efficient reading. Eden et al. (1996) testing visuospatial and phonological abilities in 39 normal readers and 26 reading-disabled children, found that when verbal and visuospatial variables were combined in a multiple regression analysis, 71% of the reading variance could be accounted for. This result suggests that "reading disability cannot solely be attributed to left hemisphere dysfunction resulting in phonological impairment" but that often behavioral deficits such as visuospatial abilities, possibly caused by a common mechanism contribute to reading disability.

Finger Gnosis

This is the ability to localize correctly by touching, showing, or naming, tactile stimulation of the fingers, or by localizing fingers correctly in the subject or in the pictorial model of the hand, in response to verbal commands designating the fingers by name or number. Along with right-left discrimination, it is part of the central representation of the model of the body, the schemata of Head (1926/1963), and the body image as described by Schilder (1935). It is said to require the integrity of the parietal-occipital area of the dominant hemisphere. Disturbance in finger gnosis (i.e., finger agnosia), implies that despite intactness of the somatosensory functions of touch and kinesthesia and despite the ability to understand verbal directions, the stimuli to the fingers cannot be age-appropriately localized.

Essential to the study of finger gnosis is the method of testing for it. Benton stated (1959, p. 13), "Finger localization, like right-left discrimination, comprises a variety of types of performance related to the awareness of the finger schema, which differ greatly with respect to complexity and level of difficulty." Gerstmann's early studies (1924, 1927, 1930) asked for indicated fingers to be named and named fingers indicated. Benton (1955a, 1955b, 1959) used a 50-item battery assessing (a) with the aid of vision, identification of single fingers that have been touched, (b) without the aid of vision, identification of fingers that have been touched, and (c) without the aid of vision, identification of pairs of fingers subjected to simultaneous tactual stimulation. The stimulus on that part of the battery, "without the aid of vision," was made on the subject's fingers. The identification of that stimulus was made on a pictorial, two-dimensional model of the hand and fingers by means of pointing, naming, or numbering of the fingers. A verbal response was not required. The subject had to project the mental schema of his own fingers to that of a model. Satz and Friel (1973) and their associates used a similar procedure: a hidden unilateral stimulation on the back of the hands required the subject to point to his own fingers that had been touched and to a corresponding diagram of a hand. Satz's battery required a verbal mediation.

Kinsbourne and Warrington (1962, 1963), in their original study of finger gnosia in 12 adult neurological patients, used a different procedure with five separate components.

1. *In between test.* Two fingers of one hand are simultaneously touched. The patient is asked to state the number of fingers "in between" those touched.
2. *Two-point test.* The same finger or two different fingers of the same hand are touched. The patient designates whether one finger or two fingers are touched.
3. *Matchbox test.* One or two matchboxes are placed between the fingers. The response designates awareness of the sides of the fingers.
4. *Finger block test.* The patient's hands are molded around a test block and the patient is required to pick out the corresponding block.
5. *Finger strip test.* Strips of paper that have the names of fingers written on them must be arranged in sequence.

Kinsbourne and Warrington (1963) concluded that finger gnosia involves "specific difficulty in relating fingers to each other in correct spatial sequences" (p. 136).

Pontius (1983) studied representation of the fingers in different cultures (New Guinea, Indonesia, and Western Europe) by the pictorial representation of the fingers as seen in a drawing of the human figure. Pontius, a foremost proponent of an ecological (cultural) evolutionary neuropsychiatry (ECEN), found that there is a quantitatively inaccurate pictorial representation of the fingers in 78% of the New Guinean islanders and 70% of Indonesians living in remote areas as compared with 16% in western Europe. "A specific link" is noted between low skills in arithmetic and inaccurate pictorial image of the fingers. Pontius theorizes that because the counting system of New Guinea is done concretely by looking and touching the hands, fingers, and other lateral parts of the body "no mental representation of the fingers appears to be necessary and no concept of number is employed as a symbol."

Kinsbourne and Warrington (1963) stated that by age 7½ the criteria for finger gnosis was met by more than 95% of children. Using the same group of 158 children examined in his study of right-left discrimination, Benton (1959) studied them with the 50-item protocol described in the preceding paragraphs. He found that (a) total scores rose progressively from ages 6 to 9; (b) the level of performance of 6-year-olds was considerably above chance expectations, indicating that initial development of the finger schema begins in early childhood; (c) the level of performance of 12-year-olds was roughly that of adults; (d) finger gnosis under visual guidance was relatively easy (this finding is in contrast to right-left discrimination where performance under visual guidance does not appear to be significantly better than when the hands are hidden); (e) double simultaneous discrimination was difficult even for 9-year-olds; and (f) mental age played an important role in developing accuracy of finger localization but not as great as in accurate right-left discrimination.

In contrast to the methods described for testing finger gnosis (those of Gerstmann, Benton, Kinsbourne, & Warrington, and Satz & Friel) in which the child is asked to identify fingers touched with eyes open and with eyes closed or for which a verbal

Table 7.10   Protocol for finger gnosis

Single stimulus (5 years or under)
　R1
　L3
　L5
　R4

Bilateral symmetrical (6 years)
　R2-L2
　R4-L4
　R5-L5

Bilateral asymmetrical (8 years)
　R3-L5
　R2-L4
　R3-L4
　R4-L3

Score:

Single stimulus	number correct $\times$ 1 =
Bilateral symmetrical	number correct $\times$ 2 =
Bilateral asymmetrical	number correct $\times$ 3 = _____
Total score	

Note: Adapted from A. A. Silver and R. A. Hagin. SEARCH 1998 (2nd ed., p. 55). Cranford, NJ: Shoestring Press.

mediation is required to identify fingers by number in a pictorial representation of the hand, we have adopted a protocol that is relatively simple to administer but that encompasses a developmental sequence in maturation of the finger schema (Table 7.10). The child sits across the table from the examiner, her hands placed on the table, palms down fingers spread apart, eyes closed. The examiner says, "I will touch some of your fingers while your eyes are closed. Then you will open your eyes and point to the fingers I touched. Would you close your eyes please?" The examiner touches lightly the middle phalynx of each finger to be tested. Three groups of stimuli are used: (a) single stimuli (R1, L3, L5, R4); (b) double simultaneous, bilateral symmetrical stimuli (R2-L2, R4-L4, R5-L5); and (c) double simultaneous, asymmetrical stimuli (R3-L5, R2-L4; R3-L4 and R4-L3), which are used for children 8 years old or older. A developmental sequence may be found; 5-year-olds can easily identify single touch on digit 5 or digit 1; 6-year-olds identify double simultaneous bilateral symmetrical stimuli of digit 5 and digit 1; the 7-year-olds identify double simultaneous bilateral symmetrical stimuli of digit 2 and digit 4. It is not until 8 or 9 years of age that children can identify double simultaneous bilateral asymmetrical combinations of digit 4 and digit 2, and not until age 10 can children identify the asymmetrical combinations of digit 4 to 3 combinations. In scoring, weighted credits are given—1 point for each correct single stimuli, 2 points for each correct bilateral symmetrical stimulus, and 3 points for each bilateral asymmetrical stimulus. Quantitative norms for kindergarten and first graders in various educational settings are included in the *Search* manual (A. A. Silver & Hagin, 1981).

Table 7.11 summarizes the finger schema norms for kindergarten in three different settings: highly selective private independent schools (*N* = 384), inner city schools

Table 7.11 Finger gnosis in kindergarten children in three different socioeconomic settings

Stanine	Distribution of Scores in a 14-Item Test: Number of Items Correct		
	Private Independent (*N* = 384)	Inner City (*N* = 311)	Suburban (*N* = 949)
9	14	14	14
8	14	14	14
7	12–13	13	12–13
6	10–11	11–12	10–11
5	9	9–10	9
4	7–8	8	7–8
3	6	6–7	5–6
2	4–5	4–5	4
1	0–3	0–3	0–3

Note: From "Spatial orientation and temporal organization in three socioeconomic groups" by A. A. Silver and R. A. Hagin, 1989. Presented at the annual meeting of the American Academy of Child and Adolescent Psychiatry, October 11–15, New York, NY.

($N = 311$), and suburban schools ($N = 949$). Despite the superior IQs of the children in the independent schools and the socioeconomic differences in the three settings, the development of finger gnosis abilities in 5- and 6-year-olds appears to be independent of these variables (Figure 7.3). In the A. A. Silver and Hagin follow-up study (1964), finger gnosis along with visual finger-ground perception was resistant to spontaneous maturation.

In the management of the clinical examination for finger gnosis, while the child is sitting across from the examiner, hands on the table, eyes closed, it is simple matter to test for *extinction phenomena*. Extinction means that in the double simultaneous stimulation test the subject reports only one of the two stimuli. Thus, a definite impairment in perceptual awareness is present. However, if the same areas are stimulated separately and singly, the stimulation will be perceived. The extinction phenomenon has also been described as "inattention" (Critchley, 1964). Oppenheim in his examination of adult neurological patients reported that "in certain brain disease which cause unilateral disturbance of sensibility . . . stimulate simultaneous two symmetrical points.

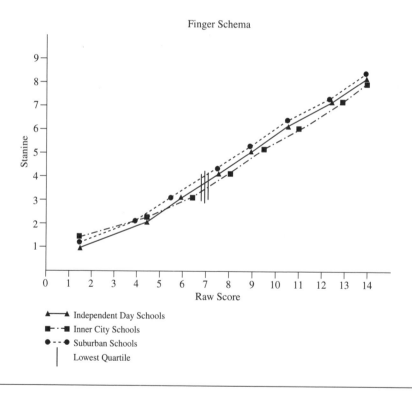

Figure 7.3   Finger schema in 5- and 6-year-olds. There is no significant difference in distribution of scores among the three socioeconomic groups; the lowest quartile is the same for all groups. *Source:* **Silver and Hagin (1989).** *Spatial orientation and temporal organization in three socioeconomic groups.* **Presented at annual meeting, American Academy of Child and Adolescent Psychiatry, New York, October 1989.**

The patient will . . . detect it only on the affected side." M. B. Bender (1952) has adopted this technique in a series of investigations with Hans Teuber, involving penetrating wounds of the brain, adult patients with a variety of neurological disease, children with cerebral palsy, and normal adults and children. The technique of double simultaneous stimulation has been applied in various perceptual modalities—visual, auditory, tactile, and haptic. It is the basis for studies of hemisphere specialization including dichotic listening testing in which different verbal stimuli are applied to the ears simultaneously and in which there is a normal suppression of stimuli from one ear.

In our examination, we use tactile stimulation. In effect, in our double simultaneous stimulation of the fingers, as we test for finger gnosis, we have already tested for extinction phenomena. We have used double simultaneous symmetrical (i.e., homologous) stimuli and double simultaneous asymmetrical stimuli. Two additional stimulus sites, however, are specifically directed at the study of the extinction phenomena: double simultaneous stimulation of homologous areas of the wrist (wrist-wrist) and double simultaneous stimulation of the forehead and the wrist (wrist-head). With the child's eyes closed, the dorsa of the wrist are lightly touched. The child is asked to open her eyes and point to the places where she was touched. The wrist and lateral aspect of the forehead are then touched and the question is repeated. In the wrist-head test, both ipsilateral (right wrist, right forehead; left wrist, left forehead) and contralateral (right wrist, left forehead; left wrist, right forehead) stimuli are used. In testing for extinction, several variables must be considered: intensity and duration of the stimulus, type of stimulus, sensory area to be tested, and age and general intelligence of the subject. Increasing intensity or duration can push the stimulus into awareness and extinction phenomena may be obliterated. In our examination for extinction, the wrist and forehead are lightly brushed and the stimulus is applied for only a fraction of a second.

Just as in the development of finger gnosis, there is a maturation in the ability to distinguish both the wrist and forehead stimuli on the face-hand test. M. B. Bender, Fink, and Green (1951), using a slightly different method for examination, found that 90% of normal children ages 3 to 6 ($N = 56$) responding to contralateral face-hand stimulation, would identify only the face stimulus, and in normal children aged 7 to 12 ($N = 76$), only 38% correctly reported both stimuli. In all, there was the relative dominance of sensation in the face over hand.

In our work, a similar developmental pattern was observed. Half the children in kindergarten reported only the head stimulus on the face-hand test, but by the first grade (ages 6 to 7) at least 75% of the children in the entire first grade were able to report both stimuli. Extinction of the wrist stimulus in second graders was considered abnormal. There was, however, an additional important finding: In approximately 20% of the 5-year-olds, either the head stimulus was displaced to the homologous contralateral side (allesthesia) with extinction of the point to which the head stimulus was applied, or the head stimulus was referred to both sides (synchiria). These phenomena, allesthesia, and synchiria, were also observed in older children where there was evidence for an organic disturbance of the central nervous system. The possible relationship of the direction of displacement to the development of hemisphere specialization has yet to be studied.

Praxis is "the ability to carry out purposeful movements by an individual who has normal motor strength, reflexes, and coordination and has normal comprehension of the act to be carried out" (Hecaen, de Ajuriaguerra, & Angelergues, 1963). Liepmann (1920) described apraxia as a dissociation between the idea of the movement and its motor execution. It is conventional to describe three types of apraxia: (a) *ideomotor,* the disruption of simple gestures used to convey symbolic meaning (e.g., to wave good-bye, stir coffee with a spoon, or hammer a nail); here the response to the verbal command is disrupted while the response to imitate gestures may be preserved; (b) *ideational apraxia,* the disruption of complex gestures that together make up a co-ordinated act; although the individual elements of the act can be performed, there is "disruption in the logical and harmonious succession of separate elements" (Hecaen et al., 1963); and (c) *constructional apraxia* (Kleist, 1934), "a disorder of formative ac-tivities in which the spatial part of the task was disturbed although single movements were not affected" (Hecaen, De Agostini, & Monzon-Montes, 1981, p. 264). This may be seen clinically in the inability to reproduce a drawing of a house. Rutter, Graham, et al. (1970) used reproduction of matchstick designs in their test for praxis. Construc-tional apraxia may also be seen in the visuomotor tasks that are in common use in bat-teries of neuropsychological tests and that we also use in our routine examination. The meaning of visuomotor difficulty may not be so clear, however. It may suggest defect at any point from problems in visuospatial discrimination through difficulty with the ability to establish or sequence a program for a desired action, to difficulty with the motor execution of the task. Visuomotor function is thus a complicated task that re-quires careful analysis.

Ideational praxis requires the ability to mature beyond a concrete and egocentric level of performance to an abstract allocentric level. Nijiokiktjien, Vranken, et al. (2000) in testing 357 normally developing children, 2½ to 9½ years old with six named actions that had to be performed on verbal request, found that the 6-year level marked that point where abstract commands could be performed. O'Hare, Gorzkowska, and Elton (1999) found that children ages 3 to 12 years from families with low income, had difficulty with performance on task for which verbal commands were given but there was no problem in imitating gestures. This result was also found by Cermak, Morris, and Koomer (1990). Fifteen children with "learning disorders" (not specified) scored lower than "normal" children on ideational or ideomotor tasks. The *American Journal of Occupational Ther-apy* devoted its July issue to study of the Jean Ayres tests (1989) of Sensory Integration and Praxis (SIPT). The papers in the issue review the standardization, reliability, valid-ity, and interpretation of the SIPT and reports its value in diagnosis of the learning-disabled. The interrelationship between the test SIPT and other tests of sensory integration, (e.g., for form and space perception, constructional abilities, and motor clumsiness) were also reviewed (Murray, Cermak, & O'Brien, 1990). Twelve delinquent-prone adolescents with learning problems were compared with 114 nondelinquent ado-lescents ages 12 through 18 years. The delinquent-prone group performed "more poorly" on all of the praxis-related tests and on tests of vestibular function (Fanchiang, Snyder, Zobel-Lachusa, et al., 1990). In children ages 6 through 8 years with praxis difficulty, 6 months of twice weekly occupational therapy resulted in "significant improvement" in the scores of praxis or sensory integration tests (Kimball, 1990).

As part of our routine examination for praxis, we use a test that Schilder (1931) called constructive finger praxis, the ability to imitate positions of the fingers given an intact motor apparatus. With the subject standing facing him, the examiner successively touches his own thumb to digit 3, digit 5, digit 2, and digit 4, first with the right hand then with the left. As each finger is touched, the subject is asked to imitate that motion. Just as the test for finger gnosis, this requires the development of a central schema of the fingers. It is more difficult than our test for finger gnosis in that the child must be able to visualize the correct spatial representation of the examiner's fingers, transfer that spatial image into her own body schema, and then correctly execute the movement of the fingers. According to Schilder, the inability to indicate fingers on command (finger agnosia) is related to a defect in the angular gyrus. The inability to name the fingers (finger aphasia) is related to a defect of the Wernicke's area. Visual finger agnosia (an inability to identify the examiner's finger) is related to a posteriorly placed occipital lesion; apraxia of finger choice (an inability to move finger on command), and constructive finger apraxia are related to defects in the region of the supramarginal gyrus. At any rate, our examination for praxis appears to measure related but different functions of the body image, including elements of visual finger agnosia and constructive finger praxis. In young children ages 5 to 6 years 6 months (kindergarten and first grade) the pencil grip is taken as a measure of praxis.

These tests—right-left discrimination, finger gnosis, double simultaneous stimulation to test extinction phenomena and constructive finger praxis—are manifestations of the development of the concept of body image in space and as such are an important part of our theoretical formulation that spatial orientation is an essential foundation for academic learning, particularly in writing and in arithmetic.

Visual Discrimination and Visual Recall of Asymmetries

The examination for soft neurological signs is not complete without evaluation of visual discrimination and recall of asymmetrical figures, visuomotor function, and auditory temporal sequencing. In addition, although not specifically included in the protocols for examination of soft signs (Table 7.3), the receptive, associate, and emissive aspects of language are informally evaluated and studied more intensively as indicated.

Our own routine testing for visual discrimination and recall of asymmetrical figures is based on the Lamb Chops Test: The ability of the child to match the orientation of asymmetrical figures (the lamb chop) as the axis of the figure is rotated 90, 180, 270, and 360 degrees in random fashion. The test requires the child to match stimulus cards, each containing an asymmetrical figure in various degrees of rotation, with response cards from which the child must select the correct orientation. In the matching part of the test, the child is given unlimited time to make his choice. In the recall part, the stimulus is flashed for a limited time (4 seconds for 5- and 6-year-olds), and the child must *recall* the position of the stimulus figure by indicating its orientation on the response card. Norms for children ages 5 years through 6 years 6 months appear in *SEARCH* (A. A. Silver & Hagin, 1981): Three correct recall responses of eight trials are normal for these ages. It is of interest that the tests there is no significant difference in distribution of scores among three socioeconomic groups (Figure 7.4).

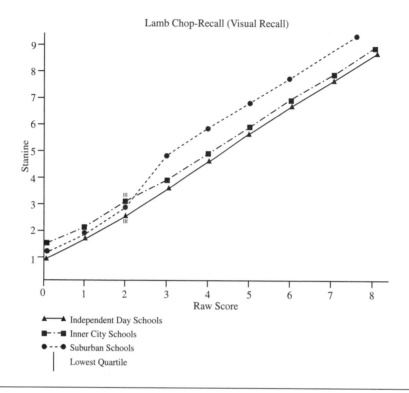

Figure 7.4 **Visual recall in 5- and 6-year-olds. There is no significant difference in distribution of scores among the three socioeconomic groups; the lowest quartile is the same for all groups.** *Source:* **Silver and Hagin (1989).** *Spatial orientation and temporal organization in three socioeconomic groups.* **Presented at annual meeting, American Academy of Child and Adolescent Psychiatry, New York, October 1989.**

Bender Visual Motor Gestalt Test

One of the most frequently used techniques involving the ability of the child to copy written patterns is the Bender Visual Motor Gestalt Test (VMGT). Although the visuomotor function involves many functional elements (visual perception of spatial relationships, praxis, and fine motor coordination), it is a basic for writing and is a skill needed for written work in school. L. A. Bender (1938) wrote, "The visuomotor gestalt function is a fundamental function associated with language ability and closely associated with various functions of intelligence such as visual perception, manual motor ability, memory, temporal and spatial concepts and organization or representation" (p. 112). This test had its origins in the work of Max Wertheimer (1923), a German psychologist, who used a variety of line drawings and configurations as stimuli for his subjects to elicit verbal descriptions of their perceptions. L. A. Bender adapted these figures. She first used them to elicit drawings from otherwise inaccessible, mute schizophrenic women at Springfield State Hospital in Maryland. When she moved to New York City, she realized the potential of this drawing technique in understanding the development of children. In describing Gestalt psychology, L. A. Bender wrote (1938) that it "teaches that whatever we perceive, we experience as a global whole or gestalt. The organized whole is more immediately experienced than any of its parts or details, which are recognized later by a process called differentiation" (p. 5).

Published in 1938 as a monograph of the American Orthopsychiatric Association, Bender's VMGT is a well-defined method for evaluating the gestalt function: "that function of the integrated organism whereby it responds to a given constellation of stimuli as a whole, the response being a motor process or patterning the perceived Gestalt" (p. 3). The aim of the test is to determine the individual's capacity to experience visuomotor gestalten in a spatial and temporal relationship.

As we use it for children, test administration is relatively simple. The examiner presents cards each containing one of nine figures, one at a time, and asks the child to copy them on a white sheet of paper 8½ by 11 inches (copy paper). The examiner is asked to discourage turning of the cards ("I have to show them to you this way") and to encourage but not to insist on drawing the first figure in the upper left-hand quadrant of the page. However, instruction should be noncommittal, with no time limit indicated. This is a clinical technique in which formalization would destroy its function. The aim of the test is to obtain a record of the perceptual-motor experience that is unique and often retains its characteristic quality over the years.

However, as Tolor and Brannigan (1980) summarize their review of administration and clinical application of the Bender Gestalt test, "The research reviewed attests to the incredible ingenuity of psychologists who continue to develop modifications in the administration of the Bender Gestalt Test" (p. 20).

Spraings (1966) for example, developed a multiple choice Bender Gestalt in which the subject inspects each Bender card and then selects the one figure from 12 alternatives that best matches the individual card. Allen and Frank (1963), noted the difference in the way the stimulus cards are presented (each stimulus on a separate card) and the way they are reproduced (all on a single 8½ × 11 sheet of white paper) and modified the administration by having each stimulus drawn on a separate 4″ by 6″ sheet piece of paper. Canter (1966, 1968) had his subjects first reproduce the designs on a blank sheet of paper and then on a specially designed paper on which curved interesting lines are printed (background interference).

Tachistoscopic presentation (Rosenberg & Rosenberg, 1965), as expected, was found to lower the discrimination power of the copy mode. Tachistoscopic presentation is used by Rosenberg and Roseberg to discriminate between "organics" and "normals."

Each of these modifications, however, appears to test functions other than the Gestalt visuomotor function for which the test was intended: Spraings testing visual discrimination; Allen and Frank altering the Gestalt by changing relationship of the figures to each other; Canter adding a visual figure-background task, similar to that of the Gottshalt test; tachistoscopic adding a temporal constraint to the subject's appreciation of the stimulus.

L. A. Bender's manual (1938) and later writing (L. A. Bender, 1970) described the principles that determine maturation of visuomotor perception. The first of these principles is vortical movement, which is biologically determined and gives rise to the most primitive circles and loops. Movement is always present and always directional.

At first, this movement in space may be clockwise or counterclockwise; later, as the child works in the horizontal plane, it takes on sinistrad or dextrad directions. As control of vortical movement emerges at about age 3, the child begins to produce closed circles and arcs. These figures help her organize the foreground and background aspects of the visual field. Gradually, boundaries of the figures are delineated. At about age 5, the phenomenon of verticalization in drawings appears. Gradually crossed lines and diagonals emerge at a later level of maturation, usually at ages 7 and 8.

The "niceties" of the perceptual-motor relationships of the Bender VMGT are not usually completed until about age 11, but the main principles are recognizable in the normally developing child certainly by age 8. L. A. Bender (1958) also drew on the field of embryology to relate perceptual-motor development to the principle of plasticity. On the VMGT, this principle is represented in the lack of stabilization of form, particularly with those figures of the test that consist of a constellation of dots. Plasticity is the state of being as yet undifferentiated, but capable of being differentiated. Plasticity has both negative and positive implications for development.

In the negative sense, it may appear in the tendency to revert to more primitive forms; whereas in the positive sense, it may represent the promise of increased maturation.

The VMGT standardization data include cross-sectional studies of 800 normal children. These data show characteristic drawings of the figures at ages 5 through 11 (L. A. Bender, 1938), as well as the ages at which a majority of children produce a mature figure. Table 7.12 is based on these cross-sectional studies. As can be seen from this table, age of mastery of the figures ranges from 7 through 11 years.

Some of the current clinical uses of the VMGT violate the theories of Gestalt psychology and the rationale on which the test was based. The following four misuses indicate the attempt to use the VGMT as a cookbook, rather than as the thoughtful consideration of developmental parameters intended by the test's author:

1. The "30-second squint" in which the drawings are viewed hastily and then pronounced as "a good Bender" or a "bad Bender." This method of interpretation is without documentation and is of little use in understanding the child's problem.

Table 7.12   Ages of mastery of figures of the Visual Motor Gestalt Test (VMGT)

Figure	Age
A	7 years (75%)
1	9 years (75%)
2	10 years (60%)
3	11 years (60%)
4	10 years (80%)
5	7 years (65%)
6	10 years (60%)
7	11 years (75%)
8	7 years (60%)

2. The use of the VGMT to determine the presence of brain damage. Koppitz (1975) and L. Small (1980) listed peripheral behavior characteristics that are "indicators of brain damage," giving the mistaken impression that the Bender test is sort of a neurological examination.

3. The futile attempt to force the VGMT into a psychometric mold. There have been complaints that the VMGT is not an acceptable measure to use with learning-disabled children because it lacks statistical evidence of test-retest reliability. L. A. Bender has stated repeatedly that she did not intend the VGMT to be used as a psychometric measure but as a developmental technique.

4. Minute examination, sometimes even with a protractor used to measure angles, to detect errors that are then summed to obtain an age score. Given the range in age of mastery of the test figures (as shown in Table 7.12) and also the large standard deviation of the means of the error scores of one such scoring method (Koppitz, 1975), the lack of validity of this approach is obvious.

Even more significant to the clinician who seeks to understand a child's learning disorders through the use of the VGMT is that these misuses fail to take into account the gestalt—the global nature of the task. L. A. Bender (1938) wrote cogently to this point in the manual of instruction to the VMGT:

> However a child produces the gestalt test, it is a perfect, complete, and correct projection of that child's experience at that time and at the level of his total maturation, including whatever personality, maturation, and organismic problems he may have. A child cannot make an error in reproduction.

Based on Bender's formulation of the development of gestalt function in children, the following questions can be used to guide the interpretation of VGMT drawings:

• What is the motor pattern of the gestalt along which the figures of the test are organized?
• What signs of circular movement and plasticity are present?
• How are directional orientation of figures and directionality handled?
• What signs of verticalization of diagonal lines are present?
• How are angles and parts of figures differentiated?

In short what signs of disorganization in the gestalt and what signs of immaturity in the development of the gestalt, are found.

Each of the functions described in this section (right-left discrimination, finger gnosis, extinction constructive finger praxis, visuomotor) has its own normal sequence of maturation, in response to its innate biological trajectory and the environmental stimuli acting on that biological substrate: Form (biological) plus appropriate and sufficient stimulus (environmental) yields function. Delay in the course of maturation may thus result from a deviation in the biology (genetic polymorphism), and/or in the environment (effects of inappropriate and/or inadequate stimulation of that function).

The concept of "developmental lag" suggests that maturational delay may spontaneously be overcome; that if we just wait, the function will spontaneously mature. Unfortunately for any individual child this may not occur, or if it does, maturation may not occur until it is too late for the child to keep up with his peers. We cannot wait for maturation to occur, but we can provide the appropriate stimulation in the development of that function. Brian is an example.

CASE STUDY: BRIAN

Brian was just 9 years of age, in the third grade of a private, parochial school, when he was evaluated in our clinic. He was referred by his pediatrician because, following his grandmother's death approximately one year earlier from complications of diabetes Brian started clicking his teeth and blinking his eyes. His parents report that these symptoms had not appeared before then; he had not been hyperactive, but his writing and math were problems at school. During the course of our visit, his father was noted to have eye blinking. He said that he had this symptom since he was a child, but that it had not interfered with his life. His parents however are concerned about Brian's tics, and they asked repeatedly if the tics were curable.

On our examination, Brian is a pleasant, verbal, cooperative child with round chubby face, round glasses, close-cropped hair; his voice is husky but his verbal replies are clear and relevant, with good syntax and understanding. Eye blinking, clicking of his teeth, and shaking of his head were all frequent and severe, occurring at least once every 5 to 10 seconds. Vocal tics, wheezing, and sniffling are also frequent and loud. Impulsive touching was described, touching "anything I pass by," accompanied by counting, a minimum of 5, maximum over 12. He is irritable at school and at home; sometimes at home he slams his cup on the kitchen counter, or when angry throws his shoes at the closet door. He feels that the tics are a punishment because he did not pay enough attention to his grandmother. He talks about his school problems; he has no trouble reading, he does not understand why his writing is so bad and he cannot seem to understand math. He feels the teachers think he is stupid and he is beginning to think so himself.

There are severe neuropsychological processing defects, particularly in visual motor function and in body image. In drawing a diamond figure, for example, he has difficulty deciding which way to move the pencil, to make acute angles. As a result, his diamond figure becomes stellate. On a Bender-Gestalt drawing at age 9 years, the primitive angulation is seen along with verticalization. He cannot decide which is his right hand and cannot tell right-left directions. Constructive finger praxis and finger gnosis are each at about a 7-year level. His fine motor coordination, as in finger-to-finger testing, is poor; and on extension of the arms in this right-handed child, the left arm is clearly elevated. In contrast to these immaturities, his vocabulary (Van Alystine, picture vocabulary) is easily at a 10 year 2 months level; phonic ability is good, he could read with ease at a third-grade level. His figure drawing however gives evidence of severe body image difficulty.

Brian has Tourette's syndrome. However, the neurological examination including soft signs is severely impaired, with specific body image immaturity and resulting writing disability. The relation between Tourette's syndrome and these body image and visuomotor dysfunctions is not clear, although Schroeder, Richter, Geiger, et al. (1993) associate these "soft signs with size of the basal ganglia as measured with CT scan."

Brian has been followed from age 9 years to 13 years of age. During that time, there has been gradual maturation of all immature soft signs, until at age 13 years, his Bender-Gestalt figures are almost normal, his right-left discrimination, praxis, and finger gnosis are now close to a 13-year level. Brian was approximately 10 years of age when remedial training particularly in visuomotor function and in writing was recommended and finally implemented. He was transferred to another school that understood and compensated for his problems and recognized his high verbal ability. At age 13, his visual motor function, although not yet at his age level, is markedly improved, and his writing is no longer a problem in school (see Figures 7.5 and 7.6).

Brian illustrates the tenacity with which visuomotor and body image immaturities persist. This is particularly true where other developmental disorders, such as Tourette's syndrome or ADHD are present. Brian also illustrates the importance of appropriate diagnosis and intervention.

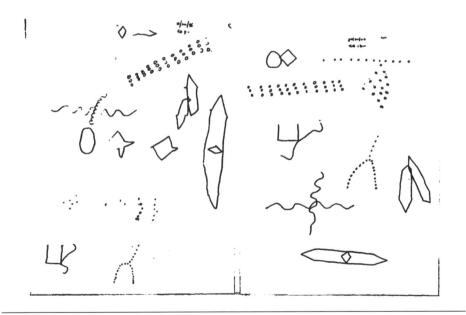

Figure 7.5   Brian. Bender-Gestalt drawings at age 9 years and at 13 years illustrating improvement with remediation, but with remnants of visual-motor dysfunction persisting.

7/20/85
CA-9

Charlie is standing on a stool.

Figure 7.6   Brian. Figure drawing at age 9 years, illustrating significant body-image immaturity with suggestive finger gnosis problems.

Auditory Rote Sequencing

Auditory rote sequencing assesses the extent to which the child has memorized commonly heard verbal sequences and to which he can order the elements within these sequences. Ten items are included in the sequencing test used for kindergarten and first-grade children (Table 7.13).

The scoring for this test varies with the developmental difficulty of the item so that the items involving the capacity to order sequences are weighted. Of the 15 possible points a child earns on this item, norms for ages 5 to 6 years 6 months and for specialized groups (independent day school, suburban, and inner city) appear in *SEARCH* (A. A. Silver & Hagin, 1981). It is on this test, which requires verbal mediation, that experiential factors are most important, with distribution of scores of the inner-city children far below that of suburban children who, in turn, are significantly lower than those from the independent day schools. Of a possible 15 items correct on this test, the lowest quartile of the inner-city kindergartners falls at 3 correct, the suburban children at 6 correct, and the independent day school at 8 correct. A similar discrepancy appears in first grade with no improvement in distribution of scores for the inner-city children (lowest quartile at 3 correct), while the suburban first graders are significantly improved (lowest quartile at 9 correct) (Figure 7.7).

Table 7.13 Auditory rote sequencing

	Value	Score
1. Count my fingers as I touch them.	(1)	
2. What number comes after 5?	(1)	
3. What number comes before 3?	(2)	
4. What number comes after 6?	(1)	
5. What number comes before 9?	(2)	

Examiner says:
Today is ————————————————

6. What day will tomorrow be?	(1)	
7. What day was yesterday?	(2)	
8. Name the days of the week starting with Sunday.	(2)	
9. What day comes after Monday?	(1)	
10. What day comes before Thursday?	(2)	

Total weighted score 15

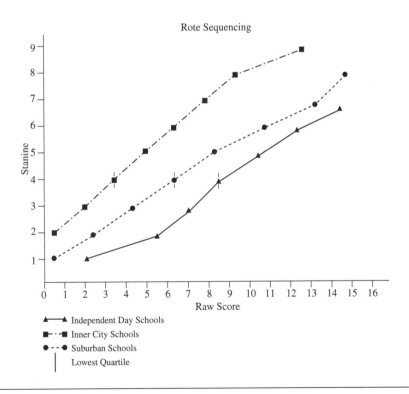

Figure 7.7 Auditory rote sequencing in 5- and 6-year-olds. There is a wide difference in distribution of scores among the three socioeconomic groups; the lowest quartile is significant for each group. *Source:* **Silver and Hagin (1989).** *Spatial orientation and temporal organization in three socioeconomic groups.* **Presented at annual meeting, American Academy of Child and Adolescent Psychiatry, New York, October 1989.**

INTEGRATION OF DATA OF THE PENTAXIAL EXAMINATION

While the description of the neurological examination for children with learning disorders in this chapter may appear to indicate that each detail of the examination exists independently of all the others, in practice each bit of data has its place in completing the comprehensive profile of the assets and deficits we are building for each child. Each bit of data adds to the picture, which, in sum, is greater than any of its parts. In Charles, the child reported as a case example at the beginning of this chapter, the soft neurological signs dramatize the difficulty he has in orientation of the body image in space (finger gnosis, praxis, and extinction phenomenon). The spatial disorientation may well be the biological basis for his visuomotor immaturity, which, in turn, portends poor written work and resistance to demands for him to do such work. His immaturity in the placement of sequences in time may be the biological underpinning to putting sounds in proper sequence to make words—thus his reading difficulty. And all of these signs are seen against a background of diffuse disorder in impulsive control and in motor coordination, a lowered threshold for anxiety, a less than supportive family, and a less than understanding school. Charles illustrates the need for pentaxial study at least for every child whose learning problem has not responded to educational measures. It would be optimal for each child with a learning disorder to have the advantage of such a comprehensive evaluation before he or she is long on the road to failure, and the data thus obtained needs to be integrated into an appropriate plan for management.

SUMMARY

Psychiatric and neurological examinations are part of the pentaxial scheme for evaluation of children with disorders of learning. The psychiatric examination explores the content, dynamics, genesis, and structure of the child's thoughts, wishes, conflicts, and reactions to stress; it evaluates the supports and stresses of the environment and the development and structure of the child's personality. The clinical interview most commonly in use assesses affect, object relations, impulse control, reality testing, identification, thought content, defense mechanisms, and behavior. There is increasing use of a more standardized approach to assessment with a series of structured interview scales. Five of these are described in this chapter.

The neurological examination investigates the integrity of the central nervous system and the level of its maturation and integration, including neuroperceptual function. It is an important component of the pentaxial scheme and of the examination of children with disorders of learning. The classical neurological evaluation is here supplemented by study of soft neurological signs, including kinetic patterns; postural responses; the so-called higher cortical functions, such as spatial and temporal organization in visual, auditory, and body image modalities; and receptive, associate, and emissive aspects of language. Soft signs are viewed as an index of maturation in the central nervous system, responsive to genetic laws of maturation, modified by factors from within or from the environment that may interfere with such maturation. Soft signs may not spontaneously disappear with maturation, and lagging function may not spontaneously became age-appropriate. A standardized procedure for testing is only now beginning to evolve. Procedures for standardized examination are described for the arm extension test, right-left discrimination, finger gnosis, and praxis. The arm extension test offers clues for the establishment of hemisphere specialization. Right-left discrimination, praxis, and finger gnosis are components of the awareness of the body image in space, a function frequently impaired in children with learning disorders. Visual discrimination and recall tests visuospatial orientation; the Visual Motor Gestalt Test relates to the ability to reproduce the spatial orientation of visual symbols and as such is a basis for writing; auditory rote sequencing assesses the function of temporal organization.

The neuropsychiatric examination completes the sequence of study of the child with learning disorder—academic achievement, educational opportunity, sensory acuity, cognitive function, and neuropsychiatric-neuropsychological-social evaluation.

Chapter 8

EDUCATIONAL REMEDIATION

Is it not proper and right that every human being, by the time he has reached his tenth year, should be familiar with the holy gospels, in which the very core and marrow of his life is bound?

—Martin Luther

PRINCIPLES OF EDUCATIONAL REMEDIATION

Although the etiologies of learning disorders are varied and the diagnosis is multidisciplinary, the responsibility for remediation is primarily educational. Inevitably, whether children learn to listen, speak, read, write, spell, and do mathematical calculations depends on what and how they are taught. While the chapters of this book dealing with the various learning disorders focus on special educational provisions for each of these disorders, this chapter deals with general educational issues common to all: (a) organizational patterns for delivery of services and evaluation of education placements, (b) the educational impact of learning disorders, and (c) recommended intervention principles and models of intervention approaches.

ORGANIZATIONAL PATTERNS FOR SERVICE DELIVERY

Marked changes have occurred during recent years in patterns of service delivery. These changes are reflected in Table 8.1.

As can be seen in this table, there is an increase from 16.2% in 1986 to 1987 to 42% in 1995 to 1996 in the percentage of students with learning disabilities placed in regular classes as a result of the movement toward inclusion. There are corresponding decreases in the percentages of students enrolled in resources rooms (from 60.7% to 39% and modest decreases in enrollment of students with learning disabilities in separate classes (from 20.9% to 17%) in separate schools (1.9% to 0.006%), and in the more restrictive settings, such as residential centers, homebound, and hospital settings. These changes have been explained and rationalized in various ways. Some educational and

Table 8.1   Percentage of children ages 6–21 served in different educational environments

Setting	1986–1987 (%)	1995–1996 (%)
Regular class	16.2	42
Resource room	60.7	39
Separate class	20.9	17
Separate school	1.9	0.006
Residential setting	1.9	0.001
Correctional institution	0.2	0
Homebound/hospital	0.1	0.001

Source: Adapted from Table AB8: Number of Children Served in Different Educational Environments Under IDEA, Part B by Disability, U.S. Department of Education (1998), *Twentieth Annual Report to Congress on the Implementation of the Individuals with Disabilities Education Act.* Washington, DC: U.S. Department of Education, p. A157.

governmental administrators perceive them as necessary budgetary economies. Some educators find that regular class placement provides social and educational gains not available in more restrictive settings. Some people see inclusion as a civil right that should be available to all students. Whatever the reasoning behind this change and however schools choose to structure instructional services, the education of children with learning disabilities (and other children with special educational needs) continues to be the legal, professional, and ethical responsibility of schools.

Educators have accepted the reality of this changed configuration of educational services and have struggled to devise ways of meeting the needs of students with learning disabilities, as they are included within regular classrooms. Consultation services have been developed to assist regular classroom teachers in implementing the educational recommendations for special students in their classes. Team teaching also is being used to increase the collaboration between regular and special educators. Provisions for inservice training of regular education teachers in principles of special education are also beginning to appear in local and state requirements for teacher certification. A project of the Professional Preparation Committee of the Learning Disabilities Association of American has taken steps to improve the preservice training of teachers at the source by encouraging collaboration by teacher educators in regular and special education. This project has for the past four years provided stipends for two-person teams representing special education and regular education who participate in the annual conference of the Association. Some schools experiment with a blend of inclusion and resource room services, as described in the personal report of a special educator in Chapter 1.

Evaluation of Educational Placements

Nevertheless, many professionals and parents question whether the special teaching procedures, especially in the skills areas of reading, written language, and mathematics, can be taught effectively to all children with learning disorders in inclusive class-rooms. Parental doubts on this issue are reflected in backup operations, such as the proliferation of commercial tutoring services and widely promoted games such as *Hooked on Phonics* or *The Phonics Game* that advertise money-back guarantees for multiyear gains in reading.

While the quantitative data provided in the annual reports to Congress of the Office of Special Education and Rehabilitation Services show that the variety of service mod-els projected in the legislation continue to exist, these data tell little about the quality of such services. The Collaborative Study of Children with Special Needs, a 5-year study funded by the Robert Wood Johnson Foundation (1988), was an effort to fill the need for qualitative information on special education provisions. The major research question in this study was: What differences have the special education laws made in the lives of handicapped children, their families, their teachers, and their nonhandi-capped classmates? Answers were sought in five large metropolitan school districts: Milwaukee, Wisconsin; Houston, Texas; Charlotte-Mecklenburg, North Carolina; Santa Clara County, California; and Rochester, New York. Reviews of school records and interviews with children, parents, teachers, and key informants representing a sample of 2,000 elementary school special education students constituted the database for this study.

The Collaborative Study of Children with Special Needs resulted in both positive findings and what was called "an unfinished agenda." The study found that the proce-dural guarantees of the special education law were generally in place. The report saw as one of the law's most profound effects the schools' acceptance of their roles as a thera-peutic agent and their commitment to the principle of the least restrictive environment.

Variations in local practices and in the frequency with which different handicap-ping conditions were identified were noted. For example, the percentage of learning-disabled children identified in the five school districts ranged from 31% to 58%. Specific placements may depend on many factors, some of which appeared to be inde-pendent of the child's needs: economic conditions within the school district, the child's level of social adjustment, and the wish to avoid certain stigmatizing classifi-cations. Learning disability was one of the conditions that showed the highest degree of variation in placements among the cities studied. The majority of special education students were mainstreamed, attending regular schools and spending at least part of the day with regular classes.

The review of the cost basis for the various placements indicated that the main-streaming ideology supported the least costly approach. However, the report cautioned against the application of mainstream placements only for the economic rather than the education benefits it promised.

A follow-up of 1,184 students 2 years after the original data collection yielded some salient results on return to regular education (Walker, Singer, Palfrey, & Orza, 1988). There was very little movement back to regular classes reported, with 72% of the stu-dents remaining in the same classification and 12% receiving placement in different special education classes and these were usually young children whose original classi-fication had been for speech and language disorders.

Although the Collaborative Study of Children with Special Needs offers some reas-surance that the organizational structure mandated by the special education legislation is in place, even cursory contact with parents and professionals in the field leads to a sense of uneasiness about the quality of educational services that are being provided. Satisfactory ratings were given by 80% to 85% of the respondents on such variables as social integration, school administration, teachers, facilities, transportation, and related services, but only 60% of the respondents rated the *academic* progress of their learning-disabled children satisfactory. This finding is particularly striking in that it is precisely for increased academic progress that the children were placed in special education programs in the first place. Some parents show this discomfort in a lack of trust in their relationships with school personnel. Results of diagnostic studies and triennial evaluations are sometimes viewed with suspicion; relationships at educational planning conferences take on a legalistic, sometimes adversarial tone. The Individual Educational Programs parents are asked to approve may be lists of canned computerized behavior objectives that bear little relationship to what their children tell them happens in the classroom every day. Parents' worries about educational and vocational outcomes for their children leave them vulnerable to promises of magic cures through unconventional interventions unsupported by rational theory and research (L. B. Silver, 1989).

Policy makers also express a sense of discomfort about provisions for students with learning disabilities. At times, school administrators seem more worried about complying with the letter of the laws than with understanding and implementing the spirit in which these laws were made. Even the administrators who have dealt adequately with compliance issues may face budgetary problems in financing services. They worry about "overidentification" of children as learning disabled.

The concept of overidentification provides a facile solution to the increasing numbers of children who are identified as learning disabled. A shortsighted approach to this problem is to blame someone—the parents "who don't spend enough time with their children to get them ready to learn at school" or the school's diagnostic team that "sees children only as individuals and does not understand how many children the schools have to deal with." More enlightened administrators avoid the blame game and try constructive approaches. They might investigate more carefully the effectiveness of the regular education program in the early grades; or they might strengthen the preschool services available to moderate- and low-income families; or they might institute a preventive program in the kindergarten. Finally, they might consider the possibility that there *just might be* that many children with learning disabilities who need special school services.

Teachers are also frustrated in their attempts to work with children with learning problems in their classes. Opportunities for consultation with school psychologists, social workers, or learning-disabilities specialists may be limited by the need for services, first of all, to the already-identified children with special educational needs. If they try to find answers in the professional literature, they may receive, instead of clear-cut answers to their questions, mixed messages as different researchers pursue their own points of view in discussions of the issues. Even the best-intentioned teacher can sense that alienation between research and the actual decisions one must make in the classroom each day. An example of this alienation between research and practices is seen in Lyon and Moats's (1988) discussion of critical issues in instruction of students with learning disabilities. On the basis of what they described as "a selective rather than an exhaustive review" of the literature of the field, they reached the following conclusions:

- Theory-based instruction is a necessary, but not totally sufficient condition for improved academic outcomes.
- Even the most efficacious instructional approaches rarely remediate academic deficits.
- Instructional outcomes are difficult to quantify accurately because remediation may not lead to changes in cognitive and academic outcomes.
- The outcomes of instructional decisions evade understanding through conventional research methodologies; to address these methodologies in a meaningful way would require research methodologies that are dynamic, fluid, and flexible. (pp. 832–833)

According to these investigators in 1988, the field of learning disorders should not look to the then-current research for guidance. They observed that the then-current research in the field of learning disabilities seemed to lead only to more research. Some efforts to improve the situation have occurred recently. One such effort is that of the National Reading Panel (2000), which produced a major meta-analysis of existing research on alphabetics, fluency, comprehension, computer technology, and teacher training. Research that met high standards of design and generalizability was analyzed to answer questions about major findings, implications for classroom instruction, teacher preparation, and directions for further research. As panel members are currently engaged in dissemination of the final report, the impact of this well-designed analysis is yet to be seen.

EDUCATIONAL IMPACT OF LEARNING DISORDERS

The discomfort with current educational provisions and the confused communication among researchers, professionals, policy makers, and parents result from the nature of the problem they are attempting to deal with. Learning disorders are complex conditions. The characteristics vary from person to person and from stage to stage in the development of an individual. People with learning disabilities compose a very heterogeneous group. This generalization has been repeated many times, but nowhere is it more relevant than in educational management. Anyone who hopes to help students with learning disabilities must accept the fact that these individuals are different from their nondisabled schoolmates. They are not just the low end of the curve of the distribution of educational test scores; they are different in the ways they learn. Experienced clinicians have observed these differences as they work with individuals with learning disabilities. Technological advances in the neurosciences, such as functional magnetic resonance imaging, are beginning to reveal differences in brain functioning between people with learning disorders and adequate readers. People responsible for educational planning for students with learning disabilities must understand these differences and provide for them appropriately.

What are these differences? While the characteristics may differ among individuals and within individuals at different stages in their development; some specific characteristics can be recognized:

- When compared with their general cognitive abilities, they have unexpected difficulty in learning basic skills in reading and the language arts and, less frequently, in mathematics. They have difficulty remembering what words look like. After having worked out a word on one line of text, they may not recognize the same word when they meet it two lines later. These students often come to the attention of teachers and parents because of their difficulties in early reading.

- These students represent a heterogeneous group of children; diagnostic assessment will reveal unique patterns of strengths and deficits that provide clues for educational management. One-size-fits all approaches are doomed to failure. Careful initial assessment and ongoing monitoring of changes as intervention progresses are essential to successful planning for these students.

- Their language development may lag behind that of their peers. Age of beginning to talk may be delayed in some. Oral inaccuracies in pronunciation and more primitive syntax may persist in their language. Use of language may be inaccurate, although logical and reasoning abilities may be strong. Their language limitations may cause people to underestimate their abilities.

- Preacademic skills may be delayed so that the neuropsychological foundations of reading may not be in place when they reach first grade. They may present problems in phonological processing, rote sequencing of sounds within words and words within sentences, correct orientation of symbols, fine motor control, development of clear-cut laterality, figure-background perception, and memory.

- They do not learn basic literacy skills from casual exposure. They need *explicit, systematic, code-based instruction* in reading; experience-based reading approaches just do not work for them.

- Even when they have been taught effective word attack skills, their reading will not be fluent. They will continue to read slowly and will need extended time to demonstrate their full knowledge on timed examinations.

- The order of steps in directions will be difficult for them to learn. This problem may be seen in learning such sequences as time and measures. They have difficulty learning the order of the days of the week and the months in a year. In mathematics, the multiplication tables and the steps in long division often present problems.

- Any set of new symbols presents problems, whether it is learning the Morse Code or a foreign language. Years of study in secondary school will not result in any degree of fluency with a foreign language.

- With any kind of associative learning task, they need opportunity for repeated practice to the point of overlearning. Computerized activities have proved invaluable for this purpose because they provide privacy and rapid feedback of correct responses.

These difficulties require hard work on the part of the student with a learning disability, who may find that his efforts are not recognized and rewarded by some teachers. The full range of defensive reactions may appear: anger, depression, blame, withdrawal, isolation. Teachers and parents need to be able to separate the basic learning problems from the emotional overlay that may result when a student does not have appropriate educational management. These general management principles cut across subject areas: The following discussion will focus on the three skill areas that present most problems to students with learning disabilities: reading, written language, and mathematics.

INTERVENTIONS FOR PROBLEMS WITH READING

Reading is the skill area that presents problems for the greatest proportion of students with learning disabilities. Lerner (1988) estimated that 80% of the children diagnosed as learning disabled have problems in this area. Also, problems in reading soon impact on other curriculum areas, so that their effects are inescapable. Finally, reading is a complex task—probably the most difficult one our culture asks in the education of young children.

Skilled reading is a complex multilevel system that includes letters, graphophonemic patterns, words, and syntactic units. The divergence among theoretical models of the task lies in the weight and relationships ascribed to these components by various investigators. Inevitably, these theoretical models of the task of reading influence the materials and methods that find their way into classrooms. One theoretical dichotomy is that of the *bottom-up* model versus *top-down* model of reading. The bottom-up model is based on the idea that the analysis of smaller units, (such as graphophonemes and words) is essential to the processing of larger conceptual units. In contrast, the top-down model assumes that readers use knowledge of higher order language structures to anticipate oncoming text. K. S. Goodman (1967) described this process as the "psycholinguistic guessing game." An additional formulation, somewhere between the two extremes, is the *parallel interactive* model that suggests that all sources of information—from signal cues of the perceptual features of words to syntactical and semantic information—are used simultaneously.

These models can be used to classify the instructional methods represented by the major approaches to teaching reading, although it should be acknowledged that few methods are applied in the "pure" sense in the classroom. Also, English combines words from many different sources; it is not phonetically regular. Nearly any "rule" offered by a teacher can be countered with exceptions by a diligent student. The bottom-up approach is best illustrated by phonics methods that teach grapheme/phoneme relationships, encourage the synthesis (or blending) of sounds into words, and use phonetically regular text insofar as it is possible to do so in English. The top-down models are exemplified by language experience approaches in which sentences often dictated by the children are introduced as meaningful wholes, with later practice with identifying individual words by referring back to the original sentences. Little work is done with the smaller components of the text because it is assumed that the correspondence between the text and the child's own language will provide adequate word recognition cues. As progress in reading is made, the student moves on to trade books, in which the meaning of the story carries the burden for word identification. Conventional basal reader approaches used in typical classrooms represent the parallel-interactive model. These approaches expect the learner to master approximately 200 words as "sight" words on the basis of signal cues in the configuration of the word and/or the language and context of the story in the textbook. Most teachers supplement this work with workbooks or work sheets dealing with phonic generalizations and word structure. However, unlike the synthetic phonics methods, these practice materials require the child to apply visual manipulations by copying or underlining words already met as sight words.

The Job Analysis of Reading (described in Chapter 6, Table 6.1) represents the model of reading used in this book. This model posits four skills areas for effective reading: prereading neuropsychological skills, word attack, comprehension, and study skills. Children with learning disorders may experience difficulties with any aspect of the reading process and require directive teaching of subskills that other children learn form casual experiences. This is particularly true of the prereading skills of visual and auditory perception and directionality. Both clinical observations of people with learning disabilities and meta-analyses of the relationships between perceptual skills and reading support the inclusion of visual and auditory perceptual skills (Kavale, 1981, p. 545, 1982, p. 51). Word attack skills include versatile use of sight words, contextual cues, language cues, phonics, and structural analysis, all of which are necessary because of the phonological and orthographic variations of written English. Comprehension skills draw on the oral language background the student brings to the task, literal comprehension, inferential reasoning, and appreciation of meaning. Study skills include the strategies necessary for locating, selecting, organizing, and retaining the content one reads. Each of the following interventions can be analyzed in terms of its contributions to the comprehensive model of the reading tasks in the Job Analysis of Reading.

Interventions Using Regular Classroom Methods

Interventions using regular classroom methods have their basis in the belief that learning disorders are primarily pedagogic in nature, that children with learning disorders are not very different from the range of children within the regular classroom. This viewpoint holds that learning disorders are merely the tail end of the distribution of reading achievement among large samples of students and concludes that learning problems result from inadequate and ineffective teaching. This is not the viewpoint of the authors of this book, but nonetheless it is reported because it exists in some schools and among some teachers and administrators. Since ineffective teaching is believed to cause the problems, the solution is seen to lie in more intensive reteaching using the same content and same methods.

Grade Repetition

Recommendations for a child to repeat a grade are the most obvious application of this approach. This provision may help in cases in which the child has not had the opportunity to attend school because of chronic illness, family mobility, or family disorganization, but its efficacy in improving the academic fate of children with learning disorders has yet to be documented. Nonpromotion also carries with it emotional burdens of guilt and loss of self-esteem that proponents of this alternative need to consider before implementing this superficially easy solution.

Administrative Provisions

Many administrative arrangements have been suggested in connection with this dyspedagogic point of view. Transitional classes to intensify instruction have been tried with limited success. Cross-age grouping for reading instruction, cross-age tutoring, and buddy-reading are all examples of experimental measures offered to meet the needs of low-achieving children within regular classrooms. These programs, too, need careful long-term evaluation.

Oral Reading Techniques

Some specific techniques use regular classroom materials to focus on specific skill deficits in reading fluency. Moyer (1982) developed a technique called *multiple oral reading (MOR)* in rehabilitation work with a patient with acquired alexia. Text is chosen at a level that presents little difficulty in word recognition for the reader. The selection is read once at a pace that permits a high degree of accuracy. The selection is repeated, usually three or four times, with speed increasing with each repetition. Moyer says that "daily practice has consequently resulted in an increase in the rate of reading new material" (p. 619). Repeated reading in remedial instruction provides the degree of redundancy necessary to extract the system of correspondence between written and spoken language. Other methods also draw on the principle of redundancy for their basic premise. The *neurological impress method* (Hechelman, 1969) uses choral reading by student and instructor. Massive *oral decoding* (R. J. Johnson, Johnson, & Kerfort, 1972) uses the repetition of phonetically regular text. The simplicity and economy of these methods is attractive. However, all three methods are designed to encourage fluency in oral reading only *after* the learner has acquired accurate word attack skills. Moreover, no objective data are presented to indicate their effective transfer to the complete reading process.

Repeated Reading to Enhance Fluency

Recent research on the characteristics of effective readers focused attention on fluency—the ability to read connected text rapidly, smoothly, automatically with little consciousness of the mechanisms of decoding. It has been shown that even when students with learning disabilities have learned decoding skills, their reading tends to be slow and dysfluent. Several theoretic explanations have been advanced: (a) Verbal inefficiency seen in a slow rate of decoding obstructs the efficient operation of higher conceptual functions involved in comprehension; (b) difficulties in orthographic recognition of sight words, in combination with limited working memory capacity, result in the need to reread to obtain meaning from text; (c) there is a separate factor-slow retrieval of verbal data that can be seen in difficulties with rapid naming. Because research indicated that intensive decoding instruction utilizing phonemic skills does not necessarily improve fluency in young children, some researchers have designed methods to use a direct approach to develop fluency. Although the basic approach involves repeated reading, these experimental methods are somewhat more sophisticated. RAVE-O (Wolf & Bowers, 1999b) is a comprehensive approach involving perceptual, phonological, and word retrieval skills, as well as application of fluency practice in reading. The investigators use direct teaching and computerized materials in a well-designed experiment that assesses the educational impact of different intervention conditions with low-achieving young children. *Great Leaps* (K. Campbell & Mercer, 1995) is designed to supplement classroom reading programs. The reading tasks consist of phonemic awareness skills, systematic decoding, and stories. Students read for brief periods of time from a list of phonetically regular words, phrases, and text. Tutors (who may be community volunteers, paraprofessionals, or parents) review skills, model fluent reading, correct errors, and graph progress. The goal is to read the selection in a minute with less than two errors. When it is accomplished, the student "leaps" forward to a higher level within the program. *Decoding Pilot Program* (Hecker & Gunter-Mohr, 1999) is an experimental program designed at Landmark College. Actually a comprehensive retraining program in many aspects of reading and the language arts at the postsecondary level, it involves the use of computer software and the Kurzweil Ultimate Reader-3000 for specific training in reading fluency. These cutting-edge experiments in an important aspect of reading remediation are described in an excellent paper by Meyer and Felton (1999) that also places this research within the context of current reading methodology.

Reading Recovery

The Reading Recovery program developed by Clay (1985b) is a broad-based application of classroom procedures. This approach targets the lowest 20% of the first-grade children identified by their teachers and by a diagnostic survey that includes six measures: letter identification, word test, concepts about print, writing vocabulary, dictation test, and text reading level. In addition to regular classroom activities, 30-minute individual tutoring sessions by specially trained tutors consist of (a) reading easy stories, (b) reading a story aloud while the tutor keeps a "running record" of errors, (c) working on letter identification, (d) constructing written messages in the child's own writing book, (e) reconstructing the written message after it has been transcribed on a strip and cut apart, (f) talking about a new book selected to support the child's strategies, (g) reading a new book with assistance from the tutor (Pinnell, 1985). Results of the Reading Recovery Program in New Zealand reported by Clay (1988) indicate that children at risk for failure made accelerated progress while receiving individual tutoring. "After an average of 12 to 14 weeks in the program, almost all Reading Recovery children had caught up with their peers and needed no further help. Three years later the children still retained their gains and continued to make progress at average rates" (Clay, 1988, p. 2). Reading Recovery has been replicated in the United States through Ohio State University and has been selected as an exemplary program by the U.S. Department of Education's National Diffusion Network on the basis of data on educational impact in model programs in Ohio. It is difficult to determine the effectiveness of this program with children with learning disabilities, because the selection methods from the lowest 20% in the classes do not include diagnostic information. Should students with learning disabilities be included in the program, 12 to 14 weeks of intervention in first grade appears to be a meager intervention to produce the results described by its developer.

Inclusion Models

These models have been discussed in detail in Chapter 1. The impact of early studies used to justify this model were unimpressive (Biklen & Zoellers, 1986; Hallahan et al., 1988). However, the wide acceptance of this model provides the opportunity for careful study of the long-term effects of its effectiveness.

Models Emphasizing Language Development

The relationship between general language abilities and reading achievement has been recognized for some time. The apparent logic of this relationship was confirmed in early correlational studies (Artley, 1950; Peake, 1940; W. W. Young, 1936). In a clinical study of contrasting groups of retarded and nonretarded readers matched in terms of age, IQ, and sex, Hagin (1954) found clear-cut differences between the groups in a large number of language variables. The groups differed significantly in their perception of verbal stimuli as assessed through auditory measures of discrimination, blending, rhyming, and matching initial sounds. Measures of verbal fluency, as assessed through word association, articulation, and length and complexity of sentences also differentiated the groups, as did measures of conceptual use of language, such as analogies, and level of abstraction on an object sorting test. Breadth and accuracy of vocabulary differentiated the two groups, but vocabulary measured by pictured responses did not. Other investigators have emphasized the relationships between learning disorders and various aspects of language development. One of the most recent was the report of the Committee on the Prevention of Reading Difficulties in Young Children commissioned by the National Academy of Science (Snow, Burns, & Griffin, 1999). This meta-analysis of the research on early reading instruction found that the correlation between early vocabulary development and reading comprehension at sixth grade was .60. Acknowledging the contributions of other factors (e.g., motivation, appreciation of literacy, phonological awareness, letter recognition, and general world knowledge), these investigators emphasized the primary importance of rich language experiences to success in learning to read.

Language Enrichment Programs

Most textbooks on children's language development or learning disabilities are rich sources of methods for enhancing language development (Dudley-Marling & Searle, 1988; D. J. Johnson & Myklebust, 1967; Lerner, 1988) and offer guiding principles and practical methods for enriching the language environment of the classroom. Classrooms that provide a physical setting that promotes talk stimulate children to use language for a variety of purposes. Interaction that responds to talk in ways that encourage continued communication are preferable to classrooms in which children sit isolated at their desks working on workbooks in solitary silence.

Whole Language Approach

The classroom instructional strategy called the "whole language approach" has been recommended by Brand (1989) who believes it can alleviate some of the difficulties of learning-disabled children, including problems in memory, cognition, anxiety, inadequate self-esteem, locus of control, and attentional problems. This approach requires the teacher to establish a literate environment in the classroom, demonstrating how language is used for real communication in functional activities. There is an emphasis on free choice of books, usually trade books of stories, rather than basal readers. Student authorship of reading materials is encouraged so that the language arts are integrated in natural ways with the reading process. Reading and writing involve communication that is meaningful to students. Organized so that the physical, intellectual, and social-affective components of the setting emphasize communication, this environment contrasts with the classroom that emphasizes isolated worksheets, memorized rules, and skill tests (G. G. Duffy & Roehler, 1989).

All this sounds ideal for children with learning disorders until one considers how this approach accomplishes the teaching of word attack skills, one of the major difficulties these children encounter in learning to read. G. G. Duffy and Roehler (1989) explain this process in their textbook on reading instruction. Teachers are told to teach children to recognize words by having them read the words to be learned in phrases on flash cards "until students instantly recognize the word." For some students with learning disorders, this lesson might last for a long, long time, because a basic characteristic of these children is that they cannot remember what words look like. With otherwise unfamiliar words, the student is encouraged to use contextual cues (guessing on the basis of the words around the unknown word) or structural analysis (using structural units such as prefixes, suffixes, roots, and inflectional endings). As a last resort, the student might use phonics to "sound out" the unknown word, but G. G. Duffy and Roehler apparently take a dim view of these methods: "Phonics is the slowest of the three decoding methods because it requires that each separate letter-sound unit be retrieved from memory and then blended together. . . . Further, phonics is not always reliable because letter sounds are not always consistent and predictable" (G. G. Duffy & Roehler, 1989, p. 108). This point of view is maintained in the face of a substantial body of research to the contrary (Chall, 1983; Stanovich, 1986b).

The G. G. Duffy and Roehler (1989) textbook, intended for use in the training of teachers, makes few suggestions for adaptations for children who have trouble learning to read. About special education students, they write: "Sometimes teachers have the expectation that such different students require different instruction. This is not so. You must adept your instruction to the level at which such students are working, but your basic instructional techniques remain the same" (pp. 76–77).

Despite this inflexibility in the recognition of differences among students, the whole language approach has merit in its emphasis on the natural interrelationships among language skills, its recognition of the importance of meaning in the development of communication skills, and its adaptability for use with word processing systems as computers become part of regular classroom equipment. Because of its inadequate provision for direct teaching of word attack skills, however, the whole language approach does not offer much promise for success in teaching students with learning disorders.

Fernald Tracing Technique

Fernald's tracing technique is a venerable remedial method that uses student authorship and language context to teach beginning reading (1943/1988). Fernald developed this method in a clinical setting with bright retarded readers, described its use, and documented it with painstaking case studies. The steps in the procedure are as follows:

- The student writes a brief story without assistance.
- The student and the teacher rewrite the story, making corrections in terms of mechanics, but preserving the student's own words.
- As misspelled words or omitted words are encountered, they are rewritten in large cursive writing by the teacher on paper approximately $4\frac{1}{2}$ by 11 inches.
- The student traces each word with his or her finger, saying the word (not individual letters or sounds) aloud as it is traced.
- When the student feels the word has been learned, he or she writes the word from memory on a small piece of paper and then compares it with the large copy written by the teacher.
- If the student wrote the word correctly, it is then written in the copy of the story that is being rewritten; if incorrect, the student resumes tracing the word until it can be written correctly from memory.
- The large copies of words are filed to serve as an informal dictionary for the student when writing other stories.
- The teacher types the rewritten stories for use as text for oral reading practice by the student.

The tracing technique is used to build a sight word vocabulary of 200 to 300 words. With this personal vocabulary of sight words, the student then moves on to direct, systematic instruction in phonics and structural analysis skills that permit development of independence in word attack.

The reasons for the effectiveness of the tracing technique with some children have not been established. Fernald's hypothesis about the effects of kinesthetic-tactual stimulation seems improbable in the light of more recent information about brain function. It may be that the use of language generated by the student provides more salient cues to the beginning reader than text like "Come Spot and Puff, come and run." It may also be that the tracing and rewriting impose detailed, directionally accurate inspection of the words, so that the student is given more cues and more practice than with the conventional classroom approaches to beginning reading. Whatever the reasons, the Fernald Tracing technique appears to be one the few "top-down" methods that hold promise for children with severe reading disorders.

Models Emphasizing Code-Based Word Attack

There is probably no aspect of reading instruction that has given rise to greater controversy than that dealing with phonic analysis in word attack. Orton cited this controversy in the Salmon Lecture in 1937:

> There has been in recent years a striking swing toward the use of the sight or flashcard method of teaching reading and away from the use of phonetics. The writer is not in a position to offer an opinion as to the efficacy of either of these methods as a general school procedure, but their effect on children suffering from varying degrees of strephosymbolia has come under his immediate attention and he feels that there can be no doubt that the use of the popular flash method of teaching reading is a definite obstacle to children who suffer from any measure of this disability. (Orton, 1937, p. 104)

The subject of diatribes (Flesch, 1981), carefully reasoned research analyses (Chall, 1983), and policy statements (D. Anderson, 1985; National Reading Panel, 2000) the value of phonics instruction is not debatable at this time. However, the heated discussions of reading approaches in the state of California (discussed in Chapter 1) show that the differences of opinion continue.

Orton-Gillingham Approach

Despite continuing debate about the teaching of phonics to improve reading competence, the modest description Orton wrote more than 60 years ago is equally true today: "The hallmark of specific reading disability or strephosymbolia is a failure in recognition of the printed word even after it has been encountered many times" (1937, p. 175). Orton described the teaching of sound/symbol correspondences in the Language Research Project at Neurological Institute in New York City in the following manner:

- Use of kinesthetic-motor patterns to teach graphic forms of letters.
- Teaching phonetics equivalent of printed letters through cards containing the printed letters.
- Teaching the process of blending auditory sequences of such equivalents to produce the spoken form of the written word.
- Using associative linkages of vision, audition, and kinesthesis to ensure transfer to written spelling.

With admirable restraint, he added: "We have tried to avoid overstandardization lest the procedure become too inflexible and be looked upon as a routine method applicable to all cases or non-readers, which would be clearly unwise in view of the wide variations in symptomatology and hence in training needs" (1937, p. 175).

These procedures were developed with Gillingham, who later organized, expanded, and recorded this approach so that it could be used by other teachers (Gillingham & Stillman, 1968). These modest beginnings, now known as the Orton-Gillingham approach, have influenced a large number of teachers and inspired many related teaching systems (Childs, 1973; Enfield, 1988; E. T. Hall, 1976; R. E. Saunders, 1973; Slinger-land, 1971; Traub, 1972). It has been emphasized that Orton-Gillingham is an approach, rather than a standardized program of lessons. While specific applications of the approach may differ, common themes are derived from the principles elucidated in Orton's early work. Recent years have seen the organization of the Orton-Gillingham Academy among members of the International Dyslexia Society (the current name for the Orton Dyslexia Society that was organized in memory of Samuel T. Orton by his friends and students). The Academy offers training courses, supervision, and certification of tutors using the Orton-Gillingham approach.

Despite widespread acceptance and application of this approach, there has been little educational research to assess its efficacy or to compare it with other approaches. However, continuing research may eventually provide a different kind of validation for code-based teaching approaches. Research by such investigators as Stanovich (1982), A. A. Silver and Hagin (1964), and Perfetti and Hogaboam (1975) has through varying paths shown the essential role of accurate decoding processes in reading comprehension.

Phonological Processing

The recognition of the importance of accurate decoding to the reading process has resulted in research focusing on phonological processes. J. P. Williams (1984) pointed out that in the past this area was known as *auditory skills*. Today some of the current terms used to refer to this area as a whole (or subparts of it) include phonological awareness, linguistic awareness, linguistic insight, phonemic segmentation, and phonemic recoding in lexical memory. Some complex terms are used to designate familiar processes; for example, *phonemic synthesis* is used to describe the activity most classroom teachers call "blending" *and phonological recoding in lexical access* is used to designate what teachers call "sounding out words." Whatever terms are used, they indicate studies to understand how children learn to identify and use correspondence between letters and sounds in word recognition in reading. To do this, the student must be able to identify the units, both graphic and phonetic, and to blend these units in accurate temporal sequences into recognizable words. These processes of analysis and synthesis are complex because of the variations and irregularities of sound-symbol correspondence in English words.

According to Williams, some of the earliest work relating phonemic analysis to reading was done by two Russian psychologists: Zhurova (1963) found that many children between the ages of 3 and 6 could not isolate the first phoneme of simple words and later had difficulty in learning to read; Elkonin (1973) taught children to identify the number of phonemes in words by using discs to represent separate phonemes. When the discs were replaced with letters, these children showed improvement in the various aspects of literacy (J. P. Williams, 1984, p. 219).

Some American investigations have focused on the relationships of various aspects of phonological processing to reading: differences in development of syllable segmentation and phoneme segmentation (I. Y. Liberman, 1973); sound deletion and language arts achievement (Rosner & Simon, 1971); ceiling levels at age 4 years for word and syllable segmentation and at age 6 for phoneme segmentation (Fox & Routh, 1975). All investigators found significant relationships between phonological skills and word recognition in reading. P. Bryant and Bradley (1983), using an odd-word-out paradigm, found that, when asked to recognize and to produce rhymes, "backward readers" in schools in England had more difficulty than younger children who were reading at the same achievement level. They concluded that these difficulties resulted from phonological weakness.

J. P. Williams (1984) conducted one of the most carefully designed training studies in a decoding program that included lessons in phonemic analysis and blending. Evaluation after training showed that the program children were able to decode both familiar words and nonsense combinations, indicating transfer effects of the skills taught. The results suggested to her that phonemic training made instruction more effective, but she added the caution that it was impossible to evaluate the effects of phonemic training apart from the effects of all the other components of the experimental program. Thus, while this work is valuable in that the experiment was placed within the natural context of reading instruction, additional research is necessary to focus on the contribution of specific phonological skills.

Williams' caution is a reasonable one, especially if one considers a series of experiments that used an interference condition to isolate visual and phonological skills as children solved two matching tasks, one involving rhyming and the other involving conceptual grouping (R. Baron & Baron, 1977). The interference condition, which blocked out use of phonological cues, interfered with reading and recognizing rhymes, but did not interfere with reading and completing a conceptual task. The investigators concluded that in the early stages of reading, many children adopt a visual strategy that takes them directly to the meaning of words without having to build them up from phonic elements—without translating symbols into sounds at all. The paradox is that while good readers seem to acquire the skills of phonological analysis as part of their language development, they also seem to be able to read without using them. In contrast, children with reading disorders have difficulty acquiring these skills, but they need to be taught to use these skills in reading.

It seems premature to suggest, as R. K. Wagner (1986) and others have done, that phonological factors are the *cause* of reading disorders. At least two alternative hypotheses suggest themselves. The first is that there may be a circular effect: While phonological awareness enhances the process of learning to read, knowing how to read enhances one's awareness of phonology. This interaction might explain why the phonemic segmentation skills do not develop fully until age 6, when children have had some experience with sound-symbol correspondences in beginning reading. A second hypothesis is that the difficulties with phonological tasks may be part of general difficulties with the associative aspects of language, apparent also in spatial orientation and in temporal sequencing problems that children with learning disabilities experience.

The National Institute of Child Health and Human Development has supported an extensive program of research on instructional applications of research findings on the role of phonological processing in reading. This program responds to the strong belief that the difficulties of most children with learning disabilities involve a dysfunction in the phonological components of their natural capacity for language (Liberman,

Shankweiler, & Liberman, 1989, p. 1). Of this group of investigators, Torgeson has provided carefully documented results of two experimental programs: a preventive study with kindergartners and a remedial study with 8- to 11-year-olds.

The preventive study provided intensive intervention with individual one-to-one sessions totaling 80 minutes per week for 2½ years. Subjects were children nominated by their teachers as being "at risk" and verified on the basis of tests of alphabetic knowledge and phonemic awareness by the project staff. Scores for these skills predicted that these children would place within the lowest 10% of their classes in reading by second grade. All earned estimated IQ scores higher than 75. Four instructional conditions were contrasted: (a) Oral motor training of phonological awareness (using the Lindamood program *Auditory Discrimination in Depth*) plus synthetic phonics instruction for decoding words and little books of phonetically regular stories (PASP); (b) embedded phonics and implicit phonological awareness (EP); (c) regular support with the classroom reading program; (d) no treatment control condition. Preliminary evaluation at the end of 2 years showed that alphabetic reading skills of the PASP condition children approached average levels for the age-group as a whole and that fewer of them had repeated first grade than the children in other conditions. This group of children had a significant advantage over the other groups on several measures of phonological awareness and on a spelling measure that assessed use of phonic knowledge in spelling. Overall differences in word identification and in a standardized measure of reading comprehension had not reached the required level of statistical reliability (Torgeson, 1998, pp. 211–212). He also reported the variability within the PASP group and the need for continuing monitoring of the effects of these skill changes as the children continued in school.

A remedial program offered to 8-to 11-year-olds, nominated by their teachers and validated through measures of phonological processing and alphabetic skills, provided similar intervention conditions to those of the preventive project. Intensive training was provided for 2 hours per day for 5 days a week for 8 weeks. Following the intensive instruction, students were seen in their learning disabilities classroom for one hour a week for 8 weeks to ensure application of the newly developed skills in classwork. Preliminary results show that children in both intensive instructional conditions made striking gains in the accuracy of their alphabetic reading skills. The change is equivalent to 1½ to 2 years of growth in the skills after 80 hours of tutoring. The investigator comments that "the children also experienced substantial growth in their ability to recognize real words and to comprehend what they read, though changes have not been so dramatic as those for alphabetic reading skill" (Torgeson, 1998, p. 214). However, changes in fluency continued to lag behind in both groups. Torgeson concluded that these studies showed that it is possible to intervene successfully with alphabetic skills and that explicit teaching, rather than indirect and embedded approaches, are more effective. As other investigators have concluded previously, Torgeson states that "phonetic reading skills are probably a necessary but not sufficient cause of growth in sight word ability. They will not be helpful if they are not routinely applied when children are reading text" (p. 216). He also pointed out that the present results are based on a relative short time period that does not permit the skills to be developed to the point of automaticity.

Interventions Involving Strategy Training

Interventions involving cognitive strategies are being used to improve academic achievement, particularly with students at the secondary school level. Many students, despite the goals of competent independent learning and intrinsic motivation set for them in earlier school programs, have failed to realize these objectives by the time they reach high school. Many of these students reach a plateau in skill development at approximately fifth-grade level. Deshler, Schumaker, Levy, and Ellis (1984) have shown that these students have been in programs with a strong remedial emphasis for several years and need to explore other than traditional remedial approaches. They describe these students as "inactive learners" who fail to attend selectively, do not know how to organize material to be learned, do not use mnemonic strategies in learning, and have difficulty maintaining on-task behavior. Despite these maladaptive habits, these investigators have found that the students could behave strategically if they were taught how to do so. Indeed, many of these youngsters could be taught to use effective learning strategies (Palinskar & Brown, 1987).

The purpose of the strategies approach is to enable adolescents with learning disabilities to use their existing academic skills in a strategically optimal fashion. These students are taught task-specific strategies for such activities as monitoring of errors in written work, test-taking skills, retrieval of information from textbooks, and self-questioning and paraphrasing as aids in reading comprehension. Deshler's group, which has accomplished exemplary work in this area at the University of Kansas Institute for Research in Learning Disabilities, use the following seven steps in teaching strategies:

1. *Task-Related Pretest.* This step establishes the need for the strategy to be taught by assessing the student's current achievement with the specific task. Results of the pretest are discussed with students so that they are aware of their instructional needs.

2. *Rationale.* The teacher provides a rationale for using the skill and a description of its use in current school activities.

3. *Modeling.* The teacher models the skills with appropriate demonstration and explanation.

4. *Verbal Rehearsal.* The student rehearses the skill verbally using the steps involved in the skill to the level of mastery.

5. *Controlled Practice.* The teacher provides practice material at the student's instructional level, so that practice can occur without interference caused by content difficulties.

6. *Advanced Practice.* When the student is able to apply the strategy with material at a modified level, he or she is given grade-level material for further practice.

7. *Task-Related Posttest.* These teaching methods have been validated with 90 students with learning disabilities enrolled in the upper years of high school (Deshler et al., 1984). Educational impact was demonstrated in scores on classroom tests and district competency examinations, improved course grades, and

positive teacher ratings of students' progress. One caution is offered by the designers of this approach: Students must have some basic reading competencies (approximately fourth-grade reading level) if they are to profit from strategy training.

One of the important applications of strategy training has been with memory. Since learning and memory are inseparable, it is not surprising to find memory problems associated with learning disabilities. Gelzheiser and associates (Gelzheiser, Solar, Shepherd, & Wozniak, 1983) have provided a rationale for teaching memory strategies to students with learning disabilities. Three processes are involved in their training: mnemonics (e.g., categorization, rehearsal, and elaboration), monitoring, and evaluation. Successful learners apply these strategies without specific training, unlike many people with learning disabilities. These researchers hypothesized that cognitive resources are finite and, therefore, central processing is limited. Differences between novices and experts in memorization may be due to differences in the way they allocate limited central processing capacity. The proficient memorizer organizes a plan and remains conscious of the goal. Often people with learning disability are found to fail to plan how to deal with a memory task; they also tend to remain at a stage of consciously directed practice for long periods of time. It may be that they need more practice (i.e., opportunity for overlearning) to reach the stage of automaticity.

The strategy training approach represents very thorough and efficient teaching and precise analysis of the tasks to be taught. It has been found helpful in ensuring transfer by teaching students to use, maintain, and generalize the study skills that many students with learning disabilities need to be taught if they are to succeed in secondary school and beyond.

General Principles

Thoughtful consideration of intervention models in reading inevitably leads to the conclusion that there is no single structure or model that is suitable for every child in the vast, heterogeneous population of learning disorders. There is no one best model that will work in all cases with all children. Furthermore, there is no way of borrowing the "double-blind" design from pharmacology to set up comparisons of intervention models and placebo conditions to find the teaching method of choice for children with learning disorders. In such research, the independent variables would be so variable and the dependent variables so complex to measure, that the experiment would be difficult to conduct and outcomes difficult to interpret. This is not to suggest that results of studies of intervention models are irrelevant to educational planning—far from it. Studies that highlight the strengths and weaknesses of the various models available in the field are especially helpful in guiding appropriate educational choices. Intervention models need to be considered in terms of their strengths and the unique needs of the individual for whom the plan is being made. This analysis should relate each intervention model to a conceptualization of the reading process, such as the Job Analysis of Reading. Planners can then consider the question: "What aspects of the complex process of reading does this model address?" This kind of analysis is useful in targeting the strengths of the wide range of intervention models and in guarding against either a mismatch with the student's needs or unreasonable expectations about a particular model.

DEVELOPMENTAL WRITING DISABILITIES

Writing has been conceptualized as a problem-solving process whereby the writer attempts to produce visible, understandable, and legible language reflecting his or her declarative knowledge of topic. *DSM-IV-TR* provides diagnostic criteria for a disorder of written expression, but the definition does not operationalize the criteria (see Table 8.2). *DSM-IV* offers no standardized instruments for assessment, nor does it state what functions other than generalized "writing skills" are to be measured. It does not describe the neuropsychological foundations for writing.

In general, there are three areas of function in which problems are found in individuals with a developmental writing disability: (a) the content and organization of ideas; (b) the mechanics of written expression, including spelling, grammar, capitalization, punctuation, and diction; (c) the handwriting itself.

Content and Organization of Ideas

Poor writers are more likely than good writers to have limited vocabulary and to produce shorter and less interesting essays. Text may be disorganized. Mechanics of writing may be inaccurate with poor spelling, incorrect grammar, and missing punctuation. Handwriting may be labored, with letters poorly formed or intentionally illegible to obscure uncertainties in the writer's spelling. This group of functions has been labeled by Berninger and Abbott (1994) as *composition disability, spelling disability,* and *handwriting disability.*

While there is apparent lack of concern about the importance of handwriting in school curricula (Sheffield, 1996) and there is relative scarcity of research studies on

---

Table 8.2   Diagnostic criteria for disorder of written expression

A. Writing skills, as measured by individually administered standardized test (or functional assessments of writing skills), are substantially below those expected given the person's chronological age, measured intelligence, and age-appropriate education.

B. The disturbance in Criterion A significantly interferes with academic achievement or activities of daily living that require the composition of written tests (e.g. writing grammatically correct sentences and organized paragraphs).

C. If a sensory deficit is present, the difficulties in writing skills are in excess of those usually associated with it.

Coding Note: If a general medical (neurological) condition or sensory deficit is present, code the condition on Axis III.

Note: Reprinted with permission from the *Diagnostic and Statistical Manual of Mental Disorders,* Fourth Edition, Text Revision. Copyright 2000 American Psychiatric Association.

handwriting, the components of the content of written expression in students who do not have learning disabilities has received some attention. Hierarchical phases in broad mental operations required in their types of written expression have been described: planning (generating ideas, retrieving information stored in long-term memory, organizing ideas into meaningful structures, goal setting); translating (putting ideas into writing, guided by the mechanics of syntax, vocabulary, grammar, spelling, and punctuation); and reviewing (polishing text, proofreading for errors in mechanics) (J. R. Hayes & Flower, 1980).

Mechanics of Written Expression

Specific types of errors in handwriting, spelling, syntax, organization of text, and "sense of audience" have been discussed by Gregg (1992). Syntactical errors include word omissions, errors in word order, lack of subject/verb agreement, absent or incorrect punctuation and capitalization, and problems with cohesion. In evaluating spelling, Gregg emphasized the importance of error patterns containing phonological, visual, and orthographic errors.

The utility of these models in the evaluation of writing is seen in a factor analysis of quantitative indices in the writing of elementary schoolchildren (Tindal & Parker, 1991). These indices included number of words written, words spelled correctly, words sequenced correctly, words sequenced incorrectly, total number of sequenced words, percentage of correctly sequenced words, story idea, story organization, and written language conventions. In this factor analysis, three factors accounted for 81% of the variance: (a) production and sequence of words (37% of the variance), (b) conventions including punctuation (26% of the variance), (c) idea/cohesion/organization (18% of the variance).

Efforts have been made to move from a description of the content and analysis of grammatical errors to a description of the neuropsychological processes that underlie the component functions of written language. Roeltgen (1985) traced the development of graphemes as they emerge from the auditory and visual input needed for the production of word engrams and the development of oral language and reading. The grapheme, together with nonverbal visual-spatial orientation, is then translated into motor programming and written language. Roeltgen proposed that, instead of classifying students based on the clinical manifestations of their disabilities, classifications should be based on the neuropsychological functions that are assumed to disrupt the writing process. In a sample of 300 first, second, and third graders, Abbott and Berninger (1993), Berninger and Rutberg (1992), found a significant relationship on a battery of neuropsychological tests with measures of spelling, handwriting, and composition. This battery included orthographic coding, neuromotor functioning, visuomotor integration, phonological coding, word finding, syntax, verbal IQ, word reading and nonword reading, and passage comprehension. In the primary grades, measures of orthographic and phonological coding, fine motor function, and orthographic-motor integration correlated highest with handwriting, spelling, and composition. Of these measures, automaticity in the production of alphabet letters, rapid coding of orthographic information, and speed of sequencing finger movements were the best predictors of handwriting and composition skills. These "lower level" neurodevelopmental abilities may influence the ability to transcribe ideas into letters, words, and sentences. While these factors also influence the ability of older students to transcribe letters, words, and sentences into writing, linguistic factors and working memory are needed for written expression in the intermediate grades; and higher order cognitive abilities begin to determine the level of writing at the secondary school level.

Written expression is thus a complex process that requires interaction between variables intrinsic to the child (neuropsychological, linguistic, genetic) and variables that are extrinsic to the child (family, school, and teacher demands) Hooper et al. (1994). Writing draws on many brain systems: oral language, orthographic coding, orthographic-motor integrations, working memory, reading and verbal reasoning (Berninger, 1994). With such variations in intrinsic and extrinsic factors, not all aspects of written language are impaired in any one child. For example, a sample of 99 children, 9 to 15 years of age, referred to medically oriented school problems clinic was found to have writing disability. The diagnosis was based on teacher information, ratings of writing legibility, mechanics, rate of linguistic sophistication, and spelling. Sixty-three children without writing disability served as controls. Q cluster analysis revealed four distinct subtypes and two nonwriting disability clusters in controls. The four writing disability clusters had characteristics of reading and writing that were significantly different ($p = <.0001$) from each other to derive empirical subgroups:

- *Group 1* ($n = 50$) evidenced fine motor and linguistic deficits with poor phonetic spelling, slow motor output, and problems with mechanics.
- *Group 2* ($n = 35$) predominantly manifested visuospatial deficits; their writing was characterized by poor legibility and poor spatial organization. In contrast to Group 1, these subjects had adequate spelling and idea generation.
- *Group 3* ($n = 9$) had prominent problems with attention and memory including poor spelling and frequent omissions, insertions, and inconsistencies in legibility. Mechanics and rate were generally intact.
- *Group 4* ($n = 11$) showed primary problems in sequencing with written output characterized by poor automatization of letter production, poor mechanics, and poor legibility. (Sandler et al., 1992)

It is not clear from this study what comorbid factors are present in their sample. For example, does Group 1 also have reading problems? Does Group 2 also have significant body image problems? Do attentional deficits characterize Group 3? Group 4 appears to have a multitude of motor and language processing problems. Results of cluster analysis alone do not offer a clinical picture of these children and do not tell us the etiologies of their difficulties. However, this study is an effort at clinically based classification of children with writing difficulties and suggests the overlapping deficits and clinical presentations seen in these children.

Handwriting

The third function, the handwriting itself, in our opinion has not received sufficient attention. This apraxic-agraphic group has not been well understood in terms of underlying etiology. These children have a basic problem with the postural model of the body and with the orientation in space. This is seen in immaturity in right/left orientation, and inability at age 6 years to identify correctly their own right and left hands or to perform crossed commands or identify the examiner's right and left hands at age 8 years. In addition, they often cannot identify correctly the position of their own fingers nor localize tactual stimuli to their fingers when their eyes are closed (finger gnosis). They have difficulty imitating with their fingers the position of the examiner's fingers (constructive finger praxis). These functional immaturities, together with dyspraxia, appear in children who have difficulty forming written letters and words. There is evidence that these functions are subsumed by the area between the angular gyrus and the second occipital convolution of the left hemisphere. Benton (1992) reported the syndrome complex to occur on electrocortical stimulation of "small areas" in the left parieto-temporal cortex.

Right-left discrimination, finger gnosis, and constructive finger praxis have normal sequences of maturation. It is when maturation is disturbed, as in the developmental language disorders—when there is perturbation in the development of hemispheric specialization—that their functions do not mature appropriately and their functioning is impaired. From a functional perspective, these immaturities will prevent accurate transcription of the phoneme into the grapheme and also, conversely, translation of the written symbol to the phoneme. Children with spatial orientation and body image problems will, therefore, have difficulty copying other written material, writing from dictation, and (as older students) taking notes during lectures.

This child may, but most often does not, have problems with visual perception; they are aware that they cannot write the form they see. Berninger (1994) states "visual perception cannot be equated with orthographic skills for processing the letters in written words. Orthographic abilities probably are important for processing the letters in words not only for reading, but also for writing" (p. 422). It is the very awareness that their writing hand cannot reproduce what their eyes see that intensifies the frustration they feel. When children have an accompanying reading disability, the problem of writing is further intensified. When they can translate the dictated word into its phonemes, they must translate the phonemes into graphemes. This brings into play the same difficulties in spatial orientation and in awareness of position of the fingers as does transcribing the grapheme from the visual symbol in reading. With a reading disability, the phoneme may not be perceived accurately or may not be sequenced correctly. This adds another layer on the problems of children learning writing skills.

Writing disability may also be found in children with problems of attention and impulse control. These symptoms may aggravate the frustration of children who are already angry and depressed because of their difficulties in decoding in reading. In the secondary school years, teachers judge students' work primarily in terms of what they put down on paper. Writing problems will show up in the failure to complete independent work, test responses on which they write as little as possible, and the inability to take effective notes during class discussions. Teachers may perceive such behaviors as indications of poor motivation and respond with low marks and complaints to parents. The students respond with anger and resentment toward teachers and school. In many cases, the outcome will be a cycle of failing grades, tension between parents and children, school refusal or truancy, and dropping out when school-leaving age is reached. For these reasons, difficulties with written work should be taken very seriously.

Assessment

The evaluation of a child with developmental learning disability is incomplete without a study of the intactness of body image skills including right-left discrimination, finger gnosis, constructive finger praxis, and fine motor control. These functions are basic to handwriting, an essential part of literacy. Children with disorders of writing deserve the same pentaxial evaluation described in Chapters 6 and 7 of this book. Educational planning for them requires an understanding of the cognitive, educational, neuropsychological, emotional, and social factors affecting their learning. Assessment of their specific problems requires the examiner to evaluate their writing in terms of the three areas described at the beginning of this section by both formal and informal measures. These evaluations should include a careful review of current school papers and notebooks to determine (a) what the school expects of this student, (b) the extent to which the student is meeting those expectations, (c) what assistance has already been given. Some formal measures of written work are available, such as the Writing Samples and Dictation Sections of the Woodcock-Johnson Tests of Achievement III, the Wechsler Individual Achievement Test, and the Test of Written Language.

Intervention Methods

Graphic Organizers

Teaching students to use mapping for planning the content and organization of written work is an important approach for students who need help with this aspect of written work. Unlike outlining, mapping provides flexibility in charting ideas, yet is really the first step toward organizing ideas in a logical outline. Used consistently, it requires with careful questioning, modeling, and verbal rehearsal of the planned content. Mapping can result in gradual shifting of the responsibility for generating and organizing content to the student. It also provides a structure for teaching college students who need help in organizing papers and responding effectively to essay type examinations.

Handwriting

Hagin (1983) has designed a handwriting approach called *connected print* that is suggested for use with students who have great difficulty learning conventional cursive handwriting patterns. It is based on the vertical downstroke, rather than the diagonal slant and retracing necessary for cursive writing. It builds on the motor patterns of manuscript letters taught in the early grades, but adds connecting pencil strokes that permit faster writing than is possible with the separated letters of printed manuscript. Connected print assumes that handwriting is a complex visuomotor/body image/verbal skill that must be automatic to be effective. A skill is acquired through repetition of a series of motor patterns until they become easily accessible to the writer.

The chalkboard is used as a medium for introducing new letter forms for several reasons. Work in the vertical plane is easier than in the horizontal plane at a desk, because developmentally vertical planes precede horizontal ones. The vertical plane also provides firmer cues for correct left-to-right orientation. Finally, writing on the chalkboard permits the writer to observe the results as the various elements of the letter patterns are joined. Connected print uses manuscript letters as a bridge to simplified writing style with connections between the letters made by the writer's natural movement to the next vertical downstroke. The vertical line is emphasized because it is easier than the diagonal line necessary for conventional cursive writing. The importance of this distinction is documented by persistence of printing with many youngsters, long after cursive writing has been taught in their classroom. However, print becomes less serviceable as more rapid written work is required at school. The need to lift the pencil after each letter makes printing too slow for work beyond the primary grades. Few people can produce rapid print that is not untidy or illegible.

In the connected print approach, letter forms are taught through some simple motifs on the chalkboard, using methods first learned at Newell C. Kephart's Glen Haven Camp in Colorado (Kephart, 1960). These motifs include Ferry-boats (used to teach smooth pivoting movements across the page) and four motifs that serve as foundations for lower case letters:

1. Waves (foundation for the letters *a, c, d, g, p, q*)
2. Pearls (foundation for the letters *e, i, h, j, m, n, u, y, z*)
3. Wheels (foundation for the letters *b, o, v, w, x*)
4. Arrows (foundation for the letters *f, k, l, r, s, t*)

A motif and its associated letters are first practiced on the chalkboard, and then transition is made to the desk. Details necessary for teaching connected print are contained in a paper titled "Write Right—or Left: A Practical Approach to Handwriting" (Hagin, 1983).

Computers

The most powerful form of assistance for people with writing disabilities is learning to use computers. Computers can be of help with all three aspects of their problems: organizing content, dealing with the mechanics of written English, and the handwriting process. Wanderman has said: "Without a computer, composing and printing are wed. This means that there is no temporal or mechanical separation between recording ideas, working with them to get them right, and printing to save and share them" (Wanderman, 2000, p. 3). The effect is that the writer feels immense pressure to express his entire thought, correctly ordered, and right the first time—or otherwise to endure the pain of writing and rewriting. The computer eliminates this kind of pressure, as well as the frustration of writing by producing perfectly formed letters by hitting a few keys. Wanderman also points out that the computer becomes an extension of memory by "moving ideas from your head onto a medium" that permits you to see them and store them. Moreover, writing on a computer offers flexibility so that one's writing can be stored for later editing and revision. Editing and reorganizing on a computer is easy; it is never necessary to recopy the whole document because of a change. The spelling checks on software programs make spelling and typographical errors much less of a problem. Although they aren't much help in dealing with homonyms, they prevent the blocking of ideas that occurs as the writer tries to select words he can spell and avoid those he cannot.

As the development of computer advances, other ways of getting information recorded appear. Different keyboard arrangements are being developed, such as membrane keyboards and one-handed keyboards. Word prediction software augments spelling and syntax to help the user make choices, find alternative words, complete sentences. Specialized software translates the writer's speech by microphone into text that appears on a screen. The synthetic speech of such programs reads back the writing that has been dictated so that the writer can hear what he has written.

The opportunity that computers present for revising and editing frees the writer from worry about making mistakes and encourages fuller expression and more writing. Structured writing tools like outliners and semantic web programs help writers to work more easily as they develop their ideas for written text. Although the writer is still responsible for the content of what he is trying to say, these tools provide structure for the creative process. Finally, the range of resources available electronically is vast: dictionaries, thesauri, encyclopedias, and the search capabilities on the Internet place information within easy reach of the writer.

MATHEMATICS DISABILITIES

Disabilities in mathematics have not received as much attention from researchers in the field of learning disabilities as disabilities in reading and the language arts. This may be due to the pervasive nature of skills in reading and writing in the school curriculum and the relative independence of mathematics. It may also result from the relatively lower incidence of the problem. Most authorities place the incidence of mathematics disabilities at about 6% (Lerner, 1988; Geary, 2000) with about one-half of these students estimated to have problems with literacy skills as well. This lack of recognition of mathematics disabilities may also result from the failure of some educators to recognize aspects of learning disability that interfere with learning mathematics and to attribute the problems as evidence of carelessness, laziness, and deficient motivation just as reading failure was explained in the past. Because mathematics is not regarded as drawing on verbal abilities, it was not expected that any special instructional provisions in mathematics were needed for students with reading disabilities since their problems were assumed to be confined to verbal academic skills. Actually, these assumptions are unwarranted. Present-day mathematics curricula draw on many abstract verbal skills that youngsters with reading disabilities find difficult. In schools of the past, when students with reading disabilities excelled in mathematics calculation, this skill was probably the result of much practice with computational skills that they and their teachers resorted to because there were few provisions for appropriate work in reading and language available for them. It is clear now that some learning-disabled students have specific disabilities in mathematics and that their teachers need to understand the impact of learning disability on mathematics and to consider the educational management principles described earlier in this chapter.

Types of Problems Encountered

Early signs of delays in development of mathematics skills can appear in preschool and kindergarten years. Difficulties with counting, matching, sorting, and comparing, all observable in the classroom, are signs of possible future difficulties. Avoidance of tasks such as puzzles, blocks, or other manipulatives, failure to learn sequences such as the numerals in counting or in calendar tasks, difficulties in matching accurately the finger pointing to objects being counted and the order of the numerals are all signs for an alert observer. Failure to understand quantitative concepts such as *more, bigger, smaller, nearer, farther, before, after, over, under* are also part of the preacademic language background for quantitative learning. Parents and early childhood educators should be alert for children who differ from their classmates in their abilities to deal with space, form, time, order, and quantity.

Geary (2000) has described three problem areas frequently seen in school-age children with mathematics disabilities.

Semantic Memory Problems

In this group are students who have difficulty retrieving the addition and subtraction combinations, and even when some facts are retrieved, the rate of errors is high. They may also confuse signs in computation, so that they may add when the sign calls for multiplication or subtract when the sign requires addition. Even with simple counting tasks, they sometimes experience trouble in keeping the count in working memory. They also have difficulty with any interruptions in the rote sequences in counting (when working on the addition combinations, they need to start at the beginning with both numbers, rather than using the cardinality principle to start counting with the second number; e.g., in adding the combination 4 + 2, they cannot start with 4 and say 4, 5 to find the sum, but must say 1-2-3-4-5-6). This has been called a problem in working memory that slows down and impairs the learning of basic combinations. In computation, they will also tend to use extraneous cues that show a lack of basic concepts of quantity. For example, in column addition they will count four single points in the numeral four or three single points with three, rather than the abstract quantities represented by these numerals. Because of the cumulative nature of knowledge in mathematics, inadequate mastery of early skills interferes with these students learning more advanced complex processes. The student who is uncertain about early combinations in subtraction will make errors even though he understands the principle of exchanges in borrowing, and the student who is uncertain about times tables will be lost when asked to estimate quotients in long division or to reduce improper fractions or to deal with factoring in algebra.

Procedural Deficits

Some children with mathematics disabilities make adequate progress at the beginning of schooling, but experience difficulties when a series of operations is required. For example, they may appear to be ready for long division. They may have fairly accurate multiplication and subtraction skills and may be able to understand the principle of division well enough to deal with short division. However, these students may be unable to follow the order and sequence of the series of steps required in long division. Both the sequencing of operations and the mathematical insights involved in estimating quotients and comparing remainders will elude them.

These students also have trouble with word problems. Often it is assumed that people with learning disabilities find word problems difficult because they are poor readers. This may explain some errors. However, it is possible to read the words of a problem accurately, but to be unable to translate the relationships described in the problem verbally to a series of mathematical operations. This represents a more challenging instructional problem for both the teacher and the student.

Visuospatial Problems

This group of problems includes errors in dealing with place values in multiplication, division, and decimals; illegible or untidy handwriting that misaligns columns in basic computational processes; misinterpretation of numerals in decimals; inability to deal with spatial relationships in geometry. This content tends to be taught in the middle school and early secondary school grades, although spatial difficulties can also affect a young child's ability to appreciate numbers and to deal with number sets.

These subgroups of difficulties are not mutually exclusive; an individual may experience difficulty with different aspects of mathematics. Because of interrelationships implicit in mathematics, ongoing assessment of the student's status with regard to all of these areas is advisable.

Assessment

Formal assessment of achievement is usually based on a sampling of content in as wide an area as time permits. Because the content domain in mathematics is very broad, the validity of results on any test depends to a large extent on the *match* between the student's past educational experiences and the content of the test. Mathematics skills tend to be specific; furthermore, when not used currently, there is opportunity for decay unless intensive mastery skills have been developed. In contrast, both word attack and comprehension skills in reading tend to be more generally applicable. If one knows how to decode or to comprehend effectively, content does not make much difference provided one is acquainted with the vocabulary being used. Thus, formal achievement tests can provide information about general achievement levels in skill areas such as computation and solving of word problems, but these scores do not give specific cues for instructional planning for the teacher. An examiner can be more helpful to the teacher by offering an appraisal of how the student goes about computation or problem solving. Individual achievement tests, such as the Woodcock-Johnson Achievement

Batteries, can offer richer information than group tests, provided the examiner observes and inquires as the student deals with the items. In addition, careful review of work samples from the child's school (with the child present to explain the tasks) is essential. Finally, ongoing curriculum-based assessment as teaching proceeds is an important source of guidance for assistance to a student with mathematics disabilities.

General Principles for Remedial Assistance

The cumulative nature of content in mathematics requires a broad-scale assessment of strengths and needs. With older students, examiners should evaluate not only the presenting problems, but also determine whether earlier, supporting skills have also been mastered. It is especially important to assess preacademic understanding of space, time, form, order, and quantity with younger children. With older students with problems in algebra, it is important to determine whether the necessary basic arithmetic skills have been mastered.

For students with learning disabilities, verbal concepts usually need to be supported by direct experiences with practical examples, diagrams, manipulatives, models, and field trips. Without concrete, visual, experiential backup, the verbal problem-solving approaches (Etheredge, 2000) may leave these students lost and confused.

Some students with learning disabilities who have had appropriate intervention will begin to demonstrate giftedness in specific areas of mathematics, such as computer programming and accounting. Teachers should be alert for positive signs of strengths and provide encouragement and vocational counseling to enhance what may be signs of emerging career goals.

SUMMARY

Systems of service delivery for students with learning disorders have changed in recent years with larger numbers of them being included in regular education classrooms than in resource rooms or special classes. These changes in the location of instruction do not preclude the need for special provisions for these students, particularly in the skill areas of reading, written language, and mathematics. Instructional provisions for students with learning disabilities need to be considered in relationship to the individual assets and deficits that comprehensive diagnosis has outlined. Without such modifications, traditional classroom methods will not ensure successful learning for these students. Teaching approaches in reading that provide systematic teaching of word-attack skills, enhancement of language development, guided reading comprehension, and practice in application of these strategies as tools for learning in the content subjects are more likely to be successful than more passive teaching approaches that center on student motivation. Written language skills also require directed teaching of (1) organization of ideas, (2) mechanics of written expression, and (3) legible, convenient handwriting. Compared with disabilities in reading and written language, disabilities in mathematics are fewer in number and narrower in their effects on the school curriculum. However, their effects in adult life can be equally disabling. Mathematics disabilities may be apparent in problems with counting, matching, sorting, and solving puzzles even in preschool youngsters. Mathematics disabilities in school-age children center around three areas: semantic memory in counting and computation, procedural deficits in mathematical operations, and visuospatial problems. Assessment in mathematics needs to consider the match between school curriculum and the content domain tapped by formal achievement measures. Ongoing assessment in all skill areas is important not only in charting remedial progress, but in highlighting signs of strengths for emerging career goals.

Chapter 9 ———————————————————————

DRUGS AFFECTING LEARNING AND MEMORY

Memory is the glue that holds together our thoughts, impressions, and experiences. Without it, past and future would lose their meaning and self awareness would be lost as well.

—Hans J. Markowitsch, 2000

In 1973, at a symposium of the biochemical correlates of learning and memory, Nakajima and Essman noted that "the enhancement of intellectual function by drug administration has been one of the most formidable tasks presented to the student of the function of the brain." Despite the significant advances in the use of medication in child psychiatry since that time, there is still no practical way of increasing intelligence by use of drugs.

Medication is of course available for the relief of symptoms that may be associated with some learning disorders. Chapter 13 of this book describes the successful use of stimulant drugs (dextroamphetamine, methylphenidate, and pemoline) in reducing overactive, inattentive, and impulsive behaviors in children with attention deficit disorder, and improving performance in tasks that require sustained attention. Antidepressant medication has been helpful in restoring affective balance in depressive children; anticonvulsive medication has been effective in abating seizure discharges (Chapter 14); and psychotropic medications such as dopamine blockers have helped bring the psychotic child back into this world, and have been able to reduce overactivity of basal ganglia motor disorders. (Chapter 15). Where the symptoms of each of these conditions (ADHD, depression, seizures, Tourette's syndrome) contribute to impairment in learning, relief of the symptoms may free the child to learn. There is no evidence, however, that these drugs have a direct effect on the processes of learning and memory themselves. There is as yet no compelling evidence that medication is effective as a treatment of disorders involving the neural processes that accompany learning and memory (Sarter et al., 1996).

One reason for this is that only within the past two decades are we beginning to understand the molecular events that accompany learning and memory. Although clinical reports of the amnesias and the agnosias have been available for over 100 years, only in the past 20 years have the complex connections and interconnections among neural structures involved in the reception, storage, and retrieval of memory been traced.

THE ANATOMY OF MEMORY

Learning is defined as the process of acquiring new information; memory is the persistence of learning in a state that can be retrieved at a later time. Memory involves a persistent change in the relationship among neurons through biochemical events within neurons that change the way neurons communicate. Learning most often originates as sensory impressions, gathered by peripheral sensory receptors and transmitted via neural pathways to primary areas, specialized for the reception of the particular sensory stimulus, in cerebral cortex. For example, visual stimuli are gathered by the retina and are transmitted via the optic nerve and the optic tract to the lateral geniculate body and from there to the primary occipital visual cortex. Similarly, auditory stimuli are transmitted from the cochlea to the auditory nerve, to the central cochlear nuclei, and then via the acoustic striae and trapezoid body to form the opposite lateral lemniscus that courses through the superior olivary to reach the posterior quadrigeminal and the medial geniculate body. From there, impulses are transmitted to the primary auditory cortex in the superior temporal gyrus. Each primary cortical area reflects a systematic image of the peripheral sensory field, and each small region of the field activates a distinct cluster of neurons in the cortex. But from each primary cortex, impulses are transmitted to secondary and tertiary cortical stations; the visual, for example, to the inferior temporal cortex, the posterior parietal cortex, and the angular gyrus. While individual neurons in the striate cortex respond selectively to a single stimulus presented at a specific location in the visual field, the inferior temporal neurons receive data from large segments of the visual world, suggesting that information is processed at each station, becoming progressively more comprehensive in complexity of the information they admit, until at the final station, a complete representation of the stimuli is synthesized. This progression has been traced for response to visual, auditory, and tactile stimuli. The posterior parietal cortex also has a visual role, receiving impulses from the primary visual cortex, but mediating visuospatial relationships. The role of the posterior parietal cortex in mediating the body image has long been known (Schilder, 1935), but only recently have positron emission studies linked this area to brain activity in tasks related to vision.

The neural circuits involved in memory, however, do not stop at the secondary and tertiary cortical relay stations. Information from patients undergoing brain surgery and from experimental surgical, pharmacological, and behavioral studies (particularly in primates), have indicated that medial temporal structures, diencephalic structures, and prefrontal cortical areas are involved in the transformation of short-term learning to long-term memory. In 1953, a patient, H. M., then a 23-year-old, right-handed man, now classic in the literature of learning and memory, became amnesic as a result of bilateral surgical excision of the medial temporal region to relieve severe epilepsy (Corkin, 1984; Scoville & Milner, 1957). This amnesia had four characteristics: (a) it was global, involving memory from experiences of all senses; (b) it was anterograde;

(c) there was a patchy retrograde amnesia extending for approximately 3 years before surgery, but his early memories were retained clearly and vividly; and (d) there was preservation of perceptual, attentive, language, and motor skills.

H. M. had normal language skills and a good vocabulary; he could perform tasks he had learned before surgery; and his IQ on the WAIS was 118. Yet, when tested 13 years after the surgery, he was virtually unable to recall or to learn any new verbal or visual material. He could manage short-term memory. He could learn material within his short-term memory span, but he could not remember that material. For example, he could retain the digit span of six that he had preoperatively, but he could not increase the length of that span even with repetition. If given a series of 10 words, he could not recall the words at the beginning of the list but could recall only those from the end of the list. He could rehearse and keep material in mind for several minutes, but no longer. "He forgets the episodes of daily life as rapidly as they occur" (Squire, 1987, p. 138). H. M. stated, "Every day is alone in itself, whatever enjoyment I've had, whatever sorrow I've had . . . At this moment everything looks clear to me, but what happened just before? That's what worries me. It's like waking from a dream. I just don't remember" (quoted in Rozin, 1976, p. 6). Magnetic resonance imaging (MRI) (Corkin, Amaral, Gonzalez, Johnson, & Hyman, 1997) revealed that H. M.'s brain damage is confined to the amygdala, para hippocampal-entorhinal cortex, and the anterior hippocampus.

These findings are interpreted to indicate that short-term memory was spared, provided the information does not exceed immediate-memory capacity, but that short-term memory could not be transformed into long-term memory. The medial temporal structures, particularly the hippocampus, are essential for the development of long-term memory. In primates, surgical destruction of both hippocampus and amygdala are needed to produce a global anterograde amnesia (Mishkin, 1982). In humans, Mishkin and Aggleton (1981) suggested that the severity of memory loss may vary in proportion to the amount of damage sustained jointly by the amygdala and the hippocampus.

The hippocampus and amygdala, however, do not function in isolation. Efferent fibers from each course to limbic diencephalic structures, the dorsomedial nucleus of the thalamus and to the mammilary complex. In turn, nuclei from these structures send fibers to limbic structures and then to specialized areas of the cortex. Long-term memory may be interrupted at any of these stages. The hippocampus and the amygdala, the thalamus and the hippothalamus, normally participate in memory storage without being the site of that storage (Markowitsch, 2000).

A case illustrating the role of the dorsomedial nucleus of the thalamus is reported by Squire (1987). The patient, N. A., sustained a penetrating wound of the brain when a fencing foil was accidentally thrust through the right nostril and entered the left forebrain, producing an initial right-sided paresis and a right oculomotor weakness. The paresis subsided and he was left with a mild paresis of upward gaze, a mild diplopia, and a severe memory impairment for verbal and conceptual material. He now has difficulty remembering the events of each day. For example, he forgets what he has just done and whom he has just seen. It is as though his memory is intact up to the time of his accident: his past extends up to that time only. In 1981, 21 years after the accident, his IQ was 124 on the WAIS and he earned superior scores on vocabulary and visuo-motor function. He has an obsessive concern with keeping everything in his house in fixed locations, and his personality is rigid—"single-minded" and inflexible in thought. On examination, CT scan revealed a small lucency in the position of the left dorsomedial nucleus of the thalamus. He has a severe anterograde amnesia. His mother says, "you've got to have a memory to remember."

Clinical and experimental data thus have identified neural stations within the brain in which sensory information is processed from elementary units into global perception of the information and from short-term information to long-term memory. Children with learning disorders may have impairment at any one point of these pathways. In specific developmental reading disability, for example, subgroup studies have identified varied patterns of information-processing deficit. We also stress the importance of temporal organization in the auditory-verbal area and spatial orientation in the visual and body-image area. The problem for these children is not in long-term memory but in the correct perception of their world. The findings of morphological abnormality in the cellular patterns of the temporal lobe in specific developmental reading disability would suggest that the functions normally subsumed by these cortical areas are impaired. These functions relate to decoding information. Our remedy should attempt to correct these basic functions rather than approach remediation at higher levels of memory. On the other hand, children with structural damage of the central nervous system resulting, for example, from hypoxia or from birth trauma may well have, in addition to perceptual impairment, difficulty with higher levels of memory, with long-term memory, and with retention and retrieval of stored information. Brain damage occurring in early development may alter the pattern of relationships among surviving neurons. These children need help over and above the basic perceptual remediation. In children with Attention Deficit/Hyperactivity Disorder (ADHD), who do not have the perceptual distortion of the specific developmental disability, the emphasis in remediation need not be educational but the modulation of poor impulse control and the difficulty with sustaining attention so characteristic of these children.

MOLECULAR MECHANISM(S) OF LEARNING AND MEMORY

Cellular Mechanisms

Although there is general agreement about the anatomy of learning and of long-term memory, the molecular mechanisms of these events are now beginning to be defined. Work on vertebrate systems such as the isolated spinal cord and skeletal muscle of chickens and on higher invertebrates such as *Aplysia* (Kandel & Schwartz, 1982; Kandel et al., 1983), *Hemirssenda* (Farley & Auerbach, 1986), and Drosophila (Dudai, 1985, 1988) identified cellular mechanisms for short-term learning, as in habituation and sensitization, and for longer term memory, as in conditioning.

Hawkins and Kandel (1984) summarized the common features of these findings as follows. Elementary aspects of learning are not diffusely distributed in the brain but can be localized to the activity of specific nerve cells. Learning induces alterations in membrane properties and synaptic connection of these cells. Memory storage lasting days and weeks in the systems studied has not involved formation of new synaptic contacts but results from changes in already existing contacts. These profound and prolonged changes in synaptic strength can be achieved by modulating the amount of chemical transmitter released by presynaptic terminals of the neurons (presynaptic facilitation). Finally, in several instances the molecular mechanisms involve cyclic nucleotide second messengers and modulation of specific ion channels.

In *Aplysia,* sensitization involves activation of facilitator neurons that synapse on the terminals of sensory neurons and use serotonin as the dominant neurotransmitter. Activation of serotonin receptors on the sensory cell initiates a series of biochemical events that phosphorylate a membrane protein, which closes a particular type of K^+ channel, increasing the duration of the action potential and increasing the influx of Ca^{++}, thus permitting an increase in transmitter release. The biochemical cascade involves the activation of an adenylate cyclase in the terminals of the sensory neuron, increasing the level of cyclic adenosine monophosphate (cyclic AMP), which in turn, activates a second enzyme, a cyclic AMP-dependent protein kinase, by combining with its regulatory unit, thus freeing the catylic unit for protein phosphorylation. In turn, the change in protein closes K^+ channels and opens the Ca^{++} channel. Classical conditioning is described as resembling sensitization, in that a response to stimulus in one pathway is enhanced by activity in another, leading to selective enhancement of responses to stimuli (the conditioned stimulus) that are temporarily paired with the unconditioned stimulus. Hawkins and Kandel (1984) stated that the mechanism(s) of learning used by lower forms of animals may be a cell-biological alphabet to be put together by higher forms: "Where individual neurons may possess only a few fundamental types of plasticity that are utilized in all forms of learning, combining the neurons in large numbers with specific synaptic connections . . . may produce the much more subtle and varied processes required for more advanced types of learning" (p. 391). In 2000, Eric Kandel received the Nobel Prize for his work in beginning to understand the molecular mechanism(s) of learning.

Protein Synthesis

While the biological cascade described for *Aplysia* may be a basis for elementary "learning," the relationship between this mechanism and long-term memory still needs to be explored. In long-term memory, terminals of the sensory neurons undergo striking morphological change, increasing the number and size of active zones. It is generally agreed that encoding experiences of short-term memory into long-term memory requires new structural proteins, underlying any permanent changes in synaptic connections and/or in axonal or dendritic morphology. Evidence for a macromolecular change in long-term memory is gathered from three major sources: (a) the plasticity of the neuron responding with structural change to stimulation and to deprivation, (b) the increase in neuronal RNA and the change in base ratio of RNA in cells involved in training, and (c) the interference with long-term memory by inhibitors of RNA and protein synthesis.

Neuron Plasticity

Morphological changes in brains of rats reared in a stimulating environment with toys and interaction with other animals, in contrast to those reared in standard laboratory cages, show an increase in gross cortical weight and thickness, in size of neurons, and, most important, in number and length of dendritic branches and dendritic spines (Turner & Greenough, 1985). The terminals of the dendritic spines also undergo striking morphological changes. The sites on the axon terminals from which neurotransmitter vesicles are released undergo a marked increase in number and sensitivity (Bailey & Kandel, 1995). Conversely, where there is a deprivation of stimulation, there is a decrease in complexity and number of dendrites and dendritic spines (Valverde & Ruiz-Marcos, 1970). Riesen (1970) kept newborn monkeys in the dark for the first 3 to 6 months of their life and found that when they were brought into a normal visual world, they could not discriminate even simple shapes. Direct evidence that sensory deprivation in early life can alter cellular structure of the cerebral cortex was obtained by Hubel and Wiesel (1979). In a series of ingenious experiments, Hubel and Wiesel found that when they deprived a newborn monkey of vision in one eye for 6 months by suturing the eyelids closed, that eye had permanently lost useful vision when the sutures were removed. Electrical recordings from the retina of that eye and from cells of the lateral geniculate body that received projections from the eye were normal. Electrical recordings from the visual cortex corresponding to those projections, however, were not obtained. Further, the cellular architecture of the visual cortex corresponding to the occluded eye was altered, with the size of the ocular dominance columns reduced. There appears to be abundant evidence that stimulation is necessary for function and that stimulation can change the morphology of the cortex, the number and complexity of dendritic connections, the number of sites for neurotransmitter release, and the sensitivity of receptor sites. These changes require new macromolecules.

The development of ultraviolet microspectographic and microelectrophoretic techniques (Hyden & Egyhazi, 1963) to determine the quantity and base percentages of RNA in single neurons dissected from a mammalian brain, contributed to the evidence that macromolecular change accompanies long-term memory. In one of their early experiments, Hyden and Egyhazi (1963) found total RNA to be significantly increased in cells of the vestibular nucleus of rats trained to obtain food by balancing on a 1 meter steel wire set at an angle of 45 degrees. Control animals subject to passive vestibular stimulation without having to learn to balance also showed increased RNA in the vestibular nucleus. Control animals, who did not undergo the learning or the stimulation experience, did not. RNA based composition changes, however, were seen only in the learning group and there only in neuronal and glial nuclei. The finding that RNA was increased during stimulation was confirmed by others (Booth & Sandler, 1967; Zemp, Wilson, Schlesinger, Boggan, & Glassman, 1966). The base composition changes, increases in adenine (35.7% in experimental animals and 21.0% in controls), and decreases in uridine (4.4% in experimental animals and 21.3% in controls), however, seemed to be specific to the learning process. Using a different species (goldfish) and a different paradigm (the fish had to learn to overcome being forced to swim upside down), Shashoua (1968) found the cytosine/uridine ratio doubled because of decreased uridine after the learning experience. These data suggested that in learning, the functional site of the gene is permanently altered, thus directing the formation of new proteins that are theorized to act in altering the excitability characteristics of the neuron.

Neuronal RNA

At about the time the RNA and RNA base composition experiments were reported, a startling series of observations appeared, in which a learned conditioned response in one animal could be transferred to another animal by extracts of the brain of the trained animal. In a series of reports, McConnel (1966) described the transfer of light-shock conditioning to untrained planaria that had cannibalized trained worms or in which was injected a crude RNA extract of the trained worms. These phenomena were repeated in intraperitoneal injection to untrained rats of donor (trained) rat brain homogenates, from animals conditioned in various paradigms (Ungar, 1970, 1971). That RNA was the active ingredient for this transfer was suggested by the inability of planaria to be trained after they had been in a solution of ribonuclease for 10 days. Also, if the synthesis of RNA were blocked with actinomycin, the transfer was unsuccessful. Similarly, ribonuclease injected into the hippocampus of rabbit and rats will inhibit their training in food-gathering. What was surprising in these experiments was not only that training could be transferred by brain homogenates from trained animals, but that the *specific* learned experience could be transferred. By the early 1970s, however, a review of approximately 250 investigations of this phenomenon (Dyal, 1971) found that fully half of them failed to demonstrate the transfer of training. It was suggested that RNA is not the only substance extracted from brains of trained animals: DNA, proteins, peptides, and complex carbohydrates may also be found. These substances themselves may activate the synthesis of RNA in untrained animals. Although a specific peptide effective in transfer experiments was later reported by Ungar, Desiderio, and Parr in 1972, the hypothesis that specific information is encoded in correspondingly specific molecules is not now generally accepted. The death of Ungar in 1977 and the demise of the *Worm Runner's Digest* in 1979 stilled active proponents of the specific molecule for specific training theory. Rejection of the specific encoding hypothesis, however, does not reject the importance of protein synthesis for the formation of long-term memory. As Rosenzweig and Bennett (1984) stated, researchers are "convinced that there is one obligatory process: the formation of long-term memory requires synthesis of proteins" (p. 264).

Protein Synthesis Inhibitors

Evidence that protein synthesis is necessary for long-term memory also stems from studies that use protein synthesis inhibitors. The basic design of these studies, recapitulating the early work of J. B. Flexner, Flexner, and Stellar (1963), involves brief training of the animal; retests done at varying times after training; administrations of a protein synthesis inhibitor at varying times after training; and comparison of test performance of experimental and control animals. It was expected that memory of the training would be retained at the retests. In the early studies in the 1960s and early 1970s, puromycin, a drug that becomes incorporated into the carboxyl ends of growing polypeptides, was used in goldfish (Agranoff, 1981) and in mice (Barondes & Cohen, 1966; L. B. Flexner, Flexner, & Stellar, 1965). The toxic and side effects of this drug, including the induction of abnormal hippocampal EEG's, clouded interpretation of results. Puromycin was soon replaced by cyclohexamine, acetocyclohexamide, actinomycin D, and anisomycin. Antibiotic memory loss of a learned discrimination (Squire & Barondes, 1973), of passive avoidance (H. P. Davis & Squire, 1984), and long-term habituation (Squire & Becker, 1975), all in mice, have been reported. A retention deficit for a motor task, active avoidance learning, and tasks that are interpreted as requiring memory storage are reported in goldfish (Shashoua, 1968). Anisomycin, which blocks protein synthesis at the level of translation, is reported to be markedly less toxic than the other protein-synthesis inhibitors mentioned earlier and can produce 80% inhibition of protein synthesis in the brain for about 2 hours (Bennett, Rosenzweig, & Flood, 1977). Thus it can be repeated at 2-hour intervals and can extend the inhibition to 14 hours.

Using the repeated injection paradigm, it was found, in rodents, that the stronger the training, the longer the inhibition had to be maintained to prevent the formation of memory for a one-trial passive avoidance training (Flood, Bennett, Orme, & Rosenzweig, 1975). The timing of the inhibiting injection relative to the time of training suggested that "under appropriate training conditions, protein necessary for establishing long-term memory can be synthesized within minutes after training" (Bennett et al., 1977). With chicks, the inhibitor can be administered as long as 20 minutes after training and still be amnesic. The conclusion from the time interval studies, is that once a brief critical period is past (and its exact time course may vary with task and species), even prolonged subsequent administration of anisomycin will not prevent formation of memory.

The effect of protein synthesis blockers is that "animals (fish, mice, and chicks) under the influence of a block in brain protein synthesis demonstrated [acquired] the learned behavior as do uninfected controls. On subsequent testing, however, they are partially or totally amnesic" (Agranoff, 1981). Thus protein synthesis selectively blocks the formation of long-term memory or perhaps accelerates the forgetting process. Other protein synthesis inhibitors have also been shown to block retention. Camptothecin, which blocks synthesis of ribosomal RNA; alpha amanitin, which blocks RNA polymerase II; and 5 bromoturberciden, an adenine analog, which blocks mRNA and rRNA—all have amnesic action. There is evidence that protein synthesis inhibition in the entire brain is not a requisite for memory deficit. Small amounts of cyclohexamine injected bilaterally into the hippocampus, amygdala, or striatum of mice after training impaired memory formation, whereas injection into midbrain reticular formation, thalamus, and cortex did not (cited by Agranoff, 1981).

Increasing RNA

There have also been attempts to facilitate memory by increasing the synthesis of RNA. An early report by Cameron and Solyom (1961) that the memory of geriatric patients could be improved by oral administration and by intravenous injection of RNA stimulated the search for improvement of memory by administration of ribonucleic acid. At that time, Cameron was a well-respected figure in psychiatry, director of the

Allen Memorial Institute of Psychiatry and chairman of the Department of Psychiatry at McGill University. The 1961 paper received much attention. Forty-one patients, 19% of them suffering from what was diagnosed as "brain arteriosclerosis," 8% of them as "senile dementia," were orally given slowly dissolving RNA tablets in doses from 3 to 18 grams daily for an average period of 6½ months, for a total mean dose of approximately 1,200 to 1,300 grams. Unfortunately, this group of patients was also given intravenous injections of RNA for a total of approximately 164 grams. The effectiveness of oral RNA alone is not clear. A second sample of 43 patients from a geriatric ward of a provincial mental hospital were divided into medication and placebo groups. The paper is scant in the details we now expect. The authors concluded, however, that RNA has a favorable effect in general on memory retention failure in the aged because it increased alertness, interest, initiative, and confidence. The Cameron and Solyom results could not be confirmed clinically, and results of animal experiments were equivocal. Research using this direct approach has faltered. High doses of brewer's yeast, however, a source of ribonucleic acid, is till a folk remedy to improve impaired memory.

In 1966, Glasky and Simon reported that magnesium pemoline (Cylert) increased the activity of RNA polymerase in vitro and in vivo. This effect could not later be confirmed by H. H. Stein and Yelline (1967) in the same laboratories. Clinically, magnesium pemoline is used in the treatment of ADHD. Its effects parallel those of methylphenidate in improving attention span and in reducing impulsive behavior. It does not improve academic performance unless that performance is impaired by the attention deficit itself. Experimental studies on learning in mice and in the effectiveness of pemoline in attenuating the amnesia produced by electroshock have been equivocal. However, two studies have found pemoline to improve cognitive performance. Conners (1972) found that, in a heterogenous group of 81 children, ages 6 to 12, both pemoline and dextroamphetamine improved spelling, reading, perceptual abilities, and visuomotor function at the end of 8 weeks of treatment. The improvements in cognitive function were later (Connors & Taylor, 1980) found to be modest, although significant, in improving full scale and performance IQs. The consensus in the literature, however, is that pemoline, like methylphenidate, does not appear to have a long-term effect on improving academic performance. This drug, along with methylphenidate and dextroamphetamine, is considered in more detail in Chapter 13. It may well be that pemoline exerts its action through its mildly sympathomimetic activity and not by its action on RNA polymerase at all.

MODULATION OF LEARNING AND MEMORY

The formulation of a memory trace thus appears to involve basic processes in which the stimulus induces molecular transformation as it goes from short-term perception to memory and recall.

Simultaneously with learning, however, there are neurohumeral and hormonal changes that persist into the posttraining period and that may influence learning consolidation and storage: "These agents do not affect the direct process of protein synthesis but may act by facilitating or inhibiting the transmission of neural impulses and circuits involved in processing information leading to memory formation" (Rosenzweig & Bennett, 1984, p. 275). These agents are neurotransmitters and hormones released in the "affective states" (Kety, 1976) that accompany learning, the reaction to the stress of learning, and the homeostatic responses that accompany change. Peripheral hormones (epinephrine and cortisol) peripheral norepinephrine, pituitary hormones (vasopressin and oxytocin), and endogenous opiates and central neurotransmitters (particularly but not exclusively, cholinergic, catacholamine, and GABA transmitters) have been studied as agents modulating learning and memory. Performance may thus be affected by many exogenous and endogenous factors. The concept of modulation denotes that "in addition to the neural system within which the content of memory is preserved, other systems may be involved in the memory process by serving a more trophic function" (M. Gallagher, 1984, p. 368). The concept of modulation does not depend on a single integrating system but on an interrelationship among systems, an "endogenous state dependency" (Izquierdo, 1984). Within this concept, the specific pattern of arousal present in the brain at the time of training may become an integral component of the stored information, "to promote the persistence of those circuits that have led to reward or the relief of discomfort" (Kety, 1976, p. 323). Search for the underlying mechanism(s) of modulation are still in their early stages.

The Acetylcholine Hypothesis

In 1954, Krech, Rosenzweig, and Krueckel at the University of California at Berkley reported the cholinesterase activity of the visual cortex of the rat to be 20% lower than that of either the somatosensory or the motor cortex. They questioned whether a high concentration of cholinesterase in sensory areas makes for a generally more adaptive (more intelligent) animal and whether a high concentration of cholinesterase in specific areas of the brain had relevance for the mode of adaptation the animal used. In a series of investigations with rats solving spatial and visual mazes, they concluded that learning capacity is related to levels of acetylcholine and of cholinesterase, so that within limits, the greater the amount of functioning acetylcholine at the synapse, the greater the efficiency of transmission and consequently the greater the learning ability (Krech, Rosenzweig, & Bennett, 1960). While this conclusion has proven to be an oversimplification of the effect of cholinergic activity on learning, two major lines of evidence have implicated acetylcholine as having, at least, a modulating role in learning and memory. The first is finding in repeated studies in mice, dogs, and human volunteers that, in general, drugs that increase acetylcholine levels in the brain (choline, arecoline, physostigmine, and diisopropylphosphofluoridate) increase retention of learned responses, whereas drugs that block acetylcholine receptor activity (atropine and scopolomine) decrease retention. These generalities may be modified by such variables as drug dose (where low doses of cholinergic drugs may potentiate and high doses may inhibit retention learning), relationship of time of administration of the drug to the time of training and testing, the type of training task, the method of drug administration, and the subject animal used. For example, the specific effect of physostigmine may facilitate or impair learning, depending on how long after training the drug is administered (Squire, 1987). Cholinergic drugs, said Squire "are the only ones [studied] that have been reported to have opposite effects, either facilitating or impairing, depending simply how long after training the drug is administered" (p. 47). That these effects are central rather than peripheral is suggested by a report of Drachman and Leavitt (1974), who compared the effect of scopolomine, which crosses the blood-brain barrier (1 mg subcutaneously), with that of methscopolomine, which mimics only the peripheral effects of scopolomine, and with physostigmine, which does cross the blood-brain barrier. The subjects were 20 men (volunteers, ages 19 to 25) and 20 controls; the test was that of immediate memory (digit span), storage, and recall (free recall of lists of words, and then writing lists of remembered words). While no difference among groups was found in immediate memory, the scopolomine-treated subjects were significantly impaired in measures of word storage and recall, whereas the methscopolomine subjects showed no more impairment than the controls. When the subjects were given a small dose (1 mg) of physostigmine, they performed equal to or slightly better than controls but were definitely impaired when a higher dose of 2 mg was used. Of interest in the improvement in memory related task performance in rats and in aged monkeys with low doses of mecamylamine (a ganglimic blocker) whereas higher doses impaired the same memory related tasks (Terry, Buccafusco, & Pendergast, 1999).

The second line of evidence implicating the cholinergic system relates to the anatomical and chemical findings in Alzheimer's disease, where profound and selective degeneration was found in cholinergic neurons of the nucleus basalis of Meynert (Whitehouse et al., 1982). Similarly, a 60% to 90% loss of choline acetyl transferase activity was found in the areas receiving the cholinergic projections from the nucleus basalis, namely the hippocampus, neocortex, and entorhinal cortex. While there is evidence that other transmitters systems (loss of noradrenergic cells in the locus ceruleus, loss of serotonogenic cells in the raphe nuclei) are linked to Alzheimer's disease, the importance of the cholinergic system in the dementia of Alzheimer's disease appears undisputed. Attempts to improve memory in Alzheimer's disease by use of acetylcholine precursors such as choline and lecithin (a source of choline) and by acetylcholine agonists, however have not been successful (Jorm, 1986). One study however (Summers, Majovski, Marsh, Tachiki, & Kling, 1986), reported that tetrahydroaminoacridine (THA), a potent cholinesterase inhibitor that penetrates the blood-brain barrier and has a high margin of safety, improved the cognitive function of 17 patients (mean age 71) with moderately severe Alzheimer's disease. The drug was given in doses up to 20 mg/day along with 900 to 1200 mg of lecithin for 4 to 6 weeks. Unfortunately, the effect lasted only for 8 to 10 hours after each dose and the drug did not affect the course of the disease. THA has been known since 1907, about the time Alzheimer described the disease that bears his name. The Summers et al. study has been criticized for its methodological faults (Crook, 1988). On the other hand, in the memory impairments that may accompany the use of anticholinergic drugs when given to patients on neuroleptic regimes, discontinuation of the anticholinergic drug has yielded improved performance on the Wechsler Memory Scale (Fayen, Goldman, Moulthop, & Luchins, 1988).

Acetylcholinesterase inhibitors have been clinically introduced as cognition enhancing agents in the treatment of mild to moderate Alzheimer's disease (Cummins,

2001; Emilien, Beyreuther, Masters, & Maloteaux, 2000; Mayeux & Sano, 1999). The cholinesterase inhibitors, tacrine (Cognex), donepezil (Aricept) and rivastigmine (Exelon) are currently in use for cognitive impairment and during the past 2 to 5 years have undergone extensive clinical and carefully controlled trials. Although the clinical utility of these drugs is still being debated, the general consensus is that they are useful in slowing the progression of the dementia and may also be useful in the amelioration of behavioral symptoms. Their clinical use is modified by side effects, particularly the cholinergic gastrointestinal symptoms induced by the butylcholinesterase activity of tacrine and rivastigmine. Nevertheless these new drugs may be heralding a new era in the pharmacological management of Alzheimer's disease. A more cautious viewpoint is expressed by Pryse-Phillips (1999) "Such manipulations undoubtedly can alter cognition, but neither enough or for long enough." Thus the cholinergic system is implicated in learning and in memory. Just what that role may be is still unclear. The cholinergic system may function as a modulator, or it may be important because of its synapses in those areas of the brain (the hippocampus, amygdala, and cortex) that are important in memory. A diametrically opposite approach to memory has been described by Terry, Buccafusco, and Pendergast (1999) who found that the ganglimic blocker, mecamylamine improved memory related task performance in aged monkeys. This effect was dose-specific, responding to very low doses of mecamylamine (0.03 to 0.1 mgm/kilo) but impairing memory when high doses were given.

An attempt has recently been made to ameliorate the course of cholinergic nerve atrophy by using a nerve growth factor. This experiment was done in aged rats and has no clinical relevance as yet (W. Fischer et al., 1987).

The Norepinephrine System

The norepinephrine system is involved in modulation of memory, as the following four facts show:

1. *Posttraining treatments alter norepinephrine function and thus retention of recent learning.* Sympathomimetic drugs such as amphetamine or metaraminol can attenuate the memory impairments produced by antibiotics (A. J. Dunn, 1980). Conversely, peripherally administered adrenergic receptor antagonists will enhance the memory impairments induced by antibiotics and will render ineffective other drugs, such as vasopressin, which attenuate such antibiotic-induced impairment. The destruction of norepinephrine projections from the locus ceruleus by 6-hydroxydopamine will also intensify memory impairment induced by antibiotics. The effects of norepinephrine on memory are related to dosage: There is an optimal level for maximum effect; above or below that level the effect is decreased along the familiar inverted U curve fashion.

2. *Norepinephrine may serve to enhance neuronal communication in which the primary information is carried by other transmitters.* For example, when norepinephrine is applied iontophoretically to a neuron (Waterhouse, Moises, & Woodward, 1980), the responses of the cell to other imputs, excitatory or inhibitory,

are often enhanced. The probability of lateral geniculate cells firing in response to electrical stimulation of the optic nerve is increased by application of norepinephrine to the recording site (Rogawski & Aghajanian, 1980). Long-term potentiation of lateral geniculate cell firing may be enhanced by peripheral injection of amphetamine or epinephrine (Delanoy, Tucci, & Gold, 1983). Norepinephrine has also been found to affect long-term potentiation in the hippocampus (Goddard, Bliss, Robertson, & Sutherland, 1980). These findings suggest that the threshold necessary to establish long-term memory may be reduced by adrenergic agonists and raised by adrenergic antagonists. Gold (1984) stated that the effect of norepinephrine on long-term memory appears to be mediated by peripheral alpha-2 receptors.

3. *Central norepinephrine may interact with endogenous opioids to affect memory.* There is a depth of experimental evidence to indicate that memory in rodents, as assessed in a variety of training tasks, is modulated by posttraining treatments affecting opiod receptors. Retention is generally impaired by posttraining administration of opiate receptor agonists (such as morphine and beta-endorphine) and enhanced by opiate receptor antagonists (such as naloxone and naltrexone; McGaugh, Introini-Collison, & Nagahara, 1988). These effects appear to be central, since retention is not affected by posttraining intraperitoneal naltrexonemethylbromide, which does not readily pass the blood-brain barrier. Propranolol will block the enhancing effect on naloxone in memory (Izquierdo & Graudenz, 1980). This finding suggests that since opioid peptides inhibit norepinephrine release, opioid antagonists such as naloxone may enhance memory retention by releasing norepinephrine from the inhibitory effect of opioid peptides. McGaugh et al. (1988) reported that the anatomical site for such interaction to enhance memory lies in the amygdala. Propranolol blocked the memory-enhancing effect of naloxone when it was injected into the amygdala but not when it was injected into the caudate or into the cortex dorsal to the amygdala. That both beta-1 and beta-2 receptors may be involved is seen in the blocking of the naloxone effect on memory by the beta-1 adenoreceptor blocker, atenolol, and by the beta-2 blocker, zinterol. Conversely, the posttraining intraamygdala administration of the alpha-1 antagonist, prazosin, or the alpha-2 antagonist, yohimbine, did not attenuate the memory-enhancing effects of systemically administered naloxone.

4. *Central norepinephrine appears to mediate the influence of hypophyseal peptides on the process of memory consolidation.* In 1965, DeWied found that removal of the posterior and intermediate lobes of the pituitary in rats interfered with the maintenance of shuttle-box avoidance behavior. This behavior could be reversed by injection of pitressin or by purified vasopressin. In intact animals, a single injection of vasopressin, administered during the acquisition or the extinction period of shuttle-box avoidance behavior, resulted in a long-term, dose-dependent, inhibitory effect on the extinction of that behavior; that is, memory persisted. This effect persisted beyond the actual presence of the peptide in the body (DeWied, 1971, 1976). There appeared to be an association between

concentration of vasopressin released during critical periods of avoidance learning and retention and memory consolidation. The memory effect of vasopressin was dissociated from its peripheral endocrine effects. Subsequent studies revealed that vasopressin and related peptides could prevent or reverse the amnesia for a passive avoidance response in rats induced by CO_2, by electroshock, or by pentylenetetrazol. Vasopressin could also reverse the puromycin-induced amnesia for a maze-learning task in mice. Oxytocin appears to have an effect on memory opposite to that of vasopressin. With both vasopressin and oxytocin, the familiar inverted U shape, dose related, curve on memory, was found. Systemic or intracerebroventricularly administered vasopressin will enhance norepinephrine turnover in the hypothalamus, thalamus, and medulla. Conversely, destruction of the cerullotelencephalic norepinephrine pathway by 6-hydroxydopamine prevents the facilitory effect of vasopressin, if the vasopressin is injected immediately after the learning trial but not if injected prior to the retention test. Intracerebral vasopressin affects other transmitter systems, facilitating dopamine turnover and decreasing serotonin concentration in the mesencephalon and the septum but not in the hippocampus, hypothalamus, or striatum (DeWied, 1984).

Evidence from these four sources thus appears to implicate the adrenergic systems, at least in the modulation of processes involved in learning and memory, influencing them either directly or indirectly through the effect of endogenous opioids and of hormones of the posterior pituitary.

From this evidence, it is to be expected that drugs which stimulate the release of norepinephrine would facilitate learning and memory and that those which block its action would impede learning and memory. There are reports that beta-blockers do indeed impair short-term verbal memory in nonpsychiatric hypertensive patients (Solomon et al., 1983). As with other drugs used for specific indications in psychiatric patients, however, if the specific symptom is inhibiting learning, the overall effect of the drug may actually enhance the ability of the child to focus attention on learning. Propranolol, although in itself an inhibitor of learning, may so relieve anxiety and impulsivity that the net effect is improvement in attention and behavior. There is no conclusive evidence, however, that beta-blockers or the widely used adrenergic drugs directly affect the biological cascade involved in learning or the transformation of macromolecules needed for memory consolidation.

The adrenergic agonist, methylphenidate, pemoline, and dextroamphetamine, are discussed at length in Chapter 13. Dextroamphetamine is an indirectly acting sympathomimatic, releasing biogenic amines from storage sites in the nerve terminal. The dextroisomer is three to four times more potent than the levo. Dextroamphetamine significantly counteracts the amnestic effects of anisomycin even when given as late as 90 minutes posttraining. By that time, consolidation of learning into long-term memory is probably over. Interestingly in rodents, amphetamine will do so when injected intraperitoneally. That its effect may be mediated peripherally is seen in using 4-hydroxyamphetamine, which, although it does not penetrate the blood-brain barrier, mimics the d-amphetamine effect on retention of memory in anisomycin-treated animals.

Clinically, the effect of dextroamphetamine in normal children was studied by Rapoport, Buchsbaum, et al. (1978). In 14 normal prepubertal boys of normal IQ, with no learning problems and without attention deficit disorders, the administration of a single dose (0.5 mg/kg, mean dose approximately 16 mg/day) of dextroamphetamine resulted in decreased motor activity, generally improved attention with faster reaction time, improved immediate recall, and improved vigilance. However, a marked behavioral rebound, consisting of excitability and talkativeness, occurred in about 5 hours. These boys were included in another study (Rapoport et al., 1980), which also involved hyperactive boys and young adult college men and the administration of a single dose of dextroamphetamine or a placebo. The college sample was divided into low- and high-dose d-amphetamine. All four groups responded to the drug with decreased motor activity, the hyperactivity boys most of all, a trend to increase scores on a verbal learning test, and a tendency to increase verbal output. Both groups of the prepubertal boys reported "feeling funny." The adults had the feeling of increased energy and decreased fatigue. The effects of amphetamine may result from its cortical and possibly reticular-activating system stimulation. In doses of amphetamine higher than 30 mg/day, dopamine is released from nerve terminals; in still higher doses, serotonin is released. Disturbances in gait and perception and in the development of tremor and stereotype behavior may result (Solanto, 1998).

Methylphenidate and magnesium pemoline also have adrenergic effects, blocking the reuptake of catecholamines from the synaptic cleft by the presynaptic nerve terminals. The blocking effect, however, is not on norepinephrine alone, but it is nonselective, also influencing the reuptake of dopamine. The effectiveness of dextroamphetamine, methylphenidate, and pemoline in modulating impulsivity and in enhancing attention, as well as their lack of effect in enhancing learning, memory and academic achievement, is documented in Chapter 13. While there are dissenting opinions, our general conclusion is that these drugs are not recommended for improving learning or academic achievement in children with specific language disability. The drugs do have their use in children with ADHD whose learning disorder is the result of their impulsivity. Methylphenidate is not effective in behavior, attention, memory, or processing speed in children with head injury (Plenger et al., 1996; Speech, Rao, Osmon, & Sperry, 1993; S. E. Williams, Ris, Ayyangar, Shefft, & Berch, 1998); in HIV-infected children (Van Dyck et al., 1997); or in children with anxiety in association with ADHD (Tannock, Ickowicz, & Schachar, 1995). At high doses, methylphenidate slowed performance on the most difficult high load conditions (Berman, Douglas, & Barr, 1999).

Clonidine, an alpha-2 agonist, is having increasing use in child psychiatry with reports of its effects on ADHD and in Tourette's syndrome. Studies on the effect of clonidine on learning and memory are scant. In a case report (G. Fein, Merrin, Davenport, & Buffreon, 1987), a depressed 74-year-old diabetic man is said to have had "significant" short-term memory loss on 0.1 mg of clonidine b.i.d., with low scores on immediate recall and in recall after a 5-minute delay, on an object memory test. No deficits were found in adolescents (Falkner, Koffler, & Lowenthal, 1984), while facilitative effects of clonidine on cognition of primates are reported (Arnsten & Goldman-Rakic, 1985). There is one clinical study reporting improvement in memory of patients with Korsakoff's syndrome (McEntee & Nair, 1980). At this writing, the effects of clonidine on academic achievement are unknown.

Guanfacine, which like clonidine, is an alpha-2 agonist, has less sedative effect than clonidine, but in doses of 29 micrograms/kg, is reported to improve planning and spatial memory (Jakala, Riekkinen, Sirvio, Koivisto, & Riekkinen, 1999).

Tricyclic Antidepressants and Learning

Like the adrenergic stimulant drugs, the tricyclic antidepressants have been effectively used in modulating the activity and attention of children with ADHD. Like those drugs, too, they block the reuptake of norepinephrine from the synaptic cleft. However, they also block the uptake of dopamine and serotonin. The potency and selectivity of the tricyclics for inhibition of neuronal uptake varies, with desipramine a most potent blocker of norepinephrine uptake but less potent for serotonin; clomipramine and fluoxetine are potent and selective blockers of serotonin uptake. In addition, tricyclic and the newer antidepressants have anticholinergic properties, blocking muscarinic cholinergics with a potency of $\frac{1}{20}$ to $\frac{1}{80}$ that of atropine in inhibiting the effect of acetylcholine on guinea pig ilium. In practice, this effect is not considerable since the therapeutic doses of tricyclics are higher than the effective doses of atropine. In theory, then, the tendency of anticholinergics to inhibit learning conflicts with the tendency for adrenergic drugs to facilitate learning. Of the tricyclics, desipramine is least potent in its anticholinergic activity; while amitryptyline, with its strong anticholinergic activity, impaired short-term memory in adult nondepressed volunteers (Liljequist, Linnoila, & Mattila, 1974; Mattila, Liljequist, & Seppela, 1978).

In children, while imipramine and desipramine appear to be effective in modulating impulsive behavior (see Chapter 13) there is little effect on cognitive performance (Rapoport, 1965; Waizer, Hoffman, Polizos, & Englehardt, 1974; Werry, Aman, & Diamond, 1980). Rapoport found no improvement in cognition in tests of 29 hyperactive boys given imipramine in a mean daily dose of 80 mg/day for 6 weeks; Waizer et al. found a statistically significant impairment in recalling digits forward in 19 hyperactive boys receiving imipramine in a mean dose of 174 mg/day; Werry et al. administering imipramine in a dose of 1 to 2 mg/kilo/day for 3 weeks to hyperactive children found improvement on a continuous performance test. In short, the effect of imipramine in cognition in hyperactive boys paralleled those seen with the stimulant drugs.

It is said (Quinn & Rapoport, 1975) that no adverse effect on long-term use of imipramine in a mean dose of 65 mg/day was found in cognitive or intellectual functioning. The long-term effect of the drug on receptor sensitivity should be considered, however. Long-term use, and just how long long-term is, is not clear, may result in desensitization of presynaptic alpha-2 adrenergic receptors, increased neuronal responsiveness to alpha-1 adrenergic agonists and to serotonin, and decreased numbers of serotonin receptors and beta adrenergic binding sites (Gilman, Goodman, Rall, &

Murad, 1985). Certainly enhancement of learning and memory, and improvement of academic learning, is no indication for use of tricyclics.

A review of the newer antidepressants, the selective serotonin reuptake inhibitors (SSRI), including fluoxetine, sertraline, paroxetine, fluvoxamine, and citalopram, are becoming the treatment of choice for mood disorders, obsessive-compulsive disorders, and eating disorders, with good efficacy and safety. They have side effects including gastrointestinal symptoms, headache, sedation, weight gain, paresthesias, and impaired memory (Masand & Gupta, 1999). As of this writing there have been few double-blind controlled studies on the effects of these drugs on learning and memory. A single patient report of a 14-year-old male treated with fluoxetine for depression indicated impairment on all five scales of the Wechsler Memory Scale-revised (Bangs, Petti, & Janus, 1994).

Caffeine and Theophylline

Among the stimulant drugs that are said to increase vigilance, caffeine, a methylxanthine, mediates its effects by presynaptic release of norepinephrine. It may elevate cyclic adenosine monophosphate by inhibition of phophodiesterase. Parents will frequently ask about the effects of coffee and cola drinks on activity level and on learning. A series of 10 studies, reviewed by Elkins et al. (1981) revealed little or no benefit on the vigilance and behavior of "hyperkinetic" children when caffeine was given in a daily dose of 3 to 12 mg/kilo. Elkins et al. studied the effect of a single dose of high (10 mg/kilo) and low (3 mg/kilo) doses of caffeine on the mood, activity, evoked potential, reaction time, memory, and sustained attention in 19 "normal," prepubertal boys whose mean age was 10 years, 6 months. There was significant increase in vigilance on the high dose of caffeine measured by both a decrease median reaction time and a decrease in omission errors on the Continuous Performance Test. However, there was an increase in commission errors in that test, suggesting that although vigilance was enhanced with the single high caffeine dose, impulsivity was not modulated, total motor activity increased significantly, and recall scores in the memory test worsened. The low dose of caffeine, approximately a moderate to heavy daily caffeine intake, had minimal or no behavioral effects.

The adverse effect on school performance by theophylline in therapeutic doses was cited by Rachelesky et al. (1986). After review of the data in the literature on theophylline and learning, the Pulmonary-Allergy drugs Advisory Committee of the Food and Drug Administration (FDA) concluded that present data do not support the adverse effect of theophylline on the academic performance of schoolchildren. However, the FDA (1988) concluded that further well-controlled studies are needed. A subsequent report found no adverse effect of theophylline (Theo-Dur tablets, 14 to 16 mg/kilo/day) on 27 measures of performance, behavior, and attention in 17 children receiving the drug in a crossover design (Rapoport et al., 1989).

The Dopamine System

While this section has so far emphasized the role of the acetylcholine, the serotonin system and the adrenergic system in learning and memory, there is evidence to indicate a crucial role for the dopamine system in the learning and memory of spatial discrimination in rats and primates. Injection of 6-hydroxydopamine injected bilaterally into the lateral septum of rats induced selective depletion of dopamine concentrations in the septum without damaging noradrenergic or cholinergic cell bodies. This injection into the lateral septum interfered with spatial memory in rats (Simon, Taghzouti, & LeMoal, 1986). Iontophoretically applied dopamine into prefrontal cortex of primates enchanced a task involving spatial short-term memory. Fluphenazine and haloperidol attenuated the learning of spatial short-term memory, whereas sulpride had no effect (Sawaguchi, Matsumura, & Kuboto, 1988). Neonatal dopamine in rats depleted at 3 and 6 days of age with intraventricular 6-hydroxydopamine, resulted in deficits in tasks requiring spatial alteration behavior and in a significant impairment in the ability to use spatial cues during ontogony (Feeser & Raskin, 1987).

Dopamine Blockers

These findings raise the question of the effect of frequently used dopamine blockers on learning and memory. Phenothiazines and butyrophenones have a direct effect on learning and memory by the sedative effect of these drugs, by their anticholinergic action, and by the various clinical conditions for which the drugs are prescribed. In general, neuroleptic drugs selectively inhibit the learning of conditioned avoidance behaviors in animals: motor responses are fewer, slower, and smaller and vigilance of human subjects on tapping-speed tests is impaired. On the other hand, neuroleptic drugs do significantly impair function on digit-symbol tests. In adults, in normal volunteers, and in schizophrenic patients, no significant effects on short-term memory as measured by immediate recall of word lists, random numbers, and visual designs were found. Also the ability of schizophrenic patients, hospitalized for the long term, to recall recent, mid-past, and distant events was not impaired with chlorpromazine in doses of 25 to 900 mg/day. What was related to impaired memory, however, was the serum anticholinergic level induced by low-potency neuroleptics and not by the serum level of the neuroleptic drug itself.

In children, neuroleptic medication has been used in management of symptoms of hyperactivity, aggression, heterogeneous conduct disorders, Tourette's syndrome, schizophrenia, autism, and mental retardation. The major concern in studies investigating these populations was on the target symptoms and not on learning and memory at all. For example, a 1966 placebo-controlled, double-blind clinical trial of chlorpromazine in hyperactive children of normal intelligence with a mean age of 8 years 5 months was done by Werry, Weiss, Douglas, and Martin, with the focus on hyperactivity and attention. On a mean daily dose of 106 mg of chlorpromazine, hyperactivity and attention were improved; but at the end of 8 weeks of treatment, cognition, as seen in the comprehension subtest of the WISC and on the Bender-VMGT, was depressed. Psychomotor activity was slowed in a group of 12 aggressive, hospitalized patients ages 7 years 8 months to 12 years 10 months, receiving 3 mg/day of haloperidol. On the other hand, haloperidol in doses of 0.05 mg/kg/day for 6 months did not adversely affect a battery of tests measuring scholastic achievement and intellectual function (Wong & Cook, 1971). Werry, Aman, and Lampen (1975) found that the adverse effects of haloperidol on measures of cognitive function in hyperactive, aggressive children, was largely a function of the dose of the drug; low doses (0.025 mg/kg/day) reduced the number of false responses in a continuous performance test. Compared with the placebo and with methylphenidate, high doses (0.05 mg/kg/day) of the drug impaired performance on both a continuous performance test and a short-term memory test. On an even higher dose (mean 0.096 mg/kg/day) of haloperidol given to hospitalized children diagnosed as having conduct disorders, there were no significant effects on a matching familiar figure test, short-term recognition memory, or the Stroop test. Thus in the hyperactive children of normal intelligence and in disturbed aggressive children, haloperidol, in doses that increase target symptoms, may also depress some aspects of cognition.

Since the time Fish, Campbell, and Shapiro (1970) found that chlorpromazine in autistic children was sedating in doses that had little effect on symptoms, attention has focused on the use of an alternate drug, haloperidol, in this group. Two reports coming from the New York University laboratories are relevant to learning and memory. In the first (Campbell, Anderson, Small, et al., 1982), the effect of haloperidol in doses of 0.5 to 4.0 mg/day was compared with a behavioral intervention focusing on language acquisition, and on the results of a combination of both treatments (drug plus behavioral intervention) in a group of 40 autistic children aged 2 years 6 months to 7 years 2 months, hospitalized in Bellevue Psychiatric Hospital. While haloperidol alone was effective in decreasing stereotypes and withdrawal, the combination of the drug and contingent reinforcement facilitated language acquisition in the 12-week study. There was no effect on cognition as measured by cognitive battery. The most common untoward effect was sedation, which was a function of dosage. In reviewing this detailed paper, contingent reinforcement schedules aided in enhancing language, even in the placebo-treated children. The differences between the haloperidol and the placebo groups and the effectiveness of language training in enhancing language were not statistically significant. The haloperidol-contingency reinforcement group, however, showed an acceleration in language acquisition in the second half of the project, and it is this acceleration that turned the tide. It must be mentioned, however, that language acquisition was still primitive, consisting of shaping of immature speech by successive approximation. The paper does not tell us how many children mastered that skill, going on to identification of objects, two-word chains, concepts, responsive speech, and predictive identification. The overall rates of learning (number of words mastered/the numbers of sessions) were 1.61 for the haloperidol-contingency reinforcement group, 0.77 for the placebo-contingency group, 0.46 for the haloperidol noncontingency group, and 0.32 for the placebo-noncontingency group. Details of the language acquired are not given.

In the second study (L. T. Anderson et al., 1984; Campbell, Anderson, Cohen, et al., 1982), the question of whether haloperidol facilitates learning because of improved attention was addressed. In this study, 40 children (29 boys, 11 girls) ranging in age from 2 years 3 months through 6 years 9 months, mildly to profoundly retarded, were given haloperidol or a matching placebo tablet in a double-blind crossover design, in doses individually regulated to yield optimal behavioral response with minimal sedation. The effect on learning of discrimination tasks was determined in a structured environment, in an automated operant conditioning paradigm in which correct responses to discrimination tasks were automatically rewarded with an M&M candy. The discrimination tasks were visual, flashed on the computer screen. Behavior such as hyperactivity was also automatically recorded in the structured environment by means of pressure-sensitive switches mounted every 6 inches under an indoor-outdoor carpet. The experimental design divided children into two groups: The first received haloperidol for 4 weeks, placebo for 4 weeks, haloperidol for 4 weeks; the second received placebo-haloperidol-placebo. Each treatment condition consisted of 10 learning sessions. The percentage of correct responses for each child and the mean across treatment groups and treatment periods was plotted. Learning tended to improve within each set of 10 sessions, more so in the first two sets. This improvement was seen in both the haloperidol group and the placebo group; however, an effect in favor of the haloperidol group was seen in the first 4 weeks (first 10 learning sessions) of the study. Also in that same treatment period (group I haloperidol, group II placebo), 71% of the children receiving haloperidol achieved a performance score higher than an arbitrary determined cutoff score on the discrimination tasks in contrast to 39% of the placebo group. Only two variables, verbal developmental quotient and drug, significantly accounted for performance in discrimination learning. Hyperactivity and stereotype did not appear to affect such performance adversely, suggesting that "the effect of the drug on learning was not a function of its [effect on] decreasing maladaptive behaviors, but was possibly a function of its more directly affecting attentional mechanisms" (L. T. Anderson et al., 1984, p. 1200). It is still not clear, however, what the biochemical mechanism of haloperidol-induced enhancement of discrimination learning in these autistic children might be. Certainly the work of the New York University investigators needs confirmation. At this writing, therefore, the use of dopamine antagonist is not recommended for treatment of specific language disabilities nor for enhancement of learning populations other than in autistic children, and even in autistic children the effect of dopamine antagonist on learning is equivocal.

Among the newer neuroleptics (risperidone, clozapine, olanzapine), a potential side effect, just as with the older neuroleptics, is cognitive impairment, which does not appear to be a function of the drowsiness that these drugs induce. In these drugs, just as with the SSRIs, studies on their effects on learning disabilities are scant, possibly because their use in children is limited to comorbid disorders that may accompany the learning disorders (ADHD, Tourette's Disorder) and not to the learning problem itself. There have been studies in schizophrenia however, where there is an interest in the neurocognitive effects of these drugs. Kern et al. (1999), for example, found that risperidone-treated patients, showed greater improvement than haloperidol-treated patients, in general verbal ability. McGurk (1999) in his review of 12 studies of clozapine, olanzapine, and risperidone for their effects on cognition in schizophrenia found that clozapine improves attention and verbal fluency but its effects on working memory and spatial memory were inconclusive; risperidone has positive effects on working memory, executive function and attention, while improvement in verbal learning and memory was inconsistent. Olanzapine improves verbal learning and memory, verbal fluency, and executive function but not attention, working memory, or visual learning and memory. Thus these drugs appear to produce differences in specific cognitive functions. These data need confirmation and the mechanism for these differences needs elucidation. For children with learning disabilities these findings have no direct application, except as possible relevance in their application to comorbid disorders.

Glutamic Acid, Glycine, and the GABA System

There have been numerous attempts at enhancement of learning with drugs that modify the availability of gamma-amino-buteric acid (GABA) in the central nervous system. Basing their work on the fact that 1-glutamic acid is oxidized in vitro by the brain (Weil-Malharde, 1936), F. T. Zimmerman and Ross (1944) suggested that feeding 1-glutamic acid might enhance intelligence. Indeed feeding 1-glutamic acid to rats for 2 weeks facilitated maze learning in these rats. Clinical application of this study followed. F. T. Zimmerman, Burgemeister, and Putman (1947) reported that the intelligence quotients of retarded and epileptic children were enhanced by feeding them 1-glutamic acid for 6 months, but this work was not subsequently confirmed. By 1966, Austin and Ross had reviewed 33 studies on the effect of glutamic acid on intelligence in humans; only 6 of these were controlled studies of children with mental retardation; 14 used no control group at all. In general, the studies were criticized for lack of adequate control groups, the neglect of double-blind methodology using placebo controls, and the difficulty in controlling for effects of environmental stimulation. Practically, also, the task of ingesting the recommended dose of bulky 1-glutamic acid (6 gram/day) for long periods of time, with its attendant gastric irritation, created problems in compliance. The use of glutamic acid to increase intelligence has fallen into disuse.

Nootropic Drugs

Within the past 10 years, a group of drugs has been said to enhance learning and memory in children with specific reading disability (developmental dyslexia). This group has been classified by Giurgea (1978) as "nootropic" drugs (from the Greek, *noos* = mind, *tropein* = toward) as drugs acting on the central nervous system, acting "directly on higher, integrative brain mechanisms by enhancing their efficiency, thereby resulting in a positive, direct, impact on mental, noetic, function" (Giurgea, 1978, p. 67). Thus the nootropic drug is said to:

- Facilitate learning acquisition.
- Reduce the adverse effects on memory of such factors as electroshock and cerebral hypoxia.
- Enhance transcallosal transfer of information.

In addition, these drugs do not cause sedation or affect the autonomic nervous system, and they have minimal toxicity. The nootropic drugs are claimed to have possible specific effects on the left-hemisphere language function, including vigilance, coding, short-term verbal memory, naming, and verbal learning (Dimond & Brouwers, 1976) but not on spatial ability of children with developmental dyslexia. Piracetam, the first drug if this class, chemically 2-pyrrolidine acetamine, is chemically related to gamma-amino-buteric acid. It is reported to be an activator of brain adenylate cyclase, and it is reported to enhance cerebral perfusion in dogs with induced cardiovascular insufficiency. An analog of piracetam, oxiracetam has been synthesized.

Two major studies of the effect of piracetam on the learning of children with specific reading disability have been reported. The first, a 12-week multicentered double-blind trial, involved six centers and 257 boys with dyslexia defined as a "specific written language difficulty." The subjects were otherwise normal, with average or above IQ; good school, social, and language opportunities; no visual or auditory acuity problems; and no neurological or psychiatric disturbances. Piracetam is reported to have increased their reading fluency (speed of reading) without sacrificing accuracy. In children with poor short-term memory, piracetam increased their digit span score but did not improve reading comprehension (DiLanni et al., 1985). Encouraged by this study, a 36-week double-blind, multicentered study to test the effects of the long-term administration of piracetam was initiated. The five sites for the study were the New York Columbia-Presbyterian Psychiatric Institute (R. Rudel, principal investigator), Washington, D.C. Children's Hospital (C. K. Conners), University of North Carolina (L. Feagans), Minneapolis Washburn Child Guidance Clinic (L. Hanvik), and San Diego Children's Hospital (P. Tallal). The study involved a total of 225 children (153 boys, 73 girls) ranging in age from 7 years 6 months through 12 years 11 months. The criteria for acceptance into the project were similar to those of the 12-week project. On the average, the children were 3.4 grades below expectancy in reading as measured by the Gray Oral Reading Test. The project involved double-blind placebo controls, with the experimental group receiving 3.3 mg of piracetam administered in two doses of 5 ml each, one in the morning and one in the evening. Careful monitoring of physical status, including hematology, blood chemistry, and urine analysis, was done. At 12 weeks, 24 weeks, and 36 weeks into the project, two general areas of reading achievement were evaluated: reading accuracy (WRAT, Gilmore oral reading test, Gray oral reading) and reading comprehension (Gilmore oral passage reading and Grey oral passage reading test). Two hundred children completed the project.

Results have been reported with all centers combined (Wilsher, 1987) and by the individual centers. The report of the Columbia group is representative (Helfgott, Rudel, Koplewics, & Krieger, 1987). Their major finding was improvement of the piracetam-treated children on the reading comprehension scores on both the Gilmore and Gray oral passage reading tests. On the Gilmore rest of reading comprehension, improvement was significant at 36 weeks of the project. On this test, piracetam-treated children increased their comprehension 1.5 grade levels, while the placebo-treated children increased 0.7 grade level. As measured with the Gray oral passage reading test, comprehension of the piracetam group was significantly improved compared with the control group at 12 and 36 weeks of treatment. On the other hand, while single-word reading accuracy, as measured by the WRAT and by the Gray oral reading test, improved after 12 weeks of treatment with piracetam, the improvement at the end of 24 weeks and at 36 weeks was not different from that of controls. On the Gilmore oral reading test, no significant difference between placebo and piracetam groups was found. The authors cautioned, however, that because the pretreatment comprehension scores of their children were about 1.75 grades above their accuracy scores, studies should be done with children whose comprehension scores are as low as their accuracy scores.

The differences in results among sites are expected to disappear into the combined results obtained from all five sites (Wilsher, 1987). At one of the project sites, however, the baseline differences between control and experimental groups reached statistical significance. Accordingly, group data were calculated both with and without data from that site. Of the 225 children entering the study, 25 left before the study was completed. The mean age of the original group was 10 years; 205 were white, 15 black, and 5 other. Their average full scale IQ on the WISC-R was 104 (performance IQ of 106, verbal IQ of 100). All children were randomly assigned to piracetam or control groups: 11 black children, 99 white, and 3 other were assigned to the control groups; 4 blacks, 106 white, and 2 other assigned to the piracetam group. Results of the total study, excluding those from the site with the baseline difference data, showed significant differences favoring the piracetam group in the Gray Oral Test at 12, 24, and 36 weeks, the Gray total comprehension scores at 12 and 36 weeks, the Gilmore oral reading comprehension score at 36 weeks, and the WRAT-R reading score at 24 weeks. No differences between the groups were found on the WRAT-R score at 12 weeks and at 36 weeks, the rate and accuracy of reading as measured by the Gilmore oral reading test, and the Gray comprehension score at 24 weeks. One of the project sites found a significant difference favoring the placebo group on the Gray oral passage score at 36 weeks. The major finding of the study appeared to be an overall improvement in reading comprehension seen in the piracetam-treated group compared with the controls.

Wilsher also dichotomized the entire sample by median age. The older group (10 to 13 years) proved to be homogeneous in baseline differences and in treatment by investigator interactions. This group demonstrated increased overall reading ability (WRAT, at 24 and 36 weeks, Gray oral reading at 36 weeks, Gilmore oral reading accuracy at 36 weeks, and Gray oral comprehension test). Wilsher (1987) states, "It is possible that piracetam acts differently in different age populations, i.e., increasing comprehension in the young but increasing overall reading ability in the older group" (p. 106).

Side effects to the drug were minimal, with three piracetam children complaining of irritability or nervousness, compared with none for controls and one child in the San Diego study with elevated liver enzymes after 60 days of treatment.

What is disturbing about this multisite study is the lack of information on the educational experiences of the children during the 36 weeks. Detailed data about intervention other than medication is needed.

A med-line review of the effect of nootropic drugs in learning and memory over the past decade has uncovered 99 publications, only one of which has studied these drugs in children. Ackerman, Dykman, Holloway, Paal, and Gocio (1991) had as their subjects 60 children (41 boys, 19 girls; ages 9 to 12), enrolled in a 10-week summer tutoring program that emphasized word-building skills. They were randomly and blindly assigned to a placebo group or a piracetam group. Of the 53 children who completed the program; 37 were classified as dysphonetic and 16 as phonetic. While the phonetic group improved more in word-recognition ability than did the dysphonetic, children on piracetam did not improve more than the placebo group in any aspect of reading.

The remaining 98 reports in the 2000 med-line survey were concerned with the effects of nootropic in the elderly, or in the intact animals or in those whose brain function had been impaired either by hypoxia, pentylenetetrazol kindling, strokes, or by 6-OH-dopamine. With the exception of a preventive effect on the induction of seizures by pentylenetetrazol, the data are mixed. The animal studies however are more positive in their results and the mechanism of nootropic effect is said to influence directly the energetic processes in the brain, increasing the adenosine triphosphate (ATP), phosphocreatine (P_{CR}) and 3 H-valine in cultured astrocytes (Gabryel, Trzeciak, Pudelko, & Cieslik, 1999). At this writing, piracetam is not ready for use as a therapeutic modality in the treatment of specific language disability. Educational intervention is still the way to go.

This chapter has reviewed the effect on learning and memory of various classes of drugs that are currently being used in the management of emotional and behavioral disorders in children. Many of these drugs have an adverse effect on learning and others, although used to influence academic achievement, do not do so. As our knowledge of the anatomy and biochemistry of learning and memory increases, our knowledge of the effect of drugs on these processes will also increase, offering promise of designing drugs to influence such processes.

SUMMARY

Learning is defined as the process of acquiring new information; memory, the persistence of learning in a state that can be retrieved at a later time. Memory involves a persistent change in relationship among neurons through structural change and/or through biochemical events within and between neurons. The structures of the medial temporal lobe and diencephalon (particularly the hippocampus, amygdala, and dorsomedial nucleus of the thalamus) are essential neural stations for processing sensory information into memory. Molecular mechanism(s) by which a change in neurons may occur have been identified. For long-term memory, the synthesis of proteins is required. Attempts to improve learning and memory by direct administration of RNA or by increasing the activity of RNA have not been successful.

Although they do not directly affect protein synthesis, there are drugs that may act by facilitating or inhibiting the transmission of neural impulses or the circuits involved in processing information leading to memory. Historically, levels of *acetylcholine* and of *cholinesterase* have been implicated in learning; a greater amount of acetylcholine at the synapse enhances learning. Thus choline, arecoline, physostigmine, or diisopropyl phosphofluoridate increase, while atropine and scopolamine decrease, retention of learned responses. Attempts to improve memory in Alzheimer's disease with choline and lecithin, however, have not been successful. Tacrine, donepezil and rivastigmine, potent cholinesterase inhibitors, are in current clinical use. Experimentally, *sympathomimatic amines* (norepinephrine) enhance, while *adrenergic antagonists* inhibit, cell excitability. The adrenergic response is enhanced by *opioid receptor antagonists* that appear to activate the beta 1 and 2 receptors. Hypophyseal peptides (vasopressin) facilitate norepinephrine activity on memory retention. Clinically, beta-blockers (proparanolol) impair short-term verbal memory; however, the adrenergic agonists (methylphenidate, pemoline, and dextroamphetamine) while blocking the amnestic effects of antibiotics do not enhance learning, memory, or academic achievement. The effects of clonidine, an alpha-2 antagonist, on memory are as yet unknown. Caffeine and theophylline do not enhance learning and memory. Tricyclic antidepressants, which block the reuptake of the catecholamines, but which also have anticholinergic properties, have not enhanced learning but, just as with the stimulant drugs, tricyclic antidepressants may improve attention when given to hyperactive boys. The effect of the SSRIs on learning and memory is at this writing, equivocal.

Dopamine depletion during ontogeny interferes with the ability to use spatial cues. Dopamine blockers have an effect on learning because of their sedative and anticholinergic actions. In children, chlorpromazine depresses cognition, while the effect of haloperidol varies directly with the dose: Low doses appear to enhance learning, while high doses impair performance on a continuous performance test and on a short-term memory test.

Overall, glutamic acid has been unsuccessful in increasing cognitive function in retarded children, while GABA blockers (picrotoxin, bicuculine, and pentylenetetrazol) are too toxic for use.

The one group of drug that shows promise for facilitating learning is the nootropic group. Piracetam is said to improve reading comprehension, oral reading, and in some studies, reading fluency. This group of drugs holds promise for having effects on the left-hemisphere functions.

Chapter 10 ─────────────────────────

PREVENTION OF DISORDERS OF LEARNING

> *The importance of identifying the sources of regulation of human development is obvious if one is interested in manipulation of that development, as in the case of prevention or intervention program.*

> —Arnold J. Sameroff

During the academic year 1996 to 1997 2,676,299 children, or 5.5% of the total number of children attending public schools in the United States, were classified as "learning disabled" and were being taught in special educational programs (U.S. Department of Education, 1998). This prevalence poses a problem of great magnitude in terms of not only the high cost of special education and the resources the school system must mobilize to appropriately educate these children, but equally important, the cost to each child and to his family emotionally, financially, and in the long term, socially and vocationally. In New York City, the per pupil cost in regular education in the elementary school is $6,000 to $8,000, whereas the conservatively estimated special education cost ranges from $14,000 to $18,000 per learning-disabled child (Public Education Association, personal communication, 1998). In reality, the USDE data understates the problem, with prevalence estimates of learning disorders ranging between 5% and 20% of the total elementary school population. How to prevent these children from ever developing their learning disorders becomes a task of great importance.

THE HETEROGENEITY OF RISK FACTORS

The task of prevention of learning disorders is complicated by the fact that learning failure is but a symptom and can stem from many factors acting singly or more often in synergistic combination. Some of these factors may have biological roots in genetic

Modified from: Silver, A. & Hagin, R., "Learning Disabilities: Risk and Prevention," in Raphael, B. and Burrows, G., (Eds.) *Handbook of Studies on Preventive Psychiatry* (1995) with permission from Elsevier Science.

variation or in differences in rates of maturation of central nervous system functions needed for academic learning. Others may be related to more clearly definable life experiences such as infections, drugs, toxic substances, and perinatal distress, all of which compromise the structural integrity of the developing brain. Psychological differences in cognitive abilities and emotional and personality factors also may interfere with learning. Environmental-social factors include the problems of poverty, cultural experiences that involve the quality and quantity of sensory stimulation at critical ages in development, and the reality events that may interfere with maturation, object relations, trust, and motivation to learn. Educational factors relate to the appropriateness and adequacy of teaching. With such heterogeneity of influences on learning, an almost infinite number of risk factors can synergistically prevent a child from academic achievement consistent with his intelligence. For this reason, prevention of learning disorders must start with a comprehensive analysis of the many forces influencing learning, an evaluation along a pentaxial scheme involving biological, psychological, cognitive, environmental-social, and educational parameters, as outlined in Chapter 7. With data from such an evaluation, classification of disorders of learning based on clinical evaluation of what appear to be primary etiological events may then be constructed. Such a classification may be seen in Table 5.1.

Risk factors vary for each of the groups identified in this scheme. The learning problems of children reared in a culture of poverty and disadvantage differ from those of the economically advantaged child who has received cultural benefits and educationally oriented stimulation, and risk factors inherent in each of these groups will differ from those of the hypoxic, low-birth-weight infant. However, the groups delineated by this taxonomy are not mutually exclusive. Poverty and cultural disadvantage frequently accompany maternal drug abuse and prematurity. The economically and psychologically secure child may still suffer from a traumatic birth that has a long-term effect on learning. Despite the frequent overlap in groups delineated by this taxonomy, such a classification is helpful in isolating factors that put a child at risk for a learning disorder. We can identify the risks of pregnancy and birth that may lead to learning disorder in the "organic group"; we can distinguish the central neuropsychological defects in the child with specific (developmental) learning disability, isolate the role of attention deficits in Attention-Deficit/Hyperactivity Disorder, and we can implicate poverty and cultural disadvantage as risk factors in minority groups. Some of these risk factors lend themselves to primary prevention where programs may be developed so that the risk factors themselves will not occur; in some we cannot yet eliminate risk factors but we can intervene and interpose programs to reduce the influence of the risk factor in learning so that learning disorder does not develop. This is secondary prevention. An evaluation of the child should include biological, psychological, cognitive, educational, and environmental-social parameters to tease out the heterogeneous factors that predispose to a disorder of learning.

RISK FACTORS AMENABLE TO PRIMARY PREVENTION

Examples of risk factors that lend themselves to primary prevention may be found in Chapter 14. "Healthy start initiatives" designed to ensure that all women have access to prenatal care and prenatal programs that offer special services to mothers at high risk because of health, educational, and socioeconomic factors have proliferated throughout the United States. In Florida, for example, all physicians attending pregnant women are required (as of April 1992) to complete a Prenatal Risk Survey report to be reviewed by the State Office of Health and Rehabilitative Services. This office, in turn, is mandated to provide intervention for pregnant women experiencing high-risk pregnancies. Toxicological screening of 715 pregnant women seen for 1 month at public health clinics ($N = 380$) and 12 private obstetrical offices ($N = 335$) in Pinellas County, Florida, found evidence for alcohol, opiates, cocaine and its metabolites, and cannabinoids in 14.8% with little difference in positive findings between women seen at public clinics (16.3%) and those seen in private offices (13.1%), among white women (15.4%) and black women (14.1%). Black women, however, had more frequent evidence of cocaine use (7.5% vs. 1.8%), while white women had more frequent use of cannabinods (14.4% vs. 6.8%). Discrepancies in the mandatory reporting to health authorities exist, however, with black women being reported 10 times the rate for white women (Chasnoff, Landress, & Barrett, 1990). Special services are offered in local programs (e.g., Genesis, 1991); these multidisciplinary groups help women carry high-risk pregnancies to term with minimal damage to mother and child. Specific additional funding is provided for substance abusing women. Inpatient detoxification, intensive outpatient counseling, social service, parenting classes, high-risk obstetrical care, and 3-year pediatric follow-up to detect drug-related problems such as language delay, attention disorders, learning disorders, and cognitive impairment are components of such programs (Project STRIVE, 1992). What is encountered is that "in addition to their medical and social problems, these women have emotional and mental health needs. They need treatment for depression and anxiety. Some have family history of physical, psychological and social abuse as well as drug abuse and alcoholism" (Belcher, 1992).

Teenage pregnancy compounds the problem. In the state of Florida, there were 38,000 teenage pregnancies in 1990. Twenty percent have some sexually transmitted disease including human immunodeficiency virus (HIV) (Hartsfield, 1992). The effect of HIV on neuropsychological, cognitive, motor, and emotional behavior of children is becoming clearer as research reports appear (S. Hersh, 1992). The appearance of a 2-year-old HIV infected child, appearing the size of a 6-month-old, spastic, unable to relate, with no expressive language and no apparent receptive language, is dramatic demonstration of this effect.

Toxic substances affecting the central nervous system are other targets for primary prevention. Neurotoxicity is defined by the U.S. Office of Technology Assessment (OTA) as an adverse change in the structure or function of the nervous system following exposure to a chemical agent (OTA report, 1990). Although the number of substances that pose significant risk and the extent of the risk are unknown, the inverse relationship between blood levels of lead at the age of 24 months and scores on the McCarthy Scales of Children's Abilities at 60 months has been reported (Bellinger et al., 1991). Levels of lead in the atmosphere, in paint, and in drinking water have been implicated. A congressional bill (HR 2922), The Lead-Based Paint Abatement Trust Fund Act, established a Trust Fund of approximately one billion dollars per year for 10 years for use by states and cities to develop programs for inspection, training of contractors and workers, oversight and quality assurance, and counseling of occupants of older houses in lead poisoning prevention methods. Local city and state ordinances are attempting to reduce the quantity of lead emissions in automobile exhaust. The American Academy of Child Psychiatry has a task force on lead exposure that is drafting guidelines related to children's exposure to toxic levels of lead. The U.S. Center for Disease Control recommends that screening for lead poisoning be included in health care programs for children, especially between the ages of 6 months and 9 years. A blood level of 25 µg/dl or greater and an erythrocyte protoporphyrin level of 35 µg/dl or greater, calls for medical treatment and identification and removal of the source. Because even lead levels of 10 to 15 mg/dl may have toxic effects, the CDC is currently reviewing the acceptable (safe) blood levels (Chisolm & O'Hara, 1982; Agency for Toxic Substances and Disease Registry, 1990).

The effect of drugs, food additives, and pesticides on developmental neurotoxicity is now being considered by the Food and Drug Administration, as it revises its guidelines to recommend that screening for neurotoxicity should be done routinely and systematically. The Environmental Protection Agency is requesting comment on a new ruling to require manufacturers of chemical substances to test for developmental and reproductive toxicity that would include a test for learning and memory. Japan, the United Kingdom, Italy, and France have required neurotoxicity testing for drugs since 1970.

That children of high-risk pregnancies, particularly in association with sociocultual disadvantage, are also at risk for learning disorders has solid documentation in the literature (Dorman & Katzir, 1994). In a study of 171 children in 7 mainstream first grades in inner-city schools, 5% (1 to 2 children in each class of approximately 25 children) had evidence suggestive of a structural defect of the central nervous system (A. A. Silver & Hagin, 1972). In self-contained classes for 60 severely emotionally disturbed children, A. A. Silver (1984) found that 18 (approximately one-third of the entire sample) had some organic defect of the central nervous system: three had a history of prematurely and low birth weight, three had cerebral palsy, three had identifiable chromosome abnormality, two had idiopathic seizures, two with cerebellar palsy, and one each with Rh incompatibility, lead toxicity, Tourette's syndrome, traumatic birth, and one with dyskinesia of unknown cause. The importance of identification of pre- and perinatal events is that the residuals do not simply disappear with maturation alone but that brain functions important for learning may be impaired in adult life.

SECONDARY PREVENTION FOR CHILDREN OF POVERTY AND DISADVANTAGE

Preschool Programs

While pre- and perinatal risk factors offer a wedge in which to insert programs for primary prevention, the effects of a culture of poverty are not readily accessible to primary prevention. Broad social changes and attempts to eliminate poverty have not yet reduced the high incidence of learning failure and school dropouts in minority populations. Attempts to improve urban schools and to reverse the incidence of learning disorder in these children are examples of secondary prevention, of mitigating the effect of the risk factors although the risk factors themselves (e.g., poverty) are not changed. Such preventive efforts involve broad changes in social and educational policy and may include modification of the elementary school-home culture gap and provision of special services within the schools. (See Chapter 12 for details of preschool programs.)

Bilingual Education as a Preventive Measure

The use of bilingual education in children who enter school with limited English proficiency (LEP) has been contaminated with political static (see also Chapter 1). English groups have argued that, as citizens of the United States, minority children, particularly Hispanic ones, must become literate in English, while Hispanic groups have opposed efforts to reduce the use of Spanish. Evaluation of the effectiveness of bilingual programs has also yielded confusing results with a large-scale study by the American Institutes of Research (Baker & de Kanter, 1981; Danoff, Coles, McLaughlin, & Reynolds, 1977 to 1978) concluding that bilingual programs are not effective in promoting English language and other academic skills. These studies typically compared bilingual instruction with that in which the LEP children are immediately placed (submerged) into all-English classrooms. In further analysis of the American Institute of Research data, a U.S. Department of Education Study (Developmental Associates, 1984), found that 93% of LEP first graders in the study received a "substantial" portion of their instruction in English and 26% received instruction only in English. Analyzing the same data, Willig (1985) found evidence in favor of bilingual studies. The following misconceptions were pointed out:

- The belief that bilingual education does not teach English rapidly enough. Actually, a strong native language foundation acts as a support in the learning of English, making that process easier and faster (Cummins, 1984). Most of the learning in native language transfers readily to English.
- That bilingualism retards cognitive development. In reality, bilingual children may gain cognitive flexibility, particularly where the first language is maintained rather than replaced (Hakuta & Diaz, 1984).
- The belief that if children have not mastered the second language by early school years, they never will. In reality, teenagers and adults are efficient learners, fourth to seventh graders learning English as well as first to third graders (Snow & Hoefnagel-Hohle, 1977).
- Literacy is impaired. Actually, once the basic principles of reading are mastered in the home language, reading skills transfer to a second language (Snow, 1986). However, a child with a developmental (specific) learning disability (SLD) will have problems in learning any language.

A program with native language (In class Reactive Language, INREAL) as a central focus was designed by R. S. Weiss (1980), to serve children with Hispanic background and limited English proficiency. Evaluation 3 years after the original project, using matched INREAL and control groups showed INREAL children requiring fewer remedial services and less likely than control groups to be retained in grade. In general, research supports the use of their native language in the instruction of language-minority children.

Despite the massive social and educational advances seen in the preschool programs for poor, minority children and in the successful demonstration projects, the prevention of learning disorders in these children is still elusive. Not only is there no reduction nationwide in school dropout rates, but there is a decline in the number of black high school graduates going to college (see Chapter 12). The truth is that the recent reforms have bypassed millions of students in urban schools across the nation. The future of urban schools is the primary issue facing the nation's educational system.

ADMINISTRATIVE STRATEGIES TO PREVENT LEARNING DISORDERS

While the preceding section focused on measures to prevent academic disorder in the poor, minority, and culturally different populations, schools have been attempting to find out why some schools are more effective than others in enhancing learning for all children, or for groups of children (e.g., boys or girls, children with different learning and development characteristics, social class origins, racial backgrounds). A 4-year study of 50 elementary schools randomly selected from a total of 636 schools within London, England, jurisdiction (Mortimore & Sammons, 1987), found that for many of the educational outcomes—especially progress in cognitive areas—the school was more important than background factors in accounting for variations among individuals. There were striking differences between the least and most effective schools. In reading, for example, the most effective school improved students' attainment by an average of 15 points above that predicted by the child's attainment at entry into school; in the least effective school, by contrast, each child's attainment was 10 points lower than predicted. Of the 50 schools, 14 had a positive effect on academic achievement and in noncognitive outcomes; 5 schools were ineffective in most areas. Furthermore, effective schools were effective for all students, regardless of race or social class; by contrast, the less effective schools were also less effective for all groups of children. The authors dramatize this report: "On average, a student from a blue-collar worker's family attending an effective school achieved more highly than one from a white-collar family background attending one of the least effective schools" (Mortimore & Sammons, 1987, p. 39). What in the schools could account for these differences? The policies and processes within the control of the principal and teachers were found to be crucial. Size, status, environment, and stability of teaching staff do not themselves ensure effectiveness. They do provide a supporting framework for 12 key factors of effectiveness:

1. Purposeful leadership of the staff by the principal; he/she is involved in curriculum decisions, influences teachers' strategies, and sets the stage for structure.
2. Involvement of the assistant principal in policy decisions.

3. Involvement of teachers in curriculum planning, in decisions concerning classes they are to teach, on policy issues and allocation of resources.

4. Consistency among teachers.

5. Structured sessions—Organizations within which students can work, yet allow for freedom within the structure, are effective.

6. Intellectually challenging teaching, communication of enthusiasm, encouraging creative imagination, and problem solving.

7. Work-centered environment with feedback to students.

8. Limited focus within sessions, to the level of individuals needs.

9. Maximum communication between teachers and students.

10. Written records of individual work to monitor progress.

11. Parental involvement, with an informal "open-door" policy.

12. Positive climate; a positive climate created by teachers for students and by principal for teachers creates a background for well-behaved students and effective work.

Alternative administrative provisions have been recommended to decrease the failure rate and to attempt to adapt the relatively fixed structure of school organization to the differential levels of maturation and readiness experiences of schoolchildren. Unlike the approaches directed toward enhancing the effectiveness of the total school program described in the previous section, these provisions are generally short-lived and often fall victims to the winds of educational change before definitive evaluations of their effectiveness have been conducted. However, a search of the educational research literature yields a few administrative models that have been evaluated.

Transitional First Grades

Transitional first grades (sometimes called junior first grades or prefirst grades) have been proposed as a means of adapting the lockstep organization of school grades to the needs of children who do not seem ready for first grade at the end of the kindergarten year. However, little efficacy data appeared on this provision until Zenski's study (1987) in which she compared second-grade reading, language, and mathematics scores for children who had been placed in a transition class with a group of children who had repeated first grade. No significant differences between the two groups were found, apparently since the transition program had been primarily an extension of unstructured kindergarten activities. It is also regrettable that other data, such as information on motivation and social adjustment were not also collected in the evaluation of the transition first grade.

Broadscale data were used by Kilby (1983) in a retrospective study of children enrolled in the middle grades who had participated in a junior first grade following the kindergarten year. The achievement and adjustment of the experimental children were more favorable than those of comparable classmates and there were fewer referrals to remedial programs and fewer grade repetitions among the program participants. Kilby concluded that intensive instruction in reading in the junior grade may have had positive, long-term effects.

All-Day Kindergartens

Common sense dictates that the effectiveness of educational programs bears a direct relationship to the amount of instructional time. The extended kindergarten day is an intervention provision growing directly from this point of view. However, results of evaluations are somewhat mixed. On one hand, Weissman (1985) found that the opportunity for extended kindergarten experiences did not discriminate between children who made successful and unsuccessful mainstream adjustment. On the other hand, E. Anderson (1984) reported a well-designed experiment in which increased instructional time (3h vs. 4.5h) was the contrasting condition. The programs in both full-day and half-day kindergartens drew on similar curriculum content. Ages, gender, socioeconomic levels, and entry level skills were matched. Evaluation including results of the Stanford Early School Achievement Test, administered at the end of kindergarten, indicated significantly higher scores for the full-day kindergartens in reading and mathematics. Parental support of the full-day program was strong and may have influenced ratings that indicated that the group also demonstrated greater self-confidence, independence, and ability to play cooperatively. Full-day kindergartens are especially popular with parents because they offer a partial solution to the child-care problems of mothers who are employed outside the home. Thus, no matter whether such practices prove to be efficacious, their expansion is likely because of such unrelated factors as the lack of affordable child-care facilities and the outside employment of mothers of young children.

School Placement Based on Individual Development

Admission to kindergarten on the basis of individual patterns of development has long been advocated by the Gesell Institute in New Haven, Connecticut (Ilg & Ames, 1965). The developmental age concept maintains that 50% of all school problems could be prevented or remedied by placement in terms of developmental ages. Problems later diagnosed as learning disability, emotional disturbance, minimal brain dysfunction, and underachievement are said to result from children's being asked to perform at educational levels for which they are not ready developmentally. This approach does not propose any specific curriculum, but rather that a child take another year to handle the regular school offerings. This theory opposes early intervention based on a child's needs and assumes that waiting a year in a less demanding environment will enable a child to succeed in the conventional program.

Decisions about readiness for kindergarten admission are based on the Gesell Readiness Screening Test that assesses children's performance on block construction, copy forms, interview questions, writing of names and numerals, completion of drawing of a man, and gross motor control. Although this test is widely used, little data beyond case studies about its validity have been presented. A study by C. Wood, Powell, and Knight (1984) raises questions about the statistical characteristics of the measure because slight variations in cutoff scores resulted in significant variations in false negatives and false positives. Results of this test that find a child "unready" have been used as a basis for recommending that a family postpone kindergarten entrance for a year even though the child may have reached the legal chronological age for school entrance.

The outcomes of such predictions were reported by May and Welch (1984) who located 222 second to sixth graders who had been given the Gesell Readiness Screening Test prior to kindergarten entrance. These subjects consisted of (a) "unready" children whose parents accepted the recommendation to postpone kindergarten entrance for a year, (b) unready children whose parents did not accept the recommendation and who, according to the theory were "overplaced," (c) children who earned developmental ages above 4.5 years who were considered "ready" for kindergarten. No significant differences were found among the three groups in number of referrals for special education placement, speech and language services, remedial service in reading or mathematics, or counseling. Two children in each group had been recommended to repeat a grade, and a few more of the postponed kindergarten group had been referred to adaptive motor and resource room programs. May and Welch concluded that these results do not show greater difficulties for the overplaced group and that maturation alone will not make a child more ready for school. The provision of developmental placements is attractive to some educators because it does not involve any adjustment on the part of the schools. The child merely waits at home until he fits the practices and curriculum that are already in place.

PROGRAMS FOR PREVENTION OF DEVELOPMENTAL LEARNING DISORDERS

The preceding sections have been on the primary prevention of pre- and perinatal insult to the fetus and infant, the massive social and educational reforms broadly categorized as secondary prevention that attempt to attenuate the academic and social disadvantage of culture and poverty, and on administrative modification in schools designed to promote a learning environment for all children and remedial help for children already struggling to keep up with their peers in academic achievement. The remediation programs that have been discussed may be considered tertiary prevention (i.e., the disorder is established; the program attempts to prevent further progress of the disorder).

There remains to be considered the prevention of learning disorders in children with so-called developmental or specific learning disabilities. The National Joint Committee on Learning Disabilities provides the following definition of learning disability (1981): (a) significant difficulties in the acquisition and use of listening, speaking, reading, writing, reasoning or mathematical abilities (i.e., significant discrepancy between academic achievement and intellectual ability despite adequate educational exposure and not primarily due to sensory impairment, mental retardation, social and emotional disturbances, and environmental influences such as cultural differences); (b) a disorder in one or more basic psychological process in understanding or using language spoken or written (see also Chapter 4).

These developmental disabilities have a strong familial risk, but they are also heritable. Epidemiological study suggests that the genetic fault is heterogeneous with some support for a partially dominant major gene or genes (Pennington, 1991). Familial and heritable risk are, at this writing, not susceptible to primary prevention, although the presence of specific learning disabilities in a family (particularly in parents or in siblings) should alert the clinician to the strong probability of future learning problems in younger siblings with the possibility of early detection and intervention in these children. Since our efforts are to prevent the learning disability from ever occurring, the task of prevention is to identify the child at potential risk for learning disability before he or she has failed. This places the time of identification at the latest in kindergarten or early in first grade. What measures can be used for such identification? Family history by itself is not sufficient. However, the disorder in one or more basic psychological process in understanding or using language spoken or written can be detected in kindergarten and programs of intervention for children with such immaturities may be introduced. The task is to locate in kindergarten, children with specific neuropsychological immaturities in language and accelerate the maturation of these immaturities before they affect academic learning. These programs may be considered as secondary prevention since the *anlage* for the learning disability, the neuropsychological processing defect, is already present and our preventive programs only obtund or help to eliminate the effect of the defect on learning.

In practice, neuropsychological processing defects are not exclusive to children with specific learning disabilities. Other primary risk factors, whether they are biological or experiential, traumatic or hypoxic birth, inappropriate or inadequate stimulation of poverty or cultural deprivation at critical ages of language development, all these may cause psychoneurological dysfunction that makes academic learning difficult. Identification based on the presence of neuropsychological dysfunction in kindergarten thus reveals an etiologically heterogeneous group. The identification process is not diagnosis. All a scanning instrument can be expected to accomplish is to identify a heterogeneous group of children whose members have one thing in common: that their function in those parameters assessed by the scanning instruments is immature when compared with their peers. It does not imply sickness or wellness. It does not dichotomize, categorize, or label. It looks over the entire kindergarten class finding children who in specific neuropsychological functions are quantitatively, not qualitatively, different from their peers. Nevertheless, the identification of children for whom we can predict learning difficulties is an obvious first step in prevention; detection of neuropsychological immaturities specific to language is the tool for that identification.

Ideally, diagnosis along the pentaxial lines described earlier is a next step. The diagnostic process will identify the etiological factors responsible in the first place for the neuropsychological defects found. The significance of diagnosis is that the "organic child" or the "poverty child" or the "ADHD child" will need more than educational intervention. Whatever the diagnosis, however, neuropsychological defects require educational intervention.

Programs for the prevention of learning disorders then have three components: scanning, diagnosis, and intervention. Barclay (1984) describes successful preventive programs as needing three basic components: assessment technology to identify children at risk, a set of intervention procedures, and sufficient time to assess the results. The National Joint Committee on Learning Disabilities (1985) also cautions, "Identification programs not followed by assessment, intervention and follow-up are futile."

IDEAL CHARACTERISTICS OF A SCANNING INSTRUMENT

The test or battery of tests used to identify children for whom learning failure is predicated should accurately predict educational outcomes. In addition, evidence should be provided that it has demonstrated its reliability and validity, that its content and norms are appropriate for the population studied, that the incidence of false positives and false negatives is minimal. In short, it should meet the standards for educational and psychological tests described by the American Psychological Association (1985). In addition, however, it should be brief enough to be given to a large number of children (i.e., all children in kindergarten classes) quickly and economically, be clear enough to identify children who need further detailed diagnostic services and provide guidance to the teacher in using interventions appropriate to each child's needs. Finally, the scanning instrument should be based on a rational conceptualization of the learning process.

In scanning instruments, false positives (the test score indicates failure and the child succeeds) are practical problems. Because so many factors other than neuropsychological defects influence learning, it would be overly optimistic for a brief scanning instrument to tap all the variables important in learning. False negatives are to be expected. False positives on the other hand are more disturbing, raising questions about the basic theoretical structure of the instrument, the validity of the test items, the scoring of the items, and perhaps the creation of a prophecy of failure. The level of inaccurate predictions, however, may be statistically manipulated to yield the fewest number of false positives. They may be decreased by lowering the score at or below which failure is predicted. Thus, fewer children are placed in the vulnerable category. Lowering the cutoff score, however, will increase the number of false negatives. Determination of the cutoff point in scanning batteries thus becomes an important decision in predictive tests. Most predictive batteries are composed of subtests, that are themselves usually not dichotomous but represent scores along a distribution curve. A decision as to the cutoff point for each subtest is a basis for scoring. Most predictive instruments do not include the method of arriving at vulnerable scores.

Three well-researched instruments, however, do record the method of deriving cutoff scores. Fletcher and Satz (1984) state, "Discriminant function formed the basis for classifying (predicting) children into reading groups later in school. . . . in essence this technique computes a weighted linear composite of kindergarten (predictor) variables that subsequently separate criterion reading groups" (p. 165). A. A. Silver and Hagin (1981) used base rates of third-grade reading failure in their sample schools to set cutoff scores for each of the subtests in their scanning instrument (SEARCH). The total score was then the number of subtests in which the child scored above the cutoff. Ten subtests make up the battery; the total score may vary from zero (i.e., no subtest score above the cutoff score) to 10 (all subtests above the cutoff score). Since the base rate of reading failure in the schools in the schools studied was approximately 25% to 30%, children scoring in the lowest quartile in each subtest were considered vulnerable in that subtest. With these cutoff scores as a base, the cutoff point on the total score was set at the lowest quartile of the distribution. Children whose total score fell within that lowest quartile of the distribution corresponded to the base rate for reading failure. Jansky and DeHirsch (1972) also defined the total score of their screening battery in terms of the rates of reading failure in the schools.

Other identification instruments used as their component subtests "nationally validated" instruments such as the Peabody Picture Vocabulary Test, the Visual-Motor Integration Test, the Goodenough Draw-a-Person, the Pre-School Language Scale, and a Revised Motor Activity Scale, Werner (Early Prevention of School Failure). While there are norms on each of these components of such batteries, it is not clear just how the scores of each are combined into a total score and just what total score puts a child into the vulnerable category. Meehl and Rosen (1955), using Bayesian statistics, suggest a way of determining optimal cutoff points on psychometric devices to identify true positives and true negatives. For a prediction to be more likely true than false, the ratio of the positive to negative base rates in a sample must exceed the ratio of false positive rates to valid positive rates attained in the scanning test. Decreasing the cutoff point score improves decisions only if the ratio of improvement in true positive rates to worsening false negative rates, exceeds the ratio of actual failing readers to actual successful readers in the population.

Predictive Validity of Readiness and Screening Tests

By and large, most screening tests in use have emphasized prediction of success or failure in reading rather than in predicting vulnerability to learning failure in other academic areas, as in reading, spelling, writing, and mathematics. The criteria for validation (the measures used to determine false positives and false negatives; the power of the prediction of the screening tests) vary. Yet in comparisons of screening instruments, the criteria for validation must be carefully considered. Different validating measures, not comparable across studies, may only compound any comparison. The validity of the criterion measure itself as a gold standard for level of academic achievement may be questionable and the use of the criterion measure, even if comparable and valid, must be appropriate for the normative data of the criterion measure (e.g., a test developed for testing first graders in May to June may not be appropriate for testing in September or November). Finally, even when validity measures are comparable, are in themselves valid, and are used appropriately, the cutoff point of the criterion measure must also be considered. For example, should grade expectancy level or median achievement score of the class be used as a measure, or should significant improvement be measured by a percentage an individual child improves on his academic achievement scores? That these are practical concerns may be seen in A. A. Silver and Hagin (1981). The test, SEARCH, yielded a 4% false negative rate using an expectancy criterion of fourth grade at the end of third grade. If, however, the median grade score of 4.6 were used, the false negative rate would become 13%. At the end of second grade in one school, the expectancy grade score of 3 yielded 9% false positives. Using the median achievement level, however, lowered the false positives to 3%. Further, the predictive power of any scanning instrument may be contaminated by intervention programs that may vary in impact on the academic progress of their children. Yet strangely enough, what educational experience the children had between the time of original testing and the time of follow-up is generally not stated in many validity studies.

All these considerations contribute to the practical usefulness of the scanning instrument. Predictive validity, however, is not a strong suit in the description of predictive batteries. The reading-readiness tests pioneered by Monroe (1935) and others developed by Nuress and McGauvran (1965), Gates and MacGinitie (1968), and Chew (1981) are in common use. In general, the scores of these tests correlate concurrently with reading achievement tests in the range of .60 to .75 (the Metropolitan Readiness Test reports concurrent r of .80 with Murphy Durrell readiness test).

Three well-researched scanning instruments may serve as examples of validity of scanning instruments derived from a theoretical position. The Florida Kindergarten Screening Battery (FKSB) is summarized by Fletcher and Satz (1984). Its predictive validity is based on follow-up of an original sample of 497 white kindergarten boys in Alachua County, Florida, as they went on to Grades 2 and 5. The criterion measure at end of Grade 2 included teacher's estimate of reading proficiency, the Iota Word Recognition Test, and Vocabulary Recognition scores of Gates-MacGinitie. The FKSB, using the cutoff scores previously described, identified 95 kindergarten boys at high risk for learning disability; 48 of these were severely retarded at Grade 2, 21 had mild reading retardation (10.7 months below expectancy), but 26 were average readers. Of the 67 predicted to be at mild risk, 10 had severe reading problems, 26 mild; but 29 were average and 2 were superior readers. For the total number of children for whom failure (severe and mild) was predicted (162), 105 were true positives with severe or mild reading problems, 55 were false positives (a false positive rate of 55/497 or 11%). For the total number of children for whom success was predicted (255), 217 were correctly identified, 38 were not (false negative rate 17%). The rate of false positives is high. Assuming a base rate of reading disability at 25% to 30%, the ratio of positive to negative base rates does not exceed the rates of false positives to true positives, thus not meeting the Meehl and Rosen (1955) criteria prediction to be more likely true than false. The overall "hit rate" of the correctness of prediction of this test is reported at 74%.

The Predictive Screening Index (Jansky & DeHirsch, 1972) correctly identified 77% of the kindergarten children who failed in reading at the end of second grade. Here were 19% false positives. If only the black and Puerto Rican children and the white boys were considered (and excluding only white girls), the Predictive Screening battery identified 79% of the failing readers, but had 22% false positives. These data were based on a heterogeneous sample of 401 kindergarten children in five public schools in New York City, 217 boys, 184 girls; 42% were black, 5% were Puerto Rican. Of these, 347 had a complete set of scores. At the end of second grade, criterion measures were Roswell-Chall Auditory Blending Test, Bryant Phonics Test, Gates

Advanced Primary, or Gates-McGinitie Paragraph Reading Test, Gray Oral Reading Test, Fluency of Oral Reading, guessing at words from context, written spelling from the Metropolitan Achievement Test for second grade, spelling from the Stanford Achievement Test for Grades 1 to 2, numbers and letters transposed and/or reversed from the Metropolitan Achievement Test, numbers of words in written composition, and percentage of correctly spelled words in composition. Failure in reading was defined as grade score 2.2 or lower on the silent reading paragraph reading test. Jansky and DeHirsh in a sobering note state: "In the group of 347 children, 16% of the white girls, 23% of the white boys, 41% of the black girls and a staggering 61% of the black boys had failed to read by the end of second grade" (p. 53). These rates, staggering as they appear, are not the exception in the heterogeneous population of New York City.

The predictive validity of SEARCH (A. A. Silver & Hagin, 1981) correctly placed 87% of children in one sample, 83% in another. The base rate of 30% reading failure in 31 schools located in the lower East Side of Manhattan, in Brooklyn, New York, and 22 schools in the semirural North Carolina, set the cutoff point for each subtest of SEARCH. The resulting Total Search Score (the number of subtests in which the child exceeded the cutoff score for that component) was used to predict success or failure in reading. Approximately 10% of the standardization sample of 2,319 children earned a total SEARCH score of 0 to 3; 30% between 0 and 5, 60% between 0 and 7, and of course 100% between 0 and 10. A score of 0 to 5 was predictive of reading failure. Scores for 1,136 children, representing intact groups (i.e., all children in the first grade) were evaluated over 3 successive years for false negatives; 494 of these children (Sample A) were examined at the end of Grade 1, 386 (Sample B) at the end of Grade 2, and 256 (Sample C) at the end of Grade 3. The criterion measure was the reading scores on the reading section of the WRAT. At or above grade level was considered a successful reading score, below grade level, considered failure. Of the 1,136 children, 5% of those for whom SEARCH predicted success did not make normal progress, a rate of 5% false negatives. False positives are harder to determine because of intervention programs, which are designed to invalidate the original prediction of failure. Nevertheless, two untreated samples were available: Sample D ($N = 40$) and Sample E ($N = 153$) came from schools where the intervention program was not implemented. In these schools, a false positive rate of 3% (Sample D) and 9% (Sample E) was obtained (A. A. Silver, Hagin, & Beecher, 1981). Using Bayesian theory of probability, the ratio of positive to negative base rates exceeded the ratio of false positive to valid positive rate, thus the predictions of SEARCH are more likely true than false.

With all their problems (cutoff point on the scale, criterion measures, cutoff points on criterion measures, appropriate norms for sample studies), the scanning instruments do provide a significant start in early identification of potential learning failures. This is particularly true when local norms are derived. It has been found highly desirable and practical to derive local norms for schools in sections of the country that may be socially and economically different from the standardization sample.

Content of Scanning Batteries

The earlier batteries were composed of tests that "practical judgment" indicates are related to reading (Farr, 1969). Thus, letter matching in the first week of first grade yielded at the end of first grade, a correlation of .87 with the Detroit Word Recognition Test (N. B. Smith, 1928); prereading visual discrimination, knowledge of letter names and auditory discrimination of beginning sounds were considered predictive of later reading (Barrett, 1965a, 1965b, 1965c). Intermodal integration skills were said to distinguish normal from inadequate readers (Birch & Belmont, 1964), and later studies identified skills of phonological awareness, phonological integration, and verbal encoding basic to reading. Multivariate statistics attempted to base subgroups of children with reading disabilities on combinations of neuropsychological skills. These findings were used to develop the context of predictive batteries. The content of representative scanning tests is discussed in this section.

In their earlier theoretical position Satz et al. (1978), Satz and Sparrow (1970), and Satz and Van Nostrand (1973) postulated:

> Reading disabilities reflect a lag in the maturation of the brain which differentially delays those skills which are in primary ascendancy at different chronological ages . . . skills which develop earlier during childhood (language and informal operations are more likely to be delayed in younger children. . . . maturationally immature . . . skills which have a slower rate of development during childhood (language and informal operations) are more likely to be delayed in older children developmentally immature. (Satz et al., 1978, p. 315)

Factor analysis of 14 variables used in the original testing of the 497 Alachua kindergarten boys yielded three major factors: (a) sensory-perceptual-mnemonic, (b) verbal-conceptual, and (c) verbal-cultural. Later, however, the composition of the test battery changed and the final FKSB (Satz & Fletcher, 1982) consisted of five subtests; two of which are nationally normed (Peabody Picture Vocabulary Test, Beery Test of Visual-Motor Integration). The remaining three subtests include a visual discrimination test, alphabet recognition, and finger localization. Whether these five tests are faithful to the original theoretical formulation is uncertain, but the functions implied in these five subtests range widely from vocabulary to visual discrimination and motor to body image.

The Predictive Screening Index (Jansky & DeHirsch, 1972) was developed with the concept that "the ability to comprehend and use oral language was of overwhelming importance in learning to read" (p. 45). Their final Predictive Index, derived from multiple regression procedures based on data from the pool of 19 tests given to a sample of 347 kindergarteners, consisted of five subtests, Letter Naming, Picture Naming, Gates Word Matching, Bender Visual-Motor Gestalt Test, Binet Sentence Memory. The emphasis here on language use is concordant with the theoretical formulation. It may be that the sample Jansky and DeHirsch studied was skewed to minority groups.

The content of SEARCH (A. A. Silver & Hagin, 1981) is based on the theory that the neuropsychological functions of temporal organization and/or spatial orientation must be age appropriate for the child to learn academic skills, that orientation in space and time is a basis for learning. These functions may be sampled in all combinations of visual, visuomotor, auditory, and body-image perception; and these functions may reliably be assessed in 5-year-old children. Data from intensive examination of 154 children were reduced to 20 variables and subjected to factor analysis. Five factors were found: I, Auditory-Verbal; II, Visual-Motor-Neurological; III, Chronological

Age; IV, Psychiatric Status; V, IQ as measured by the WPPSI. These factors accounted for 61.05% of the total variance. Factors I and II, accounting for 35% of the variance, contained variables designed to assess the functions of temporal and spatial orientation. In accordance with our theoretical position, variables with the highest loadings on factors I and II constituted the 10 subtests of SEARCH; 3 tests of visual-spatial function, 4 of auditory-verbal orientation, and 3 of body image concepts (right-left discrimination, finger gnosis, and praxis). This battery is designed to predict vulnerability to learning, not only reading but the language arts. The distribution of scores on SEARCH is profiled and used as a basis for intervention planning.

EDUCATIONAL INTERVENTION IN PROGRAMS TO PREVENT LEARNING DISORDERS

A program to prevent learning disabilities is not complete without intervention; the answer to "What are you going to do about the children your program identifies as having future learning disabilities?" Intervention is the bottom line, the payoff, for the child, his family, and the school. Yet, surveys of the special education or early childhood education literature yield little information concerning the operation of actual projects for the prevention of learning disabilities in young children. For example, one recent computerized literature search produced 69 references, of which 30 dealt with specific projects. Of the 30 projects, only 8 contained any outcome data that would permit evaluation of the intervention approaches (A. A. Silver & Hagin, 1990, p. 158). Descriptions of methods for identification of children to be served (Caro & Derevensky, 1991) descriptions of the roles of the various disciplines involved; and general discussions of organizational methods (Horsch, 1992; Telzrow, 1991) are more frequently discussed in these papers. There are several explanations for this gap in the professional literature:

- Current legislation offers greater support for services after a child has failed than for preventive services.
- The ongoing demands for services are so great that there is little time for research and publication; there may be many high-quality projects in operation in the field that do not appear in literature searches because their leaders are so busy providing good services that they do not have time to write about them.
- Philosophic differences between advocates of more structured early intervention programs and some traditional early childhood educators who wish to give children "the gift of time" by waiting for development to render children ready for academic work limit the number of innovative projects. D. F. Siegel and Hanson (1991) term this so-called developmental approach a "well-meaning but romantic" assumption that is inappropriate to the needs of most children today.

Given these limitations in the available reports on intervention projects, some significant trends in prevention projects can be seen.

There is one important trend in the available reports on intervention between early language development and school achievement. Skarda (1974) and her associates used communication skills as the focus of their model preventive program. Specifically, they set out to develop life-oriented language skills in language-delayed children. This group provided a 2-year oral language intervention program in public schools in Wisconsin. Complex case finding procedures were used. Intervention involved "structuring the auditory environment, reinforcing essential behaviors, fostering home-school communication." Curriculum emphasis was on art, physical movement, and music. Evaluations based on parent interviews, language tests, and case studies provided evidence that language functions improved in the participants, although follow-up data on the effects of the program on later school achievement are not available.

Studies of specific techniques (e.g., interactive approaches) in fostering the development of language in young children have been reported in two projects. In these cases, interactive skills were taught to mothers of language-delayed children and evaluations were based on discourse samples of mother-child interactions. Weistuch, Lewis, and Sullivan (1991) reported decreases in parallel talking and increases in content-related speech, but not significant differences in expansion or extension of language. Tannock and Girolametto (1992) found that although social interactions (such as turn-taking in conversation) were increased in the young language-delayed children in their study, language skill did not improve over the course of the intervention. These investigators provide detailed descriptions of their assessment and intervention methods that can be a useful model for other investigators. As part of their discussion, they noted that their group represented considerable variation in cognitive abilities and that changes in language skills were closely related to differences in cognitive functioning. It may be that changes in language skills in some children were masked in the overall analysis of their data.

Another significant group of projects is directed toward the academic needs of young children who live in large cities. Success for All is a well-designed example of such projects (Wasik & Slaving, 1990). A comprehensive schoolwide restructuring program that is designed for schools serving large numbers of disadvantaged students in Baltimore, Maryland, uses one-to-one tutoring in Grades 1 through 3 and family support services to render all children successful in acquiring the basic academic skills.

Project children are selected on the basis of informal reading inventories and reevaluated every 8 weeks. On the basis of the reevaluations, children are rotated in and out of tutoring; the amount of tutoring may vary from 8 weeks to an entire year. Tutors are certified teachers who teach a 90-minute reading class each day and spend the rest of the day tutoring three children per hour. Because of their knowledge of the general program, tutors are able to reteach what individual children have failed to learn in the class sessions. The reports of the project do not describe any innovative teaching strategies, but rather more efficient assessment and prompt, effective reteaching when a child falls behind in classroom work. Evaluations have produced impressive effect sizes in the original intervention site, as well as in replicating schools in the same city. In addition to effects on reading achievement, the investigators report "substantially reduced assignments of students to special education for learning problems and essentially eliminated grade retentions" (Wasik & Slaving, 1990).

Reading Recovery is a widely used intervention approach originally developed by Marie Clay (1985a) in New Zealand and disseminated in the United States by a group from Ohio State University. This program provides one-to-one tutoring to first graders who score in the lowest 20% of their classes on a program-developed diagnostic set of tasks that includes (a) letter identification; (b) reading words; (c) concepts about print; (d) writing vocabulary; (e) dictation; (f) test reading level. Tutors are certified teachers who have received special training of more than 2 hours a week for a year from the developers of the program. The tutoring model emphasizes "learning to read by reading" (Pinnell, 1985) with students tutored 30 minutes per day until being "discontinued" when they reach the level of their classmates or released as "not discontinued" after having had 60 tutoring sessions without reaching classroom expectations. Data provided by the Ohio State group on reading achievement tests from "discontinued" Reading Recovery children compared with control students at their respective school sites, qualified the program for selection as a Developer/Demonstrator of the U.S. Department of Education's National Diffusion Network. However, a number of questions remain concerning the fate of children who do not succeed after the 60 tutoring sessions and are presumably not included in the evaluations. Wasik and Slaving (1990) have also raised the question of long-term effectiveness on the basis of data concerning nonpromotion. One of the project developers has reported that in second grade 22% of the Reading Recovery students and 31% of the comparison students repeated the grade or were assigned to special education. By third grade, the differences had largely disappeared with 40.1% of the Reading Recovery children and 42.2% of the comparison children enrolled in third grade; the rest presumably repeated a grade or enrolled in special education.

Finally, the learning problems of the program child are not clearly defined by the initial identification methods used. These methods tap educational achievement only; one can only speculate on the reasons for their learning disorders. As stressed in this chapter, learning disorders represent a heterogeneous group of symptoms. Effective interventions would seem to be most likely when there is an appropriate match between salient factors in a child's vulnerability and the intervention approach. Research using statistical methods of path analysis to understand the contributions of the many factors that mediate the effects of early interventions (A. J. Reynolds, 1992) demonstrates just how complex intervention can be. It is not easy to define each child's disability, to match intervention to the individual child's needs, to maintain experimental treatments uncontaminated in the natural atmosphere of the school, to preserve control conditions when many children need service, and to obtain the commitment of time, resources, and funding for experimental research in schools.

Some of these barriers were overcome in the fortunate collaboration between a learning disorders unit in a medical school department of psychiatry and an urban school district in an interdisciplinary program using the SEARCH and TEACH model. Based on work begun in 1969, this model attempted to prevent learning disabilities and their emotional consequences through an interdisciplinary, school-based model. This model locates children vulnerable to learning failure with a brief scanning test, SEARCH, using interdisciplinary diagnosis with children found vulnerable, and provides appropriate educational intervention in the child's own school.

Officially known as the Prevention of Learning Disabilities: An Interdisciplinary Model, this work is more often called the Search and Teach program, the names of its two major components. Originally funded as a child service demonstration center by the Bureau for the Education of the Handicapped in 1976 to 1979 and approved by the Department of Education's Joint Dissemination and Review Panel in 1979, it continues to the present as one of the projects in the National Diffusion Network (Educational Programs That Work, 1998). This program seeks to prevent learning failure by (a) identifying vulnerable children; (b) providing diagnostic study to clarify the causes of their vulnerability; and (c) providing school-based intervention before failure has occurred.

The Search and Teach program has been modified for Spanish-speaking children and for church-related schools that requested modifications of the content of the program, to conform to their special needs. Content modification in each was assessed for reliability and for validity in identification of children at risk for academic failure (1999).

The first step, identifying the vulnerable children, using a scanning test, SEARCH, as described earlier, is based on the rationale that delays in spatial orientation and temporal organization are marker variables for learning failure in young children. These delays may appear in various combinations of language and perceptual functions; each child may be expected to have an unique pattern of strengths and needs. By surveying all the children in kindergarten or early in first grade, it attempts to identify children who are vulnerable to learning failure before they have failed.

SEARCH's database is the result of intensive clinical examinations of all first graders at an elementary school in Manhattan for two successive years (A. A. Silver & Hagin, 1972). Factor analysis of 20 variables from these examinations defined two SEARCH components (verbal-auditory and visual-neurological factors) and located the most powerful measures of each component. The test-retest reliability of SEARCH is 0.80 and the standard error of measurement of the total SEARCH score is 0.89 of a raw score unit. Prediction-performance comparisons show rates of 5% to 10% false negatives and 1% to 9% false positives.

The second step in implementation is to provide intensive diagnostic examinations to children identified as vulnerable. Results of these examinations are pooled in case conferences attended by school and clinical personnel to clarify the learning needs of individual children and to make appropriate intervention plans.

The third element of the preventive program is the provision of educational intervention. These activities are described in TEACH (Hagin, Silver, & Kreeger, 1976), a prescriptive approach designed to build the preacademic readiness skills for reading. The reading process is conceptualized as a complex one, requiring facility with four areas: prereading skills; word attack; comprehension; and study skills (A. A. Silver & Hagin, 1990, pp. 88–94). At ages 5 and 6 years, it is the lag in the development of prereading skills that identifies youngsters destined to fail. Although many children acquire these skills in the course of their development or learn them from informal educational experiences, children destined to have problems fail to do so.

The 55 tasks in the TEACH program are designed to develop these prereading skills by direct tutoring of the vulnerable children. The tasks are organized into five clusters (visual, auditory, visuomotor, body-image, and intermodal) from which teachers select tasks appropriate to the child's needs as reflected in the profile of SEARCH scores.

For most children, services are provided for 2 years, during kindergarten and first grade or during first and second grades by teachers and educational assistants in the child's own school. Two program models have been used: a resource room pullout mode, and a classroom support model in which an educational assistant works with children in the regular classroom.

The program was validated in eight core schools in Manhattan on the basis of data on its educational impact, cost effectiveness, and replicability. The original evaluation provided for a control group design and two-cohort design with varying degrees of intervention for each cohort. Analysis of variance statistics showed significant gains in reading during intervention and in the year after intervention had been completed. Follow-up at fifth-grade level showed that academic gains had been maintained and that the social adjustment of vulnerable children who had participated in the project did not differ from that of their classmates who had not been found vulnerable on SEARCH.

Data from a suburban school in which the intervention program had been replicated show that academic gains were maintained during elementary school and that few children required special education, remedial services, or grade repetition (Hagin, Thackeray, & Silver, 1991). These follow-up studies indicate that educational gains were associated with program participation, that gains were maintained after direct intervention was completed, and that early identification of vulnerable children did not jeopardize participation in the general educational enterprise.

SUMMARY

Factors that predispose children to learning disorders are heterogeneous arising from biological, psychological, cognitive, educational, and social sources, acting singly or synergistically. A comprehensive pentaxial evaluation encompassing all these sources is necessary to identify the various risk factors. Risk factors resulting from high obstetrical risk pregnancies, including teenage pregnancy and sexually transmitted diseases, from toxic substances in air, water, food, and other environmental sources, are susceptible to primary prevention—to the elimination of the risk factors themselves. To obtund the risk of poverty and social and cultural disadvantage, broad social and educational programs have been developed. Here the task is one of secondary prevention: The risk factors cannot yet be eliminated, but the impact of the risk factor predisposing to learning disorder may be reduced. Although Head Start and similar early education programs have reported favorable academic and social results, the risk of poor minority children developing a disorder of learning is still great. Administrative strategies such as lengthening the kindergarten day, creating transitional first-grade classes, and delaying entrance to kindergarten have had only partial success in preventing learning failure.

Greater success has been achieved in programs for the prevention of specific developmental learning disabilities. The developmental learning disability is characterized not only by a discrepancy between academic achievement and academic expectancy, but by the presence of central neuropsychological processing immaturities in the acquisition and use of all aspects of language. Successful programs for the prevention of developmental learning disorders have four basic components:

1. A scanning instrument with proven reliability and validity, capable of identifying early, in kindergarten or first grade, children for whom learning disorder is predicted (the scanning instrument should meet the accepted standards of the American Psychiatric Association for educational and psychological tests).
2. A diagnostic process for evaluation of vulnerable children to identify the specific needs of each child.
3. A set of intervention procedures capable of correcting and/or compensating for the central neuropsychological immaturities specific to each child.
4. Follow-up of sufficient time to permit long-term evaluation of the program.

Several preventive programs approved by the U.S. Department of Education Joint Dissemination and Review Panel are described.

PART IV

CLINICAL PATTERNS OF DISORDERS OF LEARNING

Chapter 11

DEVELOPMENTAL LEARNING DISABILITIES

Many people who fit the broad general designation of dyslexia, are notable, first of all for their seeming likeness to everybody else. Their ranges in age, IQ and social and other circumstances are just as wide as in every sense of the word "normal." Their learning, and skill problems, are specific to language.

—Margaret Rawson, 1968

Among children with disorders of learning, the most prevalent is the group said to have a "learning disability." While it is difficult to define the boundaries of this group, schools generally refer to learning disability in accordance with federal guidelines stated in the Individuals with Disabilities Education Act 1997 (Code of Federal Regulations, Title 34, Subtitle B, Chapter III, Section 300.7(b)(10)):

> Specific learning disability means a disorder in one or more basic psychological processes involved in understanding or in using language, spoken or written, that may manifest itself in an imperfect ability to listen, speak, read, write, spell or do mathematical calculations. The term includes such conditions as perceptual disabilities, brain injury, minimal brain dysfunction, dyslexia and developmental aphasia. The term does not apply to children that have learning problems that are primarily the result of visual, hearing and motor disabilities, of mental retardation, of emotional disturbances or of environmental, cultural or economic disadvantage.

The immense problems with these guidelines—their inclusionary and exclusionary criteria—have been discussed in Chapter 4 in this book. Nevertheless, it is these guidelines with which public schools contend.

Since the passage of Section 618(b) of the Individuals with Disabilities Education Act (IDEA) in 1997, school districts are required to report annually to the Office of Special Education Programs (OSEP), the number of children with disabilities served under programs mediated by that law. Under IDEA, there are 12 diagnostic categories of disability to be reported: learning disabilities, speech or language impairments, mental retardation, emotional disturbances, multiple disabilities, hearing impairments, orthopedic impairments, "other health impairments," visual impairments, autism, deaf-blindness, and traumatic brain injury (see Table 11.1). The different interpretations of the guidelines as well as the different assessment practices and educational policies of individual school districts create a heterogeneous population reported as "learning disabled," with resulting difficulty in knowing just how many individuals in the U.S. school population are indeed learning disabled, in what domain(s) their academic difficulties lie, the spectrum of their processing deficits, and the underlying causes contributing to their disability (see Chapter 5).

Nevertheless, despite the diagnostic heterogeneity of children reported as being served in special educational programs, their number has consistently increased at a rate higher than the general school enrollment since the programs were federally mandated in 1977 with the passage of PL 94-142. The number of children, ages 6 to 21 years, designated as having learning disabilities increased from 796,000 in the school years 1976 to 1977 to 1,942,304 in 1987 to 1988 to 2,676,299 in 1996 to 1997, an increase of 37.8% in the past 10 years. The total number of children served in all categories of disabilities (Table 11.1) also increased from 3,692,000 in 1976 to 1977 to 4,120,214 in 1987 to 1988 to 5,235,952 in 1996 to 1997, an increase of 46% since

Table 11.1   Number of children ages 6 to 21 served under IDEA by disability: 1987 to 1988 and 1996 to 1997

Disability	1987 to 1988		1996 to 1997		Change	
	Number	%	Number	%	Number	%
Specific learning disabilities	1,942,304	47.1	2,676,299[†]	51.1	733,955	37.8
Speech or language impairments	953,568	23.1	1,050,975	20.1	97,407	10.2
Mental retardation	598,770	14.5	594,025	11.4	−4,745	−0.8
Emotional disturbance	372,380	9.0	447,426	8.6	75,046	20.2
Multiple disabilities	79,023	1.9	99,638	1.9	20,615	26.1
Hearing impairments	56,872	1.4	68,766	1.3	11,894	20.9
Orthopedic impairments	46,966	1.1	66,400	1.3	19,434	41.4
Other health impairments	46,056	1.1	160,824	3.1	114,768	249.2
Visual impairments	22,821	0.6	25,834	0.5	3,013	13.2
Autism	*	*	34,101	0.7	34,101	*
Deaf-blindness	1,454	<0.1	1,286	<0.1	(168)	−11.6
Traumatic brain injury	*	*	10,378	0.2	10,378	*
All disabilities	4,120,214	100,0	5,235,952	100,0	1,115,738	27.1

*Reporting on autism and traumatic brain injury was required under IDEA beginning in 1992 to 1993.
[†]Represents 5.5% of total public school population.
Source: U.S. Department of Education, Office of Special Education Programs. Data Analysis System (DANS).

1997. However, when the number of children classified as learning disabled is subtracted from the total number served, the increase in the number of children classified in the other eleven categories is only 11.6%.

The number of children, adolescents, and young adults designated as having learning disabilities constitutes 51.1% of all students in the special programs and 5.5% of the total school population of the United States—a formidable number imposing great burden, not only financially, but also logistically, socially, and vocationally. Table 11.1 reports by disability the number of children ages 6 to 21 served under IDEA during the years 1987 to 1988 and 1996 to 1997.

As seen in Table 11.1, "Specific Learning Disabilities" is the most prevalent of the disabilities reported (51.1%) followed by speech or language impairments (20.1% or 1,050,975 children), mental retardation (11.4% or 594,024 children), and emotional disturbances (8.6% or 447,426 children). Not only is the prevalence of learning disabilities the highest of the disabilities reported, but the rate of increase was also greater than any category other than "other health impairment." The tremendous increase in the "other health impairment" may be a response to a 1991, Department of Education, Office of Special Education and Rehabilitation Service (OSERS) requesting that students with ADD and ADHD be included in the annual report when ADD (ADHD) is a "chronic or acute health problem resulting in limited alertness that adversely affects educational performance" (OSERS, 1991).

In reality, these statistics present a conservative estimate of the prevalence of learning disabilities. As Gaddes pointed out as early as 1976, "Service statistics, largely determined by budgetary restrictions and educational policy, are a minimum estimate of prevalence and indicate nothing about the number of neglected needy" (p. 12). A report of the Canadian Commission on Emotional and Learning Disorders (1970) estimated that the number of children in Canada needing specific diagnostic and remedial help to be between 10% and 16% of the total school-age population. The Canadian study estimated that in Great Britain 14% of school-age children had "special needs"; in France, 12.14%; in the United States, 10% to 15%. The Collaborative Perinatal Project (P. L. Nichols & Chen, 1981) was a longitudinal study of the relationship between perinatal problems and neurological and cognitive defects in infancy and early childhood. It was not designed to assess prevalence, but in a study of 29,889 children followed from birth to age 7 years, 6.5% of their population had "learning disability only," 5.8% had hyperactivity and impulsivity only, and 6.2% had "neurological signs only."

Estimates of incidence vary widely. Lyon (1996) suggests that "virtually all children scoring below the 25th percentile on standardized reading tests can meet criteria for having a reading disorder." Badian (1999) reports that 6% of the school population has difficulties in mathematics, while problems with written expression are found in 8% to 15% of the school population. Many variables enter in prevalence estimates, not only definitional ones, but also the cutoff points and the test probes used. On the basis of early data from the Connecticut Longitudinal Study, the prevalence of dyslexia in the third grade is reported by B. A. Shaywitz, Fletcher, and Shaywitz (1994) as 17.5%. Given these figures, the prevalence of learning disabilities among public school children in the United States then is, conservatively, math, 6%; written expression, 8% to

15%; dyslexia, 17.5%; the total is approximately 25%. Of course, there is considerable overlap among the academic domains of disability.

The term *learning disabilities,* however, is the language spoken in the public schools. The term *developmental learning disabilities* has come to imply that a familial, hereditary, genetic factor contributes to the cause of the disability and that these children do not have evidence of a structural defect of the central nervous system, are not intellectually retarded, and do not have defects in sensory acuity related to their learning failure. Although they may have emotional problems, these problems may be reactive to the learning disability and not the cause of it. Extrinsic factors, such as those listed in Table 5.1, and Attention-Deficit/Hyperactive Disorder may be present, but these factors (although they may be present along with developmental learning disability) are separate disorders and do not cause the disability (see Chapter 5). In this book, we use the term developmental learning disability to indicate the heterogeneous group of children who may have problems in any or all combinations of academic domains, in any or all combinations of neuropsychological processing defects that relate to the development of language, and who may have a family history of language or learning problems. Language here is considered in its broadest sense: the processing of symbols from all modalities including decoding, temporal sequencing, association, short- and long-term memory, comprehension, retrieval, and expression.

As suggested earlier, other causes of learning disorders may be present in addition to the developmental disorders, (see Table 5.1, in Chapter 5) but are not part of the developmental learning disabilities syndrome. We make this distinction to identify a group that is as homogeneous as our current knowledge permits and also because treatment of children with developmental learning disabilities has, with appropriate intervention, a favorable outcome, different from the guarded prognosis of children with ADHD, as well as of children coming from a culture where they experience inappropriate or inadequate language stimulation at critical ages and of children with an organic defect of the central nervous system. The term *specific learning disability* has been used synonymously with developmental learning disability. In the previous edition of this book, the adjective *specific* was used in two senses: (a) the medical meaning, that the cause of the disorders was unknown (e.g., *specific hypertension*) and (b) that it related to one major area of defect—the development of language. In this edition, advances in genetics have focused on the hereditary aspect of the disorder. Accordingly, the term specific has outlived half its usefulness (we are beginning to understand the hereditary origin of the developmental learning disabilities) and will not be used here in the medical sense. The *DSM-IV-TR* criteria for diagnosis of "reading disorder" appears in Table 11.2. The remainder of this chapter will consider academic domains in which developmental learning disabilities are impaired.

DEVELOPMENTAL READING DISABILITY

Among children with developmental learning disabilities, the most prevalent in the classroom are those having developmental reading disabilities, perhaps 80% of all children with developmental learning disabilities (Lerner, 1988). This group has been

Table 11.2   Diagnostic criteria for 315.00 Reading Disorder

A. Reading achievement, as measured by individually administered standardized tests of reading accuracy or comprehension, is substantially below that expected given the person's chronological age, measured intelligence, and age-appropriate education.

B. The disturbance in Criterion A significantly interferes with academic achievement or activities of daily living that require reading skills.

C. If a sensory deficit is present, the reading difficulties are in excess of those usually associated with it.

Coding note: If a general medical (e.g., neurological) condition or sensory deficit is present, code the condition on Axis III.

Note: Reprinted with permission from the *Diagnostic and Statistical Manual of Mental Disorders,* Fourth Edition, Text Revision. Copyright 2000, American Psychiatric Association.

described as having developmental dyslexia (Critchley, 1964), strephosymbolia (Orton, 1928, 1937), congenital word blindness (Hinshelwood, 1917), congenital auditory imperception (Worcester-Drought & Allen, 1929), and psychoneurological learning disabilities (Myklebust, 1968; Myklebust & Boshes, 1969). Developmental reading disability is equivalent to the primary reading disability of Rabinovitch (1968); the dyslexia pure of Denckla (1978); and the specific reading retardation of Rutter (1978). The term *dyslexia* is commonly used as a synonym for developmental reading disabilities, and major American and International Associations are dedicated to both practical and theoretical aspects of its problems. The term dyslexia is used by the European Dyslexic Association (EDA) and the International Dyslexic Association (formerly the Orton Dyslexia Society) with its International Affiliates Subcommittee. The term *developmental reading disability* identifies the academic domain in which the disorder is expressed, but in addition implies that neuropsychological processing deficits, predominantly in the language functions, are present and that there is a familial and presumably genetic basis for the disability. While for each child, the constellation of processing defects is unique, there is a unifying defect: an immaturity in development of language function considered in its broadest sense, but most frequently in the ability to make accurate sound/symbol associations (phonemic-phonological processing), sequencing the sounds to make words, retaining the sounds in short-term memory, storing the sounds in long-term memory, understanding the meaning of the sequenced sounds, and finally expressing them in oral or in written form. It is recognized that identifying processing deficits within the realm of language as conceptualized here will, in itself, yield a heterogeneous population of individuals with a variety of processing problems.

While recent thinking emphasizes the role of phonological processing in reading disabilities (Morton & Frith, 1995; Pennington, Van Orden, Smith, Green, & Haith, 1990; Stanovich & Siegel, 1994), other language and cognitive processing deficits may also be found. Stanovich and Siegel conceptualized these language deficits as a "phonological core with variable differences" (Stanovich & Siegel, 1994).

Variable differences in the phonological core model of reading disability were investigated by a consortium (Morris et al., 1998).

Morris et al. (1998) studied 376 children including 58 children with a reading disability, 87 with math disability, and 108 with both reading and math disability, along with 123 non-learning-disabled children (including 55 with ADHD, 81 without ADHD and with full scale IQ ≥ 90, and 17 children with full scale IQ < 80), with a battery designed to evaluate a broad array of cognitive skills hypothesized to be differentially related to reading proficiency. The results of these tests were subjected to cluster analysis. Eight measures were selected for testing: phonological awareness, tested by an Auditory Analysis Test (Rosner & Simon, 1971); verbal short-term memory (VSTM) (word string recall, Shankweiler, Liberman, Mark, Fowler, & Fischer, 1979); rapid naming (Rapid Naming Subtest-1, Katz & Shankweiler, 1985); lexical/vocabulary (WISC-R similarities); speech production (speed of articulation, Hulme, Thompson, Muir, et al., 1984); visual-spatial (Judgement of Line Orientation, Lindgren & Benton, 1980); visual attention (Doehring, 1968); and nonverbal short-term memory (Milner, 1971). The final cluster analysis solution resulted in 10 subtypes, well-defined statistically with a strong core of about 80% of the sample accounted for in the analysis. The remaining 20% were outliers not belonging to any clear subtype of the 10 subtypes. One of the subtypes consisting of 5 nondisabled readers was deleted for consideration, leaving 9 subtypes including 208 children. Of the 9 remaining subtypes, 2 groups ($n = 25$) were predominantly nondisabled in reading. Only 3 children in these groups were initially defined as reading disabled. The 7 remaining subtypes were composed of children identified as reading disabled. Two of these subtypes were severely disabled readers who earned scores on the 8 test variables well below those obtained by the other 7 subtypes. One of these 2 groups labeled *global deficit* ($n = 26$) had a flat profile; 35% of this group consisted of children with earned IQs below 80; all in this group had reading difficulty. The other group, labeled *global language* ($n = 35$) had better performance on visual processing measures relative to language measures. Morris et al. (1998) state that these 2 subgroups most likely represented garden-variety poor readers (i.e., they had reading scores that were not discrepant from their IQ).

There were 5 specific subtypes of predominantly reading-disabled children; four of the five shared a relative weakness on the measure of phonological awareness, varying in whether they were impaired on other measures, such as rapid serial naming and VSTM, that the authors state are "other measures involving phonological processing." These 4 clusters are labeled (a) *phonology-verbal short-term memory* (VSTM) – rate ($n = 43$); (b) *phonology-rate* ($n = 18$); (c) *phonology-VSTM-lexical* ($n = 15$); (d) *phonology-VSTM-spatial* ($n = 31$). The first 3 of these subclusters included 6 nondisabled children; 69% of the reading-disabled children in these clusters had reading scores discrepant relative to IQ. The phonology-VSTM-spatial type included 11 children with no disability who also had strength in rapid naming.

The fifth specific cluster labeled *rate deficit* ($n = 15$) was not weak on phonological awareness but was impaired in verbal and nonverbal measures associated with rapid or sequential responses. The finding of a cluster specifically impaired in rapid naming, and another with specific strength in rapid naming is consistent with the double-deficit model of Maryanne Wolf (1999); she emphasized a group of children with reading disabilities who have deficits in the fluency-related processes underlying naming speed, and not in phonological processes (this double-deficit model, to use Wolf's term, is discussed in Chapter 5).

The authors (Morris et al., 1998) conclude that "results support the view that children with reading disability usually display impairments on phonological awareness measures with discrimination variability in other measures involving phonological processing, language and cognitive skills" (p. 147). Review of the data, however, also emphasized that in evaluating the processing deficits of a child with a reading disability, evaluation of phonological awareness in the sense of symbol-sound association alone will not reveal the entire spectrum of processing deficits with which the individual child suffers. The entire range of language functions, including temporal sequencing, rapid naming, short-term memory, long-term memory, retrieval and expression, visuomotor-spatial, right-left orientation, finger gnosis, and constructive finger gnosis all need testing. As emphasized in this book, the processing deficits found in any sample of children with developmental learning problems will, in part, depend on the preconceived battery of processing deficits with which the subjects are examined and on the etiological homogeneity of the sample. Thus, unless the range of functions outlined earlier are tested, some processing problems that have implications for treatment and for prognosis are undetected. Further, unless in each child, the underlying cause(s) of the reading disability is evaluated, as outlined in Chapter 5, the sample under study may represent a mixture of etiologies and not a sample of developmental reading disabilities at all. The results of the Morris et al. (1998) study are not unlike those of the multivariate analysis reviewed in Chapter 5 of this book and are subject to the same criticism.

THE CONTINUUM OF DEVELOPMENTAL LANGUAGE AND READING DISABILITIES

We have stressed that the spectrum of neuropsychological processing deficits in developmental reading disorders is related to a disruption in the sequences involved in the development of language. If this hypothesis is valid, then the precursors of developmental reading disability should be found in preschool children who would not have yet been exposed to variations in preschool reading instruction. Scarborough and Dobrich (1990) followed three groups of children from age 30 months to age 8 years: 32 children from families in which "someone had experienced a severe childhood reading problem." Group 1 included 20 (65%) of these children from families with dyslexia who subsequently themselves became disabled readers by age 8 years. Group 2 were 12 of the 32 children selected from dyslexic families but who did not become disabled readers. The third group were 20 "normal" children selected so as to resemble the dyslexic family children in IQ, socioeconomic status, and gender. A retrospective analysis compared the early language skills of these 3 groups of children. At 2½ years of age, the 20 children who later developed reading disabilities were deficient in the length, syntactic complexity and pronunciation accuracy of their spoken language, but not in lexical or speech discrimination skills. As 3-year-olds, these 20 children began to show deficits in receptive vocabulary and object-naming abilities. At age 5 years, they were weak in object naming, phonemic awareness, and letter sound knowledge, immaturities that have characterized kindergartners who became poor readers. At age 5 years, syntactic deficiencies were no longer apparent. In short, the precursors for later phonemic awareness and letter/sound knowledge could be found in earlier defects and delays in spoken language. Further, phonological skills, as assessed by rate of consonant errors in speech production, did not account for significant variance in outcome. However, syntactic proficiency emerged as a unique predictor in Grade 2. The language deficits of children who became dyslexic were not observed in children from dyslexic families who became normal readers. Scarborough argued that the phonological hypothesis does not offer a *complete* explanation of reading failure, but that dyslexia is a general verbal problem, a broader delay in language development whose manifestations change over time with a variation both in the occurrence and severity of symptoms among disabled readers.

A similar study is reported by A. Gallagher, Frith, and Snowling (2000). Sixty-three children selected from families in which at least one member was dyslexic, were compared in cognition and language measures, with 34 families reporting no history of reading impairment, at age 45 months and at 6 years. Fifty-seven percent of the genetically at-risk group were delayed in "literacy development" (i.e., reading, spelling, phonetic spelling ability, nonword reading, alphabet knowledge, and general cognitive ability) compared with 12% of the controls. At 45 months, the "unimpaired" at-risk group were not statistically different from controls on most cognitive and language measures, whereas the "literacy delayed" group was delayed in their speech and language development, although they did not differ from controls in the draw-a-man test as a measure of nonverbal ability. Speech or language development at 45 months was measured by vocabulary, expressive language, articulation, phonological processing, phonological awareness (test of rhyme knowledge). Letter knowledge at 45 months was the strongest predictor of literacy level at 6 years. However, other early speech and language skills also predicted differences in literacy outcome. Thus, "retrospective analysis of their language development in the pre-school years suggests that literacy delayed children are subject to mild delay in all aspects of their spoken language" (p. 210). The largest group differences among the early language measures were found for vocabulary, naming, and digit span. Of interest, these findings were exactly those reported by Hagin in 1954.

Snowling, Bishop, and Stothard (2000) carry this concept further than the second grade. They assessed the literacy skills of 56 children at age 15 years. This group had specific language impairment as preschoolers. At age 15, they performed worse on tests of reading, spelling, and reading comprehension than agemate controls. More significantly, the rate of reading retardation in these early language-impaired children increased between the ages of $8\frac{1}{2}$ and 15 years, a substantial drop in reading accuracy relative to age. Children who had impaired language development at $4\frac{1}{2}$ years and still retained verbal deficits at $5\frac{1}{2}$ years had reading and spelling problems as well and persistent oral language impairment, particularly in comprehension and expression of spoken language, in the early elementary grades. In these children, reading comprehension tended to be poor. Syntactic competence in the preschool period accounted for a substantial variance in literacy skills (V. Bishop & Adams, 1990). These children fell further behind their peer group in vocabulary growth over time (Stothard, Snowling, Bishop, et al., 1998). These findings suggest that the demands of reading change over time, and that while phonological difficulties of language-impaired preschoolers place them at risk of literacy failure at the onset of reading, impairment of other language skills may compromise development to adult level fluency.

MRI studies (Gauger et al., 1997) of children with developmental language impairment have reported reversed asymmetry or symmetry of the planum temporale, consistent with MRI findings in children with dyslexia, suggesting that the same underlying neurobiological deficit is present in both developmental language disability and in developmental reading disability. Electrophysiologically, language-impaired children, like reading-impaired children, exhibit atypical patterns of evoked brain activity. However, it was not the same group of children who displayed abnormalities across the different tasks, so that there may be multiple patterns for the neurobiology of development language impairment (Mills & Neville, 1997) and by extension for the neurobiology of developmental reading disabilities. That these three groups have different diagnostic labels results from differences in language/literacy requirements at different age levels.

The continuum of developmental language disability and developmental reading disability leads to the common history reported by parents of children with developmental reading disability:

- Such children may be slower in reaching the developmental milestones for using words and sentences.
- Oral inaccuracies may persist in their speech longer than that of other preschoolers and then mature spontaneously.
- They often do not enjoy the playful rhyming that many young children do spontaneously.
- In the primary grades, their oral language may be less complex than their age and intelligence would indicate.
- They have difficulty generating rhymes and matching initial sounds.
- They have difficulty remembering the names of people and common objects.
- Vocabularies may be more limited than age, intelligence, and background experiences indicate.
- They sometimes mix up the order of syllables within words and produce spoonerisms.
- Longer than most first graders, they will continue to reverse or rotate letters and numbers when they write.
- They continue to confuse right and left directions and the orientations of the body in space.
- When they are learning to do cursive writing they find it hard to remember the motor patterns of letters.
- They have trouble remembering the arbitrary sequence of letters, months, and measures.

- They have trouble relating sound to written symbols and blending these sounds into known words.
- Written expression will be simple even though they may have complex ideas to express.
- There is generally a history of reading difficulty or of anomalies in developing clear-cut hand preferences, in the family.

CASE STUDY: LUCIEN

Lucien was first seen when he was 13 years 3 months of age and entering the seventh grade at a demanding parochial school that he had been attending since first grade. His parents were concerned that he had barely passed sixth grade, with particular difficulty in grammar and in handwriting. Although he is a good athlete, he resented his academic work, grumbling at what he felt was too much homework. He became irritable and depressed. In the seventh grade, his teachers recommended that he be tutored.

His parents report that as early as 2 years 9 months, Lucien's language development appeared "slow," that he was communicating by gestures and not by words. At that time, "articulation defects" were reported by a speech therapist. By age 7 years 3 months, when his school psychological report described difficulty with "written language and weakness in vocabulary, spelling and syntax," Lucien earned a Full Scale IQ of 112 on the WISC-III (Verbal IQ 108, Performance IQ 113). However, scores for subtests were scattered with a subtest score of 8 in vocabulary, 6 in digit span, 8 in object arrangement. The coding subtest was considered "invalid" by the examiner. On the Woodcock-Johnson Tests of Cognitive Ability, Lucien earned percentile ranks of 8 in memory for names, 9 in memory for words, 16 for the cluster of tests measuring short-term memory, 31 for long-term retrieval.

At age 13 years 6 months, retesting by the same speech and language therapists who had examined Lucien when he was 3 years old, found that he "presents language delays in areas of processing directions and questions, comprehension, auditory sentence/word memory, and written language. He exhibits strength with sentence assembly, understanding semantic relationships and formulating sentences." He earned a percentile rank of 3 in a test of Written Expression (Oral and Written Language Scales, OWLS), a percentile rank of 16 each in Concepts and Directions and in Recalling Sentences in Word Classes (Clinical Evaluation of Language Fundamentals, CELF-3). It was clear that Lucien's language problems were still present.

In our examination, Lucien was found to be good-sized 13-year-old, about 5′3″ in height weighing 110 pounds. His bones are large, giving promise of a physically solid adolescent and adult. He was pleasant in appearance, brown hair tousled, gaze direct, sitting quietly in his chair, slightly tense. Initially guarded in affect, he was soon able to relax and respond to questions relevantly and coherently. There was however, a mild articulation defect and very laconic responses. He said he does not understand things, that he has trouble "figuring out things" mostly when he reads. He said he has trouble with reading, spelling, and writing but is "okay in math." He said his writing is "kind of messy" and that he is very slow "in a lot of things," like homework, where "it takes a kid one hour but it takes me two hours." He said he feels stupid on tests because he cannot remember what he studied the night before. He feels frustrated and angry because of his inability to do well in school. He is developing a fear of failure, not only in school but in anything he does. For example, he dreams that he is playing in the NBA, but he misses the basket and leaves in disgrace. He worries about his future.

On neurological examination, he has significant areas of neuropsychological immaturity. He has a severe auditory sequencing defect such that, even at his age of 13 years, with good intelligence, he cannot sequence the months of the year or recall elements of the sequence without going through the entire sequence. He has trouble remembering the sequencing of strings of common objects and on previous cognitive testing with WISC-III he earned a subtest score of 6, on Digit Span. His visuomotor function is also immature on the Bender-Gestalt. He works very slowly, and has many primitive features (problems with angulation in Figures A and 7), rotation (Figures 2, 3, 4, 5), primitive loops (Figures 1, 3, 5). There is still hesitation in right-left orientation, although finger gnosis and construction finger praxis are excellent. On the arm extension test in this right-handed boy, it is the left arm that is clearly elevated. His palms are sweaty, blood pressure 110/62, pulse rate 66. The remainder of the neurological examination in terms of gross and fine motor coordination, power, synergy and muscle tone, deep and superficial reflexes, cranial nerves and gross sensory evaluation (including hearing) is normal. Educationally, his word recognition (WRAT) is at an early sixth-grade level with persistent difficulty with sound/symbol associations and sequencing; spelling is also at an early sixth-grade level.

In summary, this 13-year-old boy with high average intelligence, had a language disability noted in his first three years of life, characterized by moderate delay in the development of language, articulation problems evident at age 3 years; then at age 7 he was noted to have "auditory processing deficits" including auditory figure-ground perception, questionable ability to interpret verbal direction, questionable short-term memory and long-term memory retrieval with low average vocabulary. Now at age 13, he has problems with comprehension, particularly in reading, slow rate of reading, poor spelling, and slow labored writing. He has specific neuropsychological processing deficits in auditory sequencing, phonological difficulty in reading, and primitive visuomotor function. The discordance between writing hand and elevated arm on the arm extension test, suggests that hemisphere specialization for language has not been established. It is not clear whether the comprehension problem is an entity in itself or is a consequence of the neuropsychological processing deficits.

The management recommended was to provide compensatory support in his school and specific training for each of the central processing deficits contributing to his difficulty with comprehension. The principles behind these recommendations are described in Chapter 8. Lucien illustrates the aberrant development in the sequence of language functions, from delayed speech in his first years of life to articulation deficit in early preschool, to problems with sequencing, short- and long-term memory (and probably with phonology) in early school age and to persistent problems with sequencing phonics, memory, and visuomotor function in late elementary school.

CASE STUDY: RICHARD

Richard illustrates the continuum of language deficits as they merge into reading problems and academic difficulty. He was first seen at age 6 years 7 months when he was in the first grade of a demanding private school. The major complaint was behavioral: "He has not adjusted to first grade," said his mother. He clowned and became physically aggressive to his classmates when he did not get their attention. The teacher reported that he seemed to lack the understanding necessary to discuss his problems with his peers or with teachers. At home with two younger siblings aged 3 and 2, his mother reported Richard to be "hard driving, persistent, difficult to handle, and jealous of his brothers." His father, a physician, was preoccupied with his profession and at home preferred to retreat into an easy chair to read, with little verbal communication with his family. His mother was attentive, concerned, and verbal, but she had to manage the home and the children with little emotional support.

On examination at 6 years 7 months, Richard was a chubby, handsome, brown-eyed child, who came into the examining room with little overt anxiety and began immediately to play with the toy trains. He was attentive, cooperative, and motivated, but his verbal responses were laconic, with short sentences and simple sentence structure. His school reported that on the WISC-R he earned a full scale IQ in the average range (92), but there was a significant discrepancy between verbal IQ of 69 and performance IQ of 121. His strengths were in Picture Completion (scaled score 14), Picture Arrangement (17), Coding (13), and Mazes (14). His greatest weaknesses were in Information (5), Similarities (2), and Arithmetic (2). Richard's difficulty appeared to be in auditory processing and in associative learning. When questions were difficult for him, he would frown, hold his head in his hands, even grind his teeth, but would never say he did not know the answer. On the Peabody Picture Vocabulary test, he scored in the 40th percentile. The Illinois Test of Psychologystic Abilities further delineated Richard's auditory processing deficits, with auditory memory $1\frac{3}{4}$ years below chronological age, auditory association $1\frac{1}{2}$ years below chronological age, and auditory reception 1 year below chronological age. He could not sequence the days of the week. On the Aphasia Screening Test of the Halstead Reitan Neuropsychological Battery for Children, there was difficulty naming objects, and mild finger agnosia.

Classical neurological examination was within normal limits. There was, however, immaturity in right-left discrimination, in finger gnosis, and in praxis. On the arm extension test (discussed later in this chapter), the left arm was elevated in this right-handed boy, suggesting that hemisphere specialization for language was not yet established. Electroencephalogram and audiometric examinations were normal.

This was a child with a developmental language disability whose major area of deficit was in auditory reception, in temporal sequencing of auditory information, and in recall of that information. He was already reacting to his frustration with anxiety and with demands for attention and temper outbursts when his demands were not met. He could not cope with the high expectations of the school that he was attending. Accordingly, Richard was placed in a special school for children with learning disabilities where he was given specific training for his auditory and associative deficits. By fourth grade, he was doing well in a reasonably demanding private school. His father received psychotherapeutic assistance. Examination of a younger brother when he reached kindergarten age revealed the same pattern of deficits with which Richard struggled.

In the past 10 years, educators have become increasingly aware that developmental learning disabilities do not disappear when their students finally graduate from (or leave) high school or even college. Without appropriate and adequate intervention, the disability persists; people do not spontaneously outgrow their disabilities. A section of this chapter reviews the generally unfavorable outcome as seen in research investigation, of children with developmental reading disabilities (Satz, Buka, Lipsitt, & Seidman, 1998). While the prevalence of adults in the United States with developmental reading disabilities is unknown, a National Adult Literacy Survey (quoted in the *Tampa Tribune,* September 22, 2000) found 40 million adults in the United States have low literacy skills. This number may include all causes of illiteracy (non-English speaking, cognitive retardation). However, adults who have developmental reading disabilities with neuropsychological processing problems that were present in childhood, fill clinics that treat them. These individuals may have high intelligence and still have persistent problems with the sequence of maturational problems in language seen in Richard and Lucien. Mark is an example.

CASE STUDY: MARK

Mark is a 30-year-old, third-year student of an excellent medical school in the United States. Despite reports of his excellent clinical abilities and performance, he did not pass the written miniboards in surgery and in obstetrics and gynecology. Unless he can pass these examinations, he cannot go on to his fourth year and complete medical school.

On examination, Mark is essentially as he describes himself, "friendly, outgoing, hard-working, caring, reasonable, and intelligent." He is not depressed, but is appropriately anxious about his academic difficulty. He expresses himself clearly, relevantly, and appropriately. He says that he does not finish the written exams, that as they are structured with a paragraph to be read and responses to be made to the paragraph, he cannot finish on time. He reads the paragraph slowly, but then must read it again to understand the content before he can answer the questions about it. As time elapses in the examination, he realizes that he cannot finish and this in turn provokes tension. He reads slowly not only during exams but in general and must go back over what he reads to understand the content. In contrast to this reading speed and comprehension difficulty, auditory-verbal inputs present no difficulty and he can summarize and outline lectures with no problem. Similarly, he has no difficulty organizing data, presenting case material clearly and concisely.

Neurological examination reveals intact visuomotor function. The Bender-Gestalt figures are drawn slowly and carefully with no significant errors. Auditory-temporal sequencing is intact. There are no problems in fine-motor coordination or in right-left discrimination. There are mild immaturities in constructive finger praxis. On extension of the arms in this right-handed individual, the extended arms tend to diverge and the left arm is distinctly elevated. (This is an abnormal response and suggests that hemisphere specialization for language is not clearly established.) Educationally, Mark can identify single words at a beginning college level with difficulty with phonics, particularly in words that are not familiar to him. He reads slowly and with hesitation. Written spelling is at a 10th to 11th grade level. The difficulty is not concentration. On the Stroop Test (which requires concentration and freedom from distracting stimuli), he is excellent. The remainder of the neurological examination is within normal limits.

Mark is suffering from the residuals of a developmental disability, characterized by persistent phonic difficulty, resulting in slow reading, almost word-to-word reading. This has never been diagnosed, largely because his above-average intelligence, motivation, and concentration have enabled him to compensate for his processing difficulty. The demands presented by the miniboards, which require rapid reading and reading comprehension, have overwhelmed the defenses Mark has previously used. There is a family history of learning problems in two of his brothers: one was diagnosed as learning disabled and was in special classes at school; the other was identified with reading difficulty and "school problems."

EDUCATIONAL INTERVENTION

Each of these case studies provides a sampling of the varying clinical pictures of individuals with developmental learning disabilities. They demonstrate not only the basic disorder as is manifested at different ages, but the efforts of the individuals as they attempt to compensate for their problems and to deal with tasks and responsibilities expected of people their age in our society. When these efforts are unsuccessful, these individuals and their families seek assistance from clinical personnel. While clinical services are also needed, targeted, appropriate, consistent teaching is essential intervention for the student with a developmental learning disorder.

Educators may have any of several titles—tutor, special education teacher, reading specialist, educational therapist, remedial specialist—but in the final analysis their job is to teach. They are responsible for understanding the disorder and the specific strengths and weaknesses the student brings to it. This implies that they relate the student's pattern of assets and deficits seen in the diagnostic formulation to the individual's educational needs. These teachers assess what has already been learned and what needs to be taught and select the most effective methods for teaching each student. The plans for intervention are made by taking into account not only the student's personal qualities and interests, but also the requirements of the real world in which the student lives. Therefore, good teaching is highly individualized and carefully targeted. We have all seen the disappointing results of unfocused tutoring that consists of doing the students' homework with them or "going over again" whatever has been covered in class, often material that bears little relationship to the child's diagnosed needs. Effective teaching is planned, targeted, and taught to mastery. These principles can be illustrated through the educational plans made for Lucien, Richard, and Mark.

Lucien

With an almost classic history of the effects of the developmental learning disorder on language and learning, Lucien is attempting to meet the educational demands of a challenging school setting after seven years of marginal achievement. His teacher should not be misled by his apparent strengths in word attack; examination on the oral reading test record and listening as he reads aloud will convince her that there are significant gaps in his skills in phonics and structural analysis of words. His mild articulatory inaccuracy and his poor spelling suggest problems in auditory discrimination that interfere with accurate decoding in reading and encoding in spelling. His early limitations in oral language development are now mirrored in his laconic speech and limited written compositions. His delays in fine motor control are reflected in illegible handwriting—an awkward print in which malformed letters mask spelling uncertainties. Gaps in reading skills interfere with comprehension of textbooks, and gaps in written language skills interfere with note taking in the content subjects. Failure to hear the words accurately or to write them down correctly contributes to his failure to remember for unit tests at school.

Despite these complex language and learning disabilities, Lucien earned scores within the high average range of intelligence on formal testing. He is aware of his difficulties and is angered that his hard work at school is not rewarded by higher grades. His success at sports has been some compensation in the past, but even there he is beginning to lose faith in his ability to achieve. Intervention planning for Lucien involves a two-part approach (a) agreement on some general management principles with his parents and his teachers at school (b) intensive tutoring to teach basic skills necessary for school achievement appropriate for Lucien's potential.

Management at home requires counseling to help his parents understand his learning problems and the generally positive outcomes when appropriate educational opportunities and parental support are available. Because of the genetic origin of developmental learning disability, a parent or sibling may also have the disorder and may, therefore, have some understanding of its effects. While parental understanding is important, school cooperation is also essential. The tutor or other clinician must advocate on behalf of Lucien and achieve some modification of schoolwork for him:

- Modification of homework assignments.
- Extended time on unit tests and major examinations.
- Taped books for use in content subjects like social studies and science.
- Substitution of work with reading and language arts for foreign language classes.

It is also important for the school staff to recognize the need for leadership opportunities for Lucien in sports or the arts and photography, to help restore his faith in his ability to learn.

The cooperation of Lucien's parents in the provision of individual tutoring at least three times per week is also essential to intervention planning. This tutoring should involve the following components:

1. *Systematic Review and Mastery of Word Attack Skills*

Using the word lists of systematic formulation of the generalizations of phonics and structural analysis (such as Steere et al., *Solving Language Difficulties*) Lucien should be retaught word attack skills using the DOMinate method (for detailed description of method, see Chapter 8). Some of these principles are already known by Lucien, so that the work will proceed rapidly, particularly as these skills become more automatic. This method consists of interactive dictation, oral reading, and silent reading for meaning of words grouped according to a specific phonic or structural analysis principle. Dictation will help his vague or inaccurate sound discrimination and will teach him to sequence sounds into words from the model of blending provided by the tutor. Repeated oral reading of the dictated list will provide practice and improve fluent silent reading and clarify word meanings.

2. *Increase the Quality and Quantity of Language*

The first step suggested would be to use manipulatives, such as the A-blocks or the People Pieces of the *Attribute Games*. These structured materials would give Lucien practice in verbalizing similarities and differences in the attributes of color, size, and shape. When these oral skills are fluent, Lucien can move onto written language practice by completing written conversations, with responses guided by questioning by his tutor. Gradual transitions can then be made so that he learns to use graphic organizers, like webbing, to chart the main ideas and supporting details in brief compositions. These webs become the basis for learning to outline the structure of a written composition. Compositions should be carried through the four phrases of (a) planning content with webbing, (b) drafting, (c) editing draft with his tutor, (d) rewriting final copy.

3. *Improve Legibility of Handwriting*

Use the "connected print" approach to develop a more legible handwriting style. This approach builds on the manuscript he has been using, but teaches him to connect the letters for more legible and fluent handwriting. (Techniques for teaching this style of writing are explained in detail in Chapter 8.) This handwriting approach develops motifs for individual letters at the chalkboard because work in the vertical plane is closer to gross motor activity and avoids some of the directional orientation problems students encounter in working at a desk. After the letter patterns and connections are mastered, transfer is made to pencil and paper writing at a desk.

4. *Teach Strategies for Reviewing Content for Tests*

Lucien's tutor can help him prepare for unit tests at school by reviewing the material with him and guiding him in *selecting* significant terms and concepts in the content areas, in *constructing* flash cards (with the term or concept written on one side of the card and the brief definition on the reverse side), and in *self-testing* by verbalizing or writing the definitions and then checking with the reverse side of the card. Guided review will demonstrate to Lucien the need to isolate important parts of the content and to use repeated reviewing to master the concepts. Lucien's memory problems seem to result from his inability to separate important points from details and his futile efforts to try to remember everything.

Reevaluation of academic skills at 6-month intervals is recommended, as well as regular contact between tutor and classroom teachers and parents in shared support of his program of remediation.

Richard

The account of Richard's problems shows the lifelong nature in developmental learning disorders. The disability persists, although the way it manifests itself depends upon the age of the individual and the various compensations available to him. Richard's early problems were severe, both educationally and behaviorally. His family had the resources to obtain diagnosis and intervention services in a special school for children with learning disabilities. His excellent cognitive abilities permitted him to make good progress with decoding and encoding in the special setting. By age 10 years, he was able to return to a regular educational setting in a small private school. His basic language problems persisted, however. With the increasingly complex reading and writing requirements of the secondary school curriculum, it now manifested itself in difficulties in comprehension and written expression. Although the discrepancy between his verbal and nonverbal abilities is not as extreme as it was at age 6 years, his verbal abilities are still limited. He finds it difficult to follow the lectures and discussions in his classroom. His reading is accurate word-by-word, but he often must reread sentences "to see what they say." Reading assignments are burden for him; he looks for short books for the book reports that are required in his English class. He understands a good deal more about the subject than he is able to get down on paper for essay-type examinations or in occasional papers required in his classes. His teachers are puzzled because he seems inarticulate and not very bright in the verbal atmosphere of the high school classroom, yet there are flashes of sound insights and good judgment in his social and interpersonal contacts. Educational intervention for Richard should focus on three areas: comprehension strategies for reading, vocabulary development, and written composition.

1. *Reading Comprehension*
The use of taped textbooks of *Talking Books for the Blind and Dyslexic* is an immediate approach for dealing with the burden of reading that Richard's secondary school classwork requires. He needs to be taught the "bypass" method for his reading assignments: listening to the tape while following along in the textbook. It may be that his school maintains an institutional membership in this program; if so, his teachers can make arrangements for the prompt receipt of tapes to match his reading assignments. If the school is not involved in this program, arrangements can be made at his local

library by his parents for an application to borrow play-back equipment and request tapes to meet the schedule of school assignments. The bypass method can provide two benefits for Richard: (a) it can lessen the amount of time he must spend in reading his textbooks, (b) it offers a fluent language model that will gradually move him beyond the word-by-word reading he now uses and improve his word attack skills.

Teaching Richard some reading strategies would also be useful. Teaching him to move beyond single words by preview questions, observation of cues such as headings and language signals, and reading summaries or abstract first for an overview of a chapter can be helpful. The visualizing/verbalizing strategies developed by Nanci Bell (1991) would also be useful. Bell's illustration of the detailed questioning to guide visualization of text would be especially useful with Richard because it utilizes the exceptionally strong visual perceptual skills Richard displays on psychological examinations.

2. *Vocabulary Development*

Assessment indicated that Richard continued to have limited vocabulary abilities, whether measured through ability to produce verbal definitions, select multiple choice responses, or recognize pictured relationships. It is also clear that rote learning of definitions from word lists would not ensure any transfer to Richard's language abilities.

Interactive computer technology can be effective in increasing vocabulary skills. The intensive, private practice offered by a computer would be valuable for Richard.

3. *Written Composition*

Because of Richard's strong visual orientation, the use of graphic organizers would be particularly appropriate. The visual mapping of verbal relationships through diagrams and charts and the webbing methods for introducing outlining would all help enhance his verbal expressions of ideas.

The services of a teacher should be provided for individual work with Richard to move his writing beyond simple sentences to more mature sentences structure, to expand his use of relational adverbs and conjunctions, to teach him to use topic sentences to introduce paragraphs, and to organize his ideas coherently.

Mark

Mark's history illustrates the role of compensations and accommodations in the management of developmental learning disability. He has managed to complete his education and to succeed in professional training in medical school, despite the residual effects of the developmental learning disability found in the diagnostic examination: slow rate of reading, difficulties in word attack, and spelling. He has managed, on his own without professional assistance, to this point in his career. The problems that he had compensated for came to light because of the board examinations that play a crucial role in his realization of his career goals in medicine. For Mark, accommodations rather than remediation is most prudent advice he can be given.

Learning disability is recognized as a developmental disability by the federal law, under the Americans with Disabilities Act (ADA). By this law, people with learning disabilities who are otherwise qualified have the right to reasonable accommodations on professional examinations and to nondiscriminatory procedures for securing them.

Mark must petition the Board of Medical Examiners by providing recent documentation of his disability done by qualified professionals. He must provide a history of his learning problems and a specific statement of the testing conditions he needs. It is his responsibility to convince the Board of Medical Examiners that he is entitled to the protection of the law because of a disability that in the words of the law limits one or more major life activity, such as learning.

Additionally, it is recommended that, assuming he continues in medicine, he should arrange for recorded journals so that he can keep current with information in his field. While it would be ideal for Mark to have remediation of his encoding and decoding disabilities, the realities of work at medical school (and hopefully later on as a physician) make accommodations the most practical method for dealing with his disability at this point in his life.

The clinical histories of Richard, Lucien, and Mark are repeated daily in schools and clinics. In all, the thread of interruption in the normal developmental sequences in language may be found. They are not identical, any more than people are the same, differing in their biological substrate, in the timing and nature of the experience they sustained even in fetal life; and the adequacy and appropriateness of educational remediation and family support they receive. The deviations need not be static; at any given time in an individual's life, the spectrum of language deviations—their scope, their severity, their responsiveness to remediation—will vary. However, at the age where reading is to begin, the ability to recognize and remember the sound of the written symbol is critical for learning to read.

HEMISPHERE ASYMMETRY

So far in this chapter, we have considered only the first two segments of the metaphorical iceberg (Chapter 5, Figure 5.1): the academic domain of the disability, reading, and the neuropsychological processing deficits that underlie the disability. However, the spectrum of these processing deficits and their relationship to the development of language enable us to look into further depths of functional asymmetry of the brain, the specialization of the left side of the brain for language, and the contribution of the right side to language. While neuroimaging and neurofunctional imaging appear to define localized brain areas as being a repository for discrete brain functions, findings from functional MRI studies identify multiple sites of brain area activation, often involving both hemispheres during language tasks (Pugh et al., 1996). Such multiple areas may represent activation of mechanisms to compensate for left hemisphere functional deficits in processing language or alternatively may represent indications that a basic defect exists in interhemispheric transfer of information.

In the introduction to his book *Hemispheric Asymmetry* (1993), Joseph Hellige reminds us:

> When thinking about hemisphere asymmetry, it is critical to be mindful of the unity of
> the brain. That is, the two hemispheres are part of a much larger anatomically extensive
> system that encompasses both hemispheres, the connections between them, numerous

subcortical structures, and more. . . . A new awareness of the fact that information processing is anatomically extensive, has led to topics like the manner in which the two
hemispheres interact in the normal brain to produce unity of thought and action. (p. 4)

Nevertheless with these caveats, the relationship between language and cerebral localization suggests that hemisphere specialization is an area for investigation of the functional defects in developmental reading disabilities.

Studies on Hemisphere Specialization

The relationship between language and cerebral lateralization was documented by Marc
Dax in 1836 (published in 1878) and later rediscovered, apparently independently, by
Broca in 1861, but it was not until 1917 that James Hinshelwood related "congenital
word blindness" to a focal agenesis of the left angular gyrus. To Orton (1928, 1937), the
problem of hemisphere specialization was central in understanding the group of developmental language problems that included reading, writing, and spelling disabilities,
"word deafness," motor speech delay, and the developmental apraxias. He attributed
these disorders to failure to establish the physiological habit of working exclusively
from the engrams of one hemisphere, that is, the failure to establish a dominant hemisphere. Orton reasoned that visual symbols are represented in each hemisphere, oriented correctly in the dominant hemisphere, but as a mirror image in the nondominant
side. Normally, the nondominant image is elided from awareness. In the developmental
language disorders, said Orton, suppression of the nondominant engram does not occur.
The competing engrams result in twisted symbols or "strephosymbolia," creating the
one symptom "common to the entire group (of developmental language disorders) . . . a
difficulty in repicturing or rebuilding in the order of presentation, sequences of letters,
of sounds, or of units of movement" (Orton, 1937, p. 145). Orton felt there was an increased incidence of left-handedness, incomplete handedness, and/or mixed eye and
hand dominance in these children.

While the Orton explanation of confusing mirror-images in specific language
disability has not been substantiated and more recent research has failed to find a
relationship between "mixed" eye-hand preference and specific language disability
(Hagin, 1954), there has been continuing study of the development of hemisphere specialization and the specialized functions subsumed by the right and left hemispheres.
These functions were dramatically revealed by Sperry and his colleagues as they studied the abilities of patients whose brain was surgically divided by midline section of
the cerebral commissures:

> Each of the hemispheres continues to function at a high level, but most conscious experi-
> ence generated within one hemisphere becomes inaccessible to the conscious awareness
> of the other. . . . The disconnected left hemisphere retains the ability to speak its
> mind . . . whereas the right hemisphere for most practical purposes is unable to express
> itself in speech or in writing. (Sperry, 1985, p. 11)

In the child with a developmental reading disability, in the neurologically intact
brain, the competence of each cerebral hemisphere cannot be tested in isolation, yet it

is possible to examine the speed and accuracy of the individual performing tasks that we believe are functionally related to specialized areas of the brain which can process these tasks most efficiently. Such studies have been spurred by the development of noninvasive techniques in which two different perceptual stimuli within the same modality are simultaneously presented to the left and to the right sensory fields. Stimuli from the right sensory field are normally represented predominantly in the left hemisphere; those from the left sensory field in the right hemisphere. This is most true for the cortical representation of visual stimuli; it is also true, although with lesser consistency, in auditory and tactile-haptic representation. "Thus any asymmetry in hemisphere processing of particular stimuli may be reflected in response asymmetry to left vs. right stimulation as measured in accuracy or reaction time" (Witelson, 1976, p. 235). Such stimuli may be in the auditory (dichotic listening), visual (visual half fields), or tactile-kinesthetic (dichotomous tactile stimuli) areas and involve both linguistic and nonlinguistic processes. These techniques and the studies using them are not without their problems. Thus, unequivocal resolution of the question of hemisphere specialization in developmental language disorders by means of these techniques is still not available.

More recently, SPECT, fMRI, and event-related EEG have added a new dimension in the study of functional differences in hemisphere specialization in individuals with developmental reading disabilities.

Dichotic Listening Skills

The dichotic listening techniques were initiated by Broadbent (1954) and applied clinically by Kimura (1961, 1963) at the Montreal Neurological Institute. By then, the Montreal Neurological Institute was already known for the pioneering work of Penfield and Roberts (1959) in localizing, by direct electrical stimulation of the brain, areas subserving language. In addition, the Montreal Neurological Institute was known for locating the side of the brain subserving speech by the unilateral intracarotid injection of sodium amytal (the Wada Test, Wada & Rasmussen, 1960). The sodium amytal test is useful in determining which hemisphere controls speech and language, independent of the handedness of the patient. From studies of this procedure, it was found that 95% of all right-handers without history of early brain damage have speech and language controlled by the left hemisphere and in 5% of right-handers, speech and language are controlled by the right hemisphere; 70% of left-handers are left-brain dominant for speech, 15% of left-handers have speech controlled by the right hemisphere, and 15% of left-handers have bilateral speech control. For those who have a history of left-brain damage early in life, 70% of right-handers and 19% of left-handers have right hemisphere-controlled or bilateral speech. Results of the Kimura dichotic listening tests parallel, but do not entirely coincide with, results on the sodium amytal test: All patients who are left-brain dominant on the sodium amytal test do not necessarily show a right ear advantage on dichotic listening (Kimura, 1961).

The Kimura dichotic listening technique included using pairs of different spoken digits presented simultaneously via headphones to each ear in groups of three pairs. The subject is to recall in any order as many of the digits as possible. Control subjects reported the digits presented to the right ear more accurately than to the left (right ear advantage, REA): The stimuli reaching the left hemisphere are more accurately reported than those to the right hemisphere. This has also been found for words, nonsense syllables, pairs of consonant-vowel syllables formed with the stop consonants *(b,d,g,p,t),* Morse code, and processing and ordering temporal information (Noffsinger, 1985). On the other hand, when musical chords and melodies are used instead of digits or words, there is a left ear advantage (LEA), suggesting that musical symbols are more accurately perceived with the right hemisphere. Using sets of dichotic nonsense syllables as stimuli, Noffsinger (1985) found that in adults the ear advantages revealed are often small, the listening tasks are demanding, and the tasks require many stimulus presentations to establish advantage. Normally also, the size of the ear advantage is not consistent across subjects. Moreover, in any one subject, no ear advantage at all will be found in approximately 27% of the trials.

In children with specific reading disability, no clear-cut pattern of ear advantage emerges although there is a tendency for REA to be less in older (ages 11 to 15) boys with learning disability than in good readers of the same age. Zurif and Carson (1970) and Witelson and Rabinovitch (1972) found no significant REA in the learning-disabled groups as contrasted with controls and, indeed, they found a nonsignificant trend in favor of LEA in the learning-disabled groups. Using digit pairs as the auditory stimulus, Witelson (1976) found that although the overall accuracy increased with age for both reading disabilities and controls, and that each group had a significant REA, the overall accuracy was significantly greater for the normal group. These findings are consistent with the theory that learning-disabled children have "some dysfunction" in the left hemisphere.

Similar, although less significant, results were found by Sparrow and Satz (1970) in 40 learning-disabled boys, ages 9 to 12, when they were compared with a matched control group in a dichotic listening task using four-paired digits. In these studies, REA was found for both groups, but almost four times as many dyslexic boys had LEA. When groups of younger boys were studied at ages 5, 7, and 12, Darby (1978) found that in the control group (normal readers matched with the dyslexic boys), the magnitude of ear asymmetry increased with age, with increasing REA, which, however, was statistically significant only at age 12. By contrast, the dyslexic groups revealed no significant REA at any age, although there was a trend to REA observable by age 5. Normal readers tend to demonstrate a greater magnitude of REA than do children with learning disabilities particularly at older ages, at early adolescence. Satz, however, specifically stated that children with learning disability "reveal a lag in the development of ear symmetry with no significant REA at any age level" (Satz, 1976, p. 282). This finding was used to lend support for the theory that, in disabled readers, functional lateralization of the brain matures at a slower rate than in nondisabled readers.

The general conclusion of less adequate REA in poor readers as contrasted with adequate readers is reflected in a review of dichotic listening studies (Bryden, 1988) in which, of 51 dichotic listening studies, 30 "claim to show in greater or lesser extent that poor readers are less lateralized than good readers" (p. 510). Of the remainder, 14 show no difference between groups and 7 report that poor readers are more lateralized than good readers. Examination of these reports however, reveals that the ear differences usually make up only a small percentage of the actual responses made by the subject. In a task involving 100 trials, perhaps 45 correct identifications are made of sounds presented to the left ear, 55 of correct identifications of sounds presented to the right ear, and on only 10% of the trials was there an ear difference (Molfese & Burger-Judisch, 1991). A. Beaton (1985), however stated that "most experiments have shown REA for verbal material among disabled as well as normal readers . . . what is in doubt is the magnitude of the asymmetry in each group of readers and how this relates to age" (p. 208).

The relationship of blood flow to frontal, temporal and parietal areas in subjects undergoing dichotic listening tests was studied by Coffey, Bryden, Schroering, Wilson, and Mathew (1989), Gregory, Efron, Divenyi, and Yund (1983) and Rumsey et al. (1987) utilizing the Xenon (^{133}Xe) inhalation technique. In the Gregory et al. study, 9 of 14 strongly right-handed medical students (mean age 23 years) with no evidence of learning disability, had significant LEA on two-tone dichotic listening tasks, 5 had REA. There was a small but significant increase in mean regional cerebral blood flow to the temporal cortex contralateral to the ear advantage; those with REA showed activation over the left temporal region, while those with LEA showed activation over the right temporal region. C. E. Coffey et al. state, "These are the first data to provide a direct indication that perceptual asymmetry on a dichotic listening task is associated with regional asymmetries in brain functional activity measured by regional cerebral blood flow" (p. 50). The authors caution however, that because of the small number of subjects, the confounding variables inherent in dichotic auditory testing, and possible metabolic changes in subcortical structure, these results are to be considered preliminary.

In 14 adult men with "severe developmental dyslexia" and a control group, Rumsey et al. (1987) found that when given a simple cognitive task, no difference in regional cerebral blood flow was found. With tasks involving reading and comprehension, however, the dyslexic group showed more activity than controls in the left hemisphere of the brain. These findings are consistent with later studies and suggest that dyslexics do not process information as efficiently as controls.

Visual Half-Field Presentation Studies

Studies on visual half-field presentation, just as those with dichotic auditory presentations, also suffer from technical and theoretical problems. The hemifield tachistoscopic technique is based on the anatomical arrangement of fibers from the retina, in which fibers from one-half of each visual field reach the occipital cortex, contralateral to the stimulated side. Stimuli from the right visual half field, striking the nasal half of the right retina and the temporal half of the left retina, are ultimately carried to the left visual cortex, while those from the left visual half field impinge on the nasal portion of the left retina and the temporal portion of the right and are ultimately processed in the right occipital cortex. The technique requires the subject to fixate his or her gaze on a specific point positioned on a screen in front of the subject. This may create a problem since poor readers may be less likely than normal readers to fixate appropriately when told to do so. Tachistoscopic presentations are made to the right or left visual half field, or bilaterally and simultaneously. The presentation must take less than 180 msec (the time to initiate and saccade in the direction of presentation), usually 100 msec or less. The size of the stimulus must be 1 degree or more to avoid the bilateral macular projections, and the presentations to each half field must be random so that the subject cannot predict the field stimulated. Presentation of words is confounded by scanning habits. Because in English we scan from left to right, a word presented in the left visual half field is further away from the fixation point than a word in the right. Requiring a subject to read words presented to the visual half field may also be a problem since it may not be visual field asymmetry that is being studied, but simply the reading-disabled subject's difficulty in reading the word no matter in which half field it is presented. Interpretation of results may also be criticized in that differences in hemifield recognition may relate more to style of information processing than to a proposed lateralization of function. A. Beaton (1985) stated about visual field studies: "There is a surprising lack of sophistication in attempting to understand the cognitive processes which are deficient in cases of reading retardation" (p. 206).

Nevertheless, using this technique in normal adults, Kimura (1969, 1973) found superiority in right visual field recognition for English letters or words. Other studies described left visual superiority in normal adults for recognition of complex forms, recognition of dot figures, recognition of overlapping figures, face recognition, and line orientation (see E. Zaidel, 1985). D. W. Zaidel (1985) stated: "It is by now commonly agreed that letters, words or digits are better recognized in the right visual field than in the left visual field" (p. 147) and the "left visual field [is superior] for recognition of complex forms, recognition of dot figures, recognition of overlapping figures, face recognition and line orientation" (p. 148). However, unlike consistent right visual field superiority for recognizing nonverbal stimuli, left visual field superiority for recognizing nonverbal stimuli is smaller in comparison and in general is less consistent.

Because of the singular lack of information about the development of visual field superiority in normal children, however, there are problems in interpreting visual field studies in children with learning disabilities. McKeever and Huling (1970), presenting four-letter nouns, found right visual field advantage (RVFA) in recognition of words in both normal children and those with severe reading retardation. Mean age for both groups was 13 years. No difference in hemifield asymmetry between normal and reading-disabled children was also found by Keefe and Swinney (1979). Marcel and Rajan (1975) also found significant asymmetry in the right visual field for word and letter reports in both good and poor readers, but the absolute difference between left and right hemifields was greater for the good readers. This study included both boys and girls, of whom all except two, were right-handed, ages 7 years 6 months to 8 years 7 months. A methodological procedure confounds this study since the mean duration of exposure was much longer for the disabled readers than for the normal controls. Significant elevation thresholds in the right visual field than in the left were found by Gross, Rothenberg, Schottenfeld, and Drake (1978). Reduced hemifield asymmetry for four-letter words presented bilaterally was found in 19-year-old poor readers (Kershner, 1979) and in 12½-year-old poor readers (Pirozollo & Rayner, 1979). Yeni-Komshian, Isenberg, and Goldberg (1975), however, found a significant asymmetry in the right visual field for both numerals and vertically presented words in a group of black children, boys and girls, ages 11 to 13, only in *poor* readers. Finally, Witelson (1976) in 83 "dyslexic" and 86 normal boys, ages 6 to 14, did not demonstrate a right visual half field asymmetry for both groups. The stimuli in this study were two upper-case letters that were similar or different. The subjects were required to indicate whether the letters were the same or different but not to name them. When pictures of people were used, however, the normal group obtained significantly different scores for each visual field, with greater accuracy in the left visual field, whereas the dyslexic group did not obtain significantly different scores for each visual field. Witelson stated that "the lack of significant behavioral asymmetry for the dyslexic group could be suggestive of a lack of right hemisphere specialization for spatial processing in the dyslexic group" (p. 245). A review of 14 visual hemifield studies (Bryden, 1988) found 8 of them confirmed the conclusion of less lateralization in poor readers than in adequate readers. Four of the studies, however, found equal lateralization and two found poor readers more adequately lateralized.

The Witelson study was part of a larger one in which she proposed to evaluate hemisphere specialization in children with dyslexia. This project, carefully planned and implemented, studied 85 right-handed boys, ages 6 to 14 with reading disability, who had performance IQ scores of at least 85 on the WISC, difficulty in reading since Grade 1, a discrepancy of at least 1½ grades in reading between reading level on the WRAT and chronological age, with no detectable neurological damage or primary emotional disturbance, adequate sensory acuity, adequate educational opportunity, and English as the first and main language. A control group of 156 normal boys was used. Hemisphere specialization was studied by (a) tactile stimulation (nonsense shape test and a letters test); (b) lateralized tachistoscopic stimulation using pictures of people; and (c) a dichotic listening test using digits.

Dichotomous Tactile Tests

The suggestion of impaired right-hemisphere specialization in dyslexics was reinforced by Witelson's results on tactile stimulation tests. The first of these, a dichotomous tactile stimulation test, was designed to be nonlinguistic. It required spatial perception of pairs of competing nonsense shapes through touch. The subject was required to choose the two test stimuli from a visual recognition display of six shapes. In 100 nondyslexic boys ages 6 to 14, greater accuracy was observed for shapes felt by the left hand, whereas for 49 dyslexic boys the differences between the left- and right-hand scores were not significant; the right-hand score of dyslexics was significantly greater than that of the controls, however. A second dichotomous tactile stimulation test used letters (three-dimensional, presented in 10 sets of two pairs) instead of nonsense shapes with the same groups of dyslexic boys and controls. The group did not differ significantly in overall accuracy. For the normal group, the right-hand score was significantly greater than the left-hand score; for the dyslexic group, the left-hand score was significantly greater than the right. In addition, the left-hand score of dyslexics was significantly greater than the left-hand score of normals.

Witelson concluded (1976):

In contrast to the normal pattern of right hemisphere specialization for spatial processing, it is suggested that dyslexics have a bilateral representation of spatial functions. . . .

This hypothesis is based on the dyslexics' lack of left field superiority on the spatial touch test and on the visual spatial test and on their atypical pattern of left hand superiority on the "linguistic" touch test. There appears to be an association between the syndrome of developmental dyslexia and two possible neural abnormalities; a lack of right hemisphere specialization for spatial processing and a dysfunction in left hemisphere processing of linguistic functions. (p. 251)

Conclusions concerning hemisphere specialization arising from dichotic and tachistoscopic studies, however, have been challenged. First, visual and auditory measures of lateralization are not highly correlated with each other (Eling, 1981; Fennel, Bowers, & Satz, 1977; Hiscock & Kinsbourne, 1982). Second, reliability of the tests is low (Blumstein, Goodglass, & Tartter, 1975; McKeever, 1974). Such variability may mean that the laterality tests are tapping functions that can shift over brief intervals of time. Special strategies adopted by subjects and attentional biases may contribute to performance (Gregory et al., 1983; Hiscock & Kinsbourne, 1982). Third, these tests underestimate the incidence of left-hemisphere speech in right-handers as determined by the sodium amytal test. If, as determined by the sodium amytal test, the estimated prevalence of left-brain speech in normal right-handers is 95%, and 70% of that right-handed sample show a right ear advantage on a dichotic listening test, then the probability of right-brain speech when a left ear advantage is found in right-handers is small. This raises the issue of validity of these tests as measures of cerebral dominance for language.

Arm Extension as a Clinical Test for Hemisphere Specialization for Language

As part of the neurological evaluation of children with learning disabilities, arm extension is done (Chapter 7). In this examination, the child stands with his arms extended at shoulder height, palms down, fingers spread, eyes closed. He is then asked to count aloud very slowly, up to 10, so that the examiner can hear him and so that his arms are extended for 20 to 30 seconds. Normally by age 5 years, one arm gradually rises slightly higher than the other and *Prechtl* movements and other adventitious movements are minimal, although their appearance at ages 5 to 7 years is normal. By age 7, the posture is stable with one arm held slightly higher than the other. While the child is standing with his arms extended and his eyes closed, the head is gently, passively turned from one side and then the other. By age 6 years, the body does not turn to maintain head, neck, and body alignment (neck righting response) and tonic neck positions are not elicited.

In right-handed children, normally it is the right hand that is elevated on arm extension. However, in right-handed children with developmental learning problems, as defined at the beginning of this chapter, the right arm does not rise above the left; the left arm may be higher than the right or neither arm is elevated or there may be fluctuation in height of the extended arms; at one moment the right, at one moment the left is the elevated arm. In determining which extended arm is higher than the other, the examiner stands directly in front of the child, viewing the extended arms at their level and judging arm elevation at the wrist. There appears to be no advantage in quantitative measurement of the degree of elevation. In left-handed children, both normal and those with developmental reading disabilities, the evidence is not so clear-cut, for the elevated extremity may be seen in either arm.

We have extrapolated from the data of this test that in right-handers, in the absence of peripheral orthopedic defect, or centrally induced paresis, the elevated extremity is governed by increased muscle tone of the hemisphere more specialized for language. In other words, the elevation of the right arm in right-handers, suggests that a left hemisphere specialization for language has been established. When in the right-handers, the specialization of left hemisphere for language has not been established, or incompletely established, an abnormality in arm extension will be found. In left-handers, as stated, the relationship between handedness and hemisphere specialized for language is not so clear as in right-handers. It will be remembered in the Wada (sodium amytal test) Test, done at the Montreal Neurological Hospital, 70% of non-right-handers (mixed and left-handers) had speech controlled from the left hemisphere, 15% from the right hemisphere, and 15% bilaterally represented; whereas 95% of right-handers had speech controlled from the left side of the brain and even that percentage was considered an underestimate. The arm extension test suggests that if in right-handers, the right arm is not elevated, then hemisphere specialization for language has not been established.

The relationship between the extension test and oral reading and reading comprehension was suggested by an experimental study of 54 boys ages 7 to 12 from first through sixth grade, with Full Scale IQ (WISC) ranging from 80 to 132, all with intact homes, who were referred to Bellevue Hospital Mental Hygiene Clinic because of learning failure and/or behavioral difficulty. These boys were matched for age, IQ, reading ability, neurological signs, and psychological impairment and were randomly assigned to one of two groups.

The experiment was designed to study the effect of perceptual stimulation of deficit perceptual areas on perception, on reading, and on measures of cerebral dominance for language. The design was a crossover one planned for 1 year, in which, for the first 6 months, Group I received perceptual stimulation while Group II received compensatory remedial reading. For the second 6 months, Group I received compensatory reading while Group II received perceptual stimulation. All subjects were tested at the beginning of the experiment (T1), at the end of 6 months (T2), and at the end of a year (T3). In this crossover research design, both within-group and between-group (Table 11.3) comparisons could be made (Table 11.4).

At T1, the groups were not significantly different on the extension test (chi-square = .05, NS). At T2, however, measuring improvement in the extension test, a significant value for chi-square was obtained (chi-square = 15.31, $p < .01$). At this point, only Group I had received perceptual stimulation; thus there is a suggested relationship between perceptual training and normal response on the extension test. At T3, chi-square was again not significant (chi-square = 1.65, NS). At T3, both groups had received perceptual training. If the extension test is responsive to such training, both groups would show improvement at that time. Within-group comparisons show a shift to the normal extension test during the perceptual training phase in each of the groups, regardless of

Table 11.3   Arm extension test: Comparisons across groups

	Group I		Group II			
	Normal Response	Abnormal Response	Normal Response	Abnormal Response	x^2	p
T1	7	26	5	16	0.05	NS
T2	27	6	6	15	15.31	.01
T3	20	11	17	4	1.65	NS

Source: From "Effects of perceptual stimulation on perception, on reading, and on the establishment of cerebral dominance for language" by A. A. Silver and R. A. Hagin, 1972, Report to the Carnegie Corporation, New York.

the order in which perceptual stimulation was given. These results suggest that spontaneous maturation did not occur, but that perception stimulation may have influenced the direction of the elevated arm to normal.

Mean oral reading scores for Groups I and II combined, obtained before the training phase, and the mean combined reading scores, obtained after the training phase, were dichotomized in accordance with posttraining normal or abnormal findings on the arm extension test.

The group of children in whom the response to the arm extension test was normal following the perceptual stimulation phase earned a pretest mean of 2.68 and a posttest mean of 3.48 on oral reading. The difference between these means was found to be significant ($t = 5.49$, $p < .001$). For the same group, the pretest mean in reading comprehension was 2.22 and the posttest mean for the same measure was 3.02. The difference between these means is also significant ($t = 4.68$, $p < .001$). On the other hand, the group with abnormal response to the extension tests, following the perceptual stimulation phase, earned a pretest mean of 2.70 and a posttest mean of 3.33 in oral reading. On the reading comprehension test, their pre- and posttest means were 2.82 and 2.07 respectively. Comparing t-scores for the difference between these means were 2.31 for

Table 11.4   Arm extension test: Relationship with oral reading and reading comprehension, groups I and II combined

Extension Test Response	Oral Reading			Reading Comprehension		
	Test Mean Preexperiment	Test Mean Postexperiment	t-Ratio	Test Mean Preexperiment	Test Mean Postexperiment	t-Ratio
Normal ($n = 44$)	2.68	3.48	5.49 ($p < .001$)	2.22	3.02	4.68 ($p < .001$)
Abnormal ($n = 10$)	2.70	3.33	2.31 ($p < NS$)	2.82	2.07	4.68 ($p < NS$)

Source: From "Effects of perceptual stimulation on perception, on reading, and on the establishment of cerebral dominance for language" by A. A. Silver and R. A. Hagin, 1972, Report to the Carnegie Corporation, New York.

the oral reading measure and 4.68 for reading comprehension, neither ratio reaching the level of significance set for this experiment. This suggests that there is a relationship between reading and the arm extension test.

In summary, the elevated extremity in right-handed children may be an index of hemisphere specialization and appears to be related to success in beginning reading.

Hemisphere Specialization Seen in Imaging and Electrophysiological Studies

While (as reviewed in Chapter 3) Galaburda found all 6 of the dyslexic brains his laboratory had examined showed symmetry of the planum temporale—a statistically unexpected finding since symmetrical planum occur in only about one-fourth of normal brains—and while morphological imaging studies, CT and MRI, have with exceptions, found symmetry or even reversed asymmetry in brain regions that include the planum temporale in populations of dyslexic subjects—the question arises as to the relationship of these morphological findings to hemisphere specialization of function. Galaburda (1991) asks, "Does the presence of symmetry of a language area in dyslexic subjects mean that dyslexics have two symmetrical but small language areas and therefore are 'phrenologically' vulnerable to linguistic weakness?" (p. 12).

Morphologically, however, the dyslexic brain does not lose the normal asymmetry of left greater than right because the left hemisphere becomes smaller; it becomes symmetrical because the right planum temporale and surrounding language areas become larger. The total planum area, right and left, thus becomes larger than that of the asymmetrical planum of the normal brain. The question is therefore not that of morphological size, but of the functioning of the dyslexic brain. Pennington, Filipek, et al. (1999) comparing, by means of MRI morphometry, the brain structure of 75 individuals with reading disabilities with those of 22 control subjects found a significant group-by-structure interaction in the major neocortical subdivisions, with the insula and the anterior superior neocortex smaller and the retrocallosal cortex larger in the reading disability group. They conclude that "most brain structures do not differ in size in reading disability, but cortical development is altered subtly" (p. 723).

Functional imaging and quantitative EEG studies offer evidence for abnormalities in the way the dyslexic individual deals with the processing of information. PET scan measures of brain activation (and deactivation) as the brain responds to hierarchical tests of language function, reveal differences in cerebral blood flow in dyslexic and in "normal" response to these tasks. There appears to be a decreased activation of language areas in dyslexic subjects (Rumsey, 1996). Wood and Flowers (1999), like Rumsey, find that widely distributed neuronal circuits are involved in processing of language tasks. In an extensive study involving 100 subjects (50 normal readers, 50 dyslexic; male/female = 62/38, mean education 15.9 years), Wood and Flowers utilized both MRI and glucose metabolism in PET scanning, examining the glucose utilization in 22 regional areas of the brain. These were extensive areas, not only cortical temporal, frontal, parietal, and occipital cortices but also subcortical areas, thalamic and striatal. The glucose metabolism in these areas was studied as their subjects responded to three different tasks: phonemic awareness (auditory, oral tasks requiring segmentation), phonological decoding (nonword reading), and single word reading. These three phenotypes associate strongly with inferior temporal-occipital (phonemic awareness), right central frontal (phonological decoding) and thalamic (single word reading) with generally lower activation of these areas in dyslexia, in oral word reading, nonword discrimination, and rhyme detection. The various processes of language, however, normally activate all 22 regional areas of the brain studied, suggesting again the interlocking neural networks activated in reading and writing. The decreased activation of the dyslexic in various language areas of the brain suggests that hemisphere specialization in the dyslexic is not as clearly established as it is in the normal subjects during the process of reading and writing.

The difference between dyslexic and normal processing of information is further seen in brain mapping and in evoked potential studies as discussed in Chapter 3. The overall conclusion is that in individuals with reading disability, the areas of the brain that normally subserve the processes in reading are not activated, that the functions subserved by these areas are performed by other areas of the brain. The normal process of specialization of function is "subtly altered."

This chapter has so far discussed hemisphere specialization for language and has offered some evidence that, in individuals with developmental learning disorders, particularly developmental reading disabilities, there is an aberration in the normal development of such specialization. The following section traces the differentiation of function in the cerebral cortex, from the first weeks of fetal life to adolescence.

The Development of Hemisphere Specialization

In his seminal book *The Biological Foundations of Language* (1967), Eric Lenneberg stated that the cerebral hemispheres were not specialized for cognitive function at birth and that the two hemispheres had equal potential in their capacity to acquire language. Lateralization, however, was a process of increasing specialization of language by the left hemisphere in parallel with decreasing involvement of the right hemisphere; this process only begins at age 2 years, at the time the brain develops the biological capacity for language and continues until puberty when the biological structure for language attains adult form. There is a biologically determined developmental sequence to brain laterality. Lenneberg did not explain why language was subserved by the left hemisphere and not the right and his premature death prevented him from being aware of more recent work that, to quote Hellige (1993), concluded:

> The seeds of functional hemispheric asymmetries are sown long before an individual's birth and are likely to date back to the ontogenetic formation of the first neural structures, to asymmetries of the ovum or even to various molecular asymmetries. From these early origins, functional hemispheric asymmetries are shaped by the interaction of many biological and environmental factors beginning with the fetus as it develops in utero and continuing into old age. (p. 260)

Evidence for this statement is seen in morphological asymmetries in the fetal brain and in functional asymmetries, particularly auditory asymmetries, in the neonate and infant. Best (1988) has argued that the functional asymmetries found in infants, parallels a similar gradient in the embryological development of the cerebral hemispheres and that the patterns of morphological asymmetries in brain structure in adults should be attributable to embryological growth patterns. While the neurons destined to form the cerebral cortex arise from the subependymal zone of the cerebral ventricles, assemble into a multilayered laminar structure, and migrate to their destined location in the cortex during the first 10 to 18 weeks of gestation, the elaboration of cortical connections—axons, dendritic trees, and synaptic circuits—begins during the second trimester of pregnancy and continues postnatally. The process of neuronal migration and synaptic connection proceeds in determined sequence (growth gradient or vectors) moving from primary motor or sensory zones to secondary association areas and finally to tertiary association zones. The growth vector proceeds in an anterior-posterior dimension, a right-to-left direction, and a diagonal from right anterior to left posterior. Thus the right frontal-motor regions may become attenuated as growth proceeds into association areas of the left posterior regions, which emerge late in development. For example, the cortical markings surrounding the Sylvian fissure on the left appear later than those on the right, and cortical landmarks appear 1 to 2 weeks later on the left side than on the right (Chi, Dooling, & Gillis, 1977). Higher order dendritic branches in areas important for language also develop later in the left hemisphere than in the right. This development is in accord with Galaburda's morphological findings in normal adult brains, with Galaburda, LeMay, Kemper, and Geschwind's (1978) findings on fetal brains, and with Robert Thatcher's (1991) neuroimaging findings of the anatomical sequence of growth spurts in the human brain.

The morphological growth vectors should have implications for the development of perceptual and cognitive functions and for asymmetrical patterns in developmental plasticity. The earliest appearing functions, frontal motor and premotor, primary sensory regions (right hemisphere function), should mature earlier than left hemisphere functions (language functions) in homologous areas. The prenatal guidance of neuronal migrations and neuronal connections is likely to be influenced by genetic, hormonal, and environmental factors.

The abnormalities in lateralization and in cortical neuronal organization found by neuroimaging, electrophysiological, and morphological studies in developmental reading disabilities suggest that dyslexia and developmental learning disabilities in general, may represent a neuroembryological disturbance in the prenatal migration of neurons during mid-gestation.

THE GENETIC BASIS OF DEVELOPMENTAL
READING DISABILITIES

We have so far in the chapter attempted to review the hierarchical structure of developmental reading disability as seen in the metaphorical iceberg: going from the domain of academic difficulty that is clinically evident, to the neuropsychological processing deficits immediately underlying the academic difficulty, to the perturbation of normal hemisphere specialization of function, which may be the overall aberration responsible for the central processing deficits. While proceeding into the depths of the iceberg, we have reviewed the morphological and functional differences in the reading disability brain as seen in neuroimaging and electrophysiological studies. These morphological and functional differences are not yet the base of the iceberg, the motor that drives all of these hierarchical stages, the etiological factor or factors that cause the deviations in morphology, in function, in the development of hemisphere specialization, the central processing deficits, and finally the academic difficulty. As discussed in Chapter 5, the possible causes of the symptoms of learning disability are many, acting singly or in combination. However, there is evidence to believe that for developmental learning disability there is an inherited influence, most probably genetic factors, a modification in one or more genes that influence the development of function in the regions of the brain that subsume language (Hyman & Nestler, 1993).

As in the case of all research with reading disabilities, however, genetic research suffers from the perennial problems of diagnostic and etiological functional heterogeneity so that learning disorders are the final common clinical pathways for many etiological factors (phenocopies).

In addition, there are specific problems inherent in genetic studies themselves. A single genetic defect may produce markedly different phenotypes depending on interactions with other genes and/or environmental factors (*variable expressivity*); or the gene may be present, but not expressed (*reduced penetrance*). Further, many neurodevelopmental disorders may have two or more different genetic defects that may produce a similar phenotype. The mode of inheritance of neuropsychiatric disorders is complex in that they may not be inherited in a single major genetic locus as are Mendelian traits.

Despite these difficulties, however, there is strong evidence from genetic studies that reading disabilities *are* inherited. These studies may be considered in four steps: (1) family studies, (2) twin and adoption studies, (3) segregation analysis, and (4) linkage analysis.

1. *Family Studies.* These studies compare the rates of reading disabilities in relatives of probands (relatives of individuals with diagnosed reading disabilities) with rates in relatives of unaffected individuals. Many of these studies are reported in Chapter 3 in describing the work of the University of Colorado Learning Disability Research Center. In summary:

- *Comparing probands versus controls.* Composite reading score was over 2 standard deviations lower in probands versus controls; symbol-processing speed and spatial reasoning were 0.7 standard deviations lower in probands versus controls. Girls obtained higher scores on symbol processing and boys scored higher on spatial reasoning.

- *Comparing brothers of probands versus brothers of controls.* Reading score was about 1 standard deviation lower in brothers of probands than in brothers of controls, and significant differences were found in symbol-processing speed and in spatial reasoning.

- *Comparing sisters of probands versus sisters of controls.* Reading scores were about 0.4 standard deviations lower in sisters of probands than in sisters of controls.
- *Comparing parents of probands versus parents of controls.* Scores were lower for each of the three measures in parents of probands than in parents of controls; somewhat greater for fathers (0.8 sigma) than for mothers (0.5 sigma).

In general, the results of family studies

> . . . conclusively demonstrate the familial nature of reading disability, but no single-gene model was found to account adequately for transmission of the disorder. Little or no evidence for sex-linkage was obtained and complex segregation analysis of the total dataset provides no evidence for autosomal major-gene influence. . . . [When, however] data from only families of female probands were analyzed, the hypothesis of single-gene recessive influence could not be rejected. (DeFries, 1985, p. 112)

2. *Twin and Adoption Studies.* Once established that reading disability has a strong familial influence, is the similarity among family members explained by shared genes or shared environment (diet, socioeconomic status, language stimulation at critical ages, educational opportunities)? Twin and adoption studies address this issue. Comparisons of monozygotic (MZ) (identical) twins who have 100% of their DNA in common, with dizygotic twins (DZ) (fraternal) who have an average of 50% of their DNA in common can provide evidence of hereditability if the concordance for reading disability is higher among MZ than among DZ twins. Studying twins raised together does not eliminate the contribution of environment. The effect of environment may be neutralized if, when children are adopted early in life, the concordance between biological parents and adopted child is greater than between adopted parents and adopted child. Even here certain environmental factors cannot be excluded. Studies at the Colorado Learning Disabilities Research Center have found that the identical twin (MZ) of a person diagnosed with reading disability has a 68% risk of having a reading disability, whereas a fraternal twin has a 38% chance (DeFries & Alarcon, 1996). As reported in Chapter 3, use of the DeFries and Fulker equations suggest that half of the difference in reading scores between dyslexics and the general population can be explained by genetics (Plomin & DeFries, 1998).

3. *Segregation Analysis.* Whole family and twin studies can measure the hereditability of traits. They do so without identification of the kind and number of the genes involved. In segregation analysis, the pattern of transmission (segregation) of a trait or disorder is studied in extended family pedigrees, focusing on the appearances of the trait or disorder both within and between generations. Transmission in models of Mendelian inheritance may reveal a single major locus and whether the inheritance is in a dominant, recessive, or sex-linked pattern. In their early studies, S. D. Smith, Kimberling, & Pennington (1991) in 84 individuals from 9 extended families found that reading disability was inherited in autosomal dominant manner. Review of the data, however, found that 70% of the segregation was due to one family and that the autosomal dominant mode of inheritance could not be proven. Studies by Lubs and his

associates (1990, 1991) at Miami, with 20 families, did suggest an autosomal dominant mode of inheritance, but there was no consistent mode of transmission, and it was probable that the transmission of reading disabilities was polygenic.

4. *Linkage Analysis.* Definitive evidence that vulnerability to a disorder comes from demonstrating that reading disability is linked to a specific site (a known genetic marker) on a chromosome or chromosomes and identifying the specific gene or genes involved. A genetic marker is a detectable phenotypic trait or DNA sequence that has been mapped to a known location on a particular chromosome. The Human Genome project has constructed a complete linkage map of the human genome making it possible to develop a large number of novel markers, DNA polymorphisms, that contain variations in primary DNA sequences and whose locations on chromosomes are known (for technical details of linkage analysis, see Blum & Noble, 1997, or Hyman & Nestler, 1993). If genes are placed close to each other on the same chromosome, they tend to be transmitted together from one generation to the next. In contrast, if genes are either far apart on the same chromosome or on a different chromosome, chances are they will be inherited independently. Cotransmission between a disorder and a marker suggests that a gene for the disorder and the marker are in the same region of a chromosome. A gene can be localized to a specific chromosome region by comparing its transmission pattern with those of marker genes whose locations are known. The likelihood that an apparent linkage within a pedigree is true and does not occur by chance is expressed as a LOD score (logarithm of the odds for the linkage), with a LOD score of 3 representing odds of 1,000 to 1 that the linkage is not due to chance alone.

The search for gene(s) for reading disabilities has been a major concern of the Learning Disability Research Centers at the University of Colorado and at the University of Miami. There were two general approaches: (a) pedigree linkage analysis, study of individuals in extended families where members of the family have the trait under study (reading disability) and (b) sib-pair linkage analysis. For pedigree analysis, each individual in the family needs to be evaluated and diagnosis made. This must be done across a wide age range and for family members of different generations. Further, the assumption is made that the disorder is caused by a single gene with a specified mode of inheritance. Complex disorders such as reading disabilities are probably genetically heterogeneous, influenced by genes at several different chromosome locations. Sib-pair linkage is based on the concept that sib-pairs concordant for reading disabilities will tend to be concordant for the marker. Phenotypic data from one generation are required, although to determine if a marker carried by two siblings is inherited from the same parent, the parents of the siblings should also be phenotyped for the markers.

Initial studies of family pedigrees (see Chapter 3) pointed to linking of reading disability to chromosome 15 and to one or more genes at chromosome locations other than 15. Using markers on chromosome 6, S. D. Smith et al. (1991) expanded the number of extended families and individuals in the pedigree and found apparent linkage in some families to chromosome 6. The markers used for chromosome 6 are near a known region (human leukocyte antigen region, HLA) suggesting a possible relationship between reading disability and genes that affect the immune system. Using different markers, the Miami group also suggested a linkage of reading disability to chromosome 6. Data from their extended family pedigree linkage study was reanalyzed to include siblings and provided evidence for possible linkage to markers on both chromosomes 6 and 15 (Fulker, Cherny, & Cardon, 1995; S. D. Smith et al., 1991). With the same sample of 126 sib-pairs from 19 extended families, and from an independent sample of 46 dizygotic twin pairs, Cardon et al. (1994, 1995) narrowed the search to a possible locus for reading disability at chromosome 6, near the HLA complex. This finding received confirmation in a study of six extended families at the Bowman-Gray Reading Disabilities Research Center (Grigorenko et al., 1997), genotyped for chromosome markers on the short arm of chromosomes 6 (6p), 15, and 16. Five phenotypic measures were analyzed: phonological awareness, phonological decoding, rapid automatized naming, single-word reading, and discrepancy between IQ and reading performance. Researchers obtained significant linkage of phonological awareness to five DNA markers on chromosomes 6p and some evidence for single-word reading on the same region. A significant LOD score of 3.15 was found for linkage of single-word reading to a DNA marker on chromosome 15.

The linkage of specific reading-related skills to chromosome 6 was also found by Gayan et al. (1999) and by Fisher et al. (1999). Using a sample of 126 sib-pairs from 79 families in the Colorado Twin Study, Gayan et al. (1999) genotyped 8 DNA markers on chromosome 6p with PIAT subtest scores, phonological decoding, orthographic decoding, phoneme transposition, and phoneme deletion. Results suggest the presence of loci on chromosome 6 affects both phonological and orthographic skills. Whether these loci can affect other cognitive functions is still to be determined. Nevertheless, these studies offer powerful evidence there is a genetic component to the disorders termed developmental reading disabilities.

It is also yet to be determined whether the genetic linkages found in developmental learning disabilities are associated with normal variations in reading ability. In our thinking about dyslexia, we have come to consider development reading disability as a qualitative variant (one has it or does not); the degree of disability can then be described in a quantitative fashion—one can have a little bit of it or a lot of it. Shaywitz et al., however, consider learning disabilities to be the low end of a normal continuum. Plomin and DeFries (1998) have studied this question: They reason that "if reading disability is influenced by genes that also affect variations within the normal range of reading performance, then the reading scores of identical twins, one of whom is dyslexic, should be closer to those of the reading disability group than the reading scores of fraternal twins" (p. 68). As a group, identical twins who are not reading disability subjects perform almost as poorly as the diagnosed dyslexic twin on quantitative tests of neuropsychological processing defects found in reading disabilities. It is possible that dyslexia may be quantitatively rather than qualitatively different from the normal range of language processes found in reading. This study, however, may indicate that identical twins share the same genetic polymorphism but have different penetration.

Nevertheless, there is now sufficient evidence to implicate polymorphism in two or more genes as a biological mechanism that drives the morphological variation seen in individuals with developmental learning disabilities. Morphological variation in twins implies functional variation in hemisphere specialization, in neuropsychological functioning, and ultimately in academic disabilities. Just how perturbation in specific

328 Clinical Patterns of Disorders of Learning

genes causes this hierarchical progression is as yet unknown. As with most developmental functions, however, the biological basis for a function still requires appropriate and sufficient stimulation at critical ages for that function to develop. Biology is the structural framework. Structure plus stimulus equals function.

PSYCHOLOGICAL AND BEHAVIOR SYMPTOMS ASSOCIATED WITH DEVELOPMENTAL LEARNING DISABILITIES

Describing the individual with a developmental learning disability only in terms of his domain of academic difficulty and in the spectrum of his neuropsychological processing deficits provides an essential, but an incomplete description of that person. How an individual adjusts to the learning disorder, what emotional and behavioral patterns he or she develops, depends on a multitude of interacting factors: the cause, extent, and severity of the disorder; the spectrum of neuropsychological deficits; the temperamental and intellectual endowment with which the child was born; the presence of comorbid factors; and most important, the adequacy and appropriateness of the support the child receives from parents and from the school. Understanding the child with a learning disorder (and prescribing appropriate management) must begin with an evaluation of educational, neuropsychological, cognitive, psychiatric, and neurological parameters—a pentaxial scheme described in Chapters 6 and 7 of this book.

The child with a learning disability does not leave his problems in the classroom; he carries them home, affecting his relationship with parents and peers; the disability pervades adjustment of the adolescent and reaches into the social, emotional, and vocational adjustment of the adult. Hynd, Hooper, and Tekahashi (1998) describe the effects as direct and indirect, transactional and dynamic. By direct is meant the behavioral consequences arising from abnormal brain activity; the behavioral effects that arise directly from anomalous development of specific areas of the brain affecting temperament and personality. As an example, Hynd et al. describe "learning difficulty arising from frontal lobe dysfunction resulting in pronounced impulsivity, social disinhibition and poor judgment" or "right-hemisphere dysfunction in which an individual is prone to a variety of internalizing symptoms and social interaction problems" (p. 693) and in understanding gestures and facial expression.

Direct effects are also seen as results of the neuropsychological deficits with which each learning-disabled individual must cope: "the deviant performance in perceptual immaturities in perceptual, linguistic, sequencing and intercessory integration abilities" (Benton & Pearl, 1978, p. 468), the spectrum of language deficits including concepts of space and time, of temporal sequences, and of sound-symbol associations and their effects on the reading process.

While these skills are basic to learning, they may also form the basis for the hierarchical steps needed for advanced skills. Delay in temporal sequencing, for example, leads to difficulty in the correct storage of sequences. As a result, lacunae may occur in the retrieval of information—problems with word finding, the presence of expressive reversals, difficulty in organizing and sequencing ideas. Persistent problems in spatial orientation are seen in immaturity in right-left orientation, in concepts of distance and map reading, in ability to tell time or awareness of time sequences. These are direct effects of the biology of learning disabilities.

The indirect effect of these processing problems may involve the child in a problem with his own sense of identity. Piaget (1954) stated that reality is constructed out of one's multimodel contact with the external world. With perceptual lacunae and defects in the apparatus when the child makes contact with the world, with confusion in temporal organization and spatial orientation, he must perceive reality in a distorted frame. His construction of the world is not concordant with reality—at least as others see it; if his orientation difficulty includes right-left confusion and immaturity in praxis and in finger gnosis, his own body image in relation to the world must also be askew. The child with a learning disability is not exempt from the emotional problems of growing up with which all children must cope. The difference here is that the biological substrate is different, the neuropsychological apparatus is immature, and the vulnerability to anxiety increased. With learning disability, there is repeated exposure to failure, anticipation of failure, frustration that he cannot, despite adequate intelligence, learn to read, write, or spell, or do math as well as his peers, that it takes longer to do (academically) what his classmates can do. Added to this may be teasing, and/or rejection and/or humiliation by his peers—thus, in addition to his distorted body image, there is a sense of distorted self-worth and diminished self-confidence. The behavioral consequences are seen very early.

The learning-disordered child's problems may be apparent in preschool and kindergarten. At this level, visuomotor difficulties are seen in the child's inability to copy a circle or to color within lines; he may not be able to recognize asymmetrical letters, tell a coherent story, or understand directions. The pattern of failure and frustration thus is set very early. School becomes a confusing and perhaps a painful experience, something to be avoided by refusing to leave mother, crying, or complaining of stomachaches; or on the other hand, the child may become passively acceptant by simply withdrawing, regressing, and behaving much like someone with the "learned helplessness" (Seligman & Groves, 1970) of animals who, after repeated, inescapable electric shocks, fail to initiate responses to escape the shocks when they are freed. Other preschool children may become actively aggressive, clowning, disobedient, or negativistic.

The patterns established in the preschool years are intensified and aggravated in the elementary grades when the child cannot meet academic demands. Word recognition in reading, phonic sequences needed for spelling, and motor control and praxis needed for writing may be lacking. Academic failure is the consequence, and frustration once again surrounds the child. She now is convinced that she is stupid and cannot learn. Some children blame themselves for the failure, that somehow they are "bad," that they are being punished. Others project the blame to teachers, parents, and peers. The patterns of defense begun in kindergarten are clearly evident: Submission, somatization, depression, regression, negativism, clowning, and aggression are seen. Some children try very hard to conform, developing ritualistic behavior. In all, however, the normal progression of psychological maturation is interrupted, the anxiety engendered is not adequately managed, and neurotic symptoms may emerge in fears, obsessions and compulsions, nightmares, and eating and toileting problems. More generally, a study of 45 third-grade students from a suburban elementary school, 30 of whom were considered learning disabled, and 15 normal readers, found that stressed students with a learning disability have a significantly more difficult time recovering from stress than their peers in regular education.

By early adolescence, new educational demands are placed on the child. Education now emphasizes the ability to abstract, to gather and identify information, and to impart what has been learned in sequential written form. College preparatory courses require foreign languages often before the student has mastered English. Remedial programs are no longer concerned with neuropsychological processes, but with tutoring to keep up with current assignments. Cognition is expected to evolve into formal operations. Social needs also change. The adolescent is expected to understand social judgments. If by high school reading has somehow been improved, the rate of reading is generally slow and comprehension is impaired. Reading and writing are burdens, and outlining sequential material is difficult. Moreover, the consistent classroom teacher of elementary school is replaced by a series of academically oriented taskmasters. In adolescence, the learning-disordered child is more capable of acting out emotions in sexual and aggressive behaviors. This pattern is more readily seen in children who come from homes where aggression, antisocial behavior, and drugs are part of the social milieu. The pattern for delinquency emerges: early school failure, frustration, development of poor self-image, alienation, and finally being pushed out of school or dropping out as a response to an overwhelming sense of defeat.

It seems apparent that all children who have repeated unexplained absences from school and those who are truant deserve a comprehensive study to understand the reasons behind their school absence. All studies suggest that a majority of these children are suffering from severe learning problems. Not all of these problems are in the category of specific language disability; some children have borderline intelligence or a subtle organic defect of the central nervous system. But even in these children with low intelligence, an unrecognized language disorder may contribute to their low IQ. A 1992 article in the *Tampa Tribune* bemoaned the fact that truants are placed in detention centers. Although it indicated that more counselors are needed for these children, it made no mention of the need for comprehensive evaluation for these children and for remedial measures appropriate to those findings. Also glaringly absent is any mention of earlier recognition and treatment of these children, perhaps as early as kindergarten.

Truancy, school dropout, drugs, and delinquency, significant as they are, are but an end stage in the natural history of learning disorders and their emotional consequences. A learning disorder is the most frequent finding in classes of severely emotionally handicapped children (A. A. Silver, 1984). Most of the children in this study had already internalized intrapsychic problems and were severely anxious with low self-esteem; they were depressed, obsessive-compulsive, or phobic; many had conduct or behavioral problems—they ran away from school or were oppositional and aggressive. L. B. Silver (1989) emphasized that "emotional, social and family problems . . . the result (not the cause) of the frustrations and failures experiences by the parents" (p. 319). To this, we add the frustrations experienced by the teachers.

Not all children fit the dismal progression of emotional and behavioral dismay. We have briefly mentioned the mitigating factors interrupting such a progression. Nevertheless the self-ratings of students with learning disabilities were significantly lower than the self-ratings of average achievers on their perceptions of their own performance (Meltzer, Roditi, Houser, & Perlman, 1998).

Consequences for the Parents

We have so far been concerned with the direct effect of a learning disorder on the child. Equally important are the psychiatric implications of a learning disorder on the parents. With the identification of a learning disorder in their child, parents often have an immediate reaction of denial. This is true of families at all levels of the socioeconomic scale and at all intellectual levels. Those with high intellectual functioning, with their tendency to project their own needs onto the child, have great difficulty in accepting the child's deficits. Those on the lower socioeconomic scale proclaim how well they have done without education. In both groups, a common reaction is "He is just as I was when I was a boy. He will grow out of it." As a result of denial, many parents do little to obtain help for their child. Some devote time, money, and energy in pursuit of an "expert" who will tell them what they want to hear, namely, "The child will outgrow it."

As problems continue, denial, suppression, or nonacceptance of the child's difficulty are replaced by depression and guilt in the parents: depression that the child is impaired, that the future is uncertain, and that the child cannot fulfill their wishes for him; guilt if they can find at least one indiscretion in themselves to account for their learning-disordered child. Inevitably in their search for the cause of the learning disorder and perhaps as a way of relieving their own guilt, parents will project the blame onto anyone other than themselves: the obstetrician who delivered the child, the pediatrician who cares for him, the schools that have failed him, the psychologist who tested him, and finally the psychiatrist or neurologist who examined him. Anger is directed at all who are involved with the child, at the spouse, and at the child himself. With some parents, the resentment is focused in complaints about the money spent for remedial help, special schools, and special tutoring. At times, the anger is suppressed, and with a mechanism of reaction formation, the child may be overprotected and infantilized. Such overprotectiveness may not only inhibit the child's independent functioning, but also disrupt the balance of authority in the household. The spouse and siblings are relegated to subsystems generating resentment that is usually directed against the learning-disordered child whose overprotection labels her the "sick" one. She then becomes the scapegoat, responsible, not only for the reality problems of her disorder, but for all other problems within the family: the father's job, the daughter's boyfriend, and the mother's isolation. By not accepting the child as she is, parents do not give her the support she needs, adding to the child's feelings of worthlessness and guilt that she cannot seem to please even her parents.

Parents usually have made some adjustment to the effects evoked in them by the time their child reaches adolescence. Some of these adjustments are supportive: the acceptance of the learning disorder, realistic appraisal of goals, cooperative effort with schools, and special remedial help. Some are not so supportive, continuing the defeating patterns of affect and behavior, undermining the child's confidence in himself, preventing him from developing trust, stirring up conflict with schools and other professionals and, above all, making the family a dysfunctional system.

Further, the patterns of behavior the child develops at home are carried with her wherever she goes: the helplessness or the aggressive anger and the control over the household. Each may be reflected in attempts to control the school: demanding the teacher's attention, finding excuses for the child's behavior, and blaming the teachers. All of these behaviors are disruptive to academic performance and behavior and serve only to feed back increasing frustration, failure, and resentment.

Consequences in the Schools

The psychiatric implications of a learning disability, however, are not restricted to the child and parents. The school is also involved, both teachers and administration. There is still a tendency to think of a child who does not learn as stupid or lazy or negativistic; to think of the child with a behavior problem as "bad." True, there are stupid, lazy, negativistic, and rebellious children, but it is the wise teacher who is not threatened by a lack of success with this particular child and who asks what the cause of such behavior or poor learning may be. In many cases, the answer is a specific language disability, perhaps complicated with hyperkinesis, attentional deficit, poor motor coordination, or even more specific signs of organic insult to the central nervous system.

The pattern of teacher affect and response can send negative messages that are often interpreted as low ability cues, thus affecting students' self-esteem, sense of competence as learners, and motivation to achieve (Clark, 1997). The identification of a child as learning disordered, however, is only the beginning of the school's responsibility. Can the school modify the curriculum so that it can support and encourage the child's strengths, but make little academic demands on his or her deficits? Can the school provide the training so that the deficits may be overcome? Can the school provide appropriate remedial help? In terms of sheer numbers of children with learning disabilities, this is a formidable problem of logistics, money, and emotional involvement.

Moreover, if inadequately treated, the emotional reactions to learning disabilities do not disappear as the child grows up, but persist into adulthood (Mannuzza, Klein, Bessler, Malloy, & LaPadula, 1993). Even when good social support has been available, internalizing behaviors, lowered self-esteem, high-tuned anxiety, perceived stress, and depression themes tend to interfere significantly with family functioning and other interpersonal relations (Matejcek, 1994).

Management of Emotional and Behavioral Problems

While remedial educational help is the basis for management of most children with learning disorders, management of the complex emotional interrelations between child and parents, parents and school, and child and school may make the difference between educational success and failure, social adjustment and maladjustment, and vocational gratification and lack of vocational achievement. As we have repeatedly stressed, comprehensive evaluation will yield information on the psychiatric, biological, cognitive, environmental (parental), and educational dimensions. As the data unfold and the parameters for help are identified, management becomes a task of dealing with each of these parameters. It is helpful if one person takes the job of coordinator and synthesizer of all these data; one person becomes the contact person, the ombudsman to impart information to all concerned, including the child and parents, and to coordinate management. Just what professional should undertake this job is not the major issue. No matter in what discipline this professional is trained, he must have knowledge, not necessarily expert, in all the skills implied in the comprehensive data base. All too often this information is fragmented, or never obtained; remedial measures are uncoordinated, so the child and family appear in the office with a heavy load of behavioral problems, academic difficulty and, frequently, a blanket of hostility.

A clear explanation to the family and to the child within the capacity of her understanding is a first step in practical management. These explanatory visits help lay out the problems and clear the air for further help. To the parents and to the child, these visits provide a comprehensive overview and an intellectual understanding of the problem. They define the relationship between specific neuropsychological deficits and academic difficulty. They detail the overall assets and capabilities of the child and suggest educational help needed. They confront the parents with their psychological defenses, and they offer continued support of a knowledgeable professional.

Practically, one of the most immediate problems requiring help is management of school adjustment. Here the family and the child need help in evaluating the appropriateness of the school and its curriculum for the child. In addition, however, the academic goals of the parents may be forcing the child into a no-win situation. The needs of the school, the desires of parents, and the abilities of the child must be reconciled.

CASE STUDY: EVAN

A 15-year-old boy, a 10th grader in an academically demanding, college preparatory school, was beginning to fail the five classes he was taking. His parents complained that he was not studying, was rebellious, and had no friends. On examination, he was a small, thin child with a face covered with acne. He was truculent, grandiose, and negativistic, replete with mechanisms of denial. However, he was very depressed and anxious. He had severe perceptual problems with visual discrimination and recall of asymmetrical figures, visuomotor function, and auditory sequencing all at an 8 to 10 year level. His performance IQ on the WISC-R was 65, verbal 105. Academically, he could recognize words at the sixth-grade level, but his rate of reading was slow and his comprehension was poor. Written work was an impossibility. He blamed the school and his parents for his problem, but inwardly he was overwhelmed, with little self-esteem or hope for the future. Discussion with the school revealed their inability to individualize their curriculum to modify the demands made on the child.

Discussion with the parents helped them see the child's real difficulties and to accept his placement in a small school for learning-disordered children. Incidentally, in the year after he was relieved of the constant pressure of classical academic demands, he grew at least two inches, and his acne responded to treatment. The parents however, need continued visits to help them cope with their rapidly shifting expectations, varying from grandiose high-level profession to despairing low-level clerk. Now, 5 years after his leaving high school, this young man did manage to get a high school equivalency diploma and is graduating from a small college with a degree in criminal justice. He is seriously considering graduate school. During these years, he has had intensive remedial educational help and continued psychotherapeutic support.

It is difficult to separate effective educational modification and remediation from the emotional problems of the child and parents. It is essential to reemphasize, however, that, although therapy of whatever type for the child and parents will not cure the learning disorder and although education is still a basic component of any management plan, the emotional tensions within the child, within the parents, and between the child and parents cannot be neglected.

Learning-disordered families, with their tendency toward overprotection, enmeshment, lack of conflict resolution, and scapegoating and rigidity, resemble in many ways the "psychosomatic families" described by Minuchin, Rosman, and Baker (1978). Family therapy has been an effective, relatively economical way of relieving the dysfunctional tensions within such families. The goal is to encourage conflict resolution by developing appropriate communication between parents and child and between parents.

Parents, however, have additional groups with which to identify and within which to work for support of specific programs for learning disabilities within the community. There are local chapters of the Association for Children and Adults with Learning Disabilities (now called the Learning Disability Association) and of the International Dyslexia Association. These groups have been helpful in helping parents understand that they are not alone with this problem, helping them find appropriate educational programs for their own child, maintaining lists of qualified special education teachers who are available for private tutoring, and making them part of a group to encourage community understanding and overcome community prejudice. The Learning Disability Association may be reached at 4156 Liberty Road, Pittsburgh, PA 19234; The International Dyslexia Association at 8600 La Salle Road, Chester Building, Suite 382, Baltimore, MD 21286-2044; Telephone (410) 296-0232.

Therapy for the Child

If we consider psychotherapy as encompassing a spectrum from psychoanalysis, on the one hand, through supportive psychotherapy to counseling, on the other, and if we consider management of the children by their parents and teachers using dynamic understanding also as psychotherapy, we must conclude that virtually every child with a learning disorder requires some form of psychological understanding and management.

Indications for psychotherapy include: (a) where the disturbed affect and behavior interfere with educational measures; (b) where the child is in emotional pain; (c) where the defenses the child has adapted are maladaptive, getting her into difficulties with parents, teachers, and peers and interfering with psychological maturation; and (d) where the environment does not offer the emotional support the child needs for maturation and/or where the child becomes the expression of the parent's unconscious needs, and as a corollary to this indication, where the child's behavior must be interpreted to teachers so that they may work with him successfully when comorbid disorders (depression, AD/HD) interfere with educational progress.

The literature advises that a clear explanation of the child's problem must eventually be presented to the child and his parents; for the child this means emphasis that he is not unique, that his problems are relatively common, and that he is not stupid or a freak, abnormal or a "retard," but that he is more than his problems and has skills and assets.

However, the timing and manner of this explanation must be an individual thing. A depressed 12-year-old, with potentially average intelligence was told that he was failing in school because his brain just was not hearing sounds in the proper order, and that this was not his fault but that he was just born this way. Rather than reassure him, this explanation only convinced him that his brain was no good and intensified his depression. The explanation must obviously be geared to the capacity of the child for understanding and must be buffered by an emphasis on positive function.

Another example: A first-year medical student could not master the sheer volume of material presented to him. He was falling farther and farther behind in his work, becoming depressed, and was ready to quit medical school. Our examination revealed the persistence of an old specific language disorder, with a rate of reading expected for a seventh grader. An explanation of his difficulty only convinced him that he never could master the academic demands of medical school and he became more depressed. Only vigorous intervention, including special help in organizing his work, selecting priorities, obtaining supportive reassurance from the medical student dean, and supportive psychotherapy enabled him to carry on.

Most important is the awareness in the therapist of the lowered threshold for anxiety in these children, the decreased stimulus barrier, and the specific perceptual and cognitive deficits.

Basic rules in the conduct of psychotherapy for children with perceptual-cognitive immaturities may be summarized as follows:

- Use the intact perceptual areas in communication.
- Present stimuli as simply as possible concordant with the child's perceptual and cognitive ability, a single stimulus at a time, repetitiously with immediate feedback.
- Avoid the chaos of distracting stimuli.
- Respect the psychological defenses the child has developed.

These principles are most important in the preschool and elementary school years, but they are still valid in working with adolescents. These principles, by protecting the child from stimulus overload, will also decrease anxiety, help sustain attention, and may help decrease hyperactivity and impulsivity.

MANAGEMENT OF SPECIFIC LANGUAGE DISABILITY

All the foregoing data represent results of studies from many disciplines. While the cause (or causes) of specific language disability (or disabilities) is still elusive, these studies have broadened the breadth and increased the depth of our understanding of the central processing problems of the child and the adult with developmental learning disabilities, providing appropriate and sufficient treatment, and following him through the years of his life. These practical problems have already been addressed in previous chapters of this book: diagnosis in Chapters 6 and 7, management in Chapters 8 and 9. This section uses two case studies to apply recommended management guidelines.

Rawson (1968) wisely observed, "The many, many people who fit the broad general designation of dyslexia are notable, first of all, for their seeming likeness to everybody else. Their ranges in age, IQ, and social and other circumstances are just as wide, and in every sense of the word 'normal.' Their learning and skill problems are specific to language" (p. 179).

In some ways, their very normality creates problems for the children with developmental language disability. Nearly a century since it was first identified clinically and 50 years after Orton wrote about it so insightfully, dyslexia is still regarded as a myth by some writers who say these children are just like all the other poor readers and even not very different from mentally retarded children. This could be an interesting theoretical debate, except that some of these writers are educators whose writing can have grave consequences for the educational interventions available to children with developmental language disabilities.

Although the presenting symptom (reading difficulty) may be similar in all these cases, the etiology, clinical course, and prognosis are different. This book is based on that understanding. Even brief clinical experience should convince the most obstinate critic, but research evidence is also available in an aptly entitled paper, "Is There a Thing Called Dyslexia?" (Aaron, Kuchta, & Grapenthin, 1988). These investigators provide sound evidence that children with dyslexia are different from those they call "garden variety retarded readers." Furthermore, if Galaburda's dyslexic brains are in any way representative of the population of dyslexics in general, these children are different in the way they develop the brain functions that serve language. Each new set of language symbols and each step in the language arts sequence holds new hazards for them. Most of the time, conventional classroom methods will be ineffective for them.

CASE STUDY: JANE

The following progress notes from her teachers recount the sad school history of Jane, a bright, seriously depressed youngster who was seen at age 13.

Teacher's Report of Progress: End of Grade 1

"Jane is a student of fine ability. She has insatiable curiosity. She thinks rapidly and logically. Her ability to reason and draw conclusions is superior. She is ever alert and strove to do her best this year, but there were areas beyond her reach because of her level of developmental maturity. Initially, Jane required a period of extended readiness for formal reading instruction. Now, although Jane has made progress, her skills have not reached grade level, nor has she reached her potential. My recommendation is to retain Jane in first grade, which I feel would be the most appropriate placement at this time."

[Translation: We don't know what we did wrong, but we want to do it over again.] The parents did not agree to nonpromotion. Reading achievement test score: 14th percentile.

Progress Report: End of Grade 2

"Jane has been working a bit harder lately and is showing improvement in all academic areas, particularly math. Jane still does not show as much interest in reading as she must in order to be able to be a more proficient reader. She struggles with words, even in a primer, and becomes restless when her small reading group is at the reading table. She likes to look at the other children while they are reading when she should be following along in her book. She looks at the pictures for clues much too often at this time of year. She should have broken away from that rather questionable reading aid by now. In my professional opinion, Jane has not made sufficient progress in reading this year to ensure success in third grade where so much additional reading will be required. Jane is a bright youngster who deserves a chance to be the best she can be. I recommended retention in second grade."

[Translation: I don't know how to teach her either, but I think whatever it is that is wrong is your fault, because you should have let her repeat first grade.] The parents agreed to having Jane repeat second grade. Reading achievement test score: 9th percentile.

Progress Report: End of Grade 2 (repeated)

"Jane has successfully completed second grade this year. Her math improved tremendously. She is still having difficulty with her reading, but hopefully this also will continue to improve. Jane is a very creative and imaginative girl as exemplified by her writings, drawings, and storytelling. She is very outgoing and friendly. She usually has a very good relationship with her classmates. Jane still needs to work on increasing her self-confidence. When she feels she is 'smart,' things go well. When she feels she is 'dumb,' she starts having difficulty in all areas."

[Translation: Since we can't teach her to read very well, let's work on self-confidence, now that we've taken that away by having her stay back.] Reading achievement test score: 25th percentile.

Progress Report: End of Grade 3

"Since Jane is still experiencing difficulty with her classroom work, she will continue remedial reading classes in order to support Mrs. _____'s efforts."

[Translation: We've given up.] Reading achievement test score: 15th percentile. Records do not contain further end-of-year reports. However, the reading achievement test score for fifth grade was recorded at the 16th percentile.

The records show that the typical administrative approaches (retention in grade and remedial reading consisting of reteaching the basal reading series used in the classroom) did not help Jane read better. Even more striking is the emotional attrition from failure. In 3 years, the interested, motivated youngster became acutely sensitive to slights about her intellectual abilities, which even in her depressed state at age 13 were respectable (WISC-R: full scale IQ, 116; verbal IQ, 106; performance IQ, 124). After third grade, she was placed in a resource room program under special education auspices. That the combination of workbook exercises and homework help she received there was not particularly effective is indicated by achievement test scores at age 13:

Wide Range Achievement Test	Percentile
Oral Reading	1
Spelling	8
Arithmetic	6

Woodcock-Johnson Psychoeducational Battery

	Grade Scores	Percentile
Reading Cluster	3.0	5
Mathematics Cluster	3.4	7

Despite daily sessions in the resource room, she has not mastered decoding skills. When she met an unfamiliar word, she guessed at it on the basis of its visual configuration and initial grapheme. Thus *form* was read as "from," *grunt* as "garnet," and *theory* as "through." The Phoenician Spelling Test showed that she was uncertain of the short vowels but knew most consonant blends and digraphs. She did not know such serviceable generalizations as the long vowel/silent *e* rule or the closed syllable rule, but she knew *r*- controlled vowels, and soft *g* and *c;* she reversed the letter *b* twice:

Jane: Phoenician Spelling Test

Word Dictated	Response	Word Dictated	Response
mag	mag	muttin	motin
fid	fed	noy	nowy
vol	val	tort	tort
pub	pud	cim	cim
plat	blat	theet	thet

Decoding and encoding skills were so limited that it was difficult to assess Jane's reading comprehension and writing skills. It is not surprising that she felt lost and discouraged when faced with classwork in a large suburban middle school.

The discouraging outcome with Jane illustrated how her normality and reasonableness did her disservice. Had she demonstrated some negative behavior, she would have called attention to her problems and perhaps received more effective assistance. Her defense was one of withdrawal and self-devaluation.

Not all youngsters with developmental language disabilities respond as Jane did (see previous section of this chapter). Some youngsters respond with anger and hostility; others become dependent and passive; some use denial and isolation; some become almost sociopathic in their skill at cheating on tests, copying homework, and beating the system. When these children get to the clinician's office, the diagnostic problem is complicated by the need to separate the primary problem from the defensive system the youngster has had to construct to survive. Therefore, a major management principle is the need for early, comprehensive, multidisciplinary diagnosis. On the basis of the information elicited, an intervention plan should be developed so that one professional becomes responsible for intervention strategies. This kind of individual educational plan is mandated by special education legislation in the schools; it is no less necessary in the private practice of psychiatrists, educators, and psychologists working with children with specific learning disabilities. This disorder is a lifelong condition. A brief diagnostic conference or a few months of tutoring to "catch up" in a subject area will not suffice. While direct services may be necessary at some critical times in an individual's development, at other times consultation may be need at pivotal decision points (e.g., a change of schools or vocational plans), or support may be required in documenting history of a learning disorder in order to obtain accommodations such as extended time on tests for various qualifying examinations. For effective implementation, this plan should be arrived at in cooperation with the parents and the youngster involved. Children who have had past experiences like Jane's may express some reservations about any plan for remediation. Time spent dealing openly with those reservations and in building understanding of the intervention plan is certainly time well spent. Some students who bear the scars of many previous unsuccessful interventions may require some negotiation before they agree. Setting a time-limited trial period is one method of providing such youngsters the control they feel they must have before they can make commitment to an intervention plan. One can understand students' reluctance to trust still another program that promises to teach them to read, having felt disappointment in the past. This is particularly true when students have some doubts about their ability to learn; they may be reluctant to make a great investment in a program that will prove, in the final analysis that they really do not have the ability to learn to read.

Once the intervention plan has been agreed on and the responsibilities for intervention have been assigned, the program is ready to begin. Whether it is a relatively modest arrangement for tutoring, a resource room program, a special class, or a special school, it should be understood that educational decisions are under the control of the teacher. Although they may be therapeutic in effect, these programs differ markedly from psychotherapy in this respect. Rapport in this setting is based on the teacher's designing the work in such a way as to give student opportunity for successful learning. This sense of accomplishment will be a most powerful motivation force. Used successfully, it will make rewards in the form of extrinsic motivation unnecessary.

For the child with a specific language disability, the program activities should be embedded in the total language sequence. Content of the lessons should be based on the child's level of development in that sequence and move on from there. Although students may request it, help with school homework is not very useful unless it is appropriate to the level and the type of skills being taught. Frequently, homework assignments will be far beyond the student's actual language skills. Sacrificing the time needed for practice with these skills to complete what may be inappropriate busywork is an unwise choice. This problem can be met by asking that homework requirements be modified by the teacher in terms of the child's actual educational needs. One exception to this advice might be the use of the textbooks in the content subjects when teaching reading comprehension strategies. For example, if the SQ3R comprehension technique (survey, question, read, review, recite) is being taught, using the child's science or social studies textbook will improve transfer of the techniques to real-life requirements.

Particularly at the secondary level, other accommodations in the school program may be necessary. This might have meant the substitution of one type of skill for another (i.e., the substitution of a computer language for a traditional foreign language requirement) or the choice of a more phonetically regular foreign language (Spanish, Russian, or Hebrew rather than French). The use of the word processor (and spelling checker) for written compositions is an important skill for secondary school students to learn and to use with regular assignments.

The major problem with most students with specific language disabilities is in the area of decoding. Teachers working with them should not assume that all aspects of these skills are in place, no matter how old the student is. A careful survey of the student's skills through examination of oral reading, formal spelling, and a spontaneous writing sample is essential. Any aspects of these processes that have not been mastered should be given major priority in intervention. Reading comprehension is seriously hampered by word attack skills that are not automatic; written expression is constricted if the student must take time from expressing her ideas to select words she can spell and avoid those she cannot.

Finally, the teacher of the child with dyslexia should be alert for special abilities the child may have that are not addressed by the current school program. In our descriptions of the language problems of these children, it is easy to lose sight of their strengths. These talents may begin to show up in art and design, in mechanical abilities, in mathematics, in leadership and management skills, in computer applications, in sports abilities, and in countless other fields. During the school years, they represent a respite from the drudgery of learning to deal with the language. As the youngster enters adolescence, these interests may assume a more important role than that of hobby or compensatory activity. They may point the direction for vocational choices in adult life.

CASE STUDY: MATT

The case of Matt illustrates some principles in education intervention with a boy who has a specific language disability.

Matt was referred for psychological testing and educational planning by a child psychiatrist whom his family had consulted because of Matt's lack of progress in learning to read. Matt's family was acquainted with dyslexia, because his older brother had similar problems. In addition, his father, although he had graduated from an Ivy-League college and was now a successful professional, had had difficulty in learning to read. The signs were recognized early in Matt and help was sought when he was a 7½-year-old second grader in a challenging independent school.

On the WISC, Matt earned a full scale IQ of 124, placing cognitive functioning at the 94th percentile. The performance IQ of 135 (99th percentile) was superior to the verbal IQ of 110 (75th percentile), although one of the highest scores on the record occurred with the verbal scale test of Vocabulary. The only significantly low score was with rote sequencing of digits:

WISC Scaled Scores

Information	12	Picture Completion	12
Comprehension	11	Picture Arrangement	20
Arithmetic	11	Block Design	15
Similarities	12	Object Assembly	15
Vocabulary	16	Coding	13
Digit Span	8		

In addition to Vocabulary, Matt also did well with the subtest tapping the building of a story sequence from pictures. On this test, he showed skill in sequencing ideas and insight and alertness to the subtle behavioral cues in the pictures. This easy sequencing of ideas contrasted with his difficulties with the arbitrary sequences of digits, on which he was only able to handle a sequence of four digits forward and three digits reversed.

Matt related well in the session. He was honest with himself about what was hard for him. He tended to undervalue his efforts, however, and needed encouragement to improvise with items on which he was not completely certain of the answer, particularly with manipulative or numerical items.

Because of Matt's superior cognitive resources, his educational expectancy was estimated to be at the high third-grade level at the time of testing. This expectancy estimate is a rough standard that can be compared with the scores he earned on the following education tests:

Wide Range Achievement Test	Grade Scores
Oral Reading	1.4
Spelling	1.6

Peabody Individual Achievement Test	Grade Scores
Mathematics	3.2
Reading Recognition	1.2
Reading Comprehension	(untestable)

As can be seen from these scores, learning of mathematics is appropriate to expectancy. The only difficulties he experienced occurred with such arbitrary verbal sequences as measures (inches, pints, quarts, etc.) and with place values of some numbers.

Oral reading places Matt at the beginning reading level on both the PIAT and the WRAT. Matt has some idea of phonic analysis, but did not associate all sounds and symbols accurately. Furthermore, phonic knowledge was not used with any consistency in reading. When Matt met an unfamiliar word, he was apt to guess at it on the basis of its configuration, rather than to use sounds even when he knew them. Spelling reflected the same mixed approach. It was not possible to assess reading comprehension at that time because Matt recognized too few words. The impression, however, was that once he learned to decode the words, he would have no trouble dealing with the ideas.

On assessment of perceptual skills, Matt found auditory tasks easier than the visual and visuomotor tasks. His articulation was precise. He blended sounds into words well but had difficulty matching initial sounds and recognizing or supplying rhymes. The Bender VGMT was difficult for him, with integration and orientation of figures somewhat below his age level. Even when the motor aspect was removed from the task (as it was on the Lamb Chop Test), he tended to rotate the figures. He was able to indicate right and left on himself, but not on the examiner. He was also uncertain of the finger schema. Our arm extension test suggested that for Matt laterality for language had not been firmly established.

Despite superior cognitive abilities, a diagnosis of specific language disability was made and tutoring was recommended along the following lines:

1. Training in prereading skills to build a basis for beginning reading:
   a. Visuomotor.
   b. Visual orientation.
   c. Rhyming.
   d. Locating sounds within words.
   e. Finger schema.
2. When perceptual skills permit, teaching of independent word attack skills with emphasis on a code-based approach and use of phonetically regular text.
3. Written language activities to teach accurate mechanisms and to encourage fluent written expression.

The first step in tutoring was goal setting. Added to the original three instructional goals was an additional one, that of reaching consensus with Matt, his parents, and his school about the recommended intervention program. Matt's parents were intelligent, sensible, and supportive. Matt himself had not experienced devastating failure and, although he may have had some reservations, he went along with the plans quietly. His school was also cooperative, albeit overoptimistic about what Matt had accomplished with the conventional program. Exchange visits were arranged so that we had some idea of classroom activities and his teacher had an opportunity to observe a tutoring session. Responsibilities were apportioned so that some skills that required daily practice (e.g., Rhythmic Writing on the chalkboard) could be done at school. Observation of the reading lesson at school indicated that some modification of the basal reader sight-word approach was needed to reinforce the code-based approach used in the tutoring sessions. The suggestion for this change required tact, but it was received and implemented with materials already available in the classroom.

The first work with Matt centered around building the prereading skills. Matt enjoyed Rhythmic Writing on the chalkboard, adapting himself to the precision in motor control required by the task, even inventing motifs of his own to be added to the collection we were getting ready for publication in *Teach*. The purpose of Rhythmic Writing was to provide practice with directional orientation and to help him overlearn the motor patterns needed for handwriting. The latter purpose was crucial because his school curriculum made the transition from print to cursive writing at the end of second grade. It was important to Matt to keep up with his classmates with this skill, although it was not easy for him; he often complained that he could not remember "how the letters went." These handwriting techniques (and the neuropsychological principles underlying them) have been described (Hagin, 1983).

Work with rhyming provided a supportive skill for learning phonic analysis. The idea of rhyming was taught using paired associate learning, practice with games (such as Concentration and Rhyming Dominoes), and poems. This skill needed to be automatic if it were to be of any use in word attack. Matt enjoyed this work, seeming to find comfort in its repetitiveness. He soon began trying his hand with writing simple rhymes like this one that turned into a valentine after much help with the spelling:

A valentine heart
In my best art.
Made for you
With paper and glue
Because
Parents are
Good skiers
&
Sight see-ers
Great cooks
And they help us with books
And tons of fun
Your happy son

Matt

Work in decoding reviewed all consonant sounds to mastery and began introducing various phonic elements, more or less in the sequence presented in Gillingham's *Jewel Box*. Activities in this area included (a) rapid review of sound cards from previous lessons, (b) introduction of the new sound element, (c) dictation of words containing a high frequency of the sound element being taught with much emphasis on Matt's blending sound elements as he wrote them, (d) oral reading of the dictated words, (e) rapid silent reading of the dictated words in response to a Guessing Meanings game, and (f) reading aloud from phonetically regular text (i.e., from such series as the SRA Basic Reading Series). This pattern of activities (called *DOMinate*) was used to teach all phonic elements. As word attack skills were mastered, there was gradual introduction of natural text from conventional remedial materials and, with them, generalizations and procedures for syllabication. This work was not accomplished easily or rapidly; it spread over 4 years, with many frustrating hours for Matt as the sound-symbol associations almost mastered at one session eluded him completely on his return.

When dealing with words he could decode, Matt had little difficulty understanding meaning. His exceptionally broad vocabulary was enriched by the many travel experiences his family provided and by the broad-based, sometimes very challenging curriculum at school. Matt read his first book independently while in fourth grade, in connection with a history unit on the Middle Ages at school. We had found a simplified version of *Men of Iron,* and he set to work enthusiastically. During the next session, he explained the game plan he used on each chapter: "First I read the words: then I read it to see what it says; then I close the book and think about what happened." An effective, if rudimentary study strategy!

Spelling and written composition work moved most slowly of all goals. There was such a gap between Matt's ideas and his ability to deal with the written language code that many of his early efforts were almost unreadable:

> *Wen we went ot apan we had fund and do you*
> *Know wut the most fun wun sking.*
> *And my big —————— got a ————— fi ————— —————*

Using the Fernald tracing technique (Chapter 8), Matt rewrote the story:

> *Aspen*
>
> *When we went to Aspen, we had fun, And do you*
> *Know what was the most fun? Skiing.*
> *My big brother got a pair of moon boots*
> *And I tried them on, but they did not fit.*
> *I was sad!*

Fernald tracing helped Matt build a private dictionary of words he used in his own writing. We also used written conversation rehearsals of letters he would be writing from camp, and letters to other children, thank-you notes—any and all excuses were used to give Matt functional use of communication skills. Eventually, spelling generalizations were taught in the sessions. Matt's school allowed him to substitute the Plunkett speller for the one used in the classroom because the former was more consistent with the code-based approach we were using in his tutoring sessions.

Revaluation of educational progress was an integral part of the work. It helped Matt gain confidence in his ability to learn and it helped us assess the effectiveness of the teaching approach. This information was shared with parents and school staff, as shown in the following letter:

Dear Mr. & Mrs. Blank:

This is a progress note on Matt's work with me. I am enclosing a copy in order that you can share it with Miss Jones and Matt's school.

Matt did retests of reading and spelling this month. The scores are listed below together with results on the same measures six and twelve months ago:

	Baseline	At 6 Months	At 12 Months
Wide Range Achievement Test			
Oral Reading	1.4	2.5	3.4
Spelling	1.6	2.2	2.4
Peabody Individual Achievement Test			
Reading Recognition	1.3	2.4	3.1
Reading Comprehension	untestable	2.0	3.1

As you can see there is progress in all areas since last year, although Matt has not reached the level that his cognitive abilities predict.

Matt has made progress with the basic perceptual skills underlying reading and spelling. One area in which he will continue to need work is with Rhythmic Writing, which Miss Jones continues to do at school. This is most important work in making cursive writing motifs automatic. As you probably have noticed, Matt still complains about "forgetting how the letters go." I've noticed this with the formation of cursive capitals. Other perceptual skills have been learned and are being used to support word attack in reading.

It has been very helpful to hear from Miss Jones from time to time in order to coordinate our efforts. I have noticed such a difference since Matt has been working with the code-based series at school also. In addition to this growth in cracking the code, Matt is also making better use of contextual cues in reading. This was especially apparent in his work on the PIAT comprehension section and his comments about whether what he reads "makes sense."

I have added some composition to our regime here, so that Matt can build a core vocabulary to use in written work. He has a second set of his "word file" at home—his own idea, I might add. Words are added each week, taught by multisensory cues. The entire file is reviewed and alphabetized to incorporate the week's new words.

Matt's motivation is improved. He is gradually becoming confident in his ability to learn and to try new skills. This confidence will, of course, facilitate further progress.

I will continue to keep you informed concerning our work. Please let people at Matt's school know I appreciate hearing from them and look forward to continue cooperative planning on Matt's behalf.

Sincerely yours,

Matt's achievement continued to improve, so that by the end of sixth grade, the following scores were earned in the Woodcock Reading Mastery Test:

Woodcock Reading Mastery Test

	Grade Scores	Percentile
Letter Identification	6.2	50
Word Identification	11.0	80
Word Attack	12.9	83
Word Comprehension	11.2	79
Passage Comprehension	8.7	64
Total Reading	9.6	82

Tutoring was concluded at that point, although informal contact was continued with him and his family. When he applied for admission to boarding school at Grade 9, acceptances were received from all schools to which he made application. He chose a rigorous one and worked hard through the 4 years. He met the foreign language requirement with Spanish, managing to survive with the help of tutoring during the summer. A this point, he has completed college and is working in a small law office and reviewing for the Law School Admissions examinations.

Matt's case makes a number of points about the clinical management of specific language disability. It documents the positive outcomes when the problem is identified early and when appropriate support is provided as long as the youngster needs it. Matt was fortunate in his family's choice of schools; these schools, in turn, offered him challenges that he met without any attempt to avoid hard work. Finally, it illustrated that specific language disability does not inevitably doom the individual to learning failure and emotional distress.

LONG-TERM PROGNOSIS OF LEARNING-DISABLED CHILDREN

For any individual child with a learning disorder, the outcome in terms of persistence of linguistic and perceptual deficits and in academic, social, vocational, and psychological adjustment will vary with many factors: the causes, extent, and severity of the learning disorder; the presence of complicating attentional deficits, hyperactivity, and neurological signs; the cognitive substrate with which the child comes into the world; the psychological defenses the child has established; and most important, the adequacy and appropriateness of the environmental and educational support he or she has received. With this complex interplay of forces, it is not surprising that long-term reviews of outcomes of children with learning disorders are varied.

The most recent review of prognosis of learning disabilities (Satz et al., 1998) focuses on reading and learning problems and draws on the methodology used by Schonhaut and Satz (1983) to evaluate the scientific merit of the studies that have been in print from 1959 through 1993; 21 studies between 1959 and 1978; and 12 additional studies from 1981 through 1993. The 1993 review found 4 follow-up studies with good outcomes, 3 mixed, and 14 poor; the 1999 review added 3 studies reporting good outcomes, 1 mixed, and 8 poor. These 33 reports were subjected to 5 criteria considered by Schonhaut and Satz to be necessary, to determine the validity of the outcomes reported; (a) an adequate follow-up period, (b) a sufficiently large sample at baseline and at follow-up, (c) a satisfactory method of sample selection, (d) an adequate comparison group, and (e) a valid and objective measure of reading/learning ability. Each criterion was, in turn, scored by subcriteria to identify 12 methodologically stronger studies. Of these, 3 reported good outcomes, and 9 poor outcomes. Even the stronger studies however, had significant variability. For example, in one favorable report, Rawson (1968) studied only occupational and educational outcome. Her sample moreover was drawn from a private school, with students from high-income families, with mean IQ (Stanford-Binet) of 130 and with every educational support. Satz et al. (1978) on the other hand, studied the entire male population of a public school in a rural area in Florida in which IQ scores were not specified and educational intervention not mentioned. In the Satz study, of 49 severely retarded readers at the end of second grade, only 6% were rated as average or better readers at the end of fifth grade. Thus, with two different samples from different socioeconomic and IQ levels and presumably with different educational interventions, these studies came to completely different conclusions. Two studies other than that of Rawson, report favorable outcome. The first Bruck (1985, 1987) compared the academic, occupational, social, and emotional status of 101 adolescents and young adults who had been diagnosed as learning disabled during childhood with 50 non-LD peers and 51 non-LD siblings matched for age, sex, and social class. The LD group was drawn from children who had been diagnosed as LD at McGill-Montreal Children's Hospital. All subjects had difficulty with written language, 75% with math, 45% with problems in visuospatial processing. Although the childhood learning problems of many persisted at follow-up, most had sufficient skill to continue their schooling and further their occupational status. Bruck found childhood IQ and family SES were the best predictors of educational outcome.

The second study with good outcome was that of Finucci, Gottfredson, and Childs (1985). This was a long variable follow-up of two groups of students: one group attended a private school for dyslexics (Gow) and the other was a combined nondyslexic group from another private school (Gilman); 472 out of 965 Gow alumni and 351 out of 753 Gilman alumni were followed. Although the long-term academic and occupational outcomes were generally good for both groups, the Gow alumni had greater academic difficulty, (95% Gilman vs. 50% Gow attaining college degree; 3 times as many Gow took 5 years to earn the bachelor degree, Gow majoring in business, Gilman in science and liberal arts).

Poor outcomes were found in 12 methodologically stronger studies using the Shonhaut and Satz criteria. Houden followed 53 children who attended fifth and sixth grade classes in Springfield, Oregon in 1942 for an average of 19 years. Poor readers did not do well in years of formal schooling and in occupational status. However, as Satz et al. (1999) points out, the poor readers came from lower SES families than good readers. Spreen (1987) followed 203 LD children referred to the University of Victoria for an average follow-up period of 10 years, then approximately 6 years later when subjects were 25 years of age (Spreen, 1987, 1989; Spreen & Haaf, 1986). Spreen divided the sample into 3 groups depending on neurological signs: Group 1 ($n = 88$) had at least one hard neurological sign and 3 soft; Group 2 ($n = 95$) children with one or two soft signs; Group 3—no neurological signs. At the 6-year follow-up in terms of educational, occupational, social, and psychological adjustment, the outcomes of the LD group were worse than that of the control group. Female LD subjects had more social and emotional problems than male LD. A second follow-up of this sample, done when the subjects were at age 25, used cluster techniques to identify similar neuropsychological subtypes at baseline (linguistic, visuospatial, and anticulo-graphomotor). The linguistic subgroup had poor outcome in terms of cognition and academic performance; the visuospatial remained stable over time. There was stability also for those with soft and hard neurological signs. The number of neurological signs during childhood predicted poorer outcomes for grade completion, college attendance, monthly income, and employment. The LD children with neurological signs were considered disorganized, emotionally dependent, and lacking appropriate social skills.

Satz et al. (1999) reviews in detail the remaining 6 studies, all with poor outcome (DeFries & Baker, 1983; Korhonen, 1991; McKinney, Osborne, & Schulte, 1993; Rutter et al., 1976; Satz et al., 1978; Zigmond & Thornton, 1985).

The overall findings suggest that while childhood reading or learning problems persist over time, the generally pessimistic outlook for children with learning disabilities must be tempered by diagnosis, severity, intelligence, and by environmental support including remedial education and parental and school understanding. Despite "adequate" adjustment, the neuropsychological problems are tenacious and tend to persist throughout adolescence and early adulthood. This is particularly true of children who have neurological signs (see also A. A. Silver & Hagin, 1964, 1985). One can no longer say that children will spontaneously outgrow their learning disorder.

Satz et al. (1998) conclude that larger and more epidemiologically based studies are needed. They suggest that the National Collaboration Prenatal Project, launched in the late 1950s represents a potential cohort with approximately 55,000 children followed from birth to age 7. The NINCDS and March of Dimes has funded prospectively all children from the Providence cohort (4,140) who at age 7 years meet the criteria for LD. "It is hoped that this project will help resolve many of the problems found in this review" Satz et al. (1998).

SUMMARY

The essence of the dysfunction of developmental language disability lies in the brain's ability to process, store, and retrieve symbols when this dysfunction appears to be the result of developmental processes (other than general cognitive retardation, autism, or schizophrenia), the cause of which appear to emanate from genetic polymorphism. Although, in general, the dysfunction relates primarily to the processing of information from visual, auditory, and tactile modalities, and although the majority of children with developmental learning disabilities appear to have language processing deficits, the pattern of dysfunction for any individual child is unique, so that clinically the developmental learning disability group itself appears to be clinically heterogeneous.

The academic difficulty is but the tip of the iceberg; the neuropsychological deficits are just below the surface. To offer a mechanism for the neuropsychological deficits, the concept of an abnormality of hemisphere specialization has been advanced. Studies of lateralization of brain function have been spurred by the development of noninvasive neuropsychological and neuroimaging techniques. Asymmetry in processing bilateral, simultaneous presentation of auditory, visual, and tactile stimuli have, in general suggested that hemisphere specialization in children and adults with developmental language disability is not as well developed as in normal controls. This inference, drawn from dichotic listening, visual half field, and bilateral symmetrical tactile studies, has been challenged. Nevertheless, the concept of developmental aberration in the neuropsychological functions necessary for learning reading, spelling, writing, and arithmetic continues to be advanced as an explanation for the deficit functions. This concept does not necessarily mean that maturation will spontaneously occur, and there is evidence that unless the disorder is adequately and appropriately treated, processing deficits persist into adult life.

Genetic factors have been advanced to account, at least in part, for developmental learning disability. Family and twin studies offer strong presumptive evidence of a genetic factor in the expression of developmental LD. There is high prevalence of developmental LD within families, and twin studies demonstrate a significantly higher prevalence of developmental LD in monozygotic twins than in dizygotic twins. The genetic mode of inheritance, as seen in segregation and linkage analysis, appears to involve chromosomes 6 and 15.

Morphologically, the normal pattern of asymmetry in the cerebral cortex does not appear to be present in specific language disability, and microscopic findings consistent with cell dysplasia and ectopia, particularly in the left temporal lobe, were found in the few patients studied. Neuroimaging scans also find the more usual pattern of cerebral asymmetry to be absent or reversed in the brain of dyslexics. Electroencephalographic studies have revealed many different patterns in children with developmental LD. The relationship between each of these wave patterns and developmental LD is controversial. EEG patterns have been studied with computer assistance so that plots of the wave frequencies (spectra) and their quantity (power) may be obtained for each electrode position on the scalp and then displayed on a computer screen (brain electrical area mapping, BEAM). Such maps have revealed suggestive differences between developmental LD and normal readers.

Functional asymmetries found in infants may have their origins in parallel morphological gradients in the embryological development of the cerebral hemispheres, and the patterns of morphological asymmetries in brain structure in adults should thus arise from embryological growth patterns.

Emotional and behavioral responses to learning disabilities depend on the cause, extent, and severity of the disorders, the innate coping mechanisms, and most important, on the adequacy appropriateness of support the child receives from parents and school. Failure and frustration may appear early in the child's school experience where reactive behaviors of avoidance, depression, aggression, and disobedience set the stage for subsequent emotional and behavioral problems. Parental reactions, denial and nonacceptance, depression and guilt, projection for blame to the school, all undermine support for the child. Teachers may see the child as stupid and lazy and may not understand the child's special needs. Psychotherapeutic management of the complex emotional interrelations between the child and the parents, parents and school, and the school and child is described.

Remedial education, however, as described in Chapter 8 and in the management of the children described in this chapter, is the basis for management.

The long-term prognosis in terms of academic, vocational, and social achievement, for the child with a developmental reading disability, will vary with many factors: the extent and severity of the disorder, the presence of complicating comorbid disorders (ADHD, OCD, Tourette's syndrome), the cognitive abilities of the child, the psychological defenses and most important, the adequacy and appropriateness of the environmental and educational support he secures. While the success in reported studies, based on research criteria, is generally pessimistic, many individual case reports seen in schools and in private remedial clinics, present a more optimistic future. Remediation must be specific, appropriate, and continue long enough to teach the brain to overcome its processing deficits.

Chapter 12 ―――――――――――――――――――――――――――――

EFFECTS OF POVERTY, CULTURAL DIFFERENCES, AND INAPPROPRIATE STIMULATION

America's most glaring domestic inequality is the life-blighting failure of inner-city public schools to serve poor, mostly minority children.

—George F. Will, 2000

CASE STUDY: WYN

Wyn was already 16 years old when he was referred to us from the juvenile justice system with a history of having been involved in an armed robbery. He had been on homebound instruction because he could not be contained in a day-care program for children with severe behavioral and learning difficulty, and even on homebound, he refused to be available for his tutoring sessions. He was involved with drugs, sex, and behaviors that his father said will "either get him killed or him killing someone else."

Wyn has a long, distressing history of aggression and learning disorder going back to first grade. Repeated psychological testing revealed a full scale IQ on the WISC-R in the low normal-borderline range with a verbal IQ of 75 and a performance IQ of 94. Psychological study revealed an impoverished vocabulary but no specific areas of defect. Although he received remedial services in Grades 1 through 3, his oral reading level at age 16 years (WRAT) was Grade 4.0 and his spelling Grade was 3.0. Neurological and electroencephalographic examinations were normal. Perceptual study revealed good visual discrimination and recall of asymmetrical figures, poor visuomotor function with primitive verticalization, and body image immaturity in right-left discrimination and in praxis. The major area of defect, however, was in auditory processing, with difficulty in auditory discrimination and auditory rote sequencing. It was questionable whether these were actual auditory perceptual defects or a function of his black dialect reaction to Standard English. On psychiatric examination, he was verbal and appeared intelligent and

351

cooperative, but his was a hedonistic personality with no guilt over his behavior. He has never learned to control his impulses and beneath his overt cooperation was a readily mobilized anger. He projects his anger to his parents, stating that they do not love him, never did love him, and thwart his every wish. He says that he becomes angry when he is restricted unfairly or when someone talks about him. There is a mild paranoid flavor in his thinking. He says his father talks about his school problems, and everyone knows about them. He would very much like to learn in school, but feels he does not understand the teacher's instructions.

He is one of seven children, the oldest four of whom are in difficulty with the law. His background is one of poverty and disadvantage. His father, a broad-chested man, appearing physically powerful, has not worked for years because of a "back injury." His mother has always worked, according to Wyn, and is emotionally distant from him. The relations at home are mutually distrustful. The image of his father is a macho one, a powerful male whom Wyn is trying to emulate; the image of his mother is vague and nonsupportive.

Can Wyn's behavior and academic difficulty be dissociated from the social reality of the environment surrounding him?

LEARNING DISABILITY AND SOCIOECONOMIC DISADVANTAGE

The preponderance of evidence points to the reciprocal relationship between poverty and learning disorders. In 1997, the Washington State Learning Disabilities Research Project estimated that of all individuals on welfare in the entire state, 54% were learning disabled, 34% were slow learners, 4% were mentally retarded, and 5% had other learning problems. The Coutinho Study (1995) found that 65.4% of households with individuals with "specific learning disabilities" had an annual income of less than $25,000, while 38% of the general population earn less than $25,000 per year. Thirty-five percent of students with learning disability drop out of high school, twice the rate of their non-LD peers. In 1999, young adults living in families in the lowest 20% of income distribution of all families in the United States were five times as likely to drop out of high school as their peers coming from families in the top 20% of income. Comparable data over the past 25 years provides continued evidence that income (and social factors affected by income) is correlated with high school dropout rate; in families with income in the lowest 20%, the dropout rates ranges from 4.5 to 11 times the rate for students from families with income in the highest 20% (National Center for Education Statistics, 1999). Among students with learning disabilities, 62% were unemployed one year after graduation from high school (M. Wagner, 1991) and difficulty with reading comprehension, even for following a birth control plan, are among the top reasons reported by teenage girls for not using birth control aids (Adult Committee, Speical Populations Subcommittee, 2000).

Thus, in the United States poverty itself is a potent risk factor in predicting the occurrence of learning disabilities, and learning disability itself is a risk factor in perpetuating the cycle.

Here in the United States, in the beginning of the twenty-first century, children are more likely than any other age group to live in poverty. During the past two decades, there has been a substantial increase in the number and percentage of poor children under the age 18. Over 13 million children live in poverty, and the number of children living in poverty has increased by 15% (3 million) from 1979 to 1998. Nineteen percent of children under the age of 18 live in families below the federal poverty line ($13,003 for a family of three in 1998); 8% of children live in extreme poverty with incomes 50% below the poverty line ($6,562 for a family of three in 1998); finally 40% of American children live in or near poverty with incomes below twice the poverty line ($26,006 for a family of three). Many of the concerns of the near-poor families overlap with those of the poor (need for well-paying jobs and access to affordable child care and health care; National Center for Children in Poverty, 2000).

Analyzing these data by race, the poverty rate is highest for African Americans (37%) and Latino (34%) children, it is also high for white children (11%). These relative percentages have remained stable since 1980. The United States child poverty rate is often two or three times higher than that of most other major Western industrialized nations (National Center for Children in Poverty, 2000). In the United States, the top 1% of income earners receive 12% of the country's pretax income and hold 37% of the wealth, while there is evidence that "the social and economic structure of a society may fundamentally determine the health of its members," and that "absolute wealth or income is a less important determinant of health than the relative disparity in income or the income gap between the rich and the poor" (McCally, 2000, in his review of Kawachi, Kennedy, & Wilkinson, 1999). While this thesis and its social consequences may be debatable, there is no debate about the widening of the income gap between the poor and the affluent in the United States.

Where the effects of poverty and social disadvantage are compounded by race, the child's educational achievement has a "double deficit." Over the decade 1990 to 1999, between 347,000 and 544,000 tenth- through twelfth-grade students left school each year without completing high school. As of October 1999, 3.8 million young adults, 11.2% of the 16- through 24-year-olds in the United States had not completed high school. In October 1996, the total dropout rate was 11.1% (22.1% from lowest 20% income level, 10.8% from middle income, and 2.6% from the high 20% income level). Table 12.1 shows the dropout rate by income and race-ethnicity, as of October 1996.

In 1999 when Asian/Pacific Islanders were included, the dropout rate for Asian/Pacific Islanders was 4.3%; Hispanics, 28.6%; blacks, 12.6%; and whites, 7.3%. Of the Hispanics, 44.2% born outside the United States were high school dropouts; those born in the United States were "less likely" to drop out (National Center for Education Statistics, 1999). The effect of poverty and race on academic achievement was dramatically demonstrated 30 years ago in what was termed the "Coleman Report" (Youth in the Ghetto, Harlem Youth Opportunities Unlimited, 1964). By first grade, the scores of minority groups (African American, Indian American, Mexican American, and Puerto Rican) were already one standard deviation below national norms on standard achievement tests. At Grades 6 and 8 they were 2.5 years below national norms on reading comprehension, word knowledge, and arithmetic. The Coleman report spurred impressive socioeducational reforms such as busing to equalize racial representation in schools and early compensatory programs such as Head Start. As early as 40 years ago

**Table 12.1   Status dropout rate, ages 16 to 24, by income and race-ethnicity
(October 1996)**

| Family Income | Total | Race-Ethnicity[1] | | |
		White, Non-Hispanic	Black, Non-Hispanic	Hispanic
Total	11.1	7.3	13.0	29.4
Family Income[2]				
Low income level	22.1	13.9	21.9	42.4
Middle income level	10.8	8.3	9.0	24.9
High income level	2.6	2.0	2.5	11.0

[1] Due to relatively small sample sizes, American Indian/Alaskan Natives, and Asian/Pacific Islanders are included in the total but are not shown separately.
[2] Low income is defined as the bottom 20% of all family incomes for 1996; middle income is between 20 and 80% of all family incomes; and high income is the top 20% of all family incomes.
Source: U.S. Department of Commerce, Bureau of Census, Current Population Survey, October 1996, unpublished data.

in 1966, Leon Eisenberg, in what is now a classical study found that 28% of the children in inner-city schools were 2 or more years retarded in reading with respect to their grade placement. Even in the same schools, black children were reading at a lower level than their white peers. In schools with parents who were predominantly white-collar workers, 15% of the children were similarly below grade in reading and, in suburban public schools, 3% were. In independent private schools, whose students were carefully chosen, there were no children 2 or more years below grade level in reading. Where data permitted race to be studied, especially in the predominantly white-collar workers' schools, 12% of the white children, in contrast to 36% of the black children in the same schools, were 2 or more years retarded in reading. While the tests used for criterion measures were not the same across schools, the trend was clear: Reading retardation was more prevalent among children from lower than from upper socioeconomic groups and among black than white children.

The importance of socioeconomic status and ethnic factors in level of achievement may be seen in the study of Lesser, Fifer, and Clark (1965). Middle- and lower-class samples of first-grade children in four different ethnic groups (Chinese, Jewish, Puerto Rican, and blacks) were studied with a specially constructed scale to yield ratings on verbal ability, reasoning, numerical ability, and conceptualization of space. For the entire sample, the middle-class children were significantly superior to the lower-class children on all scales and subtests. The pattern of abilities, the distribution of assets, and deficits, however, differed among ethnic groups. In verbal ability, for example, Jewish children rated first, followed by blacks, Chinese, and Puerto Ricans. On numerical ability, however, the Chinese children rated first. Social-class differences were most striking in black children where there was a greater difference in scores between middle- and lower-class blacks than between social classes of other ethnic groups. Lesser et al. concluded that while the *pattern* of abilities tested may vary with ethnicity, the *level* of scores is affected by social-class status (Stodolsky & Lesser, 1967).

While the data in the previous sections of this chapter consider the effects of socioeconomic status and ethnicity on overall academic achievement, Silver and Hagin studied differences among children from three different socioeconomic groups on neuropsychological skills related to beginning reading, writing, and arithmetic. These neuropsychological measures were drawn from early studies devising a screening instrument to identify kindergartners who the test predicts will fail in learning (A. A. Silver & Hagin, 1981). The predictive instrument called SEARCH was standardized on 2,319 children from 31 schools with a wide range of socioeconomic and ethnic backgrounds. Ten neuropsychological functions are sampled by SEARCH including visual discrimination, visual recall, visuomotor, right-left discrimination, temporal sequencing, auditory word discrimination, articulation, intermodal dictation, and pencil grip (as a measure of finger gnosis). In 1989, this battery was administered to 1,654 kindergarten children; 384 from private, independent day schools (high socioeconomic, 95% white, high IQ), 311 from inner-city schools (low socioeconomic, multiethnic, average to low IQ), and 959 from schools from the suburbs of New York City (predominantly middle- to high-middle socioeconomic groups, predominantly white, average to high IQ).

Table 12.2 charts the scores attained by the lowest quartile of each socioeconomic group in each of the neuropsychological processes studied; that is 25% of each group falls at or below the scores entered in the table; thus the lower the score, the poorer the group performance. What these data tells us are that while inner-city (poor, multiethnic) children are equal to their white middle- and upper-economic class peers in their development of visual discrimination and recall, visuomotor, and body image skills, they lag significantly behind these peers in the development of language skills involving auditory discrimination, temporal sequencing, articulation, and sound and symbol association (dictation). These are significant differences that predict difficulties in academic achievement, which will be apparent by second or third grade. It is also clear that these differences in language skills of the inner-city child will affect his verbal scores on commonly used intelligence tests. The Wechsler Intelligence Scale

Table 12.2   Three socioeconomic groups scores on SEARCH, lowest quartile

	IDS	Suburban	Inner City
N	384	959	311
Visual matching	5	3	4
Visual recall	2	2	2
Visual motor	3	2	3
Right-left discrimination	5	3	5
Finger gnosis	7	7	7
Auditory discrimination	16	15	10
Temporal sequencing	8	6	3
Dictation	6	1	0
Articulation	17	17	12

for Children Revised, for example, was found to yield a significantly lower Full Scale IQ and significantly lower verbal IQ in "disadvantaged black" third graders than in their white classmates. There was no difference, however, between these groups on the Kaufman Assessment Battery for Children (K-ABC) (Skuy, Taylor, O'Carroll, Fridjhon, & Rosenthal, 2000). The question arises as to whether the SEARCH data is similarly culturally biased. Whether SEARCH data reflects a cultural bias or a defect in language development in the poor minority children, however, the fact is that these children develop learning disabilities particularly in reading and spelling. The question might better be asked what combinations of nature and nurture are involved in the production of the verbal skills needed for academic achievement in the present culture of our schools? These are important questions, the answers to which may well influence social policy and educational intervention and prevention.

CONDITIONS OF SOCIOECONOMIC DISADVANTAGE IN RELATION TO LEARNING

It is not sufficient, however, to implicate social-cultural and economic disadvantage as a potent determinant of later educational failure. What is it in the setting of such disadvantage that predisposes to failure? Does the statistical association represent a causal connection, or are there possible alternative explanations, such as heredity or the effect of the child on the family and on the school, and not the family and the school on the child? What are the *conditions* of the external social and cultural world in which the child lives? What are the *adaptive consequences* that adults in the environment acquire in their interaction with the system? In what specific forms do these *adult orientations* appear in interactions with children? What are the *behavioral outcomes* of these experiences in children? What is there in the setting of socioeconomic disadvantage that predisposes to failure?

In reviewing the culture of the economically disadvantaged, Hess stated, as early as 1970, that being "powerless is one of the central problems of the poor" (p. 465). It limits the poor's ability to influence their own lives and to make changes within their community, and it encourages dependency on society and on chance. Their poverty offers few resources with which to face disaster and restricts the range of alternatives to action. Their relationships tend to be structured in terms of power. Their own low status and inability to command their own lives evokes a low self-esteem and a sense of inadequacy and passivity.

In general, "disadvantaged" poverty-ridden homes have more than their share of family discord and disruption: single-parent or many-fathered homes; child neglect; possible abuse; many different caretakers; exposure to crime, alcohol, and drugs; low levels of parental educational achievement; lack of role models relating to education with consequent poor motivation for academic success; possible poor nutrition; general patterns of disorganization within the home; depression and discouragement in the mother; physical illness; and large family size with overcrowding and lack of adequate and appropriate stimulation at critical ages, to name a few. L. B. Murphy and Moriarty (1976) emphasized that in poor households there is a general lack of appropriate stimulation and feedback. The houses are characterized by bare walls, with no patterned visual stimuli; mobiles, if present, are not within the range of vision. There is no variety in the environment, no suitable toys within reach. There is nothing to explore or discover. Most important, however, there is no response to individual differences, few individual tolerances to stimulation, and inappropriate auditory feedback. There is little response to need cues from the infant.

The grim reality of the environment of minority group poverty is described by Kondracke (1989): "Besides abysmal education, illegitimacy, welfare-dependency, unemployment, bad housing, insufficient health care and crime, the black underclass is being raked by drugs, AIDS and an upsurge in child abuse connected to drug addiction" (p. 20).

The difficulty in isolating these various socioeconomic factors as predictive of learning disorders is further complicated by the finding that prenatal and perinatal complications are more frequent in populations that are both poor and black. Pasamanick and his associates (Pasamanick, Rogers, & Lilienfeld, 1956) found that the proportion of infants with some problem associated with pregnancy and labor increased from 5% in the white upper social class to 15% in the lowest white socioeconomic group to 51% among blacks. Parenthetically, the studies of Pasamanick, implicating the effect of poverty and minority group status on learning, earned him recognition by the American Psychiatric Association in 1986 as an outstanding contribution to the prevention of emotional disorders in children.

While perinatal difficulties, particularly low birth weight (<1000 grams), have greater effect than socioeconomic status on severe learning disorders, sociodemographic factors (poverty, male gender, low maternal education, minority group) have an overall greater total impact on adverse educational outcomes than perinatal factors, between 5 and 10 times greater than the perinatal factors of low birth weight, congenital anomaly, or prenatal care (Resnick et al., 1999).

While studies have tended to implicate one or more of the general characteristics of poverty, a comprehensive longitudinal investigation of environmental risk (and protective) factors was conducted by Sameroff and his associates in what was called the Rochester Longitudinal Study. The premise of this study was that "socioeconomic status (SES) operates at many levels of the ecology of children. It impacts on parenting, parental attitudes and beliefs, family interactions and many institutions in the community" (Sameroff, 1998, p. 1288). Ten environmental variables, correlates of SES but not equivalents, were tested to determine whether poor cognitive and social-emotional development of preschool children were a function of the environmental risk factors identified. These factors were:

1. History of maternal mental illness.
2. High maternal anxiety.
3. Parental perspectives that reflected rigidity in the attitudes, beliefs, and values that mothers had in regard to their child's development.
4. Few positive interactions with the child observed during infancy.
5. Head of household in unskilled occupations.

6. Minimal maternal education.
7. Disadvantaged minority status.
8. Single parenthood.
9. Stressful life events.
10. Large family size.

Two phases of the Rochester Longitudinal Study are described. In the early childhood phase, children and their families were assessed at the child's birth and at 4, 12, 30, and 48 months; a second phase carried the assessments of children and families to when the children were 13 and 18 years old. From the 10 environmental risk factors, a multiple risk score was devised (the total number of the risk factors for each individual family). At the 4-year-old assessment, while each of the variables was a risk factor influencing cognitive and social competence development, it was the *total number* of risk factors for any child that significantly increased the magnitude of the effects on cognitive and social factors, increasing the effect three times relative to the effect of single variables. Similarly on an intelligence test, children with no environmental risk scored > 30 points higher than children with eight or nine risk factors. On average, each risk factor reduced the IQ score by 4 points (p. 1289). Assessments of the same children and their families at ages 13 years and 18 years, found:

- Few families had major changes in the number of risk factors. Mothers without a high school diploma or equivalent dropped from 33% to 22%. However, the number of children raised by mother alone increased from 21% to 41%.
- Mental health at 4 years correlated significantly with mental health at 13 years.
- Intelligence at 4 years correlated even more significantly with intelligence at 13 years.

Whatever the child's individual capabilities, the environment continues to limit or expand opportunities for development for that child. The stability of the environmental risk scores between the child's age of 4 to 13 years was $r = .77$; between 4 and 13 years IQ scores, $r = .72$. Sameroff concludes that "single environmental or child risk factors alone may have statistically significant effects on cognitive and emotional development but these differences are small in comparison with the effects of the accumulation of multiple negative influences that characterize high risk groups" (1998, p. 1291). No single risk factor could be identified as a cause of low levels of social-emotional and cognitive competency but acting together, the risk factors are significant predictors of cognitive, emotional, and social competency. The pattern of risk was less important than the total amount of risk. Further there is little change in the environmental picture presented by families as the child grows from birth to late adolescence; thus there is continuity in exposure to environmental risk.

   M. Gittelman and Joyce (1999) also found that the total income of all family members, adjusted for family size, differed very little during the decade of the 1980s from that of the 1970s. Individuals in families headed by a young person, or a person without a college education were less likely to experience upward mobility. McLoyd (1998) reports that persistent poverty has more detrimental effects on IQ, school achievement, and socioemotional functioning than transitory poverty. He links the effects of socioeconomic disadvantage and the child's socioemotional functioning to be mediated partly by "harsh inconsistent parenting and elevated exposure to acute and chronic stressors." Longitudinal data from centers other than the Rochester Longitudinal Study are in general, similar to those obtained by Sameroff (1998) and his colleagues. Duncan, Brooks-Gunn, and Klebanov (1994), with data from their Infant Health and Development program, found that family income and poverty status are powerful correlates of the cognitive development and behavior of children. Black, Dubowitz, and Starr (1999) examining the role of fathers in low-income African American families found that fathers who were satisfied with parenting and were employed had children with fewer behavior problems. Luster and McAdoo (1994), with data from 378 African American children between the ages of 6 and 9 years (the National Longitudinal Survey of Youth), found a positive relation between the number of risk factors to which children were exposed, and the probability they were experiencing academic or behavioral problems. Brooks-Gunn and Duncan (1997) found that the timing of poverty to be important for school completion; children who experienced poverty during preschool and early school years have lower rates of school completion than those who experience poverty only in later years. Brooks-Gunn and Duncan found as did Sameroff that children who live in extreme poverty for *multiple* years, appear, all other things being equal, to suffer the worst outcome.

The attempts to derive some quantitative measure of evaluating the continuum of socioeconomic stressors on the developing child, antedated the studies of the past 10 years. A generation of parental questionnaires, structured and semistructured interviews, and most important, direct observations of the home have been developed to tap such information. A brief review of the development of scales for assessment of the environment is contained in Caldwell, Bradley, and Staff (1984). As early as 1954, Barker and Wright described a narrative account of objects and actions occurring in the child's life during a given time frame. The accounts are subsequently coded into a scheme of categories depending on the requirements of the investigation. The Barker-Wright method was used in the Harvard Preschool Project to analyze the role played by the person interacting with the child (Human Interaction Scale) and the child's involvement with objects in the environment (Object Interaction Scale). In the Harvard studies for well-developing children in contrast to the poorly developing ones, the sheer quantity of interaction between child and parent was greater, more time was spent with the children in intellectually valuable activities, and participation in the activity was more common with more overt encouragement.

In their review of research on relationships between the environment and development, Caldwell et al. (1984) theorized that the environmental characteristics likely to influence early development include the following: frequency and stability of adult contact, amount of developmental and vocal stimulation, need gratification, emotional climate, avoidance of restriction on motor and exploratory behavior, available play materials, and home characteristics indicative of parental concern with achievement. With these characteristics as a guide, the Home Inventory for Measurement of the Environment (HOME) was developed (R. H. Bradley, 1982). There are three such inventories: one for families of infants and toddlers (to age 3), the second for preschoolers (ages 3 to 6), and the third for families of elementary-age children. Each requires a home visit. The infant and toddler scale, in use the longest, contains 45 items, each of which is scored as present or absent, yes or no. The 45 items are grouped into six subscales: emotional and verbal responsivity of parent, acceptance of child, organization of physical and temporal environment, provision of appropriate play materials, parent involvement with child, and opportunities for variety in daily stimulation.

HOME scores obtained at 6, 12, and 24 months of age are said to be better predictors of the Binet IQ at 54 months than the Bayley Infant Development Scores and a better predictor of IQ than standard social indices (R. H. Bradley & Caldwell, 1981). In a black sample, HOME scores accounted for approximately three times as much variance in IQ than did socioeconomic status alone. This predictive validity was higher for low-income and minority populations than for higher income groups (R. H. Bradley & Caldwell, 1981). However, a discriminate function composed of HOME scores at 6 months is reported to predict retardation (IQ below 70) at 3 years, with 71% correctly identified, and to predict average to above-average IQ (above 90) at 3 years with 70% accuracy. Twelve-month HOME scores also were more efficient predictors of school achievement than were indices of socioeconomic status.

The HOME inventory for preschoolers (ages 3 to 6) consists of 55 items clustering into eight subscales: learning stimulation, language stimulation, physical environment, warmth and affection, academic stimulation, modeling, variety in experience, and acceptance. While the number of investigations completed on the preschool version of HOME is less than that for the infant version, HOME preschool scores appear to be significantly related to measures of cognitive development during early childhood and the primary grades. The total HOME score attained between 3 and 5 years of age had correlations ranging from .51 to .58 with SRA Achievement Test Scores in reading, language arts, mathematics and in composite achievement score obtained between 6 and 10 years of age. The HOME subscale score that showed the strongest correlation with academic achievement was toys, games, and experience ($R = .41$ to .49).

The HOME observation requires a home visit of at least 1 hour. For more rapid study, Coons, Fandal, Kerr, and Frankenberg (1981), using HOME as a basis, developed a multiple-choice, fill-in-the blanks, yes/no questionnaire that may be completed in about 20 minutes. Called the Home Screening Questionnaire (HSQ), it is a parent-answered questionnaire designed to sample social, emotional, and cognitive aspects of the home that relate to the child's growth or development. Correlations between total score on the HSQ and HOME inventory is .81 (Coons et al., 1981). A concurrent measure of HSQ validity was obtained through the ability of HSQ to correctly identify sibling school status: special class placement, one or more grades repeated, low achievement test scores, failures in core subjects, and repeated concerns expressed by teachers. The HSQ was 75% accurate in identifying the problems and 44% accurate in identifying no problem, with 28% false positives and 13% false negatives.

Attempts have also been made to assess the risk factors of socioeconomic disadvantage together with those arising from prenatal distress, prematurity, and low birth weight. Tableman and Katzenmeyer (1985) described the Borgess Interaction Assessment (BIA) derived from the Michigan programs in prevention of emotional disorders.

The BIA is based on previous infant scanners such as the Neonatal Perception Inventory (Broussard, 1979), which compares the mother's perception of her baby at 1 day after birth and at 1 month after birth in items such as crying, spitting, feeding, elimination, sleeping, and predictability. A negative perception was related to abuse, neglect, injury related to lack of care, and failure to thrive. The Borgess Interaction Assessment (named for the hospital in which it was developed) has three sections: the first, a situational section with 16 items, contains information on the condition of the infant at birth (Apgar rating and irritability) and on the mother's experiences that may impair bonding (i.e., single parent, age of mother, family employment, history of mental illness, drugs, retardation, and family support systems). The second section of 7 items is concerned with the mother's response to the infant immediately after delivery; the third section of 12 items looks at the mother's interaction with the infant during the hospital stay. Tableman and Katzenmeyer reported on 1,062 successive live births. The BIA identified 19.5% of the infant-mother dyads as at risk for later emotional problems; of these, more than one-half were related to situational factors. At the end of 1 year, the BIA achieved a correlation of .86 with the HOME inventory. The Michigan study did not study their subjects beyond one year, thus its predictive validity for learning disorders is still uncertain. L. S. Siegel (1982, 1983) also developed a risk index based on demographic, reproductive, and perinatal factors to predict test scores on selected scales (the Bayley, Uzgeris-Hunt, and Reynell scales of language development) at age 5.

However, when the HOME scale was used to evaluate 118 middle- and low-income mothers and their low birth weight or very low birth rate infants, income alone was found to account for 41% of the variance in the sample (Lotas, Penticuff, Medoff-Cooper, Brooten, & Brown, 1992).

Returning now to our original question about the relationship of socioeconomic and cultural factors to Wyn's learning disorder: The evidence suggests that we cannot dissociate his learning disorder from his environment. We find no evidence for a structural defect of the central nervous system. There is evidence for the specific spatial disorientation and temporal disorganization that underlie the neuropsychological processing dysfunction of the specific learning disability. Wyn grew up in an atmosphere in which academic achievement was unimportant; where his role model skirted the fringes of and frequently encroached on the law; where life was hazardous; and where drugs were seen as one way out of poverty and helplessness. He was sporadic in school attendance at best. As the fourth of seven children, in a poverty household with the mother working, it is questionable how appropriate and adequate were the affection and cognitive stimulation he received during his early years. Using the strict definition of learning disability of PL 94-142, Wyn is not classified as learning disabled; yet if any child needed help in learning, it is Wyn. Although his learning disorder was recognized early, his behavioral problems led him into classes for the emotionally handicapped and consistent remedial education was not offered. The school could not overcome the lifestyle into which Wyn was born.

The studies previously reported cumulatively implicate elements of socioeconomic status as factors that determine the cognitive, academic, emotional, social, and even the vocational achievement and adjustment of children. These studies however stress the factors in the social economic and cultural environment that act on the child. Outcomes are a combination of the individual and his experience, the child himself affects his environment, just as the environment affects the child in a continuous series of dynamic interactions, a transactional model as described by Fiese and Sameroff (1989) and by the "goodness of fit" between the child and his family as described by A. Thomas and Chess (1980). A home interview conducted by Feagan, Merriwether, and Haldane (1991) evaluated the mother's rating of how her child fit into the family's expectations. There were 63 families with a child with learning disabilities, 53 with a "comparable" child without learning disabilities. For both groups of families, children who had a "poor fit" in the home demonstrated less positive behavior in the classroom and poorer achievement over the elementary school years. As this book has repeatedly emphasized to understand a child with a learning disability, a pentaxial evaluation, including biological, emotional, cognitive, social, and educational parameters is needed.

In a book that has evoked intensive interest as well as intensive criticism (*The Bell Curve*, 1994), Richard J. Herrnstein, a professor of psychology, and Charles Murray, a political scientist at Harvard, examined evidence from analysis of data compiled in the National Longitudinal Study of Youth (NLSY), an ongoing federal project that tested over 10,000 Americans in 1980 with follow-up interviews regularly thereafter. Each participant completed the Armed Forces Qualifying Test (AFQT), which was used as a measure of intelligence and was then evaluated for subsequent social outcomes (high school graduation, level of income, likelihood of being in jail or divorced). As a rule, intelligence predicted these outcomes more strongly than did the parental socioeconomic status. "This relationship held for all ethnic groups; indeed when intelligence was statistically controlled, many outcome differences among ethnic groups vanished" (Chabris, 1998, p. 34). Herrnstein and Murray concluded that American society was becoming increasingly meritocratic; wealth and other positive outcomes were being distributed more and more according to people's intelligence and less and less according to their social backgrounds. Further, intelligence was not easily subject to environmental control and even is, in part, inherited. Genetic differences, then, contribute significantly to an individual's future.

Putting aside the controversy about what is measured by an intelligence test and the nature and even the existence of a common factor (*g* factor) in intelligence, Chabris states that the conflict is about a side-issue of the book: the difference in intelligence among groups, particularly between whites and blacks and the degree to which these differences might be explained genetically. The political implications evoked from this concept is that African Americans are genetically predisposed to intellectual ability which is inferior to that of whites and that genes for intelligence are "so correlated with class that the lower-class children have virtually no hope of bettering their lot" (J. R. Flynn, 1998). In commenting on *The Bell Curve,* a panel of the American Psychological Association (1996) refute certain of its central assertions: (a) that differences in intelligence explain economic inequality (psychometric intelligence is only one of a great many factors that influence social outcome); (b) that differences in intelligence explain racial inequality (differences in IQ scores among racial groups, whatever their origin, are within the range of effect sizes that can be produced by environmental factors);

(c) that intelligence because it is genetic is largely immutable (school itself can change mental abilities including abilities measured on psychometric tests).

Thus while there is argument about the conclusions that Herrnstein and Murray derive from the data of *The Bell Curve,* there is little argument about the data themselves. The application of their conclusions as they relate to learning disorders, however do require refutation: (a) that the score on standard IQ score is not culture free and in children of the inner city, standard IQ tests do not give a true evaluation of the child's potential. We have pointed out the lower Standard English verbal skills of the inner-city child may arise from causes other than low verbal ability; (b) that the use of African American English in the early years critical for language learning inhibits the skills in Standard English use. It is true that inner-city children, particularly African American children do score lower on standardized intelligence tests than do children from high- and average-income families and there are more African American children than white children in the lower income families. Thus formal testing of poverty children speaking African American dialect will create the impression that these children are not intelligent, and that it is all a problem of heredity as Herrnstein and Murray suggest. As Rutter pointed out (1983), "In no case is the heredibility of psychological attributes so high that there is no room for environmental effects" (p. 295).

The Language of Social Disadvantage

The significantly low scores in tests of language abilities found in inner-city kindergartners and the persistently lower verbal than performance scores throughout the educational experience of inner-city children, particularly African American children, need explanation.

As early as 1960, Bernstein described differences in "language facility" between two extreme social groups. He described these differences in what he called an "elaborated" and a "restricted" code or style of language. Bernstein stated that the "differences in language facility result from entirely different modes of speech found within the middle class and the lower working class . . . the organization of the two social strata is such that different emphasis is placed on language potential which orient the speakers to distinct and different types of relationships to objects and persons, irrespective of intelligence" (p. 27). Middle-class, or elaborated speech, facilitates verbal elaboration of subjective intent, has complexities of syntax at command, is aware of semantic nuances, and has a large vocabulary and experiential store on which to draw. The "working class," however, has a limited, restricted form of language that discourages elaboration of subjective content and orients the user to descriptive rather than abstract concepts. Bernstein's formulations stemmed in part from his early work in which he compared 61 "working class" boys, ages 15 to 18, with 45 "public school" boys on Raven's Progressive Matrices and on the Mill-Hill Vocabulary Scale and found a significant difference on each of these measures between the two groups.

The 1960s and early 1970s saw intensive studies of the language of lower socioeconomic status groups. Major contributions came from the Institute for Developmental Studies, headed by M. Deutsch (see M. Deutsch, 1973). A core sample of 292 children and an extended sample of 2,500 children were available. A cross-sectional study of first and fifth graders found that by first grade the groups with lower socioeconomic status were associated with poorer scores on intelligence tests (tests of verbal identification) that require abstract reasoning, on CLOZE tests, on several rhyming and fluency tests, and on verbal explanations than the groups with middle socioeconomic status. By the fifth grade, additional tests involving association and manipulation of language, syntactical control, and logical sequencing further revealed poverty of language. If race was added to low socioeconomic status, additional problems (word knowledge and sentence fluency) were also apparent. M. Deutsch (1973) summarized as follows:

> As complexity of language increases from labeling to categorizing, the negative effects of social disadvantage are enhanced . . . the cumulative deficiency is failure in development of an elaborated language system that has accurate grammatical order and logical modifiers, which is mediated through a grammatically complex sentence structure which has frequent use of prepositions and impersonal pronouns and a discriminative selection of adjectives and adverbs. This gives direction to thinking. The restricted code of the lower [socioeconomic status] is grammatically simple, often unfinished sentences; poor syntactical form; simple and repetitive use of conjunctions; inability to hold a formal topic through speech sequences; a rigid and limited use of adjectives and adverbs. (p. 84)

Labov (1969) in an extensive longitudinal study of language development in elementary-school children, found differences in the complexity of language used by lower-class and middle socioeconomic groups.

These cumulative studies have led to the conclusion that when ghetto children have a verbal deficit, this deficit does not allow for the expression of complex or logical thinking, and it is a major cause of poor performance at school.

It is noted, however, that these studies were done in the 1960s and 1970s. Since that time, there has been recognition that the nonstandard language of the poor, particularly nonstandard African American English (AAE) reflects the survival of phonological, grammatical, and semantic forms from the African languages spoken by slave ancestors. The language forms spoken by today's African Americans were documented as rule-governing systems that conformed to language universals (Kamhi, Pollock, & Harris, 1996). However, recognizing the legitimacy of AAE, the black children, particularly the poor black children, are still at a disadvantage in the school, which teaches, speaks, reads, and writes Standard English. Despite this growing concern and a long-standing recognition of the need for culturally fair language tests, there continues to be a critical shortage of valued and reliable language assessment instruments for individuals communicating with AAE. For example, using the Peabody Picture Vocabulary Test-Revised (Dunn & Dunn, 1981) which was standardized nationally and included poor African American children within the normative sample, Washington and Craig (1992) found that when given to 105 apparently typically developing low-income African American preschoolers and kindergartners, 91% scored below the mean of the normative sample. They concluded that PPVT-R was unsuitable for this population. Several other norm-referenced tests were also judged to be biased and unsuitable for use with poor African American children (S. Adler & Birdsong, 1983). These tests include:

- Illinois Test of Psycholinguistics-Revised (ITPA; Kirk, McCarthy, & Kirk, 1968).
- Northwestern Syntax Screening Test (NSST; Lee, 1971).
- Utah Test of Language Development (UTLD; Mecham, Jex, & Jones, 1967).
- Wepman Auditory Discrimination Test (WADT; Wepman, 1973).
- Goldman-Fristoe-Woodcock Test of Auditory Discrimination (G-FW TAD; 1970).

There have been efforts to extend the norms of other tests for language assessment to include African American children. For example, on the Test of Language Development (TOLD; Newcomer & Hammill, 1977), F. D. Wiener, Lewnau, and Erway (1983) found that all 198 African American children ages 4 years to 8.5 years scored below the mean of the original normative sample. Kercher and Bauman-Waengles (1992) found that 77% to 100% of the test items penalized children who use AAE. The lack of performance spread in these studies, made TOLD inappropriate for renorming or scoring adjustment. Norms were established for Black English Sentence Scoring (BESS; N. W. Nelson & Hyter, 1990) to supplement the Developmental Sentence Analysis (DDS; Lee, 1971). This, too, proved invalid, because scoring AAE responses of children was largely based on adult data and because DDS was normed on Standard English usage. These investigations illustrate the difficulty in modifying for existing expressive and receptive language tests for AAE. Washington (1996) points out that on an expressive and receptive language test, a single grammatical feature that is affected by AAE may be found in many test items. The more items the AAE speaker fails, the more items in which scoring is modified and the "more dubious the test's original content validity becomes" (p. 44).

Rather than norm-referenced assessment, criterion-referenced assessment is suggested. The criterion-referenced model compares the child's performance with an operationaized performance criterion (Watkins & Rice, 1991). Criteria are based on development data that, although available for SAE, is not available for AAE. Language performance may, however, be matched to that of parents or caregiver or to that of a child of the same age who is least competent in the use of AAS (Stockman, 1996a, 1996b). Craig and Washington (1994) identified complex syntax as an important clue to language development in AAE children. Because in AAE, complex syntax in use of a clause is largely unaffected, it should be possible to identify AAE speakers who use such clauses in an atypical manner. Until developmental norms for AAE children are determined, however, testing of these children is limited.

A test designed to differentiate between typical phonological and atypical phonological production among AAE-speaking children was devised by Wilcox and Anderson (1998; Wilcox African American English Screening Test of Articulation, WAAESTA). A list of sounds and the syllable positions in which they occurred in a set of 50 stimulus words, was selected to include sound and sound clusters that are part of

AAE phonology. The sound combinations had been reported as differentiating between children with normal and disordered phonologies (Bleile & Wallach, 1992) and are used by children between the ages of 5.0 and 6.6 years of age (Hielot & Howard, 1997). In addition, the sounds have been described as particularly problematic for both SAE- and AAE-speaking children. In 26 AAE-speaking children 5.0 to 6.6 years of age, this test found significant group differences between children with typical and atypical phonological development, with accuracy of 84.6 %. A list of the test words and the observed error patterns are described in the Wilcox and Anderson paper (1998).

A quantitative index of linguistic growth was described by Craig, Washington, and Thompson-Porter (1998) using average length of communication units (C-units) in words and in morphemes in their sample of 95 African American boys and girls (ages 4 to 6½ years) from low-income homes. The syntactic complexity of language correlated with increases in C-unit length, increasing across the ages in the sample. Kindergartners produced significantly longer C-units than preschoolers. Washington, Craig, and Kushman (1998) also evaluated low-income African American children (ages 4.5 to 6.5 years) in context of C-units in language samples evoked by free play and picture description. Picture descriptions were useful in determining dialect usage. The problem of testing AAE children, however, has not yet been solved.

Emotional Resistances to Standard American English

Among the risk factors inherent in the sociocultural environment of the African American population is a wariness and mistrust of the white community, its political structure, and its institutions. This mistrust includes the public school system, which is the carrier of white aspirations, behavior, and customs. The use of African American dialect, the deficit in attaining early language skills needed for reading, the rebellious behavior, has caused black children to be disparaged by their teachers in ability and desire to learn.

African American/white conflict must still be seen historically emanating from emancipation in the mid-1860s to the civil rights, equal opportunity, affirmative action struggles almost 100 years later. The perceived and often real attitudes of the established white world, in relation to the black population have evoked in blacks, poor self-esteem, anger, hostility, mistrust, and an attempt to identify with their own culture (F. Terrell & Terrell, 1996).

In schoolchildren, hostility may be acted out in many ways as they refuse to identify with white behavior and values and reject the standards of the school. Even learning becomes a symbol of identification with the school, so that these children may feel they are traitors to their own culture if they succeed in learning and may resent their own peers who do conform (Oreos). The retention of African American English and disruption behavior in the classroom may be an outcome of this mistrust, underlined by repeated academic failure, the feeling of powerlessness and lack of self-esteem. Other children express their hostility and fear in withdrawal, an "invisibility" syndrome that keeps them mute in the classroom—nonresponsive, nonparticipating—so that they are considered retarded and may even be placed in classrooms for the retarded, failing to get the stimulation of the regular classroom (Franklin & Boyd-Franklin, 2000). While these children are monosyllabic at school, they are verbally expressive at home, with all criteria for use of complex language. These complexities include comparisons, similarities and differences, recall of events, linking events in time, describing purpose of objects, giving reasons, explanations of purposes, or results of actions, and concerned with hypothetic events (Tizard, Hughes, Carmichael, & Pinkerton, 1983).

Anyone who has worked with immigrant Puerto Rican children in New York City can testify to this behavior. As pointed out earlier, it is only 40 years ago that the language of poorer socioeconomic groups was considered inferior to that of the more affluent. The self-fulfilling prophesy of these behaviors is stressed by Tuakli-Williams and Carrillo (1995), "Particularly for children of color one's productivity and prosperity as an adult depends to a significant degree on one's education as a child; education is both the development of skills and the attainment of character." The National Academy of Science reports (*Lost Generations: Adolescents in High Risk Settings,* 1993) that the single common pathway to high-risk adolescent behavior is early academic failure. Indeed it should be no surprise that gifted black adolescents hold significantly higher goal attitudes and perception than regular education students and accept, more readily, academically successful peers (D. Y. Ford & Harris, 1996).

To measure the level of mistrust among African Americans and to evaluate the impact of mistrust in clinical and educational settings, F. Terrell and Terrell (1996) developed a 19-item questionnaire, a Children's Cultural Mistrust Inventory (in Appendix B of F. Terrell & Terrell, 1996). In a study with samples of African American adolescents, one group with high mistrust scores, the other with low mistrust scores, half of the number in each group having intelligence tests administered by a white examiner, the other half by an African American examiner, found that students with a high level of mistrust who were tested by the white examiner, had lower intelligence test scores than any other group. In elementary-school children, similar results were found. The authors concluded that mistrust of whites can have an adverse effect on intelligence test performance. Mistrust of whites has been found to affect the refusal of African American students to go for counseling if the clinician they are assigned to is white.

L. R. Campbell states:

Barriers to provision of quality educational services to children from African-American (and from other minority groups) include ethnocentric attitudes of professionals, low expectation and negative attitude toward African-American students, their families and communities, lack of professional training regarding cultural and linguistic diversity, test bias and misdiagnosis, monocultural education materials and inappropriate curricula with inadequate instructional techniques; different disciplinary and reward systems. (1996, p. 74)

Admirable as these requirements are for education of poor black children, they are not enough. The problem is more extensive than the education system, but must grapple with problems of poverty and health—problems of great magnitude, importance, and difficulty that demand commitment and effort, not only from education, but from social, welfare, economic, health, and mental health institutions.

It would be a gross mistake however to dismiss *all* children who speak and cling to AAE as having language *different* from what is taught and used in schools. Some do have a *deficit* in their language abilities. As many poor black children have developmental language disorders as do white children. Unfortunately, the federal definitions of developmental learning disability specifically exclude children of low socioeconomic families. So by definition, poor black children may be placed into classes for emotionally handicapped or educable mentally retarded and, as pointed out, be deprived of the special education instruction they sorely need.

EDUCATIONAL PROGRAMS FOR THE DISADVANTAGED

Overall, solutions to the educational problems of children of poverty and of social-cultural disadvantage have yet to be found (Chapter 10). A 5-year collaborative study of children with special educational needs (Robert Wood Johnson Foundation, 1988) found that more than one-third of the children served in special education programs are poor and that more than one-third of their mothers have not completed high school. Special education programs may include classes for the emotionally handicapped and classes for various degrees of severity of mental retardation as well as special programs for remediation of developmental language disabilities.

In their study of five large metropolitan school districts (Milwaukee public schools; Houston independent school district; Charlotte-Mecklenburg, North Carolina, schools; Santa Clara County, California, schools; and the Rochester, New York, school district), Palfrey et al. (1986) found that in schools that serve poorer children, the diagnosis of "emotionally handicapped" is made more often than that of "learning disability." This placement may reflect the exclusionary criteria for SLD, but as pointed out, placement in classes for the emotionally handicapped may deprive children of the remedial education that may make the critical difference in keeping them in school and in achieving subsequent academic, social, and vocational adjustment. Further, more than half the poor black children in the Robert Wood Johnson study did not complete high school.

Four general approaches have been made to attempt to fill the educational needs of children and families living in poverty:

1. Modification of the first 3 years of life in Head Start and in other early education programs and in the continuation of these services in preschool education programs for 3- to 5-year-olds.
2. The identification, no later than in their kindergarten years, of children for whom academic failure is predicted and the provision of appropriate and sufficient remediation (see Chapter 10).
3. Modification of the curriculum of the early elementary grades to provide education in the language the child brings to the school (bilingual education) (Chapter 8).
4. Modification of the cultural gap between home and school in the early elementary years and as needed in the junior high and senior high years.

The Head Start and Early Education Programs

Broad social and educational planning that attempts to modify the environment of the first 3 years of life, to alter the effects of poverty and inappropriate stimulation on the child, have been made in the Head Start program (Cicirelli, 1970; Datta, 1969; M. S. Smith & Bissell, 1970) and in the early education programs such as those of Bereiter (1972), Bereiter and Engelmann (1966), the Perry High Scope Preschool Project (Weikart, 1967, 1972), the Early Training Project (Klaus & Gray, 1968), and the Comparative Urbana Illinois Study (Karnes, Hodkins, & Testa, 1969). These programs were developed in the belief that the sensory inputs to the child were inappropriate and/or inadequate to develop specific functional areas of the brain at critical times when the biological development was optimal for the acquisition of function. As we have seen from the SEARCH data, the function most vulnerable to inappropriate and/or inadequate stimulation is language. The conditions of poverty, the patterns of speech and language surrounding the child, the poor education of the child's mother, the burdens of single parenthood, the frequent change in caretakers, the exposure of the infant to chaotic sounds from television or CDs, leaves the infant with inappropriate stimulation to enhance the development of the biological substrate for language. It was the intention of Head Start to prevent a poverty of language and enhance the child's biological potential.

A critical review of these early programs appeared in Meier (1987), and a 10-year outcome study was reported by Gray et al. (1982). The Gray et al. study, following 86 children who were in the Early Training Project in the 1960s, suggested that the intervention program did have a measurable lasting effect; more enduring, however, on school requirement indices than on standardized tests. Insofar as school performance was concerned, however, the favorable effect reached statistical significance only in females.

The High/Scope Perry Preschool program, a high-quality research study that began in 1962 has followed its children through age 27. What is important that when compared with a randomly assigned nonparticipating group of children, 123 High/Scope children, now adults, have significantly improved social responsibility, educational performance, earning and economic status, commitment to marriage, and a financial return to society on the investment made in early childhood. Weikart concludes, "Early childhood, ages 3 to 5 is a highly effective time to provide support and opportunity to improve an adult behavior and life chances" (1998, p. 237).

The experimental early intervention efforts of the 1960s are an excellent example of programs with enhancement objectives. These programs with their target population of poor, disadvantaged preschool children, their clearly defined interventions, and their long-term follow-up research culminated in the collaborative report of the Consortium for Longitudinal Studies (1983).

A more recent review of three early intervention programs—the Abecederian program, Project Care, and the Infant Health and Development Program—was reported in 1994, as the proceedings of the International Conference on Child Day Care (Ramey & Landesman-Ramey, 1998). The 1998 review attempted to determine whether mental retardation thought to be caused by inadequate (and/or) inappropriate environment can be prevented by providing intensive high-quality preschool programs, along with medical and nutritional support, beginning shortly after birth and continuing at least until the children enter kindergarten. While the report concludes, in general, that early educational intervention can substantially improve intellectual performance and academic achievement, it raises two important questions: Who is at the greatest risk for being cognitively delayed or mentally retarded among extremely economically disadvantaged families? Who shows the greatest benefits of participating in a high-quality intensive early environment?

Extensive data, even before the child's birth, were collected and included family income, parental education, maternal IQ score, marital status, number of children in the family, mental health status of the mother and data relevant to the family's child-rearing practices. This information was predictive of the children's developmental progress, especially intellectual development (Ramey, Yeates, & MacPhee, 1984). The single, strongest predictor, however was the mother's level of intelligence. Children whose mothers had IQs below 70 were studied at age 3 in two groups. For the first group, the children received medical, nutritional, and social services, but did not receive daily early intervention services from birth to 3 years. The second group received a full-day, early education program 5 days a week, 50 weeks per year. Of Group 1, all but one of the children whose mothers had an IQ of 70 or below, also had IQs in the retarded or borderline range (70 or 71 to 85). In contrast, the education intervention group whose mothers also had IQs of 70 or below, all had IQs in the normal range by the time they were 3 years of age. It was concluded that the families in most need of intervention and who also appear to benefit most in outcome, are those with mild and moderate retardation whose families have low resources and also have limited intellectual resources.

A successor to Abecederian, called Project Care, was designed to determine the effect of teaching mothers to carry out, in the home, the same curriculum that trained personnel in the center-based program used (the same center-based intervention used in the Abecederian project). A three-group randomized protocol assigned one group to the full center-based program 5 days a week, supplemented by home visits; the second received home-based treatment; the third (or control group) received free health and social services. The intellectual benefits derived by Group 1 (center-based plus home visits) were almost identical to those of the Abecederian project. The intellectual gain for the home-based group however did not improve. F. Campbell and Ramey (1994), suggests that one reason for lack of improvement in intellectual performance is that the home-based treatment was not significantly intensive, on a day-to-day basis, to produce the same benefits of a formally organized and monitored center-based program that was provided throughout the year.

The third study (Infant Health and Development Program, IHD), like the Abecederian project and Project Care, included a center-based enhancement program and home visits throughout the first 3 years. It differed however in that it was for premature infants, at less than 37 weeks gestation and birth weight less than 2,500 grams. These are children at risk for poor cognitive development. The subjects for this study, in contrast to the Abecederian and Care programs, were drawn from a wider range of socioeconomic groups, although most families have "very low income and educational resources." Families were randomized into a control group (medical care and social services) and an educational intervention group.

At age 3 years, babies with birth weight 2,001 to 2,500 grams in the education group had IQs that were 13.2 points higher than controls; babies with birth weight less than 2,000 grams in the education group had IQs that were 6.6 points higher than controls.

With further analysis of the data of these studies, researchers found that the more the level of participation of subjects in the programs, in terms of number of scheduled home visits completed, number of parent meetings attended, and daily attendance of the child at the center, the better the cognitive outcome. In the control group 17% of the children scored in the mentally retarded range (IQ, 70); in the intervention group, 13% of low-level participants earned IQ scores < 70; 4% of median-level participants and 2% of the high-level participants scored in the < 70 group.

Families in the Abecederian group were followed until the children were 12 years of age, when intelligence tests (Wechsler Intelligence Test for Children) and academic achievement tests (Woodcock-Johnson) were given to the children. Forty-four percent of the control children had IQ scores below 86, compared with 13% for children who had been in intervention. Fifty-five percent of the control group failed one or more grades during the elementary grades; 28% of the intervention group.

Similar, although not identical outcomes, were found in an analysis of 38 studies that estimated the effects of early childhood education programs on cognitive development in school success of children. Fifteen studies were of research-sponsored model programs as described in the preceding pages of this chapter; 23 investigated the effects of large-scale public programs provided by Head Start in the public schools. These were primarily half-day preschool programs, with Head Start providing also medical and dental care and parent education and counseling. In contrast to the studies described previously, IQ test scores tend to fade out after entry into elementary school, suggesting that as expected, intensive programs may produce more persistent effects on IQ than the public school programs beginning at age 3 or 4. However, the average effects on cumulative rates of grade repetition and high school graduation are not significantly different for both types of programs. There are significant cumulative rates of special education placement.

Over the past 40 years, early education programs to modify the environment of the first 3 years, to offer enhancement in functions that lag in development, and to train mothers in providing sensory and emotional stimuli the infant and child needs have consistently demonstrated encouraging developmental outcomes in children of low-income and undereducated families. In contrast to comparable control youngsters, a high proportion of program graduates avoid special education placement or repetition of grades in school and earn fewer scores within the retarded ranges on intelligence tests; they reflect positive attitudes toward education, have a greater likelihood of graduating from high school, and demonstrate more productive behaviors in the classroom. Older program graduates reflect the indirect effects of greater educational and social competency in improved vocational expectations and status. However, these programs seem less effective in producing and maintaining specific educational skills in reading and to a lesser extent in mathematics in about 20% of program participants. This percentage is interesting in that it corresponds to the usual incidence estimate of specific learning disability. One is tempted to speculate whether this subgroup may be composed of learning-disabled youngsters who require more specific interventions for their special learning problems than enhancement programs provide.

How to identify children who will benefit from programs, how early to begin programs, and how long to continue them are still unanswered questions (Ramey, 1994). Public law (PL) 99-457 creates a federal program (the Handicapped Infant and Toddlers Program) that provides financial assistance to states for services for 0 to 2-year-olds. This law suggests that public will and political will exist to maintain the early education programs. PL 99-457 also extends educational services to 3 to 5-year-olds, the age at which they emerge from Head Start and before they enter kindergarten. What is needed is the recognition that poverty itself is a handicapping condition and that our educational, social, mental health, and physical health systems must combine resources and skills in a unified effort at interrupting the cycle of poverty school failures and recurrent poverty.

Programs for Early Identification
Intervention of Learning Disabilities

In addition to the work of Head Start and the Pre-K experience, programs for the prevention of learning disorders are needed. Preventive programs involve three major components: (a) reliable and valid identification of children, no later than age 5 or 6 years, in kindergarten or in first grade, for whom learning failure is predicted, (b) evaluation of these children, and (c) introduction of a successful intervention for these children so that failure does not occur. The identification system must be a practical one, so that it can be implemented on a large scale, can scan large numbers of children quickly, and can be administered and interpreted reliably by school personnel with minimal training. It must meet the statistical constraints set by the American Psychological Association with a minimum of false positives and false negatives, be based on a documented theoretical foundation, and be integrated with the intervention part of the program. Identification alone is not enough. Intervention is essential. The intervention program, just as the identification component, should have a firm theoretical base and be tested in school-based projects with sufficient longitudinal observation to prove its effectiveness. Well-researched identification and interventions programs are available. These have been discussed in Chapter 10 of this book.

What has impeded the implementation of these programs is not their degree of success in preventing learning failure, but the difficulty in committing resources of money and staff, a willingness to accept the training a new program requires, and the patience to work out the kinks that must inevitably develop. The ultimate cost for the education of the learning-disabled child and for the emotionally/behaviorally impaired child is immense compared with the cost of a preventive program. The average annual cost for education of a learning-disabled child is approximately $12,000 to $16,000, in contrast to the $6,000 per public cost in regular education. Approximately 2 to 5 million children in the public schools of the United States receive special services because of learning disabilities. Assuming savings of $4,000 per child for each of the 2.5 million children who are receiving these special education services, the annual savings would be close to $10 billion! Further, the dollar cost of the emotional, behavioral, social, and vocational burdens of learning disorders cannot be estimated.

Preventive programs are particularly important for children of poverty who have not had the opportunities of the middle-class child. It is self-defeating to wait until the poor, minority-group child has failed, has developed emotional reactions to academic failure, is already a behavior problem by the time he is in third grade, and by sixth or seventh grade is already effectively dropping out of school.

Programs Modifying the Social Environment of the School

In addition to programs that focus on the basic skills needed for reading, writing, and arithmetic, there are programs that build on the development of supportive bonds that draw together children, parents, and school. The concept behind such programs is stated by Comer (1988): "The contrast between a child's experiences at home and those at school affect the child's psychological development, and this in turn shapes academic achievement . . . the failure to bridge the cultural gap between home and school may lie at the root of poor academic performance" (p. 43). The attitudes, values, and behavior of the family and its social network affect the development of social, emotional, moral, and cognitive values in the child, values critical to academic learning. As discussed earlier, the child of a poor black family may already resent the mainstream white (and even mainstream black) attitudes the school represents; his or her parents, resentful and/or defensive, also avoid contact with the school staff. Thus a basic problem is the correction of the sociocultural misalignment between home and school, the mutual distrust between home and school.

A school intervention project growing from these concepts was initiated as early as 1968 by the Yale Child Study Center and the New Haven school system. Two model schools were chosen—one with 300 children from kindergarten through fourth grade, the other with more than 350 children from kindergarten through fifth grade. In both schools, 99% of the children were black and more than 70% were from families receiving Aid for Families with Dependent Children. In an attempt to involve parents, a governance-management team was initiated. The function of the team, in addition to offering parent involvement, was to provide cohesiveness and direction in school policy and teaching. The team, led by the school principal, was made up of elected parents and teachers, a mental-health specialist, and a member of the nonprofessional support staff. It involved parents in shaping policy and encouraged them to participate in school activities by supporting programs and attending school events. In addition to the management group, a mental health team of psychologist, social worker, and special education teacher worked together in reviewing and managing troublesome behavior among the children, to tease out what the school might do to decrease the incidence of such behavior, and in recommending policy changes to the governance team. Behavior problems were viewed as resulting mainly from unmet needs, not necessarily from "willful badness," and steps were undertaken to meet those needs. Special projects (such as a discovery room for children who have lost interest in learning), social activities, and parent involvement as teachers' aides round out the program.

Within 10 years of the initiation of the project, the two elementary schools, once ranked the lowest in academic achievement among the 33 elementary schools in New Haven, now had children in the fourth grade who had caught up their grade level; and by 1984, fifteen years after initiation of the project, pupils in the fourth grade in the two schools ranked third and fourth highest among the 33 elementary schools in the Iowa Test of Basic Skills. Attendance was high, first or second in the city, and there were no serious behavior problems. By 1980, twelve years after initiation of the project, the program was fully integrated within the schools and the Yale group was able to leave the schools to develop their program in other sites. The program has been replicated in Prince George's County, Maryland; Benton Harbor, Michigan; Norfolk, Virginia; Lee County, Arkansas; and Leavenworth, Kansas.

Programs of Special Services for Specific Groups within the Span of Elementary and High School Years

While the Yale school intervention project dealt with early elementary age, poor, and predominantly black children, a school-based mental health program, administered by the Children's Hospital National Medical Center's Department of Psychiatry, is aimed primarily at refugee children and families from Central America. The program is under contract with Multi-Cultural Services Division of the Washington, DC, Commission on Mental Health. There are approximately 85,000 Central Americans, most from El Salvador, now living in Washington, DC. Their problems are at least threefold: academically delayed, traumatized by war, and adjusting to a strange country. In many cases, families are separated. The program attempts to combine the mental health system with the school system, offering a wide range of services that include direct patient care; prevention; mental health consultation to the schools; and working with children, families, and teachers in school, in home visits, and at the Children's Hospital. The services of the program staff are directed at children and their families who are referred by the school staff in need of help. Thus in contrast to the Yale program, which deals with systems in an entire school, the Children's Hospital project is directed at individual cases. Since 1987, 160 children from participating schools have been referred. The psychiatrist directing this program, Edgardo J. Menvielle, believes that a key to working with the Central American refugee group is having an understanding of the families and of their culture.

In contrast to the provision for the services for the immigrant refugee sample in Washington DC, a program, broad in concept, to address the problems of all children in the school district who, because of emotional and/or behavior problems, could not be contained in the mainstream was introduced in the state of Florida. While these children were not primarily diagnosed as learning disabled, a sampling of the classes for severely emotionally disturbed children revealed that at least 70% of them were functioning at an academic level 2 or more years below their grade placement and while they were not primarily directed at serving the poor and minority group children, at least one-third of children in the classes for emotionally handicapped came from the lowest socioeconomic groups. The special classes are full-time programs, most housed in a wing or in portables, physically a part of schools for "normal children." They comprise the severely emotionally disturbed (SED) classes. Comprehensive neurological, psychiatric, psychological, educational, and social evaluations of samples of these classes revealed them to consist of a heterogeneous group of children, differing in diagnosis and in function, demanding the cooperative efforts of many disciplines for comprehensive management, particularly the educational and the mental health systems (A. A. Silver, 1984).

Accordingly, a joint program, the cooperative product of the State Department of Education and the state mental health system (Health and Rehabilitation Service) was initiated to strengthen the multiagency network to integrate the school systems, social service-welfare systems, and the mental health providers in services to severely emotionally disturbed children and to extend the facilities of the multiagency to those counties in which networks have not been developed. Initially, the state provided $150,000 for each of 3 years to each social service administrative district to develop the mental health and school network. The state legislature, however, has continued funding beyond the 3 years, and it appears that such funding will continue.

Administratively, most social service districts encompass a vast geographic area, rural and urban, possibly involving a number of counties each. The school administration of one of the counties accepted responsibility for acting as fiscal agent; a steering committee composed of a representative from each school district and a psychiatrist from a mental health center (in this case a medical school) composed the governing body. The mental health component was to provide a comprehensive evaluation for each child and his family in the program, to mobilize the team needed to develop and implement a comprehensive treatment plan for each child, to prescribe medication as needed and follow the effects of the medication, to offer psychotherapy to selected children, to meet with individual parents and with parent groups, to help teachers in the management of crisis situations, and to be available to them for in-service training. To accomplish these tasks, a psychiatrist was to devote one-half day each week throughout the school year, directly in the classroom; family workers were to devote full time to the SED centers; psychologists and social workers, employees of the school system, were to be assigned part time to each center. A school coordinator was responsible for each center, and overall, the SED funding was to enable a school coordinator to be responsible for the entire SED program within each district. Essentially, the SED network brought together the skills of mental health with those of special education to work as a coordinated team in school-based projects. The success of this integration may be judged by its continued funding by the state legislature.

While these special programs are being developed, the school system itself has developed alternative programs to capture the children who are dropouts or potential dropouts, to try to interrupt the vicious cycle of poverty-dropout-poverty, with all that this implies. In one county in Florida (Hillsborough County) with 125,000 children in public schools, the state funded approximately $5 million in 1987 to 1988 to develop such alternative programs. The county school district has six such programs for adolescents:

1. Intensive learning programs for potential dropouts in 16 junior high schools to offer individualized academic support and counseling to improve self-concept and attitude toward schools.

2. Intensive learning programs for potential dropouts in senior high schools parallel to the junior high school intensive learning programs.

3. Programs for pregnant teenagers, designed to keep students in a school program and to work with them toward the most feasible way to complete their education.

4. Intensive English in secondary schools for students whose English proficiency is limited.

5. Non-school-based programs. There are seven sites for adolescents who are runaways, dependent, delinquent, or adjudicated. The objective is to provide education for children in those centers.

6. Alternative school programs for adolescents who cannot function in the regular school. Those classes are similar to the SED classes for younger children.

There is nationwide recognition of the academic, emotional, social, and behavioral problems of the poor, particularly of the child from a minority ethnic group. Programs to address these problems range from the preschool age in enrichment programs of Head Start and preschool early education social interventions to programs designed to redirect the focus of early elementary schools into a cooperative society that bridges the cultural gap between home and school. Programs to prevent the development of learning disorders, while permitting the ego to become a strong point around which to rally are available and need only the will and the effort to be discriminated throughout the school system. Past the point of kindergarten and first grade, where children have already failed, the integrated efforts of mental health, social, and school systems are being mobilized in a network of special services to bring the child back into the mainstream and to function to the limits of his or her potential.

Yet despite these advances and innovations, there is much to be accomplished. Not only is there no decline, nationwide, in the dropout rate, of children from poverty families, but there is a decline in the number of African American high school graduates going to college; and of the African Americans who do enter college, only 42% graduate. The economic reality in this day and age is that a high school diploma is not a ticket out of poverty. More intensive thought and effort is needed to move the poor child, into a "kinder and gentler" America.

INTEGRATION OF SOCIAL, EDUCATIONAL, AND HEALTH SYSTEMS

The problems of poverty in the United States are problems of great magnitude, difficulty, and concern, requiring more than the education system to solve, demanding commitment and effort, not only from education, but from social, welfare, economic, health, and mental health systems and institutions. An important initiative to integrate all of these systems into a coordinated team was launched in 1992 by the Child, Adolescent and Family Branch of the Center for Mental Health Services within the Substance Abuse and Mental Health Services Administration, U.S. Department of Health and Human Services. The program is called the Comprehensive Community Mental Health Services for Children and Their Families. This goal of this initiative is to "promote the provision of mental health services within the context of a system of care that involves mental health and other supports into a coordinated fabric of services to meet the diverse, highly individual and changing health, educational and supportive needs of children with severe emotional disturbance" (National Institute of Mental Health, Report to Congress, 1998); to build and sustain family-centered systems of care. It does so by provision of grants to states, communities, territories, Native American Tribes, and tribal organizations to improve and expand local systems of care to meet the individualized needs of the estimated 4.5 to 6.3 million children and adolescents with serious emotional disturbances and their families. Grants, such as that given to the Childrens' Board in Tampa, Florida, are for $7 million for 5 years; after 5 years the agency receiving the grant, is expected to be able to continue the network it has put in place with its own funding and those of the agencies in the service network. Starting with four grants awarded in the first cycle in 1993—East Baltimore Mental Health Partnership, Stark County (Ohio) Family Council and Southern Consortium, the Village Project (South Carolina), and Access (Vermont)—with an initial appropriation of $2 million, the Comprehensive program has now funded 68 sites nationally with an appropriation of $92 million for the 2000 to 2001 fiscal year. In addition, for the first 3 years of its grant, each grantee must match one-quarter of the amount of its grant in services, until in its fifth year, the local match goes up to 50%.

The systems of care envisioned by the program have three basic concepts; (a) The needs and *preferences* of the child and his family are involved in the choice of services offered; (b) services are community based, their management built on multiagency collaboration; and (c) the services offered, the agencies participating, and the programs generated are both responsive and sensitive to the cultural context and other characteristics of the population being served. Agencies and system must work together, with families participating in their own service decisions, with minority interest and desires respected. In Hillsborough County, Florida, systems involved in the community of services include the Children's Board (which receives county tax dollars for social services), the School Board, the Department of Juvenile Justice, the Department of Children and Families, the Human Services Board, and the Agency for Health Care administration. Within the framework of the federal grant, these agencies have come together collectively to provide comprehensive services, as a unified team, centralized in its organization to build and sustain family-centered services, integrated across delivery and funding. The goals and objectives of this program: (The Tampa Hillsborough Integrated Network for Kids, THINK) as outlined by THINK (1998) are:

THINK Goals and Objectives

Goal 1.   To implement an organized, community-based system of care that provides services, which are integrated across delivery and funding systems for children and adolescents with serious emotional disturbances and their family.

Objective 1.1. Close service gaps; increase service capacity, particularly for case management; offer wraparound and nontraditional services; and increase services to undeserved populations and geographical areas.

Objective 1.2. Ensure the full involvement and partnership of families in planning, implementing, evaluating, and advocating for the system of care and the care of their children.

Objective 1.3. Assure the cultural competency of the system of care by providing opportunities for meaningful participation in the program by representatives of the minority and rural communities.

Objective 1.4. Expand and complement the existing service delivery directly accountable and responsible to health and welfare authorities with effective structures for managing services planning and delivery processes, and fully involving families.

Objective 1.5. Develop a service delivery system that consolidates existing fragmented, categorical funding streams for the target population.

Objective 1.6. Create a single system of care that will be financially sustained through collaborative and integrated funding investments from State and/or community-based child-and family-serving agencies.

Goal 2.   Complete required evaluation of THINK, including both descriptive and longitudinal studies and any other requested evaluation data. Conduct local evaluation studies to inform future direction.

Objective 2.1. Provide data for the national multi-site evaluation.

Objective 2.2. Conduct several site-specific evaluation studies in geographical areas, school-based clusters, or other project-based locations once funding is awarded.

Goal 3.   Conduct a communication and dissemination campaign to gain state and local commitments to sustain the program beyond the five-year federal funding period.

Objective 3.1. Increase awareness in the community about the need for and benefits to be gained from system of care services.

Objective 3.2. Disseminate information about the cost-effectiveness of system of care services to Administrators and elected officials at the state and local level.

THINK Systems of Care Initiatives

Project RELIEF, a collaborative initiative to provide respite services, composed of five provider agencies and the Federation of Families, was formally approved for funding in October 1999. The initiative addresses the major service gap identified by family members of the Federation of Families. Family members continue to serve on all implementation sub-committees to operationalize Project RELIEF.

THINKids, is a demonstration project to pilot a system navigation initiative for 25 children with the most serious needs. This initiative also serves as the Child and Adolescent Interagency System of Care Demonstration Model for the Department of Children and Families, District 6. Contract awarded February 2000.

Hillsborough County Youth Advocate Program. Responding to the needs of teenagers with serious emotional disorders who are involved with multiple systems, and living in overcrowded foster homes, a contract was awarded in February 2000 to provide in-home supports, wraparound and flexible, and nontraditional services for this population.

Family and School Support Teams Project (FASST). Based on extensive demographic data and several meetings with community, family, and school personnel, four sites were selected for the development of a school/community partnership initiative. Communities agreed that an enhanced model of the FASST teams would improve the system of care for children through a school/community partnership.

The Comprehensive Community Health Services for Children and Their Families Program has reviewed outcome statistics, collected in August 1999, from 22 sites initially funded in FY 1993 or FY 1994, involving 34,377 children and their families (Report to Congress, 1998). The number of children with severe emotional-behavior problems, as indicated by a Total Problem Score above 90% on the CBCL, decreased from 76.9% to 60.2% in one year; the number of children considered to be clinically improved went from 13.4% to 27.3%; the number of children with average or above average grades increased by 11% over the levels observed at intake; law enforcement contacts were reduced; residential stability improved. Demographically, 62% of children in the programs were boys, 38% girls; average age was in early adolescence, the racial-ethnic population was mixed with 54% Caucasian, 17% African Americans, 24% Hispanic, 2% Native Hawaiian, 2% Native American, 1% Asian or Pacific Islander, 1% other; 54% of the children lived in single-parent homes, 25% in two-parent homes, 7% lived with a guardian, 1% were wards of the state, 4% other. Sixty-one percent of the families reported income below $15,000.

The results appear promising. The integration of services, so obvious in the thinking, may yet prove to be a reality.

CASE STUDY: JOEY

Joey, whom we have been able to follow from age 3 through age 18, illustrates a positive outcome with a family that experienced the complex problems associated with urban poverty. It points up the need for coordinating services and agencies: medical and psychological treatment, appropriate educational services, and long-term support from interested professionals.

Joey was referred by Bellevue Hospital Social Service Department at age 3 because he was speaking very little. His mother (who was seen for treatment by the social workers) had great difficulty managing him. He entered the playroom with some reluctance, but soon headed for the toy shelves. He examined the toys quickly, losing interest in each one he picked up after a very short time. Single words and a few short, unelaborated sentences were used in a mixture of English and Spanish. There was a minimal cooperation in any play or aspects of the psychiatric examination. Joey was no more enthusiastic about psychological examination, although over several sessions the Stanford-Binet Intelligence Scale, Form L-M was completed. He earned a mental age of 2 years, 10 months and an IQ of 72. He earned a social quotient of 80 on the Vineland Social Maturity Scale. These scores were regarded to be a minimal estimate of his abilities.

Joey is the only child of Sara and Angel. His birth history as obtained from hospital records revealed normal parturition and neonatal course. Little is known about Angel, although he is reported to have been a waiter, Sara said he was abusive to her and that he left her soon after Joey was born. There is, on the other hand, much information about Sara. Her parents were separated when she was 8 years old; her father, now dead, was said to have been an alcoholic. At the time Joey came to our Unit, Sara and Joey were living with Sara's mother in a small apartment. Sara has two siblings; Milagros, who is deaf and mute, and Manuel, a mentally retarded resident at one of the large state institutions. Sara is reported to have had meningitis at age 6. At age 11, Sara had a grand mal seizure. She is being followed at the Neurology Clinic and is receiving various seizure medications that control the grand mal seizures. Psychological study done when she was 11 years old placed her functioning within the moderately retarded range (WISC full scale IQ, 50; verbal IQ, 48; performance IQ, 61). Because of aggressiveness, self-abusive behavior, and what were called "anti-social tendencies," Sara's mother requested that she be placed at Willowbrook State School for retarded children. Although Sara remained at Willowbrook for more than 10 years, little is known about her treatment there because Sara refuses to talk about it. The discharge from Willowbrook describes her as "cheerful and affectionate, but craving attention, sulky, and quarrelsome." She appeared at the walk-in clinic at Bellevue at age 23 and has remained in contact with various Bellevue services since that time.

Despite his mother's traumatic history, the Unit staff felt that Joey had a normal intellectual potential and that his delayed language development might be due to inappropriate stimulation and ineffective management. Strengths were seen in the good physical care he had received and Sara's active search for help for her son. It was decided to admit him to the Unit's nursery so that his development could be observed over an extended period of time in a program that provided intensive social, language, and perceptual stimulation. It was also decided that Sara would work with the Unit's social worker to make some consistent plans for the household and to learn more effective parenting with Joey.

Joey adjusted well to the nursery group. The teacher noted that he related well and freely to the adults. He liked group activities and entered dramatic play with the other children, although he did not talk much. He was sometimes aggressive, hitting out hard over a toy or a coveted role. However, he would accept adult intervention and compromise solutions and rarely held a grudge. His language was more limited than that of other children in the group. He could name familiar objects and had some simple concepts (big-little, night-day), but did not use any adjectives without help. He had difficulty in drawing forms: He was able to draw a circle but had trouble getting his hands to make circular motions. He seemed to be left-handed, but switched occasionally to his right. Joey continued in the nursery, although attendance was uneven because Sara overslept.

There were signs that Sara was beginning to trust us, but building an ongoing relationship with her was not easy. Minor crises occurred. Joey was denied admission to kindergarten. Sara had failed to register him during the kindergarten roundup because she was unable to read the announcements. The Unit staff members found an alternative kindergarten and taught Sara how to get there with Joey by public transport until an additional kindergarten class was organized in Joey's neighborhood school. The housing problem was a recurrent one; Sara's mother neutralized gains Sara was making in managing Joey and dealing with issues of independence. As a result, the Unit staff wrote to the Department of Welfare on Sara's behalf, documenting the need for separate apartment. Through some minor miracle, the request was granted. The next task for the social worker was to prepare Sara for the responsibility of housekeeping on her own. As it turned out, Sara took on these responsibilities easily and, apart from minor setbacks, continues to the present time to discharge these responsibilities very well.

Joey made progress, although it was not rapid. Reevaluation at the beginning of first grade showed marked improvement in both expressive and receptive language. On the WPPSI he earned a full scale IQ of 87, with a verbal IQ of 77 and a performance IQ of 100. Slight immaturity was seen on the neurological examination, but no real dysfunction was noted. When his class was scanned with *Search*, he earned a score of 5, which falls in the vulnerable range. His teaching plan provided perceptual stimulation activities in the Auditory Sequencing, Auditory Discrimination, Visual Recall, Visual-Motor, and Body Image areas. All tasks were completed by the middle of his second-grade year and a code-based approach to reading (SRA Basic Reading Series) was begun in the classroom. By the end of second grade, he was reading at the beginning second-grade level. Joey was well integrated in the school setting and there were few complaints about behavior. Even his attendance improved. By the end of third grade, his reading was approximately at grade level and he earned an oral reading score of 4.0 on the WRAT.

Sara continued her contact with the Unit, although she no longer saw the social worker on a regular basis. Rather, she would initiate contact with the Unit when she had a specific problem or concern. These concerns ranged widely. Her mother threatened to take Joey away from her. (Unit staff assured her that we would offer evidence of her good care if any court action was brought.) She did not have enough money for presents at Christmas time. (She was put in touch with some of the hospital charities.) She had sent Joey to camp but could not find the address. (A call to the agency helped locate him.) There was a PTA fashion show for children at school and she wanted Joey to participate. (A word to the organization committee helped open this opportunity.) As time went on, there were less frequent crises or, at least, Sara was better able to handle life's trials on her own. When Joey graduated from sixth grade, he did not earn any special academic honor, but the Units staff was pleased to see him listed with nine others who had also achieved perfect attendance that year.

Sara's contact with the Unit staff became less frequent when Joey entered junior high school. At one point, Sara decided he must have a problem because he was so quiet. A telephone call to his guidance counselor indicated that all was well—in fact, he was one of the students the counselor called in when she needed a group of the boys to help with some project. The last follow-up occurred in the spring of Joey's senior year in a chance meeting on the street. Sara said that he was graduating and that he was "filling out the papers to go to college downtown." Her information was vague, but it turned out that she was referring to a 2-year community college that prepared people for civil service jobs in the city.

SUMMARY

The preponderance of evidence points to the determining influence of poverty and inappropriate and/or inadequate stimulation on the development of learning disorders, with poor minority children having the lowest scores on academic achievement tests. As these children move into higher grades, they fall farther and farther behind their peers in academic achievement, a "cumulative deficit." The conditions of disadvantage that appear to predispose to failure are, in general, the lack of appropriate stimulation and feedback. The environmental characteristics likely to influence early development are referred to as a "continuum of caretaker casualty" and include frequency and stability of adult contact, amount of developmental and verbal stimulation, gratification of needs, emotional climate, avoidance of restriction on motor and exploratory behavior, available play materials, and home characteristics of parental concern with achievement. Inventories to measure these characteristics have been developed, with inventories for toddlers, preschoolers, and elementary-age children. Some studies suggest that the verbal deficit seen in some ghetto children does not allow for expression of complex or logical thinking. On the other hand, there is evidence that the English of poverty or social disadvantage is not an inferior language but a different dialect, capable of mediating the complexities of thinking and reasoning.

Broad social and educational programs have attempted to modify the environment of the first 3 years of life. Contrary to early reports of Head Start's ineffectiveness, the Consortium of Longitudinal Studies, reviewing long-term pooled data of Head Start programs, "clearly demonstrated positive effects of these programs throughout childhood and adolescent years." Long-term studies of preschool programs other than Head Start also yielded favorable outcomes.

At the elementary school level, programs to bridge the cultural gap between the demands of the school and the experiences of the home, special programs for refugee children, and comprehensive programs to develop a multiagency network for emotionally disturbed children have functioned with reported success. At the junior and senior high school levels, alternative programs are mobilized to keep potential dropouts in school. Although there is a national recognition of the academic, emotional, social, and behavioral problems of poor children, the academic problems of that group are still with us. The integrated efforts of mental health, social, and school systems are needed if these problems are to be solved. The development of integrated programs and services is made into a reality through a federal program for Comprehensive Community Mental Health Services for Children and Their Families.

Chapter 13 ─────────────────────────────────

ATTENTION-DEFICIT/ HYPERACTIVITY DISORDERS

Everyone knows what attention is. It is the taking possession by the mind, in clear and vivid form, of one out of what seems simultaneous objects or trains of thought.

—William James, 1890

Although the term "hyperkinetic reaction" was codified in 1968 in *DSM-II,* the term "attention deficit with hyperactivity" emerged in 1980 with *DSM-III* in which the essential features were described as "developmentally inappropriate attention and impulsivity." In the past, a variety of names had been attached to this disorder: Hyperkinetic Reaction of Childhood, Hyperkinetic Syndrome, Hyperactive Child Syndrome, Minimal Brain Damage, Minimal Brain Dysfunction, Minimal Cerebral Dysfunction. In the historical development of the concept of developmental learning disorders, these same terms have been applied to children with learning problems (see Chapter 4, Table 4.1), suggesting that as early as the 1920s the coexistence of the two syndromes of hyperactivity and learning disability was recognized. Although the relative independence of the core symptoms of inattention, impulsivity, and hyperactivity were recognized, *DSM-III-R* (1987) retained the inclusive diagnosis of ADHD with the criteria for that diagnosis being met by the presence of at least 8 of a list of 14 symptoms.

It was soon recognized, however, that while observational studies found a clear differentiation between normal and hyperactive children in the hyperactivity dimension, activity level was not significantly related to measures of attention (Hinshaw, 1992; Luk, 1985). Further, on a battery of teacher ratings, peer ratings, and self-report measures, there were markedly different patterns of behavioral characteristics between inattentive children (ADD) and ADHD (hyperactive) children (Lahey, Schaughency, Strauss, & Frame, 1984):

> Children with ADD with hyperactivity exhibited aggressive conduct disorders and bizarre behavior, were guiltless and very unpopular, and performed poorly in school. In

contrast, ADD children without hyperactivity were found to be anxious, shy, socially withdrawn, moderately unpopular and poor in sports and school performance. Both groups exhibited depression and poor self concepts . . . these different patterns suggest the ADD/H and ADD/WO are dissimilar syndromes and perhaps should not be considered to be sub-types of the same disorder. (p. 302)

In preparation for *DSM-IV* field trials (Lahey et al., 1994), were able to establish a consensus for the two core dimensions of behavior previously subsumed under the label of ADHD: an inattentive dimension and a hyperactive-impulsive dimension. The criteria for the presence of these dimensions are codified in *DSM-IV-TR* (2000). Thus, an inattentive (ADD) type, a predominately hyperactive type (ADD/HD) and a combined type (ADHD) are now recognized (Practice Parameters, 1997). The diagnosis, however, is still made by a checklist of symptoms: 6 or more of 9 symptoms for inattention; 6 of 9 symptoms for hyperactivity and inattention. Symptoms must have "persisted for at least 6 months to a degree that is maladaptive and inconsistent with developmental level" and there must be clear evidence of clinically significant impact in social, academic, or occupational functioning. Also, "the symptoms do not occur exclusively during the course of a pervasive developmental disorder, schizophrenia or other psychotic disorders, anxiety disorders, dissociation disorder or a personality disorder" (*DSM-IV-TR,* pp. 92–93 and Table 13.1).

Table 13.1   Diagnostic criteria for Attention-Deficit/Hyperactivity Disorder

A. Either (1) or (2):
 1) six (or more) of the following symptoms of **inattention** have persisted for at least 6 months to a degree that is maladaptive and inconsistent with developmental level:

 Inattention
  a) often fails to give close attention to details or makes careless mistakes in schoolwork, work, or other activities
  b) often has difficulty sustaining attention in tasks or play activities
  c) often does not seem to listen when spoken to directly
  d) often does not follow through on instructions and fails to finish schoolwork, chores, or duties in the workplace (not due to oppositional behavior or failure to understand instructions)
  e) often has difficulty organizing tasks and activities
  f) often avoids, dislikes, or is reluctant to engage in tasks that require sustained mental effort (such as schoolwork or homework)
  g) often loses things necessary for tasks or activities (e.g., toys, school assignments, pencils, books, or tools)
  h) is often distracted by extraneous stimuli
  i) is often forgetful in daily activities
 2) six (or more) of the following symptoms of **hyperactivity-impulsivity** have persisted for at least 6 months to a degree that is maladaptive and inconsistent with developmental level:

(continued)

Table 13.1   (Continued)

Hyperactivity
a) often fidgets with hands or feet or squirms in seat
b) often leaves seat in classroom or in other situations in which remaining seated is expected
c) often runs about or climbs excessively in situations in which it is inappropriate (in adolescents or adults may be limited to subjective feelings of restlessness)
d) often has difficulty playing or engaging in leisure activities quietly
e) is often "on the go" or often acts as if "driven by a motor"
f) often talks excessively

Impulsivity
g) often blurts out answers before questions have been completed
h) often has difficulty awaiting turn
i) often interrupts or intrudes on others (e.g., butts into conversations or games)

B. Some hyperactive-impulsive or inattentive symptoms that caused impairment were present before age 7 years.

C. Some impairment from the symptoms is present in two or more settings (e.g., at school [or work] and at home).

D. There must be clear evidence of clinically significant impairment in social, academic, or occupational functioning.

E. The symptoms do not occur exclusively during the course of a Pervasive Developmental Disorder, Schizophrenia, or other Psychotic Disorder and are not better accounted for by another mental disorder (e.g., Mood Disorder, Anxiety Disorder, Dissociative Disorder, or a Personality Disorder).

Code based on type
 314.01   Attention-Deficit/Hyperactivity Disorder, Combined Type: if both Criteria A1 and A2 are met for the past 6 months
 314.01   Attention-Deficit/Hyperactivity Disorder, Predominately Inattentive Type: if Criteria is met but Criterion A2 is not met for the past six months
 314.01   Attention-Deficit/Hyperactive Disorder, Predominately Hyperactive-Impulsive Type: if Criterion A2 is met but Criterion A1 is not met for the past 6 months

Coding note: For individuals (especially adolescents and adults) who currently have symptoms that no longer meet full criteria, "In Partial Remission" should be specified.

Note: Reprinted with permission from the *Diagnostic and Statistical Manual of Mental Disorders,* Fourth Edition. Text Revision. Copyright 2000, American Psychiatric Association.

HETEROGENEITY OF THE SYNDROME

It would appear that the diagnosis of ADHD using the checklist of *DSM-IV-TR* should be a simple task. Such is not the case. First, ADHD symptoms may not be observed in a highly structured or novel setting with interesting tasks or one-to-one attention (Practice Parameters, 1997) and may require observations in a variety of settings. Porges and Smith (1980) state, "A description of behavior that constitutes hyperactivity is not meaningful without reference to a situational context." Second, *DSM-IV-TR* criteria describe only a cluster of symptoms. These symptoms may arise from different causes and represent heterogeneous groups with clusters of children who have similar symptoms, but that differ in etiology, natural history, and treatment. Conditions in which symptoms of inattention and of impulsivity have been reported are listed in Table 13.2.

Structural and/or physiological deficit of the central nervous system, arising from a multitude of causes including prenatal, natal, and postnatal trauma; hypoxia, prematurity,

Table 13.2   Conditions associated with symptoms of inattention and/or impulsiveness

1. Structural defects of the CNS (see also Chapter 14).
   - (a) Prenatal, natal, postnatal injury to the CNS, including trauma, prematurity, hypoxia, toxins, infections
   - (b) Metabolic disorders
   - (c) Known genetic disorders
   - (d) Seizure disorders—particularly petit mal and partial complex seizures

2. Developmental disorders with no known etiology
   - (a) ADD/HD
   - (b) Tourette's syndrome
   - (c) Specific learning disorders
   - (d) Developmental language disorders

3. Disorders associated with inappropriate or inadequate stimulation at critical ages
   - (a) Cultural differences
   - (b) Education inappropriate or inadequate
   - (c) Pathology in the formation of object relations
   - (d) Nutritional deprivation

4. Exclusionary factors as listed in *DSM-IV*
   - (a) Pervasive development disorders
   - (b) Autism
   - (c) Schizophrenia
   - (d) Mood disorders (bipolar disorder)
   - (e) Anxiety disorders
   - (f) Dissociation disorders
   - (g) Personality disorders

5. Miscellaneous
   - (a) Temperament
   - (b) Tasks described as "too boring" or "too difficult"

toxins, and infection; known genetic, metabolic, and seizure disorders, all have been described with symptoms of inattention and impulsivity (see Chapter 14). Developmental disorders with no known etiology such as Tourette's syndrome, disorders associated with inappropriate and/or inadequate stimulation at critical ages as well as mental disorders in which inattention and/or impulsivity occurs, may have comorbid impulsivity and hyperactivity. Developmental learning disorders themselves may cause restless and fidgety behavior that teachers may find disturbing. The difficulty of an academic task may not match the child's abilities, development, or cultural background. There may be inadequate motivation or inadequate reinforcement (D. Shaffer et al., 1983). As Mirsky states, "The etiology of disordered attention in children is as varied and complex as the manifestations of attention disorders themselves" (1996, p. 98). Ostrom and Jenson (1988) point out, "ADHD may not be a unitary condition defined by an attention defect but may include a loosely defined set of common childhood problem behaviors . . . noncompliance, academic difficulties, social skills deficits, aggression, overactivity and attentional defects" (p. 264).

Even with these exclusionary and restrictive factors, there is no certainty that the residual group of children represents a homogeneous entity with a known common etiology and natural history. There remains, however, the group of children for whom no etiological factor for their inattention and or impulsivity can be found.

The problem of heterogeneity is reminiscent of the problems in the definition and diagnosis of "learning disabilities." Children with learning disabilities, just as those with ADHD, may have a group of symptoms in common. Learning disabilities, however, may arise from varied causes. It is these final neuropsychological processing deficits to which all etiological factors lead, but the natural history, treatment, and prevention of each may be entirely different (see Chapter 5). We have attempted along with others (Denckla, 1978; Keogh, 1988) to define a more homogeneous group of learning disabilities or a "dyslexic pure" group. Similarly, we attempt to isolate a "pure ADD/HD" group by evaluating each child along a pentaxial scheme that includes psychiatric, neurological, cognitive, educational, and social parameters. The *DSM-IV-TR* criteria do not isolate a pure ADD/HD (to use Denckla's term), and further diagnostic work is needed to identify the many possible factors that may lead to the clusters of symptoms described in *DSM-IV-TR*. It would appear that diagnostic criteria are still fluid and that taxonomy will respond to the findings of new research. McCracken points out the importance of new findings since "diagnostic differences clearly influence prevalence rates and the associated clinical and even cognitive characteristics of the disorders" (1998, p. 484).

CASE STUDY: DAVID

David illustrates the comorbidity of learning disabilities with ADHD, the need for educational intervention for the learning disability, and the emergence of motor tics with stimulant medication. David was 10 years 4 months of age and scheduled to enter fifth grade at a private elementary school in the fall semester. Although going into fifth grade, David will be placed academically with the fourth graders. This is important to David, because at his school, the fifth graders are physically placed in a building across the campus from the fourth graders, thus effectively separating David from his friends of the previous semester.

David is an only child, his mother gravid 3 para 1, with 1 pregnancy resulting in a miscarriage, another in an ectopic. His birth is reported by his mother as being without complications. Gross developmental milestones are also reported as normal except that by age 2 or 3 years, he was considered to have a short attention span and was diagnosed by a psychologist as having ADHD, combined type, and separation anxiety disorder. On an educational and neuropsychological examination done at age 7 years 8 months, David earned a full scale IQ of 108 on the WISC-III (verbal 115, performance 99) with significantly low subscale scores of 7 (16th percentile) in arithmetic, 9th percentile in picture arrangement, 25th percentile in coding. His academic achievement at that time (Woodcock-Johnson Educational Battery, revised) was 36th percentile in reading, 16th percentile in math, and 21st percentile in written language. The psychologist concluded that David did have ADHD, Anxiety Disorder, and disorders of written expression and mathematics. David has received private tutoring for reading with improvement in word recognition, but he has not had specific remediation in writing or in math. Since the age of 5 David has received medication in gradually increasing doses so that now he is receiving methylphenidate, Tenex, clonidine, and Prozac: Each morning he receives methylphenidate 20 mg SR and 15 mg regular, Tenex 2 mg, clonidine 0.025 mg; methylphenidate 20 mg SR and 5 mg regular at 11:30 A.M.; and clonidine 0.075 and Paxil 10 mg h.s. An EEG done when David was 7 years of age is reported as normal. An EKG done at that time is also reported as normal.

On examination, David had received his usual morning medication about three hours previously. He is slender, slightly small for his 10 years, pleasant; he has no overt anxiety in coming into the examining room without his mother. He has, however, a serious expression, an air of intensity, and immediately gets down to business, telling me that he has to find the best medicine to help him stay on task. His speech is slightly rapid, under pressure, articulation clear, but with much elaboration and explanation with elements of fluid association, one thought flowing into the other so that in his very first paragraph he says, "I need medicine to stay on task, kids make fun of me because I'm not ready for fifth grade, I would struggle in fifth grade, one of my friends is staying back, it's hard for me to focus, I daydream, I try to work so hard I get frustrated, I would say, I'm not doing this, it's too hard, I'm not as good as other people and not so smart, I am scared that I won't pass." It is clear that David finds life a struggle, feels that he cannot cope, and is ready to give up. However, there is much fight in this child and no sign that he would injure himself; instead, his depression is hidden in anxiety. He sees little things in the darkness coming at him, some of them with a knife, shadows at night that move, ghosts of which he says he is not scared because if they come, he will say, "I'm going to kill you." Sometimes he gets his stuffed bear from the top of his bunk and the bear makes him feel secure and he can fall asleep. He has introjections of a bad guy and a good guy: The bad guy whispers bad things for him to do; the good guy has a gentle voice. He has never seen these guys, but imagines what they would look like.

David is at the verge of understanding that the voices are a part of himself and the conflicts within himself. He is a sensitive child with sympathy for "poor people" and for "old people with problems." Seeing them makes him feel unhappy. He feels secure with his parents but he does say that he is worried about their going away and of something happening to them.

During this part of the examination, David could sit in his chair without undue gross restlessness. There were occasional bouts of eye blinking, sniffing, and blowing and a constant pulling and adjusting of his clothes, a constant wringing of his hands. When given specific tasks to do, his ticlike movements were decreased, he was able to focus and to maintain attention on what he was supposed to do. He is right-handed with a two-finger pencil grip, directing the pencil away from his body. On extension of the arms, Prechtl movements are marked with a choreic quality. There is no clear-cut elevation of either arm. Fine motor coordination as in finger-to finger testing is impaired in the right hand, but normal in the left. Synkinesis is also marked in the right, less so on the left. There is a terminal tremor on finger-to-nose testing and constructive finger praxis is impaired in the right hand, but normal on the left. He still confuses right-left orientation and exhibits extinction of the hand stimulus on the face-hand test with synesthesia of the head stimulus, that is, the head stimulus is identified as being at the point of the stimulus, but also at a contralateral homologous point of the forehead. This is a primitive response seen in 4-year-olds. There is marked impairment of visual motor function with a Bender-Gestalt drawing that has characteristics of specific language disorder (verticalization, angulation immaturity), which in addition becomes impulsive with erasures suggesting David's own dissatisfaction with what he has done. His oral reading is at beginning fifth grade, but there are still phonic and sequencing problems along with problems with comprehension. Spelling is at best at third grade with no concept of phonology or orthography. Static reversals are still seen.

These findings add up to an anxious child with poor self-esteem who is phobic and in conflict with his compulsivity and in efforts at control. He feels that the world is a struggle that he cannot win. He has a severe learning disorder with specific neuropsychological processing defects (visual motor, laterality, phonics, orthography, and somesthesia). He has problems with attention and distractibility. In addition to the learning disorder, he is beginning to develop tics, possibly resulting from stimulant medication. Management for David included intensive remediation of this learning disorder at his school; adjustment of medication (gradual discontinuing methylphenidate and Prozac, rearranging doses of clonidine and quanfacine, and adding morning dose of mecamylamine).

THE DEFINITION OF ATTENTION AND HYPERACTIVITY

Difficulty in objective measurement of attention and hyperactivity may be a reflection of the difficulty in defining just what is meant by attention, attention deficit, vigilance, and executive function. Barkley (1996, p. 50) has stated, "The staggering range of measures used to assess attention has been limited principally by the creativity of the investigators, the available technology and the particular theoretical models driving research." William James states:

> Everyone knows what attention is. It is the taking possession by the mind, in clear and vivid form, of one out of what seems several simultaneous possible objects or trains of thought. Focalization, concentration of consciousness are its essence. It implies withdrawal from some things in order to deal effectively with others and is a condition which has a real opposite in the confused, dazed, scatterbrain state which in French is called *distraction* and *Zerstrutheit* in German. (1950, pp. 403–404)

In 1890, James had already abstracted the essence of what we mean by attention, characterizing the concept by its functions. So, too, by its functions, did S. Freud identify the concept of the ego (1940). Barkley refers to attention as "the relationship of behavior to its environment" (1996, p. 45). Environmental events may stem from external and/or internal environment. Voeller (1998) states, "Attention is a dynamic process by which the brain modifies its representation of the external world on the basis of what is important to the organism" (p. 489). She sees the overall concept as an array of behavioral processes: the processing of sensory information in the context of previous experience and relevance, selective attentiveness to these stimuli, the ability to filter out distractions, "disengaging, shifting, reengaging" with sustained attention and alertness across time. The functions of attention may also involve a motor component "tightly integrated with the perceptual side, both at a behavioral and a neural (psychophysiological) level involving activation, selection of responses, preparation of response, initiation of response, inhibition, switching, persistence and stopping the response" (Voeller, 1998, p. 449).

Thus an array of cascading neuropsychological functions describe the attentional and executive functions. The multiple functions are subserved by multiple neurophysiological systems, widely distributed, involving multiple sites in the brain. Current imaging and electrophysiological techniques are attempting to identify the brain areas and systems subserving the functions of attention and impulse control. While at this writing, there is progress in identifying the brain systems underlying the visual, auditory, somatosensory, and motor systems involved in attention and in execution function, the coordination of these operations into a network system is required for task performance (Posner, 1988). Attention, then results from the coordinated actions of several elements linked into such a system (Mirsky, 1987). To investigate such a system, Mirsky (based on Zubin's 1975 work on attention deficits in schizophrenia) focused on three elements of attention—focus/execute, sustain, and shift. To these, he has added a fourth function, encode—a capacity to hold information briefly in mind; and possibly a fifth element—the reliability or stability of attention effort (Mirsky, Anthony, & Duncan, 1991). Using the five-process paradigm, Mirsky (1996) hypothesizes brain regions subsuming each:

1. *Focusing/execution.* Superior temporal, inferior parietal, and structures that comprise the corpus striatum.

2. *Sustaining a Focus.* Rostral midbrain, including mesopontine reticular formation and midline and reticular thalamic nuclei.

3. *Stabilizing.* Midline thalamic and brain stem.

4. *Shifting.* Prefrontal cortex, including anterior cingulate gyrus.

5. *Encoding.* Hippocampus and amygdala.

Posner and Petersen (1990) describe three major functions that make up attention: orienting to sensory events, detaching signals for focal (conscious) processing, and maintaining a vigilant or alert state. These functions have two major loci in the human brain: (a) a posterior attention system that lies in the dorsal (magnocellular) visual pathway and has its primary cortical projection area in V1 (striate cortex, Broadman's area 17) extending into the parietal lobe, and (b) an anterior attention system in the anterior cingulate gyrus and supplementary motor cortex responsible for signal detection. A third anatomical area functions to maintain vigilance and is not so clearly defined, comprising the norepinephrine innervation system extending from the locus coeruleus rostally to the posterior attention system. We anticipate that the new techniques of functional imaging will define the areas of the brain involved in the functions of attention and impulsivity.

EXECUTIVE FUNCTION AND THE STIMULUS BARRIER

The definition and objective measurement of impulsivity, like that of attention and vigilance, suffers from lack of consensus in conceptualization. As far back as 1920, Freud conceived problems in the modulation of impulses coming from within the child and of stimuli from without, as a function of the stimulus barrier. Just as the ego is a metapsychological construct, defined by its function, so too is the stimulus barrier a metapsychological construct whose function is to modulate within limits tolerable to the organism, the impulses coming both from within and from the world around him; to prevent him from being overwhelmed by stimuli, and to enable him to achieve a dynamic equilibrium between his own needs and the capacity to satisfy those needs. It thus functions in the modulation of psychological and physiological stimuli.

In the modulation of physiological stimuli, the stimulus barrier regulates the *milieu interieur* (Bernard, 1858), homeostasis (Cannon, 1939), and "the constant satisfactions and dissatisfactions which occur in a polyphasic colloidal solution" (Stunkard, 1932). In modulation of physiological stimuli, there is a balance, with feedback mechanisms allowing physiological variability with limits tolerated by the organism.

Psychologically, S. Freud conceived the stimulus barrier both as a protection against external stimuli and as a modulator of internal drives. As a protection against external stimuli, he said (1920/1955): "The perceptive apparatus of our mind consists of two layers, an external protective barrier against stimuli whose task is to diminish the strength of excitations coming in and of a surface behind it which receives the stimuli." Freud felt that failure of the protective barrier against external stimuli was clinically important in the development of anxiety and the traumatic neurosis. As a modulator of internal drives, S. Freud later (1940) considered the stimulus barrier as a significant function of the ego, a "special organization to act as an intermediary between the id and the external world" (p. 15). Of the stimulus barrier, Frosch (1983) stated that "it incorporated multiple ego functions such as the capacity for reality testing, judgement and delay among others. All of these not only facilitate the mastery of stimuli, but also defensively control the impact on the psychic apparatus" (p. 287). Silverman proposed (cited in Frosch, 1983) that the very development of defenses and the methods of coping with stress is` phase related to the development of the stimulus barrier.

Individual differences in the stimulus barrier may be detected early in a child's development (Brazelton, 1973; Paine, 1965; Prechtl & Beintema, 1964). These observations find individual differences in "state" of the infant—differences in state of consciousness with variations from deep torporous sleep (Gesell, 1945/1969) to alert, bright look with a focus on the source of stimulation. Brazelton (1973) suggested, "The pattern of states as well as the movement from one state to another, appear to be important characteristics of infants in the neonatal period and this kind of evaluation may be the best predictor of an infant's receptivity and ability to respond to stimuli" (p. 5). In the mid-1940s, Fries (1944) filmed a series of neonates demonstrating a "constitutional" activity level characteristic for each child. Wolf (1959), observing neonates for protracted periods in the first few days of their life, found specific but characteristically different reactions appearing in regular or irregular sleep, with the infant demonstrating temporally organized rhythmical motor patterns, an inner physiological clock for serial ordering of adaptive function. Individual variability in temperament was described by A. Thomas and Chess (1980) in nine categories: activity level, rhythmicity of biological function, approach or withdrawal to new stimuli, adaptability to new or altered situations, the sensory threshold of responsiveness to stimuli, the intensity of the reaction, quality of mood, distractibility, and attention span and persistence. These characteristics really describe functions of the stimulus barrier, including the rhythmicity of autonomic and impulse control.

The genetic capability of the stimulus barrier, however, may be modified by several factors: organic insult to the central nervous system, experiential factors that prevent realization of the full potential of the stimulus barrier from being attained, manic-depressive disorder, and elusive syndromes that we call severe developmental disorders, including autism and schizophrenia. Organic insult may vary as to cause, severity, extent, and time of life occurrence. Its effect may depend on all these variables and on the support and understanding the child receives from her environment. Experiential factors—stimulation from the environment appropriate to the needs of the child—are essential for the normal development of the stimulus barrier. Biological maturation and genetic potential by themselves are not sufficient for it to function; appropriate and adequate stimulation impinging on the biological substrate is necessary. Form requires appropriate stimulation to evolve into function. Thus, an infant deprived of maternal interaction at the time she is beginning to separate herself as distinct from her mother at about 5 months to about 18 months of age, does not develop a barrier to her primitive drives or impulses. She does not develop an inner modulating structure. She demands immediate gratification. Her behavior is impulsive, hyperactive, demanding, and clinging. She cannot form meaningful object relations. She does not anticipate danger and does not learn from repeated failure. Such a child is suffering from primary maternal acathexis, an affectionless psychopathic personality (L. A. Bender, 1953); more recently, she is termed a borderline personality (E. R. Shapiro, 1978).

The child with an attention deficit disorder also suffers from a thin or deficient, stimulus barrier. As we have defined ADHD pure, impulsivity in these children must be found in factors other than in structural insult to the central nervous system or in experiential factors. Gorenstein and Newman (1980) found a parallel in the behavior of impulse-driven children and the behavior of "psychopathy, hysteria, antisocial personality and alcoholism," all of which belong to a group of disorders labeled as "disinhibitory psychopathy," which has a parallel in the syndrome produced in animals by lesions of the septal-hippocampal frontal system.

The term *stimulus barrier* is rarely heard here in the beginning of the twenty-first century. The functions of the stimulus barrier have now become executive function, control functions involving modulations of attention and its efferent functions, the control processes involving inhibitions and delay, "anticipatory set, preparedness to act, freedom from previously established response tendencies, the ability to sequence behavioral outputs." These functions "hover close to the motor border" (Denckla, 1996, p. 265) when described as initiate, sustain, inhibit/stop, and shift. Historically, the anatomical substrate of executive function is the frontal lobes and/or frontally interconnected subcortical regions. Disorders of executive function may, as do the symptoms of ADD/HD, result from damaged, diseased, or disordered development.

THE MEASUREMENT OF ATTENTION AND HYPERACTIVITY

Definitions of attention and of impulsivity are thus characterized by their function, and their function is described in terms of the brain areas and systems presumably serving them. At this writing, however, they are accessed by probes of neuropsychological processes utilizing neuroimaging and electrophysiology and, clinically, by scales tapping behavior. These scales are, in practice, rating scales, questionnaires completed by parents, clinicians, teachers, peers, even the child himself. Essentially statements on the scales are based upon clinical impressions or subjective observation (Halperin, 1991). Early studies (Langhorne, Loney, Paternite, & Bechtoldt, 1976; Sandberg, Rutter, & Taylor, 1978) have demonstrated that rating scales of the hyperactivity dimension, obtained from different sources such as parents and teachers, correlated poorly with one another. Correlation of the hyperactivity factors between parents and teacher versions of the Connors scale, for example, have ranged from 0.18 to .36 with a cross-study average of 0.26 (Sandberg et al.,1978). Deson (1998) investigated the concordance of reports of distractible and hyperactive behavior among 93 elementary school children from three different sources: parents, teachers, and the child, using two different instruments, the ADHD Rating Scale and the Continuous Performance Test of the Gordon Diagnostic System (GDS). When the incidence of attentional problems was calculated in this naturalistic setting, percentages of subjects identified varied widely. Parents identified more children as hyperactive and distractible (23%) than either teachers (9%) or the GDS (4%). However, no child was identified by all three data sources. Further qualitative analysis indicated that some degree of concordance occurred for 56 of the subjects, but overall findings emphasize the low levels of agreement between parents and teachers for both hyperactivity and distractibility among the children and the situational nature of diagnosis based on behavioral reports. As Henker and Whalen (1980) and Rutter (1983) pointed out, there may be several reasons for this lack of agreement: (a) Situational or environmental variations may generate differences in the child's behavior; (b) different observers may have different expectations for the child, different tolerances for the child's behavior, or different interpretations of the questions asked on the scales; (c) the scales themselves may have low reliability. Actually, all of these factors may be relevant. Diagnosis made on the basis of scales indicating that the child has ADHD because the scale indicates that he has attentional problems and is hyperactive, confirms only that, *under the observed or recollected conditions,* the child demonstrated attention problems or hyperactivity. This is indeed a diagnosis created by circular reasoning. They are inadequate for identification of specific deficiencies of the attentional processes or of impulsivity (Ostrom & Jenson, 1988).

Early investigation of the component functions of attention and impulsivity in terms of neuropsychological processing is seen in the, by now, classic work of Virginia Douglas reviewed in her "Attention and Cognitive Problems" (1983, pp. 280–329), whose tests and scales are organized in terms of vigilance and reaction times, perceptual search, perceptual discrimination and retention, logical or conceptual search, avoidance learning, inhibitory control (see Table 13.3). Because many of these tests and their modifications are not currently in clinical use they are outlined in Table 13.3. For details, please see V. Douglas, 1983.

These studies suggest:

> Attentional problems represent one of a constellation of closely related deficits, all of which have far reaching effects on the children's behavior, academic achievements and cognitive functioning. A tentative list of defective processes includes: 1) the investment, organization and maintenance of attention and efforts; 2) the inhibition of impulsive responding; 3) the modulation of arousal levels to meet situational demands; and, 4) an unusually strong inclination to seek immediate gratification. (Douglas, 1983, p. 280)

Further, these primary deficits may lead to secondary ones: limited development of higher order cognition schemata, impaired metacognition, and diminished effective motivation.

The accuracy of various screening methods currently in use in the evaluation of attention and impulsivity among children 6 to 12 years of age was studied by M. Green, Wong, Alkins, et al. (1999) in a report for the Agency for Health Care Policy and Research. One section is a review of evidence from current ADHD literature in four areas: prevalence of ADHD and its "comorbidities" in the general population; prevalence in primary care (pediatric) settings; the accuracy of screening methods; and the prevalence of abnormal findings on selected medical screening tests. To determine accuracy of screening scales for ADHD two types of scales were examined: Specific Scales and Broad-Based Checklists (Table 13.4). Quantitative information on each

Table 13.3   Tests of attention and cognition to measure ADHD behavior

I.   For Tasks Involving Vigilance and Reaction Time
  A. Continuous Performance Test (CPT; Rosvold, Mirsky, Sarason, Bransome, & Beck, 1956)
  B. Reaction Time and Delayed Reaction Time Tasks (DRT)
  C. Response to Specific Auditory Signal (Hoy, Weiss, Minde, & Cohn, 1978)

II. For Tasks Involving Perceptual Search
  A. Matching Familiar Figures Test (MFF; Kagan, Rosman, Day, Albert, & Phillip, 1964)
  B. Embedded Figures Test (EFT)
  C. Subject-Paced Viewing Tasks (Ain, 1980)
  D. Picture Recognition Tasks (PRT; Sprague & Sleator, 1977)
  E. Recall of videotaped lessons (R. A. Barkley, 1977)

III. For Tasks Involving Perceptual Discrimination and Retention

IV. For Tasks Involving Logical or Conceptual Search
  A. Demands for Sustained Strategic Effort
    1. Extended Digit Span
    2. 34-word list
    3. Categorization Learning Task (CLT; Kinsbourne, 1977)
    4. Paired-associative learning (Benezra, 1980)
  B. Concept-Discovery and Rule-Learning
    1. Wisconsin Card Solving
    2. Diagnositc Problem Solving (Niemark & Lewis, 1967)

V.   For Tasks Involving Avoidance Learning, Inhibitory Control, and   Pull of Immediate Award
  A. Lykken Maze Test (Lykken, 1957)

Note: Adapted from "Attentional and Cognitive Problems" (pp. 280–329). V. I. Douglas (1983). New York: Guilford Press.

scale is presented, including subscales included in each, comorbid conditions addressed, numbers of items, ages for which norms are available, computer scoring availability, ordering information and costs, and reliability and validity (M. Green et al., 1999, pp. 26–30).

The ability of the scales to discriminate abnormal from normal behavior was determined by "effect size" based on scores in case and control populations, calculated as the difference in mean scores between two samples divided by an estimate of individual standard deviations (Hedges & Olkin, 1985). Results indicate that the 1997 Revision of the Conners Rating Scales contains two highly effective indices (Parent Rating Scale, Teacher Rating Scale) in detection of ADHD versus controls, in overall symptoms of ADHD and in hyperactivity. Sensitivity and specificity are reported as greater than 94%. By contrast, the Barkley school questionnaire was weak with matched sensitivity of less than 86%. The hyperactivity and impulsivity subscales of SNAP were also high. The only hyperactivity subscale to perform poorly was AETeRS. However,

Table 13.4   Scales used in diagnosis of ADHD

I. ADHD Specific Scales
  A. Comprehension Teaching Rating Scale ACTeRS (Wellman, Sleator, Sprague et al., 1977)
  B. Barkley Questionaires (Breen & Altepeter, 1991)
    1. Home Situations (HSQ)
    2. School Situations (SSQ)
    3. ADHD Rating Scale (ADHDR)
  C. SNAP checklist (Atkins, Pelham, & Licht, 1985; Horn, Wagner, & Ialongo, 1989)
  D. Vanderbilt AD/HD Diagnostic Teacher Rating Scale (Vanderbilt Child Development Center)
  E. Gordon Diagnostic System (GDS) (Loge, Staton, & Beatty, 1990)
  F. Conners Rating Scales (Conners, 1990, 1997)

II. Broad-Based Checklist
  A. Burks Behavior Rating Scale (BBRS) (Burks, 1996)
  B. Child Behavior Checklists (CBCL) (Achenbach, 1991)
  C. Devereau Scales of Mental Development (Naglieri, Le Buffe, & Pfeiffer, 1994)
  D. Pediatric Symptoms Checklist (PSC)
  E. Ontario Child Health Study Scales (OCHS) (Boyle et al., 1993)
  F. Yale Children's Inventory (YCI) (Epstein, Shaywitz, Shaywitz, & Woolston, 1991)

the effect may have been in part due to an older sample (ages 6 to 14 vs. 7 to 11). M. Green et al. (1999) warn, however, that several subscales are represented by only one study.

The global broad-based scales, in this literature review, were relatively consistent across the various studies, but the effect size relatively small, representing a sensitivity and specificity of about 80%, while none of the tests had good estimated effect size for discriminating between referred and nonreferred populations.

Prevalence

The prevalence of ADHD in school-age children in the United States is estimated by *DSM-IV-TR* to be 3% to 5%. Using criteria of *DSM-III,* however (Szatmari, Offord, & Boyle, 1989), the prevalence of ADHD is reported as 10.1% in males and 3.3% in females, ages 4 to 11 years, and 7.3% in males, 3.4% in females, 12 to 16 years. Workers using *DSM-III-R* criteria (Wolraich, Hannah, Pinnock, Baumgaertel, & Brown, 1996) to evaluate teacher ratings of 8,000 children, found a total of 11.4% of these children with ADHD. Using *DSM-IV* subtype criteria, 214 teachers completed questionnaires on 4,323 children K-5, attending 10 schools in a Tennessee county. These teachers classified 11.5% of the boys and 5.8% of the girls as predominantly inattentive type; 3.9% boys, 1.3% girls predominantly hyperactive type, and 7.4% boys, 2.1% girls combined type. The total prevalence for all ADHD diagnosis was 22.8% boys, 9.2% girls. If, however, impairment (defined as performance at or below the 5th percentile in academic or classroom function as measured by a teacher rating scale developed by the authors) was considered, the percentages dropped significantly, 3.2% (boys and girls) inattentive type, 0.6% hyperactive impulsive, 2.9% combined type for a total prevalence of 6.8% (Wolraich et al., 1996).

A meta-analysis from 10 studies, estimated the prevalence rates of ADHD in school-age population by gender, setting, and criteria (M. Green et al., 1999). The overall prevalence rate was: males, 9.2%; females, 3.0%; school sample, 6.9%; community sample, 10.3%; *DSM-III,* 6.8%; and *DSM-III-R,* 10.3%. The results suggest that gender, diagnostic criteria, and setting are significant contributors to prevalence estimates, but age (5 to 9 years vs. 10 to 12 years) is not a significant factor. If the 1998 data are valid indicators, prevalence using *DSM-III* is higher than that of *DSM-IV,* perhaps 10% to 15% of the school-age population; and the inattentive type is higher than the hyperactive type. The male/female ratio as given by *DSM-IV* is 9 : 1, in clinical settings and 4:1 in community settings.

Comorbidity

"Comorbidity is present in as many as two-thirds of clinically referred children with ADHD" (*Practice Parameters,* 1997). Meta-analysis of five studies provided the data for prevalence rates of five diagnoses comorbid with ADHD; oppositional defiant disorder, conduct disorder, anxiety disorder, depressive disorder, and learning disability (M. Green et al., 1999). The estimated prevalence of oppositional defiant disorder in children diagnosed with ADHD is 30.2% to 44.3% with a mean estimate of 35.2%; conduct disorder, 15.6% to 48.3%, mean 25.7%; anxiety disorder, 24.0% to 35.7%, mean 25.8%; depressive disorder, 14.3% to 18.8%, mean 18.2%; learning disability, 12%. These estimates are slightly lower than reported in *Practice Parameters:* 50% for oppositional defiant disorder; 30% to 50%, for conduct disorder; 15% to 20%, mood disorders; 20% to 25%, anxiety disorders.

The prevalence of learning disabilities in children with ADHD has been estimated at approximately 12% (August & Garfinkel, 1989). It has been noted for many years that these two common disorders tend to co-occur, appearing together as a sequel of the influenza pandemic in the early 1920s and joined together in the definition of Minimal Brain Dysfunction (Clements, 1966). The comorbidity prevalence rates depend on definition, source of sample (clinical or school based or epidemiological), and the criteria used to identify "reading disability." In 1988, S. E. Shaywitz and Shaywitz used a regression-based IQ/achievement based discrepancy and a 1.5 standard deviation cutoff to classify children as learning disabled, for inclusion in the learning-disabled group. In that study, "11% of children with attention disorder were classified as learning disabled (LD) in either reading or arithmetic, whereas 33% of children with learning disabilities satisfied the criteria for ADHD" (S. E. Shaywitz et al., 1994a, p. 111). In this study, the prevalence rate of LD in ADHD is similar to the rate of LD in the general population. When the criteria for learning disability were broadened in a second study to include children not only with IQ/achievement discrepancy, but also with reading achievement below the 25th percentile, there was a marked increase in percentage (36.4% of LD in children with ADHD and a decrease to 15% in children with learning disability who have ADHD (Shaywitz et al., 1994). The finding of a prevalence of 36.4% of LD in ADHD is higher than that found in other studies: Holborow and Berry (1986) 27%, Frick (1991) 13%, Lambert and Sandoval (1980), 16%, Semrud-Clikeman et al. (1992), 23%. One outlier of 92% (L. B. Silver, 1981) was reported in a highly selected referred group.

As A. C. Schulte, Conners, and Osborne state: "Comorbidity prevalence rates must be considered from two perspectives, prevalence of reading disabilities in children with attention disorders and the prevalence of attention disorders in children with reading disabilities" (1999, p. 168). These rates have important implications for causal hypothesis. Four possible models are reviewed by Hinshaw (1992):

1. Poor reading leads to attentional problems.
2. Attentional problems lead to poor reading.
3. Both domains lead to each other.
4. Underlying variables result in both problem domains.

Both support and rejection for each of these models may be found in the literature. Given the heterogeneity of the population of learning disabilities and of attention disabilities, these models are not mutually exclusive; attention disorders and specific learning disabilities may influence each other. Common sense in addition to empirical observation (Rowe & Rowe, 1992) suggests that children with attention problems have more difficulty acquiring academic skills than those without attention problems, and that specific learning disorders may increase inattention in situations requiring academic skills.

B. A. Shaywitz, Fletcher, and Shaywitz (1994b), as part of their mandate by the National Institute of Child Health and Human Development have explored the relationship between ADHD and SLD (specific reading disability). The prevalence data quoted previously was one outcome of their reports (B. A. Shaywitz & Shaywitz, 1988; B. A. Shaywitz et al., 1991; B. A. Shaywitz, Fletcher, et al., 1992). In addition, their subjects were assessed with a variety of tests of academic ability, cognitive skills, and behavioral adjustment; comparisons were made on neuropsychological processing skills, word decoding, oral reading, listening comprehension, and silent reading. Four groups were considered: RD (reading disability) only, ADHD only, RD and ADHD, and control. The cognitive profiles for reading-disabled children with and without ADHD (the RD only and the RD & ADHD) were similar with a large proportion of the variance explained by linguistic measures and the attention variables resulting in only a small additional proportion of the variance. These linguistic defects *were not* characteristic of ADHD only. Thus, B. A. Shaywitz et al. conclude, "ADHD and LD, more specifically RD are separate disorders that frequently co-occur . . . linguistic disorders are not characteristic of ADHD unless attention disorder is associated with reading disability" (1994, p. 114).

These conclusions receive support from Lahey, Schaughency, and Hynd (1988) who, utilizing factor analysis, found separate LD and hyperactivity factors. Felton et al.

(1987) found RD children to have difficulty with rapid automated naming, ADHD with word-list learning and recall; August and Garfinkel (1990) found that ADHD and RD contribute "separate sources of cognitive morbidity"; Pennington (1991) and Pennington, Grossier, and Welsh (1993) found ADHD to have executive functioning defects, while RD was found to have phonological processing defects.

These findings are not only important in the pathogenesis of ADHD but are most important in the intervention(s) needed in management. Stimulant medication will not remediate the processing defects of a child with specific learning disabilities; on the other hand, stimulant medication will help improve attention and impulsivity problems. This difference is discussed in the sections on medication in ADHD.

However, as suggested earlier, children with pure ADHD may not be a homogeneous group (see also Halperin, 1997). There may be two distinct subgroups of attention deficit disorders, one of which is characterized by both attentional and reading problems. Light, Pennington, Gilger, and DeFries (1995) in a study of identical and of same-sex fraternal twins found that a genetic factor in reading disabilities influenced attention disorders. Halperin et al. suggested that there may be two groups of children, one with deficits in the frontal attentional system and one with defects in the posterior attentional system, as described by Posner (1988) and Posner and Petersen (1990), and that overactivity of the locus coeruleus and the posterior cortex and thalamic regions related to language processing occurs in the language disabilities while reduced norepinephrine leads to inhibitory dyscontrol in ADD. Halperin et al. (1997) support this view, finding higher plasma levels of MHPG in children with RD plus ADHD, than in ADHD without RD. Children with ADHD and RD have a double deficit.

POSSIBLE BIOLOGICAL MECHANISMS IN ADHD

Genetic Factors

Early family and twin studies have suggested a genetic component in the biology of ADHD. Stewart (1980) found a connection between hyperactivity in children and alcoholism, antisocial personality, and hysteria in their adult relatives. This finding is reminiscent of the family history of "disinhibiting psychopathy" of Gorenstein and Newman (1980):

- Hyperactivity in childhood may predispose to these disorders in adult life.
- Hyperactive children tend to have relatives who were or are hyperactive.

There is evidence from family studies (Francone & Biederman, 1994) that ADHD and reading disabilities or arithmetic disabilities are transmitted independently in families suggesting that ADHD is likely to be etiologically independent from learning disabilities. Concordance rates for ADHD have been reported as ranging from 51% to 80% for monozygotic twins versus 29% to 33% for dizygotic twins (R. Goodman & Stevenson, 1989; Sherman, 1977). Twin studies have also estimated heritability for hyperactivity to be between 64% and 77%; for inattention and related behaviors between 76% and 98% suggesting that hyperactivity and inattention are independently heritable. This finding (Hudziak et al., 1998) supports the separation of the ADHD syndrome into hyperactive-impulsive and inattentive types. S. G. Ryan (1998) states:

> The/these disorders clearly has/have a major genetic component as indicated by family and twin studies . . . which suggest a polygenetic mode of inheritance, and although evidence for a major locus has been presented it has not been confirmed. The direction of research has been to examine the hypothesis that genetic variation in protein involved in dopaminergic function, influences risk for ADHD. (p. 192)

An association between a specific allele at the D4 receptor gene and the personality trait "novelty seeking" has been reported in adults. In children with ADHD, an allele of D4 with a sevenfold, 48 base pair repeat sequence was found. A genetic variance in the base pair repeat sequence in the dopamine transporter gene DAT1 has also been identified (Cook, Stein, Krasowski, et al., 1995). Smalley et al. (1998) found that presence of the 7 allele attributes a 1.5 fold risk for developing ADHD over noncarriers of this allele while Gill, Daly, Heron, Hawi, and Fitzgerald (1997) replicated the work of Cook, Stein, Krasowski, et al. finding a significant association between ADHD and the 48 bp DAT1 variable number of tandem repeat (VNTR) allele. However, using four analytic strategies to examine the association and linkage of the dopamine transporter gene (DAT1) and ADHD, Waldman et al. (1998) found that levels of hyperactive-impulsive symptoms but not inattentive symptoms were related to the number of DAT1 high-risk alleles. However, the DAT1 polymorphism accounts for about 3% of the variance of ADHD traits in the general population and 90% of the population carries at least one or two copies of the high-risk gene. Currently, therefore, assay of DAT1 polymorphism is not considered helpful in the diagnosis of ADHD.

Biochemical Factors

There is recent evidence to suggest that immaturity in the maturation of neurotransmitters may be the developmental basis of the ADHD syndrome and that these neurotransmitters may be monoaminergic mechanisms. Wender (1973), impressed with the behavioral parallel between the behavior disorder of post von Economo encephalitis in children and the behavior disorder of ADD, postulated a defect in catecholamine, particularly dopamine metabolism, in each of these conditions. In adults, Parkinsonism, a clearly defined lesion of dopaminergic neurons, may follow von Economo encephalitis. In children, a similar lesion may yield the hyperkinetic, impulse disorder of childhood (see review in Chapter 4).

S. E. Shaywitz, Shaywitz, Cohen, and Young (1983) pointed out that although our present understanding of the anatomy of the brain monoamines is fragmentary, there is evidence to suggest significant variation in both catacholaminergic and indolaminergic mechanisms with normal maturation. Norepinephrine mechanisms tend to increase with age during childhood and adolescence and dopamine activity appears to decrease as the organism matures, whereas serotonin either declines or stays relatively consistent. Serum dopamine beta hydroxylase (DBH), urinary MHPG

(3-methoxyl-4-hydroxphenylglycol), and urinary VMA (3-methoxy-4 Hydroxyman-delic acid) increase with age in childhood; platelet MAO (monoamine oxides) decreases. Cerebrospinal fluid concentrations of 5-HIAA (5-hydroxyindoleacetic acid) appear to be stable throughout the life cycle. Girls tend to have lower accumulations of dopamine metabolites and a higher accumulation of serotonin metabilites than boys. S. E. Shaywitz et al. (1983) stated, "These findings suggest that girls tend to have relatively more mature or modulated CNS functioning, particularly in relation to central inhibiting mechanisms. It is possible that variations in disease prevalence (i.e., ADD, autism, and Tourette's syndrome occur more frequently in boys than in girls) might relate to observed differences in monoamine concentrations" (p. 336).

More recent studies (Teicher, Andersen, & Hostetter, 1995) have reported that in adolescence there is a normal "pruning" of dopaminergic synapses in the striatum. This is marked in boys, but less so in girls. The question is the relationship of these findings to ADHD. Is there indeed a difference in concentration of neurotransmitters and/or their metabolites in the central nervous system of children with this syndrome? The evidence so far is mixed, plagued by technical difficulties in measurement, in understanding the source (whether it is central or peripheral) of the metabolites measured, in ethical considerations in experimental procedures with children, and in diagnostic heterogeneity. When compared with normal controls, urinary MHPG, for example, is found to be decreased (Shekim, DeKirmenjian, Chapel, Javid, & Davis, 1979), increased (A. U. Kahn & DeKirmenjian, 1981) and not different (Rapoport, Mikkelson, et al., 1978; Wender, 1971).

Comparisons of platelet MAO-B in normal and hyperactive children are also inconclusive, because they have been determined to be both lower (Shekim et al., 1982) or perhaps in excess (Brown et al., 1984). The finding of decreased platelet serotonin in early studies has not been replicated and, indeed, was later found to be increased (Irwin, Belendink, McCloskay, & Freedman, 1981). Plasma 5-H1AA was reported to be low. No difference in urinary HVA or 5-HIAA was detected between normal and hyperactive children, and there was no relationship between DBH and hyperactivity.

Spinal fluid studies, which may more accurately reflect CNS monoamineric function than do urine and plasma studies, are still in preliminary stages. B. A. Shaywitz, Cohen, and Bowers (1977) using techniques of probenecid loading, found concentrations of HVA relative to probenecid significantly reduced in the cerebrospinal fluid of 6 hyperactive boys, aged 5 to 9, over that in the 20 controls, aged 2 to 16. Levels of 5-H1AA were not altered. However Castellanos, Elia, Kauesi, Gulotta, Mefford, et al. (1994) studying CSF plasma and urinary metabolites in 29 boys, ages 6 to 12 years, with ADHD found CSF 5-H1AA to correlate positively with a history of aggression and HVA positively correlated with hyperactivity.

Zametkin and Rapoport (1987) reviewed the evidence for "pharmacological dissection" of possible neurotransmitter abnormality in hyperactive children. Dopamine agonists (L-dopa, amantadine, and pirabidel) have not obtunded the symptoms of ADHD, whereas dopamine antagonists (chlorpromazine, haloperidol, and thioridazine) do decrease the inappropriate motor activity and inattention. These actions appear to be additive with methylphenidate. The importance of norepinepherine in ADHD is suggested by the decreased excretion of MHPG with drugs effective in decreasing inattention and impulsivity (i.e., dextroamphetemine and desipramine). However, fenfluramine, which also decreases urinary MHPG, is without benefit in ADHD. Fenfluramine also depletes brain serotonin. Increasing serotonin with L-tryptohan results in no behavioral change. Thus, it appears that a single neurotransmitter hypothesis is no longer tenable. That urinary MHPG decreases in responders but not in nonresponders to d-amphetamine (Shekim, Javid, Davis, & Bylund, 1983), and that the decrease in MHPG, VMA, NE, and total NE turnover correlated with improvement with MAO inhibitors, suggests that norepinephrine may be a necessary but not a sufficient condition for understanding the biochemical mechanism for the ADHD syndrome.

McCraken (1991) and Pliszka, McCracken, and Mass (1996), also utilizing the concepts of "pharmacological dissection," found that medication, robustly effective in treatment of ADHD, enhanced dopamine availability and inhibited noradrenergic locus coeruleus. The importance of the dopamine system is further seen in the production of an animal model (hyperactivity) of ADHD by destruction of the ascending mesolimbic dopamine tracts by 6-OH dopamine and by overactivity of the locus coeruleus to impede modulation of behavioral responses. Thus, increasing dopamine availability and inhibiting noradrenrgic activity are hypothesized to be required for maximal therapeutic effect. Further, theories of dopamine hypofunctioning are also supported by the single gene mutated mouse, which shows increased dopamine receptor density, and by the spontaneously hyperactive rat, which exhibits both regional dopamine reductions and increases in norepinepherine in hypothalamus and septum. This theory is not consistent with the effectiveness of dopamine blockers in ADHD (W. H. Green, 1995), since dopamine blockers are less effective than other medication in controlling ADHD symptoms.

Breese and his associates at the University of North Carolina School of Medicine (1981) agreed that hyperkinesis may not have a single pathophysiological base, but that, chemically, hyperkinesis is a heterogeneous syndrome which may involve, in varying combinations, dopamine, norepinephrine, and serotonin systems. These opinions are based on both clinical and laboratory evidence. Clinical data show that the serum levels of methylphenidate in hyperkinetic children who do not respond therapeutically to that drug are no different from levels in those who do. Laboratory data, examining the mechanism of action of stimulant drugs in rats, suggest that all monoamine transmitter systems are involved in the action of d-amphetamine, so that it is impossible to identify any specific monoamine as the vehicle for the therapeutic action of d-amphetamine (Pliszka et al., 1996; Rogeness, Javors, & Pliszka, 1992).

Neuroimaging Studies

Neuroimaging and functional studies have found differences in metabolism and in morphology of the brain in ADHD subjects. PET scans of adults with ADHD (who had a history of childhood ADHD and who have never received stimulant drugs and who have at least one child with ADHD) were done at the National Institute of Mental Health (Zametkin et al., 1990). Brain studies of this sample, compared with controls, showed reduced glucose metabolism bilaterally with significant reductions in superior prefrontal and premotor cortices. This was subsequently replicated in a sample of adolescents by Zametkin et al. (1993). However, Ernst, Liebenauer, and King (1994) found the reduced glucose metabolism (PET) only in females.

Morphological (MRI) studies reported reduced right anterior frontal width and absence of normal right greater than left asymmetry of the caudate nucleus (Hynd, Hern, & Novey, 1993). Castellanos et al. (1996) found total cerebral volume of 57 ADHD boys to be 4.7% smaller than in 55 normal controls and cerebellum and the right globus pallidus smaller than controls. Also the right greater than left caudate asymmetry was not found. Filipek, Semrud-Clickeman, et al. (1997) contrasting MRI examinations of 15 male subjects (ages 12.4 ± 3.4 years) with ADHD matched without comorbid diagnosis with 15 normal male adolescents (ages 14.4 ± 3.4 years) matched for IQ and handedness found ADHD subjects do have smaller volumes of total left caudate head, right anterior superior (frontal, bilateral anterior-inferior and bilateral retrocallosal areas), findings concordant with theoretical models of abnormal frontostriatal and parietal function. Inconsistencies in these findings have been reported. The significance of these findings, the relationship to symptoms, and the effect of treatment has yet to be determined. For example, stimulant medication does not produce a consistent increase in glucose metabolism (Ernst, Gonzalez, & Campbell, 1993).

MEDICATION TO MANAGE THE ADHD SYNDROME

Stimulant Medication

The use of medication in the management of the child with ADHD has a long clinical and experimental tradition. It is over 60 years since C. Bradley (1937) reported on the effect of Benzedrine on the behavior of 30 children, ages 5 to 14, of normal intelligence, hospitalized at Emma Pendelton Bradley Hospital for severe behavior disorders of varied etiology. With Benzedrine, 14 of his patients were "dramatically improved." Six years later, L. A. Bender and Cottington (1943), picking up the thread of Bradley's work, treated 40 children, ages 5 to 13, all inpatients at Bellevue Psychiatric Hospital, with amphetamine sulfate (Benzedrine). Thirty of these children with "neurotic diagnosis" improved, and aggressiveness diminished in four children with "psychopathic personality." Since that time, literally hundreds of reports on the use of stimulant drugs in hyperactive, impulsive, and aggressive children have appeared and additional classes of drugs—alpha agonists, buproprion, selective serotonin reuptake inhibitors (SSRIs), tricyclic depressants, and monoamine oxidase (MAO) inhibitors—have been reported to be effective. Reviews and summaries of the efficacy and safety of these drugs have appeared in Zametkin and Rapoport (1987); Richters, Arnold, and Jensen (1995); Practice Parameters (1997); McCraken (1998); NIH Consensus (1998); L. S. Goldman, Genel, Bezman, and Slanetz (1998); Jadad, Boyle, Cunningham, Kim, and Schachar (1999); Arnold et al., MTA Cooperative Group (1997); Pliszka et al. (2000a, 2000b).

By the late 1970s, stimulants were prescribed for approximately 1% of all American schoolchildren (Sprague, 1978). Ten years later, Safer and Krager (1988) found that since the mid-1970s stimulant medication use had increased steadily so that by 1987,

6% of all public elementary schoolchildren were receiving stimulants, primarily methylphenidate, primarily prescribed by pediatricians. Using time-trend findings from two large population-based sources, three pharmacological databases, and physician audit, Safer, Zito, and Fine (1996) found that between 1990 and 1995 there had been a 2.5 fold increase in the prevalence of methylphenidate in treatment of youths with ADD, so that approximately 2.8% or 1.5 million U.S. children and adolescents were receiving methylphenidate in mid-1995. Safer et al. attributed this to increased duration of treatment, more girls, adolescents, and inattentive children being treated with the drug, and possibly increased public acceptance of the medication. Safer et al. state, however, that their findings do not clarify the issue of appropriateness of this treatment. In 1988, S. E. Shaywitz and Shaywitz were concerned that methylphenidate was "prescribed for children who may not require it" and that "rather then reflecting real studies in our conceptualization of neurobehavioral disorders, current treatment practice represents a return to an antiquated simplistic approach that views all school and behavioral problems as one" (p. 227). In England, stimulants so widely prescribed in the United States, were given to 1% of the children referred for outpatient neuropsychiatric disorders (E. Taylor, 1983).

The Jadad, Boyle, et al. (1999) study is a report funded by the Agency for Healthcare Research on Quality, U.S. Department of Health and Human Services, to review the evidence on the effectiveness and safety, both short and long term, of pharmacological and nonpharmacological interventions for ADHD for children and adults. A total of 2,405 relevant citations were identified; of these, however, only 92 papers were randomized control trials and met the criteria for detailed study and analysis. Even these had methodological deficiencies sufficient to limit their validity, relevance, and precision and, therefore, clinical application: Outcome measures across studies were heterogeneous; comorbid disorders were not indicated; sample size was small; compliance with treatment was not indicated; characteristics of patients' families were not reported. Albeit reluctantly, the study concludes:

- There are few, if any, short-term differences in effectiveness among methylphenidate, dextroamphetamine, and pemoline.
- Stimulants are more effective than nonpharmacological interventions.
- Combined treatment, however, offers modest additional treatment effect for non-ADHD areas of functioning. (This conclusion is not explained in detail).
- Desipramine is more effective than placebo; results evaluating imipramine are inconsistent.
- There is little evidence for improvement in academic performance with stimulants.
- Methylphenidate or antidepressants may be effective for treatment of ADHD in adults.
- Side effects associated with stimulants appear to be relatively mild and of short duration. (Tics are not discussed.)

Equally important as these conclusions, culled from detailed analysis of the literature, are the limitations of the available evidence. The report cites the Multimodel

Treatment Study of Children with Attention-Deficit/Hyperactivity Disorder (the MTA Cooperative Group Study), described by Arnold et al. (1997) and Greenhill et al. (1996) as the direction of the future and states, "If this field continues to produce small incompletely reported studies with heterogeneous designs, instead of the high quality collaborative efforts required, research in this area will continue to be abundant but will be of little value to guide most clinically relevant decisions" (1999, p. 7).

In clinical usage, there is general agreement that in the short term (the exact limits of which are unknown) methylphenidate, amphetamines, and related drugs are of established potency in reducing overactive, inattentive, and impulsive behavior; improving laboratory tests requiring sustained attention; improving ability to play and work independently; reducing off-task behavior in the classroom; improving academic work dependent on sustaining attention; and improving peer social status. These effects have been documented with rating scales and in more effective measurements of vigilance, reaction time, and perceptual search. Objective measures of activity level (Teicher, Ito, Glod, & Barber, 1996) suggest an important effect of stimulant drugs is reduction of activity across various situations. The change in activity is not the same in all situations; the results will vary depending on the situations and the type of activity measured. Barkley (1997) sums up these effects, "The primary impact of stimulant drugs on hyperactive children is increased concentration or attention span or improvement in ability to stop, look and listen" (p. 152).

In a meta-analysis of 39 studies involving 2,303 children receiving stimulant medicine, Barkley (1977) reported that an average of 74% of the hyperkinetic children improved on amphetamine; 26% did not change, or their symptoms were exacerbated. The range of improvement reported was from 44% to 96%. Similar rates were found for methylphenidate and magnesium pemoline (range 51% to 94%). The average improvement for placebo groups was 39% (8% to 67%) In a meta-analysis involving 4,777 subjects, Wilens and Biederman (1992), extending and including preschoolers and adolescents and outcome measures of targeted behaviors, found a mean response rate of 70% and the proportion of subjects responding to methylphenidate, amphetamines, and pemoline was similar. Why one child responds to stimulant drugs, however, and another does not, is as yet difficult to predict. Neurological soft signs, immaturity in EEG, reported as nonpredictors of response to stimulant medication (Halperin, Gittelman, Katz, & Struve, 1986; Zametkin, Linnoila, Karoum, & Sallee, 1986). The presence of neurological signs suggestive of structural brain damage are signs that stimulants will not be effective (personal observation; see Chapter 14). Children with "more severe" inattention and with a better "mother-child" relationship may have greater response to stimulants (Barkley, 1990). Comorbid aggression in ADHD does respond to stimulants (Hinshaw, 1991), whereas children with ADHD and comorbid anxiety did not respond to stimulants, having responders no higher than that from a placebo (Pliszka, 1989). Gadow, Nolan, Sprafkin, and Sverd (1995) and R. L. Livingston, Dykman, and Ackerman (1992) found that children with comorbid anxiety responded to stimulant medication as well as those who did not have comorbid anxiety.

Response to the different stimulant drugs may also be difficult to predict. Elia, Borcherding, Rapoport, and Keysor (1991), in a sample of boys with ADHD tested with methylphenidate and with dextroamphetamine, found that 25% responded to one of these drugs and not to the other. In practice, a clinical trial of each may be done to determine the most effective drug for a particular child (Karniski, personal communication, 2000; Strayhorn, 1995). The specific stimulant medication and the form in which it is prescribed (i.e., regular or sustained release) is dependent on clinical indications, recognizing that prolonged biological actions also have the disadvantage of reduced bioavailability, erratic absorption, and difficulties with dosage titration. Combinations of regular and sustained release forms may be optimal for a given child. Interindividual variability in plasma concentrations, despite equivalent doses of methylphenidate and dextroamphetamine, are significant. Significant association between plasma levels and behavioral measures have not been found (Gualtieri, 1984).

Stimulant Medication and Learning

Despite the effect of stimulant medication on the improvement on laboratory measures of attention and on the ability of the ADHD child to contain his restless motor activity, these changes are not reflected in improved academic performance. Rie, Rie, Stewart, and Ambuel (1976a, 1976b) found that the academic achievement of children receiving methylphenidate for 6 months was not different from their achievement during a control period on placebo. Sixty-one children with learning problems without hyperactivity were studied by Gittelman-Klein and Klein (1976) over a 12-week period using random assignment to placebo and methylphenidate. Measures of academic achievement were no different for the two groups. Performance on tests that required speed of "mental processing" was improved, but performance on untimed complex verbal tasks was not. In a later study, Gittelman-Klein and Feingold (1983) combined methylphenidate or a placebo with remedial reading or "academic tutoring." Sixty-six children, whose earned IQs ranged from 90 to 115 on individual intelligence tests, were randomly assigned to three groups: Group 1 received reading remediation and the placebo; Group 2 received academic tutoring and the placebo; and Group 3 received reading remediation and methylphenidate. The drug was given at a mean daily dose of 1.19 mg/kg up to 60 mg/day for 18 weeks. At 2 months and 8 months after treatment, there was no difference between groups in basic reading skills, in reading achievement, or in academic skills other than reading. Gittelman et al. concluded, as did Douglas (1983) and Swanson and Kinsbourne (1976), that the use of stimulants in conjunction with a training program was problematic.

These conclusions were underlined by Aman and Werry (1982), who compared the effects of methylphenidate and diazepam in 15 children, ages 6 years 8 months to 12 years, who earned IQs ranging from 81 to 135 and who were at least 2 years retarded in reading relative to their mental age. In a crossover design, each drug was given for 6 days followed by 1 day washout between conditions. The methylphenidate dose was 0.35 mg/kg/day; that of diazepam, 0.10 mg/kg/day. Each child was given a series of behavioral and learning tasks. Significant reductions in omission errors in the continuous performance test were found with each drug. No effects were seen on a manifest anxiety scale, in matching familiar figures, or in audiovisual integration. A slight nonsignificant improvement was found in letter recognition and in a psycholinguistic analysis. Word recognition actually deteriorated. Aman and Werry concluded that "drug-related changes occurred mostly in areas unrelated to basic cognitive deficits" (p. 36).

A number of studies reporting improvement in academic achievement in children with hyperactivity, behavior problems, and academic difficulty have appeared since the early optimistic data of Bradley. Two of these papers are early ones (Conners & Eisenberg, 1963; Conners, Eisenberg, & Sharpe, 1964) and three appeared in 1985 (Pelham, 1985; Pelham, Bender, Coddell, Booth, & Moorer, 1985; Pelham & Murphy, 1985). In a placebo-controlled study of 42 children, mean age 10 years, whose primary complaint was some form of learning disorder, Conners et al. (1964) found that d-amphetamine given at a dose of 10 mg/day over a 4-week period improved arithmetic achievement, but there was only a nonsignificant trend in reading improvement. Conners noted, however, that his d-amphetamine group had improved performance on the Porteus maze, in ability to copy geometric designs, and in ability to sequence phonemes to make words. Pelham et al. (1985), using a double-blind, controlled crossover design, tested methylphenidate in doses of 0.15, 0.3, and 0.6 mg/kg/day in a 7-week summer day program. There were 24 boys and 5 girls ranging from 5 years 5 months to 11 years 5 months of age; 26 of these children were diagnosed as having ADHD, 3 as having ADD. Eight had additional conduct disorders. Pelham stated that during the methylphenidate phase there was increased performance in number of arithmetic problems done and attempted and an increased comprehension of questions answered correctly. In contrast to the findings of Sprague and Sleator (1977), Pelham found that a dose higher than 0.3 mg/kg/day was needed to obtain improvement in these parameters. In a review of six studies on the effects of stimulant drugs on learning, Aman and Werry (1982) summarized: "While most investigations can be faulted on diagnostic heterogeneity, dose or duration of medication, it seems reasonable to conclude that at present, stimulants have no clear role to play in [improving] learning disabilities" (p. 37). Where the academic difficulty is a function of inattention and vigilance, then stimulant medication will be helpful, but where there is a learning disability with recognized neuropsychological deficits, these deficits will not improve with stimulant medications alone. For children with ADHD and comorbid learning disabilities, remedial education, adaptation of the school program, and support at least to parent and child are indicated. E. Taylor states:

> Improvement in ability to attend would only be of overall benefit if it were the limiting factor in achievement . . . attention deficit is not usually the limiting factor in school learning. . . . It is possible that there is a subgroup of children with learning disabilities for which attention deficit is a crucial problem, but this has not been established. (1983, p. 448)

Adverse Effects of Stimulant Medication

Medication also is not without its problems. Barkley (1977) reviewed 29 studies that have reported side effects of stimulant medication. The most frequently noted are insomnia or sleep disturbances, decreased appetite, weight loss, irritability, and abdominal pain.

Less frequent are headaches, drowsiness, sadness, dizziness, nausea, proneness to crying, euphoria, nightmares, tremor, dry mouth, constipation, lethargy, tics, anxiety, and suppressed gain of height and weight. Although most of these side effects are not serious, and may be temporary and respond to decrease in medication, some are potentially serious. A number of reports have associated the emergence of Tourette's syndrome with stimulant medication (Denckla, Bemporad, & MacKay, 1976; Erenberg, Cruse, & Rothner, 1985; Golden, 1984; Lowe, Cohen, Detlor, Kremenitzer, & Shaywitz, 1982; Mitchell & Matthews, 1980). More recently, there has been a trend to use methylphenidate in Tourette's syndrome if ADHD symptoms are troublesome (Gadow et al., 1995; Gadow & Sverd, 1990; Law & Schachar, 1999). Whether methylphenidate can induce tics or whether the drug brings out the tics that are latent is still not clear. The tenacious and disturbing symptoms of Tourette's syndrome demand careful monitoring for emergence of tics. In our clinic, even a family history of chronic tics is reason enough for not giving stimulant medication (see Chapter 15 for discussion of stimulant drugs and Tourette's syndrome).

Effects on growth have been a concern since the report by Safer, Allen, and Barr (1972), in which a dose-related decrement in rate of growth was described in children receiving methylphenidate or amphetamine over the school year. No growth suppressant effects were found, however, when the daily dose of methylphenidate did not exceed 20 mg.

A special committee of the FDA Psychopharmacological Drug Advisory Committee (Roche, Lipman, Overall, & Hung, 1979), reviewing reports on the long-term effect of stimulants on growth, concluded that there appears to be a decrease in weight gain and in rate of growth during the first 2 years of medication. By the third year, a tolerance appears to develop so that there is no effect on long-term (adult) stature or weight. In contrast to the FDA committee, however, Safer and Allen (1973), found that no tolerance to the height and weight effects developed. They recommend discontinuing medication during the summer months. When medication was discontinued during the summer, a "rebound" effect on weight was found during that time.

Growth suppression in hyperkinetic boys has been found with all three of the stimulant drugs used: d-amphetamine (Greenhill, Chambers, Rubinstein, Helpern, & Sacher, 1981), methylphenidate (Mattes & Gittelman, 1983), and pemoline (Dickinson, Lee, & Ringdehl, 1979). Greenhill (1981) reviewed the literature to 1981. The Columbia group found that 13 boys receiving a mean daily dose of amphetamine of 21 mg/day (10 to 30 mg: 0.84 to 0.1 mg/kg/day) for 1 year, lost 16 percentile points in weight and 10 percentile points in height. Mean sleep-related prolactin concentrations fell significantly during treatment. Mattes and Gittelman found inhibition of growth (height velocity) when methylphenidate was given in doses of 1.3 mg/kg/day for prolonged periods up to 4 years. Greenhill et al. (1984) found that in 10 boys receiving a mean dose of methylphenidate of 1.3 mg/kg/day (mean amount 39 mg/day) for 1 year, there was a loss of 13 percentile points in weight, but only a 3 percentile point loss in height. Mean sleep-related prolactin concentrations were unchanged, although there was a 34% increase (drug related) in mean sleep-related growth hormone. In a study of the acute effects of methylphenidate, Gualtieri et al. (1981) and Gualtieri et al. (1982) found that 1 hour after a single dose of either 0.3 mg/kg or 0.6 mg/kg, significant elevations of growth hormone were found, whereas prolactin was significantly depressed with higher doses of methylphenidate. Greenhill et al. (1981) suggested that the short half-life of methylphenidate as contrasted with d-amphetamine may be related to the lesser growth-inhibiting effect of methylphenidate. Growth inhibition in stimulant-treated children may be the result of inhibition of somatomedin, thus altering cartilage metabolism. Whatever the cause, it is not only prudent to monitor the height and weight curves of children receiving stimulant medication but also to prescribe the lowest dose possible over the shortest period of time to attain the desired therapeutic effect.

There has also been concern that children who receive psychostimulants become addicted to stimulus as adolescents or may more readily become drug abusers as they grow older. Published evidence suggests that such is not the case, with only one report (Goyer, Davis, & Rapoport, 1979) of a young adolescent abusing a prescribed stimulant. This 13-year-old boy had been receiving methylphenidate for approximately 3 years for hyperactive and behavioral difficulties. He responded to 10 mg t.i.d. Within a year, however, he required a dose of 20 mg t.i.d. He began to take medication more often, so that before admission to NIMH he had been taking 40 mg approximately every 2 hours. He claims the drug made him feel "high" or gave him a "numbness" or a "buzz." There was absence of dysphoria following the drug. In fact, such reports that are available (Beck, Langford, MacKay, & Sunn, 1975; Blovin, Bornstein, & Trites, 1978) found less drug use in adolescents who had received stimulants in childhood than in a so-called normal group. There is one report, however, of the mothers of two children abusing the methylphenidate prescribed for their children (Fulton & Yates, 1988). The authors pointed out that where "alcoholism, substance abuse and antisocial personality disorder" exist in families of children with attention deficit disorder, the structure for misuse of the prescribed drug exists. The $5.00 street value of a 10 mg methylphenidate tablet, in contrast to the prescription price of 35 cents, may also encourage such families to attempt to get multiple prescriptions for the drug.

There are more subtle stimulant drug effects. Whalen and Henker (1980b), in a paradigm involving peer interrelationships and social communication, found that some hyperactive children on placebo seemed happier, were less self-derogatory, and gave more positive feedback to peers than when on medication. Whalen and Henker described the "emanative" effects of psychostimulant medication as a series of concentric circles, starting from the inner direct effect of medication, spreading to the psychological effect on the child, family, teachers, and peers, outward to include institutional, subcultural, and societal effects. Medication modifies the child's perception of himself and the way others view him; it conveys the message that the child's problems are biologically based and may interfere with attempts to modify personal effort, interfamily tensions, and educational aspects of management.

The short-term effect of these drugs may also increase the tendency to label a child as hyperactive, may obscure many of the situational influences on behavior, and may perpetuate the fallacy that because the child responds to a drug he is classified as having an attention deficit disorder. A series of studies extending over a 2-year period at the National Institute of Mental Health (Rapoport, Buchsbaum, et al., 1978) compared the response to a single dose of d-amphetamine of normal prepubertal boys, hyperactive boys, and normal college-age males. The college-age subjects were divided into two groups: one given the same per weight dose as was given to the children, the second half given a per weight dose to approximate the absolute dose given to the children. All groups (except the high-dose adults) tended to decrease motor activity and increase vigilance, but the hyperactive children had a greater response to medication. In one task requiring sustained attention, the hyperactive group improved significantly in contrast to the other three groups. Affectively, adults experienced "euphoria" on the medication, whereas children reported feeling "funny" or "tired." In a double-blind, crossover design, using methylphenidate and a placebo given to a group of boys, ages 6 to 12, with a variety of conduct disorders, all showed positive changes in ratings of behavior and in tests of attention when on stimulant medication (E. Taylor, 1983). Thus, the effect of stimulant drugs is nonspecific and is not confined to a particular pathological state; there does not appear to be a diagnostic specificity in the use of stimulants.

It has also been a frequent practice to titrate the dose of medication with its effect on hyperactivity. However, ratings of attention and behavior responded differently to varying doses of methylphenidate. The error rate on a continuous performance test improved on low doses (10 to 20 mg), but progressively deteriorated with higher doses. The teacher rating scales showed decreased hyperactivity and improved behavior with higher doses. In the average preadolescent boy, a dose of 10 to 20 mg/day appears optimal for cognitive tasks. The target for treatment should help define the dose.

Serious psychotic symptoms have occurred with use of methylphenidate or of dextroamphetamine with 20 cases reported as of 1992 (Greenhill, 1992; Wilens & Biederman, 1992). These may have resulted from high doses or from an activation of an underlying predisposition to psychosis. Hepatotoxicity and choreoathotoid movement have been reported in patients receiving pemoline. In 1990, Neha, Mullick, Ishak, and Zimmerman analyzed 100 cases of pemoline-associated hepatic toxicity observed from 1976 to 1990. Approximately half of these were linked directly to pemoline, occurring primarily in children and adolescents taking less than 100 mg/day and manifesting itself after 10 to 12 months of treatment. Symptoms varied from asymptomatic variation in liver function tests to jaundice, hapatomegaly, and hepatic necrosis. A patient who had methylphenidate together with pemoline succumbed to fulminant hepatic failure (Berkovich, Pope, Phillips, & Koren, 1995). Sallee, Stiller, Perel, and Bates (1985) found only one of 691 ADHD patients treated with pemoline, to have elevated liver enzymes, which normalized 4 months after pemoline was discontinued. Sallee states that "data suggests that liver enzyme elevation related to pemoline is a rare adverse event that occurs in less than 1 in 1,000 treated patients" (Sallee, Stiller, Perel, & Bates, 1992). Baseline liver function tests with monitoring at least every month are recommended (Greenhill, 1992).

Tricyclic Antidepressants

Despite their narrower margins of safety than the stimulant drugs, TCAs have been effective and "may be indicated as second-line drugs for patients who do not respond to stimulants or who develop depression, or have other side effects to stimulants" (*Practice Parameters,* 1997, p. 965). ADHD patients with comorbid anxiety disorders or depression may respond better to TCAs than to stimulants (Spencer et al., 1998).

Imipramine, desipramine, and nortriptyline have been found to be effective in improving attitude, increasing attention span, and decreasing impulsivity (Saul, 1985; Wilens et al., 1993). Rapoport, Zametkin, Donnelly, and Ismond (1985) studied 28 boys ages 6 to 12, who had been referred to a day hospital program because of their hyperactive, impulsive, and inattentive behaviors, in a 3-week, random assignment, double-blind, placebo-controlled paradigm. Sixteen boys received desipramine at one dose per day up to 125 mg/day for 14 days; 12 boys received the placebo. Five of the group are reported as having a learning or language disorder. Between baseline, day 3, and day 14 testing, there was a significant decrease in scores on the Connors Abbreviated Teacher Rating Scale in the drug group, but no difference in the Continuous Performance Test. Clinical improvement was seen by the third day of treatment but clinical effects did not correlate significantly with plasma concentration of desipramine or its metabolites. Decrease in urinary MHPG, however, paralleled improvement in behavior.

Children may require a higher weight-corrected dose of the TCA than adults and are prone to rapid swings in blood levels, resulting in uneven clinical response. Divided doses are recommended (N. D. Ryan, 1992). The side effects of TCAs, however, particularly their slowing cardiac conduction time and repolarization, require careful monitoring. Conduction defects, seen as lengthened PR interval that may progress to a first-degree atrioventricular heart block, and occasional widening of QRS complex may be seen. Increased pulse rate and blood pressure may occur (*Practice Parameters,* 1997). Prolongation of the QT interval is a sensitive indication of cardiac effect (Wilens et al., 1996). Sudden unexplained death in 5 children receiving TCA (3 prepubertal, one girl, age 12; one boy, age 14) following exercise has been reported.

MAO Inhibitors

MAO inhibitors (Rapoport et al., 1985), clorgyline (MAO-A inhibitor), and tranylcypromine (A and B inhibitor) were studied in 14 boys (mean age 9 years 2 months ± 1 year 5 months) in a 12-week, double-blind crossover design in which 2 weeks of placebo were followed by 4 weeks of the active drug. After a 2-week washout period, another 4 weeks of the drug was received. With each of these drugs, there was an immediate reduction in impulsive, hyperactive behavior, comparable to d-amphetamine. Deprenyl (MAO-B inhibitor), however, was less effective than clorgyline, tranylcypromine, or d-amphetamine. While the use of desipramine appears practical in children with attention deficit disorders, the use of MAO inhibitors, with their need for controlled diet and the possibility of adverse reaction with other drugs, makes their practical use problematic.

Alpha Adrenergic Agonists

Clonidine, an alpha-2 adrenergic agonist that inhibits norepinephrine release has been used in ADHD. In doses up to 0.3 mg/per day, given in divided doses, it is reported effective in treatment of the highly active, oppositional and aggressive children and adolescents with ADHD (R. D. Hunt, Capper, & O'Connell, 1990). However it has a hypotensive action, and a relatively short half-life of 2.5 hours, which limits

its usefulness. It also is sedating, so that morning doses may cause drowsiness in school. There is a report of sudden death in four children treated with methylphenidate and clonidine (R. R. Fenichel, 1995) and the death of a 10-year-old with congenital heart disease treated with the same combination (Cantwell, Swanson, & Connor, 1997). It is only prudent to have a pretreatment EKG and to follow blood pressure. In our experience, we have found that children with ADHD who do not respond to stimulants may well be controlled with clonidine. This is particularly true for children whose impulsivity is part of a neurological syndrome. Guanfacine, also an alpha-2 agonist, is less sedating and less hypotensive than clonidine, and also has a longer half-life than clonidine, 18 hours in adults (Sorkin & Heel, 1986). While clonidine binds equally well at alpha 2a, 2b, and 2c receptors, guanfacine has selective binding to alpha 2a. In a preliminary study R. D. Hunt, Arnsten, and Asbell (1995) report encouraging improvement with guanfacine on Connors Parent rating scales in 13 children and adolescents, ages 4 to 20 years, with ADHD.

Allergy and the Feingold Diet

In 1974, Feingold, emeritus chief of the Department of Allergy at the Kaiser-Permanente Medical Care Program in San Francisco, published an anecdotal report of the role of allergy as a precipitating factor in what he called the Hyperkinetic Learning Disability syndrome. Feingold specifically indicted salicylates, food colorings, preservatives, and additives. The foods containing proscribed salicylates included a long list of fruits and two vegetables (tomatoes, cucumbers), foods containing synthetic (artificial) color or flavor, "junk" foods, manufactured candy and ice cream, and practically all pediatric medications and vitamins. Eliminating these foods makes up the Feingold or the KP (Kaiser-Permanent) diet.

Objective studies of the effect of food additives have centered largely on eight synthetic food dyes, certified as safe by the Food and Drug Administration: Red #46, Yellow #5 and #6, Red #3 and #4, Blue #1 and #2, and Green #3. These substances share no one particular chemical component that might be identified as precipitating behavioral symptoms. Kinsbourne (1984), reviewing the few objective studies, concluded that "a reasonable summary . . . admits that food colors can impair some hyperactive children's ability to learn. However, we regard the therapeutic efficacy of the Feingold diet is still lacking corroboration . . . the demonstrated effects occurred only after high doses of colors, contrary to the often heard clinically based assertions that "trace amounts upset the children" (p. 495). Two types of studies led to this conclusion. In one, diet comparison studies, the effectiveness of an additive-reduced diet is compared with a control diet. In the second, "challenge studies," response to a food dye is compared with that of a placebo. In a diet comparison study, Goyette, Conners, and Petti (1978), reported 10 mothers of 10 preschoolers who rated an adverse response to additive diet in 2 of 22 children, ages 2 years 8 months and 3 years. Harley, Matthews, and Eichman (1978) failed to find any adverse effect of reintroduction of food dye into diets of children who had previously benefited from an additive-free diet. Conners (1980) and Conners, Goyette, Southwick, Lees, and Andrulonis (1976), in a study involving 142 hyperactive children, found that when children were on an additive-reduced diet, about half had a significant improvement as measured by the Conners Rating Scale. Just as did Harley et al. (1978), however, they found no clear pattern of response to reintroduction of food dyes. What was of interest was that, when the additive-reduced diet was given first, there was a decrease in symptoms of hyper-activity, but in the control diet phase symptoms did not return. When the control diet was given first, decrease in symptoms also occurred; but when the additive-reduced diet was then given, symptoms were further reduced.

Results of challenge studies reflect the dose of additive used. With low doses of tartrazine (Yellow #5), there was little support of the Feingold hypothesis. Kinsbourne (1984), in a carefully controlled study, found significant impairment in paired associate learning test in 20 of 40 children, 1½ and 3½ hours after ingestion of the dye. The 20 children who did not react to the dye also did not improve with medication. In a 1-year follow-up study, Swanson, Kinsbourne, Roberts, and Zucker (1978) found 8 of 25 children had a long-term benefit from the Feingold diet. The beneficial effects of this diet have been attributed to its low sugar content. No objective challenge study of the effect of sugar on hyperactivity has been done to date.

While the efficiency of the Feingold diet as a treatment for hyperactivity is still under scientific consideration, families ask for it and some may indeed be able to fol-low this diet without psychological trauma to the child or to themselves. It should not be rejected out of hand, but after considering the psychological effects of the diet on family relationships, it should take its place among the therapeutic possibilities for specific children and families.

EDUCATIONAL MANAGEMENT FOR ADHD

Although research in pharmacological intervention has produced positive results in symptoms of inattention and hyperactivity, findings have been less optimistic with educational interventions.

Seidman, Biederman, Weber, Hatch, and Faraone (1998) have shown the effects of ADHD on the lives of adults. Their study of 64 unmedicated adults (ages 19 to 59 years) who had met the criteria for ADHD as children showed that, compared with non-ADHD clinical controls of similar age and gender, the ADHD group was signifi-cantly impaired on measures of semantic encoding for verbal memory, written arith-metic, and level of occupational attainment. Despite comparable educational level and IQ, these ADHD adults reported significantly more academic problems when they were in school than members of the clinical control group.

Learning is not easily controlled in terms of experimental variables for children with ADHD. These children represent a heterogeneous group with complex inter-actions of educational needs, personality characteristics, neurological status, comor-bidity, and interpersonal dynamics. Instruction must take into account not only the complex personal characteristics of each child, but also the varying educational needs that these youngsters present. These needs are best determined through comprehensive multidisciplinary diagnosis as outlined in Chapters 6 and 7.

Unlike the other disorders children experience, attentional problems and problems in impulse control are often already recognized by the parents and teachers who refer them for clinical services. It is the role of the clinical team to look beneath the surface behaviors and to bring to light the *causes* for the behaviors that bring the child to the attention of the service providers, whether they be child psychiatrists, pediatricians, school or clinical psychologists, school social workers. As shown in Table 13.2, the behaviors subsumed in the description of ADHD may have their roots in a wide range of disorders including structural defects of the central nervous system, developmental deviations, environmental factors, and emotional and personality deviations. Careful diagnostic study provides understanding of the etiology of the behaviors to guide the selection of appropriate intervention approaches.

After data from these various sources have been assembled, a clinical conference provides review of the data and decisions concerning diagnosis. If, on one hand, the data suggest that the problems in attention and impulse control that generated the referral are due primarily to the exclusionary factors described in *DSM-IV* (e.g., pervasive developmental disorders, autism, schizophrenia, or mood, anxiety, disassociative, and personality disorders), referral to appropriate mental health facilities can be made. On the other hand, if clinical findings indicate that the symptoms of inattention and/or impulsiveness are due to developmental disorders, structural defects of the central nervous system, or inappropriate or inadequate stimulation at critical ages, the team can consider a diagnosis of ADHD and can move forward with intervention planning. One member of the clinical team (as case manager) should be responsible for continuing clinical contacts (a) to discuss the findings with the child's family and school personnel, (b) to plan intervention approaches, (c) to plan follow-up measures to ensure implementation (and necessary modifications) in treatment plans including medication, supportive counseling, and education.

Where to Educate Children with ADHD

Although established procedures in mental health practices are usually well understood by families, the educational interventions with children with ADHD are not so clearly defined. A frequent recommendation (often made by clinicians who are not responsible for its implementation) is for a "structured classroom." This advice may be accepted uncritically because most people agree that a common characteristic of these children is their lack of structure. According to this thinking, it would follow that it is necessary to provide a structured framework for learning because children with ADHD are unable to provide it for themselves. Except for experiments early in the history of special education in which these children were taught in classrooms that had been cleared of any decorations or in study carrels that isolated students from environmental distractions (Cruickshank, Bentzen, Ratzeburg, & Tannhauser, 1961), few studies of educational alternatives have been conducted. Indeed, the trend toward inclusion in educational management has resulted in the placement of most students with ADHD in regular classes. One study has attempted to answer the question of effective placements of children with ADHD. DuPaul and Eckert (1998) categorized a range of current educational approaches: peer tutoring, computer-assisted instruction, task and instructional modifications, and strategy training. Two approaches, peer tutoring and task modification, were found to enhance both academic performance and attentional behavior. These investigations concluded that educational interventions that addressed directly the academic difficulties experienced by students with ADHD must be part of the treatment package. The choice of specific approaches was found to be more successful when it took into account the academic strengths and weaknesses documented in careful diagnostic evaluations.

How Should They Be Taught?

The administrative structure would seem to be less important than the match between the students' needs and the teaching content. Children with ADHD need persistent, patient instruction in systematic ways in organizing assignments and learning materials. This means that methods for keeping track of books, notebooks, disks, assignments, lockers, and backpacks need to be part of the lesson content on a regular basis. Beginning the school year with intensive training in organization would be valuable, not only for students with ADHD, but for most of the students in classes in which they are included. This training would need to be reviewed and reinforced throughout the year with the students with attentional and impulse-control problems.

Such training in organization may also require some modification in teaching behaviors. Teachers need to give clear directions in classes and to provide organized media for communicating assignments. Entreaties to "Read the next chapter" as the students troop out the door will not suffice. The successful teacher will require organized notebooks and assignment books and provide time for their consistent use. Assignment schedules, duplicated and distributed at regular intervals, encourage effective students to plan effective time management. The prudent teacher will also stockpile a few extra copies of assignment schedules, textbooks, and other materials to avoid the inevitable confrontations that occur when the student with ADHD announces that he or she cannot work because materials have been left in the locker (which he may not visit during classes) or at home.

Some teachers may attempt to place the responsibility for training in organization on the parents. This transfer of authority is implemented by having parents sign assignment books, returned test papers, and checkoff sheets. Experience shows that these systems break down after a few weeks, not so much because students circumvent them but because the mechanics of implementation become burdensome for the adults involved. Teachers should understand that at home, parents of children with ADHD have organizational problems of their own to deal with. Expecting them to manage their children's work at school by remote control is unrealistic.

The habits of effective organization need to be taught, whatever the subject matter of the course. The DuPaul study cited earlier implies that individualized, personalized approaches have some chance of success; humor and encouragement will contribute meaningfully to the student's chance for successful learning whatever the content. This does not mean that the teacher permits noncompliant behavior in students with ADHD. From the onset, some things are nonnegotiable: attendance, promptness, and class participation. Initial discussions should clarify students' responsibilities and agreements for provisions of any approved accommodations, such as time extensions for formal tests or assistance from consulting teachers. These ground rules need to be established at the beginning of the term and may need review as the year progresses.

Who Should Teach Them?

Teachers who work successfully with students with ADHD tend to be those who view nontraditional students as a challenge, rather than a burden. They seek to find ways of engaging them in class activities. They have a repertoire of techniques on which to draw to develop in the students sufficient organizational skills to permit them to achieve within the regular curriculum. They see their role as one that not only includes imparting knowledge, but encompasses skills in socialization as well. They have a high threshold for frustration and the ability to look beyond the annoying behaviors to the human being they teach. They offer a role model of acceptance and support for students with ADHD, whose impatience and talkativeness may make them less than popular with their classmates. They do not see these children as enemies to be conquered by marshaling the rest of the class against them. Students with ADHD are easy targets for scapegoating or being made the object of mirth in the classroom. They are able to build a relationship with atypical students so that they sit down and learn with their classmates. They are team workers who utilize the suggestions of clinicians and special educators who may be available to provide better understanding of the children placed in their classrooms.

There is no instructional single recipe for students with ADHD. In the final analysis, no specific kind of class placement, no single set of curriculum objectives, no special list of teaching techniques exist for teaching students with ADHD. Successful teaching must be grounded in careful clinical analysis of etiology, strengths, and weakness and sharing of those understandings with the individuals responsible for their care at home and in the classroom. Armed with this understanding, these students will fare best with teachers who accept the responsibility for teaching them, set reasonable goals, possess a repertoire of methods and techniques on which to draw, and meet the challenges they present in the classroom with skills, ingenuity, respect, and integrity.

The following case study is summarized to illustrate some basic points in the education of children with attentional disorders:

- Clinicians need to give serious consideration to parents' and teachers' reports describing typical behavior in the natural settings in which the child lives; behavior seen in the clinician's office may not be typical because it is strongly influenced by the novelty of the situation and the one-on-one attention paid during the examination.
- Educational achievement cannot be judged only in terms of test scores; low achievement test scores do not, in themselves, constitute a diagnosis of learning disability.
- Specific clinical and educational recommendations are necessary if behavioral changes are to occur.

- Even when a diagnosis of ADHD is made and appropriate medication provided, educational support is necessary to ensure successful learning at school.

CASE STUDY: KENNETH

Kenneth, an 8-year-old who would be entering third grade in a small private school in the fall, was referred by his parents because he did not do well at school.

The Initial Psychological Study

A psychological study had been done the previous year. Nevertheless, the parents felt that, although they knew something was wrong, they had no clear idea of what it was and what they could do about it. Kenneth's first-grade teacher had not been concerned about his school achievement, but reported that he "rocked from side to side during morning prayers, swayed back and forth on his feet, and occasionally rocked while seated at his desk." Both his parents and his teacher noticed some decline in achievement as the year in first grade progressed. They consulted a psychologist and, over the course of six sessions scheduled from April to the middle of June, an extensive battery was administered:

Wechsler Intelligence Scale for Children III
Bender Visual Motor Gestalt Test
Drawings
Wide Range Achievement Test
Gates-McKillop Diagnostic Reading Test
Wepman Auditory Discrimination Test
Tests for Gross Motor Development
Tests for Lateral Dominance
Sentence Completion

The psychologist's recommendations were as follows:

Kenneth's Grade 2 placement in September should be in a small class size with less disruptive children and an experienced teacher. He would benefit from individual tutorial work over the summer months and during the school year. In addition, Kenneth would benefit from specific training to strengthen auditory and visual perceptual skills. Once he is in Grade 2, his restless behavior should be reevaluated.

Continued Concerns

Kenneth continued in the same school in a class of 16 children for second grade. He was tutored in reading during the summers after both first and second grades. At the end of second grade, his teacher commented on his report card that, while his progress was satisfactory, "He is very sporadic in reading. He has improved and I believe if he focuses more, he will do better." This comment, together with the scores of the group achievement tests given in May (which placed his achievement within the first and second stanines in reading and language and the third and fourth stanines in mathematics) caused the family to request further help. They requested psychological consultation to explain the uneven school progress and to obtain recommendations for further intervention.

Because of the extensive amount of testing that had been done the previous year, it was decided to utilize whatever data could be retrieved from the report of the previous psychological study and to limit new testing as much as possible. Thus, only the Woodcock-Johnson Tests of Achievement-Revised, a figure drawing and writing sample, and a few items from the neuropsychological battery were administered to Kenneth and the ADHD Rating Scale (Home Version) was completed by his parents.

Data in the previous report made it possible to reconstruct and interpret for his parents the results of the Wechsler Intelligence Scale for Children III. Kenneth earned a full scale IQ of 116 (86 percentile), a verbal IQ of 115 (84 percentile), and a performance IQ of 113 (81 percentile). Overall scores presented a stable record, with no significant differences between abilities to handle language and nonlanguage tasks. However, the subtest scores showed some variability. Kenneth earned a very superior score on the subtest tapping speed and accuracy in associating symbols. In contrast, his score on the Block Design subtest (a measure of the ability to analyze and synthesize complex visual configurations) was low average. All other subtest scores placed well above average for his age, indicating that Kenneth had substantial cognitive resources for academic achievement.

Individual achievement test results from the Woodcock-Johnson Tests of Achievement-Revised confirmed his parents' concerns about his educational progress on completion of second grade:

	Grade Equivalent	Percentile
Letter-Word Identification	2.4	36
Word Attack	1.6	21
Passage Comprehension	3.3	70
Dictation	2.2	70
Calculation	2.5	36
Applied Problems	3.3	69

The two word-analysis tests (Letter-Word Identification, Word Attack) show that, although Kenneth knew some words as "sight words," he had very limited skills in decoding unfamiliar words by using phonic cues or structural analysis. He tended to guess at all words on the basis of the initial letter and the general configuration. Thus, the word *shoulder* was read as "shattered" and the word *experiment* as "excitement." His lowest score was earned on Word Attack, a measure of the ability to sound out words phonetically. He knew the sound equivalents of most initial consonants, but he did not know vowels, consonant blends, and digraphs. Examples of errors made on the Word Attack subtests were as follows:

Zoop read as "zap"

Lish read as "lash"

Feap read as "fap"

Kenneth earned one of his highest scores on the Passage Comprehension subtest, placing at Grade 3.3 (70 percentile). His use of contextual cues, strong cognitive abilities, and sense of language helped him to deal with these items. Despite miscalling errors (library read as "liberty" and turtle read as "travel") he was able to puzzle out the missing words to complete the cloze paragraphs of this subtest.

As might be expected, Dictation (a measure of spelling, capitalization, punctuation, and grammar) was not easy for Kenneth. He spelled some words correctly (*green, walked*), and he knew the plural forms of some regular and irregular nouns, but he did not know contractions and other mechanics of written language.

Kenneth's skills in mathematics were stronger than those in reading and language arts. He was able to deal with addition and subtraction operations, but used his fingers to count out many of the combinations. Good understanding of concepts was seen in his score of Grade 3.3 (69 percentile) on the Applied Problems subtest.

Strengths on the neuropsychological examination were seen in the following areas:

Auditory memory (94 percentile)

Auditory discrimination (perfect score)

Auditory sequencing (perfect score)

Right/left discrimination (accurate)

Visual recall (7/9 Bender figures recalled)

Rhyming (perfect score)

Lagging skills were seen in the following areas:

Fine motor control (Bender Visual Motor Gestalt Test, handwriting)

Errors in sound/symbol associations (Phoenician Spelling Test)

Time concepts (Clock Test)

Some interference in attention was seen on the Stroop Test and in his restlessness during the examination. The ADHD Rating Scale was completed separately by his parents, with a high degree of agreement in the results:

	Mother	Father
Inattention	18	16
Hyperactivity	16*	15*
Total	34*	31*

The starred scores place above the 90 percentile on the norms for this measure supplied by DuPaul, Ervin, Hook, and McGbey (1998) for boys of Kenneth's age. A good deal of restlessness was seen during the testing session, although he remained seated at the table and did not wander about the room or use excuses to divert attention from the task at hand.

Summary and recommendation were as follows:

Psychological study shows Kenneth to be a bright youngster who earned scores on the WISC III within the highest 20% of the youngsters his age in the test standardization sample. Although the tasks presented were not easy for him, he worked effortfully, despite some restlessness. His achievement is stronger in mathematics than in reading and the language arts. The problems center around his inconsistent decoding and encoding skills. His good intelligence and strong language skills enable him to do well in reading comprehension, despite his miscalling errors. Restlessness occurred during testing and was also reported at home in the ADHD Rating Scale completed by his parents. Recommendations in four areas were made: tutoring, modifications of schoolwork, home management, medical treatment of attentional problems:

1. Systematic tutoring to teach word attack skills to mastery.
2. Modification of school assignments until Kenneth's reading skills catch up with the third grade curriculum. For example, in spelling lessons it would be helpful if Kenneth were assigned only the phonetically regular words; with written work he should be graded with separate marks for content and spelling. Close communication between tutor and classroom teacher will enable Kenneth to take increasingly greater responsibility for his schoolwork.
3. At home, some practice with addition and subtraction combinations through games and computer programs would be useful so that they can become automatic. This extra drill will enhance his work in mathematics, a potential area of strength for him at school.
4. Kenneth's parents should discuss with his pediatrician the advisability of stimulant medication to help him deal with his restlessness and attentional problems.

Follow-Up

Kenneth was seen for reevaluation almost exactly a year after these recommendations were made. His parents reported that he had a good year in third grade, was achieving in the upper half of his class and even received a merit award at the end of the school year. Medication to control his hyperactivity was being monitored by a child psychiatrist to whom the family was referred by the pediatrician. Tutoring continued for the school year. Although the tutor has told the parents that it is no longer necessary, they have asked her to return for a few sessions when school starts in September.

Woodcock-Johnson Tests of Achievement were readministered to assess changes. Scores from the previous year are included for comparisons:

	Entering Grade	
	Three	**Four**
Letter-Word Identification	2.4	3.8
Word Attack	1.5	3.8
Passage Comprehension	3.7	4.6
Dictation	2.2	3.3
Calculation	2.5	5.2
Applied Problems	3.3	5.4

As can be seen from these scores, Kenneth has made progress in all areas tested. Spontaneous writing samples, done in association with human figure drawings were used to assess gains in written language. The follow-up sample was written in well-formed cursive; last year it was written in an untidy print. Mathematics continues to be a high point with scores for both Calculation and Applied Problems appropriate to his educational expectancy. Although his reading also improved, Kenneth's parents were supported in their belief that tutoring in reading and language arts should continue into fourth grade until automaticity of word attack skills has been attained.

LONG-TERM OUTCOME OF ADHD

The early studies of Laufer and Denhoff (1957) suggested that in the course of its natural history, hyperactivity tended to wane in adolescence and disappear in adulthood. This optimistic prognosis was soon modified. Menkes, Rowe, and Menkes (1967) in a 25-year retrospective follow-up of 18 children with hyperactivity and learning disabilities, found that 2 still complained of restlessness, 4 were in mental institutions, and of the 8 who were self-supporting, 4 had spent some time in institutions. By 1971, Laufer modified his opinion when parents of 100 of the children he had seen in the mid-1960s reported their children, now grown, were "still having difficulties" (quoted by G. Weiss & Hechtman, 1993, p. 384). Borland and Heckman (1976) found that a majority of 20 adults who in their childhood, conformed to a diagnosis of hyperactivity were self-supporting but fully half of them still had difficulty with attention and hyperactivity. As a group, they did not attain the social or economic level of their brothers. It is now estimated that more than 70% of hyperactive children continue to meet criteria of ADHD in adolescence and up to 65% as adults (Barkley, 1996; Goldman et al., 1998). G. Weiss and Hechtman (1993) review in detail the fate of their original group of hyperactive children seen at the Montreal Children's Hospital and 45 normal controls over 5-, 10-, and 15-year follow-up. At the 5-year follow-up with children 11 to 16 years old, the initial symptoms of hyperactivity, distractibility, impulsive behavior, and aggression were generally decreased but still were greater than in the normal controls. Further, the hyperactive children, now young adolescents, were considered immature, had difficulty maintaining goals, failed more grades in school, and had lower academic achievement than their matched controls. Twenty-five percent

of them were considered antisocial. At the 10-year follow-up, 76% of the original subjects and 45 normal controls matched for age, sex, social economic status, and IQ were
evaluated. The group was then at mean age 19 years. They were tested on a series of
variables including biographical data, psychiatric assessment, physiological measures
(height, weight, blood pressure and pulse rate, and EEG) and psychological tests (California Psychological Inventory, a social skills test, Means-End Problem Solving Test,
cognitive skills test such as Matching Familiar Figures and Embedded Figures). Of the
76 subjects, 6 had received dextroamphetamine for 6 to 48 months, 27 received Tho-
razine for 6 to 48 months, 9 had received various medications, and 35 had received no
drug longer than 6 months. The results suggest:

> While few hyperactive children become grossly disturbed or chronic breakers of the law
> and none were diagnosed as being psychotic or schizophrenic, the majority continue as
> young adults to have . . . continued symptoms of the hyperactive child syndrome . . .
> lower educational achievement, poorer social skills, lower self-esteem . . . continued im-
> pulsivity and restlessness. (G. Weiss, 1983, p. 428)

At the 15-year follow-up, 63 of the original group and 41 controls were available for
examination. As a group, the hyperactive children had less formal education than
the controls; 44% in contrast to 10% of the control group were considered restless and
distractible; 66% versus 7% were considered impulsive, and 23% versus 2.4% were
considered antisocial. The hyperactive children, now adults, had "more neurotic" and
interpersonal problems. Weiss and Hechtman concluded:

> The hyperactive child syndrome is a pervasive condition in childhood, affecting behav-
> ior, social functioning, learning and self esteem. While about half the hyperactive chil-
> dren seem to outgrow the symptoms of the syndrome, half continue to be disabled to a
> varying extent by continuing symptoms. The childhood condition predisposes to various
> psychiatric diagnoses (but not to schizophrenia or alcoholism) and to increased symp-
> toms of psychopathology. It leads to Antisocial Personality Disorder in a significant mi-
> nority of the subjects. (1993, p. 82)

These conclusions, summarized in 1986, were valid in 1993 where most studies indicated that core symptoms (inappropriate restlessness, attention difficulties, and impulsivity) were still present in adolescence, albeit somewhat muted. While poor school
performance, social deviancy, and difficulties in relationships with peers and with
adults were prominent, with 10% to 50% of the ADHD group having a history of antisocial behavior, approximately 50% were indistinguishable from normal peers. However, the remaining 50% had a history of antisocial behavior, used alcohol and
marijuana, and 20% had a *DSM-III* diagnosis of Antisocial Personality Disorder. They
were employed, but their work status (Hollingshead Scale of Work Habits) was inferior
to that of normal controls. The use of stimulant drugs does not alter this prognosis.
Drugs so effective in the short term to reverse the core symptoms of ADHD were not
effective in the long term with adolescents, still failing in school, having behavior problems and poor self-esteem, still at high risk for academic and social difficulty. G. Weiss
(1983) reviewed four reports on the long-term outcome of hyperactive children who

received stimulant medication. Blovin et al. (1978) compared hyperactive children with children who had school difficulties without hyperactivity in a 5-year follow-up study. Their conclusion is similar to that of the Weiss, Hechtman reports. No long-term beneficial effects of methylphenidate were detected on academic achievement, intelligence tests, or behavioral measures of hyperactivity and conduct disorder. K. D. Riddle and Rapoport (1976) followed 72 hyperactive middle-class children who were "optimally treated" with stimulants or tricycle antidepressants for 2 years. The outcome was disappointing. Most continued on medication and had continuous academic and psychiatric problems. G. Weiss, Kruger, Danielson, and Elman (1975) found that 26 hyperactive children treated with methylphenidate for 3 to 5 years did not have a more favorable outcome in adolescence than did two matched groups of hyperactive children, one group of which had received no medication and the other of which had received chlorpromazine.

In more recent studies, Biederman et al. (1996) reexamined children with ADHD and controls 4 years after their initial evaluation, finding there were significant differences between the groups in rates of behavioral, mood, and anxiety disorders with the disorders "increasingly marked" from baseline to follow-up. In addition, ADHD children had significantly more impaired cognitive, family, school psychosocial functioning than did controls. Baseline diagnosis of conduct disorder predicted major depression and bipolar disorder. Baseline anxiety disorders predicted anxiety disorder at follow-up. Biederman et al. (1996) also found that children with ADD without CD at baseline did not progress to CD at 4 years follow-up, whereas ADHD subjects with co-morbid OCD and CD did progress to more severe symptoms of ODD and more comorbid psychiatric disorders including bipolar disorder.

SUMMARY

In *DSM-IV-TR,* the group of children with inattention, distractibility, impulsivity, and hyperactivity were classified into 3 types, the attention deficit (AD), the hyperactive, and the combination (ADHD). Thus, the *DSM* underwent a transition from the hyperkinetic disorder of childhood in *DSM-II* through the ADHD child in *DSM-III,* to an awareness of the difference between ADHD types in *DSM-IV.* The diagnosis, however, is still made by a checklist of symptoms, providing a symptom cluster, which may represent heterogeneous groups. Since the symptoms of inattention and of impulsivity are difficult to define, objective measurement of the key symptoms is also difficult. The key symptoms are currently defined by their functions, a cascading array of postulated neuropsychological functions subsumed by multiple neuropsychological and neuroanatomical systems. These functions are clinically assessed by rating scales (questionnaires completed by parents, teachers, peers, and even the children themselves). More recently, neuroimaging and functional imaging studies have found differences in metabolism (reduced glucose utilization bilaterally with significant reduction in superior frontal and premotor cortices) and in morphology (reduced anterior frontal width and smaller volume of left caudate, frontal inferior bilateral retrocallosal). Evidence from family and twin studies suggests heritability of 64% to 77% for hyperactivity and 76% to 98% for inattention, suggesting also that hyperactivity and inattention are independently heritable.

Although *DSM-IV-TR* reports the prevalence of ADHD as 3% to 5% of the school-age children in the United States, other studies have found an overall prevalence of 9.2% males and 3.0% females, with comorbidity present in two-thirds of clinically referred children. The prevalence of learning disabilities in children with ADHD is estimated at 12%.

The hypothesis that immaturity in the maturation of neurotransmitters may be the developmental abnormality precipitating the ADHD syndrome has not changed since the first edition of this book. A hypothesized defect in a single neurotransmitter is no longer tenable. There is evidence that in varying combinations, dopamine, norepinephrine, or serotonin systems may be involved.

Stimulant medication (methylphenidate, d-amphetamine, and pemoline) will relieve inattention and restless behavior in approximately 75% of hyperkinetic children. The primary effect of stimulant drugs is increased concentration or attention span, with improvement in the ability to "stop, look, and listen." Where academic difficulty is a consequence of restlessness and inattention, stimulant medication may help improve academic achievement. However, most studies do not find clear evidence of improvement in academic learning. This is particularly true when ADHD is accompanied by the central nervous system dysfunction described for the SLD child where "it seems reasonable to conclude that stimulants has no clear role to play in learning disabilities." Tricyclics and monoamine oxidase (MAO-A) inhibitors, the alpha-2 adrenergic agonists, clonidine and quanfacine, have been used where stimulant drugs are ineffective or where side effects of stimulant drugs are disturbing. While most side effects of stimulant medication are more annoying than dangerous, the emergence of Tourette's syndrome has been reported and evidence for growth suppression on prolonged (years) administration of stimulants, particularly d-amphetamine, continues to exist. While sleep-related prolactin concentration fell during treatment with d-amphetamine, such change was found with only high doses of methylphenidate. The effect of stimulant medication is not specific to the ADHD syndrome; normal children and young adults, too, incurred decreased motor activity and vigilance. With d-amphetamine, children reported feeling tired. Response to stimulant drugs thus cannot be used as a confirmation of the diagnosis of ADHD. It is also noted that with high doses of methylphenidate, the error rate on a continuous performance test increased. The use of the Feingold diet has not received scientific confirmation.

The synergistic effect of medication, training to remediate specific immaturities in spatial orientation and temporal organization, and appropriate management in his school classes is illustrated in the treatment of a child who had both ADHD and a specific learning disability.

The long-term outcome for children with ADHD is generally disappointing. As young adults, approximately half of the children studied show continued symptoms of decreased impulse control, lower educational achievement, poorer social skills, and low self-esteem.

Chapter 14 ——————————————————————————————

LEARNING DISORDERS WITH AN ORGANIC BASIS

Unfinished, sent before my time into this breathing world scarce half made up—

Richard the Third, Act one, Scene one

Traditionally, the diagnosis of structural defect of the central nervous system is inferred from history, clinical examination, and laboratory data. Traditionally, too, the neurological examination includes the classical evaluation of nervous system functioning: muscle tone, power, coordination, and synergy; motor impulse control and kinetic patterns; deep, superficial, and pathological reflexes including the development of postural and righting responses; cranial nerves; sensation of touch, pressure, temperature, pain, joint position, and vibration; and the capacity for age-appropriate modulation of sensory stimulation as seen in the presence of extinction phenomena, allesthesia, and synchiria and in age-appropriate aspects of cortical function involving gnosis, praxis, language, memory, and executive function. The neurological examination also includes observation for possible "minor physical anomalies," which are often part of diagnosable congenital disorders. A history of trauma, anoxia, infection, neoplasm, seizures, metabolic disorder, toxicity or prematurity, and low birth weight adds corroborative detail to the clinical examination; laboratory findings (EEG, brain imaging, chemical studies, and chromosome morphology) may further confirm the diagnosis and may aid in identification of focal areas of abnormality.

The question for the child with a learning disorder, however, is how many and how strong must the findings be to make a diagnosis of organic defect of the central nervous system? The problem is compounded because early neurological signs of organic deficit in children may be obtunded or may disappear entirely during maturation, and the only objective signs of such injury may be found in delays in the maturation of function, particularly in neuropsychological processing defects and in

426

learning, memory, or behavior. Conversely, damage to cortical or subcortical sites occurring during pregnancy or labor may not affect function until a later age, when the abilities mediated by the affected site would normally be called on to perform particular function; a delayed evidence of brain injury (Dorman & Katzir, 1994). Either event, the gradual obtundation of the neurological signs or the later emergence of neurological signs, may obscure evidence that some injury that affects learning and/or behavior did indeed occur (L. J. Harris, 1991; Sarnoff, Mednick, & Baert, 1981). Further, there is increasing evidence that in at least one subgroup of children with developmental language disability there is a structural difference in their central nervous system compared with that of normal children (see Chapter 3) and that children with attention deficit disorder may have a functional immaturity in their neurotransmitter systems. Should SLDs and ADDs therefore be considered as "organic"?

Although in the ultimate sense, there is a biological abnormality in children with developmental learning disability, we do not, in this book, consider them to be suffering from an *organic* defect of the central nervous system. In the first place, these biological abnormalities are still elusive. Second, and most important, the mechanism of the abnormality is different from that of the children we call "organic." Developmental disorders have their genesis, we believe, in a polymorphism in gene or genes, which, in its aberrant expression, interferes with normal maturation of specific function or functions of the central nervous system. Organic defects of the central nervous system do not have genetic polymorphism, but result from the action of agents on an organism that, until the appearance of the pathogenic agent, is proceeding on a normal trajectory of maturation. This dichotomy is not as clear-cut as we would like it to be. There are important groups of developmental disorders that are caused by known genetic abnormalities that induce profound structural and physiological aberration in the central nervous system, for example; Down syndrome, Turner's syndrome, Fragile X syndrome; or behavioral phenotypes associated with genetic metabolic disorders as phenylketonuria, the mucopolysaccharidosis, galactosemia. These disorders, in our definition, are developmental disorders, yet they are qualitatively different from normal. Conversely, there are organic disorders such as reading disabilities that, in their neuropsychological processing deficits, mimic the neuropsychological deficits found in developmental reading deficits and in whom unequivocal evidence of the pathogenic agent cannot be found. Yet as stated in Chapter 5, the distinction between organic and developmental learning disabilities is important since the developmental disorder and the organic disorder differ in clinical manifestations, natural history, and management.

The question of qualitative and quantitative criteria needed for an organic diagnosis does not lend itself to easy answers. The neurologist will generally insist on some objective evidence on neurological examination and greater or less documented history. The psychiatrist will generally be satisfied with equivocal neurological signs, soft signs (see Chapter 7) and greater or less history. The neuropsychologist may infer brain damage and the possible brain localization of that defect, from neuropsychological tests. In many children, there is evidence for a structural defect of the central nervous system; in others the evidence is not so clear, but there is enough for a presumptive diagnosis of organic deficit of the central nervous system.

CASE STUDY: STEVE

Steve was 11 years old, a small, towheaded, disheveled, and unkempt child, when he was referred to our clinic because of academic difficulty and restless, inattentive behavior. He had gross choreiform movements; very poor fine motor coordination; difficulty with equilibrium; suggestively positive Romberg; hypotonia; mild dysmetria, with mild rebound phenomena; and marked difficulty with alternating opposite movements (dysdiadochokinesia). In addition, there were severe perceptual immaturities with difficulty in the visual discrimination and recall of asymmetric figures, in visuomotor function, in auditory rote sequencing, and in right-left discrimination. On the WISC-R, he earned a full scale IQ of 88 (verbal IQ of 94, performance IQ of 84). Educational assessment revealed his word recognition to be at about early third grade level, his spelling and arithmetic each at beginning second grade (WRAT). He was emotionally immature. He had a great need for affection. His anxiety was seen in an introjected voice of the devil who, in a lady's voice says, "I'm going to kill you if you are bad." He worried about his grandfather and said, "If he dies, I die. I'll kill myself."

The history reveals that his was a prolonged, difficult labor with mid-forceps being used. He was cyanotic at birth and required resuscitation, but appeared to recover. It was noted that he was a clumsy child, feeding himself with difficulty, physically holding onto his mother even by the time he entered kindergarten. His mother, however, was less concerned with her child than with her three marriages. Steve never did see his own father and was not sure just who his father was. His only stable relationship was with his maternal grandfather.

There was evidence of emotional deprivation and lack of physical support that left this child with emptiness in the gratification of elementary needs and added to his marked anxiety in relation to the adults in his life. He reacted to rejection with his own aggression. In addition, however, the neurological findings were consistent with a cerebellar palsy, the cause of which was presumed to be his difficult birth. In Steve, there appeared to be ample evidence to describe him as having structural defect of the central nervous system possibly resulting from perinatal trauma and hypoxia.

Christopher is an example of a child in whom the neurological findings are not as defined as those in Steve, yet his neurological status is not normal and offers presumptive evidence that there is a structural defect in the central nervous system.

CASE STUDY: CHRISTOPHER

Christopher was 7 years 9 months of age and in the second grade of a self-contained class for emotionally handicapped children when he was referred to us. The school reported that he was "constantly on the move, has problems with fine and gross motor skills, and has difficulty adjusting to the routine of the classroom." At school, at age 5 years 4 months, he earned a full scale IQ of 77 (verbal IQ of 72, performance IQ of 86) on the WPPSI.

On our examination, Christopher was a gaminlike, small child, unkempt, and with festering sores on his left elbow and on the palm of his left hand. He had an upper respiratory infection with enlarged, reddened tonsils. There were many old, healed scars on his face and right forearm. He had an esophoria of the right eye and his ocular pupils were unequal, with the right pupil 1 mm smaller than the left. His muscle tone and power appeared normal, but his fine motor coordination (as in finger-to-finger testing) was so awkward he could not touch his thumb to any designated finger but moved all of his fingers at the same time. His gross motor coordination was also awkward, and he had difficulty maintaining his balance. There were occasional choreiform movements, particularly in his upper extremities; synkinesis was marked. In addition to these neurological signs, he had severe praxic difficulty. This finding may not be related to perception, but to his very poor fine motor coordination, which may prevent him from executing praxic movements even though he may perceive the spatial orientation correctly. The motor problems were also evident in articulation difficulty, which appeared to stem from a lack of synergy in the movements of the muscles of speech. A major perceptual immaturity, however, was found in the auditory area. Although auditory discrimination was intact, his auditory rote sequencing scored at the lowest stanine of his age group. His capacity for intermodal association was also in the first stanine so that he could not decode any words. His score on the PPVT was at 5 years 9 months. In all our examinations, Christopher was not hyperactive and maintained attention throughout. Educationally he could name only single letters of the alphabet and could read no words on the WRAT. Auditory acuity was normal.

Despite his mispronunciations, he was articulate and could verbalize many of his problems. He was anxious, particularly in relation to his father's aggression. He related specific episodes at home, and finally he concluded, "My daddy doesn't like God. He curses." His anxiety was seen when he talked about his parents' arguments. He would like very much to rush to his mother's defense, but feels helpless to do so. Added to his anxiety was a depression. Overall, however, it was impressive how well this child could relate in an open, coherent manner, despite his difficult home and limited resources.

Christopher was the third of three children. His mother reported that after a 15-hour labor, a cesarean was done. Although he was jaundiced at birth, he did not require transfusion but was placed under ultraviolet light. His mother stated that, as far as she knew, smoking (two packs/day) and drinking alcohol (unknown amount) were the only abnormalities of her pregnancy. Christopher's electroencephalogram was described as abnormal with diffuse, high-voltage slow waves.

What puts this child in the "organic" category are the unequal pupils, the extremely poor motor coordination, the choreiform movement, and the dysarthria, together with his severe perceptual deficits. The diagnosis of organic nervous system defect, presumptively from the neurological evaluation, receives some support from the history and further consideration from laboratory data. The entire picture is consistent with nonprogressive defect of the central nervous system.

To treat this child as an emotional problem and/or as a child with borderline intelligence is not to do justice to his real motor handicaps or to the severe auditory sequencing and intermodal association problems he is experiencing. In management, he needs occupational therapy for his motor handicaps and specific educational train-ing for his cognitive deficits. Buffering his anxiety with involvement of this family in therapy would be helpful, but it alone will not reach the underlying biological problems.

There are many children with problems similar to those of Steve and of Christopher. In Hagin, Beecher, and Silver's (1982) study, 5% of children in a "normal" classroom on the East Side of Manhattan had such signs. The specific neurological problems of these children are generally unrecognized in the classroom. By the time they have reached fourth grade, they may have already experienced repeated failure and have de-veloped a spectrum of behavior and academic difficulties. In a study of all 60 children in two self-contained classes for severely emotionally disturbed children, A. A. Silver (1984) found 18 (approximately one-third of them) to have problems similar to those of Christopher and Steve. Of the 18 children diagnosed as having organic defects of the central nervous system, 3 had a history of low birth weight, of whom one child had fetal alcohol syndrome; 3 had cerebral palsy; 3 had identifiable chromosome abnormal-ity (1 mosaic trisomy 21, 1 fragile X, and 1 Treacher-Collins syndrome); 2 had idio-pathic seizures; 2 had cerebellar palsy; and 1 each had Rh incompatibility, Tourette's syndrome, lead toxicity, a traumatic birth, and dyskinesia, unknown cause. It seems clear that a severe learning problem, resistant to conventional educational remediation, demands comprehensive evaluation along the pentaxial scheme described in Chapter 7.

CLASSIFICATION OF NEUROLOGICAL DYSFUNCTION

The causes of neurological dysfunction are many and varied. These may be catego-rized as to:

- *Time of Insult.* Did it occur during pregnancy, at birth, in the neonatal period, in early or midchildhood, or in adolescence?
- *Type of Insult.* Included are low birth weight with or without prematurity, hy-poxia, trauma, toxic, infectious, nutritional, metabolic defects as a result of ge-netically determined enzyme defects, seizure disorders, or neoplastic disease.
- *Progression of Insult.* Are we dealing with a progressive disease in contrast to one in which that damage was done and no further structural damage is incurred over time?
- *Severity of Insult.* Pasamanick and his colleagues (1956) documented a "contin-uum of reproductive casualty," a spectrum of defects ranging from the most severe insult, resulting in fetal or neonatal death, to a series of clinical neuropsy-chiatric syndromes depending on the severity and location of damage.
- *Location of Insult.* A. Towbin (1980), reviewing neuropathological studies in children with cerebral palsy and organic mental retardation, described two main forms of cerebral damage: the deep cerebral lesions affecting the basal ganglia and neighboring structures, and the cortical cerebral lesions affecting mainly

surface structure of the convolutions. A mixed type exists, and the structures involved in each of these general areas of damage may vary. Disorders of the basal ganglia may result in many varieties of dyskinesia; disorders of the cortex will present a variety of symptoms depending on the area or areas involved. Thorburn et al. (1982, quoted by Stewart, 1983) reported that ultrasound brain scan has been able to detect hemorrhage in the periventricular region, including intraventricular bleeding, in infants with very low birth weight, short period of gestation, and serious respiratory illness. Follow-up studies have shown these abnormalities to be associated with neurodevelopmental sequelae (Stewart, 1983). More recent (Krageloh-Mann et al., 1999) MRI findings in 29 high-risk preterm children, examined at age 5.5 to 7 years, were compared with MRI findings in 57 normal controls. Abnormal MRI, mainly periventricular lesions, particularly leucomalacia, was found in 19 high-risk children. The very preterm children had severe cerebellar atrophy in addition to periventricular abnormalities. MRI revealed specific morphological correlates: motor tracks with the presence of spastic cerebral palsy; extensive white matter reduction or cerebellar atrophy with mental retardation; mild MRI abnormalities with attention deficit disorders. Severe impairment of memory for events was found with bilateral hippocampal atrophy (Gadian et al., 2000).

- *Appropriateness of environmental support.* This not only includes the reaction of the parents to the child's behavior, motor, and cognitive difficulties, but the adequacy of the school in understanding the child and providing appropriate remediation. The importance of optimal social support systems in permitting optimal compensation for incurred perinatal hazards cannot be overemphasized. These support systems must, for premature, low birth-weight neonates, and very low birth-weight infants (weighing 1,500 grams or less), start at the moment of birth and in the neonatal intensive care unit (NICU) where noise and light intensity, temperature, flavors and odors, air quality, handling and other tactile stimuli, frequency of parental visits, and maternal handling also have significant effect not only on the survival of these infants, but also on the neurological, intellectual, and neuropsychological problem, they will incur later in life (Graven et al., 1992). (See also Chapter 10.) Environmental support does not stop with the neonatal nursery. R. H. Bradley et al. (1994), examining 243 premature, low birth-weight children living in poverty, found that their outcome in terms of cognitive, social/adoptive, health, and growth parameters at age 3, depended on the responsive, accepting, stimulating, and organized care they had received and were living in safer, less crowded homes (see Chapter 12).

NEUROANATOMIC CONSEQUENCES OF BRAIN INJURY

During fetal life, the brain is most vulnerable, susceptible to genetically directed sequences of maturation as well as to toxic, infectious, and hypoxic injury. Children with learning disabilities probably escape abnormalities in the formation and closure of the neural tube but aberration in further brain development. Cell proliferation and differentiation, cell migration, dendritic growth, and normal neuronal pruning may well result in disorders of learning.

The division of cells into neurons occurs primarily in the cells lining the walls of the ventricles (see also Chapter 11, on the development of hemisphere specialization), the ventricular zone immediately adjacent to the ventricles and the subventricular zone. The majority of cortical cells come from the subventricular zone; cells destined for the phylogenetically older structures such as hippocampus, come from the ventricular zone. The proliferation of neurons declines rapidly at 26 to 28 weeks of gestation. There is, however, evidence that the number of neurons in the brain is not fixed at that time but that neurons may continue to be formed in the subependymal lining of the ventricles throughout life. From the ventricles, neurons migrate to cortical and subcortical areas. In most cortical regions, migration is normally complete by the 26th to 30th week (Kadhim, Gadisseux, & Evrard, 1988), but the migratory cells are most vulnerable from the 8th to the 15th week. Infants exposed in utero to atomic radiation in Japan (World War II) before the 8th or after the 15th week of gestation were less likely to be retarded than those exposed during the 8th to the 15th week (Otake & Schull, 1984; Otake, Shull, Fujikosh, et al., 1988, cited by Dorman & Katzir, 1994). The failure of neurons to migrate from the ventricular zone to form the normal cortex has been termed migration disorder; where the migrating cells are abnormal or where the normal lamination of the cortex is disordered, the term cortical dysplasia is used. Galaburda has found these deviations in his morphological study of adults with reading disabilities. Abnormally migrating neurons may fail to make normal connections with their target cells or make abnormal connections with other cortical neurons. In any case, functional aberration occurs. The causes for migrational failure are heterogeneous and may include destruction of the migratory neurons or death of the neuron if it does not establish a synapse.

Following cell proliferation and migration, neurons develop characteristic patterns of dendritic branches. Alterations in dendritic patterns may have a profound effect on cognitive function. Scheibel, Conrad, Perdue, Tomiyasu, and Wechsler (1990) found that the degree of complexity in dendritic branching in a particular cortical area is related to the behavioral complexity in activities mediated by that area. There appears to be interdependence between afferent innervation and dendritic differentiation and growth, suggesting that afferent input is a stimulus to dendritic complexity and growth. Dendritic growth (numbers and shapes of dendritic spines) is "highly sensitive to the number of influences and may be a prime target for impairment by early brain injury" (Dorman & Katzir, 1994, p. 9).

The vulnerability of the ontogenetic pattern of migration of neurons and the proliferation of dendrites and dendritic spines, is paralleled by the vulnerability of the fetal vascular system as it develops from longitudinal neural arteries, to the *anlage* of the circle of Willis, at about 5 to 6 weeks of gestational age to increased branches penetrating the cortex at 24 weeks, and to large capillary subependymal areas of the ventricles situated mainly over the head and body of the caudate nucleus. The vascular bed of this subependymal area is the source of more than 80% of intraventricular hemorrhages in the newborn. One of the major causes of brain damage in the fetus, and the prematurely born neonate, is hypoxic induced hemorrhage (F. J. Schulte, 1988). The reason for this vulnerability is the inability of the hypoxic premature newborn to maintain homeostasis of blood pressure, resulting first in hypotension and then to a compensatory hypertension, resulting in a breakdown of the subependymal capillary bed. Hypotension promotes hypoxic ischemic infarction; blood pressure increase leads to periventricular hemorrhage, which spreads into the infarcted tissue.

Isaacson (1976) outlined physiological and anatomical consequences of brain injury that influence behavior and cognition. The initial effects of brain damage include actual destruction of cells at the location of the damage, with astrocytic reactions at the border and sometimes well beyond the lesion, phagocytosis and invasion of the lesion by microglia, proliferation of blood vessels about the lesion, edema and the development of irritative reactions at the edge of the lesion. As these events occur, there is disruption of activity in nearby tissues as a result of edema (and/or bleeding) and denervation sensitivity in areas to which the damaged regions no longer send impulses. Later retrograde changes occur in cells whose axons have been destroyed, and there is loss of trophic influence in neurons normally reached by processes from the damaged cells. In further delayed effects, new axon collaterals proliferate into cellular regions that had been supplied by fibers from the damaged regions. If the damage occurs in infancy, aberrant fiber tracts may form and changes in the size and cellular composition of the brain may occur.

Globus (personal communication, 1936) likened the effect of brain injury to a fire on the corner of 42nd Street and Broadway: police and fire trucks rush to the flames; traffic is stalled and is backed up for blocks around the fire (edema); electrical conduits may be broken, and no power is delivered to distant buildings (trophic changes and denervation sensitivity). The immediate effects of injury thus go far beyond the initial area of insult. As the fire is brought under control, fire trucks leave, traffic is resumed, and power is restored; what remains is the burned-out area. This simple analogy is not quite accurate because in the brain, the distant effects may have more permanent impact. The proliferation of axons into areas deprived of their normal synaptic input may result in a new abnormal pattern of synaptic input. This could be helpful in providing trophic influences and in reducing denervation hypersensitivity, but it may be deleterious in creating abnormal regulatory influences on remaining systems.

Similarly, with early natal damage, new "sometimes abnormal, sometimes peculiar" (Isaacson, 1976, p. 40) fiber connections may occur, and the nerve fibers in the infant brain may accept unusual sites of termination. On the other hand, damage to one hemisphere may, in the infant, evoke compensation, such as the development of an uncrossed corticospinal pathway. Thus, "the permanent consequence of brain damage . . . must include the direct effects produced by destruction of cells at the site of damage and all of the permanent secondary changes as well" (p. 42). Experimental studies, particularly in rodents and primates, suggest, or in Isaacson's words, "it seems clear that damage to the infant brain produces greater anomalies in structure and behavior than are found after damage to the brain of the mature or juvenile animal" (p. 58).

The implication is that recovery or sparing of function is not necessarily greater the earlier in life the lesion occurs. Indeed, Hebb (1949) felt that brain damage early in life is more severe and has more profound effects than that occurring later in life. This conclusion is based on the generalization that an intact and functional cerebrum is important in the development of language and other cognitive abilities, but once language and cognitive skills have been attained, their retention does not require an intact brain. Brain damage in the adult most often produces specific defects, and depending on the area of localized injury, there may or may not be loss in intelligence as measured by standardized tests. In the infant, however, brain damage produces a more generalized defect that affects overall cognition. Kornhuber, Bechinger, Jung, and Sauer (1985) supported this conclusion, finding that, when brain trauma (bleeding, infarction), occurred in children under 4 years of age, their intelligence was impaired to a greater extent than it was in children in whom trauma occurred after 5 years of age, even though the lesions, as measured by CT scan, were the same or smaller in extent and similar in location to the lesions occurring in the older children. Of the 51 children studied, the average age at examination was 11 years 5 months and the time interval between injury and examination was an average of 9 years 6 months. Thirty-seven of the children had perinatal lesions. Kornhuber et al. (1985) stated, "Possible explanations for lower intelligence after early lesions are: cumulative training deficit in children with early lesions and an internal deficit of stimuli for growth and connectivity" (p. 132). Thus, small differences in early lesions may, in the developing brain, result in large differences in intelligence and behavior. For children who had incurred lesions after the age of 5 years, there was a correlation between extent of lesion and IQ as measured by the Wechsler scale and behavior as tested by the Conners scale: a 1% increase in extent of the lesion corresponded to a decrease of 4 IQ points. Equally important are the specific deficits in the processing of information that may be found in children who, despite perinatal brain trauma, have normal intelligence.

There does appear to be a difference between adults and children in recovery of language and localized brain damage. Infants and young children with localized brain damage "almost always recover the ability to speak." The reason for this is that early in life, both sides of the brain can subserve language function. Thus with injury to the left side early in life, the right side may take over language functions. The frequency of language-related problems after damage to the left hemisphere slowly increases with age (Isaacson, 1976, pp. 48–49).

A GENERALIZATION OF CLINICAL FINDINGS

It has been stated repeatedly that in any one child, the clinical picture is the result of reciprocally acting biological, psychological, and environmental forces. The biological dysfunction itself, the conditions subsumed under the term "organicity," has infinite variations, and the ultimate prognosis depends on the nature and extent of the dysfunction, the age at onset, the child's temperamental and intellectual resources and, to a great extent, the nature, appropriateness, and adequacy of the support he or she receives from the environment, family, and school. It may be misleading, therefore, to attempt to synthesize or create an artificial composite of the great variety of symptoms that may result from brain damage, organicity, in childhood. No one finding or pattern of findings is symptomatic of the brain-damaged child (H. G. Taylor, 1987). In general, however, the biological substrate is altered by the imposition of organic defect and the resulting symptoms, clinically observed, may be understood as an interruption in the normal progression of maturation, delay in the acquisition of new functions, and retention of more primitive ones. They may be seen in disorders of perception, cognition, and language; problems in the initiation and control of impulses, problems in muscle tone, coordination, and synergy, and in posture and equilibrium. While we may examine these areas separately, they really function in concert, each influencing the other, all contributing to the child's behavior, his response to the environment and, in turn, how the people in his world respond to him. As a group, the functions of perception, motility, and impulse control are part of the autonomous function of the ego (Hartmann, 1964) forming the barrier against excessive external and internal stimulation, action, and inhibition.

Perceptual, Cognitive, and Language Deficits

Just as the child with developmental language disability has a spectrum of neuropsychological deficits, so does the child with structural damage to the central nervous system. The pattern of deficits may indeed be similar to those of the developmental disability and can be reflected in any combination of dysgnosia, dyspraxia, and dysphasia. The difference, however, is that in general the deficits of the organic child are more severe, involve more perceptual modalities, and are more tenacious, requiring more intensive and more lengthy training than those of the developmental disability. Further, the deficits in the organic child tend to involve visuomotor-spatial and temporal sequencing functions and body image maturation as seen in finger gnosis, praxis, right-left discrimination, and immaturity in tactile representation of the body image as seen in single and double simultaneous symmetrical and asymmetrical stimuli. In the face-hand test, the hand stimulus is frequently obtunded and there is even a tendency to displace the face stimulus to the homologous, contralateral point (allesthesia) or to indicate that the face stimulus is felt both at the point of stimulus *and* at the homologous, contralateral points (synesthesia). There may be difficulty with figure-ground perception in both the visual and tactile field (marble board of Strauss & Lehtinen, 1947). The frequent visuomotor defects are compounded by dyskinesias and fine motor coordination difficulty, all of which contribute to poor handwriting. The body image immaturity is seen on the draw-a-person test. Many of the nonverbal learning disabilities described by Rourke and his colleagues are children who have a static encephalopathy.

The case of Van illustrates motor and perceptual deficits in a child born prematurely with birth weight of 3 pounds, followed by pneumonia and atelectasis.

CASE STUDY: VAN

Van was first seen at age 5, brought primarily because of unintelligible speech. He was slightly obese at that time, in constant clumsy motion, with a persistent dyskinesia, consisting of choreic and athetoid movements, poor fine motor coordination, increased muscle tone in the left with increased deep tendon reflexes, ankle clonus, and questionable Babinski on the left. He was dysarthric. His comprehension of language, however, was excellent. On the Stanford-Binet he earned an IQ of 108. Severe perceptual immaturity was found in all areas: He had difficulty with the visual discrimination of asymmetrical figures; he could not draw a recognizable circle; and he could not identify a single tactile stimulus to any finger. On testing for visual figure-ground perception with the marble board, Van's responses were chaotic; he could not even reproduce a straight line. His EEG was abnormal with bitemporal paroxysmal features. Psychologically, he was apprehensive, phobic, clinging, and ritualistic.

Van was one of the children in our follow-up study (A. A. Silver & Hagin, 1985). He had the benefit of an upper middle-class professional home, with great support, speech therapy, private schooling, tutoring in reading, and psychiatric counseling for his parents. Repeat evaluations at age 8 years, 12 years, and 18 years found his overall cognitive ability to improve (Table 14.1): Stanford-Binet at age 8 years, IQ of 119; WISC at age 12 years, full scale IQ of 112 (verbal IQ of 120, performance IQ of 100); WAIS at age 18 years, full scale IQ of 116 (verbal IQ of 128, performance IQ of 98). At the same time, with intensive tutoring, his word recognition improved from Grade 3.3 at age 12 years, to Grade 14.8 at age 18 (WRAT). His reading comprehension at age 18 was in the 57th percentile (Diagnostic Reading Test). His reading speed, however, was at the 2nd percentile and signs of perceptual deficits he exhibited at age 5 could be detected at age 17. His Bender-Gestalt drawings and his Goodenough Draw-a-Person Test each showed little maturation as Van grew older, retaining at age 17 years the characteristics seen in his 8-year-old drawings and actually scoring no higher than 8 years on the Goodenough scale. His visuomotor function improved during adolescence. Yet the tendency to verticalization

Table 14.1   Van's changes in cognitive function

	Age			
	5 Years	8 Years	12 Years	18 Years
	Stanford-Binet	Stanford-Binet	WISC	WAIS
IQ	108	119	112 V120 P100	116 V128 P98
Reading				
Word recognition (grade)			3.3 (Jastak)	14.8 (WRAT)
Comprehension (grade)			4.1 (California, primary)	57th percentile (DRT)
Spelling			2.6 (Jastak)	5.2 (Jastak)
Speed				2nd percentile

may still be seen. With much support, Van was able to complete college and become successful in his own business.

Van illustrates significant and tenacious deficits in perception, together with incoordination in the muscles of articulation and in synergistic movement. His native intelligence and the excellent support he received combined to develop a well-functioning adult. His record also illustrates the significant difference between verbal and performance scores on the WISC, with verbal abilities at least 20 IQ points higher than performance abilities. Although this pattern is sometimes stated as characteristic of a neurological defect, this generalization may be misleading. Organic insult is capricious in the areas of brain at which it strikes and the expected high-verbal/low-performance pattern may be reversed in some children. Scott's record illustrates this point.

CASE STUDY: SCOTT

At age 5 years 9 months, Scott earned a full scale IQ of 82 on the WWPSI with verbal IQ of 66, and performance IQ of 103. At that age also, the ITPA revealed auditory reception at 4 years 1 month; visual reception at 5 years 10 months; visual memory at 5 years 1 month; auditory association at 2 years 10 months; auditory memory at 4 years 8 months; visual association at 5 years 6 months; verbal expression at 2 years 7 months; visual closure at 4 years; grammatic closure at 3 years 7 months; and, manual expression at 3 years 11 months.

A statistical analysis of subtest findings indicated a substantial discrepancy in auditory association skills and in verbal expression. The school psychologist stated in her report that "the total picture suggests a pronounced defect in auditory association that can perhaps be compensated for in some measure by utilizing his relatively strong visual reception skills." Severe perseveration in all testing was noted.

It was not until Scott was 11 years 1 month of age and in the sixth grade of a class for severely disturbed children that he was referred to our clinic. At that time, he was a good-sized 11-year-old, with dark, curly hair and with head circumference of 23 inches. He wore glasses for myopia. His clothes appeared to have been thrown on him. He had a sad, deadpan expression but became animated when he was more at ease or when affective material was introduced. He exuded a faint urine odor. There was a fresh bruise on his forehead and scrapes on his right elbow.

His gait was clumsy and stiff, and his fine motor coordination was very poor, particularly in the left hand. There were gross choreiform movements with marked synkinesis and coarse intention tremor. Muscle tone appeared increased in the lower extremities. His deep reflexes were brisk but unequal with increased knee jerk and ankle jerk on the left. Ankle clonus was also present on the left. Cranial nerves revealed eccentric pupils, persistent coarse nystagmoid movements, and a refractive error. A major area of pathology was in emissive speech with scant verbalization, laconic responses, poor vocabulary, mild dysarthria, and respiratory speech dissociation.

There was evidence from his drawings, however, that concept formation was adequate (Figure 14.1). His sensitive use of detail suggested greater cognitive resources than he was able to demonstrate with formal verbal measures. His difficulty appeared to be in finding words for his understanding and his thoughts. Perceptually, visual discrimination, and recall were intact. Visuomotor function was impaired.

The impairment, however, was different from that seen in the specific learning disability and even in the organic problems that Van displayed. In Scott, there were no verticalization errors or angulation immaturities, but his intention tremor made writing difficult. Auditory discrimination and auditory sequencing were both intact. Body image, however, was markedly impaired with severe defects in finger gnosis and in praxis. He did not demonstrate extinction phenomena. On extension, the arms converged to the point of overlapping. Academically, his reading and spelling were about 1 year below his grade placement.

Figure 14.1   Figure drawing. Scott: Age 11 years. (WISC-R verbal IQ 66, performance IQ 103) with severe expressive language difficulty. His sensitive use of detail suggests greater cognitive resources than are demonstrated on formal verbal measures.

His major problem, in addition to his motor difficulty, was in the storage and retrieval of verbal material. Thus, he had difficulty expressing his thoughts. Unless one were patient, allowing him time to find ways of expressing himself, he became frustrated, angry, and withdrawn. Emotionally, he was already an anxious, sad child who had developed mechanisms of rigidity, withdrawal, compulsivity, passivity, and dependency. His anxiety was great. He had many somatic sensations, and felt he was a bad person with many sins.

Past history revealed that he was 10 pounds 5 ounces at birth, the product of an unplanned pregnancy, and the oldest of four boys. His mother was a nurse, his father an automobile mechanic. His developmental milestones were slow with delays particularly in language, and he was still eneuritic. At age 4, with a high fever, he had a grand mal seizure, but the sequence of the convulsive patterns was not known. There were three subsequent seizures in his fourth year, this time unaccompanied by fever. For the next 2 years, he received phenytoin, but he received no anticonvulsant medication after age 6.

Although the history affords only presumptive corroboration of the perinatal injury, the findings on neurological examination, the history of seizures, and the EEG place Scott in the organic category. It was noted that he had a learning disorder, but its nature and extent differed from that seen in a specific learning disability. He did not have the phonological processing problems of SLD. His academic disability relates to his emissive language deficit as well as to his motor incoordination. His placement in a class for severely emotionally damaged children was inappropriate. He should be mainstreamed and provided with supplementary work in language development. He needed physiotherapy for his motor coordination difficulties, consideration for resumption of anticonvulsant medication, and psychotherapeutic support for himself and his family.

While the perceptual, cognitive, and language deficits in the child with structural damage to the central nervous system are not to be minimized, these children suffer from other effects of the biological damage. There are problems with initiation and control of impulses and with muscle tone, posture, and equilibrium.

Problems with the Initiation and Control of Impulses

The prototype for problems with the modulation of impulses may be seen in the Moro response, the startle reaction. It is evoked by any sudden stimulus, such as loud noise or quick passive movement.

Most of us, even as adults, will startle at a sudden loud noise or a sudden change in equilibrium. Our reaction, however, is largely a controlled one, and we restore equilibrium quickly on our recognition of the source and nature of the stimulus. For the child with an organic brain defect, the return is not as rapid. The physiological concomitants of the startle response—increased heart rate, sweating, changes in gastrointestinal tone, pupillary dilation, increased muscle tone, and metabolic changes—all reverberate in persistent waves that subjectively reach awareness as anxiety.

Theoretically, we can postulate a defect in the ability to screen out and dampen stimuli. Wender (1973) considered this defect to be a major one in children designated as having minimal cerebral dysfunction. He stated the defect as "an apparent increase in arousal, accompanied by an increased activity level and a decreased ability to concentrate, focus attention, or inhibit response to the irrelevant" (p. 20). The defect may well be a decrease in inhibition. Inhibition is a vital function in the central nervous system and is evidenced at successively higher levels of function: from the motor reflex, through the brain stem reticular formation, to the pathways to thalamic, hypothalamic, and cortical areas (Japer, 1958) (see also Chapter 13).

The result is that the organism is flooded with stimuli that it cannot control. This may well be the "predisposition to anxiety," "the physiological sensitivity which heightened the anxiety potential" that Greenacre (1952) described in patients with a history of organic insult at or before birth. She stated, "This is a genuine physiological sensitivity, a kind of increase of reaction to experience which heightens the anxiety potential and gives greater resonance to the anxieties of later life" (p. 54). In Freud's terms, there is a decreased "stimulus barrier" against a flood of stimuli. Clinically, anxiety and social withdrawal in late adolescence were found in children who had soft neurological signs in early childhood (D. Shaffer et al., 1983). Electrophysiologically, Lorente de No (1947) postulated "reverberating circuits" in which a stimulus, once reaching sensory neurons in the diecephalon or in the cortex, maintains a circus rhythm that perpetuates itself. More recent investigation has tended to focus on immaturity in the inhibitory pathways involving neurotransmitters, the catecholamines, and possibly the gamma-amino-buteric acid (GABA) system (Wender, 1973; see also Chapter 13).

The stimulus, however, need not always be external, as in the startle response. It may arise from within the organism at any and every level of function from reflex, automatic level to that involving complex psychic stimuli. At a reflex level, autonomic lability is characteristic of cerebral dysfunction. This can be detected clinically in vasomotor responses, in pupillary responses, and sometimes in visceral responses. The entire homeostatic mechanism is alert and sensitive. In the framework of Selye (1956), this individual is more vulnerable to stress, overreacting initially but reaching the stage of stress exhaustion more readily. The manifestations of homeostatic dysequilibrium (increase in hippuric acid and steroid hormone excretion, decreased white blood count, and decreased electrical skin resistance) all correlate highly with the factor designated as anxiety (R. B. Cattell, 1963a). In addition, these physical sensations of homeostatic dysequilibrium may in themselves create subjective anxiety and perpetuate the physiological response. Hypochondriasis, complaints about somatic sensation, may be a specific clinical manifestation of this dysequilibrium. When combined with problems with impulse control, the anxiety may be released in aggression. There is some evidence to suggest that interrupting the feedback loop with use of peripherally acting beta-adrenergic blockers or with ganglionic blockers will decrease anxiety and help control impulsive behavior in children and in adults with "brain damage."

Problems with impulse control are not only seen in the inability to dampen external sensory stimuli, to control voluntary motor movement, and to maintain autonomic and endocrine homeostasis; impulse control problems are also seen in difficulty in emotional homeostasis, in controlling psychological impulses. As already implied, the child with a dysfunction in the central nervous system is not exempt from the psychological problems of growing up. The difference is that his ego apparatus is immature; it cannot readily inhibit psychological impulses, which may then appear undisguised in thought or action. He may then appear as a primitive personality with incessant demands, need for immediate gratification, and labile affect. Depression, explosive rage, and clinging attachment may appear in response to minor external affective events or in response to tasks that the child feels are confusing or beyond her ability to control. The "catastrophic reaction" of K. Goldstein (1938, 1954), described as a sequel to head injury, may be in this category; this results when unmodulated stimuli impinge on an organism that cannot inhibit overwhelming autonomic and motor impulses that, in turn, produce overwhelming anxiety. Pathological rage reaction has also been described in children with temporal lobe epilepsy (Lindsay, Ounstead, & Richards, 1979; Ounstead, 1955). D. Lewis et al. (1979) reported a high incidence of "brain disorder" in institutionalized delinquents.

The child does not escape the consequences of his primitive thinking. Guilt is a frequent accompaniment, and many children internalize guilt as the voice of the devil versus the voice of God. Clinic experience suggests that the presence of introjections well into latency may be a reaction to a defect at the biological level. Nine-year-old George, for example, with a history of postmeasles encephalopathy, could not control his aggressive behavior in school. He told us how he hears the devil talking to him in a low, deep voice, telling him to hit or to throw chalk, and how God tells him not to do it. These voices are heard inside his head, but he is afraid that the devil always wins. In treatment for this child, we must be a substitute for his weakened ego on the spot—the teacher telling him that when he hears the devil he must come to her and she will help him control his feelings. Medication also may be of help. Only when George can feel the strength of his ally can we begin to explore the source of his anger, not only his frustration and feelings of doubt and inadequacy, but also the needs for affection and care that he feels he does not get. With a higher level of personality development than that demonstrated by George, depression after head injury is not uncommon. D. Shaffer et al. (1985) found an excess of affective symptomatology in children with head injury localized to parietal and parieto-temporal lobes.

Other children attempt to control impulses by imposing on themselves the most rigid type of defense: obsessions and compulsions. In discussing the "option of neurosis," Freud speaks of the interaction between "constitutional and accident" factors (i.e., biological and experiental). Organic dysfunction of the central nervous system may be the biological basis for a subgroup of obsessive-compulsive symptoms starting in childhood and continuing into adult life. Schilder (1938a, 1938b) stated this, and L. A. Bender (1956) said, "Unsolved impulse problems in childhood may have a more or less outspoken connection with compulsive and obsessive neurosis of later life" (p. 25). From a therapeutic viewpoint, the obsessive-compulsive defense may represent not only a defense against anxiety but also an attempt to contain the disorganizing effect of poor impulse control. As such, it commands the respect of the therapist.

The Moro response, then, is the prototype of a reaction from which subsequent anxiety develops an inability to inhibit or modulate stimuli whether they are external or internal, autonomic or voluntary, motor or psychological. A breaching of the stimulus barrier, anxiety, disturbing somatic sensation, hyperkinesis, primitive lack of control over instinctual impulses, guilt, introjections, rigidity, obsessions, and compulsions may all be psychological consequences.

The symptoms of inattention and hyperactivity have in the past been considered a manifestation of brain damage in children and characteristic of the minimal brain dysfunction syndrome. As pointed out in Chapter 4, these behaviors were seen after the influenza pandemic of the 1920s. Reasoning by analogy, children who were hyperactive and inattentive were considered to have some form of brain damage. Although it is true that hyperactivity and inattention may be seen as a consequence of an organic defect of the central nervous system in some children, it may not be true of most. The Collaborative Perinatal Project found that children with neurological signs were not characterized by hyperactivity and that the reverse was also true: Hyperactive children did not necessarily have neurological signs (P. L. Nichols & Chen, 1981; see also Chapter 13). The specific damage induced by specific etiological agents, however, may be an important determinant in the production of hyperactivity. The pathology in the periaquaductal gray regions involved in viral encephalitis, for example, may indeed induce a hyperactivity similar to that of the postinfluenzal child described so many years ago; toxic (lead) encephalopathy yields an impulse-driven child, as does fetal alcohol exposure and fetal cocaine exposure, whereas the child with a head injury with trauma to the superficial cortical areas may not be hyperactive. Indeed, such a child may have an inhibition of activity, although the perseveration he shows indicates that there is a problem with modulation and control of impulses. Involvement of the subthalamic and caudate nuclei, as in Sydenham's chorea, results in an inability to control the characteristic choreiform movements, but also in the frequent development of obsessive and compulsive symptoms (Swedo et al., 1989; see also Chapter 15).

Problems in Muscle Tone, Coordination, Posture, and Equilibrium

Problems in muscle tone, coordination, posture, and equilibrium may be epitomized by the child's reaction to antigravity play. Holding the preschooler upside down, swinging him from side to side, and tossing and bouncing him evoke pleasure in the normal child. Disturbance of the equilibrium is normally pleasurable. This is not true of the child with a central nervous system dysfunction. In her, disturbance of equilibrium evokes panic, a clinging, frantic resistance, and attempt to realign the physical orientation of her body with the world. Subjectively and objectively, this is fear. Maintenance of posture and equilibrium is a function that is normally performed every minute of our waking hours. It is normally automatic and has an important influence on our muscle tone and even on autonomic functioning. Why should the child with an organic defect of the central nervous system display a precarious orientation in space, and how does this contribute to anxiety?

By the end of the second month of life, equilibrium problems may be found (Paine, 1964). Holding the child upright and tilting his body forward, backward, and laterally evokes, in the normal infant, a reflex depending on the integrity of the otolith-righting reflexes. Righting responses to linear acceleration, dependent on the labyrinths, are evoked by the sixth month of life. In the child with damage to the central nervous system, these labyrinthine reflexes may not appear until much later and are inconsistent and uncertain. Thus, the very biological apparatus for maintaining head alignment in space is inadequate.

There are problems also in muscle tone relative to spatial orientation. The tonic neck and neck-righting responses are also evoked; the tonic neck reflex may be found in the first month of life and although normally it is not elicited by the end of the first year, it may persist as late as the third year. The neck-righting response is said by F. R. Ford (1937) to disappear by the fifth year, but in our experience, it may persist until the seventh year (A. A. Silver, 1952). As the child develops, these responses are not lost but are buried in the nervous system, constantly exerting their tonic influence, constantly influenced in turn by suprasegmental impulses. In the child with central nervous system dysfunction, these tonic neck and neck-righting responses may be clinically persistent, exerting their tonic force and making posture less responsive to volitional command. Paine (1964) suggested that abnormality in the tonic neck responses is often followed by emergence of motor defect. A persistent tonic neck response may be one of the earliest factors affecting bonding between the infant and her nursing mother. The extended chin extremity that follows rotation of the head to grasp the nipple may be interpreted by the mother as the child physically pushing her away. In reality, it is a persistent tonic neck response in a biologically immature infant.

The child with structural brain damage, therefore, has basic biological problems in maintaining spatial orientation and in muscle tone relative to posture. He cannot automatically and smoothly adjust to changes in posture and equilibrium. Phylogenetically, this is a fundamental necessity for getting food and for defense. The survival of the individual may depend on his ability to orient his head and limbs with respect to the world. Behaviorally, the clinging of the organic child may be understood as an attempt to maintain physical support and to obtain reference points for position in space. Psychologically, the need for physical support could well be the basis for dependency needs that are often greater than can be met and in themselves then become a source of secondary anxiety (M. Shaffer, 1979).

So important in the consideration of anxiety are postural and equilibrium problems, together with tonic influences of the vestibular apparatus, that Schilder (1938b) considered these basic to the development of what he called anxiety hysteria in adults. L. A. Bender (1956) stated, "Motor problems are part of development no less important then psychological ones. . . . In psychoanalysis of anxiety neurosis, one often finds recollections of experiences of insecurity in equilibrium from the earliest childhood" (p. 25).

Problems with equilibrium, then, contribute an additional biological impetus to anxiety, leading to a physical dependency that may readily become a lifelong personality trait of dependency and anxiety.

SPECIFIC ETIOLOGICAL FACTORS

With this background of neuropsychological deficits, difficulties in impulse control and in homeostasis, in muscle tone, coordination, posture, and equilibrium together with their emotional consequences, this section reviews causes of brain damage that result in these symptoms and that underlie many of the learning and emotional disabilities seen in the classroom. The etiological factors reviewed here include the effects of prenatal and perinatal injury, seizure disorders, toxic factors (fetal alcohol syndrome, fetal exposure to cocaine), viral (HIV), bacterial infections (*H. influenzae*), head injury, and CNS radiation.

Effects of Prenatal and Perinatal Injury

Although the survival of premature infants has progressively improved over the past 30 years and the incidence of crippling conditions such as cerebral palsy, major sensory defects, and mental retardation for very low birth weight infants (VLBW, 1,500 grams or less) has decreased from 35% in the 1970s to 5% to 10% in the 1990s, there has been little decrease in the number of VLBW infants. The increased survival rates have actually increased the rates of learning, emotional, and behavior problems within the school system. These especially true for low birth weight boys. E. O. Johnson and Breslau (2000) found that low birth weight boys with IQs equal to or less than 85 developed a reading disability 3.3 times as frequently as normal weight boys and developed a math disability 6.5 times as frequently. The increased risk of learning disability in male children applied to the entire range of low birth weight and was found in both inner-city and suburban communities.

As indicated earlier in this chapter, the major pathology in the brain of premature and low birth weight infants was hypoxia.

In the neuropathological studies of neonatal deaths in the Collaborative Perinatal Project, Towbin (1980) found the following:

- Although genetic, metabolic, infectious, and toxic processes appeared in the neonate, they were relatively rare and most cases of cerebral damage in the newborn were due to perinatal hypoxia. Mechanical injury was also common but less significant than hypoxia.

- Deep basal ganglia damage was observed mainly in the premature neonate, whereas cortical damage was observed in the mature, at term, neonate. The deep form of damage was more frequent than the cortical form.

- The degree of damage was governed essentially by the intensity and duration of the perinatal hypoxia. Hypoxia may lead to focal necrosis with resulting cavitation and scarring, but even mild hypoxia resulted in cellular damage with patchy or diffuse neuronal loss.

So important is the problem of hypoxia that Skov, Lou, and Pederson (1984) stated, "Neonatal ischemia is a critical determinant for later neurological and intellectual development and may be the most important single factor" (p. 356). Skov and her associates correlated neonatal cerebral blood flow with behavior at age 4 in a sample of 19 neonates that included 14 prematures. At age 4, children with cerebral blood flow equal to or less than 20 ml/100 gram/min. had problems with praxis, coordination, muscle tone, tendon reflexes, attention, articulation, understanding of hypothetical questions, visual perception, and memory for numbers—the very problems found in a random selection of children with learning disorders. Krageloh-Mann et al. (1999), also found evidence that hypoxia was a critical determinant of brain injury. Twenty-nine high-risk preterm infants with cerebral blood flow measurements in the first 2 days of life were reexamined at 5.5 years to 7 years of age and compared with 57 control children. Abnormal MRI was found in 19 of the 29 prematures. Low oxygen delivery to the brain was found in 63% of the 19 in contrast to 12.5% of the 10 prematures with normal MRI. The MRI abnormalities in all 19 had periventricular lesions, with periventricular leucomalacia in 17.

The importance of perinatal hypoxia in later cognitive development was further documented in the series of reports by Broman and her associates (Broman, 1979; Broman, Nichols, & Kennedy, 1975). These reports, based on findings of the National Collaborative Perinatal Project, focus on overall cognitive function as determined by the Bayley scale at 8 months of age, the Stanford-Binet at 4 years, and the WISC at 7 years. These tests are supplemented by a gross motor score on three tests of balance and eye-hand coordination at 4 years and Bender VMGT at 7 years. Perinatal hypoxia is documented clinically by fetal heart rate in the first stage of labor, Apgar score at 1 and at 5 minutes, meconium staining at delivery, primary apnea, single or multiple apneic episodes, resuscitation required during birth and after 5 minutes, and respiratory difficulty in the neonatal period. Children with these early signs of perinatal hypoxia were compared with those who had no such difficulty, with the groups stratified by ethnicity, sex, and socioeconomic status. Data were studied in a linear multiple regression model with hypoxic variables along with other predictive variables introduced in a stepwise manner. In the second study, retarded children were retrospectively compared with those with normal IQ, using perinatal hypoxia as the dependent variable.

At age 8 months, consistent deficits were found among infants who had respiratory difficulty in the newborn nursery and among those with multiple apneic episodes, with their test score differences averaging about ⅘ of 1 standard deviation. At age 7 years, the test differences were smaller, with a 5.5 IQ point difference in the WISC between hypoxias and controls. At age 8 months, 27% of the White hypoxic sample and 31% of the Black, had Bayley scores 2 standard deviations below the population mean in contrast to 2% to 3.6% of the respective control groups. At age 7, 4% to 7% of the hypoxic sample had WISC scores below 70 (9% to 13% of whom were Blacks) compared with 1% in the controls (5% of which were Black). Retrospectively, the retarded children at 8 months, 4 years, and 7 years of age had a greater number of hypoxic signs than the nonretarded group. Children with significant errors on the Bender VMGT, as measured by the Koppitz score, had a significantly higher frequency of respiratory difficulty (those with 18 errors had 4% to 7% frequency of respiratory difficulty vs. 1.5% in the controls; those with 16 to 17 errors had 11% low [1-minute] Apgar scores vs. 5% in the controls; and those with 10 to 15 errors had 4% single episodes of apnea compared with 0.4% in the controls).

Broman (1979) concluded that:

> Anoxic groups, particularly those with a clinical judgement of respiratory difficulty as newborns, one of the most consistently significant signs, had lower cognitive scores

than nonanoxic groups in infancy and at age 7. The differences were undramatic at either age but consistent within ethnic, sex, and socioeconomic subgroups. . . . Anoxic groups as a whole were not found to be mentally retarded but the probability of retardation was increased as much as 12-fold in infancy and 6-fold at age 7. Viewed retrospectively, the frequency of most signs of anoxia decreased dramatically as cognitive score levels increased among school children as well as among infants. . . . Research from all analysis indicate that newborns with clinical signs of anoxia are at risk for less than normal development. It is clear, however, that the risk for serious cognitive deficits is greater when other signs indicative of central nervous system impairment are also present. (pp. 51–52)

Broman and her associates have focused on overall, cognitive deficits. Deficits that are less global, however, are equally important in the management of children with learning disorders. J. M. Hunt (1961), summarizing subsequent developmental problems in low birth weight children, noted higher incidence of visuomotor problems independent of IQ scores, in preterm children than in full-term children at 4 and at 8 years. L. S. Siegel (1982, 1983) found that very low birth weight (less than 1,500 grams), preterm children were found to perform significantly differently from a demographically matched group of full-term children on perceptual-motor tests at 5 years. The variable associated with prematurity appears to be linked with specific impairments of perceptual-motor functioning in childhood. There were no significant differences between the groups in language comprehension. Siegel (1982) went on to state that infant test scores on selected scales (Bayley, Uzgaris-Hunt, and Reynall scales of language development) at 4, 8, 12, 18, and 24 months, together with a risk index based on demographic, reproductive, and perinatal factors, could be used to predict test scores at 5 years.

M. A. Stewart (1983) reported a prospective study of 382 infants, the survivors of 694 infants with a birth weight of 638 to 1500 grams who had been admitted to the neonatal intensive care unit at University College Hospital (London), from 1966 to 1977. During this time, technological improvements to care resulted in improvement in survival from 52% in 1966 to 75% in 1977. Of the 382, 121 infants required mechanical ventilation for respiratory failure and 25 had one or more exchange transfusions. At age 2 years, 11% of the 382 children (41) had major handicaps; of these, 22 (54%) had cerebral palsy, 15 (6%) were mentally retarded, 14 (34%) had sensory neural hearing loss, 4 had hydrocephalus, 3 had retrolental fibroplasia, and 1 had congenital cataracts. At age 3 years 5 months and at 8 years, there were no dramatic group differences in cognitive attainment. However, at age 8 years, 14% of the children, although they attended regular schools, were receiving additional academic help and 5% were in special schools for the mentally or physically handicapped. Twelve percent had perceptuomotor disorders, 1 standard deviation below normal on Koppitz scoring of the Bender VMGT. The proportion of handicaps depended on birth weight, period of gestation, and the presence of respiratory failure and/or convulsions. Twenty percent of the infants who required treatment for respiratory failure and almost half of those who had convulsions in the neonatal period had handicaps at follow-up.

That perinatal events may foreshadow later development should not be a surprise. As early as 1861, Little described the influence of abnormal parturition, difficult labor, premature birth, and asphyxia neonatorium on the mental and physical condition of the child. The literature has continued to document the effect of perinatal stress on development. Extensive reviews may be found in Field and Sostek (1983); Field, Sostek, Goldberg, and Shuman (1979); and Tjossen (1976). A review of the prenatal and perinatal even specifically relating to reading disability is found in Balow, Rubin, and Rosen (1975).

Littman (1979), believing that medical events beyond the neonatal period were also important in the development of the infant, extended the time period of observation of biological events in the life of 126 preterm infants to the age of 2 years. Four medical event scales (recording obstetric complications, postnatal complications, and pediatric complications at 4 months and at 9 months) were correlated with Parmelee Newborn Neurological Examination, the Gesell at 4, 9, and 24 months, and the Bayley at 18 and 25 months. Although the only significant correlation between early (prenatal, perinatal, and neonatal) events and developmental outcomes was seen in the Bayley motor performance at 18 months, a significant relationship was found between medical events occurring during later infancy and developmental outcomes at 9, 18, and 24 months. Littman stated, "It is now clear that medical events [of the perinatal and neonatal period] associate themselves with other medical events; and to single out [e.g., low birth weight or hypoxia] in order to relate the impact of its occurrences on development excludes other complications of possibly equal import to the infant" (p. 55).

The importance of these findings is that, not only do perinatal events affect development, but that the residuals of these events simply do not disappear with maturation alone and that brain function important for learning may be impaired into adult life. As early as 1964, A. A. Silver and Hagin reported a 10-year follow-up of 41 children with learning disorders who initially were referred to the Bellevue Hospital Mental Hygiene Clinic for behavior problems at 8 to 10 years of age. The emphasis of this study was on the maturation of perceptual functions, particularly those relating to orientation in space and sequencing in time. A control group of adequate readers was matched with a learning-disordered group for age, sex, IQ, and socioeconomic class. The groups differed in academic achievement and in the presence of the neuropsychological problems described. Within the group of children with learning disorders, there were five children who, in addition to the basic perceptual deviations in spatial and temporal organization, had neurological signs including marked choreiform motility or poor fine or gross motor coordination.

On follow-up examination 12 years later, when the children had grown into young adults, the five with neurological findings were the least adequate readers and retained the neuropsychological deficits they had as children. There was no significant perceptual maturation in that group. These findings suggest that, for these children with organic central nervous system deficit, the compensatory training done was not effective and that an alternate therapeutic approach was needed.

The relatively poor academic, occupational, social, and psychological prognosis for learning-disordered children who have neurological signs has been documented more recently by Spreen (1987) in a 10-year follow-up of a sample of learning-disordered children from a neuropsychological clinic. A. A. Silver and Hagin (1985), with a sample of 79 children drawn from a private practice of psychiatry and psychology, also found that 26% of the 19 children who had evidence for structural deficit of the central nervous system, in contrast to 7% of the specific language disability group, had poor or marginal occupational and educational outcome after 25 years of follow-up. Conversely, 14% of the specific language disability group had excellent outcomes in contrast to 5% of the organic children. All of these 79 children drawn from private practice had the advantage of middle- and upper-income families and received what was then considered optimal treatment.

There is thus a tenacity in the neurological deficits found in the organic child. The old dictum of "he will outgrow it" is outmoded, incorrect, and potentially disastrous for the academic and psychological fate of the child.

CASE REPORT: MARIA

Maria was 9 years 1 month of age when first seen in our clinic. She had been admitted to the third grade of an excellent private school, having been attending a special school for children with learning problems for the first three years of her schooling. Because of her problems with learning, the principal of the private school requested an evaluation.

Two years before her visit to us, Maria had been diagnosed with attention deficit disorder and had been receiving stimulant medication, first methylphenidate and then adderall for two years. During the past 6 months, she had developed a persistent grunting vocalization. She had been diagnosed as learning disabled since first grade.

Her past history revealed that Maria was 5 weeks premature, low forceps delivery with a birth weight of 2,670 grams. Tachycardia persisted after birth. After 24 hours in the ICU, her rapid heart rate decreased and she was transferred to the neonatal nursery. Pregnancy was complicated by the death of her father from liver cancer. Maria has never seen him. There is a history of academic difficulty in both her mother and father and in two half-brothers (paternal). An aunt and three cousins are said to have Tourette's syndrome. An aunt and a cousin are left-handed.

On examination, Maria is a small, slender, dark-haired 9-year-old girl weighing 48 pounds. There are no dysplastic facial features, but the thumb of each hand is short and stubby and fifth digit of each hand is small. The fourth digit of each toe is larger than the fifth. An occasional grunting vocalization is heard. She comes into the examination room with no apparent anxiety, seating herself cross-legged in the chair. She is not hyperactive and there are no rocking or dystonic movements. She relates well to the examiner, responding to verbal questions in a soft tone of voice, clearly and relevantly. She says her main trouble is math and reading. She wonders about this because she says she is smart. She says she does remember her father but goes on to say that she must be with her mother to be sure her mother is safe.

On neurological examination there are severe neuropsychological processing defects; visuomotor function (Bender-Gestalt) is severely impaired with stellate angulation errors, 45° verticalization, separation of figures, and overall gross disorganization. Visual discrimination and visual recall of asymmetrical figures are at about a 6-year level. There are static and kinetic reversals. Temporal sequencing of auditory and visual strings are impaired. She still has significant phonic difficulty. She is confused in right-left orientation, has gross errors in constructive finger praxis, and poor fine motor coordination. Synkinetic activity is marked. Her pencil grip is grossly abnormal. On the extension test, the left arm is elevated in this right-handed girl. Awake, drowsy, and sleep EEG is normal.

Unresolved emotional problems relate to her protective identification with her mother, her anxiety about her, and a magic feeling that she can protect her mother. She has never recovered from the loss of a father.

At 9 years 4 months, she earned a Full scale IQ of 97 (verbal 104, performance 90) on the WISC III, with subtest scores of 5 in Block Design and in Mazes; 5 in Digit Span (see Table 14.2). On the Woodcock-Johnson Tests of Achievement-R, calculation achievement was at a 1.6 grade level, writing 1.8, broad written language 1.9; on the W.-J. Tests of cognitive ability there were problems with memory for sentences, (Grade 1.9), visual auditory learning (Grade 1.9). On the Gordon diagnostic tests, Maria had no evidence of attention difficulty.

The extent of the neuropsychological processing deficits, the minor neurological signs, and possible stress at birth suggests that this was more than a developmental learning disability. The mild trauma (hypoxia?) at birth increased the severity of a familial defect in learning.

Table 14.2   **Wechsler Intelligence Scale for Children-III: Maria at 9 years and at 11 years, illustrating the persistent processing deficits of a child with static encephalopathy**

	1998	2000
Full scale IQ	97	82
Verbal IQ	104	85
Performance IQ	90	81
Verbal Subscale		
Information	9	8
Similarities	11	7
Arithmetic	10	5
Vocabulary	12	8
Comprehension	11	9
(Digit span)	5	8
Performance Subscale		
Picture completion	8	9
Coding	13	11
Picture arrangement	8	5
Block design	5	3
Object assembly	8	7
(Symbol search)	7	7
(Mazes)	5	

In management, stimulant medication was gradually reduced and clonidine substituted. Educational management was most important, however; in addition to compensatory measures in school, she needed direct training for each processing deficit.

Two years later, the neuropsychological processing deficits found two years before were still persistent and severe. Anxiety was more evident in dreams and in behavior. On psychological testing done two years after her previous testing, her Full Scale IQ had decreased from 97 to 82, verbal from 104 to 85, performance from 90 to 81. Broad written language on the Woodcock-Johnson Tests of Achievement (revised) was now at Grade 3.4; broad math, 4.7; and broad reading, 3.0; still at least 2 grades below her class placement. Maria was well aware of her persistent learning difficulty and of the homework battles with her mother, yet she was most comfortable in her school, felt she was liked there by classmates and teachers, as indeed she was, and enjoyed much of her school day. Her mother considered removing her from her school. It was felt that removing Maria from this school would be traumatic for her. The intensive remediation of her processing deficits that had not been done all these two years was finally started. In lieu of the after-school tension with her mother, her school day was extended and homework and tutoring were done at that time. Now 6 months later, her handwriting has improved, she is beginning to understand math concepts; she now is beginning to enjoy her reading.

Maria illustrates that the child with a learning disability that has an organic basis (static encephalopathy) in a family with a strong history of learning disability will not simply outgrow her deficits. Specific training of the neuropsychological processing deficits as outlined in the management section of this chapter is needed to overcome the deficits.

Effects of Seizure Disorder

This section does not attempt to provide an exhaustive survey of seizure disorders in childhood but focuses on aspects of seizure disorder with relevance to learning. It has been estimated that the prevalence of seizure disorders in the general school population may be as high as 4 per 1,000 children (Hauser & Hesdorffer, 1990), and prevalence of 4 to 9 per 1,000 in 10-year-old children (C. C. Murphy, Trevathan, & Yeargin-Allsopp, 1995). Seizures my be primary (idiopathic), occurring without any known structural defect, or secondary, associated with an identified structural central nervous system defect. The primary seizure is sometimes called uncomplicated in contrast to the secondary seizure, termed complicated.

Clinical and laboratory data (EEG, MRI) permit classifications of seizures as partial or generalized (Table 14.3). Partial seizures include simple partial seizures generally without impairment of consciousness and complex partial seizures, generally with impairment of consciousness. Partial seizures are also called focal seizures, with symptoms emanating from the temporal, frontal, parietal, or occipital lobes. Generalized seizures are bilaterally symmetrical and include grand mal and petit mal (absence) seizures and akinetic type seizures with a sudden loss of consciousness, followed by language impairment particularly word finding. Word-finding difficulty may last into a lengthy postictal period. Seizures may thus appear without the dramatic

Table 14.3 Classification of epilepsy and epileptic syndromes

Localization-Related Epilepsies

Partial (focal)
> Temporal lobe
> Frontal lobe
> Parietal lobe
> Occipital lobe

Idiopathic
> Benign Rolandic epilepsy with centrotemporal spike
> Childhood epilepsy with occipital paroxysms
> Primary reading epilepsy

Syptomatic
> Chronic progressive epilepsia partialies continua of childhood

Generalized Epilepsies and Syndromes

Idiopathic
> Benign neonatal familial convulsions
> Benign neonatal convulsions
> Benign myoclonic epilepsy in infancy
> Childhood absence epilepsy
> Juvenile absence epilepsy
> Juvenile myoclonic epilepsy
> Epilepsy with grand-mal seizures on awakening
> Other generalized epilepsies not defined above

Cryptogenic or symptomatic
> West syndrome (infantile spasms)
> Lennox-Gastaut syndrome
> Epilepsy with myoclonic-astatic seizures
> Epilepsy with myoclonic absences

Symptomatic
> Epilepsies and syndromes undetermined whether focal or generalized
> Neonatal seizures
> Severe myoclonic epilepsy in infancy
> Epilepsy with continuous spike-waves during slow wave sleep
> Acquired epileptic aphasia (Landau-Kleffner syndrome)

Special Syndromes
> Febrile convulsions
> Isolated seizures or isolated status epilepticus
> Seizures with acute metabolic or toxic event

Source: R. Caplan (1998). Epilepsy syndromes, pp. 978. In C. Coffey and R. Brumback (Eds.), *Textbook of Pediatric Neuropsychiatry.* Washington, DC: American Psychiatric Press. Reprinted by permission American Psychiatric Association.

appearance of a generalized convulsion, yet symptoms of partial epilepsy may be equally dramatic.

Seizure disorders as a group may influence learning for the following reasons:

- *Emotional Problems.* Children with seizure disorders have the tendency to develop more emotional problems than do the general school population. For example, in an epidemiological survey of the Isle of Wight, Rutter, Graham, et al. (1970) found 29% of 63 children suffering from uncomplicated epilepsy to have "psychiatric disorder" compared with 7% in the general population; this figure rose to 58% in "complicated" epilepsy. Mellor (1977, quoted in Corbett & Trimble, 1983) found the rate of psychiatric disorder in 308 children with epilepsy from schools in northeast Scotland to be 27% compared with 15% in matched controls. In the past, an "epileptic personality," with rigidity, irritability, and impulsive aggressive behavior, was described for these children (Keating, 1961). On the other hand, Corbett and Trimble felt that psychological disorders of children with seizure disorders are "of similar nature" to those found in nonepileptic children. However, as discussed in the section on medication for the control of impulse problems of organic children in general, there is evidence that some aggressive, impulsive behavior may indeed be due to complex partial seizures, particularly to psychomotor, temporal lobe seizures (D. Lewis et al., 1979). Baer, Freeman, and Greenberg (1984) described the "heightened intensity" of feelings and ideas as central to the interictal behavior of individuals with temporal lobe epilepsy; these include increased sensitivity, emotional lability, lowered threshold for anxiety, emotional clinging to teachers, unwillingness to relinquish ideas, difficulty in shifting ideas, compulsive behavior, hypergraphia, and possibly paranoid ideation (Hoare & Kerle, 1991).

  Partial seizures in general may herald their onset with a wide spectrum of motor, sensory, or autonomic symptoms. In the classroom, the complaint of unpleasant epigastric sensation, including nausea; sudden auditory, visual, or olfactory illusions (unpleasant odors) or déjà vu feelings; sudden arrest of a motor act in midstream; the development of automatism such as lip smacking, unusual hand movements, body movements or gestures all suggest a partial seizure particularly of temporal lobe origin. Frontal lobe epilepsy may involve unilateral focal motor movements; choreic movements, turning of the head and eyes, but no loss of consciousness (Salanova et al., 1995); or unilateral or bilateral posturing; tonic movements; vocalizations; laughing or crying (P. D. Williamson, 1995; A. Williamson, Spencer, & Spencer, 1995); tingling or pins and needles sensations (Quesney, Constain, Rasmussen, Olivier, & Palmini, 1992); emotions of fear or panic and changes in sympathetic tone (Swartz et al., 1990). In children with partial seizures, sexual disinhibiton, pressured and tangential speech, aggression, and disorganized behavior have been described (Stores, Zaiwalla, & Berger, 1991). These symptoms are many and varied depending on the anatomical origins of the seizure.

- *Memory, Learning, and Language Functions.* With overt seizures, a postictal confusional state, varying in duration is usual. Memory for events immediately preceding the seizures is effectively erased. In subclinical seizures, too, memory suffers and what may have been recently learned can no longer be recalled. In addition to ictal and postictal memory loss, interictal changes in memory are frequent and are particularly well documented in temporal lobe seizures. Word-finding difficulty is the most frequent language difficulty experience, although recall of visual spatial material is also impaired (D. F. Benson, 1991). While children with uncomplicated epilepsy are said to have a normal distribution of full scale IQ scores (Rutter, Tizard, et al., 1970), there is a greater variability in the *pattern* of subtest scores, with large verbal-performance discrepancies on the WISC. As a group, by the time children with uncomplicated epilepsy reach the age of 10, they tend to be reading about 1 year behind expectancy. Corbett and Trimble (1983) stated, "This masks the more serious findings that one in five such children are likely to show severe reading retardation and that children with complicated epilepsy have even higher rate of reading retardation" (p. 115). What is significant for learning is the memory defect associated with even subclinical seizures and that the pattern of perceptual and cognitive assets and deficits must be determined for each child.

- *Anticonvulsant Drugs.* Many of these have both overt and more subtle effects on cognition, memory, and attention (E. Reynolds, 1982). Phenobarbital, primidone, phenytoin, ethosuximide, and sodium valproate can impair attention, psychomotor speed and performance, memory, and mood. Phenobarbital may cause drowsiness, depression, irritability, and hyperkinetic behavior; phenytoin may decrease psychomotor performance and impair memory; clonazapam may induce drowsiness; and sodium valproate may induce weight gain, decrease platelets, cause liver toxicity, and impair psychomotor function. Carbamazepine appears to have fewer effects on cognition and memory, but it, too, must be closely monitored for hematological toxicity (Aman, Werry, Paxton, Turbott, & Stewart, 1990; E. Reynolds & Trimble, 1981). The effects of these drugs on cognition and memory are only one aspect of the widespread physical effects they may have. Indications for use of these drugs in the control of seizures will be considered later in this chapter. In our experience in a psychiatric clinic where children with difficult-to-control seizures who receive multiple combinations of drugs are referred, the reduction of medication will in selected children improve cognition and mood and may also reduce the frequency of seizures. The newer anticonvulsant medications topiramate, gabapentin, lamotrigine, felbamate, and vigabatrin are also not without their problems in the classroom. Each of these drugs may induce dizziness, nausea, ataxia, and drowsiness; with long-term use, they may impair cognition and, as indicated earlier, aspects of behavior. The anticonvulsant drugs will be discussed in greater depth in the medical management section of this chapter.

Fetal Alcohol Syndrome

Although suspected for centuries, the fetal alcohol syndrome has been fully described only relatively recently (Jones, Smith, Ulleland, & Streissguth, 1973; Warren & Bast, 1988). Ethanol may be the most frequent cause of teratogenetically induced mental deficiency in the Western World (J. E. Hardman & Limbird, 1996). Depending on the population studied, the incidence of full-blown fetal alcohol syndrome ranges from 1 to 300 to 1 in 2,000 live births, and in infants of alcoholic mothers, it is as high as 1 in 3 births. Stillbirths and spontaneous abortions occur two to three times more frequently in women who have three or more drinks daily during pregnancy than in those who have less than one drink each day. Seventy-five ml (2.5 oz) taken daily during pregnancy appears to be smallest quantity of alcohol associated with the fetal alcohol syndrome, and although it is not certain that there is any safe lower limits of alcohol drinking during pregnancy, a single glass of wine daily (15 ml, 0.5 oz) appears to have no adverse effect on the fetus.

The fetal alcohol syndrome encompasses a spectrum of deficits including physical, cognitive, and behavioral abnormalities (see Table 14.4).

Table 14.4   Features observed in Fetal Alcohol Syndrome/Fetal Alcohol Effects

Growth
   Prenatal and postnatal growth deficiency[†]
   Decrease adipose tissue[‡]

Performance
   Mental retardation[†]
   Developmental delay
   Fine-motor dysfunction
   Infant irritability,[†] child hyperactivity,[‡]
     and poor attention span
   Speech problems
   Poor coordination, hypotonia[‡]
   Cognitive, behavioral, and psychological
     problems

Craniofacial
   Microcephaly[†]
   Short palpebral fissures[†]
   Ptosis §
   Retrognathia in infancy[†]
   Maxillary hypoplasia[‡]
   Hypoplastic long or smooth philtrum[†]
   Thin vermillion of upper lip[†]
   Short upturned nose[‡]
   Micrognathia in adolescence[‡]

Skeletal
   Joint alterations including camptodactyly,
     flexion contractures at elbows,
     congenital hip dislocations
   Foot position defects

   Radioulnar synostosis
   Tapering terminal phalages, hypoplastic
     finger and toe nails ‖
   Cervical spine abnormalities
   Altered palm crease patterns §
   Pectus excavatum §

Cardiac
   Ventricular septal defect ‖
   Atrial septal defect §
   Tetralogy of Fallot, great vessel
     anomalies ‖

Other
   Cleft lip and/or cleft palate ‖
   Myopia, ‖ strabismus §
   Epicanthal folds §
   Dental malocclusion
   Hearing loss, protuberant ears
   Abnormal thoracic cage
   Strawberry hemangiomata §
   Hypoplastic labia majora §
   Microophthalmia, blepharophimosis
   Small teeth with faulty enamel ‖
   Hypospadias, small rotated kidneys,
     hydronephrosis ‖
   Hirsutism in infancy ‖
   Hernias of diaphragm, umbilicus or groin,
     diastasis recti ‖

From *Developmental Neuropsychiatry, Volume II: Assessment, Diagnosis and Treatment of Developmental Disorders* by James C. Harris. Copyright 1995 by Oxford University Press. Used by permission of Oxford University Press, Inc.

Principal (†, ‡) and associated (§, ‖) features observed in 245 affected individuals. † > 80%; ‡ > 50%; § 26% to 50%; ‖ 1% to 25% of patients.

CASE REPORT: DONALD

Donald was 11 years 4 months of age, in a residential home for emotionally disturbed children coming from dysfunctional families, and attending the 4th grade of a special school on that campus, when he was referred to us because of his aggressive behavior to peers, his resistance to authority, and his lack of response to the therapeutic milieu of the residential center.

He was born to an alcoholic mother, unmarried, in her early 20s when Donald was born. She dropped out of school when she was 16, pregnant with her first child, who now, at age 17, is in a juvenile detention center for robbery and assultive behavior. It is difficult to abstract from the records of the residential home in which Donald is placed, the amount of alcohol ingested while his mother was pregnant with Donald. She has however a history of alcoholism, admits to drinking daily, but denies cocaine or heroin. He was delivered at term in a precipitous delivery, with a birth weight of 3 pounds 7½ ounces. As an infant he was fretful and colicky, did not establish rhythmic patterns of sleeping, or eating, and had frequent respiratory infections. His developmental milestones: talking, walking, elimination were all significantly delayed and he remained irritable and verbally uncommunicative. He attended a preschool program for language-impaired children, was delayed until age 6 in his entrance to a kindergarten. By age 8 years, on the Stanford-Binet-R he earned an IQ of 65, one year later he earned a Full Scale WISC-R of 65 (verbal 60, performance 73). At that time, he was examined by a psychiatrist, a pediatrician, and a neurologist all of whom remarked on his small stature, his tremor, his difficulty in verbal communication. Equally important was the chaotic nature of his home. Residential placement was suggested.

At his visit with us, Donald had been in the residential center for two years. He was physically a small child appearing no older than 9 years of age. His head circumference was at the edge of normal limits. The right eye is distinctly smaller than the left, and indeed may be microphthalmic; there is an internal strabismus of the left eye. His upper lip is thin, pulled upward because of a short philtrum. His chin is small and retracted. He has an excoriation of the left corner of his mouth. His size and appearance give him a gaminlike quality. He is grossly restless, with continuous rhythmic movement of his legs, and a gross course intention tremor, which on extension of his arms is continuous. His fine motor coordination, as in finger-to-finger testing is poor with gross synkinesis. Gait is awkward; deep tendon reflexes are brisk in the lower extremities with transitory ankle clonus but appear normal in the upper extremities. There is mild dysdiadochokinesis and poor balance in tandem walking but normal Romberg and no dysmetria. Right-left discrimination, finger gnosis, and constructive finger praxis are each at about an 8-year level.

On neuropsychological testing, he has a severe deficit in the receptive and associative aspects of language, with a major problem in the temporal sequencing of sounds. As a result, his immediate auditory recall is poor, his auditory sequence ability is at about a 7-year level, and his capacity to sequence sounds in words is at a first-grade level. On the other hand, his vocabulary as measured by a picture vocabulary test is good, at a 10-year level. Visuomotor function is severely impaired, with primitive verticalization and perseveration on the Bender-Gestalt Test. These processing deficits interfere with his academic achievement and are symptoms of his overall impairment.

Emotionally, this child makes an effort to be liked, needing reassurance. His speech is under pressure, mildly circumstantial but relevant with no articulation defect. He dreams of monsters that "grab you" and try to get a "knife in you," about "cars running over you," about his brother "being punched." He is depressed and anxious. He likes the Children's Home because "it is safe." His feelings toward his mother are mixed. On the one hand, he is apprehensive of her explosive impulsive behavior, describing a time when she threw a beer bottle at his "father" requiring him to go to the emergency room for sutures. At the present time, he says he has a "new father" who apparently has a seizure disorder. Donald is aware that he, too, cannot control his temper; he tries to control his behavior, but he says he "gets scared" and then hits. There is aggression toward his mother and his new father. He feels physically and intellectually capable of dealing with his peers, but also feels that he is bad and certainly will be punished. In his head, he hears God telling him to be good and not hit other children.

Donald embodies the problems of the child with a fetal alcohol syndrome: physically small, dysplastic features; eyes small; chin small and receded; upper lip thin and tented; gross problems with fine motor condition; gross problems with equilibrium with language and visuomotor dysfunction; intellectually mildly retarded; poor impulse control, yet sensitive and aware of his deficits. The environment of his home intensified his anxiety, fears, and depression, provided little security and safety. Despite excellent emotional and educational care at the Children's home, his emotional and educational problems are resistant and persist.

As individuals like Donald grow into adolescence and adulthood, Streissguth, Aase, Clarren, et al. (1991) found that after puberty the facial features of fetal alcohol syndrome are not as distinctive as in childhood, but these individuals remain short, with small head, and although IQ varies, average IQ is 68, with academic achievement at about fourth-grade level. There are persistent problems with compulsivity, distractibility, and emotional lability, and continued unstable family environment.

The physical features of the syndrome are thought to be due, at least in part to a direct inhibitory effect of alcohol or acetaldehyde on embryonic cellular proliferation in the early months of gestation. Selective fetal malnutrition may also occur secondary to nutritional deficits of the alcoholic mother. Of interest is the report of Tsukahara, Eguchi, and Kajii (1986) who found that the 5 alcoholic mothers they studied all were positive for aldehyde dehydrogenase-2, yet 4 of the 5 girls with fetal alcohol syndrome, children of these alcoholic mothers, did not have this enzyme. This suggests that a genetic factor may be responsible for the missing enzymes, leading to susceptibility to alcohol. Morphologically, underdevelopment or absence of the corpus callosum and enlarged lateral ventricles have been reported. Microscopic study of a 4-month-old with fetal alcohol syndrome revealed decreased numbers and abnormal morphology of the dendritic spines of cortical pyramidal cells.

The child with fetal alcohol syndrome, like the cocaine baby and the premature, poses special problems to the school system. First, there must be recognition that the learning disabilities of these children are not purely developmental, nor developmental ADHD, but that there are structural abnormalities of the central nervous system, requiring comprehensive diagnosis including neuropsychological testing for assets and deficits. Second, management must also be comprehensive, collaborative, interdisciplinary, depending on the needs of each child. Educational management must be modified in occurrence with the principles discussed in Chapter 8 and in the final section of this chapter.

Prenatal Exposure to Cocaine

It is estimated that, each year in the United States, 375,000 newborns or approximately 10% of all live births will have been exposed to their mother's use of illegal drugs during pregnancy. Of these drugs, cocaine has been found to be the one most commonly detected in the peripartum period and accounts for more than half of the drug-associated births. Epidemiological surveys find a dramatic increase in illicit use of cocaine in the past decade, with a corresponding increase of cocaine use in females in their childbearing years, 18 to 34 (Church, Crossland, Holmes, & Overbeck, 1998; Hutchings, 1989).

The effects of cocaine on the fetus and on the infant and young child are complicated by the amount and frequency of the drug use in pregnancy, the frequent use of drugs other than cocaine, the generally poor parental care given by drug abusers, and the lack of consistent and appropriate parenting in a unstable drug-taking household. The effects of the drug on the pregnant mother include poor nutrition, weight loss, hypertension, cardiac arrhythmias, myocardial ischemia, anxiety, depression, exposure to trauma, and infection.

There is evidence that the use of cocaine during pregnancy is associated with increased rates of spontaneous abortions, abruptio placenta, preterm labor, and delivery of infants small for gestational age and with small head circumference. Hemorrhagic lesions confirmed by ultrasound, cerebral infarction and, in the retina, vascular disruptive lesions (hemorrhages with rounded, domed contours suggestive of venous occlusion) and retinal ischemia were found, all of which took longer time to resolve than did neonatal hemorrhages due to birth trauma. In one study, 38% of 28 cocaine-exposed infants had such lesions (Silva-Araujo, Tavares, Patacao, & Caroliono, 1996). Congenital malformations (craniostenosis), pre-, and postnatal death have been reported.

Nassogne, Evrard, and Courtoy (1998) report epidemiological surveys and experimental animal studies implicating cocaine in induction of teratogenic effects on the developing brain selectively affecting neuronal cells. Using cultures of embryonic brain cells, cocaine caused a dramatic reduction in the number and length of neurites, then extensive neuronal death. Cocaine did not affect the abundance of astroglial cells nor their glial fibrillary acidic protein content. These effects were not due to cocaine metabolites.

In addition, the cocaine-exposed neonate and infant exhibit a range of physiological disturbances, including tremor, irritability, and startle; abnormal cardiorespiratory patterns (greater duration of periods of apnea, periodic breathing, high respiratory rate, and abnormal respiratory patterns in sleep) and poor state control, increased extensor muscle tone, and persistence of primitive postural responses. State control difficulty may be seen in a variety of behaviors: deep sleep in response to external stimulation; agitated sleep in the labile awake-sleep state with a rapid change from agitated crying to deep sleep; and a panic state when awake. Even when the infant is awake, there are only brief periods of relating to a caretaker before gaze aversion, increased respiration, and disorganized motor activity occurs. There is increased risk of seizures (Keller & Snyder-Keller, 2000). The increased and persistent extensor tone interferes with normal motor development and even development of the body image. Other anomalies have been reported in the neonate: dilated tortuous iris vessels; generalized seizures; necrotizing enterocolitis (bowel ischemia secondary to vasoconstrictive properties of cocaine); and congenital malformations (Schneider, Griffith, & Chasnoff, 1989) involving hearing, vision, and language disorders (L. C. Mayes, Granger, Frank, Schottenfeld, & Bornstein, 1993; L. T. Singer, Garber, & Kleigman, 1991).

The difficulty with regulation of arousal and with attention seen in the cocaine infant is also seen in the preschooler. There is a "disruptive arousal regulation in the face of novel challenges, increased distractibility, and consequent impaired attention to novel, structural tasks" (L. C. Mayes, Grillon, Granger, & Schottenfeld, 1998). The regulation of arousal, serving as it does as a gating mechanism, has implications for ongoing information processing, learning, and memory and predisposes children to a lower threshold for stress, increasing their vulnerability to stress and to the environmental conditions often found with substance abusing families. In early school age, this child may be identified as ADHD, without recognition of the underlying organic cause of the behavior.

Studies on neuropsychological process in longer-term outcome of cocaine exposure during pregnancy are scant. Chasnoff, Griffith, Freir, and Murray (1992) found that head circumference of the cocaine children remained significantly smaller at ages 2 and 3 years and that although there was no difference in overall performance between drug-free and cocaine-exposed children on the Stanford-Binet Intelligence Test, approximately one third of the cocaine children had delays in language development and/or difficulties with attention and self-regulation (quoted by Harris, 1996a, p. 371). Earlier studies (Rodning, Beckworth, & Howard, 1989) found that at age 2 years, cocaine-exposed children were disorganized in their play and in social, cognitive, and affective areas. At 18 months, they showed an abnormal affective blandness on separation from their mothers.

Easton and Bauer (1996) evaluated neuropsychological differences among four groups of men and women ages 15 to 61 years. The groups were defined on the basis of urine toxicology screen, indicating recent use of cocaine ($n = 12$), cannabis ($n = 14$), multiple drug use ($n = 7$), or no such use ($n = 21$). The Wechsler Adult Intelligence Scale-Revised, Trail Making Tests, and Porteus Man Test were given to all subjects. No significant differences in age, gender, histories of alcohol/drug use, or Anti-Social Personality Disorder were found. However, the cocaine positive groups had statistically significant impairment in Verbal IQ, as well as in Information, Vocabulary, Comprehension, Picture Completion, and Trails B Subtests. The other two experimental groups did not differ from the urine negative group. Although this study does not deal specifically with cocaine exposure during pregnancy, it suggests specific effects of cocaine. An unanticipated complication of the drug traffic is the swallowing of packets of cocaine by teenage couriers when they are confronted by customs officers. Aldrighetti, Paganelli, Giacomelli, and Villa (1996) report on 61 teenagers who swallowed packets containing cocaine as they were apprehended at Milan International Airports. Signs of acute cocaine toxicity is described, but no follow-up had been done.

The disturbed physiological, behavioral, and cognitive effects of cocaine represent a direct response to cocaine and are not a cocaine withdrawal syndrome. Cocaine readily crosses the placental barrier, and is metabolized slowly by the fetus and the neonate; an active metabolic product, norcocaine, readily penetrates the central nervous system. A recycling of norcocaine through the amniotic fluid may permit long exposure to the drug. Cocaine may also be ingested by neonates, when they are breast-fed by cocaine-taking mothers.

Cocaine, a short-acting (15 to 30 minutes) stimulant of the central nervous system and of the peripheral sympathetic portion of the autonomic system, is a potent blocker of the reuptake of norepinephrine, dopamine, and serotonin from the synaptic cleft, acutely potentiating the catecholamine effects. Activation of the central dopamine system results in stimulation of the central reward system. This effect is abolished by pimozide (dopamine receptor blockade) but not by phentolamine (norepinephrine receptor antagonist); and is reinforced by apomorphine (dopamine receptor agonist) but not by clonidine (alpha 2 agonist), suggesting that dopamine activation is related to the euphoric effect of cocaine. With chronic exposure to cocaine, however, there is a depletion of catecholamines and a compensatory increase in both the number and sensitivity of their receptors. It is postulated that the catecholamine blocked in reuptake is rapidly metabolized by catechol-O-methyltranferase, rendering the catecholamine unavailable for reuse. In addition, cocaine appears to inhibit catecholamine vesicle binding, exposing the catecholamine to intracellular metabolism. A compensatory increase in synthesis cannot overcome the chronic depletion, leading to the hypothesis of catecholamine depletion, particularly dopamine, as a physiological mechanism for cocaine dependency with withdrawal (Extein & Dackis, 1987).

It would be reasonable to expect that cerebral infarction will have long-term effects on learning and behavior and that the effects of hypoxia on the central nervous system would not be different from those described in an earlier section of this chapter. Hypothetically, the sensitivity of the neonate to external stimulation certainly suggests an effect of cocaine on sensorineural processing, which may have long-term cognitive sequelae and/or persist as problems in impulse control.

Human Immunodeficiency Disease (HIV) in Children

At the end of the year 1997, it was estimated that one million children, worldwide, were living with the HIV virus and suffering from the physical and psychological consequences of that infection. The number of children, worldwide, who have died from the consequences of HIV since the beginning of the epidemic in the late 1970s is estimated to be 2,700,000, and by the year 2020 another 40,000,000 will die from AIDS. Throughout the world, 1,000 babies a day become infected with HIV (M. G. Fowler,

1997). In the United States, approximately 15,000 children are currently infected with HIV and its consequences, AIDS. In 1996, AIDS was ranked as the seventh leading cause of childhood mortality in the 1 to 4 years age group and the sixth leading cause of death among 15 to 24-year-olds. In states with the highest prevalence of HIV/AIDS (New York, Florida, New Jersey), it was one of the leading causes of death in childhood. The prevalence of HIV is disproportionally large in children of minority populations, with 58% of the reported cases African American; 23%, Hispanic; and 18%, White.

Each year, approximately 7,000 women infected with HIV deliver live-born infants. The number of perinatally acquired HIV infection in children less than 13 years old rose rapidly from less than 100 new cases reported in 1979 to 500 new cases in the year 1992, as reported annually in the CDC. Since then, there has been a gradual decline to approximately 300 new cases in 1996 (Simonds, 1999).

Approximately 90% of HIV children have acquired their infection through perinatal (vertical, or mother-to-child) transmission, 10% from infected blood products in transfusions or in the treatment of hemophilia. HIV may be transmitted in breast-feeding. It is estimated that 3% to 4% of HIV women breast-feed their infants. Assuming that the risk of acquiring HIV from breast-feeding is 5% to 10% among infants who are not infected from perinatal exposure, an estimated 20 to 40 infants in the United Sates become infected annually from breast-feeding. There have been cases of HIV infection acquired through sexual abuse and very rarely through blood exposure in household settings. Simonds (1999) cautioned that cases of blood transmission in household settings, "must be kept in perspective . . . several studies of more than 1,000 household contacts with persons infected with HIV have documented no HIV transmission within these settings and no cases of transmission within school or day care settings have been reported" (p. 6).

Because the preponderance of pediatric HIV occurs by vertical transmission from HIV-infected mothers, during pregnancy, during delivery, or through breast-feeding, preventing these infections involves three strategies: (a) preventing HIV infection in women of reproductive age, (b) preventing unwanted pregnancies in HIV-infected women, and (c) preventing transmission of HIV from HIV-infected pregnant women to their infants. Prevention of HIV from mother to child during pregnancy has in the United States resulted in significant decline in rates of perinatal transmission, from 25% in an untreated group to 8% in the treated group (Sperling et al., 1996). These results first reported in 1996, involved the oral administration of antiviral medication (Zidovudine, ZDV) to known HIV-infected mothers, starting at 14 to 34 weeks of gestation, intravenously during labor, and to the newborn for the first 6 weeks of life. This regimen has been approved by the U.S. Food and Drug Administration, and the Centers for Disease Control and Prevention (Center for Disease Control and Prevention, 1994, 1995). It is effective despite maternal viral load, immune status, and other risk factors; maternal smoking, illicit drug use, nutritional factors, and social factors.

Determining the best approach to HIV testing of pregnant women however has been controversial, whether testing be voluntary or mandatory, whether the focus should be on testing pregnant women or testing the newborn. The U.S. Public Health Services recommends that testing should be voluntary. The acceptance rate of testing by women in pregnancy has been high ranging from 80% to 90% (E. J. Abrams & Bateman, 1995; Immergluck, Cull, Schwartz, & Elstein, 2000).

So effective are the prevention measures that H.R. 4426, introduced in Congress on May 11, 2000, mandated that a universal routine testing of pregnant women and newborns be the standard of care. This bill was supported by the American Medical Association and Institute of Medicine.

Modifications of the original Sperling et al. (1996) protocol have been introduced. The administration course of antiviral prophylaxis has been shortened to starting at 36 weeks of gestation and given orally during labor, has been effective in reducing transmission risk by approximately 50% in a non-breast-feeding population in Thailand (cited in Molfenson & Wilfert, 1998). Alternate or combinations of antiretroviral regimes are in progress and surgical procedures to reduce peripartum exposure to HIV in genital secretions have been in use. Reports of a small number of serious events of newborns to antiretroviral prophylaxis are under investigation (Thorne & Newell, 2000).

These preventive procedures have led to rapid implementation and dramatic decrease in new perinatal HIV infected new borns in the United Sates and in Europe since 1994. This is not the practice in the developing countries where 600,000 neonates continue to be infected by mother-infant HIV transmission each year. (M. G. Fowler, Simonds, & Roongpisuthipong, 2000). Further medical efforts are now shifting from caring for children with advanced immunosuppression and severe opportunistic infections to early maintenance of the immune system and prevention of opportunistic infections. Laufer and Scott (2000) report that although published data are limited, physicians have observed a dramatic improvement in quality of life and length of survival of these children.

The severity of symptoms and signs of the disease, and level of immune suppression in general, determines the longevity of the child with HIV. In 1994, the Centers for Disease Control and Prevention provided a clinical classification for children, which classifies the HIV-infected child in accordance with severity and immune suppression into stages: N = no signs or symptoms of the disease, A = mild signs or symptoms, B = moderate signs or symptoms, and C = severe signs or symptoms. Criteria for each stage is defined; the criteria for immune suppression is based in age-specific CD4 cell counts. A minority of HIV-infected newborns deteriorate rapidly; mortality rate in the first year of life is approximately 10%. In the 2nd year of the infection, most progress to stage B (moderate) and typically remain at this stage for over 5 years, before progressing to stage C where the mortality percentage was 83%. However median survival age is now estimated to be 9 years of age (Grubman, Gross, Lerner-Weiss, et al., 1995). There are long-term pediatric survivors who are over 9 years of age and into their teenage years. Why these children survive is not yet clearly understood. Inheritance of genes (HLA and others) may be associated with relatively rapid or delayed progression of the disease. Children whose HIV infection stemmed from HIV-infected blood or from blood products (hemophilia) usually acquire the infection at a later age than did the children with perinatally acquired infection, and the mean age of these children is early adolescence. Since 1985 when blood donors were first screened for HIV and heat treatment of clotting factors was introduced, the annual incidence of HIV in children with hemophilia declined from a high of 35 infections per year in 1988 to 3 in 1996. Transfusion-acquired HIV decreased from a high of 50 per year in 1987 to 30 in 1996.

Neurodevelopment and Neuropsychological Function in Children with HIV-1 Infection

Approximately 50% of children with HIV infection will develop some degree of CNS disease (Englund, Baker, Raskino, et al., 1996), about 13% to 23% with the most severe form—progressive encephalopathy. While astrocytes, macrophages, and microglia appear to be affected by HIV, neurons appear to be unaffected. Where immune deficiency occurs, secondary complications (tumors, infections, and cerebrovascular disease) may appear, occurring mostly in older children. The prevalence and severity of CNS disease is greatest in infants (66% to 75%), while adolescents (33%) tend to have less severe manifestations. Specific criteria for classification of HIV-related CNS dysfunction used by the HIV and AIDS malignancy branch of the National Cancer Institute, are presented in Wolters and Brouwers (1998, pp. 212–213) divided into four main patterns:

1. Encephalopathy characterized by pervasive and severe dysfunction with global impairment in cognitive, language, motor, and social skills and in significant neurological findings that affect day-to-day functioning. Encephalopathy may be progressive (most severely common in infants and young children), either subacute with progressive global deterioration or slower in progression (plateau), in which the acquisition of new skills becomes slow and there is a decline in neuropsychological test scores. Children with static encephalopathy do gain new skills and abilities, but at a slower rate than normal peers.

2. HIV-related CNS compromise, characterized by overall normal cognitive function, but with impairment in selective rather than global neuropsychological function. Children who were functioning within normal limits at baseline and who have improved after 6 months of antiviral drugs are also classified in this group. CNS compromise is not listed in the CDC classification for pediatric HIV/AIDS.

3. Apparently unaffected; cognitive function at least normal without decline in function and without neurological abnormalities that affect day-to-day function and without medication related improvement.

4. Non-HIV-related CNS impairment (drugs, prematurity, other medical risk factors). Children may have both HIV and non-HIV-related impairments.

Overall measures of general cognitive function are sensitive to changes in CNS function and correlate well with brain imaging, cerebrospinal fluid analysis and viral and immunological data (Wolters & Brouwers, 1998). However, domains of neuropsychological function such as language, attention, memory-adaptive behavior, hearing, and visuomotor function may be differentially affected. Tardieu, Mayaux, Seibel, et al., 1995, examined 33 vertically infected children, born before 1985. They were followed to the age of 6 years and tested with a battery evaluating cognitive ability, fine motor and language skills, and emotional adaptation. Of the 33 children, 22 (67%) at mean age 9.5 ± 1.6 years, had a mean IQ of 95 ± 11. However 44% had delayed language development and/or articulation defects and 54% had visuospatial problems and difficulty with time orientation. Grubman et al. (1995) found that of 42 vertically infected children, ages 9 to 16 years, approximately 25% were asymptomatic with relatively intact immune systems, while the remaining children had significant symptoms of HIV infection. Fifty-eight percent of the 42 children had normal neurological examination but 5% had isolated hearing loss. Twelve percent had problems with attention. Most of the sample (76%) were in regular education classes, but half of those children were behind in academic achievement and 25% of the total were in special education programs. McClowry (2000), reviewing the literature relating to neuropsychological processing defects in HIV-infected children, also found a heterogeneous spectrum of deficits, including communication and language, thought and emotion, and written language disorders. Communication problems included hearing loss (less than 10%) believed to be a sequel of recurrent otitis media (Mintz, 1998), dysphagia or dysarthria with drooling when the disease is severe, articulation problems (H. J. Cohen, Papola, & Alvarez, 1994), poor vocabulary, phonemic difficulty and receptive language better than expressive (Wolters, Brouwers, Moss, & Pizzo, 1995). Wolters, Brouwers, and Perez, 1999, however suggested that the underlying deficits in language may be related to difficulty in retrieval of information, semantics, or syntactic structure. Wolters and Brouwers (1998) also found that children with HIV encephalopathy have less ability than children with HIV without encephalopathy to express themselves by nonverbal means (facial expression and expressive symbolic language). Expressive language problems may be the first sign of decline. Caplan (1998) stated: "Language deterioration is seen frequently in the absence of abnormalities on neurological examination or CNS imaging and may precede evidence of deterioration in global cognitive ability" (p. 8, quoted in McClowry, 2000).

That the child with central nervous system problems associated with cognitive defects would have some difficulty with learning should come as no surprise. In a sample of 48 children mean age 11.5 months who acquired their HIV infection through neonatal blood transfusion, S. E. Cohen et al., 1991, found that when compared with a control group of noninfected children with similar transfusion histories, the HIV-positive group has significantly lower reading scores across time. Most vertically infected children of school age have age-appropriate learning and academic performances but their level of functioning is below that expected from their global IQ (Wolters et al., 1999). However, motor impairment in this group may interfere with visuomotor function and any written language.

Neuropsychological functions in children with hemophilia and HIV infection were studied. Six domains of neuropsychological function (motor, language, memory, attention, visual processing, and problem solving) were measured in 63 children and adolescents with hemophilia (25 HIV-positive, 38 HIV-negative) all with similar age, race, and socioeconomic status. A high incidence of subtle neuropsychological deficits relative to age norms and cognitive potential was found on measures of motor performance, attention, and speeded visual processing within both the infected and noninfected groups. Whitt et al. (1993) concluded, "It seems premature to attribute early neuropsychological deficits in seropositive children with hemophilia to the central nervous system effects of HIV infection." In 1996, S. D. Mayes et al. reviewed psychological and educational data of 66 school-age boys with hemophilia, HIV-infected, at the Hemophilia Center of Central Pennsylvania and found the mean IQ to be 113.5. There were, however, 28.3% with ADHD and 15.8% with learning disabilities and graphomotor weakness. These findings were not statistically associated with HIV status or type and severity of the coagulation disorder. In a large study of 277 HIV-positive and 126 HIV-negative boys with hemophilia, S. Nichols et al. (2000) found declining Vineland communication scores for boys with declining immune function but "considerable resilience in adaptive behavior."

Behaviorally a Q sort behavioral rating for pediatric HIV patients was devised by H. A. Moss et al. (1994). As we would expect, children (mean age 7.8 years) with symptoms of encephalopathy had higher scores measuring depression, irritability, and withdrawal than peers without evidence of CNS infection.

Public Education for HIV-Infected Children and Preventive Education

Public schools have two major responsibilities responding to the epidemic of HIV infection in children and adolescents: (a) education of children who are infected with the HIV virus and (b) the continuing responsibility for the education of all students, K-12, with the goal of prevention of HIV and all sexually transmitted diseases.

By law, public schools are required to provide education, in the least restrictive environment, for children with HIV, to the extent that the child's health permits. These children fit into the broad classification of handicapped and as such their civil rights are protected by Public Law 94-142, the Education of all Handicapped Children Act, which was reauthorized in 1990 and again in 1997 under the name of Individuals with Disabilities Education Act (IDEA). As recommended by the Committee on Pediatric AIDS of the American Academy of Pediatrics and also by the Center for Disease Control, "Infected children should be admitted without restriction to child care centers, and schools, and allowed to participate in all activities to the extent that their health and other recommendations for management of contagious disease permit" (Committee on Pediatric AIDS, 2000). As treatment for HIV infection becomes more effective, more children with HIV are living to school age and even well into adolescence, high school age; thus more children with HIV infection will be enrolled in schools.

For the schools, the imposition of this legal, moral, and humane responsibility has posed problems as well as opportunities. In the late 1980s and early 1990s, parents' disclosure of the HIV status of their child resulted in their child being isolated, ostracized, being treated like a pariah, "the leper syndrome" (J. Adler, Greenberg, McKillop, & Namuth, 1985). Communities even united in violence against the families of HIV children. It will be recalled that Ryan White was denied admission to his local high school and the home of the Ray family was burned to the ground. These reactions were based on fear of contagion to their own children and even to themselves. Although knowledge of the disease has, in part, quelled such reactions, fears still remain, not only of the child transmitting HIV to his schoolmates but also fears of the teachers and other school personnel being vulnerable to the infection. The sexual nature of transmission of the virus also brought on the child the wrath of the sins of his father. It is understandable that parents would be reluctant to inform the school of their child's HIV, fearing the ensuing hysterical backlash. With the present knowledge of HIV, however, parental disclosure of their child's HIV infection is most important, not only for appropriate educational placement and management but also for the child's physical well-being in receiving timely medication from the school nurse and in being protected from the usual infections of childhood. Disclosure to principal, teacher, and nurse, however, does not mean disclosure to all the school; confidentially must be respected; all medical knowledge of the particular child must be kept confidential, unless released by the child's parents. Disclosure to the child, too, must be withheld until his parents agree that the child is capable of bearing the disclosure. In schools where there has been smooth integration of HIV-infected children, specific policies and procedures based on collaboration between health providers and education have been helpful: expedited clinical evaluation of each case; an interagency review panel; strict protection of confidentiality; appropriate restricted, if needed, placement for certain children; a school site visit for each placement; and continued monitoring by school nurses and avoidance of media reporting (Santelli, Birn, & Linde, 1992).

HIV transmission from infected child to classmates or to school personnel has never been documented to take place in school. However, the guidelines for infection control developed by the Occupational Safety and Health Administration (OSHA) in 1991 are required to be implemented by schools. These guidelines are not directed specifically at control of HIV infection but are recommended for all blood-borne pathogens. Risk for transmission of HIV is directly related to exposure to contaminated body fluids, preferentially those containing cells expressing a specific antigen (CD4, T-lymphocytes, and monocytes). Although the HIV virus has been recovered from many body fluids, (blood, genital secretions, amniotic fluid, breast milk, saliva, tears, throat swabs), it is the splatter or spraying of contaminated material onto nonintact skin or mucous membrane that is the concern of school safety. Transmission through oral secretion (children putting objects and fingers in their mouths) or by children biting without breaking the skin has been investigated and transmission from these events is said to exponentially rare, if it occurs at all. Nevertheless even with these events, OSHA procedures need to be followed. Blood resulting from fights, injuries, nosebleed, shed teeth, menstruation, and from any other causes must be managed in accordance with OSHA guidelines.

It is fortunate that HIV virus does not survive for an extended time on environmental surfaces; it is highly susceptible to many disinfectants, including bleach diluted at 1:10 to 1:100 concentration of bleach to water. Appropriate materials for cleaning up and disposal of the used materials should be available.

Detailed guidelines for universal, now called standard, precautions for prevention of blood-borne infection may be found in OSHA 1991 and in Hospital Infection Control Practice Advisory Committee, 1996. The principles of prevention of transmission of blood-borne pathogens include barrier to contact with blood or other body fluids and the handling and disposal of blood and body fluids. For example in schools, gloves are to be used when in contact with blood, bloody fluid secretions, mucous membrane, and nonintact skin of all children; hands should be washed immediately after contact with any of these fluids, and after removal of gloves. Table 14.5 lists the standard precautions against HIV that should be practiced in schools.

In addition to accepting and providing appropriate education for children who are infected with HIV, schools also have the responsibility, as part of their health education program for preventive education for all children K to 12. This education "should be developmentally appropriate, ethically and culturally sensitive and should be mandatory for graduation" (American Academy of Pediatrics, 1993, p. 935). The National Association for State Boards of Education (NASBE; 2000) has also provided guidelines in the task of schools to promote "healthy behaviors," particularly since HIV education, which includes sex education, may provoke controversy among those concerned with schools interfering with rights of parents in sex education, particularly in promoting safe sex in addition to advocating abstinence. The NASBE, in addition to "promoting the teaching of HIV prevention within the context of a broader, sequential and age appropriate health education program," requires the involvement of students, parents, faith-based organizations, and other community members in the designs and implementation of HIV prevention and health promotion programs. The NASBE policy update recommends a strong and engaging academic program, comprehensive health education, effective HIV education, a "balanced message" concerning the prevention of sexually transmitted disease and of pregnancy, staff development and building of public understanding and support. Data from a Youth Risk Behavior Survey (Chanock, 1999) indicates that 90.6% of the nation's high school students have received HIV/AIDS prevention instruction in schools. The 1999 survey also reports a decline in the number of students who have been sexually active, and among those who are sexually active there has been an increase in condom use and a decrease in number of sexual partners.

Table 14.5   Standard precautions against HIV

Precaution	When Used
Handwashing	Before and after contact with body fluids Always after removing gloves
Gloves	When contact with body fluid is anticipated
Mask/eye protection	When splattering of body fluid is likely
Nonsterile gown	To protect skin/clothing from splashes when splashes of blood or infected body fluids are anticipated; dispose of properly for cleaning
Patient equipment	When exposed to blood or body fluids; handle carefully to avoid splattering
Linen	Change and dispose of without exposure to others
Surface cleaning	Thorough cleaning of exposed surface Removal of blood and other fluids Disinfect with bleach solution

Effects of Head Injury

Head injury due to falls and to traffic accidents is a common event in school-age children, and accidents at home account for a significant proportion of head injury in preschool children. In closed head injuries, there may be contusion and laceration at the point of impact, with *contre coup* injury most marked in temporal and orbital regions. Subdural bleeding may occur and the events described in the neuropathological section of this chapter ensue. In open injuries with local laceration, intracranial bleeding is generally more severe and involves fracture of the bone. Cognitive and behavioral dysfunction, resulting from head injury and recovery from that dysfunction, is of importance in learning.

An intensive study of dysfunction after head injury and its persistence was done on a sample of 5- to 14-year-old children obtained from regional neurosurgical units in southeast England and consisting of consecutive admissions of children with acute head injury (Chadwick, Rutter, Brown, Shaffer, & Traub, 1981; Chadwick, Rutter, Shaffer, & Shrout, 1981; Chadwick, Rutter, Thompson, & Shaffer, 1981; Rutter, 1977, 1981) reviewed by Rutter, Chadwick, and Shaffer (1983). Basing the severity of head injury on the duration of posttraumatic amnesia (PTA)—the period of time following the injury during which recent events are not remembered reliably, consistently, or accurately—the London group found the duration of PTA to be a reasonably good predictor of long-term cognitive, physical, and emotional recovery. Three groups of children were studied, one with posttraumatic amnesia of seven days or more; the second with a PTA of less than seven days but of at least 1 hour duration; and the third a control group of hospital-treated children who also suffered severe accidents but with orthopedic rather than cranial injuries. All children were examined with detailed psychological testing immediately after the accident and then at 4 months, 1 year, and 2½ years after the injury. The study concluded:

- The intellectual deficit is greatest immediately after acute brain damage, and progressive improvement occurs mostly during the first year.
- Severe injuries cause intellectual impairment, but mild injuries do not. With a posttraumatic amnesia of less than 2 weeks, there was only one child (of 8) with transient impairment as seen on performance IQ score of the WISC, and none with persistent impairment; transient impairment was characteristic of the children with PTA between 2 to 3 weeks; but persistent intellectual impairment, at 2½-year follow-up, was found in those with PTAs of at least 3 weeks. Other indices of severity (duration of coma or prolonged unconsciousness) also were predictive of residual impairment.
- Timed visuospatial tests showed more marked impairment and more resistance to recovery 2 years after injury than did verbal tests, regardless of which brain hemisphere was damaged. There was a slight but consistent tendency for all tests of scholastic attainment to show greater impairment with left-hemisphere lesions, and this tendency was more marked in children who were under 5 years of age at the time of injury.

- The rate of psychiatric disorder in the severe head injury group had markedly increased at the 4-month follow-up period and remained more than double that for the control group over the entire 2½-year follow-up period; the rate of psychiatric disorder in the mild injury group was not significantly different from that of controls over the follow-up period.

- Although, in general, most psychiatric problems in the head injury group resembled those in the control group, a pattern of social disinhibition, resembling the frontal lobe disinhibition found in adults, was found in children after severe head injury. This pattern included showing general disregard for social conventions, asking embarrassing questions, and making personal remarks—all behaviors considered socially unacceptable. The early findings of a generalized hyperactivity, impulsive behavior, and resistance to discipline as reported by earlier writers were not confirmed.

- No relationship was found between site of injury and symptoms of overactivity, inattention, aggression, or antisocial behavior. However, there was an association between depression and lesions in the right frontal and left posterior regions.

- Psychological adversity when combined with severe head injury increases the vulnerability to psychiatric disorder.

Effects of *Haemophilus Influenzae* Meningitis

Early reports of the sequelae of *Haemophilus influenzae* meningitis were characterized by high morbidity, with hemiparesis, sensorineural hearing loss, perceptual deficits, and learning and behavior problems found in over 20% of survivors (Sell, Merrill, Doyne, & Zimsky, 1972; Sproles, Azerrad, Williamson, & Merrill, 1969). More recent studies have tempered the pessimistic reports. Follow-up review of subjects and their control siblings found comparable educational achievement and intellectual function (Emmett, Jeffrey, Chandler, & Dugdale, 1980; Tejani, Dobias, & Samburskey, 1982), and a 1984 study (H. G. Taylor, Michaels, Mazur, Baver, & Linden, 1984), of the intellectual and neuropsychological outcomes of 24 children, 6 to 8 years after *H. Influenzae* meningitis, found these children performed as well as their siblings on individually administered tests of reading, spelling, and arithmetic.

Despite the adequate academic achievement, however, the postmeningitis children were not without problems. First, although the mean IQ was within the normal range for both postmeningitis and sibling groups, the full scale IQs and performance IQs were lowered significantly; enough to lower the IQ scores for the postmeningitis group relative to that of their siblings. Second, there were significant group differences in favor of the sibling controls on the Token test (sequential auditory language), in memory and retrieval of a list of spoken words, and in tasks of fine motor and perceptual motor abilities. Third, in terms of frequency of handicapping conditions, defined as low IQ or academic scores or requiring special education help, 47% of the postmeningitis children, compared with 29% of their siblings, were considered mildly handicapped. Although the academic and behavioral performance of children who had had *H. influenzae* between 1973 and 1975, at an average age of 1 year 4 months, was similar to that of their siblings, for the most part, these children had subtle neuropsychological deficits for which they received some compensatory additional school help. Predictors of outcome were a combination of medical variables (age at time of the disease, cerebrospinal fluid glucose and protein levels, and fever duration). The younger the child, the poorer the outcome.

The same 24 children of the 1984 Taylor study were retested by Feldman and Michaels (1988) 4 years later, approximately 10 to 12 years after the original infection. By 1988, the children were at a mean age of 12 years 7 months, with a grade placement of 6.9; mean age of control siblings was 14 years 6 months, with a grade placement of 9.8. The postmeningitis children had no greater academic, behavioral, or attentional problems in school than did their control siblings; and as determined by scores on a child behavior problems checklist completed by parents, they had no greater behavioral or attentional problems at home. Only four postmeningitis children had hearing loss or neurological sequelae. One child with seizures who had tested in the retarded range in the 1984 study remained in a special program for educable retarded children at the time of the 1988 study. There was a general finding, however, that the postmeningitis children received more academic support in school, used more remedial services and, at home, received more homework help from parents.

What is apparent from these studies, is that *H. influenzae* meningitis is associated with persistent neuropsychological sequelae that, although for the most part mild, require comprehensive evaluation and increased academic and family support. Animal studies (Konkol et al., 1987) suggest that *Haemophilis influenzae* meningitis causes a significant elevation of forebrain norepinephrine and dopamine levels in the rat and that the behavioral changes in surviving rats could be explained by "long-lasting perturbation of central monoamine neuronal transmission" (p. 253).

Effects of Radiation to the Central Nervous System

Modern radiation for malignancies in childhood has increased the overall long-term survival rate, so that by now there is a group of children who may be evaluated for the presence of delayed neuropsychological effects (Meadows & Silber, 1985). This is particularly true for children with acute lymphatic leukemia who have received 2,400 RAD of cranial or craniospinal radiation given in combination with five or six doses of intrathecal methotrexate. In a group of 18 children so treated in 1975, reexamination 3 to 5 years after termination of treatment found 11 of the 18 to earn IQ scores 10 or more points lower than their premorbid IQ scores, with the greatest declines in children younger than 5 years of age and in those with an initial IQ greater than 110 (Meadows et al., 1981). Retrospective studies are consistent with the Meadows' prospective one; treatment with radiation (2,400 RAD) to the cranium resulted in lower IQ scores than treatment with intrathecal methotrexate, with or without other agents, intravenous methotrexate, or no central nervous treatment at all (Copeland et al., 1985; Rowland et al., 1984). Radiation also appears to induce cerebral calcification, 5 to 7 years after onset of treatment (Riccardi, Brouwers, Dichiro, & Poplack, 1985).

Cranial irradiation for brain tumors may also in the long term contribute an overall low level of intellectual function with impairment of short-term memory.

What is significant is that the increased survival rate will permit more children who have been treated for acute leukemia and for brain tumor to return to classrooms. Careful evaluation of their impairment as well as their impact functions is necessary for adequate and appropriate management of their ensuing learning problems.

MEDICAL AND EDUCATIONAL MANAGEMENT

In this section, we consider the management of children whose central nervous system pathology is chronic rather than acute, resulting from some type of trauma (hypoxia) that occurred early in the child's life or from some acute process (head injury or infection) later in childhood. Both leave some residual imprint on information processing and/or on behavior. These children have been described by S. Carter (personal communication) as suffering from a "static" (nonprogressive) encephalopathy. In accordance with the position in this book, appropriate and adequate management must rest on careful evaluation, not only of the etiological factors responsible for the organic state but also of the neurological, emotional, cognitive, social, family, and educational factors within which the child must function; in short, a pentaxial evaluation as outlined in Chapters 6 and 7. Of particular relevance to learning problems is a detailed analysis of the child's abilities and disabilities in dealing with information and of the ability to modulate impulses.

In general, intervention is indicated to help with the three general groups of symptoms stemming from organic central nervous system defect discussed earlier in this chapter: the modulation and control of impulses; the processing of information; and the problems with muscle tone, coordination, and synergy. In addition, the emotional reactions and defenses to these basic problems within the child and within his or her family and school frequently require intervention. Psychotherapy, behavior management, medication, physiotherapy, and education all have a place in planning for these children. The use of medication and the principles of educational management are of concern here.

Effects of Medication

Except in the presence of seizure disorder, medication is *not* the first line of management for the child with a structural central nervous system defect who has a learning disorder. Specific remedial education is essential. Effective remediation of perceptual defects, the support of psychotherapy, and an understanding environment will improve academic function and reduce impulsivity so that medication may not be needed. Nevertheless, there are children in whom impulse control is so poor that psychopharmacological control is helpful. There are two general groups of symptoms relating to impulse control. Most frequent are children who resemble the child with pure Attention-Deficit/Hyperactivity Disorder, except that in the organic child definite or presumptive evidence for brain damage is found. These children appear confused by the perceptual stimuli about them, responding to the slightest change in the environment, the movement of other children, the rustle of papers, and the instruction of teachers.

These are the children for whom Cruickshank (1967) devised his "stimulus-free" environment, attempting to protect them from the confusion of the schoolroom by having them work in semi-isolated carrels. The second group of children with problems in impulse control, usually but not always, have the same restless quality of the first group but, in addition, have impulsive outbursts that are sometimes aggressive, violent, and destructive and other times involve inconsolable fear or weeping, all evoked by what appears to be minor provocation—or indeed may appear spontaneously, seemingly without any provocation. This group is said to be suffering from the "syndrome of episodic dyscontrol," the Intermittent Explosive Disorder of *DSM-IV* that is possibly related to the "catastrophic reaction" of K. Goldstein (1938). There is the question whether these outbursts are associated with undiagnosed psychomotor epilepsy, either as ictal or interictal phenomena. D. Lewis et al. (1979) and D. Lewis, Pincus, Shanok, and Glaser (1982) reported that of the 97 delinquent boys they examined, approximately 20% did have evidence of psychomotor seizures. There are reports that the presence of an abnormal EEG, even though clinical seizures are not seen, is associated with episodic aggressive behavior (Rickler, 1982). Anticonvulsant medication has been suggested as helpful for this group. Carbamazepine has been reported to decrease disruptive behavior, overactivity, and abnormally elevated mood in mentally retarded adults with or without EEG abnormalities (Reid, Naylor, & Kay, 1981).

In our own clinical experience, admittedly anecdotal, the presence of focal or paroxysmal EEGs suggest the use of anticonvulsants. When focal or paroxysmal EEGs are not found, and where psychomotor symptoms are not elicited clinically, the decision for anticonvulsant medication may be more difficult. The presence of diffuse high-voltage slow waves, consistent with "diffuse cerebral dysfunction," adds weight to the use of anticonvulsants. With normal EEGs and with significant clinical symptoms relating to impulse control, beta-adrenergic blockers are considered; where an affective component is present, lithium may be helpful. The use of nicotinic acetylcholine receptor antagonists, such as mecamylamine, has been found to be effective for the irritability, emotional lability, and aggression of children with diffuse organic defect of the nervous system (Silver, Shytle, Sheehan, et al., 2001).

Phenytoin (Dilantin)

First used for control of seizures by Merritt and Putnam in 1938, phenytoin has been reported to control aggression (Bogoch & Dreyfus, 1970). Open trial and controlled studies, however, have not found conclusive evidence for its effectiveness in controlling aggressive and disruptive behavior. It is not clear how many children in these studies suffered from an organic defect of the central nervous system. Looker and Cooners (1970), in a double-blind, placebo-controlled, crossover study of 14 children with severe tantrums, found no significant differences between the effects of phenytoin and a placebo. Almost half of the children had abnormal EEGs (41%) and abnormal birth records (47%). It is noted that a small number of children—too small to affect group results, did respond "dramatically" to phenytoin. In a later double-blind study, Conners, Kramer, Rothschild, Schwartz, and Stone (1971) contrasted phenytoin and methylphenidate in 43 incarcerated delinquent boys and found no therapeutic effect for either drug.

Because of its long history and relative safety in the treatment of seizure disorders, however, phenytoin deserves a closer look when used in children with structural defects of the central nervous system who have clearly defined EEG abnormality. In practice when given orally in a dose of 5 to 8 mg/kg/day, the drug is slowly absorbed, and several days may be required to attain therapeutic plasma levels of 12 to 20 mcg/ml. Toxicity results from cerebellar and brain stem dysfunction (diplopia, slurred speech, vertigo, ataxia, and headache). Long-term use may produce cognitive dulling hirsutism, hypertrophy of gums, and folate deficiency. Peripheral neuropathy has been reported after years on the drug. In animals, high doses have resulted in loss of Purkinje cells. In humans however, Dam (1972) reported that "therapeutic and even toxic doses does not lead to any changes in the density and substructure of Purkinje cells unless the doses are so high that coma with hypoxia results" (p. 234).

Carbamazepine (Tegretol)

Derived from iminodibenzyl antihistamines and having the ring structure of the tricyclic, imipramine, carbamazepine was first used as an antiepileptic in the early 1960s (E. Davis, 1964) and to treat trigeminal neuralgia (Blom, 1962). In the 1970s, it was shown to be particularly valuable in partial complex seizures (Dreifus & Sachellares, 1979) and in generalized seizures thought to arise from the temporal lobe and the limbic system (R. H. Mattson et al., 1985). A review of carbamazepine use in 800 children with behavior disorders (Remschmidt, 1975) found evidence for beneficial effects of carbamazepine on psychomotor function, drive, and mood. Groh (1978) concluded that children with emotional lability, irritability, and paranoia who tended to react violently with minimal provocation were most likely to have a favorable therapeutic effect with carbamazepine. Nineteen of the 20 patients studied by Groh had abnormal EEGs. Dalby (1975) found improved mood and behavior and attention in children treated for seizure disorder with carbamazepine. An oral dose up to 25 mg/kg/day will bring the plasma level to therapeutic range, 5 to 12 micrograms/ml. Side effects (gastrointestinal complaints, drowsiness, ataxia, and visuomotor disturbances) are dose related. More serious are bone marrow depression (leucopenia or aplastic anemia) and hepatic toxicity. There have been case reports of carbamazepine precipitating a behavior that resembles paranoid schizophrenia. Although other reports found carbamazepine effective in improving impulsive aggressive behavior in children, a clear definition of type of organic defect, its parameters as described earlier in this chapter, together with the type of EEG found, are needed. Such studies should better define the indications for the use of anticonvulsants in children with organic brain damage. O'Donnell (1985) stated "There is as yet no clear basis for treating even severely aggressive conduct disorder with anticonvulsants in the absence of clinical seizure disorder, with or without abnormal EEGs" (p. 274). Of a group of 75 children, ages 6 to 13, admitted to an inpatient service, 12 of them (17%) had abnormal EEG (type not stated); 9 of these improved on anticonvulsants, "predominantly carbamazepine," while 4 children with normal EEGs did not significantly improve (O'Donnell, 1985).

In addition to its effect on seizure disorder, carbamazepine has been found to be an effective alternative to lithium in bipolar disorder and related psychotic states, and in blocking the development of seizures kindled by lidocaine or cocaine.

Valproate Sodium (Depakene)

A carboxylic acid designated as a propylpentonoic acid or dipropylacetic acid, valproate sodium has been used in Europe since the early 1960s, but only since January 1997 has it found FDA acceptance in the United States for absence epilepsy and for complex partial seizures. It appears to exert its anticonvulsive effect by limiting sustained repetitive neuronal firing and also by stimulating the activity of glutamic acid decarboxylase and inhibiting GABA degenerative enzymes, GABA transaminase, and succinic semialdehyde dehydrogenase. Although the most common side effects are transient gastrointestinal symptoms (anorexia, nausea, vomiting), it also induces sedation, ataxia, and tremor. Hepatic enzyme elevation is observed in 40% of patients and fulminating hepatitis has occurred particularly in infants 2 years of age and younger, and in those given multiple antiseizure drugs. Goodman and Gillman's report (Hardman & Limbird, 1996) shows the incidence of hepatic failure to be about 1 in 50,000 patients of all ages. The drug brochure warns of hepatic failure and pancreatitis, and warns that liver function tests should be performed prior to therapy and at "frequent" intervals thoroughly. Valproate also has a teratogenic effect, producing neural tube defects. Valproate has also been used in the management of bipolar disorder, in depression, and in aggressive behavior in children.

Gabapentin (Neurontin)

Gabapentin was approved by the FDA in 1993 for partial seizures in adults; no data is available in pediatric patients under 18 years of age. Despite its design as a GABA agonist, gabapentin increases the release of GABA by an unknown mechanism (Honmou, Kocsis, & Richardson, 1995). Double-blind, placebo-controlled trials have supported its use as an adjunct to other antiseizure drugs, with a reduction of seizures by 27% compared with 12% for placebo. There have been no controlled studies of gabapentin in children. Like other anticonvulsant drugs, the most common adverse effects are somnolence, dizziness, ataxia, and fatigue, although these symptoms usually abate during continued treatment. Gabapentin is not metabolized in humans but is excreted unchanged by the renal circulation so that renal monitoring is indicated. Animal studies have found pancreatic acinar cell carcinoma using doses of gabapentin at 10 times the plasma concentration in humans. Fetal toxicity, with delayed ossification of bone, has been found in rodents. There are no adequate studies in pregnant woman.

Lamotrigine (Lamictil)

Lamotrigine was approved in 1994 as adjunctive therapy for complex partial seizures and for Lennox-Gastaut syndrome (akinetic seizures). Its therapeutic action appears to be related to its ability to block repetitive firing induced by depolarization of spinal cord neurons, consistent with blocking voltage-dependent Na^+ channels (as do phenytoin and carbamazepine). It is completely absorbed from the gastrointestinal tract and is metabolized primarily by glucuronidation. Its half-life when used as monotherapy is 24 hours, but when used with phenytoin, carbamazepine, phenobarbital, or primidone, the half-life is reduced to 15 hours. Lamotrigine reduces valproic acid concentration by 25% over a few weeks, and increases carbemazebine to clinical toxicity levels. Valproic acid reduced the clearance of lamotrigine so that with valproic acid, the dosage of lamotrigine is reduced by 50%. Dizziness, ataxia, blurred vision, nausea, vomiting, and rash are common side effects. Because the rash is potentially serious, and the rate of serious rash is greater in pediatric patients than in adults, it is recommended that lamotrigine is only approved for use in patients below the age of 16 who have Lennox-Gastaut seizures. Rashes leading to hospitalization included Stevens-Johnson syndrome, toxic epidermal necrosis, angioedema, and rash associated with fever, lymphoadenopathy, facial swelling, and hematological and liver abnormalities. Hematological problems included disseminated intravascular coagulation. The manufacturers warn that lamotrigine should ordinarily be discontinued at the first sign of a rash.

Topiramate (Topamax)

The FDA approved topiramate in 1996 as an adjunctive drug for partial seizures. Its action, like lamotrigine, blocks sustained depolarization of neurons suggesting a sodium channel blocking action. It potentiates the action of GABA and it blocks the glutamate receptor. Topiramate is not extensively metabolized and is primarily eliminated unchanged by the kidneys, though renal impairment reduces clearance. Adverse effects include psychomotor slowing, difficulty with concentration, word-finding difficulty, somnolence or fatigue, dizziness, imbalance, confusion, memory difficulty, irritability, and depression. Kidney stones may occur.

Evidence of teratrogenic effect (craniofacial defect, limb malformation) was found in mice; there also was an increase in urinary bladder tumors. Safety and effectiveness in children have not been established.

Felbamate (Felbatol)

In 1993, the FDA approved felbamate for generalized tonic-clonic epilepsy, partial epilepsy, and Lennox-Gastaut syndrome. It is not the first line of antiepileptic drugs. This is essentially because of its marked toxicity; its use is associated with a marked increase in aplastic anemia, a pancytopenia with bone marrow depletion of hemopoetic precursors, at a rate 100-fold greater than seen in the untreated population. Hepatic failure is also a risk with this drug. Felbatol, however, is effective in control of atonic seizures and generalized tonic-chronic seizures.

Beta-Blockers

Propranolol was reported (Elliot, 1977) to be beneficial in controlling outbursts of rage that followed acute brain damage in seven adults and outbursts in assaultive adults with organic brain disease (Greendyke, Schuster, & Wooten, 1984). J. M. Silver et al. (1996) found 7 patients of 20 hospitalized adults, to respond with a 50% decrease in aggressive behavior with propranolol. Ruedrich, 1996 found "beta adrenergic blocking" drugs effective for the treatment of "rage outbursts" in mentally retarded adults. There have been scattered reports on the effect of *beta adrenergic blockers* on impulse disorders in children with organic brain disorder. M. A. Riddle et al. (1999) reviewing all controlled trials of anxiolytic medication (including beta-blockers) for children through 1997, found "virtually no controlled data that support the efficiency of most of these drugs for the treatment of psychiatric disorders in children and adolescents." However, beta-blockers are recommended for aggressive dyscontrol. Haspel, 1995, also in reviewing the literature finds support for beta-blockers in decreasing the frequency and intensity of aggressive outbursts. As early as 1979, Schreier, found that 100 mg/day of propranolol controlled rage outburst after acute encephalitis in a 12-year-old. Of four patients that Yudofsky, Williams, and Gorman (1981) treated with propranolol, one was an adolescent with "chronic organic brain dysfunction." D. T. Williams, Mehl, Yudofsky, Adams, and Roseman (1982) treated a diagnostically heterogeneous group of 30 patients who had "uncontrolled rage and organic brain dysfunction" with propranolol in doses of 50 to 160 mg/day. Of these patients, 11 were children and 15 were adolescents. Diagnostic categories included those with MBD and those with a history of uncontrolled seizures. Each had not responded to one or more anticonvulsants, neuroleptics, or stimulants. While propranolol did not control seizures, the overall results yielded a 75% posttreatment improvement in control of rage outburst. The authors report the duration of treatment with propranolol from 1 to 30 months (median 3 to 5 months). From this paper, however, it is difficult to understand the factors that correlated with a successful outcome. Gillette and Tannery (1994) have warned that propranolol will inhibit the metabolism of imipramine so that, when given together, imipramine may reach toxic levels.

While propranolol has both peripheral and central actions, nadolol, a long-acting peripheral beta-blocker, has been reported as effective in reducing aggressive behavior in a 36-year-old retarded man who had been institutionalized since adolescence because of his impulsive, assaultive behavior. Nadolol in a dose of 120 mg/day proved to be more effective than propranolol (Polakoff, Sorgi, & Ratey, 1986). The authors speculated that beta-blockers may decrease peripheral somatic reactivity and thus break a "powerful behavioral/feedback loop" (p. 126). This is of interest since the homeostatic lability found in many children with organic brain disorders may promote subjective anxiety, and as pointed out in the review of the symptoms section of this chapter, anxiety may be discharged as aggression. A more recent open trial found nadolol to be helpful in control of aggression in 12 developmentally delayed children, adolescents, and young adults (Connor, Ozbayrak, Benjamin, Ma, & Fletcher, 1997).

Pindolol has also been reported (Greendyke & Kanter, 1986) effective in management of 11 adults whose impulsive and explosive behavior is said to be a consequence of brain disease or injury. Pindolol does not have the antihypertensive or bradykinetic effect of propranolol.

Lithium

Although lithium has been reported to be of benefit in children with cyclic mood swings, manic-depressive illness, and severe explosive or aggressive behavior, the effect of lithium on the impulsive behavior of children with organic brain disorders has not been explored. The chronic impulsive aggression of 66 prisoners, ages 16 to 22, 34% of whom received lithium, was evaluated by Sheard, Marini, Bridges, and Wagner (1976) in a well-designed, placebo-controlled study. The lithium group had significantly fewer aggressive rule infractions than did the placebo group. Fourteen boys, ages 7 to 13, with sporadic, unprovoked physical aggression were maintained on a therapeutic dose of lithium and compared with a matched control group who did not have aggressive behavior. Aggression in the lithium group "declined dramatically," only to return again when lithium was discontinued. The effect of lithium was compared with that of haloperidol and a placebo in reducing the aggressive, explosive, and disruptive behavior of 61 children, ages 5 years 2 months to 12 years 9 months, who were diagnosed in accordance with *DSM-II* as a conduct disordered, undersocialized, aggressive type, and who were hospitalized at Bellevue Psychiatric Hospital in New York City (M. Campbell, Perry, & Green, 1984; M. Campbell, Small, et al., 1984). Both lithium and haloperidol were significantly superior to the placebo in reducing the angry affect, bullying, distractibility, fighting, negativism, and temper tantrums. The authors noted, "The primary action of lithium was to decrease explosive affect. . . . haloperidol merely made the child more manageable" (p. 655). There is some evidence, too, that the aggression of disturbed, mentally retarded adolescents may also respond to prolonged (months) administration of lithium (Dostal, 1972). With the exception of three of the retarded boys who had grand mal seizures and two with lower limb paresis, the question of lithium in organic brain disorders specifically is not considered. This is an area that warrants further investigation.

Nicotinic Acetylcholine Antagonist

The safety and efficacy of mecamylamine, a ganglionic blocker, in the ability to decrease irritability, mood lability, rage, and aggression in children with Tourette's syndrome and in children with impulsive aggression has been reported in open trial studies (Sanberg et al., 1997; A. A. Silver et al., 2001). The safety of low doses (2.5 to 7.5 mgm) of mecamylamine and its effectiveness in obtunding mood aggression warrant further trial and investigation.

Educational Principles

Many of the general principles of educational remediation that were discussed in Chapter 8 are relevant to the educational management of children with organic learning problems. However, the nature of their disorder results in some special requirements that the educational planner must keep in mind to serve their educational needs appropriately.

Early work in the field of learning disabilities focused on improved methods for teaching these children. Lehtinen's work at the Cove School provided not only an understanding of their handicaps but also teaching procedures that enable these children to learn (Strauss & Lehtinen, 1947). Cruickshank, a pioneer in defining the services these children require, offered leadership in the education of children with special learning problems. Cruickshank (1967) and Cruickshank et al. (1961) demonstrated how instructional variables could be organized in a program within the public school setting to provide for the perceptual and cognitive problems these children experience. Much that is done in special education programs today draws on the work accomplished in these early programs.

As in any planning for educational intervention, comprehensive, multidisciplinary diagnostic information must be available. In the case of children with organic defects of the central nervous system, such information is essential for several reasons. First of all, there is a high degree of variability within the group. Even though their ages and overall levels of achievement may be similar, a program designed for one student may be completely inappropriate for another student who has different patterns of functioning. The qualitative information gained from sensitive clinical assessment can contribute information about strengths and needs, personality, and learning styles that is crucial to an effective plan.

Not only are there substantial interpersonal variations within this group of children, but there are also marked intrapersonal variations. Organic children frequently have significant interscale variations on the WISC-R. In the case of a child who earns a verbal IQ of 100 and a performance IQ of 70, it creates a completely misleading impression for a psychologist to report an overall level of function as an 84, which falls within the dull-normal range. The generalization does not take into account the significant amount of intrapersonal variation that the test scores demonstrate. The high points these variations signal, as well as the deficits, must be considered in planning.

The student's emotional response to her learning problems is another aspect of the diagnostic formulation that has implications for teaching. The emotional lability and tenuous impulse control that characterize many children with organic learning disorders makes it more difficult for these children to build easy relationships with teachers and other authority figures. The teacher must be able to recognize the effects of these characteristics and respond to them with tact and understanding, rather than to deal with them as behavioral infractions. The pervasive anxiety that is the psychological substrate must also be recognized. Awareness of the high level of anxiety that characterizes many of these children can help their teachers understand their mercurial mood swings, their sensitivity to stress, and the fatigue that can be misunderstood as anger and stubbornness. There may be a perseverative quality in their behavior, and teachers may lose patience when the same question is asked for the nth time. Some compulsiveness may also show up in their schoolwork; it may mark the youngster who will become a tenacious student. It also means that these children do not adapt easily to rapid transitions. Teachers will find that a warning about an end of an activity or an impending schedule change may help them adapt to shifts in activities.

The teacher must help these students learn ways to protect themselves from the intrusion of external stimuli on the educational process. Although each child may have unique patterns of functioning, difficulties with any aspect of information processing—stimulus input, storage, and retrieval—can be expected to occur. It is important for teachers to understand that the child's work requirements may be different from their own and to avoid insisting on procedures that may be comfortable for the teacher but less comfortable for the individual child. Some of these students find that background noise or music facilitates concentration; the quiet workplace that most adults insist on, actually creates anxiety in these youngsters. Teachers should not insist on the quiet workplace they may prefer when the student really needs the sound of background music to sustain attention on work.

Fast, inaccurate workstyles frequently characterize these youngsters. There is real question about the extent to which this style can be transformed into the methodical accuracy that many teachers admire in their students. One thing is certain, this transformation will not occur through direct confrontation. Instruction that makes use of metacognitive knowledge and skills may be a more appropriate approach. The strategy training procedures developed by Deshler and his associates (1984) are recommended instructional models for this purpose.

The level of instruction must take into account the range in abilities these youngsters demonstrate. Some of them may demonstrate superior verbal abilities, but have such poor fine motor control that they write illegibly, uncomfortably, and as infrequently as possible. As the burden of written work increases in the school years, this problem will affect their grades on composition, their ability to take notes in class, and the fluency with which they express their ideas in written examinations. Understanding the problem and providing typing and word processing equipment at the upper grade levels are essential if these youngsters' written work is to reflect their abilities.

Sometimes specific cognitive limitations must be recognized, particularly among the more severely impaired children in this group. These youngsters may have considerable difficulty in making generalizations, both in terms of academic learning and behavior. They need to be taught many things that other children learn from casual experiences. These children may require much more practice at a given level before reaching mastery. With the rapid pace of many current school curricula, these children experience frustration and failure. As one young woman described her experiences in high school: "I would just begin to understand something and the teacher would go to something else." Ellen illustrates the problem of a girl with an organically based learning disorder.

CASE STUDY: ELLEN

Ellen was a quiet, dark haired, gentle, 6-year-old girl when we first saw her. She was referred to us because her parents were concerned that she was slow in development of speech and appeared to be clumsy. The history revealed that although she was thought to be 1-month premature, her birth weight was 6 pounds 3 ounces. As an infant she slept "constantly." At age 3 months, she had severe croup, became cyanotic, and was hospitalized for a week. The hospital noted repeated episodes of protracted cyanosis. Her developmental milestones were delayed; standing at 17 months, walking at 18 months, single words at 2 years, and still at age 6, having urinary and bowel "accidents" during the day. She had numerous urinary tract infections that required urethral dilatation.

On examination, she was alert and cooperative, right-handed but with a grossly abnormal pencil grip, fine motor coordination, poor praxis, and visuomotor function at just about a 3-year level. Her gait was clumsy, and she had a mild articulation defect. She was not overly active, and the remainder of the classical neurological examination was within normal limits. An electroencephalogram was "abnormal with evidence of paroxysmal slow wave and spike activity appearing in both occipital leads, compatible with cortical alteration in that area and possible convulsive disorder."

Her intellectual functioning ranged from dull-normal to borderline levels, with a full scale IQ of 79, verbal IQ of 81, and a performance IQ of 81 on the WPPSI. She had severe visual and visuomotor problems, moderately severe body image and auditory sequencing problems, and short-term memory problems. She was then attending a small private school, supplemented with tutoring directed toward teaching preacademic skills. Our impression at that time was that Ellen was indeed suffering from diffuse, "static encephalopathy," affecting her overall cognitive functioning with specific problems in memory and perception.

Emotionally she was immature and was already reacting to the impatient demands of her intellectually gifted parents. Recommendations for management were made to the school and to the tutor.

When seen for reevaluation a year later, she said, "I grewed up . . . I got bigger." During the year Ellen had made progress with prereading perceptual skills, but difficulties in integration of skills in a productive fashion and in comprehension and use of language were now more evident. When Mrs. L was cautioned about expecting too rapid academic progress, she expressed doubts about the structure that the small private school offered. She was encouraged to investigate the newly formed class for neurologically impaired children in the local public school.

At the start of the next school year Ellen was enrolled in that class. This class proved to be academically oriented, beyond Ellen's ability at that time. On reevaluation, she brought along a basal reader that was difficult for her to read and a towering stack of workbooks—phonics worksheets for a wide variety of sounds she did not recognize, a handwriting workbook, a reading comprehension workbook, Frostig worksheets, and some mathematics worksheets (which she understood best of all the material). Her comment on the schoolwork was to spread her arms out wide and say, "I hate it this much." She seemed to handle all this seatwork by making written responses in an indiscriminate fashion, incorrect as often as not. Discussion or verbal rehearsal of directions seemed limited; therefore, Ellen had little opportunity to integrate the skills into her repertoire responses.

As a result of these generally unhappy experiences, Ellen, now 8-years-old, began individual weekly tutoring sessions to provide stimulation in oral and written language. Oral language stimulation work started with very elementary work in generating questions. Ellen did not know *how* to find out the things she didn't know; when people did not understand her awkwardly framed questions, she would shrug and say, "Forget it." Language work went on to transforming questions into statements and dealing with conversational exchanges. Manipulatives, such as the Attribute Games were used to deal with logical tasks. Simple reading comprehension materials were used to apply the phonics skills she was working with in school and to give her practice in following written directions. During these sessions, her mother was invited to join us for a brief period, either to admire something Ellen had accomplished or to join us in a review game. This helped Mrs. L understand what Ellen could do and to learn to set more realistic goals for her.

A repeat neurological examination at age 8 revealed persistent visuomotor, fine motor coordination, and praxic problems, but improvement in gait and articulation. Her EEG was still abnormal with "irregular slow activity over the posterior hemispheres and diffuse peroxysmal slow activity during and after hyperventilation, suggesting diffuse cerebral dysfunction."

The following school year Ellen was placed in a class that gave excellent social stimulation and opportunity for participation in a variety of activities. She began to enjoy school for the first time. In marked contrast to her previous class, there was an underemphasis on academic work and little reinforcement of skills in reading and mathematics. Her language skills had improved and so tutoring in academic areas helped to compensate for the more casual program at school, because it was felt the socialization there was valuable for her.

During the next year, Ellen moved to junior high school where the class offered, as far, as could be determined, an ideal program. The class was well integrated into the life of the school. Educational activities were well planned and appropriately structured. For the first time, it seemed that Ellen felt some responsibility for learning at school. Tutoring was directed toward making the transition to active classwork and self-directed work on her own.

Reevaluation at the end of that school year showed that WISC-R scores were within the same range as they had been in the past (Full Scale IQ of 80, Verbal IQ of 80, Performance IQ of 82). Thus while there had been no acceleration of IQ, Ellen had held her own within her age group. Her approach to testing was matter-of-fact and uncompetitive. Her subtest scores were less variable than in the past, with high points seen in the Similarities subtest (which taps abstract verbal relationships) and with Object Assembly (a measure of spatial relationships). She exceeded the ceiling for the Illinois Test of Psycholinguistic Abilities with a language age of 10 years (her original score 2 years before had been 7 years 8 months). Gains had been made in all areas; although grammatical closure was the most difficult subtest for her, even there she had gained 20 scaled score points. Achievement test scores were stable, all placing within the fourth-grade range. Ellen continued in the special education program through her high school years.

After high school, she entered a 2-year vocational program in which she was trained to work as an educational assistant in a nursery school. As a young adult, she is poised and outgoing, proud of her productive employment. Her parents are pleased, also. They are comfortable and effective in the supportive role they have taken as sponsors of a social group for young adults with learning disabilities, of which Ellen is a part.

Ellen illustrated important principles in the management of children with structural defects of the central nervous system. First, diagnosis was necessary to formulate the unique patterns of Ellen's functional deficits, as well as her strengths. Second, remediation was most effective when it matched her developmental level; it was ineffective when she was overwhelmed by the difficulty and the amount of required activities. Third, the deficits were tenacious, requiring patience and restraint on the part of the tutor and the parents. Fourth, youngsters like Ellen need support, particularly at major life transition points. Fifth, her emotional reactions to pressure for achievement beyond her current level of capability resulted in continued tension within the family.

SUMMARY

Approximately 5% of the children in mainstream first-grade classes have presumptive evidence of a structural defect of the central nervous system. When comprehensive examination, along the pentaxial scheme described in Chapters 6 and 7 of this book, is done on children in self-contained classes for severely emotionally handicapped children, approximately one-third of them will have such evidence. All of these children have some degree of learning disorder. Structural dysfunction of the central nervous system may be categorized as to nature, severity, and location of the insult; the time in the child's life it has occurred; and the appropriateness of the environmental support. Acute effects of injury include destruction of cells at the site of the trauma, astrocyte reaction, proliferation of blood vessels, invasion by microglia, and edema; long-term effects include retrograde axonal degeneration, scarring, loss of trophic influence and, most important, proliferation of new axon collaterals that may form aberrant fiber tracks. Secondary structural changes with more severe and profound effects on overall intelligence are greater in the infant brain than in the mature or juvenile brain. Following an injury, language acquisition, as well as recovery of language after it has developed, is more prone to occur the younger the child. In general, behavioral effects of brain trauma are seen in disorders of perception, cognition, and language; in the initiation and control of impulses; and in problems in muscle tone, coordination, and synergy.

In the newborn, infectious and toxic processes are not common, while hypoxia is most significant and more prevalent than mechanical injury. Deep basal ganglia damage was observed mainly in the premature, and is more frequent than cortical damage, which occurred in the mature, at-term neonate. Even mild hypoxia results in cellular damage with patchy or diffuse neuronal loss and is stated to be a critical determinant for later neurological and intellectual development. Infants with clinical signs of anoxia are at risk for less than normal development. Infant test scores on selected scales at 4, 8, 12, 18, and 24 months, together with a risk index based on demographic, pregnancy, and perinatal factors can predict cognitive test scores at 5 years of age. Although the effects of neonatal hypoxia are obtunded with maturation and with environmental support, the residuals do not disappear with maturation alone. Seizure disorders may affect learning by memory loss in the postictal state and even in subclinical seizures. In temporal lobe seizures, a word-finding problem is not unusual and in general there is a variability in subtest patterns with verbal-performance discrepancies in the WISC-R. Even with uncomplicated seizures, there is a tendency for a reading disorder to be evident by the age of 10. Anticonvulsants have a depressing effect on cognition and memory. Emotional problems of the child with seizures—impulsivity and rigidity—interfere with learning.

Fetal alcohol syndrome encompasses a spectrum of deficits including physical, cognitive, and behavioral abnormalities. Physically, the child is small, with small head, thin upper lip, pulled up by a small philtrum, and small eyes. The chin is usually receded and there may be asymmetry of the two sides of the face. Cognitively, there are problems with language and visuomotor function, with overall mild retardation. Behaviorally, he is usually impulsive yet sensitive and aware of his defects.

The public schools are mandated by law to accept the child with HIV infection into the class most appropriate for him. The cognitive defect presented by these children depends on the severity of the infection. Children with HIV may have average overall IQ, but there are usually delays in language development, with lower verbal IQ and low scores in block design subtests of the WISC. Behaviorally, these children may have difficulty with control of impulses, difficulty with attention. The child with hemophilia who acquires his infection at a later age than the vertically infected child, may have a normal IQ and function well until and if the disorder progresses and the central nervous system is involved. The management of these children in school is no different from the OSHA regulations for infection control of any blood-borne infection.

Schools are also mandated to provide preventive education appropriate to each group in elementary and high schools.

Basing severity of head injury on the duration of posttraumatic amnesia and duration of coma, mild head injury does not cause persistent cognitive impairment; severe head injury, however, may result in marked impairment, particularly in visuospatial and visuomotor tasks. With left-hemisphere lesions, all tests of scholastic attainment may be impaired. Severe head injury also tends to result in an increased rate of psychiatric disorder. Although children who have survived *H. influenzae* meningitis do not as a group suffer academic impairment, they appear to need more support, remedial services, and help with homework than their noninjured siblings. Radiation to the cranium for childhood malignancies contributes to a lowered level of intellectual function or impairment of short-term memory. Because of these findings, routine prophylactic cranial irradiation is being phased out.

The management of children with structural defects of the central nervous system must be based on comprehensive evaluation; psychotherapy, behavior modification, physiotherapy, medication, and special education each has a role. Anticonvulsant medication even in the absence of seizure disorder, but in the presence of episodic dyscontrol, has been recommended; propranolol and lithium have also been helpful in reducing aggressive and impulsive outbursts in organic children.

A case study illustrates the principles of management of children with structural defect of the central nervous system: comprehensive diagnosis and matching of remediation with the child's developmental level, the tenacity of the deficits, the involvement of parents, and the need for continued support of the child at major life transition points.

Chapter 15

TOURETTE'S SYNDROME

For students with TS, learning can be tough. Teaching them can be tougher.

—Tourette's Association, 2001

CASE STUDY: ROBERT

Robert was 10 years 10 months of age in the regular fourth-grade class of a good public school when he was referred to us, 3 months into the academic year. For the past 2 months, he had refused to go to school and was becoming increasingly demanding at home, hostile, snarling, negativistic, explosive, and even destructive of objects when his demands were not instantly met. He was an only child, the product of a normal pregnancy and labor with a birth weight of 9 pounds. His development, except for delayed speech, was said by his parents to be normal. However, he was described as "always a difficult child," very active and impulsive, so that by age 5 he was diagnosed as hyperactive. For the next year or more, he received methylphenidate up to 30 mg daily. By age 7, eye blinking and throwing motion of his arms was added to his hyperactivity. The Valium and Tranxene he received for these symptoms only appeared to increase their severity, with eye blinking, head shaking, shoulder shrugging, and dystonic movements of abdominal and back muscles. He developed vocalizations, grunting and yelling, and episodes of coprolalia in which he kept repeating "son of a bitch." Compulsive behavior—holding his knees together, grabbing his crotch with his right hand, touching and stacking furniture, and touching people as he went by them—was evident.

At age 8, a diagnosis of Tourette's syndrome was made, and since that time he received haloperidol at 1.5 mg daily. This medication did not fully control his symptoms, but increasing the dose to 2.0 mg daily induced drowsiness, extrapyramidal side effects, and akathisia. His EEG and CT scan were reported as normal. The school psychologist reported that on testing at age 8 years 5 months, Robert earned a Full Scale IQ of 93 on the WISC-R (verbal IQ of 95, performance IQ of 93). He earned a scaled score of 12 in Information and 10 in Similarities and in Vocabulary, but a scaled score of 6 on Digit Span, 7 in Arithmetic, an 8 in Comprehension. On the performance scale, he had marked difficulty with Block Design (scaled score 6). He refused all graphomotor tasks. He had limited word-attack skills in reading and could not go beyond addition and subtraction combinations in arithmetic. Rotation and poor integration of juxtaposed figures were evident on the Bender VGMT.

After the diagnosis of Tourette's syndrome was made, Robert was placed in a class for emotionally handicapped children where, with a combination of haloperidol and support to the family, he was reported to have done well behaviorally but had not progressed academically. Accordingly, for his second and third grades he was placed in a full-time class for children with learning disabilities. The IEP review summary at the end of third grade stated that "significant progress was noted and trial mainstreaming in the third grade appeared successful," and regular class was recommended for fourth grade.

This proved disastrous. Within a month he refused to go to school. His teacher stated that "because students in fourth grade must work more independently, have fewer oral assignments and increased written assignments, must do copying assignments from the chalkboard involving cursive writing, have increased spelling lists and are more socially perceptive, Robert is experiencing great difficulty. His grades have dropped from A to F, his task completion is greatly reduced, and he has become socially aggressive due to teasing by his peers." At this point, he was referred to our clinic.

Examination in our clinic revealed a handsome, slender, 11-year-old with flushed cheeks, perioral pallor, and braces on his teeth. He was in continual motion with tics of the left shoulder and right hand, body torsions, rolling on the couch, lying with his feet in the air, and clearing his throat. The day before the neuropsychiatric examination, psychological testing was to have been done. Robert refused to cooperate on any psychological tests. Reason, coercion, bribery, and threats were all to no avail. Having learned from that experience, we conducted the neuropsychiatric examination in an informal, relaxed manner and, as long as he was given no task that would expose his deficits, Robert was affable, pleasant, verbal, and showed the examiner pictures of himself seated in a large bulldozer, gutting a deer he and his father had shot. Except for rapid, staccato speech, marked synkineses, and autonomic lability, classical neurological examination was essentially normal. On extension of the arms in this right-handed boy, the left hand was elevated. There was hesitation in responding to tests of right-left discrimination in himself and gross confusion in identifying right and left in the examiner facing him. Praxis, too, was mildly impaired.

Examination of perceptual skills revealed visuomotor immaturity with the presence of angulation difficulty, primitive verticalization, and perseveration. He demanded a ruler (which was not given to him) to copy the Bender VGMT figures and became increasingly anxious, finally erasing the designs that were unacceptable to him. He tried very hard, but any written work must be frustrating to this child. Auditory rote sequencing was markedly immature, not higher than an 8-year-old level. He also could not recall the Binet sentences beyond the 8-year-old level.

Emotionally, Robert was under stress. He was emotionally labile, quick to erupt in the face of any stimulus he viewed as threatening, but friendly and reasonable

Figure 15.1   Figure drawing. Robert: Age 10 years 10 months. His impulsive drawing and his dissatisfaction with his production is seen in the upper part of this figure. Finally, he did manage an immature stick figure.

when all went as he wished. There was a sense that one must tread very lightly with Robert. His lability evoked tension in the people around him. There was a cost to his immediate demands, however. Robert felt guilty about all the "bad things" he did, felt he should be punished, and wondered if Tourette's is his punishment. Anxiety was always lurking beneath the surface of his feelings. He feared someone would get into his house—"an insane guy"—to hurt him. He said, "I cannot go to sleep unless I tell my mother to close the closet door. I convince myself that if I hide under the blanket with my dog, I can't be shot by some insane guy." His mother reported that she must sleep in Robert's room so that he can sleep. Robert said his main problem is that he cannot get to sleep. As a result, how could we expect him to get up in time to go to school? He talked about his school difficulty but blamed it on the school for not having a proper teacher for him. He worried about Tourette's symptoms, saying that he did not know how to get rid of them and if they got worse, "I would do something." He was unsure of the future.

This case vignette is reported in some detail because it illustrates important issues that must be considered in the diagnosis and management of the child with Tourette's syndrome: his prekindergarten hyperactivity, diagnosed as an attention deficit hyperactivity disorder (ADHD) and treated with stimulants; the emergence of motor tics by age 7, and vocal tics by age 8; compulsive behavior characterized by touching and stacking, with genital grabbing soon after; the diagnosis of Tourette's syndrome made by age 8 years; his learning disability characterized by visuospatial and visuomotor deficits; the anger, anxiety, and fear, and equally important his inner psychological turmoil; his social and school problems; the effect on his parents; and the problems of medication and comprehensive management.

DESCRIPTION OF THE SYNDROME

Tourette's syndrome is described as a neuropsychiatric disorder, a complex behavioral disorder that is poised between mind and body, governed by innate vulnerabilities and environmental circumstances, with an underlying genetic diathesis combined with a variable set of epigenetic stressors that constrain the potentialities of the developing brain (Leckman & Cohen, 1999). Although its pathognomonic symptoms are defined by *DSM-IV-TR* (see Table 15.1) and by the Tourette's Syndrome Classification Study Group (1993) as the presence of motor and phonic tics in various combinations of anatomical location, number, frequency, severity, complexity, and type, the vast majority of individuals with Tourette's syndrome have accompanying neuropsychiatric disorders, such as obsessive compulsive disorders and behavior, attention deficit disorders, learning disabilities, mood disorders, and behavioral symptoms of irritability, anger, and aggression. So prominent are these accompanying disorders that we have come to think of Tourette's syndrome as a spectrum disorder involving a range of neurodevelopmental disorders and the behaviors that accompany them.

Tics have been described as sudden rapid, repetitive motor movements or phonic sounds that involve discrete muscle groups. Motor tics are most often first noted between the ages of 5 and 7 years. R. D. Freeman et al. (2000) in a review of 3,500 individuals with Tourette's syndrome, reporting from 65 sites representing 22 countries (42% from Canada, 27% from the United States, 31% outside North America), found the mean age of onset of tics to be 6.4 years. Most often, tics make their appearance in a caphalad-caudal progression, starting with simple tics such as eye blinking or eye movements, grimacing, nose twitching, mouth movements, to head jerking, shoulder shrugs, arm jerking, finger movements, to trunk movement, kicking, fist extension. Complex tics are slower in motion than simple tics and appear purposeful: They include gestures of face, arms, or fingers (copropraxia); hitting, touching, bending, rotating; and dystonic postures. Simple phonic tics frequently are throat clearing, coughing, sniffling, spitting, barking, clucking; complex phonic tics are verbal, words, phrases, echolalia, palilalia, coprolalia. There are attempts to hold back words that

Table 15.1   Diagnostic Criteria for 307.23 Tourette's Disorder

A. Both multiple motor and one or more vocal tics have been present at some time during the illness, although not necessarily concurrently. (A tic is a sudden, rapid, recurrent, nonrhythmic, stereotyped motor movement or vocalization.)

B. The tics occur many times a day (usually in bouts) nearly every day or intermittently throughout a period of more than 1 year, and during this period there was never a tic-free period of more than 3 consecutive months.

C. The onset is before age 18 years.

D. The disturbance is not due to the direct physiological effects of a substance (e.g., stimulants) or a general medical condition (e.g., Huntington's disease or postviral encephalitis).

Diagnostic Criteria for 307.22 Chronic Motor or Vocal Tic Disorder

A. Single or multiple motor or vocal tics (i.e., sudden, rapid, recurrent, nonrhythmic, stereotyped motor movements or vocalizations), but not both, have been present at some time during the illness.

B. The tics occur many times a day nearly every day or intermittently throughout a period of more than 1 year, and during this period there was never a tic-free period of more than 3 consecutive months.

C. The onset is before age 18 years.

D. The disturbance is not due to the direct physiological effects of a substance (e.g., stimulants) or a general medical condition (e.g., Huntington's disease or postviral encephalitis).

E. Criteria have never been met for Tourette's disorder.

Diagnostic Criteria for 307.21 Transient Tic Disorder

A. Single or multiple motor and/or vocal tics (i.e., sudden, rapid, recurrent, nonrhythmic, stereotyped motor movements or vocalizations)

B. The tics occur many times a day, nearly every day for at least 4 weeks, but for no longer than 12 consecutive months.

C. The onset is before age 18 years.

D. The disturbance is not due to the direct physiological effects of a substance (e.g., stimulants) or a general medical condition (e.g., Huntington's disease or postviral encephalitis).

E. Criteria have never been met for Tourette's Disorder or Chronic Motor or Vocal Tic Disorder.

Specify if:
Single Episode or **Recurrent**

307.20 Tic Disorder Not Otherwise Specified

This category is for disorders characterized by tics that do not meet criteria for a specific Tic Disorder. Examples include tics lasting less than 4 weeks or tics with an onset after age 18 years.

Reprinted with permission from the *Diagnostic and Statistical Manual of Mental Disorders,* Fourth Edition, Text Revision. Copyright 2000 American Psychiatric Association.

are unacceptable. In a review of 11 studies encompassing a total of 2,463 patients with Tourette's syndrome, drawn from varied geographic areas, Bruun (1988) found the main age of onset of tics to be 7 years 2 months, with a range of 5 years 8 months to 9 years 4 months. In a sample of 350 patients drawn from her private practice and from clinics in two large hospitals in New York City, Bruun found that 53% of the patients described an eye tic as their first symptom, either blinking or rolling the eyes; 13% had facial tics such as grimacing, nose twitching, licking or biting the lips as their first symptom, while another 13% had vocalizations, such as sniffling, throat clearing, coughing, or grunting as their first symptom.

The prevalence of Tourette's syndrome has been studied in epidemiological investigations using different sampling strategies, different population samples, and different diagnostic procedures. Early in clinical based studies (A. R. Lucas, Beard, Raiput, & Kurland, 1982) found that of all patients seen at the Mayo clinic between 1968 and 1979, three were diagnosed with Tourette's syndrome, a prevalence of 0.046/10,000, a rare disorder. Sampling from school populations, however, Caine et al. (1988) found a rate of 5.2/10,000 for boys and 0.6/10,000 for girls in Monroe county, New York, while Comings, Hines, and Comings (1990) in a school district in California, found higher rates, 105/10,000 for boys, 13.1/10,000 for girls. An examination of 28,000 17-year-olds, consecutive subjects undergoing military service in Israel, identified 4.9/10,000 for boys, 3.1/10,000 for girls; while Costello et al. (1996), examining 4,500 children ages 9, 11, and 13 years in rural North Carolina, found 13/10,000 for boys and 7/10,000 for girls met criteria for Tourette's syndrome. Tourette's syndrome is no longer a rare disorder, and given the rapid increase in the number of children diagnosed with Tourette's syndrome in clinics, the recorded prevalence may need to be increased.

The case of Marquise de Dampierre was first described by Itard (1825) and more fully by George Gilles de la Tourette in *Archives of Neurology* in 1885 (translated by Goetz & Klawans, 1982; Robertson & Reinstein, 1991) and from which is derived the eponym, Tourette's syndrome. (A brief biological sketch of Georges Gilles de la Tourette may be found in *Review Neurologique,* 1996, and is discussed in Kuschner, 1999.)

It is recognized now that the syndrome may appear in all degrees of severity from mild to severe; changing in any one individual from one anatomical site to another, changing in severity, frequency, or complexity. The bouts of tics may "wax and wane" possibly in response to stress, increasing with increased stress; relieved when stress is less. Stress may rise from any source, environmental and/or intrapsychic. It is said that the symptoms are aggravated in early adolescence usually attaining most severity in mid- to late adolescence, when there may then be a decline in tic frequency and severity, (Leckman et al., 1998) until in young adulthood, follow-up studies report a remission rate of 20% to 50%. However, these studies also report an "improved" rate of 40% to 80%, no change in approximately 50%, worse in 4% to 30%. Bruun (1988), in a study of 251 patients followed for 5 to 15 years found 3% in remission, 44% improved, 45% no change and 8% worse; Park, Como, Cui, and Kurlan (1993) in a 0.5 to 7 year follow-up of 100 patients, ages 8 to 21 years, found 2% in remission, 81% improved,

17% no change or worse. A review of 15 follow-up studies, from Mahler and Luke (1946) to Park et al. (1993) appears in Leckman, King, and Cohen (1999). The presence of comorbid disorders is indicated in two of these reports: Corbett, Mathews, Connell, and Shapiro (1969) state that prognosis is worse with comorbid depression or OCD; and Mak, Chung, Lee, and Chen (1992), find that poor social progress is associated with lower IQ, abnormal EEG, and poor school adjustment. There is no data on the relationship between tic severity or response to medication, to outcome. Jonathan is an example of a child with severe motor and vocal tics at age 13 who at age 23 no longer has motor-vocal tics.

CASE REPORT: JONATHAN

Jonathan was 14 years 6 months of age when he first appeared in our clinic, referred by a psychiatric hospital where he had been for the past three weeks, unresponsive to perfenazine, 3 mgm, and clomipramine, 25 mgm daily, given to control motor and phonic tics. When we first saw Jonathan, he was a physically small child, pleasant in appearance not at all dysplastic, but acutely distressed, trying to talk to us between loud barks, which could be heard throughout the clinic corridor. The barks were accompanied by head thrusts and jaw extensions and by continuously forcibly striking his thigh with right fist. On videotape, he had 1,250 tics in 10 minutes. He had been diagnosed as having Tourette's syndrome at about age 8 years, treated by his pediatrician with acceptable success; but never reducing compulsions of redoing, checking, touching of other children, and at times, fears. Approximately 2 months before his visit to us, his tics became severe. No specific episode was temporally related to the exacerbation.

Jonathan was the first child to whom we applied a 7 mgm transdermal nicotine patch, keeping him on the same dose of perfenazine and clomipramine he had been receiving. Within 3 hours after application of the patch, his motor tics dramatically subsided, the bark was no longer heard, and the thigh hitting was not seen. The patch was removed in 24 hours; not until 4 days later did the thigh punching return. The head extension, jaw thrust, and bark had not recurred. Tic count was 585 in 10 minutes. With application of a second transdermal nicotine patch, all tics again subsided and Jonathan was able to return to school. When seen 3 weeks later, tics had not returned. Over the next month, perfenazine was gradually discontinued and haloperidol 1 mgm daily was substituted. Transdermal nicotine patch was applied on a prn basis. During the next few years, compulsions were troubling but not bad enough to keep him from school. At age 16 years, Jonathan, now a sturdy, acned adolescent, began to experience loud, noisy, coprolalia that prevented him from going to school. Transdermal patch dose was increased to 14 mgm and the coprolalia stopped. Over the next two years, medication was gradually reduced, the frequency of TNP gradually decreased and by age 19 to 20, medication was no longer needed. Now age 22, Jonathan is a responsible paramedic, recently married, with no overt symptoms of Tourette's syndrome.

Whether the history of Jonathan's illness reflects a spontaneous remission, unrelated to any medication or therapy he received throughout the years, or whether the medication contributed to the remission, is an intriguing question.

COMORBID OBSESSIVE-COMPULSIVE DISORDER

We have indicated that the majority of patients with Tourette's syndrome also suffer with comorbid disorders: obsessive or compulsive disorders, attention deficit and/or hyperactivity disorders, learning disability, mood disorders and behavioral symptoms, increasing anxiety, irritability, anger, and aggression. It is estimated that only 12% of patients with Tourette's syndrome (range among study sites, 2% to 35%) had only motor or verbal tics without accompanying comorbid disorders (R. D. Freeman et al., 2000).

A review of 12 studies from D. Cohen (1980) to Spencer, Biederman, Harding, et al. (1998) found a wide range from 11% to 80% of individuals with Tourette's syndrome also have compulsive features (Robertson, 2000). The R. D. Freeman et al. (2000), review reported a mean of 27% for OCD comorbid with Tourette's syndrome, and 32% with obsessive-compulsive behavior (OCB) comorbid with TS. It is not clear whether these figures for OCD and OCB are measuring different entities (i.e., those meeting *DSM-IV* criteria for OCD and those with obsessive-compulsive symptoms that do not meet criteria) and reported separately or together. If together, then the total rate of OCD symptoms in Tourette's Disorder is estimated at 59%. Leckman, Walker, Goodman, Pauls, and Cohen (1994), in a review of 134 patients with Tourette's Disorder find 23% with obsessive compulsive symptoms and 69% with OCD. Since the prevalence of OCD in the general population is 1.9% to 3.2%, "The high rates of OCD in Tourette's syndrome individuals are remarkable" (Robertson, 2000).

The obsessions and the compulsions associated with Tourette's syndrome, however differ from those seen in individuals without Tourette's syndrome. The obsessions seen in Tourette's syndrome deal with violence, aggressive, sexual, and religious themes with a need to get things "just right" in ordering, counting, and arranging. There is concern with symmetry, touching, and redoing. The obsessions and compulsions in OCD, without Tourette's syndrome, are usually related to contamination with dirt, or germs, washing and undoing, and fear of something happening to themselves or a member of the family. These distinctions are not absolute but may be a guide in eliciting obsessive thought and compulsive behavior from patients attempting to repress these problems (Leckman et al., 1997; Petter, Richter, & Sandor, 1998; Robertson, 2000; Zohar et al., 1997). The obsessive-compulsive symptoms of Tourette's syndrome, moreover, have an equal male/female ratio, do not respond as well as the non Tourette's syndrome-OCD to medication, are characterized by early age onset, a more frequent family history of chronic tics, higher afternoon plasma prolactin levels, and more normal CNS oxytocin levels (Leckman et al., 1994a, 1994b). These findings suggest, "Tic-related obsessive compulsive disorder constitutes a distinctive obsessive compulsive disorder phenotype." Pauls, Alsobrook, Goodman et al., 1995, have postulated three types of OCD: (a) a familial type related to tic disorders, (b) a familial type unrelated to tics, and (c) a nonfamilial type. Thus some forms of OCD/OCS are genetically related to Tourette's syndrome and may be a phenotype of the putative Tourette's syndrome gene (s) (Pauls, Raymond, Stevenson, & Leckman, 1991).

COMORBID ADHD

The prevalence of ADHD in association with Tourette's syndrome is as high as 60% (range 33% to 91% in the R. D. Freeman et al., 2000, report). This prevalence rate is slightly higher that that of OCD-OCB in Tourette's syndrome and indeed looking again at the Freeman report, ADHD is the most prevalent of the symptoms and syndromes listed by the Freeman group in association with Tourette's syndrome. Table 15.2 presents the mean end range of symptoms comorbid with Tourette's syndrome.

The review of studies by Walkup et al. (1999) includes two Comings reports, one, a clinic-based survey of 250 TS patients, in whom the prevalence of ADHD was 54%, and second, a family study using 353 TS probands in whom the prevalence of ADHD was 60.9%; an epidemiological study (Apter, Pauls, Bleich, et al., 1992) of 28,037 individuals in Israel in which 12 individuals were found to have Tourette's syndrome, only 8.3% of whom had associated ADHD. In our clinic, at least 50% of children with Tourette's syndrome also had ADHD. As illustrated by the case report of Robert, most children have the onset of hyperactivity—impulsivity in their preschool years. Equally important is the emergence of tics within a year after stimulant medication, most often methylphenidate or dexedrine, is prescribed.

This progression raises the question of whether hyperactivity is an early manifestation of Tourette's syndrome, an inevitable progression for some children in the natural

Table 15.2   Mean end Range of Symptoms and Syndromes in Association with Tourette's Syndrome

N =	1,700	Range across Sites
% Female	18%	4–31%
Adopted	2.1%	0–10%
Mean age at onset of tics	6.4 years	(Males 6.3; females 6.6)
Mean age at diagnosis of TS	13.5 years	(Males 12.9; females 16.2)
TS only, no comorbidity	11%	0–36%
ADHD comorbid	61%	31–86%
OCD comorbid	33%	0–93%
OCB comorbid	29%	7–71%
CD/ODD comorbid	16%	4–63%
LD comorbid	21%	0–44%
Mood disorder comorbid	21%	5–60%
Anxiety disorder comorbid	17%	0–61%
PDD comorbid	4.5%	0–15%
Mental retardation comorbid	3.2%	0–13%
Anger control problems	34%	0–67%

Reprinted with permission from Freeman, R. D., Fast, D. K., Burd, L., Kerbeshian, J., Robertson, M., and Sandor, P. (2000). An international perspective on Tourette's syndrome. *Developmental Medicine and Child Neurology*, p. 439.

history of the syndrome. Would tics have emerged if stimulant medication had not been given? Is the stimulant medication given for hyperactivity somehow causing tics in previously unsusceptible individuals? Or do stimulant drugs simply bring out the symptoms in a child genetically vulnerable to Tourette's syndrome? The evidence for answering these questions is mixed.

In 1984, Golden described a 9-year-old boy who developed Tourette's syndrome after administration of methylphenidate for the treatment of hyperactivity. This report was followed by a number of similar reports in which tic disorders rapidly appeared after initiation of stimulant drugs, or in which tics, already established, were exacerbated when stimulants were used. It is estimated that in children with Tourette's syndrome who receive stimulants, 30% to 50% develop an exacerbation of tics. Ten percent of ADHD children who did not have tics before stimulants develop tics (Erenberg et al., 1985; Lipkin, Goldstein, & Adesman, 1994). Borcherding, Keysor, Rapoport, Elia, and Amass (1990) however, found that 34 of 45 (76%) boys (mean age 8.6 years) subjects in a study of methylphenidate and dextroamphetamine for ADHD, developed abnormal movements. Pollack, Cohen, and Friedhoff (1977) in the very title of their paper impute the "precipitation" of Tourette's syndrome "to methylphenidate therapy." In 100 patients with Tourette's syndrome evaluated at Yale University's child psychiatry and neurology clinics, Lowe et al. (1982) described 15 children, ages 3 to 10 years, who developed Tourette's syndrome following administration of stimulant medication for hyperactivity. Symptoms of Tourette's syndrome appeared at variable times after beginning stimulant medication, from several months to 2½ years. Lowe and his associates concluded that "motor tics or diagnosed Tourette's syndrome in a child should be a contraindication to the use of stimulant medication for alleviation of hyperactive symptoms; the existence of motor tic symptoms or diagnosed Tourette's syndrome in the parents, siblings or other family members of the index patient should be viewed as a relative contraindication to stimulant therapy" (p. 1731). Golden (1988) agreed with these conclusions and added that even in the absence of tics and no family history of tic disorder, the appearance of tics after stimulant medication has been given, calls for immediate discontinuation of the stimulant drug.

Denckla et al. (1976) reported the development of motor tics in 1.3% of children receiving methylphenidate for attention deficit disorder. On discontinuing the medication, tics subsided in all but one child out of the 1,520 children with ADD who were reviewed. However, if the children being treated for hyperactivity and attention deficit disorders had tics before the use of stimulants, 13.3% suffered exacerbation of the tics when receiving methylphenidate. Thus the incidence of full-blown Tourette's syndrome emerging in children who receive stimulant medication for ADHD does not appear to be high. Nevertheless, the huge number of children receiving stimulant medication for ADHD, conservatively estimated at 6% of the estimated 40 million schoolchildren in the United States or approximately 2.4 million children receiving stimulant medication, and the devastating effect on the individual child who does develop Tourette's syndrome while using stimulant drugs, make this a problem of importance and caution for clinicians. Furthermore, the number of children with Tourette's syndrome who have been treated with stimulant drugs appears to be increasing. Price, Leckman, Pauls, Cohen, and Kidd (1986), found that of 170 patients with Tourette's syndrome, 34 had been treated with stimulant drugs. In our own group of 90 children with persistent motor and vocal tics, 30 of them (one-third) had received methylphenidate or pemoline for hyperactivity and attention problems before the onset of motor and vocal tics.

A differing opinion is expressed by A. Shapiro and Shapiro (1988). The Shapiros categorically state, "In our opinion, there is inadequate evidences that stimulants precipitate or permanently exacerbate Tourette's syndrome" (p. 277). Comings and Comings (1984), comparing children with attention deficit disorder who subsequently developed motor and vocal tics, found that those who received stimulants had a significantly *longer* time interval between the onset of hyperactivity and the onset of tics than did those who did not receive stimulants. The Comings reasoned that if stimulants are significant in causing Tourette's syndrome or in precipitating tics, then the time interval between onset of ADHD to the onset of tics should be *decreased* in children with ADHD who receive stimulants compared with the onset of tics in ADHD children who do not receive stimulants. In two successive studies, each involving 250 patients, they found no evidence that stimulant drugs hastened the time of onset of tics and vocalizations. Indeed, the time interval was actually *greater* in the children receiving stimulant drugs. Comings and Comings feel that ADHD is an integral part of the symptom complex of Tourette's syndrome and that the natural history of the majority of Tourette's syndrome cases is to begin as ADHD and then, after an average interval of 2 to 3 years, to develop tics and phonic noises. In their review of nine studies encompassing over 1,500 patients with Tourette's syndrome, Comings and Comings found that, on that average, approximately one-half of all Tourette's syndrome patients also suffered from ADHD. Further, the more severe the symptoms of Tourette's syndrome, the greater the number of such patients having symptoms of ADHD, with ADHD being prevalent in 70% to 80% of the most severe group of TS patients and approximately one-third of the very mild cases. The Comings suggested that ADHD may be the first—indeed, the only—manifestation of the putative Tourette's syndrome gene. The findings of Price et al. (1986) also suggest that stimulant medication may not substantially increase the risk for developing Tourette's syndrome. In their study with six pairs of identical twins with ADHD, only one twin of each pair received stimulant drugs, yet both twins developed tics. These twin findings suggest that there may be a genetic vulnerability to Tourette's symptoms in children who develop the syndrome after using stimulant drugs.

The use of stimulant drugs in the *course of Tourette's syndrome* is also controversial. Although they recognize that pemoline, methylphenidate, and dextroamphetamine can exacerbate tics, A. Shapiro and Shapiro (1988) stated that "the increase in tics is short-lived and the potential benefits of stimulants [in reducing symptoms of hyperactivity and attention deficit and in managing the lethargy, dysphoria, and impaired cognition of neuroleptics] often outweigh their disadvantages" (p. 277) and that "stimulants and butyrophenones have overlapping and different effects on tics" (p. 277). Comings, treating 92 patients with Tourette's syndrome with stimulant drugs, stated that in only 7 of these patients were stimulants discontinued because tics could not be alleviated with haloperidol or pimozide. Comings and Comings (1987) said that "judicious use of stimulants, kept at the lowest effective dose, can contribute significantly to overall treatment" (p. 727).

Gadow et al. (1995), finding that giving methylphenidate to 34 prepuberty children with ADHD and tic disorders, evoked a small but significant increase in frequency of motor tics and tendency for fewer vocal tics, which were not perceived by caregivers as disturbing, concurs with Comings.

Whether the tics, which arise or are exacerbated during the course of stimulant treatment for ADHD are reversible on discontinuation of the stimulant drug is also not certain. Castellanos, Giedd, Elia, Marsh, Ritchie, et al. (1997) found that such tics were revisable in 14 children who continued on methylphenidate for 1 to 3 years. In our clinical experience, however, while tic reversal does occur with discontinuation of methylphenidate or dextroanphetamine, it is impossible to predict with certainty which patient will do so.

It has been suggested that clonidine with or without stimulant medication for Tourette's syndrome may be a viable alternative to stimulants alone. In our opinion, consideration of the influence of each symptom on the adjustment and comfort of the child and his family needs evaluation of before deciding which symptoms should be medicated. Wherever possible, stimulant medication is avoided. This decision is based not only on the exacerbation of tics, but also our lack of knowledge of the factor or factors, that contribute to remission of Tourette's syndrome in late adolescence. If a factor in remission is the decrease in availability of dopamine as a result of pruning of dopamine neurons in adolescence, then the natural history of the disorder may be perturbed with the addition of dopamine producing drugs. Although the prevalence of ADHD in association with vocal tics is high, the genetic relationship is not clear. While the Comings feel that there is a common genetic relationship between ADHD and the putative Tourette's syndrome gene(s), Pauls et al. (1986) and Pauls, Leckman, and Cohen (1993) suggest that only *some* of the ADHD, particularly that which appears together with Tourette's syndrome, may be related to the Tourette's gene. However, the clinical relationship between the two syndromes suggests a related biological mechanism in terms of neuroanatomy and/or neurophysiology does indeed exist.

COMORBID LEARNING DISORDERS

The case vignette of Robert also illustrates additional problems of the child with Tourette's syndrome: school adjustment and academic achievement. There is by now general agreement that learning constitutes a significant problem for children with Tourette's syndrome. In the R. D. Freeman et al. (2000) report, a mean of 23% (range 3% to 43%) of children with Tourette's syndrome have in addition, learning disabilities. This prevalence (22%) was also found by Erenberg, Cruse, and Rothner (1986) in their survey of 200 children and adolescents with Tourette's syndrome. However in an early study, A. R. Lucas, Kauffman, and Morris, 1967 found "learning disorders in 9 of 15 children with Tourette's syndrome. Comings and Comings (1987), report that compared with their control sample, children with Tourette's syndrome are placed in special classes in significantly greater numbers and require greater special tutoring; using their own criteria, "dyslexia" was found in 26.8% of Tourette's patients compared with 4.2% in their control sample. Lerer (1987) reported that "one half of the children with Tourette's syndrome have specific learning disabilities, perceptual motor problems, attention deficit disorders, hyperactive behavior, and abnormalities of psycho-educational testing." Hagin and Kugler (1988) found that 68% of their sample of 16 children with Tourette's syndrome earned scores below their expectancy in *group* tests of reading, 52% below expectancy in tests of spelling, and 56% below expectancy in mathematics. *Individual* tests of oral reading and *individual* tests of reading comprehension, however, were in the expected range. In a later epidemiological study of 3,000 children in a single school district in California, Comings et al. (1990) identified 12% of children in special education classes as having Tourette's syndrome. Kurlan, Whitmore, Irvine, McDermott, and Como (1994) estimated the prevalence of definite or probable tics in full-time special education in a single school district in New York state to be 26%.

One problem in evaluating these diverse reports is the perennial one of understanding just what authors mean when they use the term "dyslexia," "specific learning disabilities," and "learning disorders." Perhaps more specific questions should be raised: Is there a unique pattern in the academic difficulty and in the patterns of neuropsychological dysfunction characteristic of Tourette's syndrome? Using carefully defined criteria, is the prevalence of specific learning disability greater in Tourette's syndrome than in the normal population or in a group of unselected referrals to a child psychiatric clinic? The following subsections describe academic and cognitive deficits that occur more frequently in children with Tourette's syndrome than in samples of control children.

Coding Subtest Scores

The scores on the *Coding subtest of the WISC-R* fall significantly below the individual's mean scaled scores. In the Hagin and Kugler (1988) study of 26 children with Tourette's syndrome, 40% of the children had Coding subtest scores significantly below their mean scaled scores. Ten of these children, the subjects of an earlier report (Hagin, Beecher, Pagano, & Kreeger, 1982), were recruited from the Tourette's Association to identify educational practices. The remaining 16 came as patients to the School Consultation Center at Fordham University, with diverse complaints relating to school placement, academic achievement, and behavioral adjustment. The age of the entire group ranged from 7 years to young adulthood. On the WISC-R, their Full Scale IQ was 104 ± 16 with a mean verbal IQ of 106 ± 18 and a mean performance IQ of 102 ± 15. Thirty-five percent of the group had significantly higher verbal scores and 12% significantly higher performance scores. However, although 36% of the group demonstrated an increased degree of scatter in the subtest scores, no typical pattern of subtest scores, with the exception of the Coding subtest, was found. The Coding subtest measures speed and accuracy in associating visual symbols, using a written response. This may reflect a visuomotor-praxic problem. Coding was also the lowest subtest score found by Thompson, O'Quinn, and Logue (1979) in four children with Tourette's syndrome and by Incagnoli and Kane (1982) in 13 children with Tourette's syndrome. Harcherlik, Carronara, Shaywitz, Shaywitz, and Cohen (1982) also found Coding (digit symbol B) along with handwriting and with difficulty adapting to changes in speed of the road tracking task, to be the major cognitive deviation from normal in a well-studied sample of 15 children, ages 7 to 15, with Tourette's syndrome.

Visuomotor Function

Most studies of neuropsychological function of children with Tourette's syndrome found impairment in *visuomotor function* particularly as seen on the Bender VGMT (Hagin, Beecher, Pagano, et al., 1982; Incagnoli & Kane, 1982). In a study of 25 consecutive admissions of children with Tourette's syndrome to the Child Study Center at the University of South Florida Medical School, A. A. Silver (1988) found 21 of them to have significant difficulty with visuomotor function. The age of these children ranged from 5 to 17 years; 20 of them earned a full scale IQ on the WISC-R within the normal range, 2 were borderline, and 3 were in the bright-normal range. The type of visuomotor impairment varied, however, with the majority demonstrating immature Gestalt patterns with the persistence of verticalization and angulation difficulty. Three records showed perseveration, which took their repetitive dots across the page and onto the desk; in two children a compulsive pattern—ritualistic counting or tapping—prevented accurate representation of the designs; and in two children the tics presented a jerky, uncoordinated written pattern. The immaturity of the Bender VGMT did not appear to be a visual perceptual one, because the errors were recognized. Rather, it appeared to be a praxic one, with the child's inability to make his fingers do what his eyes conveyed to his brain.

This study was extended (D. A. Harris & Silver, 1995), to 100 children, 10 years of age and older, with TS, consecutive admissions to the Child Study Center at the University of South Florida. Bender-Gestalt drawings of each of these children were reviewed independently by two reviewers, each with experience in the educational examination of children. There was 92% interrater reliability in the finding of immaturity in the Gestalt. Of the 100 children, only 25 were considered normal. Sixty-five had rotations of 45° or greater (see Case Study: Armando, later in this chapter), absence of verticalization, angulation difficulty, errors in orientation of figures. Drawings had immaturity in organization and placement of the figures included overlapping and/or separation of figures, distortion of figures in size or form, perseveration, gross immaturity (e.g., large loops or circles for dots).

Mathematics

In academic achievement, *mathematics* appears to suffer most, although in the Hagin and Kugler (1988) study using the Woodcock-Johnson Psychoeducational Battery, as noted earlier, 52% scored below expectancy in tests of written spelling, 56% were below expectancy in mathematics, and 68% were below expectancy in group tests of reading. Golden (1984), Incagnoli and Kane (1982), and Joschko and Rourke (1985) also found low arithmetic scores in their patients. Hagin and Kugler felt that problems in the test format itself accounted for the poor performance on *group* tests of reading comprehension. It is the sustained effort over an extended period that causes the children with Tourette's syndrome difficulty on that test, not the word attack skills that these children, as a group, do have. The poor spelling and arithmetic result may be due to the basic motor problems of Tourette's children, which results in slow, inconvenient, and poor handwriting, as well as their praxic difficulty.

The Woodcock-Johnson Psychoeducational Battery Testing of 100 children whose Bender-Gestalt tests were reviewed in the preceding paragraphs found written spelling, writing, and mathematics calculation to be problems; with word identification, reading comprehension, and word problem solving in arithmetic to be at age and grade expectancy (see Figure 15.2). Seventy percent were below age and grade levels in spelling, 65% below expectancy in writing, and approximately 50% below expectancy in arithmetic (D. A. Harris & Silver, 1995).

David, for example (age 13 years 5 months; 7th grade), earned (Woodcock-Johnson Tests of Achievement), percentile score of 98 and 99 in letter word identification, and reading comprehension but 64th percentile in calculation, 77 broad math and 79 in applied math problems. Allen was 14 years 4 months of age in the 8th grade earned a percentile rank of 97 in letter identification, 99 in reading comprehension and 90 in applied problems. His broad reading percentile rank was 99.9. His calculation achieved a percentile rate of 56, his written dictation 50. Dykens et al. (1990) and Schuerholz et al. (1998) also reported weakness in arithmetic and strength in single word decoding. Schultz et al. (1998) did not find poor mathematics score in a group of children with Tourette's syndrome relative to control children from the same clinic; overall, the Yale group found 4% to 16% of the Tourette's sample met their criteria for specific learning disability.

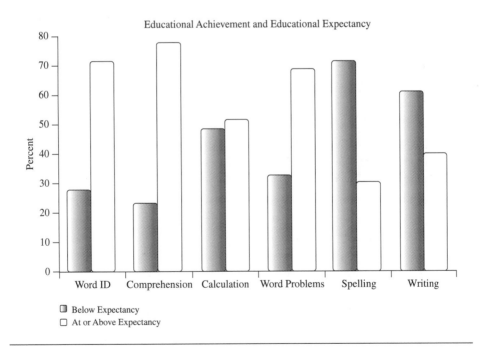

Figure 15.2 Educational achievement and educational expectancy in 100 children with Tourette's syndrome.

Attention-Deficit/Hyperactivity Symptoms

The presence of *ADHD symptoms* may be significant in the achievement of Tourette's children. In their study, Comings and Comings (1987) found "poor retention" in 41% of their 26 Tourette's sample, as contrasted with 8.3% among a control group. The presence of ADD may be a crucial factor in this finding since the distribution of reading scores in Tourette's syndrome *without ADD* was not significantly different from that found in controls, whereas the distribution of scores of Tourette's children *with ADD* was significantly impaired compared with controls. Comings and Comings used as their criteria for "dyslexia" the presence of three or more reading problems (letter, number, or word reversals; dropped words; slow reader, poor retention).

In summary, what appears to characterize most children with Tourette's syndrome is difficulty with Coding, visuomotor-praxic function, mathematics, written spelling, and handwriting. All of these deficits may be an outcome of visual-praxic immaturities. In a subset, attentional problems may be significant.

The symptoms of Tourette's syndrome may interfere with learning in ways other than by the cognitive effects of that condition. Such symptoms include:

- The tics themselves—the motor tics that make written work uncontrolled, jerky, and sloppy and that make handwriting a physically difficult chore; the vocal tics that accentuate the Tourette's child's difference from other children and call attention to her difference.

- The tendency toward restlessness, impulsivity, and hyperactive behavior.

- Obsessive thinking, which does not permit the child to move freely from one task to another.

- Compulsive behavior, which traps him into a ritual such as tapping and touching and keeps him from completing a task.

- Perseverative behaviors, which may be akin to compulsions or may be one way lack of impulse control is manifested.

- Increased anxiety, which may be reflected generally in poor sleep habits, morning fatigue, difficulty getting to school, and finally, refusal to go to school.

- The social consequences of these symptoms—teasing of classmates and demands of teachers and schools.

- The emotional consequences—poor self-esteem, guilt, and depression.

- Finally, medication used to treat the symptoms may itself contribute to decreased alertness, sleepiness, and perhaps depression and school phobia.

Thus the cognitive deficits are only one part of the many factors in Tourette's syndrome that interfere with learning. That studies report more than half of their sample of Tourette's children have some problems in learning, however, attest to their importance.

It will be noted, however, that *specific language disability* is not included in the symptoms affecting learning as we have listed them. While it is undoubtedly true that a few children with Tourette's syndrome are suffering from a specific learning disability, as does Robert, the subject of our case vignette, it is questionable whether the prevalence of specific learning disability in Tourette's children is greater than that in the normal population. To date there has been no study, using the generally accepted criteria for developmental language disability, to prove that the prevalence of SLD in Tourette's children is greater than that in the normal, unselected school population or even in children diagnosed with other emotional and/or behavioral problems.

The identification of specific language disability in children with Tourette's syndrome is important not only for management of the individual child but also for research studies. SLD and Tourette's syndrome both have a high family incidence (see Chapter 11 for genetic studies of SLD). The genetic mode of transmission for each, however, is not clear. If there is indeed a higher prevalence of SLD in children with Tourette's syndrome than in an unselected sample of their normal classmates, what is the relationship between the two? Is SLD one manifestation of Tourette's syndrome governed by the same genetic fault(s)? Are we dealing with two separate syndromes, which are synergistic? Is there a genetic linkage between the two disorders? These questions are as yet unanswered.

Nevertheless, the recognition of a specific language disorder in a given child with Tourette's syndrome is vital to his or her adjustment. In Robert the SLD was recognized, but it was not treated to the point of mastery and the contribution of his Tourette's syndrome to learning problems was not appreciated. Thus his paper tests indicated that he could adjust in the mainstream, the Tourette's symptoms said he could not. As part of the management of his school problems, Robert was returned to the SLD class, to the teacher who was familiar to him and, most important, who understood him. Just as any child with a severe specific language disability, the child with Tourette's syndrome who also has a specific language disability also needs treatment for that disability. We cannot rely on spontaneous maturation to improve perceptual deficits, as the case of Armando shows.

CASE STUDY: ARMANDO

Armando was 9 years 9 months of age when he was first seen. In addition to motor and vocal tics, he did not seem to understand directions unless they were presented to him slowly, simply, and even repetitiously. His overall cognitive ability was above average, with no significant discrepancy between verbal and performance scores; his neurological examination was normal, but he had severe perceptual difficulty in temporal sequencing, confusing events in time and being unable to place verbal meaning in proper sequences. He also had severe visuomotor problems characterized by 90-degree rotations on the Bender VGMT. Our findings were conveyed to his school. We did not see Armando for 3 years. Now he is in sixth grade, reading at about the third-grade level. Over the years, he had no special help in school, and spontaneous, maturation of his skills did not occur (see Figure 15.3).

In contrast to the specific language disability Robert and Armando demonstrated, Sam had skills in place but was unable to demonstrate what he knew in the classroom. His problems were inherent in Tourette's syndrome itself.

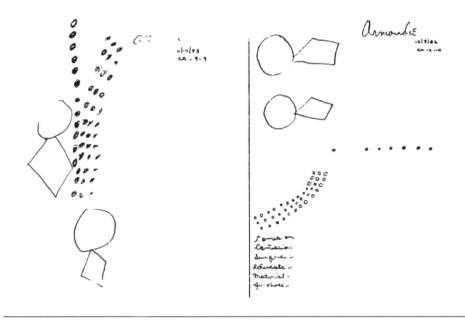

Figure 15.3   Bender-Gestalt drawing. Armando: Age 9 years 9 months and 12 years 10 months. Tourette's symptoms mild; not receiving medication; cognitive function high normal; severe temporal sequencing deficit. Educational remediation was advised but not done. The primitive features of his gestalt drawing at age 9 years 9 months are still apparent 3 years later.

CASE STUDY: SAM

At 7 years of age, Sam was referred for an assessment of the educational factors in his troubles at school by the psychiatrist who was treating him. Sam's tics were mild (blinking, shoulder shrugging, and throat clearing). He arrived clutching a sheaf of dittoed worksheets, most of them incomplete. Early in the session, he became apprehensive about the whereabouts of his mother who was providing a developmental history in a nearby office. When both office doors were opened partially and he was told he could check on her as often as he wanted to, he settled down for the morning's work. He complained bitterly about the work the teacher expected him to accomplish, the notes on his behavior she insisted he take home and the punishment for noncompletion of his seatwork—the loss of his recreation period or gym class. He asked plaintively, "What do I do if I get tired?"

Psychological study showed Sam to be a bright youngster earning a verbal IQ of 112 (79th percentile) and a performance IQ of 101 (53rd percentile) on the WISC-R. The full scale IQ of 107 was essentially an average of the disparate functions tapped by the two scales and was in Sam's case not very useful in educational planning. Sam's high score on the Vocabulary subtest reflected his good verbal ability and the wide range of experiences he had had. Sam was a well-built, redheaded, 7-year-old, who often called on language cues to help himself with nonverbal performance tasks he found difficult. For example, on the Coding subtest he named the different symbols as he located and copied them. It is questionable how much these cues helped, for the Coding subtest was a significantly low scaled score for him. Analyzed according to the factorial structure of the WISC-R, Sam's record appears as follows:

Verbal Comprehension Items	84th percentile
Perceptual Integrative Items	66th percentile
Sequencing and Memory Items	22nd percentile

Sam seemed comfortable at the Center, chatting along about related matters as we completed the test items. There were signs of self-doubts. He found the Arithmetic subtest difficult, but emphasized how much fun it was, as if he was trying to reassure himself. He also wondered several times if his mother "missed" him. When encouraged to go to the office where she was being interviewed, he did so and quickly returned to his work.

In view of the level of functioning seen on the WISC-R, Sam's educational expectancy was estimated to be at the high second-grade level or the 80th to 90th percentile range. When this estimate was compared with his achievement test scores, it was apparent that he was reading appropriately to expectance. His oral reading was rapid and accurate, placing at Grade 4.1, the 96th percentile on the WRAT. That reading was already a tool was seen in his score of Grade 3.3 (93rd percentile) on the Comprehension section of the PIAT. He had a good stock of sight words and made good use of contextual cues. Even his errors were intelligent (i.e., the word *pigeons* read as "penguins").

Handwriting was difficult for him. He worked hard to form legible letters, but had great difficulty with organization and spacing. He could spell a few words and write simple sentences. Arithmetic was the hardest skill of all for him, but he was able to handle items dealing with numeration, quantity, and simple addition and subtraction combinations.

The work samples that he had brought from school were much simpler than many of the test items he handled easily in our session. The school seatwork involved such activities as coloring tiny sections of a mosaiclike picture, connecting numbered dots to form a picture, cutting out and pasting words under pictures, and copying text from the chalkboard. It not only did not tap any of the high-level reading skills he showed on tests, but the coloring, writing, cutting, and pasting required the motor control that Sam just could not manage for any sustained period. That Sam's teacher did not appreciate this was apparent from her written comments on some of the pages: "Good, but try to stay in the boxes!" "Why didn't you finish?"

Sam's drawings of the figures of the Bender VGMT are convincing evidence of his difficulties in organization of Gestalten, immature verticalization of diagonals, and substitution of simpler figures for more complex ones (Figure 15.4). On the Purdue Pegboard, he had difficulty synchronizing his hands on the bimanual task, and the score for either hand separately fell below the 20th percentile for his age group. Right-left discrimination was borderline, accurate on him and on the

SAM:
Plate A

Figure 15.4   Bender-Gestalt drawing. Sam: Age 7 years. In first grade, evaluating difficulties in organization with impulsive, primitive qualities. At this time in his life, Sam was under great stress in school.

examiner, but errors with crossed commands. Symmetrization errors occurred on the finger schema test. Other than these problems in fine motor control and body image, there was little of note on the supplementary tests.

Sam was learning fairly well at school, despite his worries about being called "chicken nose" when his tics appeared in class, his almost phobic concern about fatigue, his dependence on his mother, and the signs of compulsive behavior that were beginning to appear. It was apparent also that his teacher understood neither his strengths nor his deficits, although Sam had been in her classroom for nearly 8 months. Attempts were made to reason with her about Sam's behavior, but these telephone calls deteriorated into a recital of Sam's misdeeds. Sam's test results and general material about Tourette's syndrome were shared with the school psychologist, who promised to work with Sam's teacher on his problem, but she was unable to effect any change in the teacher's management of the boy.

Discouraged as they witnessed the effects on his classroom on Sam's emotional state and disheartened when he was scheduled for placement in a self-contained special class with mixed diagnostic categories for the succeeding year, his parents removed him from school. This decision was appreciated by the IEP, which listed the following as the complete long-term goals the next school year.

The student will

Improve number and numeration skills.

Improve operations with whole numbers.

Increase responsiveness and appreciation of classroom structure.

Increase the ability to function independently in the classroom.

Reduce the incidence of physically disruptive behavior with peers.

Improve responsiveness to teacher intervention.

Increase awareness of personal thoughts and feelings.

Reduce the incidence of disruptive peer interactions.

Acquire basic social skills sensitivities.

This decision to remove the child from school was not one to be encouraged since it is violation of the compulsory education laws, but it can be understood as the response of intelligent, caring, and completely frustrated parents.

Sam did not return to school during what would have been his second-grade year. Private tutoring was provided 5 to 6 hours per week; his parents supplemented this education by taking him on trips to museums and by giving him a membership in the Y that provided socialization in sports, swimming, and craft activities. The family also researched schools and moved to a more hospitable school district where he had been enrolled in the third grade for 4 months when he returned for a follow-up appointment. On retesting, his fine motor control had improved (Figure 15.5) and his achievement appeared to show no ill effects:

Wide Range Achievement Test

Oral reading	Grade 6.7
Spelling	Grade 3.7
Arithmetic	Grade 3.6

Peabody Individual Achievement Test

Reading Comprehension	Grade 6.5

Sam's account of his school day, in compulsive detail, also seemed to indicate that, at least at present, all was well:

First I unpack my bag and put my books in the desk. Then we pledge allegiance. Then Mrs. A helps me with math or things I don't understand. If I do good, I get a turn at the computer with Math Mansions or I watch some other kid at the computer. Then I go back to my room. I try to listen to what the other kids are doing. If it's interesting I get involved. Or I read a book. (What do you like to read about?) Oh, lots of things,

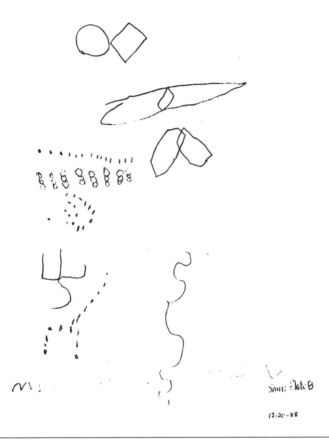

Figure 15.5 Bender-Gestalt drawing. Sam: Age 8 years. After a year of decreased school demands. The gestalt is improved in organization with decreased impulsivity and fewer primitive elements.

I'm interested in electricity, coal, Hawaii, rocks. Then we have reading groups, I'm in Stars. Then we get ready for lunch. I go home for lunch. I come back and finish my work. Then we have specials: library, gym, art. I like art best. (How are other kids in the class?) Friendly—I have two friends, K——— and M——— . And the nurse, I'm allowed to go to the nurse if I feel tense or tired. (What do you do in her office?) I read this boring book.

Sam's account of his school day illustrates some of the management principles discussed earlier in this chapter. It shows how the classroom provides support as needed, balanced by a challenging level of work in the areas where he does well. While rigid conformity in behavior is not required, social awareness is fostered by the low-key tempo of the classroom. Finally, the nurse's office is available as a temporary refuge.

MOOD DISORDERS AND ANXIETY

Prevalence of "mood disorders" and "anxiety disorders" in Tourette's syndrome is reported in Freeman et al. (2000) as a mean of 20% (range 2% to 47%) and mean of 18% (range 4% to 38%), respectively. What symptoms are included in mood disorders and anxiety disorders is not stated, however. The appearance of depression as a symptom or as major depression disorder or as bipolar disorder; or anxiety as a symptom or as a panic disorder, or separation anxiety or a general anxiety disorder, is not spelled out. From the data presented, it is not known whether these symptoms are secondary to Tourette's syndrome, and/or to OCD and/or ACHD or are comorbid to Tourette's syndrome in the sense of being a disorder as delineated in *DSM-IV-TR*. Pauls et al. (1993) compare the first-degree relatives of 85 probands with Tourette's syndrome with those of 27 control children. Compared with the first-degree relatives of the controls, the relatives of the Tourette's probands had significantly higher prevalence of major depressive disorder, panic disorder, social phobia, and generalized anxiety. However the higher than expected prevalence was significantly elevated in these relatives who themselves had tic disorder. Pauls et al. concludes that these mood and anxiety disorders are not variant phenotypic expressions of the putative Tourette's syndrome gene(s). Comings (1994) however, assessed 20 behavioral problems in a consecutive series of 361 Tourette's syndrome probands, 113 nonproband Tourette's syndrome relatives, 380 relatives without Tourette's syndrome, and 68 controls. Ranking according to the number of behaviors that was significant, indicated that mania, obsessive-compulsive behaviors, and schizoid behaviors are considered as an expression of Tourette's syndrome (Gts) genes.

Previously Comings and Comings (1987) examined 246 patients with Tourette's syndrome, 17 patients with ADHD, 15 with ADHD and Tourette's syndrome, and 47 controls, concluding that depression and manic-depressive symptoms are "common in Tourette's syndrome patients and are an integral part of the disorder, rather than being secondary to motor or vocal tics."

In a study of adult patients with Tourette's syndrome, Berthier, Kulisevsky, and Campos (1998) found that in a consecutive series of 90 patients, the "full clinical spectrum" including bipolar disorders, schizo-affective bipolar disorder, bipolar II disorders and cyclothymic disorder, was found in 30 patients. Kerbeshian, Burd, and Klug, in a series of studies from 1984 to 1996, found that the "estimated risk of developing bipolar disorder among children, adolescents and adults with Tourette's disorder was more than four times higher than the level expected by chance" (1995). There was insufficient evidence to say, as did Comings, that a genetic mechanism may play a causal role.

While relationships of these symptoms to Tourette's syndrome is as yet obscure—whether they are secondary to the motor, phonic tics, the OCD, ADHD, and learning problems, or driven by the same genetic mechanism(s) as are the motor and phonic tics, or are driven by genetic mechanisms of their own—the fact is that they do frequently appear in conjunction with the motor and phonic tics of Tourette's syndrome. Indeed, the behavior problems associated with Tourette's syndrome may be more disturbing to the child and certainly to his family than the tics themselves (Budman, Bruun, Park, & Olson, 1998; Stephens & Sandor, 1999; Wand, Matazow, Shady, & Furer, 1993).

To quantify the extent and severity of behavioral symptom on children with Tourette's syndrome, a 15-item scale (Tourette's Disorder Severity Scale, TODS), sampling lability of mood, depression, irritability, impulsivity, aggression as well as tics and compulsions has been developed by the Center for Infant and Child Development at the University of South Florida. The development reliability and validity of this scale has been described in Shytle et al. (2000).

INTRAPSYCHIC PROBLEMS

Tourette's syndrome thus involves more than phonic and motor tics, bizarre compulsive behavior, and failed control. It affects the feelings the child has about himself, the integrity of his ego, his feelings about the people around him, and his expectations from the world in which he lives. Tourette's affects the child with the disorder directly and indirectly: directly by the psychological defenses he must build to defend against the frustration of failed impulse control and the increased vulnerability to stress; indirectly in his reactions to the way family, peers, and teachers respond to his symptoms.

Tourette's syndrome is characterized by an impulse to action. The action is largely involuntary, but the impulse to the action is preceded by an awareness that the particular action will occur, a conscious sensation of specific tension building up within oneself. Bliss (1980) described the feeling as "a compelling, though subtle and fleeting itch, the moments before a sneeze explodes, the tantalizing touch of a feather" (p. 1344). Bliss continues: "Each movement is the result of a . . . capitulation to a demanding and restless urge" (p. 1345). One child in our sample (A. A. Silver, 1988) said, "I can feel it when I have to say these [bad] words. They keep coming into my mind. I say them to myself over and over and over again. I try to stop it, but it has to come out." Even at age 5, the struggle between the impulse to action and the action may be seen. Laura, a verbal, bright 5-year-old, had a grunting vocalization accompanied by spitting. She said, "I know I'm spitting but I can't help it. I think about it and I do it." Brian, age 10½, had a compulsion to tap his pencil on his mathematics paper. This is done in patterns of three, and is sometimes accompanied by stamping his foot on the floor. He said, "I know it's coming. I can feel it in my hand. It is urging me to put a dot there." Clarence, age 16, was referred to our clinic because he was disruptive in his class. He said, "Tourette's disease just maddens me. Sometimes I would like to holler out loud. I try to hold myself back, but it comes out." The discharge of tension into motor action may for a time be held back by the child, but it invariably escapes voluntary control. For a time this discharge may relieve the tension, only to have it build again. Thus the feelings preceding action may involve not only repetition of words but also the mental representation of a motor pattern. There are attempts at control over the action, but it finally escapes into involuntary behavior. Practically, this struggle is seen in school as the child attempts to conform to the teacher's instructions. The short periods of quiet the child manages to sustain are broken by a sudden dystonic movement or vocalization.

Important as the actual impulsive movement or vocalization is in affecting acceptance by peers, teachers, and even parents, the inability to control his or her thoughts and impulses is equally important to the child's own ego. Charles, age 9, put it succinctly: "I do not have mind over matter." Two types of response, frequently blurred together in the same child, may appear. In the first, the impulse and the action are projected onto some sinister force that is controlling the child. William, age 15, said, "It is an affliction of Satan who is trying to take over my life, telling me to do these things." William looks in the mirror and sometimes he sees not his image but Satan looking back at him. "I looked red and I had a knife. I thought Satan was going to stab me." When Kenny, age 11, looked in the mirror, he sometimes thought that his image was really someone else forcing him to think and say the things he considers bad. Robert, age 10, was afraid that "an insane guy" would come into his house. He said, "I convinced myself that if I hide under the blanket with my dog, I can't be shot by some insane guy." (As he told of this fear, Robert stopped and said he sometimes does crazy things that he cannot help doing and that he is afraid of the crazy thoughts he has. He was able to identify with the "insane guy" whom he fears.) The projections of Patsy, age 12, have become hallucinations of "some evil person telling me to make these faces" (her facial tics).

At the other extreme are children whose impulses are egosyntonic. They blame themselves for the behavior they cannot control. The explosive outburst, the tic, becomes a part of themselves and they are in consistent conflict over the "bad" or evil things, the uncontrolled things they do, and the good things the world expects them to do. Guilt and its consequences, depression, arise from the conflict. Kenny, age 11, talked to God "a lot." He said, "I pray to be forgiven for all the bad things I do, especially when I curse my mother." He constantly needed God's assurance that he will be forgiven. Michael, age 13, fought a constant battle between good and evil, evil argues with God, telling Michael to steal.

Andy, age 17, felt his thoughts were so bad he was afraid to say anything or bad thoughts will emerge. He sat rigidly in the chair, struggling to talk, wanting very much to communicate, yet only capable of looking to the examiner for understanding. Andy's paralyzing obsessions were preceded by a hypomanic episode that lasted about 6 months, characterized by denial of his gross perioral tics, occasional sniffing sounds, and choreiform movements of the arms and shoulders. The denial was abetted by his mother, who refused to accept the diagnosis.

Even when the child has adopted an outgoing, friendly, and apparently relaxed adjustment, the undercurrent of self-blame and depression may be seen. Jennifer, age 17, was a physically mature young woman whose Tourette's syndrome manifested itself in an occasional explosive echolalic repetition of her own affect-charged verbal responses and in an occasional jerky movement of her head. Her outgoing demeanor changed, however, when she said how bad she was or when, despite her efforts to prevent it, an explosive, expletive outburst was directed at her mother. Jennifer has been placed in a class for physically handicapped children, where she says she belongs and is most comfortable. Actually from a psychological and social point of view, this is an inappropriate placement for Jennifer. It only reinforces her feelings that she is a crippled child, that she does not belong and fears to be in the normal world, where her excellent appearance and good intelligence would help her concept of herself. Obviously, medical and psychological help is needed to change her image of herself.

The lack of balance between impulse and restraint, the difficulty in control of motor tics and vocalization, the constant battle between good and evil, the undercurrent of guilt and depression all evoke additional problems that make socialization difficult. All of the children seen by us were driven by anxiety. The cause of the anxiety, however, may not be clear. Just as the obsessions and compulsions may be multidetermined, the anxiety in these children may also be multidetermined. Anxiety may indeed spring from the conflicts created by the specific consequences of poor impulse control—the guilt and the depression. In addition, however, the biological substrate of Tourette's disease may predispose to anxiety, attenuating the stimulus barrier so that it is inadequate to deal with forces from within the organism or with those impinging on it. Physiological as well as psychological homeostasis is precariously balanced, and the child becomes a labile organism, quick to react to any stimulus viewed as threatening, and demanding immediate, sometimes irrational, gratification of needs as he or she perceives them. When these needs cannot be met, as sooner or later they cannot, the child easily erupts into a tantrum. Robert A., age 11, tried to make his parents satisfy his every whim. Robert has become a tyrant, controlling his parents and trying to get everyone else in the world to do just as he wishes.

This anxiety may emerge as specific fear. How this occurs may be seen in Kenneth, age 11. He was afraid to be in his room alone, afraid of ghosts and burglars, so afraid that he had a knife and access to his father's gun. He had terrifying dreams of being attacked and overwhelmed. He dreamed he was "in a trailer or a house, and a big thing came through the door, a wolf. I gave him something to eat but he attacked me"; and "I was living in a trailer on the beach. A big storm came and pushed me into the water." His anxiety, as well as possible ambivalence toward his mother, is seen in another dream: "Some person came and hit my mother and threw her down. They slapped her in the face. I shot this guy, but plenty others kept coming." These dreams were most disturbing to Kenny, especially since he continued to think the dreams would come true.

While the resurgence of anxiety and emergence of unresolved developmental issues are not unusual in adolescence, in Kenneth and other children we have seen, symptoms of anxiety are often severe enough to be considered an anxiety disorder. All have difficulty falling asleep and all have similar dreams. Robert D., age 9, said, "I just can't fall asleep. I just sit there and look at the moon." He dreams, "A monster is about to eat me. I took a sword and stabbed him in the side but he ran after me." Charles, a bright 10-year-old, said, "I have a wooden sword. If a monster came in, I would cut him in half." Patsy, age 12, said, "I'm afraid of being in a room by myself. A killer could bust my window with a rock." She described a dream: "White puppy dogs are biting me. I eat them for dinner." Robert, age 14, heard "noises in the ceiling." This dream evoked panic. All children we have seen attempt to protect themselves by bedtime rituals, such as checking doors, windows, closets, and under the bed, as 13-year-old James felt compelled to do for 15 minutes at a time. James was so afraid of burglars coming into his room that he slept in the linen chest at the foot of his mother's bed.

Compulsions, of course, cannot defend against the recurring anxiety, the feelings of being overwhelmed and hurt. Illusions of a face coming out of the closet or a person emerging from clothing or from the shadows of furniture are not infrequent. Thus their anxiety alone tends to make these children prisoners of themselves. They are afraid to sleep overnight with other children and many resist any change in their own routines. According to some of them (Robert D., age 9; Robert A., age 11; Kenny, age 11; James, age 13; Michael, age 13; William, age 15; Clarence, age 17), their main problem is that they cannot get to sleep. As a result, they ask, how can they be expected to wake up in time for school? This becomes an excuse for refusing to go to school. It also becomes a focal point of tension between mothers and children as they try with increasing frustrations to get them out of bed and on the school bus.

Depression is also seen in their low opinion of themselves. They are generally pessimistic about their future. Michael, who earned a full scale IQ of 109 on the WISC-R, feels that his brain is worthless and all he can ever hope to become is a garbage man. Kenneth feels he is ugly and other kids hate him. He has many somatic complaints: headaches and chest pain, "like a sword going through me." Robert says, "If my Tourette's gets worse, I would do something [to myself]." Clarence is concerned about what his disease "will do to my brain in the future." Charles says, "Why do I have to be me? Why is my soul put in this body? Sometimes I think I must be reincarnated."

Tourette's syndrome is thus more than its behavior manifestations in motor and phonic tics and dystonias. It has a profound effect on patients' thoughts, affects, and attitudes, the way they look at life and themselves, their successes and failures. The basic problem with impulse control leads to conscious struggles at control, with obsessive conscious, mental images of the emerging vocalizations or motor acts (D. J. Cohen, 1980; D. J. Cohen, Detlor, Shaywitz, & Leckman, 1982). When tension must be released, there is a feeling of being overwhelmed. The unacceptable thinking and behavior evoke guilt. There are constant battles between the good and acceptable and the bad and unacceptable. Depression and anxiety may be a by-product of these ceaseless conflicts, or they may result from the biological substrate, the pathophysiology of Tourette's syndrome, which attenuates the stimulus barrier. Anxiety is seen by day in refusal to go to school, in resistance to change, in extreme rigidity, and in infantile demands and by night in sleep disturbance, in the inability to fall sleep, and, when finally asleep, in the agony of dreams of being attacked and overwhelmed. The stimulus barrier is attenuated, and impulses and drives that normally are more or less mastered erupt in Tourette's syndrome virtually undisguised, adding again to guilt and furthering anxiety. Their self-image is low, and many fear deterioration of their brain. This psychiatric profile may be found, despite the heterogeneous nature of the overt clinical manifestations. In addition, most suffer from perceptual problems with consequence difficulty in time-limited, written assignments at school. Similar frustrations are also encountered as these children strive to complete assignments at home.

PATHOGENESIS

A model of pathogenesis of familial Tourette's syndrome: chronic motor tics, tic-related obsessive-compulsive disorder, and tic-related ADHD proposes a "reciprocal interaction between a set of interrelated genes and their microscopic and macroscopic environment" (Leckman & Cohen, 1999). These genes, as yet unknown are turned on or off at aberrant times, altering the normal sequence of the formation of neural circuits, thus perturbing the neurochemical balance needed for homeostasis and subsequently affecting function and behavior. Epigenetic risk (such as prenatal and perinatal insult) and epigenetic preventive factors (family, social, educational, environment with great support and minimal stress) may modify the impact of the vulnerability genes. The clinical presentation involving disturbed motor function, ideational function, and inhibitory functions is, it is reasoned, responding to disturbed function in the neural circuitry subsuming these functions. These neural networks reside, in part, in the loops between cortical and subcortical brain regions, the cortico-striatal-thalamic-cortical circuits (CSTC).

It has been recognized for over a century that damage to the basal ganglia (striatum) often leads to disorders of motor control (Marsden, 1982; Wilson, 1925). However the ganglia composing the striatum can no longer be viewed as a structure independent of the cerebral cortex and thalamus. In the CSTC loops, GABAergic pathways from distinct areas of the cortex (the sensory motor area, anterior-frontal and association areas) project into the striatum (caudate and putamen) where internuncial acetylcholine neurons, affect GABAergic (and somatostatin and neuropeptide) striatal neurons that project to the globus pallidus, both the external and internal segments. The internal segment of the globus pallidus projects GABAergic neurons to the ventrolateral, and ventro-anterior nuclei, and the centromedian/paravesicular nuclei of the thalamus; the external segment forms GABA connections to the substantia nigra and the subthalamic nucleus. The thalamic nuclei project back to the cortex completing the loop. There are, however, other smaller circuits within the CSTC loop. Projections from the subthalamic nucleus and the substantia nigra (pars compacta) send projections of dopaminergic neurons (possibly also neurotension and cholecystokinin) back to the striatum and to the globus pallidus; the substantia nigra (pars reticularis) also contributes GABAergic fibers to the thalamic nuclei. Normally, a balance is reached between the tonic dampening (inhibiting) effect of striatal output on the excitatory cortico-thalamic-cortical feedback loop and the inhibitory striatal (pallidal) output, which is, in turn, inhibited by input from globus pallidus, substantia nigra (compacta), and subthalamic nucleus, thus allowing thalamo-cortical activity to become disinhibited. However, the wiring of the CSTC loop is much more complicated than outlined here. The hypothesis of basal ganglia function based on summation of excitatory and inhibitory effects in a limited number of pathways, is an oversimplification (see Peterson et al., 1999; W. J. Weiner & Lang, 1989). Isolation of the CSTC circuit itself, in Tourette's syndrome is also a simplification. Structures of the limbic lobe are tied together with CSTC networks to affect essential functions such as physiological homeostasis, defense and attack, sexual and reproductive behaving, feeding and foraging. Peterson et al. hypothesize that the dense steroid hormone receptors of amygdala and related portions of the limbic lobe mediate sex-specific differences in prevalence of tics as well the sexual and aggressive content of Tourette's syndrome.

Interhemispheric coordination appears to be important for CSTC function, however, with neurons from the globus pallidus projecting via the massa intermedia of the thalamus to contralateral thalamic nuclei, and cortical projections from the areas of the CSTC cross through the corpus collosum to the contralateral striatum.

Attempts to understand the pathogenesis of Tourette's syndrome in tic-related obsessive-compulsive disorder and tic-related ACHD have involved neuropathology, neurochemestry, neuroimaging, and psychopharmacology.

A brief historical note: In 1885, Gilles de la Tourette stated, "As to the underlying lesion, we have found no anatomic or pathological cause. One can, by looking to psychology, try to interpret some of the symptoms." Meige and Feindel (1907) referred to tics as "mental infantilism" saying that "tiqueurs were big, badly reared children who never learned to bridle their will and action" (quoted by Mahler, 1949 p. 280). The psychoanalytic authors viewed tics as stemming from an inhibition of motor expression at a period in the child's life when such expression is the principal means of discharge of instinctual tension, particularly aggressive tension. Such inhibition may result in a weakening of the "motility controlling function of the ego" (F. Deutsch, 1947; O. Fenichel, 1945; Ferenzi, 1950). Mahler however, recognized that *maladie des tics* was a syndrome distinct from symptomatic tics; that symptomatic tics included transient tics and neurotic tics; *maladie des tics* was considered to be one type of tic syndrome, "genetic [in a developmental sense], dynamic, structural and economic principles of a systemic organ neurotic disease, with particular affinity for the peculiarities of infantile motor organization" (p. 282). Mahler felt that another type of tic syndrome is the tic as integral part of an "impulse or character neurosis" (p. 282). The impulse neurosis described by Mahler appears to have the characteristics of what we would now call Attention-Deficit/Hyperactivity Disorder. Mahler indicated that it is sometimes difficult to distinguish between her impulse disorder and *maladie des tics*. Indeed, as we have described, the impulse disorder may be the beginning of a Tourette's syndrome. The psychodynamic origin of tic syndrome was described by Mahler as the psychological effect of chronic suppression of aggression leading to "general and multifocal tension phenomena in the musculature, with restlessness, hyperkinetic or dyskinetic manifestations" (p. 291). Thus "generalized tics" represented an attempted drainage of a chronic state of emotional tension and is the physiological accompaniment of a chronic state of affective tension. Mahler's description of the personality characteristics of what we now call Tourette's syndrome and her recognition of hereditary or "constitutional" factors in its development are valid and accurate to this day, just as is Freud's concept of the attenuation of the stimulus barrier in disorders of homeostasis whether they be induced by genetic and/or factors acting on the organism (see Chapter 13).

MORPHOLOGICAL STUDIES

Psychodynamic theory as an explanation of etiology of *maladie des tics,* was soon submerged in the flow of new biological knowledge. In the case of Tourette's syndrome, this was impelled by the successful treatment of single patients with haloperidol by Caprini and Melotti (1961) and by Seignot (1961). Postmortem examination of three patients revealed no definite morphological pathology (Balthazar, 1956). With reevaluation of these cases, however, the findings in one case are interpreted as hypoplasia of the corpus striatum (Richardson, 1982), a failure of neuronal maturation causing an increased number of small neurons and an increased neuron-packing density in the putamen and caudate nuclei—a cytology similar to the basal ganglia of infants.

In 1993, the first neuroimaging study (MRI) of the basal ganglia in 14 non-medicated, neuroleptic naive, right-handed patients with Tourette's syndrome and 14 matched normal controls was reported (Peterson et al., 1993). In that study, the volume of the left subthalamic nucleus, putamin, and globus pallidus combined, was smaller than that of the right. This finding was independently replicated by H. S. Singer et al. (1993) in 37 children with Tourette's syndrome—29 boys, 8 girls; and 18 control children—14 boys, 4 girls. For the male only Tourette's syndrome children, an absent or reversed (right larger then left) asymmetry of the lenticular nucleus was found. In normal right-handed subjects, basal ganglia volumes are larger on the left than on the right (Castellanos, Giedd, et al., 1994; Castellanos et al., 1996). The reduced asymmetry in the globus pallidus, lenticular nucleus, and total basal ganglia suggested that the neural system in Tourette's syndrome may be lateralized. This is parallel to the findings in developmental language disorders and further suggests that the lack of, or a reduced, asymmetry may influence the emergence of developmental learning disorders in Tourette's syndrome.

Abnormalities in lateralization of basal ganglia in Tourette's syndrome were also found to be reflected in abnormalities in MRI relaxation times in the putamen and caudate of the 14 patients described by Peterson et al. in 1993.

Decreased basal ganglia volume also appeared to be fundamentally related to decreased metabolism and decreased flood flow, and both most prominent in the left cerebral hemisphere. There appeared to be inverse correlation between the severity of the disorder and decreased metabolism. T. N. Chase, Geoffrey, Gillespie, and Burrows, 1996; in a study of 12 adults with Tourette's syndrome, found a 15% decrease in glucose utilization (FDG-PET) in the inferior striatum; a second PET study (Braun et al., 1993) tended to confirm the Chase et al. findings. SPECT blood flow studies tended to find a "significant 4% reduction in blood flow to the left putamen globus pallidus complex" (M. A. Riddle, Rasmusson, Woods, & Hoffer, 1992).

Neuroimaging techniques (PET and SPECT) have also been used to quantify dopaminergic transmitter systems in the striatum. Presynaptic dopaminergic terminals, D2 receptor density, and D1 and D2 receptor availability were no different from those of controls. Dopamine transporter levels, however, were found to be increased (Malison et al., 1995).

Basal ganglia portions of the CSTS network have also been implicated in obsessive-compulsive disorder, with reports of 11% bilateral reduction in size of the caudate nucleus in adults with obsessive-compulsive disorder (Robinson et al., 1995). Just as aberrant lateralization, seen in both Tourette's syndrome and developmental learning disabilities, may influence the comorbidity between the two disorders, so the aberrant caudate volume in obsessive-compulsive disorder and basal ganglia in Tourette's syndrome suggests an anatomical relationship influencing the comorbidity of those two disorders.

The thalamus segment of the CSTS network has been studied (Peterson et al., 1998) in a functional MRI evaluation of 22 adults with Tourette's syndrome. As these subjects attempted to suppress tics, the magnitude of regional signal changes in the thalamus were reduced, a finding "consistent with our general supposition that tics occur in part, as a result of disinhibition of thalamus-cortical projections" (Peterson et al., 1999).

This section was summarized in part from Peterson et al. (1999). For a fuller discussion of neuroimaging studies involving other structures in the basal ganglia and limbic lobe, please refer to Peterson et al.

NEUROCHEMISTRY

The early finding that haloperidol, because of its ability to block the action of dopamine in basal ganglia receptors, attenuates the motor and vocal tics of Tourette's syndrome, focused attention on the position of the dopamine system in the pathophysiology of the syndrome. The hypothesis then advanced was that there was an increase in dopamine output from the nigral efferents projecting into striatal areas, or hypersensitivity of dopamine receptors in the striatum and globus pallidus resulting in disinhibition (excitation) of thalamic outflow thus releasing the symptoms of Tourette's syndrome. This hypothesis was reinforced by the exacerbation of symptoms by administration of drugs that increased DA functioning and, as indicated, by obtundation of symptoms with DA blocking agents. However, early studies measuring the CNS levels of the principal DA metabolic, homo-vanillic acid (HVA) found decreased concentration of HVA in Tourette's patients (Butler, Koslow, Seifert, Caprioli, & Singer, 1979; D. J. Cohen, Shaywitz, Caparulo, Young, & Bowers, 1978; D. J. Cohen, Shaywitz, Young, & Bowers, 1980) or unchanged (Leckman, Riddle, et al., 1988) or elevated (Takano & Ishguro, 1993). A more recent study (Leckman et al., 1995) found no mean difference in CNS HVA levels across groups of Tourette's patients and normal controls. Plasma level and urine excretion levels of HVA were also inconclusive. (M. A. Riddle et al., 1989).

The search turned to postmortem examination and to neuroimaging. Postmortem did not find levels of DA, HVA, tyrosine hydroxyleze to be different from normal in cortical and subcortical tissue, supporting the conclusion that central DA synthesis and metabolism appears within normal limits in Tourette's syndrome.

PET and SPECT imaging assays of the density of DA receptors in the basal ganglia and fluorine labeled DA accumulation in Tourette's syndrome were normal after administration of F18 labeled dopa. However, L. T. Singer et al. in a 1991 postmortem study found increased binding of a DA transporter ligand in homogenates of caudate and putamen of Tourette's patients and Malison et al. (1995) in a SPECT study also found increased binding of a DA transporter ligand, in the striatum of Tourette's patients. The implications of these findings have yet to be found. In discussing this issue, G. M. Anderson, Leckman, and Cohen (1999) feel that the "full range of DA receptor subtypes need to be studied, their relative abundance (i.e., D1 vs. D2), the decline in

DA transporter sites in the striatum with adolescence, the interaction of DA pathways and androgenic steroids." Anderson et al. caution "Whether alterations in the DA system exist in Tourette's remains an open question, whether possible alterations might be fundamentally etiologic, part of a pathophysiological cascade or of modulation influence, is also unclear" (p. 268).

The symptoms of Tourette's syndrome respond to a variety of drugs other than those directly acting on the dopamine system. The noradrenergic (NE) system is involved in the response to alpha-2 agonists (clonidine, guanfacine); the serotonin system, to tricyclics, to selective serotonin reuptake inhibitor (SSRIs) and to monamine oxidase inhibitors; the acetylcholine (Ach) system to nicotine, and nicotinic receptor blockers such as mecamylamine, calcium channel blockers; the opioid system to naloxone. Other drugs have also been used for specific symptoms: lithium, anticonvulsants, marijuana, melatonin. Although these systems, particularly NE, serotonin, and Ach, need investigation in Tourette's syndrome, these have not had the intensive investigation given to dopamine.

Early studies were inconclusive in finding any difference in plasma urinary levels of MHPG, or in plasma levels of dopamine-B-hydroxylase (DBH) in patients with Tourette's syndrome from that of controls. An interesting approach to evaluating the response of children to stress was introduced by Chappel et al. (1994), obtaining CSF levels of MHPG, NE, corticotrophin releasing factor, adrenocorticotropin hormone, in the course of lumbar puncture. A large, group mean elevation in CFS NE levels, a trend for higher levels of MHPG, and significantly higher CSF levels of corticotrophin releasing factor (CRS) and elevated plasma concentration of ACTH were found. The results suggested that Tourette's patients tend to have a sensitive stress response. G. M. Anderson et al. (1999) concluded, "The stress response systems appear more likely to be involved in influencing severity of symptoms, rather than being directly related to fundamental etiological processes" (p. 271).

Because of serotonin's general inhibitory effect on behavior and influenced by the report that the 5-HT precursor, 5-hydroxytryptophan, improved behavior in patients with Tourette's syndrome (Van Woert, Rosenbaum, & Elma, 1982) whereas behavior regressed with the 5-HT antagonist, cyproheptadine (Crosley, 1979), it was hypothesized that serotonic function was reduced in Tourette's syndrome. The effect of SSRIs on obsessive-compulsive disorder and even on depressive symptoms in Tourette's syndrome has further underlined the need for study of the serotonin system in Tourette's Disorder. Amid contradictory findings of peripheral 5-HT measures (urine indols, plasma tryptophan and kynurenine, and lower platelet 5-HT), a slight but significant lowered plasma level appears to be sustained. Some effects of tryptophan depletion on Tourette's syndrome related behavior have been reported (Rasmusson et al., 1997). Reduced levels of tryptophan, 5-HT, and 5-HIAA were also found in subcortical and cortical brain regions in postmortem studies, despite normal levels of the 5-HT transporters (Anderson et al., 1992).

The cholinergic system modulates movements and sensory-motor learning. Its tonically active internuncial neurons in the basal ganglia have significant modulatory effect on dopaminergic action of the GABA efferents emanating from the putamen and caudate and globus pallidus. S. M. Stahl and Berger (1981) reported physostigmine, a cholinesterase, to inhibit tics, but Tanner, Goetz, and Klawans (1982), could not confirm this finding. Following reports of potentiation of haloperidol-induced catalepsy in rats by systemic or intracaudate injection of nicotine (D. E. Moss, Manderscheid, Montgomery, & Norman, 1989; Sanberg et al., 1989), nicotine in the form of nicotine gum or transdermal patch, either alone or with haloperidol was found to obtund the motor and phonic tics of Tourette's patients (Dursun, Hewitt, King, & Reveley, 1996; McConville et al., 1991; A. A. Silver & Sanberg, 1993; A. A. Silver, Shytle, Philipp, & Sanberg, 1996). Double-blind placebo controlled study of 70 patients, confirmed these open trial reports (A. A. Silver et al., 2001). It is hypothesized that nicotine produces these effects by inhibition of specific nicotinic receptor subtypes (Dursun, Reveley, Bird, & Stirton, 1994; Lena & Changeux, 1997) that inhibit striatal dopamine release. This is consistent with the effect of mecamylamine, a ganglionic blocker, in attenuating behavioral symptoms of Tourette's syndrome (Sanberg, Shytle, & Silver, 1998). It is inconsistent with the hypocholinergic theory of Stahl and Berger (1981) (i.e., increasing acetycholine with a cholinesterase) but suggests instead that, rather than decreased cholinergic activity, Tourette's syndrome may reflect an increase in cholinergic activity of specific nicotinic receptors that are inhibited by ganglionic blockade and that acetylcholine may well serve as a modulating force in Tourette's syndrome.

GENETICS

There is evidence from family and twin studies that Tourette's syndrome and chronic multiple tics occur in families. Early studies suggested that simple genetic transmission models could explain family history data (Kidd & Pauls, 1982; T. Shapiro, Burkes, Petti, & Ranz, 1978). More recent evidence (Hasstedt, Leppert, Filloux, van de Wetering, & McMahon, 1995; Walkup et al., 1996) propose a more complex model of inheritance, neither dominant nor recessive, but an additive model in which the penetrance of the heterozygote is lower than that for the at-risk homozygote, but compatible with a major gene inheritance. Walkup et al., suggests that there might also be a significant polygenic background important for the expression of Tourette's syndrome and related symptoms. These recent studies (Pauls, Alsobrook, Gelernter, & Leckman, 1999) suggest that the underlying genetic mechanism for expression of Tourette's syndrome and related conditions is likely to be more complex than originally thought. Twin studies also contribute to the evidence for inheritance. In a study of 43 pairs of same-sex twins (Price, Kidd, Cohen, Pauls, & Leckman, 1985), there was a concordance rate of 53% for monozygote twins as contrasted with 8% for dizygotic twins for Tourette's syndrome. When the criteria included both chronic tics and Tourette's syndrome, the concordance increased to 77% for monozygotic and 23% for dizygotic twins.

Practically however, data from several family studies (Eapen, Pauls, & Robertson, 1993; Hebebrand et al., 1997; Pauls, Raymond et al., 1991) are consistent in their estimate that the risk for Tourette's syndrome among family members of an individual with Tourette's syndrome is about 10% to 11%; the risk for chronic tics, approximately 15%; the risk of obsessive-compulsive disorder without tics among first-degree relatives of individuals with Tourette's syndrome is approximately 11% to 12%. Thus say Pauls et al. (1999):

> There is significant risk (approximately 35%) for first degree relative of an individual with Tourette's syndrome to have either Tourette's syndrome, chronic tics or obsessive-compulsive disorder. Male relatives appear to be about three times more likely than female relatives to show tics, whereas mothers, sisters and daughters appear to be about twice as likely to have obsessive-compulsive disorder without tics as fathers, brothers, and sons. (p. 209)

Studies to localize and characterize genes at least partially responsible for the expression of Tourette's syndrome and related behaviors have not yet been found. Clinical and genetic studies of 25 families, screening more than 800 genetic marker loci have not found such genes; linkage has also been excluded between Tourette's syndrome and the D_2 dopamine receptor gene (Gelernter, Pauls, Leckman, Kidd, & Kurlan, 1994; Gelernter et al., 1990), between Tourette's syndrome and the D1 receptor gene (Gelernter et al., 1993), between Tourette's syndrome and the serotonin receptor gene (Gelernter, Pakstis, & Kidd, 1995), and the dopamine transporter gene. Other candidate loci excluded are the pro-dynorphin, the proopiomelatonin, and the gastrin releasing peptide genes. To date, approximately 85% of the genome has been excluded by pooled results from all laboratories.

The majority of these studies have been supported by the Tourette's syndrome association, in a collaborative International Genetic Consortium. Because of lack of positive results from classic linkage studies, a new approach was initiated four years ago, altering strategy to the affected gene pairs method. If two siblings have Tourette's syndrome, then their shared genetic material will likely include the genetic material that is responsible for causing Tourette's syndrome. "If a study looks at many sibling pairs and identifies areas of the genome that are frequently shared among a group of affected sibling pairs, there is a greater chance that shared areas of the genome will include the gene(s) for Tourette's syndrome" (Walkup, 2000). The first phase of the study includes 100 sibling pairs; the first report of this study appeared in the *American Journal of Human Genetics* in 1999. Two areas, one each on chromosome 4 and chromosome 8 have been identified with a maximum likelihood scores of 72 (potentially meaningful 99/100 chances these areas are important).

The genetic relationship between Tourette's syndrome and obsessive-compulsive disorder and Tourette's syndrome and ADHD will be considered. Comings and Comings in a series of papers published in 1987 proposed that a large number of behavioral syndromes in addition to OCD were variant expressions of the Tourette's syndrome gene(s). These behaviors include ADHD, learning disabilities, speech and language disorders, anxiety disorders, mood disorders including bipolar disorders, Pauls et al. (1993; Pauls et al., 1986) do not support the Comings's hypothesis. The Yale group concluded that the data was consistent with the hypothesis that a *form* of OCD is related to Tourette's syndrome. The family patterns suggest that not all forms of OCD were related to Tourette's syndrome, that there is a subtype genetically independent of

Tourette's syndrome, that there are differences in symptoms between the two types of OCD. Analysis of families with ADHD, also suggest that there might be at least two types of Tourette's syndrome probands with ADHD; those who have ADHD independent of Tourette's syndrome and those who have a form secondary to the expression of Tourette's syndrome. Pauls et al. (1999), however, are tentative about their conclusions about two types of ADHD. The relationship between Tourette's disorder and other disorders was also explored by Pauls et al. The rates of major depressive disorder, panic disorder, simple phobia, stuttering, other speech problems and specific developmental disorders were significantly elevated among probands. The prevalence of no other psychiatric disorder was increased in probands. However most depressive disorders occurred in individuals with obsessive-compulsive disorder. Pauls et al. (1999) concluded that "much" of the depression was secondary to OCD as also were panic disorders and phobias and that "these family data do not support the conclusion that ADHD, major depressive disorder, or panic disorders alone are variant expressions of the same underlying genetic factors that are important for the expression of Tourette's syndrome" (p. 202).

PEDIATRIC AUTOIMMUNE NEUROPSYCHIATRIC DISORDERS ASSOCIATED WITH STREPTOCOCCAL INFECTIONS (PANDAS)

CASE REPORT: ANN

In March 1963, Ann, age 10 years 2 months, in the 5th grade of an excellent private school in the suburbs of New York City was referred to us with a history that in December 1962, at about Christmastime, her parents noted a "marked change in personality and behavior," changing over the course of 2 or 3 weeks from a pleasant easily satisfied child, enjoying school and friends, to a "hyperactive," irritable, discontented girl, fearful of being out of her mother's sight. She could not sit still, constantly shuffling her feet, spending much time moving small objects such as ashtrays, small vases about the room, never satisfied with where they were placed. A psychiatrist in her hometown diagnosed her as suffering from schizophrenia and recommended hospitalization.

On direct questioning, her parents could not recall any upper respiratory infection preceding the onset of her present symptoms. Although she has had frequent sore throats in the past, none were diagnosed as strep infections. There is no history of rash, subcutaneous nodules, joint pain, or shortness of breath and indeed no history of any illness in the few months preceding the present symptoms. There is a history of breech delivery, with a right brachial plexus injury. In the past few months, an older boy in her school has been making sexual remarks to her.

On our examination, Ann was a pretty, alert child, appearing her stated age, relating well to the examiner, responding appropriately and relevantly to questions. However, there were intermittent bursts of choreiform movement of the upper extremities, involving groups of large muscles, each burst lasting a few seconds, but occurring frequently, perhaps every 30 seconds; her lower extremities, too, were in choreiform motion more frequently than her upper extremities. Occasionally, less frequently than the large muscle movement, her hands and fingers were involved. She appeared distressed and said she could not help these movements even though she tried. She said since the movements started, she was afraid to go to sleep at night, and feared leaving her mother, even having her mother in the waiting room was frightening and she had to interrupt her evaluation to check to be sure her mother was there. Finally, she asked her mother to come into the examining room with her to tell us of her new "habits." Her mother reports that Ann is becoming a tyrant at home, that she is constantly moving her father's ashtray, turning it in all ways until it satisfies her, but then turning it again; she demands that her family sit where she wants them to, insisting that they move at her demand; she is becoming disorganized in her schoolwork, taking hours to get dressed and to do her homework. She no longer wants to go to school saying she has a sore throat or a stomachache. Ann says that she cannot control her behavior, that the idea comes to her and she must do it. She is anxious with significant separation anxiety, but no evidence of introjections or projections, does not feel that someone is controlling her. She resents her father telling her to stop moving his ashtray and she dreams that he is sick and going to die. She complains that her mother does not talk to her.

On neurological examination, the choreic movements are obvious. The remainder of the classical neurological examination in terms of muscle tone, power, coordination and synergy, deep and superficial tendon reflexes, gross sensory evaluation of touch and pressure are all within normal limits. A physical examination including cardiac consultation was unremarkable. On neuropsychological testing, Ann worked hard to respond, but always with reluctance. Her Full Scale IQ on the WISC was 115 (verbal 121, performance 101) with scaled score of 4 on Block design, 7 on Object Assembly, Digit span (scaled score 15), coding (20) were no problems. Picture arrangement and Object Assembly were plagued with indecision and difficulty choosing her response (Figure 15.6). Her performance on Block Design suggested a figure-background problem and indeed she could not separate the ambiguous figure (vase-profile illusion), but she had no difficulty with tactile figure-ground. On the Bender-Gestalt test, there was rotation of 90° on all figures (see Figure 15.6) and angulation difficulties. There were no errors in finger gnosis or right-left discrimination. Oral reading and spelling was at 6th grade level; on reading comprehension, slightly below 6th grade level.

The sudden onset of chorea, obsessive-compulsive behavior, anxiety, and visual perceptual problems suggested Sydenham's chorea. Antistreptolysin O serum titer was high 720, Todd units. Ann was placed on penicillin prophylaxis, her parents alerted to the possible cause of her symptoms, supportive help was enlisted in school, and supportive psychotherapy started.

Improvement was slow but definite. The chorea began to subside in about 3 to 4 months, and after 12 months was not evident. Her compulsions diminished in intensity within 6 months and were not interfering with her adjustment in about 12 months. Repeat WISC testing was done in 12 months after the initial evaluation. Full Scale score on the WISC was then 133 (verbal 123, performance 139), Bender-Gestalt normal (Figure 15.6).

It has been almost 40 years since we first saw Ann. She is now a Ph.D. in psychology and is the mother of two children, with no recurrence of chorea or compulsions.

Ann demonstrates the rapid onset of chorea, along with compulsive behavior, anxiety, and visual perceptual defects, most likely as a sequel of group A Beta hemolytic strep infection, with elevated antistreptolysin titre. A protein designated as M protein has been implicated in the autoimmune response. The symptoms began to recede within 3 to 4 months but required at least 12 months for recovery. There have been no recurrences over a follow-up period of 40 years.

The association of Sydenham's chorea with obsessive-compulsive symptoms was noted by A. H. Chapman, Pilkey, and Gibbons (1958), who reported OCD symptoms in 4 of 8 children with Sydenham's chorea. In 1989, note was again made of the high incidence of OCD in patients with Sydenham's chorea (Swedo et al., 1989).

Since the time Ann was first seen, 46% of 30 children with rheumatic chorea were reported to have IgG antibody that reacted with neuronal cytoplasm of human caudate and subthalamic nuclei. This antibody was also detected in 1.8% to 4.0% in patients with a "broad variety of other disease states" (Husby, van de Rijn,

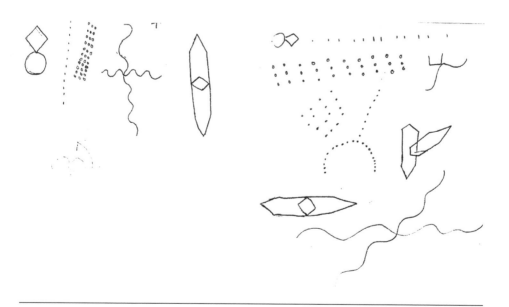

Figure 15.6   Bender-Gestalt. Left figure: Ann, age 10 years 2 months. Acute onset of Sydenham's Chorea illustrating 90° rotation of all figures and all figures placed in upper third of page; all figures were presented correctly. Right figure: Age 12 years. Approximately 2 years after onset of Sydenham's Chorea, illustrating correct orientation of figures.

Zabriskie, Abdin, & Williams, 1976). Antibody reacting with neuronal cytoplasm was completely removed by absorption with group A strep membranes or with isolated human neurons from the caudate nucleus. Husby et al. states that the antineural antibody of rheumatic chorea appeared to represent cross-reaction with antigens shared by group A strep membranes.

The similarity of clinical symptoms of Sydenham's chorea and Tourette's syndrome is apparent and indeed the question arises, Is there a subset of Tourette's syndrome that has the same relationship to group A Beta hemolytic strep as does Syndenham's chorea? Kiessling, Marcotte, and Culpepper (1993) found 44% of children with Tourette's syndrome, chorea, or choreiform movements, to have antineural antibodies and elevated streptolysin. H. S. Singer et al. (1998) found that "compared to controls, Tourette's syndrome subjects had a significant increase in the mean ($p = .006$) and median ($p = .002$) ELISA optical density levels of serum antibodies against putaman but not caudate or globus pallidus." Swedo et al. (1998) described the clinical characteristics of 50 patients with tic disorder and OCD whom they described as associated with strep (group A, Beta hemolytic) infections. They describe their course as a relapsing- remitting symptom pattern with emotional lability, separation anxiety, nighttime fears, and bedtime rituals, cognitive deficits, oppositional behaviors, and motoric hyperactivity. These criteria appear to characterize a homogeneous patient group in which symptom exacerbations are triggered by group A, Beta hemolytic strep infection. The clinical picture is similar to that seen in Ann except that with Ann, there was a gradual improvement in symptoms with no recurrence.

The presence of a B-lymphocyte antigen, D8/17 has been suggested as a trait marker for susceptibility to the group A, Beta hemolytic strep. F. Chapman, Visvanathan, Carreno-Manjarrez, and Zabriskie (1998); Swedo et al. (1997), and T. K. Murphy et al. (1997) each found that there may be a subgroup of D8/17 positive children who present with clinical symptoms of obsessive-compulsive disorder and Tourette's syndrome and who have poststrep autoimmunity as do patients with Syndenham's chorea (Swedo et al., 1997); that the average percentage of B cells expressing the D8/17 antigen was significantly higher (mean 22%) in patients with childhood OCD and/or Tourette's syndrome or chronic tic disorder than in control subjects (mean 9%) (T. K. Murphy et al., 1997).

Two possible mechanisms for this reaction are suggested: molecular mimicry and superantigen. The former suggests that host proteins share immunological epitopes with proteins in the strep; the host produces antibodies against the strep proteins and the antibodies cross-react with host tissues in basal ganglia (Kurlan, 1998). The superantigen theory postulates that the strep proteins evoke a broad range of immune responses, including a subset of T cells, some of which are autoreactive, and in turn activate antigen-producing B cells.

The differentiation of subsets of patients with Tourette's syndrome is obviously important, not only theoretically but also practically in choice of appropriate therapies (Perlmutter et al., 1999). At this writing, however, there is no clear marker to effect the differential diagnosis between Syndenham's chorea and Tourette's syndrome.

MANAGEMENT

Medication

While obtunding the symptoms of motor and phonic tics, available medication for Tourette's syndrome does not cure the disorder. Medication, however, is available if symptoms are particularly disturbing, impairing social, educational, and/or vocational adjustment. No drug is entirely free of side effects; these—long-term toxicity of the drug, and the meaning of drug use to the child and to his family—must be considered in the decision to use medication as part of the overall management. Nonspecific placebo effects, spontaneous remission of symptoms, and changes in the environment to relieve stress must also be considered in the evaluation of drug effects. Thus medication as part of the management for each child is not automatic but must be based on indications for each individual, with dosage individually titrated to achieve maximum effectiveness with minimal adverse effects (A. Shapiro & Shapiro, 1988).

In prescribing medication for the developmental disorders of childhood, the physician is always concerned about how the drug is affecting the pathophysiology of the disorder. Does long-term use of a drug induce permanent changes? If so, is the change in the direction of maturation so that remission is enhanced? Does the change simply affect the status quo; or does the change actually interrupt maturation? While at this point, there are no answers to these guidelines, the newer functional imaging techniques may help solve them. The concerns about drug effects are especially pertinent in the child whose brain is undergoing developmental change and is more vulnerable than is the adult brain, to perturbations in the timing and structure of its maturation. It must be remembered that of the entire pharmacopoeia, only haloperidol and pimozide are approved by the FDA for Tourette's syndrome.

Drugs Acting on the Dopamine System

A detailed review of medication for Tourette's syndrome may be found in Robertson (2000). In general, drugs that are potent antagonists of the dopamine receptor site (haloperidol and pimozide) decrease the motor and vocal tics, while those that increase dopamine neurotransmission by increasing the availability of dopamine (L-dopa, sinemet, methylphenidate, amphetamines, and bromocryptine) tend to exacerbate the Tourette's symptoms. Thus, alpha-methyl paratyrosine (an inhibitor of dopamine synthesis), tetrabenazine (which depletes brain stores of catacholamines), and apomorphine (which inhibits dopamine release from nigrostriatal nerve terminals) all tend to decrease tic frequency. Phenothiazines, which also block dopamine receptors, are not as effective as haloperidol or pimozide, primarily, it is theorized, because phenothiazines are more potent blockers of adenylate cylase-sensitive dopamine receptors (D1) with only a weak affinity for the dopamine-2 (3H haloperidol) receptors, while haloperidol and pimozide are potent D2 receptor blockers, with only weak affinity for D1 receptors.

A. Shapiro and Shapiro (1988) found that haloperidol improved motor and vocal tics in 78% to 91% of 141 patients reported in 41 publications between 1961 and 1975; only 8% to 22% are said to have failed to improve. In a control study, A. Shapiro et al. reported that with an average dose of 5 mg/day of haloperidol, 80% of his treated patients had decreased symptoms, compared with 24% in the nonhaloperidol-treated control sample. Shapiro concluded that 25% of patients have at least 70% reduction of symptoms at low dosage without significant adverse side effects. Approximately 50% do develop troublesome side effects to haloperidol, but these can be successfully managed. The remaining 25% are treatment failures. Shapiro uses the anticholinergic benzotrophine mesylate routinely (0.5 mg at bedtime). Haloperidol is increased by 0.25 mg every 5 days until symptoms significantly decrease or troublesome side effects occur. The dose of haloperidol is titrated to symptom relief and side effects and is monitored over time. In Shapiro's hands, the effective dose may vary from 2 to 10 mg/day and ultimately averages 5 mg/day.

Pimozide, a diphenylpiperidine, has more specific dopamine receptor blocking activity than haloperidol and is reported to have calcium-channel-blocking properties. Although it is effective as haloperidol in reducing Tourette's symptoms, pimozide is less sedative and less likely to produce dystonic effects. In a double-blind, placebo-controlled, 33-day crossover study of nine hospitalized Tourette's patients, 8 to 28 years of age (mean, 18 years 7 months), pimozide in a maximum dose of 10 to 12 mg (given 2 mg orally as an initial dose and increased 2 mg every other day for 12 days) reduced motor and vocal tics in six (75%) of the patients (Ross & Modolfsky, 1978). Nomura and Segawa (1979) found that of 31 patients who had not favorably responded to haloperidol, pimozide resulted in improvement in 90.3% of them. There is no report at this date of haloperidol in pimozide nonresponders. A. Shapiro and Shapiro (1988) found pimozide to be effective in 80% of 20 patients compared with improvement in 10% of their placebo controls. In contrast to the relatively rapid increase in doses given in the Ross and Modolfsky study, it is recommended that because of the long half-life of pimozide, the drug should be gradually increased by 1 or 2 mg every 10 days to a maximum dose of 7 to 16 mg/day. Side effects include nonspecific T wave changes and prolongation of the QT interval on the EKG. Thus, a baseline EKG with follow-up examinations is recommended. Both haloperidol and pimozide have neuroendocrine effects, decreasing the growth hormone and increasing prolactin.

Because of the adverse side effects of haloperidol and pimozide, leading to noncompliance, or because of their ineffectiveness in some patients, piperazine, the phenothiazine fluphenazine, is considered as an alternative. With fluphenazine, a good or fair improvement of tic symptoms was found in 81% of 31 children as contrasted with a similar improvement of 83% in 60 patients receiving haloperidol. Side effects accounted for withdrawal of medication in 19% of the fluphenazine group as contrasted with 33% of the haloperidol group. The mean maximum dose of fluphenazine was 5.1 mg/day. Borison, Ang, Hamilton, Diamond, and Davis (1983) and Goetz, Tanner, and Klawans (1989) report similar results.

Atypical neuroleptics, risperidone, clozepine, and olanzapine have been used in Tourette's syndrome, largely because it is felt that these drugs pose less of a risk than does haloperidol and pimozide in short-term extrapyramidcal and cognitive effects and long-term weight gain, hirsutism, and tardive dyskinesia. Risperidone has high affinity for both seratonin (5-HT$_2$) and dopamine (D$_2$) receptors and in open trial studies is said to be effective in relieving the motor and phonic tics (Bruun & Budman, 1996; Van der Linden, Bruggerman, & van Woerkom, 1994). Robertson, Scull,

Eapen, and Trimble, 1996, report "disappointing" results. Clozepine is also a potent 5-HT 2_A, 2_C 5-HT$_3$ and weaker D$_{1-A}$ receptor antagonist. Its use is cautious because of the possibility of agranulocytosis. To date, clonzepine is reported to have been successfully used in use in single patient with Tourette's syndrome who did not respond to haloperidol, pimozide or risperidone (Bhadrinath, 1998).

Drugs Acting on the Norepinephrine System

Clonidine hydrochloride, an imidazoline derivative used as an antihypertensive, is an alpha 2-adrenergic receptor agonist that preferentially stimulates presynaptic alpha-2, decreasing centrally medicated vasoconstriction of the peripheral circulation. It also inhibits spontaneous firing in the locus ceruleus, reduces brain norepinephrine turnover, inhibits ACTH and renin secretion, increases growth hormone secretion, stimulates central histamine H2 receptors (Leckman, Walkup, & Cohen, 1988), and is effective in reducing the symptoms of opiate withdrawal. The efficacy of clonidine in relieving Tourette's syndrome is still controversial. First used in Tourette's syndrome by Cohen and associates (D. J. Cohen, Detlor, Young, & Shaywitz, 1980), its effects, in the hands of the Yale group, are documented by Leckman, Sholomskas, Thompson, Belanger, and Weissman (1982). Given at a beginning dose of 0.05 mg/day, clonidine is slowly increased in 0.05 mg/day intervals over several weeks until a final dose ranges from 0.15 to 0.30 mg/day. Increasing the total dose may lead to increasing incidence of side effects, possibly because at the higher dose, the action of the drug shifts to increase postsynaptic alpha 1 activity. There is a long latency period of 8 to 12 weeks between the initiation of clonide treatment and potential response, with maximum effects seen at even longer intervals, from 6 to 12 months. The Yale experience found a 30% decrease in symptoms during the first 8 to 12 weeks and a 50% or greater decrease in symptoms over 12 months. The symptom decrease is experienced by the patient as a sense of calm or a decrease in tension, often followed by a decrease in attentional behavioral symptoms and complex tics. Simple tics, said Leckman, Walkup, et al. (1988), seem less responsive. Borison et al. (1983) found clonidine to be as effective as haloperidol after a 9-week trial. On the other hand, Goetz, Stebbins, and Thelen (1987) found no objective evidence for the reduction of motor or vocal tics after 12 weeks of clonidine. Side effects of clonidine are reported. Sedation in 10% to 20% of cases is dose related and may subside with time as tolerance is developed. Orthostatic hypotension, headache, irritability, lability of mood, and sleep difficulties can occur. Electrocardiographic changes (exacerbation of arrythmias) and decreased glucose tolerance require baseline data and monitoring. The behavioral symptoms of Tourette's syndrome (impulsivity, attention problems, and complex motor tics resembling compulsions) are said to be responsive to clonidine, whereas the motor and vocal tics appear more responsive to dopamine blockers. The reports of the effectiveness of clonidine on Tourette's syndrome have suggested a noradrenergic mechanism in the pathophysiology of Tourette's syndrome. This has yet to be delineated, since 3H yohimbine binding to alpha-2 receptors in platelets revealed no abnormalities among Tourette's syndrome patients (Silverstein, Smith, & Johnstone, 1985); MHPG levels in CSF, plasma, and urine were not consistently different (Leckman et al., 1983); and propranolol was not effective in reducing Tourette's tics (Sverd, Cohen, & Camp, 1983).

Freeman et al. (2000), however, report that in their collaborative study with 65 sites throughout the world, clonidine is the first choice as monotherapy for Tourette's syndrome and also first choice in polypharmacy. Seventeen percent of all sites report clonidine as first choice as monotherapy contrasted with pimozide 3.5%, haloperidol 5.2%, risperidone 3.6%. Clonidine also is the most prevalent drug used in polypharmacy (65.2%) with pimozide used in 41.5%, haloperidol in 56.2%, risperidone in 44.8%. Clonidine has also been reported as effective in ADHD and is finding use in Tourette's syndrome when ADHD is a comorbid symptom. Although approximately 25% of Tourette's patients respond favorably to clonidine, efforts to predict which patients will respond to the drug have not been successful. However, because it has relatively benign side effects, P. B. Chappell, Leckman, and Riddle (1995) typically recommend a trial of clonidine before prescribing neuroleptics.

Guanfacine, a newer alpha-2 adrenegic agonist selectively binds the postsynaptic alpha-2 subtype receptors in the prefrontal cortex. It causes less sedation or hypotension than clonidine and it may enhance attention and working memory (Arnsten, Steere, & Hunt, 1996). In open label studies, guanfacine is effective and well tolerated in ADHD and in Tourette's syndrome with ADHD (R. D. Hunt, Arnsten, & Asbell, 1995; P. B. Chappell et al., 1994; see also Chapter 13).

Drugs Acting on the Serotonin System

The proliferation of selective seratonin uptake inhibitors over the past 10 years, from fluoxetine to citalopram, and their effect on relief of depression and/or obsessive-compulsive behaviors, has made available a new class of drugs for use in Tourette's syndrome. Because as a group these drugs do not have the cardiac effects of clomipramine and of the tricyclics (prolonged PR, QRS and QTa intervals) and the generally marked anticholinergic effects (blocking muscarinic cholinergic receptors) and decreased sedation, they appear to have increasing use in children and adolescents. As with many of the drugs used in child neuropsychiatry, the SSRIs (although fluvoxamine, fluoxetine, and paroxetine have FDA approval for use with adults with obsessive-compulsive disorder), none of them are approved for use with children and adolescents. They have been useful however, in targeting the OCD symptoms of Tourette's syndrome. In an open trial of 32 TS-OCD patients, with fluoxetine, 6 withdrew in one week; of the remaining 26 children, treated for 3 to 8 months, 81% reported a subjective improvement (Como & Kurlan, 1991). The general conclusion of the available studies suggests that, while fluoxetine has little or no effect on the motor or phonic tics, it is helpful with OCD, with the only significant side effect being transient increase in motor restlessness (Scahill, 1997). Summaries of studies with fluoxetine and fluvoxamine have been reviewed in Robertson (2000). It is anticipated that reports of SSRIs on OCD and depression in Tourette's syndrome in children will soon proliferate.

Drugs Acting on the Nicotinic System

The role of the acetylcholine system as a modulation of transmitters in Tourette's syndrome has been briefly discussed in this chapter. Nicotine in the form of chewing gum and transdermal patches has been effective in controlling the motor and phonic tics of Tourette's syndrome; the gum effecting short-term improvement of approximately one hour after chewing; a single 7 mgm patch applied for 24 hours has a mean effect for 7 to 10 days (A. A. Silver et al., 1996) to 2 weeks (Dursun et al., 1996). Investigation of the reasons behind these effects suggested that rather than function as an agonist, nicotine in the form of transdermal patch, with its slow absorption and slowly decreasing blood level after removal, acts to inhibit a subset of nicotinic-acetylcholine receptors (nACHr). The alpha 4 beta 2 receptor emerged as a candidate. Mecamylamine, a ganglionic blocker, was chosen as a potential nAchr inhibitor. Open trial and double-blind placebo controls studies confirmed the hypothesis that mecamylamine could relieve symptoms of Tourette's syndrome, the major effect being on the lability of mood, irritability, rage and aggression, with lesser effect on the motor and vocal tics. In low doses (up to 7.5 mgm daily), mecamylamine has proven safe with occasional transient orthostatic hypotension and constipation. Replication of these studies is being planned. There is evidence from animal experiments (Newman, Shytle, Sanberg, 1999) that mecamylamine inhibits the production of cortisol releasing hormone from the pituitary. It is noted that choline and lecithin do not affect Tourette's symptoms.

Drugs Affecting the GABA System

Clonazepam, a benzodiazepine that enhances glutamate release has been reported as being effective in Tourette's syndrome (Gonce & Barbeau, 1977) and a direct GABA agonist, progabide, was effective in two of four patients with Tourette's syndrome (Mondrup, Dupont, & Braingard, 1985). Levels of GABA in CSF or in whole blood, however, did not distinguish the patients who responded from nonresponders. With or without SSRIs or clomipramine, clonazepam has been helpful in obsessive-compulsive disorder (Jenike & Rauch, 1994) and is also reported to be superior to clonidine in a study involving 20 children, 14 with chronic tic disorder, 6 with Tourette's syndrome producing fewer side effects than did clonidine (Drtilková, Balrötikova, Lemanova, & Zák, 1994). Goetz (1992) reported "a good response" in 54 Tourette's syndrome patients treated with clonazepam. Clonazepam has been used to treat seizure disorders, and other movement disorders; it may produce dizziness, fatigue, irritability, and aggression. Baclofen, which contains both GABA and phenylalanine moieties, has been found to benefit children with Tourette's syndrome, although "improvements may be related to factors other than tics" (Singer, Wendlandt, Krieger, et al., 2001).

Drugs Blocking the Calcium Channel

Calcium channel blockers are reported to bring "rapid and dramatic relief in refractory Tourette's syndrome" (Alessi, Walden, & Hirsh, 1989). Anecdotal reports describe improvement in tics and vocalization with nifedipine (Berg, 1985; A. Goldstein, 1984). The combined use of nifedipine and haloperidol was effective in a 9-year-old boy diagnosed as having Tourette's syndrome, ADHD, and specific learning disorders. Clonidine, haloperidol, pimozide, and fluphenazine were all ineffective in this patient or had unacceptable side effects. Neither verapamil nor nifedipine alone produced a major decrease in tics compared with the placebo. Verapamil caused headache, nausea, and dizziness. With the combination of nifedipine (10 mg bid) and haloperidol (1 mg bid), a significant reduction in tic frequency and a marked increase in attention and school performance occurred, "almost immediately" (Alessi et al., 1989).

Drugs Acting on the Opioid System

There are anecdotal reports of the effectiveness of opioid receptor antagonists in Tourette's syndrome. In a double-blind study of 10 Tourette's syndrome adults, Kurlan, Majumdar, Deeley, et al. (1991) reported a significant reduction in tics after naltrexone (50 mgm/day) compared with placebo; an improvement in Trail making B test is particularly noted. Methadone is said to have benefit in one patient with Tourette's syndrome after he had not responded to the more traditional drugs (Meuldijk & Colon, 1992).

Drugs affecting other systems include marijuana; buspirone (Dursun, Burke, & Reveley, 1995); and the anticonvulsant carbamazepine (Lutz & Feldman, 1977).

Reviewing the use of medication for Tourette's syndrome suggests that although we have a long way to go in understanding the pathochemistry of Tourette's syndrome, we do have significant armament to help most patients with this disorder. The very multiplicity of medication, however, reveals the neurochemical complexity of Tourette's syndrome.

Behavioral Modification

Behavioral modification is said to be helpful in reducing the feelings of stress. A variety of techniques of behavior modification for use in Tourette's syndrome has been described by Azrin and Peterson (1988). These include:

- *Massed negative practice,* in which the patient voluntarily performs the tic for a specified period of time interspersed with brief periods of rest. The object is to develop a "reactive inhibition," leading to a decrease in tic frequency in approximately half of 18 case studies.
- *Contingency management,* an approach based on operant learning theory, using (a) positive reinforcement in nine studies each involving one subject (in one study two subjects were involved) and (b) negative reinforcement in seven studies.
- *Relaxation training,* including muscular relaxation, deep breathing, visual imagery, and verbalization. This training led to temporary reduction in tics for short periods. Azrin and Peterson (1988) stated, "patients with Tourette's syndrome should be taught relaxation as a general procedure to help reduce tension and decrease frequency and severity of tics" (p. 247).
- *Self-monitoring of frequency of tics,* shown to be helpful in reducing tics in three case studies.
- *Habit reversal,* the isometric tensing of muscles opposite to the tic movements (competing response). The opposing muscles are contracted for two minutes immediately on onset of urge to have the tic. This procedure involves self-monitoring, relaxation, and contingency management as well as competing response.

Although each technique has been "somewhat effective" in reducing the frequency of tics, these treatments have been part of multicomponent treatments and thus cannot be evaluated per se. Nevertheless, positive reinforcement, praise, and encouragement may lead to improved motivation and thus improved achievement.

School Practices in Management

In her doctoral dissertation, D. Anderson (1985) surveyed the educational services provided for students with Tourette's syndrome in a six-county area in the state of Florida. Sixty-eight percent of the children with Tourette's syndrome in these counties were in regular public school classes, 10% were in classes for emotionally disturbed children, 9% were in classes for learning disabilities, 1% were homebound, 4% were in special schools for emotional, cognitive, and learning problems, and no report was received on class placement for 8%. There was no clearly defined procedure for management, with a variety of techniques used; the most frequent being a modification in classroom management to accommodate the specific learning and behavioral characteristics of each child.

A survey of positive school practices is reported by Hagin, Beecher, Pagano, et al. (1982). Seventy-two responses coming from 19 states, Canada, Australia, and Korea, were received in answer to a questionnaire included in the *Tourette Syndrome Association Newsletter*. The responses were organized according to three main headings: educational settings, sources of support, and specific educational practices.

Educational Settings

Questionnaire responses emphasized the importance of a moderate classroom structure for children with Tourette's syndrome. The degree of structure, however, elicited a variety of responses. Thirteen replies specifically mentioned a less-structured classroom atmosphere than the traditional setting. This would permit the Tourette's children freedom of physical movement when their symptoms required it, but would also offer appropriate environmental cues to guide their learning.

In contrast, two responses mentioned a highly structured boarding-school atmosphere in which "every hour of the day was programmed." These parents mentioned firm structure as being crucial to their children's learning. An additional seven mentioned small private schools with "therapeutically oriented," "patient," and "humanitarian" approaches to the pupils. While some advocated special class placements, a number of families firmly supported the mainstream class in which children had opportunities for special provisions, but worked for the major part of the school day with other children of similar ages.

An especially important provision for all the youngsters was some kind of refuge to which the child might go when the symptoms of Tourette's syndrome become severe. The opportunity to leave the class at any time without seeking special permission is an important arrangement between the child and the teacher. Refuges, such as a learning disability resource room, the school clinic, or a nurse's office are kinds of provisions mentioned.

While the physical and organizational climate of the school is important, the psychological climate is equally important. Responses mentioned over and over again the need for concerned and active efforts to assist the child to develop his or her full potential. One parent mentioned, "a teacher who never gave up on my son." Another parent mentioned, "the need for the kind of teacher who emphasized the number of correct responses, rather than errors." The need to learn to ignore the tic and focus on the child is most important.

Sources of Support

Many parents described ways of informing school staff members about Tourette's syndrome. Fifteen parents mentioned opportunities to explain Tourette's syndrome to the school staff at regular staff meetings. The publications of the Tourette's Association were distributed and the film *The Sudden Intruder* was used as the focus of these discussions. A film made for children, *Stop It—I Can't,* is a useful starting point for group discussions in classrooms in which children with Tourette's syndrome are enrolled. The publication, *Mathew and His Tics,* has been used by a number of parents as the first step toward peer acceptance for the symptoms of Tourette's syndrome. The importance of an appropriate explanation to the peers of the child or young adult is not to be underestimated. One college student stated that she experienced real acceptance for the first time when she explained to her college professor and the other students the nature of Tourette's syndrome. She said, "They then accepted my condition." Teacher support for the youngster with Tourette's syndrome was mentioned again and again in the questionnaire responses. One wise parent said, "Good teachers don't pity, pamper, or patronize." A youngster commented, "They treated me like a regular student, that helped the most." Another said, "They gave me advanced work to match my abilities." One youngster warned, "Don't let a kid cop out in school; I should have been in a college prep."

In many reports of school adjustment, there was evidence of mature, supportive parents in the background. These parents encouraged peer acceptance, but also made sure that there was adult supervision as needed during the unstructured times at school. It is during unstructured times such as in the lunchroom, in the locker room, and in the play yard that unfortunate incidents can occur.

A variety of school personnel was mentioned as having contributed a good deal to school adjustment. The teacher is a key person, but also included were guidance counselors and school nurses who not only provide teachers with information about the syndrome itself, but also can be helpful in interpreting the responses children may make to medication or to a change in medication. School psychologists were mentioned, as were the Child Study Team as a whole and the Special Education Department.

Private consultants who counseled the family and also dealt directly with the school were another source of support mentioned. Several respondents mentioned the need for careful interpretation of medication effects to school personnel, as well as the need for adjusting homework for children who may be relatively symptom-free.

The parent has a basic role in the support system. All parents should be aware of the child's right to an education in the least restrictive environment as provided in IDEA, the Individuals with Disabilities Education Act (1997). These provisions have been important in cases in which a due process hearing was necessary to have a child returned to school after he had been receiving only home instruction for several years. One parent pointed out the importance of a basically nonthreatening attitude in relation to the school. She continued, "We have assumed collegiality with those we consider professionals. We know that they are anxious to do their best and we have never been disappointed." Another parent said, "I have tried to maintain good rapport—this is an asset when you are seeking extra help and understanding. As my youngster required extra help from the teachers, I tried to help *them* when they need it as well."

The parent has a broad educational role for the youngster with Tourette's syndrome. This role may involve anticipating the next step educationally and desensitizing the child about possible failure. If long division is coming up soon, the groundwork laid by the parent at home may make it possible for the child to handle long division when the teacher introduces it.

The parent can also have a very helpful role in reviewing for unit tests with the youngster. Careful monitoring of schoolwork is useful so that the parent can fill in the gaps that occur because of attentional and organizational problems. One parent commented, "I taught him to read three times and each time he forgot; now he is an excellent reader." Parents are also helpful in encouraging the child to express feelings that may not be easily expressed in the group at school. The school can help the children by permitting them to take things at their own pace. Time is a major source of stress for youngsters with Tourette's syndrome, and stress exacerbates the symptoms.

Negative points come through in the discussion of school adjustment. Mentioned most frequently was the isolation many children with Tourette's syndrome suffer from in the classroom. Occasionally outright rejection occurs in the form of verbal abuse. One older adolescent mentioned a college professor who called attention to the symptoms. With younger children, teasing may occur by classmates in nonstructured settings like the lunchroom, the locker room, or the playing field. One parent said, "There have been no positive educational experiences. School meant nothing but harm for my child who was incorrectly diagnosed and placed with retarded children." A more subtle kind of rejection can be seen in the gratuitous advice from school personnel who attribute the Tourette's symptoms to the parent's high expectations. One parent said, "He is classed as a problem child and I am classed as a neurotic mother." Another parent characterized the ineffective and effective teachers in this fashion:

> The bad teacher is a martinet who barks out orders; the good teacher is bright and unafraid of bright people. The bad teacher teaches by rote; the good teacher teaches by developing ideas. The bad teacher is rigid; the good teacher is organized. The bad teacher destroys self-esteem; the good teacher guides it. The bad teacher stifles children; the good teacher develops them. The bad teacher takes away the child's sense of self-control; the good teacher builds confidence and self-awareness.

Responses to a questionnaire on positive educational practices sent to members of the Tourette's Syndrome Association provided a wide range of information about educational settings and climate, sources of support, and specific suggestions for instructional assistance. While no single educational approach was found to serve all children equally well, responses indicate that many families are dealing with the educational needs of their children effectively and realistically. Running through all responses is the strong conviction that appropriate educational provisions have a vital role for the child with Tourette's syndrome. The courage, supportiveness, and sense of purpose with regard to educational planning is said well in one parent's comment: "We believe so strongly in the importance of schooling that we have jumped many hurdles. It's great fun to conquer these problems; it makes us all feel so smart and so loving."

Specific Suggestions for Instruction

Some specific ideas appeared as suggestions on the questionnaires:

- *One-to-one* help with reading and mathematics is frequently essential. This may be received in a program for children with learning disabilities or in some remedial programs. Whatever the source of the instruction, it should emphasize perceptual cues, sound-symbol association, and a decoding approach to reading.
- *Small segments* of work should be taught with opportunity for mastery before the child goes on to more complex material.
- *Reasonable goals* are important; praise when they have been reached is essential.
- *The timing of schoolwork* is critical matter. Like most of us, children with Tourette's syndrome need work at their own speed.
- *The size of the class* may also be crucial. Like all children, the Tourette's child flourishes when he works in a small-individualized class.
- *Peer help* may be very useful. In return, the children with Tourette's syndrome may have the opportunity to help in subjects in which they excel.
- *Specific praise* is an important motivator for continued achievement. No child likes to receive a snow job in responses to his efforts, but all youngsters like to have good work recognized.
- *Help in following directions* is needed by most youngsters with Tourette's syndrome. Parents and teachers can help by underlying significant words to draw attention to the sequences of ideas.
- *Handwriting problems* were mentioned in nearly every response to the questionnaire. Some families have solved this problem by requesting that the child be allowed to print. A limit on the requirements of written work is also a contribution. Typing may be a solution for some youngsters, although it has been found to be a source of stress with others. Use of typing would depend on the nature of the tic and whether control would be possible as the child learns the typewriter keyboard. Use of the buddy system to cut down the amount of writing has been suggested. Someone else to help with writing, perhaps a peer who writes the assignment with carbon in order to have a copy for the child with Tourette's may be a solution. Use of a classroom aide would also be a possibility. The use of lines, color cues, and plastic pencil wedges all appeared as reasonable suggestions for use with some youngsters.
- *Exams* represent a critical issue for most youngsters with Tourette's syndrome. The possibility of taking important examinations like the Scholastic Aptitude Tests in private, untimed administration is one possibility worthy of consideration. Another solution has been to allow the youngster to take a rest between parts of the examination.

• The importance of a wide variety of *compensation activities* ran through the questionnaires. One youngster began as a Boy Scout and moved through the ranks so that he now serves as an adult leader. Several respondents mentioned the usefulness of swimming and life-saving training. A rocket club appeared to be a useful activity for one science-oriented youngster. Several musicians were reported in the sample: Some youngsters learned to play piano, French horn, and flute, and one youngster became a member of a rock group. One youngster found weight lifting an important compensatory activity, while another found jewelry making an absorbing hobby.

General Principles of Educational Management

Management of the child with Tourette's syndrome thus involves more than control of tics and vocalization; it involves the understanding of all sources of stress, whether they come from the family, from school, or from peers as well as from the Tourette's syndrome itself. With comprehensive attention of each of these sources, the majority of children with Tourette's syndrome can reach their optimal potential academically, socially, and vocationally. There is the tendency for the condition to improve by late adolescence. The resurgence of interest and the intensity of research studies to elucidate the cause or causes of the disorder offer hope for new and better methods of treatment.

As stressed in the management of all children with disorders of learning, the first step in management of children with Tourette's syndrome is understanding them and their world: A comprehensive evaluation is in order. At the least, this includes psychiatric, neurological, cognitive, educational, and family study; the content, dynamics, genesis, and structure of the child's thoughts, wishes, fears, and conflicts; the way he or she deals with anxiety in loss of motor and phonic control and in the attenuation of the stimulus barrier; the level of maturation and integration of the central nervous system; the cognitive abilities and disabilities; the academic successes and failures; and the attitudes and behaviors of parents, siblings, and teachers to the child's problem. When all these data are obtained, appropriate intervention may be offered.

A comprehensive plan of intervention involves educational, psychotherapeutic, behavioral, and medication components. Teachers, parents, siblings, neurologists, pediatricians, psychologists, and psychiatrists—the skills of many disciplines—may be a part of the management. With so many disciplines involved, management may become fragmented, and despite the sincere efforts of each, it may create confusion in parents and exacerbate anxiety in the child. A central coordinator is essential to coordinate the efforts of professionals and agencies, and to provide guidance for parents and child when problems arise.

After comprehensive study, a meeting with parents helps clarify issues, identifies their own reaction, outlines proposed treatment, and supplies them with someone who is available to them throughout the years. A similar meeting is held with the child, another with teachers and resource people at the child's school. The family most often needs support; in those who may have tics or obsessions or compulsions themselves, their guilt in the thought that they may have transmitted the disease may lead to their own depression, to anger and rejection of the child, or to overindulgence and overprotection that inhibit the child's emotional maturation. While all families need understanding and support, the extent of family counseling or therapy must be an individual matter.

The child's emotional reactions to the disorder and to the reaction of those about him or her require individual therapy. The presence of Tourette's syndrome frequently makes the resolution of stage-specific conflicts incomplete and contributes to the development of anxiety and all the defenses mobilized against it. The level and depth of therapy, however, just as with any child, depends on the child's capacity to deal with his or her emotions and may proceed from support in the face of cathartic release, through insight about feelings and behavior, and to resolution of persistent conflict. The ultimate goal is the relief of the stress that aggravates the symptoms of Tourette's syndrome and the promotion of social and vocational adjustments.

SUMMARY

Tourette's syndrome is a neuropsychiatric disorder characterized by multiple motor and vocal tics that vary in location, frequency, intensity, and complexity. Obsessions and compulsions are part of the syndrome; whether attention deficit hyperactivity is intrinsic to the syndrome or is a comorbid disorder is controversial. The age onset may vary from the preschool years to early adolescence; frequently the syndrome starts in the preschool years with hyperactivity and progresses from simple tics and vocalization to multiple, complex tics and vocalizations. Classically, coprolalia has been described. The symptoms characteristically "wax and wane," aggravated by stress and tension, frequently spontaneously improving in late adolescence or early adulthood. The syndrome has a strong family aggregation, with greater incidence in monozygotic twins than in dizygotic twins. The male/female prevalence ratio may be as high as 9 to 1 in children and 3 or 4 to 1 in adults. The genetic mode of transmission is still obscure; the mechanism through which the syndrome may be expressed is considered to be an abnormality, possibly developmental, in that part of the subcorical system involved with control of voluntary movement and involving neurotransmitter systems. The effectiveness of haloperidol in control of motor tics suggests hypersensitivity or an increased number of dopamine receptors as a mechanism. The "unitary dopamine" hypothesis, however, is becoming increasingly untenable as serotonergic, GABA, acetylcholine, and other neurotransmitters are implicated.

Tourette's syndrome has a profound effect on the patient's thoughts and feelings. The basic problem with impulse control leads to a conscious struggle to control the impulses, with obsessive mental images and feelings of the emerging tics, vocalizations, and compulsions actually preceding the motor discharge and with a feeling of being overwhelmed when the motor act escapes from voluntary control. The unacceptable thinking and behavior evoke guilt, depression, and anxiety. Anxiety may be severe, seen in phobias, difficulty falling asleep, and dreams of being attacked and overwhelmed. Some children feel they are controlled by something outside them. Their self-esteem is low; many fear deterioration of the brain, and some think their disease is a punishment for bad thoughts and behavior.

Since medication does not cure the disorder, it should not be automatic but be reserved for symptoms that impair social, educational, and/or vocational adjustment. Side effects must be considered. Dopamine receptor site antagonists (haloperidol and pimozide) are effective in decreasing motor and vocal tics in approximately 75% of patients. Patients who do not respond to haloperidol may be helped with pimozide. The favorable use of risperidone has been reported. Clonidine, an alpha-adrenergic agonist, has a long latency period (8 to 12 weeks) before response, with maximum effects seen after months of treatment. The value of clonidine in tic reduction is still controversial. Serotonic uptake blockers (clomipramine and fluoxetine) are receiving attention in their ability to reduce obsessive-compulsive symptoms. Calcium channel blockers are reported to be effective in enhancing response to haloperidol. Cholinergic drugs and GABA agonist have not been significantly helpful in treating Tourette's syndrome; however, drugs that inhibit nicotinic acetylcholine receptors may prove helpful.

School problems are significant for children with Tourette's syndrome. Most of these children have impaired visuomotor-praxic function, coding, mathematics, and handwriting. In addition, the obsessive thinking, compulsive behavior, perseveration, impulsivity, increased anxiety, and poor-self esteem; the tics themselves; and the medication—all contribute to school problems. How many children with Tourette's syndrome have a specific language disability, as defined in Chapters 4 and 11 of this book, is as yet unknown. In school management, the Tourette's Syndrome Association recommends that means be found to permit expressions of hyperactivity, to allow alternatives to handwriting, to reduce stress, to offer remedial mathematics, and, in general, to increase socialization and self-esteem. The importance of education for the parents is stressed. A survey of positive educational practices for children with Tourette's syndrome found that flexibility in educational approach, depending on the needs of the child, was indicated.

PART V

ALTERNATIVES FOR THE FUTURE

Chapter 16

EDUCATION IN A DEMOCRATIC SOCIETY

—the reforming of education, (is one) of the greatest and noblest designs that can be thought on, and for the want whereof this nation perishes

—John Milton, *Tractate on Education,* 1673 Edition

The goal of schooling is to produce literate citizens. Although there may be major disagreements about the organization, management, funding, curriculum, and methods used in schools today, there is substantial agreement on the importance of literacy as a goal of education. The 1989 Education Summit, for example, gave high priority to literacy in its goals statement describing literacy as "an individual's ability to read, write, and speak in English and solve problems at levels of proficiency necessary to achieve one's goals and develop one's knowledge and potential." Adequate literacy is necessary to manage one's affairs, to earn a living, to teach one's children, to participate fully in one's spiritual life, and to fulfill the responsibilities of citizenship in a democracy. The importance of all these aspects of literacy has long been recognized. No other area of the curriculum has been defined, described, analyzed, studied, investigated, probed, debated, researched, criticized, and written about more intensively. The PSYCHSCAN database located 5,144 references between the years 1972 and 2001, with 1,584 of these during the years 1990 to the present.

DEVELOPMENTS IN SCIENCE AND TECHNOLOGY

Rapid developments of knowledge about learning disorders have occurred in science and technology. Four areas are particularly striking:

1. *Genetics.* There is evidence of inherited defect in at least one subset of children with developmental learning disabilities. Although clinical evidence of inherited

defect was suggested in pedigrees of families as long ago as 1905, genetic studies have only recently documented some of these relationships. Twin studies, segregation analyses, and linkage patterns, such as those investigated in the Colorado Reading Study, have yielded information about the heritability of dyslexia. Advances in the molecular genetics of learning disorders will be carried along with advances in the molecular genetics of other disorders and should soon tell us more than is now known about the causes of developmental learning disability.

2. *Anatomy.* As anatomical studies of learning disorders accumulate, the possible artifacts and the contamination with other brain processes may be clarified and the true morphological structures of developmental learning disability may be better understood. Already, these studies have shown correlations, although still inconsistent ones, between gross anatomical asymmetry present in the normal brain and hemisphere specialization. In the brains of individuals who had suffered from dyslexia, such asymmetry patterns are altered and the normal cellular architecture in the left hemisphere is disturbed with dysplasias and ectopias. As these anatomical differences are found in dyslexia, we still have the problem of understanding how these changes affect function to produce learning problems. Furthermore, these anatomical anomalies do not tell us why these changes are present or what caused them, and most important how to prevent them. It is possible that these anomalies are not specific to dyslexia, but are a final common pathway of expression for many other etiological factors, one of which may be genetic. That early experiences might also contribute to these anatomical deviations is not impossible. Gross anatomical patterns may also be studied by other techniques, such as magnetic imaging. With MRI, the structure of the brain can be visualized and gross asymmetries, particularly in the temporal lobe, can be measured. Cerebral blood flow measures, positron emission tomography and magnetic imaging spectroscopy are new research tools that will be used to follow up on the basic findings of the anatomical studies.

3. *Neuropsychology.* Neuropsychological investigations have applied a variety of research paradigms designed to describe differences in children who learn well from those who do not. Among most of these studies, there is general agreement that clusters have delineated subgroups distinguished by deficits in various forms of information processing. The search for a unitary pattern, a single functional defect characteristic of all children with learning disorders, is doomed to failure, although common deficits are found in some selected samples. Subgroup studies are necessary to describe the heterogeneity of learning disorders although, with them, we are no closer to determining the causes of the differences found. Is each subgroup different in its origins or is each a different manifestation of the same underlying cause relative to the age and the educational experiences available to the subjects? What is the relationship of subgrouping to etiological factors? What is the relationship between various subgroups and intervention methods? These are all questions that further neuropsychological research may be able to address.

4. *Electrophysiological Research.* Research in this area is proceeding in several directions. First, there are studies addressing quantitative differences in the EEG patterns of children with learning disorders compared with control groups, as each responds to tasks requiring the brain to process information. Such studies look at spectral (wave length) patterns, the number of those patterns (power), and the coherence (symmetry) of those patterns in homologous portions of the recording. The results may be expressed in statistically determined deviations from reference groups and visually displayed in topographic pictures. A second direction of research is in the wave forms (event-related potentials) that appear up to 600 milliseconds or more following specific stimuli that make demands on the brain to evaluate and think as information is processed. In addition to identifying gross differences between children with learning disorders and adequate achievers, these studies may also be able to define subgroups on the basis of electrophysiological patterns. This field of study needs basic normative data defining event-related potentials in normal children. What are the electrophysiological events that normally accompany visual or auditory stimulation? What subtle differences appear as meaning of the stimuli is required, as semantic incongruities are introduced, or as arithmetic problems are solved? What is the range of normality? These studies are important to understanding brain/behavior relationships. They will become more meaningful when related to other aspects of behavior—reading, thinking, feeling. If it can be demonstrated that selected samples of learning-disordered children do indeed differ in their responses, can that potential be brought to normalization with training of the specific function related to the differences? Can it be demonstrated that training alters electrophysiology as it alters function? Here also a collaborative interdisciplinary effort is needed.

IMPACT OF THIS RESEARCH

With all this research attention, one might expect to see great progress in the provision of services to students with learning disorders and with more striking gains in the outcomes of these services. Unfortunately, this is not the case. Literacy continues to be a major problem. The National Assessment of Educational Progress (A. E. Beaton & Zwick, 1990) reported that 22% of adults in their research samples (numbering more than 3,600 individuals) performed in the lowest level on their tests of the application of literacy skills. These statistics lead to an estimate of 40 million people nationwide in the U.S. population who lack the skills necessary for adult life. Furthermore, special education programs, mandated more than two decades ago to provide services to students in the public schools, have not had much impact on the population as a whole. Except in the cases of individuals and some individual programs, such as those described in *Educational Programs That Work,* studies sponsored by the Department of Education show that special education has failed to return any sizable proportion of students with learning disabilities to regular classes or to improve the educational and vocational outcomes of those who have completed 12 years of schooling. More recently, most students with learning disabilities have been assigned to mainstream classes in the belief that their handicaps are remediable within the regular educational programs. These assignments occur often without the support of clinical services that have been shown to be necessary for effective instruction of students with learning disabilities. Professionals in the field often have difficulty agreeing among themselves on just which services are necessary and what methods are effective with these students. Inevitably, state and local governments, responsible for the major portion of the funding for services to students with learning disabilities are beginning to question the cost-effectiveness of these programs and to impose crippling economies. Enlightened legislators and administrators view these problems with alarm and frequently respond by appointing yet another task force or panel to deal with the problem. These earnest people meet, hold hearings, commission reviews of the existing literature, make recommendations based on these learned reviews, and write reports addressing the problem. These reports often contain astute recommendations that, if implemented, could help. However, changes in administrations and emerging new priorities delay or confound attempts to implement recommended changes and the problems highlighted in the past, persist.

How is it that so many good intentions have failed to have major effects on the problem of learning disabilities? How is it that a problem about which so much is known, eludes serious attempts at solution? Is the problem of literacy so complex that it cannot be solved within the public schools? Will these failures lead inexorably to the abandonment of attempts to teach children with learning disabilities within the schools? Will these services return to what occurred before 1975 with diagnostic and intervention services available only outside public school systems and available only to those families that can afford to pay for them? Should concerned people give up attempts at solution and accept illiteracy as inevitable for the substantial portion on the population known to suffer from learning disabilities?

The authors of this book do not think so. We continue to believe that solutions are within the grasp of our nation. We do not think this process will be accomplished easily or cheaply or without serious efforts on the part of all of us who are concerned that children realize their potential through education. We believe this is possible if the following conditions can be met.

If There Is Greater Collaboration between Clinicians and Educators

Effective management of students with learning disabilities requires both clinical and educational services, yet specialists in these fields operate in relative isolation from each other. It may be that the enforced cooperation between clinical personnel and educators mandated in the federal special education legislation ran into difficulties because of basic differences in training, skills, and orientation of clinicians and educators. Clinicians tend to focus on the individual; educators think in terms of groups. Clinicians are trained to focus on pathology, educators may be intimidated by pathology and may prefer to think in terms of normal development only. Educators may regard clinicians as elitist because of their additional levels of training. Clinicians, in turn, may take a superior attitude toward the educators' role in intervention and may offer recommendations that reflect their lack of real knowledge of instructional processes. Finally, both groups may fail to understand the professional literature of the other, so that their discussions may lack any real communication of ideas.

We believe that in the most literal sense, *collaboration* between clinical personnel and educators is possible. Such collaboration should have its basis in mutual respect for the contributions of each group of service providers. This respect can be fostered by opportunities for shared training within the context of the schools. Clinical personnel need to venture outside their offices and clinics into school classrooms. Educators need to abdicate their solitary role and welcome clinicians into their classrooms. The role of teacher-educator in the colleges and universities should be reserved only for people who have had successful classroom experience and provide models of sound educational practices in their classes and in the schools in which their teacher-trainees work. Most important of all, clinicians and educators should become conversant not only with the literature of their own specialties, but with all of the research in the broad field of learning disorders.

If All Service Providers Identify Their Client Correctly

Special education services have been designed for the benefit of students with disabilities and their families. Students with learning disabilities can best be served if the service providers recognize that the *students* are their clients. Too often, diagnostic decisions are made and intervention services are provided as if the client was really the school district or the local or state department regulations. Students' needs frequently are met only when those needs can fit into school district policy and budget.

Learning disabilities need to be understood not only by those responsible for classroom instruction, but by all school personnel. The variations among subtypes of learning disabilities must be recognized and related to the school curriculum requirements. School personnel should appreciate the chronic nature of learning disability and its different manifestations at different stages of development. They must be aware of the optimistic outcomes when effective programs are provided and must, therefore, entertain higher expectations for these students than they have in the past.

If Clinical Training Could Be More Realistic

Child psychiatrists and pediatricians who plan to work in schools should learn to understand the dynamics of the communities in which they work. Their high levels of training often equip them for leadership of the multidisciplinary teams that serve children with disabilities, but they need to respect the contributions of individual members of the teams and to understand the context of reality within which the recommendations will be implemented. Too often, clinicians think about schools as they existed when they were pupils decades ago, and they fail to comprehend the dynamics of today's schools and the problems faced by today's families.

Child psychiatrists and pediatricians who serve in the schools also possess unique skills for evaluating the functioning of the central nervous system of the students who may be referred for learning disorders. The neuropsychiatric examination is an important part of the pentaxial scheme for diagnosis. Although it may not be possible to provide such an evaluation to every student referred, it should be available for students whose problem behavior and learning difficulties confound their teachers and their parents and who fail to respond effectively to educational intervention measures.

School psychologists' training in research prepares them to help the diagnostic teams keep abreast of contemporary research findings in the field of learning disorders. Their training in clinical neuropsychology may also prepare school psychologists to contribute to the evaluation of the student's strengths and weaknesses in the brain/behavior relationships relevant to learning. With increased clinical contact with students, school psychologists may develop more confidence in their clinical skills, so that their recommendations are less dependent on vague generalizations and more realistic in terms of specific interventions related to the needs of individuals. More intensive clinical contacts with students will enable school psychologists to feel less like "a guest in the house of education" and to take a more responsible role in the diagnosis and treatment of students with learning disorders.

Teachers need to recognize the therapeutic value of teaching in the management of students with learning disorders. How the teacher implements the therapeutic recommendations of the evaluation team (of which they are part) will be a defining force for the child's success or failure. This implies that teachers, like other clinicians, must continue to improve their skills and advance their knowledge of the processes of teaching and learning. If they have a role in educational evaluation, they will not be satisfied with administering long test batteries and submitting print-outs of uninterpretable test scores to the diagnostic team. They will, instead, administer only those tests necessary to determine a student's needs and then draw on their instructional skills to provide a practical individual educational plan. They will avoid attachment to one method and instead will develop skills with a variety of approaches from which they can select methods suited to the specific needs of the individual children for whom they are responsible. Finally, the diagnostic teams of the schools need to move beyond petty discussions of *where* and *when* teaching is to take place and focus on how individual students can best be helped to progress on the road to literacy and independent learning.

If Parents Learn to Participate in Their Children's Education

With more realistically trained clinicians and educators, it is hoped that parents will learn to trust the services they provide in the schools. Some professionals have not always earned that trust, but conversely not all professionals have earned the suspicion and derision that is often directed toward school personnel. Parents need to be well-informed and enlightened consumers, able to sense the difference between the latest expensive "breakthrough" touted by educational hucksters and the responsible plans of professional educators. Parents need to appreciate the problems school face and to join with them to find solutions. They need to learn not to hold a protest meeting or file a suit, but instead to negotiate effective management of the education responsibilities that they share with school personnel.

If Researchers Take a Broad View of the Field of Learning Disorders

Researchers need to select research problems that truly add to existing knowledge about learning disorders. They need to read widely the work of other researchers and to view this work with caution and respect. They should not attempt to justify their own research proposals by discrediting previous work in the field; rather they should see their plans as building on earlier foundations laid by investigators who have gone before them. Finally, they should report their results in language that others outside their field can comprehend.

If Community Leaders Stop Politicizing Education

Community leaders, like all citizens in a democracy, may be expected to have opinions about education, as well as the other publicly provided services. However, recent years have seen educational issues become a part of political campaigns to the extent that decision making about school management and curriculum has been moved into the area of political debate. Educational decision making has been placed in the hands of political leaders who promise to restructure, reform, and reinvent school organization. These political leaders have little training or experience in the realities of school management. The solutions they recommend often fail to take into account the special needs of students with disabilities because provisions for these students are of only recent origin. Their plans have been made on the assumption that introducing competition will improve schools, although there is no evidence that the free market approach can be appropriately applied to education. Quick fixes such as high-stakes testing, vouchers, privatization of schools, and standards that place all students on a college preparatory track have been proposed (and even implemented in some states) without regard for the opposition of qualified professionals or parents whose children may become the victims of these untried measures. It is our hope that responsible leadership will emerge from these chaotic debates before too much damage is done, so that educators and parents can regain control of the processes of education. We hope that these leaders will seek the help of qualified advisers to survey what is already known and will trust their advice in making crucial decisions about schooling.

A FINAL WORD

These conditions are not proposed in the naive belief that the educational problems of our country can be solved easily or quickly. Our years of experience have convinced us that there is no royal road to learning and that children differ in their educational needs. A free, appropriate, public education is the right of every child in our country, but also *effective* education of all citizens is a necessary element of a democratic society.

Although these ideals have yet to be realized, their chances of fulfillment can be increased for children with learning disorders if professionals in the field collaborate along the lines suggested. This collaboration can be implemented if professionals identify individual students rather than the school system as their clients, if clinicians and educators share training experiences in the schools rather than in isolation within their own academic disciplines, if parents support and participate in the education of their children, and if educational leadership is returned to experienced and qualified professionals.

Education in a diverse, democratic, society is complex, taking place within social, political, and economic realities, difficult even in teaching children who are ready and willing to learn. Children with learning disabilities create further complexities—in their identification, in the multifaceted nature of their disabilities, in their sheer numbers, and in the resources the school must provide in terms of space, time, specially trained teachers, psychologists, and social workers needed to teach these children appropriately. Now at the beginning of the twenty-first century, there is a cumulative rich literature relevant to increasing understanding of these children and relevant also to the intervention needed to teach these children the basic skills for literacy.

In this book, we have stressed the reciprocal sharing of this new knowledge among all disciplines concerned with the education of children with learning disorders. Sadly, this integrative process has lagged. The administrative changes in the "where" children with learning disabilities are taught in the schools, and the economic and political forces mandating such changes, have not as yet improved the outcome of learning disability. What appears to be missing is recognition that the teacher or teachers who work with the child have the defining task, the ultimate responsibility as to whether the child succeeds or fails. It is the combined knowledge of education, psychology, social work, and medicine, the sharing of and the acceptance of their responsibility by all these disciplines that will offer maximum support to the teacher and the greatest chance of success for the child.

Appendix

OUTLINE FOR NEUROLOGICAL EVALUATION

Patient ID# _____ DOB _____

Name _____ Present Date _____

Examined by _____ CA _____ Sex _____

I. Time Orientation (mark only if incorrect)

		day	☐			day	☐
	Birthday	month	☐	Today's date		month	☐
		year	☐			year	☐

II. Appearance and static markers (mark any if present/or abnormal)

Head circumference, in cms ( )	☐	Epicanthal folds	☐
Interpupillary distance ( )	☐	Low bridge of nose	☐
Simian crease	☐	Attached ear lobe	☐
Clinodactyly	☐	Lowset ears	☐
Abnormal toe spacing	☐	High palate	☐
Dermatoglyphic abnormalities	☐	Other (describe)	☐

III. Autonomic tone (mark if abnormal)

Salivation	☐	Abdominal distention	☐
Perioral pallor	☐	Sweating	☐
Skin temperature cold	☐	Pulse rate	☐
Skin temperature warm	☐	Heart rhythm	☐
Flushed facies	☐	Abnormal wheal and flare	☐

Division of Child and Adolescent Psychiatry, University of South Florida, College of Medicine. Compiled by Archie A. Silver, M.D. and Gary Pagano, M.D.

IV. Perception
    A. Visual

	1 2 3 4
Discrimination (lamb chops) # incorrect	5 6 7 8
	1 2 3 4
Recall (lamb chops) # incorrect	5 6 7 8

       Visual motor:

          Gesell (developmental age years)   1 2 3 4 5 6 7

          Bender Gestalt (mark if present)

verticalization	☐	separation	☐
angulation	☐	pressure	☐
Loops for dots	☐	plasticity	☐
Poor impulse control	☐	chaotic placement	☐

    B. Auditory

       Discrimination: (Wepman) # incorrect   1 2 3 4 5 6 7
                                             8 9 10 11 12 13 14

       Rote sequencing (mark only if correct)

count to 10	☐	before November	☐
after 7	☐	months backward	☐
before 6	☐	days of week	☐
months of year	☐	after Tuesday	☐
after March	☐	before Friday	☐

       Binet sentences (developmental age)   5 6 7 8 9 10 11 12

    C. Body image

       1. Right-Left Discrimination (mark only if incorrect)

          1- R-l: single commands

a.	L hand	☐
b.	R leg	☐
c.	L eye	☐
d.	R ear	☐

          2- Ipsilateral, double simultaneous commands

a.	R hand on R eye	☐
b.	L hand on L knee	☐
c.	R hand on R knee	☐
d.	L hand on L eye	☐

          3- Crossed double simultaneous commands

a.	Touch L leg with R hand	☐
b.	Touch R eye with L hand	☐
c.	Touch L ear with R hand	☐
d.	Touch R arm with L hand	☐

          4- R-L On examiner

a.	Point to my L ear with your R hand	☐
b.	Point to my R ear with your L hand	☐
c.	Point to my L arm with your R hand	☐
d.	Point to my L arm with your L hand	☐

2. Finger-Gnosis (mark only if incorrect)
   a. Single stimulus
      (age 5 years or less)

      R1 ☐   L5 ☐
      L3 ☐   R4 ☐

   b. Bilateral symmetrical

      R2   L2   ☐
      R4   L4   ☐
      R5   L5   ☐

   c. Bilateral asymmetrical

      R3   L5   ☐
      R2   L4   ☐
      R3   L4   ☐
      R4   L3   ☐

   SCORE: a) Number correct   X1 =
           b) Number correct   X2 =
           c) Number correct   X3 =
                    Total finger-gnosis _____

3. Extinction Phenomena (mark errors)

   Wrist-wrist   ☐   L Face-L wrist   ☐
   R Face-R wrist   ☐   Synchiria   ☐
   L Face-R wrist   Displacement   ☐
   R Face-L wrist   ☐   Alesthesia   ☐

4. Praxis (mark errors)

   R   1-3   ☐   L   1-3   ☐   synkinesis   ☐
         1-5   ☐   1-5   ☐
         1-2   ☐   1-2   ☐
         1-4   ☐   1-4   ☐

V. Arm Extension Test (mark response)
   1. Cerebral Dominance
      a. Hand used for writing   R   ☐   L   ☐
      b. Extremity elevation   R   ☐   L   ☐
                       alternating   ☐   equal   ☐
   2. Hand Posturing
      Fingers maintained spread and extended   ☐
      Finger hyperextended   ☐
      Fingers flexed   ☐
   3. Adventitious Finger Movements
      Prechtl movements   R   ☐   L   ☐
      Myoclonic jerks   R   ☐   L   ☐
      Choreoathetoid movements R   ☐   L   ☐

4. Maintenance of Balance

    1. Normal ☐   2. Mild ☐   3. Moderate ☐   4. Severe difficulty ☐

5. Postural Control

    a) Horizontal drift of arms

Divergence:	None ☐	Mild ☐	Moderate ☐	Severe ☐
Convergence:	None ☐	Mild ☐	Moderate ☐	Severe ☐
Upward:	None ☐	Mild ☐	Moderate ☐	Severe ☐
Downward	None ☐	Mild ☐	Moderate ☐	Severe ☐

    b) Truncal posturing

        Frontal plane deviation   Hyperextension ☐

                                     Hyperflexion ☐

        Lateral plane deviation   ☐

VI. Postural Responses and Synergy

    a. Neck righting response and tonic neck response

	Head to R	Head to L
Standing:		
0. No movement of lower extremities	☐	☐
1. One step taken ("mild")	☐	☐
2. More than one step taken, but in stop-start pattern ("moderate")	☐	☐
3. Continuous steps taken, no stopping ("severe")	☐	☐
4. Tonic neck posture	☐	☐
Sitting:		
0. No movement of torso	☐	☐
1. 45° turning of torso ("mild")	☐	☐
2. 90° turning of torso ("moderate")	☐	☐
3. 100° turning of torso ("severe")	☐	☐
4. Tonic neck posture	☐	☐

    b. Cerebellar functioning (mark if present)

        1. Finger-Nose   mild difficulty (post pointing) ☐

                                intention tremor ☐

                                  dysmetria ☐

                                  relieved at rest tremor ☐

        2. Rapid alternating movements of upper extremity (20 pairs) (mark if abnormal)

	Right	Left
a. Rhythm:		
1. Slow irregular rhythm, but movement maintained	☐	☐
2. Irregular rhythm with frequent stops	☐	☐
3. Unable to perform	☐	☐

        3. Romberg   ☐

        4. Hyptonia   ☐

        5. Rebound   ☐

VII. Cranial Nerves (mark if abnormal)

		R	L
I	Olfactory (gross evaluation)	☐	☐
II	Acuity	☐	☐
	Visual fields (gross confrontation)	☐	☐
	Disc	☐	☐
III, IV, VI			
	EOM	☐	☐
	Convergence	☐	☐
	Nystagmus	☐	☐
	Pupils	☐	☐
	Size	☐	☐
	Shape	☐	☐
	Position	☐	☐
	React to L	☐	☐
	React to A	☐	☐
V			
Corneal reflex		☐	☐
Sensation of face		☐	☐
Masseter and temporalis		☐	☐
Jaw deviation		☐	☐
VII			
	Ptosis	☐	☐
	Brow	☐	☐
	Eye close	☐	☐
	Frowning	☐	☐
	Smile	☐	☐
	Bite	☐	☐
	Taste (ant. $^{2}/_{3}$)	☐	☐
	Other	☐	☐
VIII			
	Acuity	☐	☐
	Weber	☐	☐
	Rinne	☐	☐
	Vestibular (if needed)	☐	☐
IX, X			
Uvula		☐	
Swallowing		☐	
XI			
Shoulder shrug		☐	
Head to right and to left		☐	
XII			
Tongue		☐	

VIII. Motor Function (mark if abnormal)

		Upper Extremities	Lower Extremities
A. Musculature		☐	☐
1. Mass	R	☐	☐
	L	☐	☐
2. Power	R	☐	☐
	L	☐	☐
3. Tone			
Hyper	R	☐	☐
	L	☐	☐
Hypo	R	☐	☐
	L	☐	☐
Fluctuating	R	☐	☐
	L	☐	☐
Cog wheeling	R	☐	☐
	L	☐	☐
Other	R	☐	☐
	L	☐	☐

B. Reflexes	R	L
1. DTR		
Biceps	☐	☐
Triceps	☐	☐
Quadriceps	☐	☐
Ankle	☐	☐
Other	☐	☐
2. Superficial Reflexes		
Abdominal	☐	☐
3. Pathological Reflexes		
Babinski	☐	☐
Confirmatories	☐	☐
Hoffman	☐	☐
Other	☐	☐

C. Coordination (mark if abnormal)

1. Gross Motor		
Toe walk	☐	
Heel walk	☐	
Tandem walk	☐	
Hopping	☐	
Standing on one foot	☐	

2. Fine Motor	R	L
Rhythm	☐	☐
Pattern	☐	☐
Synkinesis	☐	☐

3. Pencil grip

Overlapping thumb ☐

2 Finger grip ☐

3 Finger grip ☐

Other ☐

D. Motor Impulse Control (mark applicable description)

1. Kinetic Pattern

  a. Age and situation appropriate ☐

  b. Rhythmus shaking of extremities ☐

  c. Wriggling, squirming, fidgetiness ☐

  d. Markedly overactive relative to situation, moves around room, touching or exploring ☐

  e. Not only (d) but increased tempo of activity ☐

  f. Underactive, little spontaneous activity ☐

  g. Underactive, rigid, anxious, fearful ☐

  h. Tics ☐

  i. Vocalization ☐

  j. Overt choreiform movement ☐

  k. Rhythmic stereotopic movements:

Rocking ☐

Whirling ☐

Head banging ☐

Toe walking ☐

Arm flapping ☐

Observing light through fingers ☐

Exploring periphery of room ☐

Other ☐

2. Persistence

  a. Persists at task until completed ☐

  b. Needs occasional prompting for completion of tasks ☐

  c. Continual prompting for completion of tasks ☐

3. Distraction

  a. Rarely, or not distracted ☐

  b. Occasionally distracted by usual stimuli or distracted by unusual stimuli ☐

  c. Distracted by usual stimuli ☐

IX. Language (vocabulary, syntax, comprehension)
(mark if abnormal, circle appropriate description)

1. Rate: rapid, slow ☐

2. Pitch: high-pitched, ventriloquist, unusually loud or soft ☐

3. Rhythm: respiratory speech dissociation, saccadic smoothness ☐

4. Articulation: difficult to understand, specific phonic errors ☐

5. Expressive speech: vocabulary limited ☐

6. Associational problems: ☐

7. Comprehension problems: ☐
8. Auditory perceptual difficulty:
   a. Sequencing ☐
   b. Discrimination ☐

X. Timed Coordination Items Note: Performance quality and simultaneous occurrence of synkinesis. Number of each performed in 20 seconds

1. Foot tap: keep heel on floor and tap toe   L   R
2. Foot-heel-toe tap: heel to toe   L   R
3. Hand pat (gentle hand taps)   L   R
4. Hand pronation and supination   L   R
5. Finger tap: tap thumb and index finger together   L   R
6. Finger succession (thumb to each finger)   L   R
7. Tongue wriggle side to side (time for 10 seconds) L   R

References

Aaron, P. G., Kuchta, S., & Grapenthin, C. T. (1988). Is there a thing called dyslexia? *Annals of Dyslexia, 38,* 33–50.

Abbott, R. D., & Berninger, V. W. (1993). Structural equation modeling of relationships among developmental skills and writing skills in primary- and intermediate-grade writers. *Journal of Educational Psychology, 85,* 478–508.

Abrams, E. J., & Bateman, D. A. (1995). Voluntary newborn HIV-1 antibody testing: A successful model program for the identification of HIV-1-seropositive infants. *Bulletin of New York Academy of Medicine, 72,* 443–453.

Abrams, J. C., & Kaslow, F. (1977). Family systems and the learning disabled child: Intervention and treatment. *Journal of Learning Disabilities, 10,* 27–31.

Ackerman, P. T., Dykman, R. A., Holloway, C., Paal, N. P., & Gocio, M. Y. (1991). A trial of piracetan in two subgroups of students with dyslexia enrolled in summer tutoring. *Journal of Learning Disabilities, 24,* 542–549.

Ackbari, H. M., Anderson, G. M., Pollack, E. S., Chatterjee, D., Leckman, J. F., Riddle, M. A., & Cohen, D. J. (1993). Serotonin receptor binding and tissue indoles in postmortem cortex of Tourette's syndrome individuals. *Society for Neuroscience Abstracts, 19,* 838.

Adams, P., & Fras, I. (1988). *Beginning child psychiatry.* New York: Brunner/Mazel.

Adler, J., Greenberg, N., McKillop, P., & Namuth, T. (1985). The AIDS conflict. *Newsweek, 106,* 18–24.

Adler, S., & Birdsong, S. (1983). Reliability and validity of standardized testing tools used with poor children. *Topics in Language Disorders, 3,* 76–88.

Adult Committee, Special Populations Sub-Committee. (2000, August). *Fact sheet: Learning disabilities and low income populations.* Pittsburgh, PA: Learning Disabilities Association of America.

Agranoff, B. W. (1981). Learning and memory: Biochemical approaches. In G. S. Siegel, R. W. Albers, B. W. Agranoff, & R. Katzman (Eds.), *Basic biochemistry* (3rd ed.). Boston: Little, Brown.

Ain, M. (1980). *The effect of stimulus novelty on viewing time and processing efficiency in hyperactive children.* Unpublished doctoral dissertation, McGill University, Montreal, Canada.

Aldrighetti, L., Paganelli, M., Giacomelli, M., & Villa, G. (1996). Conservative management of cocaine-packet ingestion: Experience in Milan, the main Italian smuggling center of South American cocaine. *Panminverva Medica, 38,* 111–116.

Alessi, N. E., Walden, M., & Hirsh, P. S. (1989). Nifedipine-haloperidol combination in the treatment of Gilles de la Tourette's syndrome: A case study. *Journal of Clinical Psychiatry, 50,* 103–104.

Algozzine, B., & Ysseldyke, J. E. (1986). The future of the learning disability field: Screening and diagnosis. *Journal of Learning Disabilities, 19,* 394–398.

Algozzine, B., Ysseldyke, J. E., & McQue, M. (1995). Differentiating low-achieving student: Thoughts on setting the record straight. *Learning Disabilities Research and Practice, 10,* 140–144.

Allen, R. M., & Frank, G. H. (1963). Experimental variation of the mode of reproduction of the Bender Gestalt stimuli. *Journal of Clinical Psychology, 19,* 212–214.

Allington, R. L., McGill-Franzen, A., & Schick, R. (1999). How administrators understand learning difficulties. *Remedial and Special Education, 18,* 223–232.

Allington, R. L., & Woodside-Jiron, H. (1999). The politics of literacy teaching: How "research" shaped educational policy. *Educational Researcher, 28,* 4–12.

Aman, M. G., & Werry, J. S. (1982). Methylphenidate and diazepam in severe reading retardation. *Journal of the American Academy of Child Psychiatry, 21,* 31–37.

Aman, M. G., Werry, J. S., Paxton, J. W., Turbott, S. H., & Stewart, A. W. (1990). Effects of carbamazepine on psychomotor performance in children as a function of drug concentration, seizure type, and time of medication. *Epilepsia, 31,* 51–60.

American Academy of Pediatrics Committee on Substance Abuse and Committee on Children with Disabilities. (1993). Fetal alcohol syndrome and fetal alcohol effects. *Pediatrics, 91,* 1004–1006.

American Educational Research Association. (2000, July). *AERA position statement concerning high-stakes testing in pre-12 education: Policies, standards, and statements.* AERA Website.

American Psychiatric Association. (1987). *Diagnostic and statistical manual of mental disorders* (3rd ed., rev.) Washington, DC: Author.

American Psychiatric Association. (2000). *Diagnostic and statistical manual of mental disorders:* (4th ed., text rev.) Washington, DC: Author.

American Psychological Association. (1985). *Standard for educational and psychological testing* (3rd ed.). Washington, DC: Author.

Anderson, D. (1985). *Educational services for students with Tourette's syndrome.* Unpublished doctoral dissertation, University of South Florida, Tampa.

Anderson, E. (1984, April). *Increasing school effectiveness: The full day kindergarten.* Paper presented at the annual meeting of the American Educational Research Association. (ERIC Document Reproduction Service No. ED 248 036)

Anderson, G. M., Leckman, J. F., & Cohen, D. J. (1999). Neurochemical and neuropeptide systems. In J. F. Leckman & D. J. Cohen (Eds.), *Tourette's syndrome–tics, obsessions, compulsions: Developmental psychopathology and clinical care* (pp. 261–281). New York: Wiley.

Anderson, G. M., Pollack, E. S., Chatterjee, D., Leckman, J. F., Riddle, M. A., & Cohen, D. J. (1992). Postmortem analyses of brain monoamines and amino acids in Tourette's syndrome: A preliminary study of subcortical regions. *Archives of General Psychiatry, 49,* 584–586.

Angold, A., & Costello, E. (1995). A test retest reliability study of child reported psychiatric symptoms and diagnosis using the child and adolescent psychiatric assessment. *Psychological Medicine, 25,* 755–762.

Angold, A., & Costello, E. (1996). Toward establishing an empirical basis for the diagnosis of oppositional defiant disorder. *Journal of the American Academy of Child Adolescent Psychiatry, 35,* 1205–1212.

Apter, A., Pauls, D. L., Bleich, A., Zohar, A. H., Kron, S., Ratzoni, G., Dycian, A., Kotler, M., Weizman, A., & Cohen, D. J. (1992). A population-based epidemiological study of Tourette's syndrome among adolescents in Israel. In T. N. Chase, A. J. Friedhoff, & D. J. Cohen (Eds.), *Advances in neurology. Tourette's syndrome: Genetics, neurobiology and treatment* (Vol. 58, pp. 61–65). New York: Raven Press.

Archibold, R. (1999, September 16). Board now says summer school was wrongly ordered for 8,600. *New York Times.*

Arnold, L. E., Abikoff, H. B., Cantwell, D. P., Conners, C. K., Elliott, G., & Greenhill, L. L. (1997). National Institute of Mental Health Collaborative multimodal treatment study of children with ADHD (the MTA). Design challenges and choices. *Archives of General Psychiatry, 54,* 865–870.

Arnsten, A. F., & Goldman-Rakic, P. S. (1985). Catacholamines and cognitive decline in aged nonhuman primates. *Annals of the New York Academy of Sciences, 444,* 218–234.

Arnsten, A. F., Steere, J., & Hunt, R. (1996). The contribution of alpha 2–noradrenergic mechanisms of prefrontal cortical cognitive function: Potential significance for attention-deficit hyperactivity disorder. *Archives of General Psychiatry, 53,* 448–455.

Artley, A. S. (1950). Research concerning interrelationships among the language arts. *Elementary English, 27,* 527–537.

Atkins, M. S., Pelham, W. E., & Licht, M. H. (1985). A comparison of objective classroom measures and teacher ratings of attention deficit disorder. *Journal of Abnormal Child Psychology, 13,* 155–167.

August, G. J., & Garfinkel, B. D. (1989). Behavioral and cognitive subtypes of ADHD. *Journal of the American Academy of Child and Adolescent Psychiatry, 28,* 739–748.

August, G. J., & Garfinkel, B. D. (1990). Comorbidity of ADHD and reading disability among clinic-referred children. *Journal of Abnormal Child Psychology, 18,* 29–45.

Austin, A. W., & Ross, S. (1966). Glutamic acid and human intelligence. *Psychological Bulletin, 57,* 429–434.

Aylward, E. H. (1996). Normal caudate nucleus in obsessive-compulsive disorder assessed by quantitative neuroimaging. *Archives of General Psychiatry, 53,* 577–584.

Aylward, E. H., Reiss, A. L., Allan, A. L., Reader, M. J., & Singer, H. S. (1996). Basal ganglia volumes in children with attention-deficit hyperactivity disorder. *Journal of Child Neurology, 11,* 112–115.

Ayres, A. J. (1989). *Sensory integration and praxis test manual.* Los Angeles: Western Psychological Services.

Azrin, N. H., & Peterson, A. L. (1988). Behavior therapy for Tourette's syndrome and tic disorders. In D. J. Cohen, R. D. Bruun, & J. F. Leckman (Eds.), *Tourette's syndrome and tic disorders: Clinical understanding and treatment* (pp. 237–255). New York: Wiley.

Badian, N. A. (1999). Persistent arithmetic, reading and arithmetic and reading disability. *Annals of Dyslexia, 49,* 45–70.

Baer, D., Freeman, R., & Greenberg, M. (1984). Behavioral alterations in patients with temporal lobe epilepsy. In D. Blumer (Ed.), *Psychiatric aspects of epilepsy* (pp. 197–228). Washington, DC: American Psychiatric Press.

Bailey, C. H., & Kandel, E. R. (1995). Molecular and structural mechanisms underlying long-term memory. In M. S. Gazzaniga (Ed.), *The cognitive neurosciences* (pp. 19–36). Cambridge, MA: MIT Press.

Baker, K. A., & de Kanter, A. A. (1981). *Effectiveness of bilingual education: A review of the literature.* Washington, DC: U.S. Department of Education, Office of Planning, Budget and Evaluation.

Bakker, D. J. (1972). *Temporal order in disturbed reading.* Amsterdam: Rotterdam University Press.

Bakker, D. J. (1979). Hemisphere differences and reading strategies: Two dyslexias? *Bulletin of the Orton Society, 29,* 84–100.

Bakker, D. J., Bouma, A., & Gardien, C. J. (1990). Hemisphere-specific treatment of dyslexia subtypes: A field experiment. *Journal of Learning Disabilities, 23,* 433–438.

Bakker, D. J., Van Leeuwen, H. M. P., & Spyer, G. (1987). Neuropsychological aspects of dyslexia. In D. J. Bakker, C. Wilsher, H. Debruyne, & N. Bertin (Eds.), *Developmental dyslexia and learning disorder* (pp. 30–39). Basel, Switzerland: Karger.

Balow, B., Rubin, R., & Rosen, M. J. (1975). Perinatal events as precursors of reading disabilities. *Reading Research Quarterly, 11,* 36–71.

Balthazar, K. (1956). Über das anatomisehe substrat der generalisierten tic-krankeit (maladie des tics, Gilles de la Tourette): Entwicklungshemmung des corpus striatum. *Arch fur Psychiatrie und Nervenkrankheiten, 195,* 531–539.

Bannatyne, A. (1971). *Language, reading and learning disabilities.* Springfield, IL: Thomas.

Barclay, J. R. (1984). Primary prevention and assessment. *Journal Personal Guidance, 62,* 475–478.

Barker, R. G., & Wright, H. F. (1954). *Midwest and its children: The psychological ecology of an American town.* Evanston, IL: Row Peterson.

Barkley, R. A. (1977). The effects on methylphenidate in various types of activity level and attention in hyperkinetic children. *Journal of Abnormal Child Psychology, 5,* 351–369.

Barkley, R. A. (1990). A critique of current diagnostic criteria for attention deficit hyperactivity disorder: Clinical and research applications. *Journal of Developmental and Behavioral Pediatrics, 11,* 343–352.

Barkley, R. A. (1996). *Critical issues in research on attention.* In G. R. Lyon & N. A. Krasnegor (Eds.), *Attention, memory and executive functions* (pp. 45–56). Baltimore: Brookes.

Barkley, R. A. (1997). Behavioral inhibition, sustained attention, and executive functions: Constructing a unifying theory of ADHD. *Psychology Bulletin, 121,* 65–94.

Barkley, R. A., & Edelbrock, C. (1986). *Attention deficit disorder with and without hyperactivity: Empirical corroboration of subtypes.* Paper presented at the 94th annual meeting of the American Psychological Association, Washington, DC.

Barnes, M. K. (1999). Strategies for collaboration: A collaborative teaching partnership for an inclusion classroom. *Reading and Writing Quarterly, 15,* 33–38.

Baron, R., & Baron, J. (1977). How children get meaning from printed words. *Child Development, 48,* 594–598.

Barondes, S. H., & Cohen, H. D. (1966). Puromycin effect on successive phases of memory in mice. *Science, 151,* 594–595.

Barrett, T. C. (1965a). Predicting reading achievement through readiness tests. In *Reading and inquiry* (pp. 26–28). Newark, DE: International Reading Association.

Barrett, T. C. (1965b). Relationship between measure of pre-reading visual discrimination and first grade reading achievement. *Reading Research Quarterly, 1,* 51–76.

Barrett, T. C. (1965c). Visual discrimination tasks as predictors of first grade reading achievement. *Reading Teacher, 18,* 276–282.

Barron, R. W. (1986). Word recognition in early reading: A review of the direct and indirect access hypothesis. *Cognition, 24,* 93–119.

Baumgardner, T. L., Singer, H. S., Denckla, M. B., Rubin, M. A., Abrams, M. T., Colli, M. J., & Reiss, A. L. (1996). Corpus callosum morphology in children with Tourette's syndrome and attention deficit hyperactivity disorder. *Neurology, 47,* 477–482.

Beaton, A. A. (1985). *Left side, right side: A review of laterality research.* New Haven, CT: Yale University Press.

Beaton, A. A. (1997). The relation of planum temporale asymmetry and morphology of the corpus callosum to handedness, gender, and dyslexia: A review of the evidence. *Brain and Language, 60,* 255–322.

Beaton, A. E., & Zwick, R. (1990). Overview of the national assessment of educational progress. *Journal of Educational Statistics, 17,* 95–109.

Beck, L., Langford, W., MacKay, M., & Sunn, G. (1975). Childhood chemotherapy and later drug abuse and growth curve: A follow-up study of 30 adolescents. *American Journal of Psychiatry, 132,* 436–438.

Belcher, H. (1992). *Project Strive.* Tampa: University of South Florida College of Medicine, Departments of Pediatrics and Obstetrics and Gynecology.

Bell, N. (1991). Gestalt imagery: A critical factor in language comprehension. *Annals of Dyslexia, 41,* 246–260.

Bellinger, D., Sloman, J., Leviton, A., Rabinowitz, M., Needleman, H. L., & Waternaux, C. (1991). Low level lead exposure in children's cognitive function in the pre-school years. *Pediatrics, 87,* 219–227.

Bender, L. A. (1938). *A visual motor Gestalt Test and its clinical use.* New York: American Orthopsychiatric Association.

Bender, L. A. (1953). *Aggression, hostility and anxiety in children.* Springfield, IL: Thomas.

Bender, L. A. (1956). *Psychopathology of children with organic brain disorders.* Springfield, IL: Thomas.

Bender, L. A. (1958). Problems in conceptualization and communication in children with developmental alexia. In P. H. Hoch & J. Zubin (Eds.), *Psychopathology of communication* (pp. 155–176). New York: Grune & Stratton.

Bender, L. A. (1970). Use of the visual motor Gestalt Test in the diagnosis of learning disabilities. *Journal of Special Education, 4,* 29–39.

Bender, L. A., & Cottington, F. (1943). The use of amphetamine sulphate (Benzedrine) in child psychiatry. *American Journal of Psychiatry, 99,* 116.

Bender, L. A., & Freedman, A. M. (1952). A study of the first three years of maturation of schizophrenic children. *Quarterly Journal of Child Behavior, 4,* 245–272.

Bender, L. A., & Yarnell, H. (1941). An observation nursery. *American Journal of Psychiatry, 97,* 1158–1172.

Bender, M. B. (1952). *Disorders in perception.* Springfield, IL: Thomas.

Bender, M. B., Fink, M., & Green, M. (1951). Patterns of perception of simultaneous tests of face and hand. *Archives of Neurology and Psychiatry, 66,* 355–362.

Benezra, E. (1980). *Verbal and nonverbal memory in hyperactive, reading disabled and normal children.* Unpublished doctoral dissertation, McGill University, Montreal, Canada.

Bennett, E. L., Rosenzweig, M. R., & Flood, J. F. (1977). Protein synthesis and memory studied with anisomycin. In S. Robert, A. Lajtha, & W. H. Gispen (Eds.), *Mechanisms, regulation and special functions of protein synthesis in the brain.* Amsterdam: Elsevier.

Benson, D. F. (1991). The Geschwind syndrome. *Advances in Neurology, 55,* 411–421.

Benton, A. L. (1955a). Development of finger-localization capacity in school children. *Child Development, 26,* 225–230.

Benton, A. L. (1955b). Right-left discrimination, finger-localization and cerebral status. *Acta Psychologie, 11,* 165–166.

Benton, A. L. (1959). *Right-left discrimination and finger localization.* New York: Harper & Brothers.

Benton, A. L. (1992). Gerstman's syndrome. *Archives of Neurology, 49,* 445–447.

Benton, A. L., & Pearl, D. (Eds.). (1978). *Dyslexia: An appraisal of current knowledge.* New York: Oxford University Press.

Berg, R. (1985). A case of Tourette's syndrome treated with nifedipine. *Acta Psychiatrica Scandinavica, 72,* 400–401.

Berkovitch, M., Pope, E., Phillips, J., & Koren, G. (1995). Pemoline associated fulminant liver failure: Testing the evidence for causation. *Clinical Pharmacological Therapy, 57,* 696–698.

Berman, T., Douglas, V. I., & Barr, R. G. (1999). Effects of methylphenidate on complex cognitive processing in attention deficit hyperactivity disorder. *Journal of Abnormal Psychology, 108,* 90–105.

Bernard, C. (1858). *Comptes Rendus d L'Academie des Sciences, 48,* 245.

Berninger, V., & Hart, T., Abbott, R. D., & Karovsky, P. (1992). Diagnosing writing disabilities with and without IQ: A flexible, developmental perspective. *Learning Disabilities Quarterly, 15,* 103–118.

Berninger, V. W. (1994). Future directions for research on writing disabilities. In G. R. Lyon (Ed.), *Frames of reference for the assessment of learning disabilities* (pp. 419–439). Baltimore: Brookes.

Berninger, V. W., & Abbott, R. D. (1994). Redefining learning disabilities: Moving beyond aptitude-achievement discrepancies to failure to respond to validated treatment protocols. In G. R. Lyon (Ed.), *Frames of reference for the assessment of learning disabilities* (pp. 163–183). Baltimore: Brookes.

Berninger, V. W., & Rutberg, J. (1992). Relationship of finger function to beginning writing: Application to diagnosis of writing disabilities. *Developmental Medicine and Child Neurology, 34,* 198–215.

Berthier, M. L., Kulisevsky, J., & Campos, V. M. (1998). Bipolar disorders in adult patients with Tourette's syndrome: A clinical study. *Biological Psychiatry, 43,* 364–370.

Best, C. T. (1988). The emergence of cerebral asymmetries in early human development: A literature review and a neuroembryological model. In D. L. Molfese & J. S. Segalowitz (Eds.), *Brain lateralization in children: Developmental implications* (pp. 5–34). New York: Guilford Press.

Bhadrinath, B. R. (1998). Olanzapine in Tourette's syndrome [Letter]. *British Journal of Psychiatry, 172,* 366.

Biederman, J., Faraone, S. V., Milberger, S., Jetton, J. G., Chen, L., Mick, E., Greene, R. W., & Russell, R. L. (1996). Is childhood oppositional defiant disorder a precursor to adolescent conduct disorder? Findings from a four-year follow-up study of children with ADHD. *Journal of the American Academy of Child and Adolescent Psychiatry, 35,* 1193–1204.

Biklen, D., & Zoellers, N. (1986). The focus of advocacy in the learning disorder field. *Journal of Learning Disabilities, 19,* 579–586.

Binet, A., & Simon, T. (1916). *The development of intelligence in children.* Baltimore: Williams & Wilkins.

Birch, H. G., & Belmont, L. (1964). Auditory-visual integration in normal and retarded readers. *American Journal of Orthopsychiatry, 34,* 852–861.

Birch, H. G., & Belmont, L. (1965). Auditory-visual integration, intelligence, and reading ability in school children. *Perceptual and Motor Skills, 20,* 295–305.

Bird, H. R., & Kestenbaum, C. J. (1988). A Semi-structured approach to clinical assessment. In C. Kestenbaum & D. Williams (Eds.), *Handbook of clinical assessment of children and adolescents* (pp. 19–30). New York: New York University Press.

Bishop, V. V. M., & Adams, C. (1990). A prospective study of the relationship between specific language impairment, phonological disorders and reading retardation. *Journal of Child Psychology and Psychiatry, 31,* 1027–1050.

Black, M. M., Dubowitz, H., & Starr, R. H., Jr. (1999). African American fathers in low income, urban families: Development, behavior, and home environment of their three-year-old children. *Child Development, 70,* 967–978.

Blackorby, J., & Wagner, M. (1996). Longitudinal postschool outcomes of youth with disabilities: Findings from the national longitudinal transition study. *Exceptional Children, 62,* 399–413.

Blank, M., & Bridger, M. W. (1967). Perceptual abilities and conceptual deficiencies in retarded readers. In J. Zubin & G. A. Jarvis (Eds.), *Psychopathology of mental development* (pp. 401–412). New York: Grune & Stratton.

Blau, A. (1946). *The master hand: A study of the origin and meaning of right and left sidedness and its relation to personality and language* (Research Monographs No. 5). New York: American Orthopsychiatric Association.

Blechman, E. A. (1991). Effective communication: Enabling multiproblem families to change. In P. A. Cowan & E. M. Hetherington (Eds.), *Family transitions: Advances in family research series* (pp. 219–244). Hillsdale, NJ: Erlbaum.

Bleile, K., & Wallach, H. (1992). A sociolinguistic investigation of the speech of African American preschoolers. *American Journal of Speech-Language Pathology, 1,* 54–62.

Bliss, J. (1980). Sensory experiences of Gilles de la Tourette's syndrome. *Archives of General Psychiatry, 37,* 1343–1347.

Blom, S. (1962). Trigeminal neuralgia: Its treatment with a new anticonvulsant drug (G-32883). *Lancet, 1,* 839–840.

Blovin, A., Bornstein, R., & Trites, R. (1978). Teenage alcohol use among hyperactive children: A five year follow-up study. *Journal of Pediatric Psychology, 3,* 188–194.

Blum, K., & Noble, E. P. (Eds.). (1997). *Handbook of psychiatric genetics.* New York: CRC Press.

Blumstein, S. E., Goodglass, H., & Tartter, V. (1975). The reliability of ear advantage in dichotic listening. *Brain and Language, 2,* 226–236.

Boder, E. (1970). Developmental dyslexia: A new diagnostic approach based on the identification of three subtypes. *Journal of School Health, 40,* 289–290.

Boder, E., & Jarrico, S. (1982). *The Boder test of reading-spelling patterns: A diagnostic screening test for subtypes of reading disability.* New York: Grune & Stratton.

Boehm, A. E. (1971). *Boehm test of basic concepts.* New York: Psychological Corporation.

Bogoch, S., & Dreyfus, J. (1970). *The broad range of use of diphenylhydantoin* (Vol. 1). New York: Dreyfus Medical Foundation.

Bond, E. D., & Appel, K. E. (1931). *The treatment of behavior disorders following encephalitis.* New York: Commonwealth Fund.

Bond, G. L., & Dykstra, R. (1967). The cooperation research program in first grade reading instruction. *Reading Research Quarterly, 2,* 101–142.

Borcherding, B. G., Keysor, C. S., Rapoport, J. L., Elia, J., & Amass, J. (1990). Motor/vocal tics and compulsive behavior on stimulant drugs: Is there a common vulnerability? *Psychiatry Research, 33,* 83–94.

Borison, R. L., Ang, L., Hamilton, W. J., Diamond, B. L., & Davis, J. M. (1983). Treatment approaches in Gilles de la Tourette's syndrome. *Brain Research Bulletin, 11,* 205–208.

Borland, B., & Hechman, L. (1976). Hyperactive boys and their brothers. *Archives of General Psychiatry, 33,* 669–675.

Booth, D. A., & Sandler, M. E. (1967). Localization of intracranial C14-orotic acid after practice at reaching for food. *Psychological Bulletin, 68,* 149–177.

Borsting, E., Ridder, W. H., III, Dudeck, K., Kelley, C., Matsui, L., & Motoyama, J. (1996). The presence of a magnocellular defect depends on the type of dyslexia. *Vision Research, 3,* 1047–1053.

Bowers, P. G., & Swanson, L. B. (1991). Naming speed deficits in reading disability: Multiple measures of a singular process. *Journal of Experimental Child Psychology, 51,* 195–219.

Boyle, M. H., Offord, D. R., Racine, Y., Sanford, M., Szatmari, P., Fleming, J. E., & Price-Munn, N. (1993). Evaluation of the diagnostic interview for children and adolescents for use in general population samples. *Journal of Abnormal Child Psychology, 21,* 663–681.

Bradley, C. (1937). The behavior of children receiving benzedrine. *American Journal of Psychiatry, 94,* 577–585.

Bradley, R. H. (1982). The home inventory: A Review of the first fifteen years. In N. J. Anastasio, W. K. Frankenberg, & A. W. Fandal (Eds.), *Identifying the developmentally delayed child.* Baltimore: University Park Press.

Bradley, R. H., & Caldwell, B. (1981). The home inventory: A validation of the pre-school scale for Black children. *Child Development, 52,* 708–710.

Bradley, R. H., Whiteside, L., Mundfrom, D. J., Casey, P. H., Kelleher, K. J., & Pope, S. K. (1994). Early indications of resilience and their relation to experiences in the home environments of low birthweight, premature children living in poverty. *Child Development, 65,* 346–360.

Brand, S. (1989). Learning through meaning. *Academic Therapy, 24,* 305–314.

Braun, A. R., Stoetter, B., Randolph, C., Hsiao, J. K., Vladar, K., Gernert, J., Carson, R. E., Herscovitch, P., & Chase, T. N. (1993). The functional neuroanatomy of Tourette's syndrome: An FDG-PET study: I. Regional changes in cerebral glucose metabolism differentiating patients and controls. *Neuropsychopharmacology, 9,* 277–291.

Brazelton, T. B. (1973). *Neonatal behavioral assessment scale.* London: William Heinemann.

Breen, M. J., & Altepeter, T. S. (1991). Factor structures of the home situations in questionnaire and the school situations questionnaire. *Journal of Pediatric Psychology, 16,* 59–67.

Breese, G., Gualtieri, T., Mailman, R., Mueller, R., Youngblood, W., & Vogel, R. (1981). Developmental psychopharmacology: Pre clinical and clinical studies of the hyperkinetic syndrome. In A. Raskin, D. S. Robinson, & J. Levine (Eds.), *Age and the pharmacology of psychoactive drugs* (pp. 63–78). New York: Elsevier.

Broadbent, D. E. (1954). The role of auditory localization in attention and memory span. *Journal of Experimental Psychology, 47,* 191–196.

Broca, P. (1861). Nouveille observaion d'aphemia produite par une lesion de la moitie posterieure des deuxieme et troisieme circonvolutions frontalas. *Bulletin de la Societe Anatomie, 6,* 398–407.

Brody, S., & Axelrad, S. (1978). *Mothers, fathers and children.* New York: International Universities Press.

Broman, S., Blen, E., & Shaughnessy, P. (1985). *Low achieving children: The first seven years.* Hillsdale, NJ: Erlbaum.

Broman, S. H. (1979). Perinatal anoxia and cognitive development in early childhood. In T. M. Field (Ed.), *Infants born at risk: Behavior and development* (pp. 29–52). New York: Spectrum.

Broman, S. H., Nichols, P. L., & Kennedy, W. (1975). *Preschool IQ: Prenatal and early developmental correlates.* Hillsdale, NJ: Erlbaum.

Brooks-Gunn, J., & Duncan, G. J. (1997). The effects of poverty on children. *Future Children, 7,* 55–71.

Brosnan, A. K. (1998). The social acceptance of children with disabilities in a fully included school district. *Dissertation Abstracts International, 58,* 4551.

Broussard, E. R. (1979). Assessment of the adaptive potential of the mother-infant system: The neonatal perception inventories. *Seminars in Perinatology, 3,* 91–100.

Brown, G. L., Murphy, D. L., Langer, D. H., Ebert, M. H., Post, R. M., & Bunney, W. E., Jr. (1984). *Monoamine enzymes in hyperactivity response to d-amphetamine.* Paper presented at the annual meeting of the American Academy of Child Psychiatry.

Bruck, M. (1985). The adult function of children with specific learning disabilities: A follow-up study. In I. E. Siegel (Ed.), *Advances in applied developmental psychology.* Norwood, NJ: Ablex.

Bruck, M. (1987). The adult outcomes of children with learning disabilities. *Annals of Dyslexia, 37,* 352–363.

Bruun, R. D. (1988). The natural history of Tourette's syndrome. In D. J. Cohen, R. D. Bruun, & J. F. Leckman (Eds.), *Tourette's syndrome and tic disorder: Clinical understanding and treatment* (pp. 22–39). New York: Wiley.

Bruun, R. D., & Budman, C. L. (1996). Risperidone as a treatment for Tourette's syndrome. *Journal of Clinical Psychiatry, 57,* 29–31.

Bryant, P., & Bradley, L. (1983). Auditory organization and backwardness in reading. In M. Rutter (Ed.), *Developmental neuropsychiatry* (pp. 289–297). New York: Guilford Press.

Bryant, T., Bay, M., & Donahue, M. (1998). Implications of the learning disabilities definition for the regular education initiation. *Journal of Learning Disabilities, 21,* 23–28.

Bryden, M. P. (1988). Does laterality make any difference? Thoughts on the relation between cerebral asymmetry and reading. In D. L. Molfese & S. J. Segalowitz (Eds.), *Brain lateralization in children: Developmental implications* (pp. 509–526). New York: Guilford Press.

Budman, C. L., Bruun, R. D., Park, K. S., & Olson, M. E. (1998). Rage attacks in children and adolescents with Tourette's disorder: A pilot study. *Journal of Clinical Psychiatry, 59,* 576–580.

Burks, H. F. (1996). *Behavior rating scales* [manual]. Los Angeles: Western Psychological Services.

Buros Institute of Mental Measurements. (n.d.). *Mental measurements yearbooks.* Lincoln: University of Nebraska Press.

Burt, M. K., Dulay, H. C., & Hernandez, C. E. (1973). *Bilingual syntax test.* San Antonio, TX: Psychological Corporation.

Butler, I. J., Koslow, S. H., Seifert, W. E., Jr., Caprioli, R. M., & Singer, H. S. (1979). Biogenic amine metabolism in Tourette's syndrome. *Annals of Neurology, 6,* 37–39.

Byring, R. F., Salmi, T. K., Sainio, K. O., & Orn, H. P. (1991). EEG in children with spelling disabilities. *Electroencephalography Clinical Neurophysiology, 79,* 247–255.

Caine, E. D., McBride, M. C., Chiverton, P., Bamford, K. A., Redliess, S., & Chiao, J. (1988). Tourette's syndrome in Monroe county school children. *Neurology, 38,* 472–475.

Caldwell, B., Bradley, R., & Staff. (1984). *Home observation for measurement of the environment.* Little Rock: University of Arkansas.

Calfee, R., Lindamood, C., & Lindamood, P. (1973). Acoustic-phonetic skills and reading: Kindergarten through twelfth grade. *Journal of Educational Psychology, 64,* 293–298.

Cameron, D. E., & Solyom, L. (1961). Effects of RNA on memory. *Geriatrics, 16,* 74–81.

Campbell, F. A., & Ramey, C. T. (1994). Effects of early intervention on intellectual and academic achievement: A follow-up study of children from low-income families. *Child Development, 65,* 684–698.

Campbell, K., & Mercer, C. (1995). *Great leaps in reading program.* Micanopy, FL: Dearmuid.

Campbell, L. R. (1996). Communication development and disorders in African American children. In A. G. Kamhi, K. E. Pollock, & J. L. Harris (Eds.), *Issues in service delivery to African American children* (pp. 73–93). Baltimore: Brookes.

Campbell, M., Anderson, L. T., Cohen, I. L., Perry, R., Small, A. M., Green, W. H., Anderson, L., & McCandless, W. (1982). Haloperidol in autistic children: Effects on learning behavior and abnormal involuntary movements. *Psychopharmacology Bulletin, 18,* 110–112.

Campbell, M., Anderson, L. T., Small, A. M., Perry, R., Green, W. H., & Caplan, R. (1982). The effects of haloperidol in learning and behavior in autistic children. *Journal of Autism and Developmental Disorders, 12,* 164–175.

Campbell, M., Perry, R., & Green, W. H. (1984). Use of lithium in children and adolescents. *Psychosomatics, 25,* 95–106.

Campbell, M., Small, A., Green, W. H., Jennings, S., Perry, R., Bennett, W., & Anderson, L. (1984). Behavioral efficacy of haloperidol and lithium carbonate: A comparison in hospitalized aggressive children with conduct disorder. *Archives of General Psychiatry, 41,* 650–656.

Campione, J. C. (1989). Assisted assessment: A taxonomy of approaches and an outline of strengths and weaknesses. *Journal of Learning Disabilities, 22,* 151–165.

Campione, J. C., & Brown, A. L. (1978). Toward a theory of intelligence: Contributions from research with retarded children. *Intelligence, 2,* 279–304.

Cannon, W. B. (1939). *The wisdom of the body* (2nd ed.). New York: Norton.

Canter, A. (1966). A background interference procedure to increase sensitivity of the Bender-Gestalt Test to organic brain disorder. *Journal of Consulting Psychology, 30,* 91–97.

Canter, A. (1968). Modified scoring method and replication. *Journal of Consulting and Clinical Psychology, 32,* 522–526.

Cantwell, D. P., Swanson, J., & Connor, D. F. (1997). Case study: Adverse response to clonidine. *Journal of the American Academy of Child and Adolescent Psychiatry, 36,* 539–544.

Caplan, R. (1998). Epilepsy syndromes. In E. C. Coffey & R. A. Brumback (Eds.), *Textbook of pediatric neuropsychiatry* (p. 978). Washington, DC: American Psychiatric Press.

Caprini, G., & Melotti, V. (1961). Una Grave Sindrome Ticcosa Guarita con Haloperidol. *Rivista Sperimentale di Freniatria e Medinina legale delle Alienazioni Mentale (Reggio-Emilia), 85,* 191–197.

Cardon, L. R., Smith, S. D., Fulker, D. W., Kimberling, W. J., Pennington, B. F., & DeFries, J. C. (1994). Quantitative trait locus for reading disability on chromosome 6. *Science, 266,* 276–279.

Cardon, L. R., Smith, S. D., Fulker, D. W., Kimberling, W. J., Pennington, B. F., & DeFries, J. C. (1995). Quantitative trait locus for reading disability: A correction. *Science, 268,* 5217.

Caro, P., & Derevensky, L. (1991). Family focused intervention model. *Topics Early Child Education, 11,* 66–80.

Carroll, J. B., & Horn, J. L. (1981). On the scientific basis of ability testing. *American Psychologist, 36,* 1012–1020.

Castellanos, F. X., Elia, J., Kruesi, M. J., Gulotta, C. S., Mefford, I. N., Potter, W. Z., Ritchie, G. F., & Rapoport, J. L. (1994). Cerebrospinal fluid monoamine metabolites in boys with attention-deficit hyperactivity disorder. *Psychiatry Research, 52,* 305–316.

Castellanos, F. X., Giedd, J. N., Eckburg, P., Marsh, W. L., Vaituzis, A. C., Kaysen, D., Hamburger, S. D., & Rapoport, J. L. (1994). Quantitative morphology of the caudate nucleus in attention deficit hyperactivity disorder. *American Journal of Psychiatry, 151,* 1791–1796.

Castellanos, F. X., Giedd, J. N., Elia, J., Marsh, W. L., Ritchie, G. F., et al. (1997). Controlled stimulant treatment of ADHD and comorbid Tourette's syndrome: Effects of stimulant and dose. *Journal of the American Academy of Child and Adolescent Psychiatry, 36,* 589–596.

Castellanos, F. X., Giedd, J. N., Marsh, W. L., Hamburger, S. D., Vaituzis, A. C., Dickstein, D. P., Sarfatti, S. E., Vauss, Y. C., Snell, J. W., Lange, N., Kaysen, D., Krain, A. L., Ritchie, G. F., Rajapakse, J. C., & Rapoport, J. L. (1996). Quantitative brain magnetic resonance imaging in attention-deficit/hyperactivity disorder. *Archives of General Psychiatry, 53,* 607–616.

Castles, A., Daha, H., Geyen, J., & Olson, R. K. (1999). Varieties of developmental reading disorder: Genetic and environmental influence. *Journal of Experimental Child Psychology, 72,* 73–94.

Cattell, J. M. (1890). Mental tests and measurements. *Mind, 15,* 373–380.

Cattell, R. B. (1963a). Nature and measurement of anxiety. *Scientific American, 208,* 96–104.

Cattell, R. B. (1963b). Theory of crystallized and fluid intelligence: A critical experiment. *Journal of Educational Psychology, 54,* 1–22.

Centers for Disease Control and Prevention. (1994). Recommendations of the U.S. Public Health Service Task Force on the use of zidovudine to reduce perinatal transmission of human immunodeficiency virus. *MMWR, 43 (No. RR-11),* 1–20.

Centers for Disease Control and Prevention. (1995). U.S. Public Health Service recommendations for HIV counseling and testing for pregnant women. *MMWR, 44 (No. RR-7),* 1–15.

Cermak, S. A., Morris, M. L., & Koomer, J. (1990). Praxis on verbal command and imitation. *American Journal of Occupational Therapy, 44,* 641–648.

Chabot, R. J., Merkin, H., Wood, L. M., Davenport, T. L., & Serfontein, G. (1996). Sensitivity and specificity of QEEG in children with attention deficit or specific developmental learning disorders. *Clinical Electroencephalography, 27,* 26–34.

Chabris, C. F. (1998). IQ since "The Bell Curve." *Commentary, 106,* 33–40.

Chadwick, O., Rutter, M., Brown, G., Shaffer, D., & Traub, M. (1981). A prospective study of children with head injuries: II. Cognitive sequelae. *Psychological Medicine, 11,* 49–61.

Chadwick, O., Rutter, M., Shaffer, D., & Shrout, P. (1981). A prospective study of children with head injuries: IV. Specific cognitive defects. *Journal of Clinical Neuropsychology, 3,* 101–120.

Chadwick, O., Rutter, M., Thompson, J., & Shaffer, D. (1981). Intellectual performance and reading skills after localized head injury in childhood. *Journal of Child Psychology and Psychiatry, 22,* 117–139.

Chalfant, J., Pysh, M., & Moultrie, R. (1979). Teacher assistance teams: A model for within building problem solving. *Learning Disability Quarterly, 2,* 85–96.

Chall, J. S. (1983). *Learning to read: The great debate* (Rev. ed.) New York: McGraw-Hill.

Chambers, W. J., Puig-Antich, J., Hirsch, M., Paez, P., Ambrosini, P. J., Tabrizi, M. A., & Davies, M. (1985). The assessment of affective disorders in children and adolescents by semistructured interview: Test-retest reliability of the schedule for affective disorders and schizophrenia for school-age children, present episode version. *Archives of General Psychiatry, 42,* 696–702.

Chanock, S. J. (1999). Medical issues in the house, day-care, school, and community. In S. L. Zeichner & J. S. Reed (Eds.), *Handbook of pediatric HIV care* (pp. 96–104). Philadelphia: Lippincott, Williams, & Wilkins.

Chapman, A. H., Pilkey, L., & Gibbons, M. J. (1958). A psychosomatic study of eight children with Sydenham's chorea. *Pediatrics, 21,* 582–595.

Chapman, F., Visvanathan, K., Carreno-Manjarrez, R., & Zabriskie, J. B. (1998). A flow cytometric assay for D8/17 B cell marker in patients with Tourette's syndrome and obsessive compulsive disorder. *Journal of Immunological Methods, 219,* 181–186.

Chappell, P. B., Leckman, J. F., & Riddle, M. A. (1995). The pharmacologic treatment of tic disorders. In M. Lewis & M. Riddle (Eds.), *Child and adolescent psychiatry clinics of North America: Pediatric psychopharmacology* (Vol. 4, pp. 197–215). Philadelphia: Saunders.

Chappell, P. B., Riddle, M. A., Anderson, G., Scahill, L. D., Hardin, M., Walker, D., Cohen, D. J., & Leckman, J. F. (1994). Enhanced stress responsivity of Tourette's syndrome patients undergoing lumbar puncture. *Biological Psychiatry, 36,* 35–43.

Chase, B. (2001). Test tosterone. *NEA Today, 19*(4), 5.

Chase, T. N., Geoffrey, V., Gillespie, M., & Burrows, G. H. (1996). Structural and functional studies of Gilles de la Tourette's syndrome. *Revue Neurologique, 142,* 851–855.

Chasnoff, I. J., Griffith, D. R., Freir, C., & Murray, J. (1992). Cocaine/poly drug use in pregnancy: Two year follow-up. *Pediatrics, 89,* 284–289.

Chasnoff, I. J., Landress, H. J., & Barrett, M. E. (1990). The prevalence of illicit drug or alcohol use during pregnancy and discrepancies in mandatory reporting in Pinellas County, Florida. *New England Journal of Medicine, 322,* 1202–1206.

Chavez, L. (1991). *Out of the barrio: Toward the new political Hispanic assimilation.* New York: Basic Books.

Chen, E. Y. H., Shapleske, J., Luque, R., McKenna, P. J., Hodges, J. R., Calloway, S. P., Hymas, F. S., Dening, T. R., & Berrios, G. E. (1995). The Cambridge Neurological Inventory: A clinical instrument for assessment of soft neurological signs in psychiatric patients. *Psychiatry Research, 56,* 183–204.

Chew, A. L. (1981). *The Lollipop Test: A diagnostic screening test of school readiness.* Atlanta, GA: Humanics Limited.

Chi, J. G., Dooling, E. C., & Gilles, F. H. (1977). Gyral development of the human brain. *Annals of Neurology, 1,* 86–93.

Childs, B., Finucci, J. M., & Preston, M. S. (1978). A medical genetics approach to the study of reading disability. In A. Benton & D. Pearl (Eds.), *Dyslexia: An appraisal of current knowledge* (pp. 301–309). New York: Oxford University Press.

Childs, S. B. (1973). *The child's spelling system.* Cambridge, MA: Educators Publishing Service.

Chisolm, J., Jr., & O'Hara, D. M. (1982). *Lead absorption in children.* Baltimore: Urban and Schwartzenberg.

Church, M. W., Crossland, W. J., Holmes, P. A., & Overbeck, G. W. (1998). Effects of prenatal cocaine on hearing, vision, growth, and behavior. *Annals of the New York Academy of Sciences, 21,* 12–28.

Cicirelli, V. (1970). Project Head Start. A national evaluation: Summary of the study. In D. C. Hays (Ed.), *Britannica review of American education.* Chicago: Encyclopedia Britannica.

Clark, M. D. (1997). Teacher response to learning disability: A test of attributional principles. *Journal of Learning Disabilities, 30,* 69–70.

Clay, M. (1988). *Reading recovery.* Unpublished manuscript, Ohio State University, Columbus.

Clay, M. M. (1985a). *The early detection of reading difficulties* (3rd ed.). Auckland, New Zealand: Heinemann.

Clay, M. M. (1985b). *Reading recovery, a guidebook for teachers in training.* Portsmouth, NH: Heinemann.

Clements, S. D. (1966). *Minimal brain dysfunction in children* (NINDB Monograph No. 3, DHHS Publication No. 1415). Washington, DC: U.S. Government Printing Office.

Close, J. (1973). Scored neurological examination (psychiatric and neurological examination for soft signs) [Special issue]. *Psychopharmacology Bulletin, 9,* 142–150.

Coates, R. D. (1989). The regular education initiative and opinions of regular classroom teachers. *Journal of Learning Disabilities, 22,* 532–536.

Coffey, C. E., Bryden, M., Schroering, E. S., Wilson, W. H., & Mathew, R. J. (1989). Regional cerebral blood flow correlates of a dichotic listening task. *Journal of Neuropsychiatry, 1,* 46–52.

Cohen, D. J. (1980). The pathology of the self in primary childhood autism and Gilles de la Tourette's syndrome. In B. Blinder (Ed.), *Psychiatric clinics of North America* (Vol. 3, pp. 383–402). Philadelphia: Saunders.

Cohen, D. J., Detlor, J., Shaywitz, B. A., & Leckman, J. F. (1982). Interactions of biological and psychological factors in the natural history of Tourette's syndrome: A model of childhood neuropsychiatric disorders. In T. N. Chase, A. J. Friedhoff, & D. J. Cohen (Eds.), *Advances in neurology. Tourette's syndrome: Genetics, neurobiology and treatment* (Vol. 58, pp. 31–40). New York: Raven Press.

Cohen, D. J., Detlor, J., Young, J. G., & Shaywitz, B. A. (1980). Clonidine ameliorates Gilles de la Tourette's syndrome. *Archives of General Psychiatry, 37,* 1350–1357.

Cohen, D. J., Shaywitz, B. A., Caparulo, B., Young, J. G., & Bowers, M. B., Jr. (1978). Chronic, multiple tics of Gilles de la Tourette's disease: CFS acid monoamine metabolites after probenecid administration. *Archives of General Psychiatry, 35,* 245–250.

Cohen, D. J., Shaywitz, B. A., Young, J. G., & Bowers, M. B., Jr. (1980). Cerebrospinal fluid monoamine metabolites in neuropsychiatric disorders of childhood. In J. H. Wood (Eds.), *Neurobiology of cerebrospinal fluid* (Vol. 1, pp. 665–683). New York: Plenum Press.

Cohen, D. J., Shaywitz, B. A., Young, J. G., Carbonari, C. M., Nathason, J. A., Lieberman, D., Bowers, M. B., Jr., & Maas, J. W. (1979). Central biogenic amine metabolism in children with the syndrome of chronic multiple tics of Gilles de la Tourette: Norepinephrine, serotonin, and dopamine. *Journal of the American Academy of Child Psychiatry, 18,* 320–341.

Cohen, H. J., Papola, P., & Alvarez, M. (1994). Neurodevelopmental abnormalities in school-age children with HIV infection. *Journal of School Health, 64,* 11–13.

Cohen, S. E., Mundy, T., Karassik, B., Lieb, L., Ludwig, D., & Ward, J. (1991). Neuropsychological functioning in human immunodeficiency virus Type I seropositive children infected through neonatal blood transfusion. *Pediatrics, 88,* 58–68.

Collaborative Study of Children with Special Needs. (1988). *Serving handicapped children.* New Brunswick, NJ: Robert Wood Johnson Foundation.

Comer, J. P. (1987). New Haven's school–community connection. *Educational Leadership, 44,* 13–18.

Comer, J. P. (1988). Educating poor minority children. *Scientific American, 259,* 42–48.

Comings, D. E. (1994). Tourette's syndrome: A hereditary neuropsychiatric spectrum disorder. *Annals of Clinical Psychiatry, 6,* 235–247.

Comings, D. E., & Comings, B. G. (1984). Tourette's syndrome and attention deficits disorders with hyperactivity: Are you genetically related? *Journal of the American Academy of Child Psychiatry, 23,* 138–146.

Comings, D. E., & Comings, B. G. (1987). A controlled study of Tourette's syndrome: VII. Summary: A Common genetic disorder causing disinhibition in the limbic system. *American Journal of Human Genetics, 41,* 839–866.

Comings, D. E., Himes, J. A., & Comings, B. G. (1990). An epidemiological study of Tourette's syndrome in a single school district. *Journal of Clinical Psychiatry, 51,* 463–469.

Committee on Pediatrics AIDS, American Academy of Pediatrics. (1998). Human immunodeficiency virus/acquired immunodeficiency syndrome education in schools (RE9741). *Pediatrics, 101,* 933–935.

Committee on Pediatric AIDS, American Academy of Pediatrics. (2000). Education of children with human immunodeficiency virus infection (RE9950). *Pediatrics, 105,* 1358–1360.

Como, P. G., & Kurlan, R. (1991). An open-label trial of fluoxetine for obsessive compulsive disorder in Gilles de la Tourette's syndrome. *Neurology, 41,* 972–974.

Conners, C. K. (1972). Psychological effects of stimulant drugs in children with minimal brain dysfunction. *Pediatrics, 49,* 702–708.

Conners, C. K. (1980). *Food additives and hyperactive children.* New York: Plenum Press.

Conners, C. K. (1990). *Conners' Rating Scale manual: Conners' Teacher Rating Scale: Conners' Parent Rating Scale: Instruments for use with children and adolescents.* Tonawanda, NY: Multi-Health Systems.

Conners, C. K. (1997). *Conners' Rating Scales–Revised: Instruments for use with children and adolescents* (pp. 94, 134). Tonawanda, NY: Multi-Health Systems.

Conners, C. K., Goyette, C., Southwick, M., Lees, J. M., & Andrulonis, P. A. (1976). Food additives and hyperkinesis: A controlled double-blind experiment. *Pediatrics, 58,* 154–166.

Connor, D. F., Ozbayrak, K. R., Benjamin, S., Ma, Y., & Fletcher, K. E. (1997). A pilot study of nadolol for overt aggression in developmentally delayed individuals. *Journal of the American Academy of Child and Adolescent Psychiatry, 36*, 826–834.

Consortium for Longitudinal Studies. (1983). *As the twig is bent: Lasting effects of preschool programs.* Hillsdale, NJ: Erlbaum.

Cook, E. H., Jr., Stein, M. A., Ellison, T., Unis, A. S., & Leventhal, B. L. (1995). Attention deficit hyperactivity disorder and whole-blood serotonin levels: Effects of comorbidity. *Psychiatry Research, 57*, 13–20.

Cook, E. H., Stein, M. A., Krasowski, M. D., Cox, N. J., Olkon, D. M., Kieffer, J. E., & Leventhal, B. L. (1995). Association of attention deficit disorder and the dopamine transporter gene. *American Journal of Human Genetics, 56*, 993–998.

Coons, C. E., Fandal, A. W., Kerr, C., & Frankenberg, W. K. (1981). *The Home Screening Questionnaire* [Reference manual]. Denver, CO: DDM.

Copeland, D. R., Fletcher, J. M., Pfefferbaum-Levine, B., Jaffe, N., Ried, H., & Maor, M. (1985). Neuropsychological sequelae of childhood cancer in long-term survivors. *Pediatrics, 75*, 745–753.

Corbett, J., & Trimble, M. (1983). Epilepsy and anticonvulsant medication. In M. Rutter (Ed.), *Developmental neuropsychiatry* (pp. 112–129). New York: Guilford Press.

Corbett, J. A., Mathews, A. M., Connell, P. H., & Shapiro, D. A. (1969). Tics and Gilles de la Tourette's syndrome: A follow-up study and critical review. *British Journal of Psychiatry, 115*, 1229–1241.

Corkin, S. (1984). Lasting consequences of bilateral medial temporal lobectomy: Clinical course and experimental findings in H. M. *Seminars in Neurology, 4*, 249–259.

Corkin, S., Amaral, D. G., Gonzalez, R. G., Johnson, K. A., & Hyman, B. T. (1997). H. M.'s medial temporal lobe lesion: Findings from magnetic resonance imaging. *Journal of Neuroscience, 17*, 3964–3979.

Corkum, P. V., & Siegel, L. S. (1993). Is the continuous performance task a valuable research tool for use with children with attention-deficit-hyperactivity disorder? *Journal of Child Psychology and Psychiatry, 34*, 1217–1239.

Costello, E. J., Angold, A., Burns, B. J., Stangl, D. K., Tweed, D. L., Erkanli, A., & Worthman, C. M. (1996). The Great Smoky Mountains study of youth, goals, design, and the prevalence of *DSM-III-R* disorders. *Archives of General Psychiatry, 53*, 1129–1136.

Coutinho, M. J. (1995). Who will be learning disabled after the reauthorization of IDEA? Two very distinct perspectives. *Journal of Learning Disabilities, 28*, 664–668.

Craig, H. K., & Washington, J. A. (1994). The complex syntax skills of poor, urban African-American preschoolers at school entry. *Language, Speech, and Hearing Services in Schools, 25*, 181–190.

Craig, H. K., Washington, J. A., & Thompson-Porter, C. (1998). Average C-unit lengths in the discourse of African American children from low-income, urban homes. *Journal of Speech, Language and Hearing Research, 41*, 433–444.

Critchley, M. (1964). *Developmental dyslexia.* London: William Heinemann.

Crook, R. (1988). Pharmacology of cognitive deficits in Alzheimer's disease and age-associated memory impairment. *Psychopharmacology Bulletin, 24*, 31–38.

Crosley, C. J. (1979). Decreased serotonergic activity in Tourette's syndrome. *Annals of Neurology, 5*, 596.

Cruickshank, W. M. (1967). *The brain injured child in home, school and community.* Syracuse, NY: Syracuse University Press.

Cruickshank, W. M. (1986). P. L. 94–142: Its making and its legacy. *Journal of Learning Disabilities, 19*, 388–389.

Cruickshank, W. M., Bentzen, F., Ratzeburg, R., & Tannhauser, M. (1961). *A teaching method for brain injured and hyperactive children.* Syracuse, NY: Syracuse University Press.

Cummins, J. (1984). *Bilingualism and special education.* San Diego, CA: College Hill Press.

Cummins, J. (2001). Cognitive and behavioral heterogenity in Alzheimer's disease. *Neurobiology and Aging, 21,* 845–861.

Dalby, M. A. (1975). Behavioral effects of carbamazepine. In J. K. Penry & O. D. Daly (Eds.), *Advances of neurology* (Vol. 11, pp. 331–344). New York: Raven Press.

Dalby, M. A., Elbro, C., & Stødkilde-Jørgensen, H. (1998). Temporal lobe asymmetry and dyslexia: An in vivo study using MRI. *Brain and Language, 61,* 51–69.

Dam, M. (1972). Dyphenylhydantoin: Neurologic aspects of toxicity. In D. Woodbury, J. Penry, & R. Schmitt (Eds.), *Antiepileptic drugs* (pp. 227–235). New York: Raven Press.

D'Amato, R. C., & Dean, R. S. (1987). Psychological reports, individual educational programs, and daily lesson plans: Are they related? *Professional School Psychology, 2,* 93–101.

Danoff, M. N., Coles, G. J., McLaughlin, D. H., & Reynolds, D. J. (1977–1978). *Evaluation of the impact of ESEA TITLE VII Spanish/English bilingual education programs.* Palo Alto, CA: American Institutes for Research.

Darby, R. O. (1978). *Learning disabilities: A multivariate search for subtypes.* Doctoral dissertation, University of Florida, Gainesville. (UMI No. 9-13.261)

Das, J. P., Kirby, J., & Jarman, R. F. (1975). Simultaneous and successive synthesis: An alternative model for cognitive abilities. *Psychological Bulletin, 82,* 887–1003.

Datta, L. (1969). *A report on evaluation studies of project Head Start.* Washington, DC: U.S. Department of Health, Education, and Welfare, Office of Child Development.

Davis, E. (1964). Clinical evaluation of a new anticonvulsant (G-32883). *Medical Journal of Australia, 1,* 150–152.

Davis, H. P., & Squire, L. R. (1984). Protein synthesis and memory: A review. *Psychological Bulletin, 96,* 518–559.

Dax, M. (1878). *L'Aphasie.* Paris: Delahaye.

DeFries, J. C. (1985). Colorado reading project. In D. B. Gray & J. F. Kavanaugh (Eds.), *Behavioral measures of dyslexia* (pp. 107–122). Parkton, MD: York Press.

DeFries, J. C., & Alarcon, M. (1996). Genetics of specific reading disability. *Mental Retardation and Developmental Disabilities Research Reviews, 2,* 39–47.

DeFries, J. C., & Baker, L. A. (1983). Colorado family reading study: Longitudinal analysis. *Annal of Dyslexia, 33,* 153–162.

DeFries, J. C., Filipek, P. A., Fulker, D. W., Olson, R. K., Pennington, B. F., Smith, S. D., & Wise, B. W. (1997). Colorado learning disabilities research center. *Learning Disabilities, 8,* 7–19.

DeFries, J. C., & Fulker, D. W. (1985). Multiple regression analysis of twin data. *Behavior Genetics, 15,* 467–473.

DeFries, J. C., Knopik, V. S., & Wadsworth, S. J. (1999). Reading and attention disorders. In D. D. Duane (Ed.), *Colorado twin study of reading disability* (pp. 17–41). Baltimore: York Press.

DeFries, J. C., Olson, R. K., Pennington, B. F., & Smith, S. D. (1991). Colorado reading project an update. In D. D. Duane & D. B. Gray (Eds.), *The reading brain: The biological basis of dyslexia* (pp. 53–87). Parkton, MD: York Press.

Delanoy, R. L., Tucci, D. L., & Gold, P. E. (1983). Amphetamine effects on long term potentiation of dentate granule cells. *Pharmacology, Biochemistry and Behavior, 18,* 137–139.

Del Dotto, J. E., Fisk, J. L., McFadden, G. T., & Rourke, B. P. (1991). Developmental analysis of children/adolescents with nonverbal learning disabilities: Long-term impact on personality adjustment and patterns of adaptive functioning. In B. P. Rourke (Ed.), *Neuropsychological validation of learning disability subtypes* (pp. 293–308). New York: Guilford Press.

Dellatolas, G., Viguier, D., Deloche, G., & De Agostini, M. (1998). Right-left orientation and significance of systematic reversal in children. *Cortex, 34,* 659–676.

DeLuca, J. W. (1991). Case studies of adolescents with nonverbal learning disabilities. In B. P. Rourke (Ed.), *Neuropsychological validation of learning disability subtypes* (pp. 356–369). New York: Guilford Press.

Denckla, M. B. (1985). Revised neurological examination for subtle signs. *Psychopharmacology Bulletin, 21*(4), 773–800.

Denckla, M. B. (1994). Measurement of executive function. In G. R. Lyon (Ed.), *Frames of reference for the assessment of learning disabilities: New views on measurement issues* (pp. 117–142). Baltimore: Brookes.

Denckla, M. B. (1996). A theory and model of executive function. In G. R. Lyon & N. A. Krasnegor (Eds.), *Attention, memory and executive function* (pp. 263–278). Baltimore: Brookes.

Denckla, M. B., Bemporad, J. B., & MacKay, M. C. (1976). Tics following methylphenidate administration: A report of 20 cases. *Journal of the American Medical Association, 235,* 1349–1351.

Denckla, M. B., Hoffman, K., & Mazzocco, M. M. (1996). Relationship between T_2-weighted hyperintensities and lower IQ in children with neurofibromatosis-I. *American Journal of Medical Genetics, 67,* 98–102.

Denckla, M. B., & Rudel, R. G. (1974). "Rapid automatized naming" of pictured objects, colors, letters, and numbers by normal children. *Cortex, 10,* 186–202.

Denckla, M. B., & Rudel, R. G. (1976a). Naming of objects by dyslexic and other learning-disabled children. *Brain and Language, 3,* 1–15.

Denckla, M. B., & Rudel, R. G. (1976b). Rapid automatized naming (R.A.N.): Dyslexia differentiated from other learning disabilities. *Neuropsychologia, 14,* 471–479.

Deno, S. (1985). Curriculum-based measurement: The emerging alternative. *Exceptional Children, 52,* 219–232.

Deshler, D. D., Schumaker, J. B., Levy, K., & Ellis, E. (1984). Academic and cognitive interventions for LD adolescents. *Journal of Learning Disabilities, 17,* 108–118, 170–179.

Deson, L. (1998). Comparison of parents' perceptions of children's behavior: A study of attentional problems in a natural setting. *Dissertation Abstracts International, 59*(4A), 1065. (University Microfilms International)

Deutsch, F. (1947). Analysis of postural behavior. *Psychoanalytic Quarterly, 16,* 195–213.

Deutsch, M. (1973). Social class and child development. In B. M. Caldwell & H. N. Ricciuti (Eds.), *Review of child development research* (pp. 233–282). Chicago: University of Chicago Press.

Developmental Associates and Research Triangle Institute. (1984). *LEP students: Characteristics and school services.* The descriptive phase report of the National Longitudinal Evaluation of the Effectiveness of Services for Language—minority/limited English proficient students. Washington, DC: U.S. Department of Education.

DeWied, D. (1984). Neurohypophyseal hormone influences on learning and memory processes. In G. Lynch, J. L. McGaugh, & N. M. Weinberger (Eds.), *Neurobiology of learning and memory* (pp. 289–312). New York: Guilford Press.

Dickinson, L., Lee, J., & Ringdehl, I. L. (1979). Impaired growth in hyperkinetic children receiving pemoline. *Journal of Pediatrics, 94,* 538–541.

DiLanni, M., Wilsher, C. R., Blank, M. S., Conners, C. K., Chase, C. H., Funkenstein, H. H., Helfgott, E., Holmes, J. M., Lougea, L., Maletta, G. J., Milewski, J., Pizzolo, F. J., Rudel,

H. G., & Tallal, P. (1985). Effects of piracetam in children with dyslexia. *Journal of Clinical Psychopharmacology, 5,* 272–278.

Dimond, D. J., & Brouwers, F. (1976). Improvement in human memory through use of drugs. *Psychopharmacology, 49,* 307–309.

Disability Rights Advocates. (2001). *Do no harm: A report by disability rights advocates.* Oakland, CA: Author.

Doehring, D. G. (1985). Reading disability subtypes. In B. F. Rourke (Ed.), *Neuropsychology of learning disabilities* (pp. 133–146). New York: Guilford Press.

Doehring, D. G., Hoshko, I. M., & Bryans, B. N. (1979). Statistical classification of children with reading problems. *Journal of Clinical Neuropsychology, 1,* 5–16.

Dorman, C., & Katzir, B. (1994). *Cognitive effects of early brain injury.* Baltimore: Johns Hopkins University Press.

Douglas, V. I. (1983). Attentional and cognitive problems. In M. Rutter (Ed.), *Developmental neuropsychiatry* (pp. 280–329). New York: Guilford Press.

Douglas, V. I., & Parry, P. (1983). Effects of reward on delayed reacting time task performance of hyperactive children. *Journal of Abnormal Child Psychology, 11,* 313–326.

Drachman, D. A., & Leavitt, J. (1974). Human memory and the cholinergic system: A relationship to aging? *Archives of Neurology, 30,* 113–121.

Drake, W. (1968). Clinical and pathological findings in a child with a developmental learning disability. *Journal of Learning Disabilities, 1,* 468–475.

Dreifus, F. E., & Sachellares, J. (1979). Treating epilepsy in children. *Current Prescribing,* 63–77.

Drtilková, I., Balaötiková, B., Lemanová, H., & Zák, J. (1994). Therapeutical effects of clonidine and clonazepam in children with tic syndrome. *Homeostasis in Health Disease, 35,* 296.

Duane, D. (Ed.). (1999). *Reading and attention disorders: Neurobiological correlates.* Baltimore: York Press.

Duane, D., & Gray, D. (Eds.). (1991). *The reading brain: The biological basis of dyslexia.* Parkton, MD: York Press.

Duara, R., Gross-Glenn, K., Barker, W., Loewenstein, D., Chang, J. Y., Apicella, A., Yoshii, F., Pascal, S., & Lubs, H. A. (1989). PET studies during reading in dyslexic and controls. *Neurology, 39*(Suppl. 1), 165.

Duara, R., Kushch, A., Gross-Glenn, K., Barker, W. W., Jallad, B., Pascal, S., Loewenstein, D. A., Sheldon, J., Rabin, M., Levin, B., & Lubs, H. A. (1991). Neuroanatomic differences between dyslexic and normal readers on magnetic resonance imaging scans. *Archives of Neurology, 48,* 410–416.

Dudai, Y. (1985). Genes, enzymes and learning in drosophila. *Trends in Neurosciences, 8,* 18–21.

Dudai, Y. (1988). Neurogenic dissection of learning and short term memory in drosophila. *Annual Review of Neuroscience, 11,* 537–563.

Dudley-Marling, C., & Searle, D. (1988). Enriching language learning environments for students with learning disabilities. *Journal of Learning Disabilities, 21,* 140–143.

Duffy, F. H., Denckla, M. B., Bartels, P. H., & Sandini, G. (1980). Dyslexia: Regional differences in brain electrical activity by topographic mapping. *Annals of Neurology, 7,* 412–420.

Duffy, F. H., Hughes, S. R., Miranda, F., Bernard, P., & Cook, P. (1994). Status of quantitative EEG in clinical practice. *Clinical Electroencephalography, 25,* vi–xxii.

Duffy, F. H., & McAnulty, G. (1990). Neurophysiological heterogeneity and the definition of dyslexia: Preliminary evidence for plasticity. *Neuropsychologia, 28,* 555–571.

Duffy, G. G., & Roehler, L. R. (1989). *Improving classroom reading instruction.* New York: Random House.

Duncan, G. J., Brooks-Gunn, J., & Klebanov, P. K. (1994). Economic deprivation and early childhood development. *Child Development, 65,* 296–318.

Dunn, A. J. (1980). Neurochemistry of learning and memory: An evaluation of recent data. *Annual Review of Psychology, 31,* 343–390.

Dunn, L., & Dunn, L. (1981). *Peabody Picture Vocabulary Test-Revised.* Circle Pines, MN: American Guidance Service.

DuPaul, G. J., & Eckert, T. L. (1998). Academic intervention for students with attention-deficit hyperactivity disorder: A review of the literature. *Reading and Writing Quarterly, 14,* 59–82.

DuPaul, G. J., Ervin, R. A., Hook, C. L., & McGoey, K. E. (1998). Peer tutoring for children with attention deficit hyperactivity disorder: Effects on classroom behavior and academic performance. *Journal of Applied Behavior Analysis, 31,* 579–592.

Dursun, S. M., Burke, J. G., & Reveley, M. A. (1995). Buspirone treatment of Tourette's syndrome [Letter]. *Lancet, 2,* 926–927.

Dursun, S. M., Farrar, G., Handley, S. L., Rickards, H., Betts, T., & Corbett, J. A. (1994). Elevated plasma kynurenine in Tourette's syndrome. *Molecular and Chemical Neuropathology, 21,* 55–60.

Dursun, S. M., Hewitt, S., King, A. L., & Reveley, M. A. (1996). Treatment of blepharospasm with nicotine nasal spray. *Lancet, 348,* 60.

Dursun, S. M., Reveley, M. A., Bird, R., & Stirton, F. (1994). Long lasting improvement of Tourette's syndrome with transdermal nicotine [Letter]. *Lancet, 344,* 1577.

Dyal, J. A. (1971). Transfer of behavioral bias: Reality and specificity. In E. J. Fjerdingstad (Ed.), *Chemical transfer of learned information* (pp. 219–263). Amsterdam: North-Holland.

Dykens, E., Leckman, J. F., Riddle, M. A., Hardin, M. T., Schwartz, S., & Cohen, D. (1990). Intellectual, academic, and adaptive functioning of Tourette's syndrome children with and without attention deficit disorder. *Journal of Abnormal Child Psychology, 18,* 607–615.

Dykman, R. A., & Ackerman, P. T. (1991). Attention deficit disorder and specific reading disability: Separate but often overlapping disorders. *Journal of Learning Disabilities, 24,* 96–103.

Dykstra, R. (1968). Summary of the second grade phase of the cooperative research program in primary reading instruction. *Reading Research Quarterly, 2,* 49–70.

Eapen, V., Pauls, D. L., & Robertson, M. M. (1993). Evidence for autosomal dominant transmission Tourette's syndrome-United Kingdom cohort study. *British Journal of Psychiatry, 162,* 593–596.

Easton, C., & Bauer, L. O. (1996). Neuropsychological correlates of urine toxicology results. *Progress in Neuropsychopharmacology Biological Psychiatry, 20,* 969–982.

Edelbrook, D., & Costello, A. J. (1984). *A review of structured psychiatric interviews for children.* Center for studies of child and adolescent psychopathology, Clinical Research Branch, (MIMEO).

Eden, G. F. (1995a). Temporal and spatial processing in reading disabled and normal children. *Cortex, 31,* 451–468.

Eden, G. F. (1995b). Verbal and visual problems in reading disability. *Journal of Learning Disabilities, 28,* 272–290.

Eden, G. F., Stein, J. F., Wood, H. M., & Wood, F. B. (1996). Differences in visuospatial judgement in reading-disabled and normal children. *Perceptual and Motor Skills, 82,* 155–177.

Educational Programs that Work. (1995). *A collection of proven exemplary educational programs and practices: Catalog of the National Diffusion Network.* Longmount, CO: Sopris West.

Eidelberg, D., & Galaburda, A. M. (1982). Symmetry and asymmetry in the human thalamus: Cytoarchitectonic analysis in normal persons. *Archives of Neurology, 39,* 325–332.

Eidelberg, D., & Galaburda, A. M. (1984). Inferior parietal lobule: Divergent architectonic asymmetries in the human brain. *Archives of Neurology, 41,* 843–852.

Eisenberg, L. (1966). Reading retardation: I. Psychiatric and sociological aspects. *Pediatrics, 37,* 352–365.

Eisenberg, L. (1978). Definitions of dyslexia: Their consequences for research and policy. In A. Benton & D. Pearl (Eds.), *Dyslexia: An appraisal of current knowledge* (pp. 29–42). New York: Oxford University Press.

Eissler, R. S., Freud, A., Kris, M., & Solnit, A. J. (Eds.). (1977). Psychological assessment: The diagnostic profile. *An anthology of the psychoanalytic study of the child.* New Haven, CT: Yale University Press.

Elbaum, B., Vaughn, S., Hughes, M. T., & Moody, S. W. (1999). Grouping practices and reading outcomes for students with disabilities. *Exceptional Children, 65,* 399–415.

Elia, J., Ambrosini, P. J., & Rapoport, J. L. (1999). Treatment of attention-deficit-hyperactivity disorder. *New England Journal of Medicine, 340,* 780–789.

Elia, J., Borcherding, B. G., Rapoport, J. L., & Keysor, C. S. (1991). Methylphenidate and dextroamphetamine treatments of hyperactivity: Are there true nonresponders? *Psychiatry Research, 36,* 141–155.

Eling, P. (1981). On the theory and measurement of laterality. *Neuropsychologia, 19,* 767–774.

Elkins, R., Rapoport, J., Zahn, T., Buchsbaum, M., Weingartner, H., Kopin, I., Langer, D., & Johnson, C. (1981). Acute effects of caffeine in normal and prepubertal boys. *American Journal of Psychiatry, 52,* 447–457.

Elliot, F. (1977). Propranolol for the control of the belligerent behavior following acute brain damage. *Annals of Neurology, 1,* 489–491.

Emilien, G., Beyreuther, K., Masters, C. L., & Maloteaux, J. (2000). Prospects for pharmacological intervention in Alzheimer disease. *Archives of Neurology, 57,* 454–459.

Emmett, M., Jeffrey, H., Chandler, D., & Dugdale, A. (1980). Sequelae of hemophilus influenzae meningitis. *Australian Pediatric Journal, 16,* 90–93.

Enfield, M. L. (1988). The quest for literacy. *Annals of Dyslexia, 38,* 8–21.

Epstein, M. A., Shaywitz, S. E., Shaywitz, B. A., & Woolston, J. L. (1991). The boundaries of attention deficit disorder. *Journal of Learning Disabilities, 24,* 78–86.

Erenberg, G., Cruse, R. P., & Rothner, A. D. (1985). Gilles de la Tourette's syndrome: Effects of stimulant drugs. *Neurology, 35,* 1346–1348.

Erenberg, G., Cruse, R. P., & Rothner, A. D. (1986). Tourette's syndrome. *Cleveland Clinic Quarterly, 53,* 127–131.

Ernst, M. (1996). Neuroimaging. In G. R. Lyon & J. M. Rumsey (Eds.), *Neuroimaging in attention-deficit/hyperactivity disorder* (pp. 95–117). Baltimore: Brookes.

Ernst, M., Gonzalez, N. M., & Campbell, M. (1993). Acute dystonic reaction with low-dose pimozide. *Journal of the American Academy of Child and Adolescent Psychiatry, 32,* 640–642.

Etheredge, S. (2000). Word problems: A structure-plus-writing approach. *Perspectives, 26,* 22–25.

Extein, I., & Dackis, C. A. (1987). Brain mechanisms in cocaine dependency. In A. M. Washton & M. S. Gold (Eds.), *Cocaine* (pp. 73–84). New York: Guilford Press.

Fagnou, D. D., & Tuchek, J. M. (1995). The biochemistry of learning and memory. *Molecular and Cellular Biochemistry, 149–150,* 279–286.

Falkner, B., Koffler, S., & Lowenthal, D. T. (1984). Effects of anti-hypertensive drugs on cognitive function in adolescents. *Pediatric Pharmacology, 4,* 239–244.

Fanchiang, S., Snyder, C., Zobel-Lachiusa, J., Loeffler, C. B., & Thompson, M. E. (1990). Sensory integrative processing in delinquent-prone adolescents. *American Journal of Occupational Therapy, 44,* 630–638.

Farley, J., & Auerbach, S. (1986). Protein kinase C activation induces conductance change in hermissenda photoreceptors like those seen in associative learning. *Nature, 319,* 220.

Farmer, M., & Klein, R. M. (1995). The evidence for temporal processing deficit linked to dyslexia: A review. *Psychonomic Bulletin and Review, 2,* 460–493.

Farr, R. (1969). *Reading, what can be measured?* [ERIC/CRIER reading review series]. Newark, DE: International Reading Association.

Fayen, M., Goldman, M. B., Moulthop, M. A., & Luchins, D. J. (1988). Differential memory function with dopamine versus anticholinergic treatment of drug induced extrapyramidal symptoms. *American Journal of Psychiatry, 145,* 483–486.

Feagan, L. V., Merriwether, A. M., & Haldane, D. (1991). Goodness of fit in the home: Its relationship to school behavior and achievement in children with learning disabilities. *Journal of Learning Disabilities, 24,* 413–420.

Feeser, H., & Raskin, L. (1987). Effects of neonatal dopamine depletion on spatial ability during ontogony. *Behavioral Neuroscience, 101,* 812–818.

Fein, G., Merrin, E. L., Davenport, L., & Buffreon, L. C. (1987). Memory deficits associated with clonidine. *General Hospital Psychiatry, 9,* 154–155.

Feingold, B. F. (1974). *Why is your child hyperactive?* New York: Random House.

Feldman, H., & Michaels, R. (1988). Academic achievement in children ten to twelve years after hemophilus influenzae meningitis. *Pediatrics, 81,* 339–343.

Felton, R. H., Naylor, C. E., & Wood, F. B. (1990). Neuropsychological profile of adult dyslexics. *Brain and Language, 39,* 485–497.

Felton, R. H., & Wood, F. B. (1989). Cognitive deficits in reading disability and attention deficit disorder. *Journal of Learning Disabilities, 22,* 3–13.

Felton, R. H., Wood, F. B., Brown, I. B., Campbell, S. K., & Harter, M. R. (1987). Separate verbal and naming deficits in attention deficit disorder and reading disability. *Brain and Language, 31,* 171–184.

Fenichel, O. (1945). *The psychoanalytic theory of neurosis.* New York: Norton.

Fenichel, R. R. (1995). Combining methylphenidate and clonidine: The role of post-marketing surveillance. *Journal of Child and Adolescent Psychopharmacology, 5,* 155–156.

Fennel, E. B., Bowers, D., & Satz, P. (1977). Within modal and cross-modal reliabilities of two laterality tests. *Brain and Language, 4,* 63–69.

Ferenzi, S. (1950). *Further contributions to the theory and techniques of psychoanalysis.* London: Hogarth.

Fernald, G. M. (1988). *Remedial techniques in the basic school subjects.* Austin, TX: ProEd. (Original work published 1943)

Feuerstein, R. (1979). *The dynamic assessment of retarded performers.* Baltimore: University Park Press.

Field, T. M., & Sostek, A. M. (Eds.). (1983). *Infants born at risk: Physiological, perceptual and cognitive processes.* New York: Grune & Stratton.

Field, T. M., Sostek, A. M., Goldberg, S., & Shuman, H. (Eds.). (1979). *Infants born at risk: Behavior and development.* New York: Spectrum.

Fiese, B. H., & Sameroff, A. J. (1989). Family context in pediatric psychology: A transactional perspective. *Journal of Pediatric Psychology, 14,* 293–314.

Filipek, P. A. (1996). Developmental neuroimaging: Mapping the development of brain and behavior. In R. W. Thatcher, G. R. Lyon, J. Rumsey, & N. Krasnegor (Eds.), *Structural variations in measures of developmental disorders* (pp. 169–186). New York: Academic Press.

Filipek, P. A. (1999). Neuroimaging in the developmental disorders: The state of the science. *Journal of Child Psychology and Psychiatry, 40,* 113–128.

Filipek, P. A., Pennington, B. F., Simon, J. H., Filley, C. M., & DeFries, J. C. (1999). Structural and functional neuroanatomy in reading disorders. In D. D. Duane (Ed.), *Reading and attention disorders* (pp. 43–59). Baltimore: York Press.

Filipek, P. A., Semrud-Clikeman, M., Steingard, R. J., Renshaw, P. F., Kennedy, D. N., & Biederman, J. (1997). Volumetric MRI analysis comparing subjects having attention-deficit hyperactivity disorder with normal controls. *Neurology, 48,* 589–601.

Finucci, J. M., Gottfredson, L. S., & Childs, B. (1985). A follow-up study of dyslexic boys. *Annals of Dyslexia, 35,* 117–136.

Finucci, J. M., Guthrie, J. T., Childs, A. L., Abbey, J., & Childs, B. (1976). The genetics of specific reading disability. *Annals of Human Genetics, 40,* 1–23.

First, M. B. (Ed.). (2000). *Handbook of psychiatric measures.* Washington, DC: American Psychiatric Press.

Fischer, W., Wictorin, K., Bjorklund, A., Williams, L. R., Varon, S., & Cage, F. H. (1987). Amelioration of cholinergic neuron atrophy and spatial memory impairment in aged rats by nerve growth factor. *Nature, 239,* 65–68.

Fish, B., Campbell, M., & Shapiro, T. (1970). Comparison of trifluperazine and chlorpromazine in pre-school schizophrenic children: The value of less sedative antipsychotic agents. *Current Therapy Research, 11,* 589–595.

Fisher, S. E., Marlow, A. J., Lamb, J., Maestrini, E., Williams, D. F., Richardson A. S., Weeks, D. F., Steen, J. F., & Monaco, A. D. (1999). A quantitative trait issues on chromosome 6p influences different aspects of developmental dyslexia. *American Journal Human Genetics, 64,* 146–156.

Fisk, J. L., Finnell, R., & Rourke, B. P. (1985). Major findings and future directions for learning disability subtype analysis. In B. P. Rourke (Ed.), *Neuropsychology of learning disability* (pp. 331–341). New York: Guilford Press.

Fiske, E. B., & Ladd, H. F. (2000, Fall). A level playing field? *American Educator,* 28–33.

Flapan, D., & Neubauer, P. (1975). *Assessment of early child development.* New York: Aronson.

Flesch, R. (1981). *Why Johnny still can't read.* New York: Harper & Row.

Fletcher, J. M., & Satz, P. (1984). Preschool prediction of reading failure. In M. D. Levine & P. Satz (Eds.), *Middle childhood: Developmental and dysfunction* (pp. 153–182). Baltimore: University Park Press.

Fletcher, J. M., & Satz, P. (1985). Cluster analysis and the search for learning disability subtypes. In B. P. Byron (Ed.), *Neuropsychology of learning disabilities: Essentials of subtype analysis* (pp. 40–64). New York: Guilford Press.

Flexner, J. B., Flexner, L. B., & Stellar, E. (1963). Memory in mice as affected by intracerebral puromycin. *Science, 141,* 57–59.

Flexner, L. B., Flexner, J. B., & Stellar, E. (1965). Memory and cerebral protein synthesis in mice as affected by graded amounts of puromycin. *Experimental Neurology, 13,* 264–272.

Flood, J. F., Bennett, E. L., Orme, A. E., & Rosenzweig, M. R. (1975). Relation of memory formation to controlled amounts of brain protein synthesis. *Physiology and Behavior, 15,* 97–102.

Flowers, D. L., Wood, F. B., & Naylor, C. E. (1991). Regional cerebral blood flow correlates of language processes in reading disability. *Archives of Neurology, 48,* 637–643.

Flynn, J. M., Deering, W., Goldstein, M., & Rahbar, M. H. (1992). Electrophysiological correlates of dyslexic subtypes. *Journal Learning Disability, 25,* 133–141.

Flynn, J. R. (1998). Does IQ matter? [Letter]. *Commentary, 106,* 14–15.

Ford, D. Y., & Harris, J. J., III. (1996). Perceptions and attitudes of Black students toward school, achievement, and other educational variables. *Child Development, 67,* 1141–1152.

Ford, F. R. (1937). *Diseases of the nervous system in infancy, childhood and adolescence.* Springfield, IL: Thomas.

Fowler, M. G. (1997). Update: Transmission of HIV-1 from mother to child. *Current Opinion in Obstetrics and Gynecology, 9,* 343–348.

Fowler, M. G., Simonds, R. J., & Roongpisuthipong, A. (2000). Update on perinatal HIV transmission. *Pediatrics Clinics of North America, 47,* 21–38.

Fox, B., & Routh, D. K. (1975). Analyzing spoken language into spoken words, syllables, and phonemes. *Journal of Psycholinguistic Research, 4,* 331–342.

Francis, D. J., Espy, K. A., Rourke, B. P., & Fletcher, J. M. (1991). Validity of intelligence test scores in the definition of learning disability: A critical analysis. In B. P. Byron (Ed.), *Neuropsychological validation of learning disability subtypes* (pp. 15–44). New York: Guilford Press.

Francis, D. J., Shaywitz, S. E., Stuebing, K. K., Shaywitz, B. A., & Fletcher, J. M. (1994). The measurement of change: Assessing behavior over time and within a developmental context. In G. R. Lyon (Ed.), *Frames of reference for the assessment of learning disabilities* (pp. 29–58). Baltimore: Brookes.

Francone, S. V., & Biederman, J. (1994). Genetics of attention deficit hyperactivity disorders. *Child and Adolescent Psychiatric Clinics of North America, 3,* 285–303.

Franklin, A. J., & Boyd-Franklin, N. (2000). Invisibility syndrome: A clinical model of the effects of racism on African-American males. *American Journal of Orthopsychiatry, 70,* 33–41.

Freeman, R. D. (1997). Attention deficit hyperactivity disorder in the presence of Tourette's syndrome [Review]. *Neurologic Clinics, 15,* 411–420.

Freeman, R. D., Fast, D. K., Burd, L., Kerbeshian, J., Robertson, M. M., & Sandor, P. (2000). Tourette's Syndrome International Database Consortium. An international perspective on Tourette's syndrome: Selected findings from 3500 individuals in 22 countries. *Developmental Medicine and Child Neurology, 42,* 436–447.

Freeman R. J. (1978). The effects on methylphenidate on avoidance learning and risk taking by hyperkinetic children. In M. Rutter (Ed.), *Developmental neuropsychiatry.* New York: Guilford Press.

Freud, A. (1977). Theory of developmental assessment. In R. S. Eissler, A. Freud, M. Kris, & A. J. Solnit (Eds.), *Psychoanalytic assessment: The diagnostic profile anthology of the psychoanalytic study of the child* (pp. 1–56). New Haven, CT: Yale University Press.

Freud, S. (1955). *Beyond the pleasure principle.* In J. Strachey (Ed.), *The standard edition* (Vol. 18, pp. 1–61). London: Hogarth Press. (Original work published 1920)

Freud, S. (1940). *An outline of psycho-analysis.* (J. Strachey, Trans.). New York: Norton.

Frick, P. J. (1991). Patterns of parent and family characteristics associated with oppositional defiant disorder and conduct disorder in boys. *Dissertation Abstracts International, 51*(8B), 4047. (University Microfilms)

Fries, M. D. (1944). Psychosomatic relations between mother and infant. *Psychosomatic Medicine, 6,* 159–162.

Frosch, J. (1983). *The psychotic process.* New York: International Universities Press.

Fulker, D. W., Cherny, S. S., & Cardon, L. R. (1995). Multipoint interval mapping of quantitative trait loci, using sib pairs. *American Journal of Human genetics, 56,* 1224–1233.

Fuller, P. W. (1978). Attention and the EEG alpha rhythm in learning disabled children. *Journal of Learning Disabilities, 11,* 44–53.

Fulton, A. I., & Yates, W. R. (1988). *Family abuse of methylphenidate.* AFP, 38, 143–145.

Gabryel, B., Trzeciak, H. I., Pudelko, A., & Cieslik, P. (1999). Influence of piracetam and oxiracetam on the content of high-energy phosphates and morphometry of astrocytes in vitro. *Polish Journal of Pharmacology, 51,* 485–495.

Gaddes, W. H. (1976). Prevalence estimates and the need for definition of learning disabilities. In R. M. Knights & D. J. Bakker (Eds.), *The neuropsychology of learning disorders* (pp. 3–24). Baltimore: University Park Press.

Gaddes, W. H. (1994). *Learning disabilities and brain function: A neuropsychological approach.* W. H. Gaddes & Dorothy Edgell (Eds.). New York: Springer-Verlag.

Gadian, D. G., Aicardi, J., Watkins, K. E., Porter, D. A., Mishkin, M., & Vargha-Khadem, F. (2000). Developmental amnesia associated with early hypoxic-ischaemic injury. *Brain, 123,* 499–507.

Gadow, K. D., Nolan, E., Sprafkin, J., & Sverd, J. (1995). School observations of children with attention-deficit hyperactivity disorder and comorbid tic disorder: Effects of methylphenidate treatment. *Journal of Developmental and Behavioral Pediatrics, 16,* 167–176.

Gadow, K. D., & Sverd, J. (1990). Stimulants for ADHD in child patients with Tourette's syndrome: The issue of relative risk. *Journal of Developmental and Behavioral Pediatrics, 11,* 269–271.

Galaburda, A. M. (1991). Anatomy of dyslexia. In D. D. Duane & D. B. Gray (Eds.), *The reading brain* (pp. 119–131). Parkton, MD: York Press.

Galaburda, A. M. (1993a). Neuroanatomic basis of developmental dyslexia. *Neurology Clinics of North America, 11,* 161–173.

Galaburda, A. M. (1993b). Neurology of developmental dyslexia. *Current Opinion in Neurology, 3,* 237–242.

Galaburda, A. M. (1993c). The planum temporale [Editorial]. *Archives of Neurology, 50,* 457.

Galaburda, A. M. (1994). Developmental dyslexia and animal studies: At the interface between cognition and neurology. *Cognition, 50,* 133–149.

Galaburda, A. M., LeMay, M., Kemper, T. L., & Geschwind, N. (1978). Right-left asymmetries in the brain: Structural differences between the hemispheres may underlie cerebral dominance. *Science, 199,* 852–856.

Galaburda, A. M., & Livingstone, M. (1993). Evidence for a magnocellular defect in developmental dyslexia. *Annals of the New York Academy of Science, 682,* 70–82.

Galaburda, A. M., Sanides, F., & Geschwind, N. (1978). Human brain: Cytoarchitectonic left-right asymmetries in the temporal speech region. *Archives of Neurology, 35,* 812–817.

Galin, D., Raz, J., Fein, G., Johnstone, J., Herron, J., & Yingling, C. (1986). EEG spectra in dyslexic and normal readers during oral and silent reading. *Electroencephalography Clinical Neurophysiology, 82,* 87–101.

Gallagher, A., Frith, U., & Snowling, M. J. (2000). Precursors of literacy delay among children at genetic risk of dyslexia. *Journal of Child Psychology and Psychiatry and Allied Disciplines, 41,* 202–213.

Gallagher, J. J. (1986). Learning disabilities and special education: A critique. *Journal of Learning Disabilities, 19,* 595–601.

Gallagher, M. (1984). Current perspectives on memory systems and their modulation. In G. Lynch, J. L. McGaugh, & N. M. Weinberger (Eds.), *Neurobiology of learning and memory* (pp. 368–373). New York: Guilford Press.

Galton, F. (1907). *Inquiries into human faculty and its development.* London: Macmillan.

Gardner, H. (1983). *Frames of mind: Theories of multiple intelligence.* New York: Basic Books.

Gastaut, H. (1970). Clinical and electroencephalographic classification of seizures. *Epilepsia, 11,* 102.

Gates, A., & MacGinitie, W. (1968). *Gates-MacGinitie Reading Tests.* New York: Teachers College Press.

Gauger, L. M., Lombardino, L. J., & Leonard, C. M. (1997). Brain morphology in children with specific language impairment. *Journal of Speech, Language, and Hearing Research, 40,* 1272–1284.

Gayan, J., Smith, S. D., Cherny, S. S., Cardon, L. R., Fulker, D. W., Brower, A. M., Olson, R. K., Pennington, B. F., & DeFries, J. C. (1999). Quantitative trait locus for specific language and reading deficits on chromosome 6p. *American Journal of Human Genetics, 64,* 157–164.

Geary, D. C. (2000). Mathematics disorders: An overview for educators. *Perspectives, 26,* 6–9.

Gelernter, J., Kennedy, J., Grandy, D., Zhou, Q-Y., Civelli, O., Pauls, D. L., Pakstis, A., Kurlan, R., Sunahara, R., Niznik, H., Odowd, B., Seeman, P., & Kidd, K. K. (1993). Exclusion of close linkage of Tourette's syndrome to D1-dopamine receptor. *American Journal of Psychiatry, 150,* 449–453.

Gelernter, J., Pakstis, A. J., & Kidd, K. K. (1995). Linkage mapping of serotonin transporter protein gene SLC6A4 on chromosome 17. *Human Genetics, 95,* 677–680.

Gelernter, J., Pakstis, A. J., Pauls, D. L., Kurlan, R., Gancher, S., Civelli, O., Grandy, D., & Kidd, K. K. (1990). Gilles de la Tourette's syndrome not linked to D_2-dopamine receptor. *Archives of General Psychiatry, 47,* 1073–1077.

Gelernter, J., Pauls, D. L., Leckman, J. F., Kidd, K. K., & Kurlan, R. (1994). D_2 dopamine receptor (DRD_2) alleles do not influence severity of Tourette's syndrome in four large kindreds. *Archives of Neurology, 51,* 397–400.

Gelzheiser, L., Solar, R., Shepherd, M. J., & Wozniak, R. H. (1983). Teaching learning disabled children to memorize: A rationale for plans and practice. *Journal of Learning Disabilities, 16,* 421–425.

Gerber, M. (1988). Tolerance and technology of instruction: Implications for special education reform. *Exceptional Children, 54,* 309–314.

Gerstmann, J. (1924). Fingeragnosie: Eine Unschriebene Storung der Orienterung am Eigenen Koeper. *Weiner Klinische Wochenschrift, 37,* 1010–1012.

Gerstmann, J. (1927). Fingeragnosie und isolierte agraphia. *Zeitschrift f.d. ges. Neurol, 108,* 152.

Gerstmann, J. (1930). Zur Symptomatologie der Hirnlasionen in Uberganggebeit der Centaren Parietal und Mitteren Occipitalwindung (das syndrom: Fingeragnosie, Rechts-Links Storung, Agraphia, Akalkulie). *Nervenartzt, 3,* 691–695.

Geschwind, N. (1965). Disconnection syndrome in animals and man [Parts I, II]. *Brain, 88,* 237–294, 585–644.

Geschwind, N., & Galaburda, A. M. (1985). Cerebral lateralization. Biological mechanisms, associations, and pathology: III. A hypothesis and a program for research. *Archives of Neurology, 42,* 634–654.

Geschwind, N., & Levitsky, W. (1968). Human brain: Left-right asymmetries in temporal speech region. *Science, 161,* 168–188.

Gesell, A. L. (1938). The tonic-neck reflex in the human infant: Its morphological and clinical significance. *Journal of Pediatrics, 13,* 455–464.

Gesell, A. L. (1969). *The embryology of behavior.* Ann Arbor: University of Michigan Microfilms. (Original work published 1945)

Gesell, A. L., & Amatruda, C. S. (1947). *Developmental diagnosis.* New York: Hoeber.

Gibb, G. S., et al. (1997). A team-based junior high inclusion program: Parental perceptions and feedback. *Remedial and Special Education, 18,* 243–249.

Gibson, E. J. (1969). *Principles of perceptual learning and development.* New York: Appleton-Century-Crofts.

Gill, M., Daly, G., Heron, S., Hawi, Z., & Fitzgerald, M. (1997). Confirmation of association between attention deficit hyperactivity disorder and a dopamine transporter polymorphism. *Molecular Psychiatry, 2,* 311–313.

Gillette, D. W., & Tannery, L. P. (1994). Beta blocker inhibits tricyclic metabolism. *Journal of the American Academy of Child and Adolescent Psychiatry, 33,* 223–224.

Gillingham, A., & Stillman, B. W. (1968). *Remedial training for children with specific disability in reading, spelling and penmanship.* Cambridge, MA: Educators Publishing Service.

Gilmore, J. V. (1968). The factor of attention in underachievement. *Journal of Education, 150,* 41–66.

Gittelman, M., & Joyce, M. (1999). Have family income mobility patterns changed? *Demography, 36,* 299–314.

Gittelman, R., Klein, D. F., & Feingold, B. (1983). Children with reading disorder: II. Effects of methylphenidate in combination with reading remediation. *Journal of Child Psychology and Psychiatry, 24,* 193–212.

Gittelman-Klein, F., & Klein, D. F. (1976). Methylphenidate effects in learning disabilities. *Archives of General Psychiatry, 33,* 655–664.

Giurgea, C. (1978). Pharmacology of nootropic drugs. In P. Deniker, C. Radouco-Thomas, A. Villanueva, D. Baronet-LaCroix, & F. Gersin (Eds.), *Neuro-psychopharmacology* (pp. 67–72). New York: Pergamon Press.

Glasky, A. J., & Simon, L. N. (1966). Magnesium pemoline: Enhancement of brain RNA polymerase. *Science, 151,* 702–703.

Goddard, G. V., Bliss, T. V. P., Robertson, A., & Sutherland, R. S. (1980). Noradrenaline levels affect long-term potentiation in the hippocampus. *Society for Neuroscience Abstracts, 6,* 89.

Goetz, C. G. (1992). Clonidine and clonazepam in Tourette's syndrome [Review]. *Advances in Neurology, 58,* 245–251.

Goetz, C. G., & Klawans, H. L. (1982). Gilles de la Tourette's syndrome. In A. Friedhoff & T. Chase (Eds.), *Advances in neurology* (Vol. 35, pp. 1–16). New York: Raven Press.

Goetz, C. G., Stebbins, G. T., & Thelen, J. A. (1987). Talipexole and adult Gilles de la Tourette's syndrome: Double-blind, placebo-controlled clinical trial. *Movement Disorders, 9,* 315–317.

Goetz, C. G., Tanner, C. M., & Klawans, H. L. (1989). Fluphenazine and multifocal tic disorders. *Archives of Neurology, 41,* 271–272.

Gold, P. E. (1984). Memory modulation: Neurobiological contexts. In G. Lynch, J. L. McGaugh, & N. M. Weinberger (Eds.), *Neurobiology of learning and memory* (pp. 374–384). New York: Guilford Press.

Golden, G. S. (1984). Psychologic and neuropsychologic aspects of Tourette's syndrome. *Neurologic Clinics, 2,* 91–102.

Golden, G. S. (1988). The use of stimulants in the treatment of Tourette's syndrome. In D. J. Cohen, R. D. Bruun, & J. F. Leckman (Eds.), *Tourette's syndrome and tic disorder: Clinical understanding and treatment* (pp. 317–325). New York: Wiley.

Goldman, L. S., Genel, M., Bezman, R. J., & Slanetz, P. J. (1998). Diagnosis and treatment of attention-deficit/hyperactivity disorder in children and adolescents. *Journal of the American Medical Association, 279,* 1100–1107.

Goldman, R., Fristoe, M., & Woodcock, R. W. (1970). *Goldman-Fristoe-Woodcock Test of auditory discrimination.* Circle Pines, MN: American Guidance Service.

Goldstein, A. (1984). Nifedipine treatment of Tourette's syndrome. *Journal of Clinical Psychiatry, 45,* 360.

Goldstein, K. (1938). A further comparison of the Moro reflex and the Startle pattern. *Journal of Psychology, 6,* 33–42.

Goldstein, K. (1954). The brain-injured child. In H. Michael-Smith (Ed.), *Pediatric problems in clinical practice* (pp. 97–120). New York: Grune & Stratton.

Gonce, M., & Barbeau, A. (1977). Seven cases Gilles de la Tourette's syndrome: Partial relief with clonazepam: A pilot study. *Canadian Journal of Neurology of Science, 3,* 279–283.

Goodman, K. S. (1967). Reading: A psycholinguistic guessing game. *Journal of the Reading Specialist, 6,* 126–133.

Goodman, K. S. (1976). Reading: A psycholinguistic guessing game. In H. Singer & R. B. Ruddell (Eds.), *Theoretical models and processes of reading.* Newark, NJ: International Reading Association.

Goodman, R., & Stevenson, J. (1989). A twin study of hyperactivity: II. The aetiological role of genes, family relationships and perinatal adversity. *Journal of Child Psychology Psychiatry, 30,* 691–709.

Gordon, M. N. (1979). The assessment of impulsivity and mediating behaviors in hyperactive and non-hyperactive boys. *Journal of Abnormal Child Psychology, 7,* 217–326.

Gordon, M. N., McClure, F. D., & Post, E. M. (1986). *Interpretive guide to the Gordon Diagnostic System.* DeWitt, NY: Gordon Systems.

Gordon, M. N., & Mettelman, B. B. (1987). *Technical guide to the Gordon Diagnostic System.* Dewitt, NY: Gordon Systems.

Gorenstein, E., & Newman, J. P. (1980). *Disinhibitory psychopathology: A new perspective and a model for research.*

Goyer, P., Davis, G., & Rapoport, J. (1979). Abuse of prescribed stimulant medication by a 13 year old hyperactive boy. *Journal of the American Academy of Child Psychiatry, 18,* 170–175.

Goyette, C., Conners, C., & Petti, J. (1978). Effects of artificial colors on hyperactive children: A double-blind challenge study. *Psychopharmacology Bulletin, 14,* 39–40.

Graven, S. N., Bowen, F. W., Brooten, D., et al. (1992). The high-risk infant environment: I. The role of the neonatal intensive care unit in the outcome of high-risk infants. *Journal of Perinatology, 2,* 164–172.

Gray, D. B., & Kavanaugh, J. F. (1985). *Behavioral measures of dyslexia.* Parkton, MD: York Press.

Gray, S. W., Ramey, B. K., & Klaus, R. A. (1982). *From 3 to 20: The early education project.* Baltimore: University Park Press.

Gray, W. S. (1955). Characteristics of effective oral reading. *Supplementary Educational Monographs, 82,* 5–10.

Green, M., Wong, M., Atkins, D., et al. (1999). *Diagnosis of attention-deficit/hyperactivity disorder* (Tech. Rev. No. 3, AHCPR Publication No. 99–0050). Rockville, MD: Agency for Health Care Policy and Research.

Green, M. Y. (2000, November). Taming the paper tiger. *NEA Today.*

Green, R. L., Hustler, J. J., Loftus, W. C., Tramo, M. S., Thomas, C. E., Silberfarb, A. W., Nordgren, R. E., Nordgren, R. A., & Gazzaniga, M. S. (1999). The caudal infrasylvian surface in dyslexia: Novel magnetic resonance imaging-based findings. *Neurology, 53,* 974–981.

Green, W. H. (1995). The treatment of attention-deficit hyperactivity disorder with nonstimulant medications. *Child and Adolescent Psychiatry Clinical of North America, 4,* 169–195.

Greenacre, P. (1952). *Trauma, growth and personality.* New York: Norton.

Greendyke, R. M., & Kanter, D. R. (1986). Therapeutic effects of pindolol on behavior disturbances associated with organic brain disorder: A double blind study. *Journal of Clinical Psychiatry, 47,* 423–426.

Greendyke, R. M., Schuster, D. B., & Wooten, J. A. (1984). Propranolol on the treatment of
assaultive patients with organic brain disease. *Journal of Clinical Psychopharmacology, 4,* 282–285.

Greenhill, L. (1981). Stimulant-related growth inhibition in children: A review. In M. G.
Hilman (Ed.), *Strategic interventions for hyperactive children* (pp. 39–63). Armonk, NY: M. E. Sharpe.

Greenhill, L., Chambers, W., Rubinstein, B., Helpern, F., & Sacher, E. (1981). Growth hor-
mone, prolactin and growth responses in hyperkinetic males treated with d-amphetamine. *Journal of American Academy of Child Psychiatry, 20,* 71–84.

Greenhill, L., Puig-Antich, J., Novacenko, H., Solomon, M., Angher, C., Florea, J., Goetz, R.,
Fiscina, B., & Sacher, E. (1984). Prolactin, growth hormone, and growth responses in boys with attention deficit disorder. *Journal of American Academy of Child Psychiatry, 23,* 58–67.

Greenhill, L. L. (1992). Pharmacologic treatment of attention deficit hyperactivity disorder.
Psychiatric Clinics of North America, 15, 1–27.

Greenhill, L. L., Abikoff, H. B., Arnold, L. E., Cantwell, D. P., Conners, C. K., Elliott, G.,
Hechman, L., Hinshaw, S. P., Hoza, B., Jensen, P. S., March, J. S., Newcorn, J., Pelham, W. E., Severe, J. B., Swanson, J. M., Vitiello, B., & Wells, K. (1996). Medication treat-ment strategies in the MTA Study: Relevance to clinicians and researchers. *Journal of the American Academy of Child and Adolescent Psychiatry, 35,* 1304–1313.

Greenhill, L. L., & Malcom, J. (2000). Child and adolescent measures for diagnosis and screening. In M. B. First (Ed.), *Handbook of psychiatric measures* (pp. 277–287). Washington, DC: American Psychiatric Press.

Greenspan, S. I. (1981). *The clinical interview of the child.* New York: McGraw-Hill.

Gregg, N. (1992). Expressive writing. In S. R. Hooper, G. W. Hynd, & R. E. Mattison (Eds.),
Developmental disorders: Diagnostic criteria and clinical assessment (pp. 127–172). Hills-dale, NJ: Erlbaum.

Gregory, A. H., Efron, R., Divenyi, P. L., & Yund, E. W. (1983). Central auditory processing:
I. Ear dominance—a perceptual or an attentional asymmetry? *Brain and Language, 19,* 225–236.

Gresham, F. M., MacMillan, D. L., & Bocian, K. M. (1997). Teachers as "Test": Differential
validity of teachers judgments in identifying students at risk for learning difficulties. *School Psychology Review, 26,* 47–60.

Grigorenko, E. L., Wood, F. B., Meyer, M. S., Hart, L. A., Speed, W. C., Shuster, A., & Pauls,
D. L. (1997). Susceptibility loci for distinct components of developmental dyslexia on chromosomes 6. *American Journal of Human Genetics, 60,* 27–39.

Groh, C. (1978). The psychotropic effect of tegretol in non-epileptic children with particular
reference to the drug's indication. In W. Birxmayer (Ed.), *Epileptic seizures, behavior, pain.* Bern, Switzerland: Hnas & Huber.

Gross, K., Rothenberg, S., Schottenfeld, S., & Drake, C. (1978). Duration threshold for letter
identification in left and right visual fields for normal and reading disabled children. *Neu-ropsychologia, 16,* 709–716.

Gross-Glenn, K., Duara, R., Barker, W., Loewenstein, D., Chang, J. Y., Yoshii, F., Apicella, A.,
Pascal, S., Boothe, T., Sevush, S., Jallad, B., Novoa, L., & Lubs, H. (in press). Positron emission tomographic studies during serial word-reading by normal and dyslexic adults. *Journal of Clinical Experimental Neuropsychology.*

Group for the Advancement of Psychiatry. (1956–1959). *Reports and symposium* (Vol. 3). New York: Author.

Grubman, S., Gross, E., Lerner-Weiss, N., et al. (1995). Older children and adolescents living with vertically acquired human immunodeficiency virus infection. *Pediatrics, 95,* 657–663.

Gualtieri, T. (1984). The persistence of stimulant effects in chronically treated children: Further evidence of an inverse relationship between drug effects and placebo levels of response. *Psychopharmacology, 83,* 44–47.

Gualtieri, T., Kanoy, R., Hawk, B., Koriath, U., Schroeder, S., Youngblood, W., Breese, G., & Pranga, A. (1981). Growth hormone and prolactin secretion in adults and hyperactive children: Relation to methylphenidate serum level. *Psychoendocrinology, 6,* 331–339.

Gualtieri, T., Wafgin, W., Kanoy, R., Patrick, K., Shen, O., Youngblood, W., Mueller, R., & Breese, G. (1982). Clinical studies of methylphenidate serum levels in children and adults. *Journal of the American Academy of Child Psychiatry, 21,* 19–26.

Guildford, J. P. (1967). *The nature of human intelligence.* New York: McGraw-Hill.

Haggerty, J., & Abramson, M. (1987). Impediments implementing national policy change for mildly handicapped students. *Exceptional Children, 53,* 315–323.

Hagin, R. A. (1954). *Reading retardation and the language arts: A comparative study of retarded and non-retarded readers in a group of behavior problems.* Unpublished doctoral dissertation, New York University.

Hagin, R. A. (1983). Write right or left: A practical approach to handwriting. *Journal of Learning Disabilities, 16,* 266–271.

Hagin, R. A., Beecher, R., Pagano, G., & Kreeger, H. (1982). Effects of Tourette's syndrome on learning. *Advances in Neurology, 35,* 323–328.

Hagin, R. A., Beecher, R., & Silver, A. A. (1982). Definition of learning disabilities: A clinical approach. In J. P. Das, R. F. Mulcahy, & A. E. Wall (Eds.), *Theory and research in learning disabilities* (pp. 45–57). New York: Plenum Press.

Hagin, R. A., & Kugler, J. (1988). School problems associated with Tourette's syndrome. In D. J. Cohen, R. D. Bruun, & J. F. Leckman (Eds.), *Tourette's syndrome and tic disorders: Clinical understanding and treatment* (pp. 223–236). New York: Wiley.

Hagin, R. A., Miranda, J. L., Beecher, R., & Kreeger, H. (1981). Busqueda: A Spanish adaptation of search. New York: School Consultation Center, Fordham University–Lincoln Center.

Hagin, R. A., Silver, A. A., & Kreeger, H. (1976). *TEACH–Learning tasks for the prevention of learning disabilities.* New York: Walker Educational Books.

Hagin, R. A., Thackeray, S., & Silver, A. A. (1991). *A program for the prevention of learning disabilities.* Paper presented at the annual meeting of the American Educational Research Association, Chicago.

Hakuta, K., & Diaz, R. (1984). The relationship between bilingualism and cognitive ability: A critical discussion and some new longitudinal data. In K. E. Nelson (Ed.), *Children's language* (Vol. 5). Hillsdale, NJ: Erlbaum.

Hall, E. T. (1976). Small group instruction for language skills improvement. *Bulletin of the Orton Society, 26,* 63–78.

Hall, G. S. (1948). The contents of children's minds. In W. Dennis (Ed.), *Readings in the history of psychology* (pp. 258–259). New York: Appleton-Century-Crofts.

Hall, M. B. (1947). *Psychiatric examination of the school child.* London: Arnold.

Hallahan, D. L., Keller, C. E., McKinney, J. D., Lloyd, J. W., & Bryan, T. (1988). Examining the research base of the regular education initiative: Efficacy studies and the adaptive learning model. *Journal of Learning Disabilities, 21,* 29–35.

Hallgren, B. (1950). Specific dyslexia ("congenital word blindness"): A clinical and genetic study. *Acta Psychiatrica et Neuroligica Scandinavia* (Suppl. 65).

Halperin, J. M. (1991). The clinical assessment of attention. *International Journal of Neuroscience, 58,* 171–182.

Halperin, J. M., Gittelman, R., Katz, S., & Struve, F. A. (1986). Relationship between stimulant effect, electroencephalogram, and clinical neurological findings in hyperactive children. *Journal of the American Academy of Child Psychiatry, 25,* 820–825.

Halperin, J. M., Newcorn, J. H., Koda, V. H., Pick, L., McKay, K. E., & Knott, P. (1997). Noradrenergic mechanisms in ADHD children with and without reading disabilities: A replication and extension. *Journal of the American Academy of Child and Adolescent Psychiatry, 36,* 1688–1697.

Hammill, D. D., & Larsen, S. C. (1974). Relationship of selected auditory perceptual skills and reading ability. *Journal of Learning Disability, 7,* 429–435.

Hammill, D. D., Leigh, J. E., McNutt, G., & Larsen, S. C. (1987). A new definition of learning disabilities. *Journal of Learning Disabilities, 20,* 109–112.

Hanna, P., Hodges, R., & Hanna, J. (1971). *Spelling structure and strategies.* Boston: Houghton Mifflin.

Harcherlik, D. F., Carronara, C. M., Shaywitz, S. E., Shaywitz, B. A., & Cohen, D. J. (1982). Attentional and perceptual disturbances in children with Tourette's syndrome, attention deficit and epilepsy. *Schizophrenia Bulletin, 8,* 356–359.

Hardman, J. E., & Limbird, L. E. (Eds.). (1996). *Goodman and Gilman's the pharmacological basis of therapeutics* (9th ed.). New York: McGraw-Hill.

Hardman, M., McDonnell, J., & McDonnell, A. (1989). *The inclusive neighborhood schools: Educating students with severe disabilities from the least restrictive environment.* Unpublished manuscript, University of Utah, School and Community project, Salt Lake City.

Harley, J., Matthews, C., & Eichman, P. (1978). Hyperkinesis and food additives: Testing the Feingold hypothesis. *Pediatrics, 61,* 818–828.

Harmony, T., Marosi, E., Becker, J., Rodriguez, M., Reyes, A., Fernandez, T., Silva, J., & Beral, J. (1995). Longitudinal quantitative EEG study of children with different performances on a reading-writing test. *Electroencephalography Clinical Neurophysiology, 95,* 426–433.

Harris, D. A., & Silver, A. A. (1995). Tourette's syndrome and learning disorders. *Learning disabilities: A multidisciplinary Journal, 6,* 1–7.

Harris, E. L., Schuerholz, L. J., Singer, H. S., Reader, M. J., Brown, J. E., Cox, C., Mohr, J., Chase, G. A., & Denckla, M. B. (1995). Executive function in children with Tourette's syndrome and/or attention deficit hyperactivity disorder. *Journal of the International Neuropsychological Society, 1,* 511–516.

Harris, J. C. (1996a). Behavioral toxicity: Cocaine. In J. C. Harris (Ed.), *Developmental neuropsychiatry: Assessment, diagnosis and treatment of developmental disorders* (Vol. 2, pp. 365–374). New York: Oxford University Press.

Harris, J. C. (1996b). *Developmental neuropsychiatry: Assessment, diagnosis and treatment of developmental disorders* (Vol. 2). New York: Oxford University Press.

Harris, J. C. (1996c). Fetal alcohol syndrome. In J. C. Harris (Ed.), *Developmental neuropsychiatry: Assessment, diagnosis and treatment of developmental disorders* (Vol. 2, pp. 361–365). New York: Oxford University Press.

Harris, L. J. (1991). The human infant in studies of lateralization of function: A historical perspective. In H. E. Fitzgerald & B. M. Lester (Eds.), *Theory and research in behavioral pediatrics* (Vol. 5, pp. 129–154). New York: Plenum Press.

Hartmann, H. (1964). *Essays on ego psychology: Selected problems in psychoanalytic theory.* New York: International Universities Press.

Hartsfield, K. (1992). *Kid's clinic: Update.* University of South Florida, Tampa.

Haspel, T. (1995). Beta-blockers and the treatment of aggression. *Harvard Review of Psychiatry, 2,* 274–281.

Hasstedt, S. J., Leppert, M., Filloux, F., van de Wetering, B. J. M., & McMahon, W. M. (1995). Intermediate inheritance of Tourette's syndrome, assuming assortative mating. *American Journal of Human Genetics, 57,* 682–689.

Hauser, W. A., & Hesdorffer, D. C. (1990). *Epilepsy: Frequency, courses and consequences.* New York: Demos.

Hawkins, R. D., & Kandel, E. (1984). Steps toward a cell-biological alphabet for elementary forms of learning. In G. Lynch, J. L., McGaugh, & N. Weinberger (Eds.), *Neurobiology of learning and memory* (pp. 385–404). New York: Guilford Press.

Hayes, A., & Silver, A. A. (1970). *Report of the interdisciplinary committee on reading problems.* New York: Ford Foundation.

Hayes, J. R., & Flower, L. S. (1980). Identifying the organization of writing processes. In L. W. Gregg & E. R. Steinbert (Eds.), *Cognitive processes in writing* (pp. 3–30). Hillsdale, NJ: Erlbaum.

Head, H. (1963). *Aphasia and kindred disorders of speech* (Vols. 1, 2). London: Cambridge University Press. (Original work published 1926)

Hebb, D. O. (1949). *The organization of behavior.* New York: Wiley.

Hebebrand, J., Klug, B., Fimmers, R., Seuchter, S. A., Wettke-Schäfer, R., Deget, F., Camps, A., Lisch, S., Hebebrand, K., von Gontard, A., Lehmkuhl, G., Poutska, F., Schmidt, M., Baur, M. P., & Remschmidt, H. (1997). Rates of tic disorders and obsessive compulsive symptomatology in families of children and adolescents with Gilles de la Tourette's syndrome. *Journal of Psychiatric Research, 31,* 519–530.

Hecaen, H., De Agostini, M., & Monzon-Montes, A. (1981). Cerebral organization in left handers. *Brain and Language, 12,* 261–284.

Hecaen, H., de Ajuriaguerra, J., & Angelergues, R. (1963). Apraxia and its various aspects. In L. Halpern (Ed.), *Problems in dynamic neurology* (pp. 217–230). Jerusalem, Israel: Hebrew University Hadassah Medical School, Department of Nervous Diseases of the Rothschild Hadassah Hospital.

Hechelman, R. (1969). A neurological impress method of reading instruction. *Academic Therapy, 4,* 277–282.

Hecker, L., & Gunter-Mohr, R. (1999). Decoding pilot program. In M. S. Meyer & R. H. Felton (Eds.), Repeated reading to enhance fluency: Old approaches and new directions. *Annals of Dyslexia, 49,* 283–329.

Hedges, L. V., & Olkin, I. (1985). *Statistical methods for meta-analysis.* San Diego, CA: Academic Press.

Helfgott, E., Rudel, R. G., Koplewics, H., & Krieger, J. (1987). Effects of piracetam on reading test performances of dyslexic children. In D. Bakker, C. Wilsher, H. Debruyner, & N. Bertin (Eds.), *Developmental dyslexia and learning disorders* (pp. 110–122). Basel, Switzerland: Karger.

Hellige, J. B. (1993). In S. M. Kosslyn (Ed.), *Hemispheric asymmetry: What's right and what's left.* Cambridge, MA: Harvard University Press.

Hermann, K. (1959). *Reading disability: A medical study of word-blindness and related handicaps.* Copenhagen, Denmark: Munksgaard.

Herrnstein, R. J. (1994). *The Bell Curve: Intelligence and class structure in American life.* New York: Free Press.

Hersh, C. A., Stone, B. J., & Ford, L. (1996). Learning disabilities and learned helplessness: A heuristic approach. *International Journal of Neuroscience, 84,* 103–113.

Hersh, S. (1992). *Neuropsychological testing for children and adults with HIV testing.* Paper presented at the annual meeting of the American Academy of Child and Adolescent Psychiatry, Washington, DC.

Hess, R. D. (1970). Social class and ethnic influences on socialization. In P. Muccen (Ed.), *Carmichael's manual of child psychology* (3rd ed., pp. 457–558). New York: Wiley.

Hess, R. D., & Shipman, V. C. (1968). Maternal attitudes toward the school and the role of the pupil: Some social class comparisons. In A. H. Passow (Ed.), *Developing programs for the educationally disadvantaged.* New York: Teachers College Press.

Hertzig, M. E. (1982). Stability and change in non-focal and neurological signs. *Journal of American Academy of Child Psychiatry, 21,* 231–236.

Heubert, J. P., & Hauser, R. M. (Eds.). (1991). *High stakes testing for tracking, promotion, and graduation.* Washington, DC: National Academy Press.

Heumann, J., & Warlick, K. R. (2000). *Memorandum: Questions and answers about provision of the individuals with disabilities education act amendment of 1997 related to students with disabilities and state and district-wide assessments.* Washington, DC: Office of Special Education and Rehabilitation Services.

Hinshaw, S. P. (1991). Stimulant medication and the treatment of aggression in children with attentional deficits. *Journal of Clinical Child Psychology, 20,* 301–312.

Hinshaw, S. P. (1992). Externalizing behavior problems and academic underachievement in childhood an adolescence: Causal relationships and underlying mechanisms. *Psychology Bulletin, 111,* 127–155.

Hinshelwood, J. (1917). *Congenital word-blindness.* London: Lewis.

Hiscock, M., & Kinsbourne, M. (1982). Laterality and dyslexia: A critical view. *Annals of Dyslexia, 32,* 177–228.

Hoare, P., & Kerle, S. (1991). Psychosocial adjustment of children with chronic epilepsy and their families. *Developmental Medicine and Child Neurology, 33,* 201–215.

Hofman, K. J., Harris, E. L., Bryan, R. N., & Denckla, M. B. (1994). Neurofibromatosis type 1: The cognitive phenotype. *Journal of Pediatrics, 124,* S1–S8.

Holman, B. L., & Devous, M. D., Sr. (1992). Functional brain SPECT: The emergence of a powerful clinical method. *Journal of Nuclear Medicine, 33,* 1888–1904.

Honmou, O., Kocsis, J. D., & Richardson, G. B. (1995). *Gabapentin potentiates the conductance increase induced by nipecotic acid in CA 1 pyramidal neurons in vitro.*

Hooper, S. R., Montgomery, J., Swartz, C., Reed, M. S., Sandler, A. D., Levine, M. D., Watson, T. E., & Wasileski, T. (1994). In G. R. Lyon (Ed.), *Frames of reference for the assessment of learning disabilities* (pp. 375–417). Baltimore: Brookes.

Horn, W. F., Wagner, A. E., & Ialongo, N. (1989). Sex differences in school-aged children with pervasive attention deficit hyperactivity disorder. *Journal of Abnormal Child Psychology, 17,* 109–124.

Horsch, P. L. (1992). School change: A partnership approach. *Early Education Development, 3,* 128–138.

Hospital Infection Control Practices Advisory Committee. (1996). Guidelines for isolation precautions in hospitals. *Infect Control Hospital Epidemiology, 17,* 53–80.

Hoy, E., Weiss, G., Minde, K., & Cohn, N. (1978). The hyperactive child at adolescence: Cognitive, emotional and social functioning, *Journal of Abnormal Child Psychology, 67,* 311–324.

Hubel, J. R., & Wiesel, T. N. (1979). Brain mechanisms of vision. *Scientific American, 241,* 150–162.

Hubert, J. P., & Hauser, R. M. (Eds.). (1999). *High stakes: Testing for tracking promotion, and graduation.* Washington, DC: National Academy Press.

Hubert, K. D. (1998). The impact of inclusive education on regular education student achievement. *Dissertation Abstracts International, 59,* 1904.

Huefner, D. (1988). The consulting teacher model: Risks and opportunities. *Exceptional Children, 54,* 403–414.

Hughes, J. R. (1985). Evaluation of electrophysiological studies on dyslexia. In D. B. Gray & J. F. Kavenaugh (Eds.), *Behavioral measures of dyslexia* (pp. 71–86). Parkton, MD: York Press.

Hulme, C., Thomson, N., Muir, C., & Lawrence, A. (1984). Speech rate and the development of short term memory span. *Journal of Experimental Child Psychology, 38,* 241–253.

Human Immunodeficiency Virus/Acquired Immunodeficiency Syndrome Education in Schools (RE9741). (1998). *American Academy of Pediatrics,* 933–935.

Humphreys, P., Kaufmann, W. E., & Galaburda, A. M. (1990). Developmental dyslexia in women: Neuropathological findings in three patients. *Annals of Neurology, 28,* 727–738.

Hunt, J. M. (1961). *Intelligence and experience.* New York: Ronald Press.

Hunt, R. D., Arnsten, A. F. T., & Asbell, M. D. (1995). An open trial of guanfacine in the treatment of attention-deficit hyperactivity disorder. *Journal of the American Child and Adolescent Psychiatry, 34,* 50–54.

Hunt, R. D., Capper, L., & O'Connell, P. (1990). Clonidine in child and adolescent psychiatry. *Journal of Child and Adolescent Psychopharmacology, 1,* 87–102.

Husby, G., van de Rijn, I., Zabriskie, J. B., Abdin, Z. H., & Williams, R. C., Jr. (1976). Antibodies reacting with cytoplasm of subthalamic and caudate nuclei neurons in chorea and acute rheumatic fever. *Journal of Experimental Medicine, 144,* 1094–1110.

Hutchings, D. E. (Ed.). (1989). Prenatal abuse of licit drugs. *Annals of the New York Academy of Sciences, 562.*

Hutt, M. L. (1945). *A tentative guide for the administration and interpretation of the Bender-Gestalt Test.* U.S. Army Adjutant General's School (Restricted).

Hyden, H., & Egyhazi, E. (1963). Glial RNA changes during a learning experiment in rats. *Proceedings of the National Academy of Sciences, USA, 49,* 618–624.

Hyman, S. E., & Nestler, E. J. (1993). *The molecular foundations of psychiatry.* London: American Psychiatric Press.

Hynd, G. W. (1992). Neurological aspects of dyslexia: Comment on the balance model. *Journal of Learning Disabilities, 25,* 110–112, 123.

Hynd, G. W., Hall, J., Novey, E. S., Eliopulos, D., Black, K., Gonzalez, J. J., Edmonds, J. E., Riccio, C., & Cohen, M. (1995). Dyslexia and corpus callosum morphology. *Archives of Neurology, 52,* 32–38.

Hynd, G. W., Hern, K. L., & Novey, E. S. (1993). Attention deficit-hyperactivity disorder and asymmetry of the caudate nucleus. *Journal of Child Neurology, 8,* 339–347.

Hynd, G. W., Hooper, S. R., & Takasashi, T. (1998). Dyslexia and language based learning disabilities. In E. C. Coffey & R. A. Brumback (Eds.), *Textbook of pediatric neuropsychiatry.* Washington, DC: American Psychiatric Press.

Hynd, G. W., Semrud-Clikeman, M., Lorys, A. R., Novey, E. S., & Eliopulos, D. (1990). Brain morphology in developmental dyslexia and attention deficit disorder/hyperactivity. *Archives of Neurology, 47,* 919–926.

Idol, L., Nevin, A., & Paolucci-Whitcomb, P. (1995). The collaborative consultation model. *Journal of Educational and Psycho-educational Consultation, 6,* 347–361.

Ilg, F. L., & Ames, L. B. (1965). *School readiness: Behavior tests used at the Gesell Institute.* New York: Harper & Row.

Immergluck, L. C., Cull, W. L., Schwartz, A., & Elstein, A. S. (2000). Cost-effectiveness of universal compared with voluntary screening for human immunodeficiency virus among pregnant women in Chicago. *Pediatrics, 105,* E54.

Incagnoli, T., & Kane, R. (1982). Neuropsychological functioning in Tourette's syndrome. In A. Friedhoff & T. N. Chase (Eds.), *Advances in neurology* (Vol. 35, pp. 305–309). New York: Raven Press.

Individuals with Disabilities Education Act. (1997). 20 U.S.C. 1402–1407 (Statute).

Ingram, T. T., Mann, A. W., & Blackburn, I. A. (1970). A retrospective study of 82 children with reading disability. *Developmental Medicine and Child Neurology, 12,* 271–281.

Irwin, M., Belendink, K., McCloskay, K., & Freedman, D. X. (1981). Tryptophan metabolism in children with attention deficit disorder. *American Journal of Psychiatry, 138,* 1082–1085.

Isaacson, R. L. (1976). Recovery (?) from early brain damage. In T. Tjossen (Ed.), *Intervention strategies for high risk infants and young children* (pp. 33–62). Baltimore: University Park Press.

Itard, J. M. G. (1825). Memoire sur quelques fonctions involontaires des appareils de la locomotion de la prehension et de la voix. *Archives of Generale Medicine, 8,* 385–497.

Itoh, L., Paolucci-Whitecomb, P., & Nevin, A. (1986). *Classroom consultant: Principles and techniques of collaborative consultation.* Austin, TX: ProEd.

Itoh, T., Magnaldi, S., White, R. M., Denckla, M. B., Hofman, K., Naidu, S., & Bryan, R. N. (1994). Neurofibromatosis type 1: The evolution of deep gray and white matter MR abnormalities. *American Journal of Neuroradiology, 15,* 1513–1519.

Izquierdo, I. (1984). Endogenous state dependency: Memory depends on the relation between the neurohumoral and hormonal states present after training and at the time of testing. In G. Lynch, J. L. McGaugh, & N. M. Weinberger (Eds.), *Neurobiology of learning and memory* (pp. 333–352). New York: Guilford Press.

Izquierdo, I., & Graudenz, M. (1980). Memory facilitation by naloxone is due to release of dopaminergic and β-adrenergic systems from tonic inhibition. *Psychopharmacology, 67,* 265–268.

Jadad, A. R., Boyle, M., Cunningham, C. E., Kim, M., & Schachar, R. (1999). Treatment of attention-deficit/hyperactivity disorder. *Evidence Report: Technology Assessment* (Summary). 1–341.

Jakala, P., Riekkinen, M., Sirvio, J., Koivisto, E., & Riekkinen, P., Jr. (1999). Effects of methylphenicate on complex cognitive processing in attention-deficit hyperactivity disorder. *Journal of Abnormal Psychology, 108,* 90–105.

James, W. (1950). *Principles of psychology* (Vol. 2). New York: Dover. (Original work published 1890)

Jansky, J., & DeHirsch, K. (1972). *Preventing reading failure-prediction, diagnosis, intervention.* New York: Harper & Row.

Japer, H. (1958). Reticular-cortical systems and theories of the integrative action of the brain. In H. F. Harlow & C. N. Woosley (Eds.), *Biological and biochemical basis of behavior* (pp. 37–63). Madison: University Wisconsin Press.

Jastak, J., & Jastak, S. (1940). *Wide range achievement test.* Wilmington, DE: Jastak Associates.

Jenike, M. A., & Rauch, S. L. (1994). Managing the patient with treatment resistant obsessive compulsive disorder: Current strategies. *Journal of Clinical Psychiatry, 55*(Suppl.), 11–17.

Jernigan, T. L., Hesselink, J. R., Sowell, E., & Tallal, P. A. (1991). Cerebral structure on magnetic resonance imaging in language- and learning-impaired children. *Archives of Neurology, 48,* 539–545.

John, E. R., Ahn, H., Prichep, L., Trepetin, M., Brown, D., & Kege, H. (1980). Developmental equations for the electroencephalogram. *Science, 210,* 1255–1258.

John, E. R., Prichep, L. S., Fridman, J., & Easton, P. (1988). Neurometrics: Computer-assisted differential diagnosis of brain dysfunctions. *Science, 239,* 162–169.

Johnson, D. J., & Myklebust, H. (1967). *Learning disabilities: Educational principles and practices* (2nd ed.). New York: Grune & Stratton.

Johnson, D. W., & Johnson, R. (1975). *Learning together and alone: Cooperation, competition, and individualization.* Englewood Cliffs, NJ: Prentice Hall.

Johnson, E. O., & Breslau, N. (2000). Increased risk of learning disabilities in low birth weight boys at age 11 years. *Biological Psychiatry, 47,* 490–500.

Johnson, R. J., Johnson, K. L., & Kerfort, J. F. (1972). A massive oral decoding technique. *The Reading Teacher, 25,* 421–423.

Johnston, R. B., Stark, R. E., Mellits, E. D., & Tallal, P. (1981). Neurological status of language-impaired and normal children. *Annals of Neurology, 10,* 159–163.

Joint Committee on Testing Practices. (1988). Code of fair testing practices in education. In A. A. Silver & R. A. Hagin (Eds.), *Disorders of learning in childhood* (pp. 564–569). New York: Wiley.

Jones, K. L., Smith, D. W., Ulleland, C. N., & Streissguth, A. P. (1973). Pattern of malformation in offspring of chronic alcoholic mothers. *Lancet,* i, 1267–1271.

Jorm, A. F. (1986). Effects of cholinergic enhancement therapies on memory function in Alzheimer's disease: A Meta-analysis of the literature. *Australian and New Zealand Journal of Psychiatry, 20,* 237–240.

Jorm, A. F., Share, D. L., Maclean, R., & Matthews, R. (1986). Cognitive factors at school entry predictive of specific reading retardation and general reading backwardness: A research note. *Journal Psychology and Psychiatry, 27,* 45–54.

Joschko, M., & Rourke, B. P. (1985). Neuropsychological subtypes of learning-disabled children who exhibit the ACID pattern in the WISC. In B. Rourke (Ed.), *Neuropsychology of learning disabilities: Essentials of sub-type analysis* (pp. 65–88). New York: Guilford Press.

Kadhim, H. J., Gadisseux, J. F., & Evrard, P. (1988). Topographical and cytological evolution of the glial phase during prenatal development of the human brain: Histochemical and electron microscopic study. *Journal of Neuropathology and Experimental Neurology, 47,* 166–188.

Kagan, J., Rosman, B. L., Day, B., Albert, J., & Phillip, W. (1964). Information processing in the child: Significance of analytic and reflective attitudes. *Psychological Monographs, 78*(1, Whole No. 578).

Kahn, A. U., & DeKirmenjian, H. (1981). Urinary excretion of catacholamine metabolites in hyperkinetic child syndrome. *American Journal of Psychiatry, 138,* 108–112.

Kahn, E., & Cohen, L. H. (1934). Organic driveness: A brain-stem syndrome and an experience. *New England Journal of Medicine, 210,* 748–756.

Kandel, E. R., Abrams, T., Bernier, L., Carew, T. S., Hawkins, R. D., & Schwartz, J. H. (1983). Classical conditioning and sensitization show aspects of the same molecular cascade in aplysia. *Cold Spring Harbor Symposium in Quantitative Biology* (Vol. 48, pp. 823–830).

Kandel, E. R., & Schwartz, J. H. (1982). Molecular biology of learning: Modulation of transmitter release. *Science, 218,* 433–443.

Kanner, L. (1935). *Child psychiatry.* Springfield, IL: Thomas.

Kaplan, E., Goodglass, H., & Weintraub, S. (1982). *Boston naming test* (2nd ed.). Philadelphia: Lea & Febiger.

Katz, R. B., & Shankweiler, D. P. (1985). Receptive naming and the dictation of word retrieval deficits in the beginning reader. *Cortex, 2,* 617–625.

Kaufman, A. S. (1979). *Intelligent testing with the WISC-R.* New York: Wiley.

Kaufman, A. S., & Kaufman, N. L. (1983). *The Kaufman Assessment Battery for Children.* Circle Pines, MN: American Guidance Service.

Kaufman, J., Birmaher, B., Brent, D., Rao, U., Flynn, C., Moreci, P., Williamson, D., & Ryan, N. (1999). Schedule for Affective Disorders and Schizophrenia for school-age children-present and lifetime version (K-SADS-PL): Initial reliability and validity data. *Journal of the American Academy of Child and Adolescent Psychiatry, 38,* 1065–1069.

Kavale, K. A. (1981). The relationship between auditory perceptual skills and reading ability: A meta-analysis. *Journal of Learning Disabilities, 14,* 539–549.

Kavale, K. A. (1982). Meta-analysis of the relationship between visual perceptual skills and reading achievement. *Journal of Learning Disabilities, 15,* 42–51.

Kavale, K. A., & Dobbins, D. A. (1993). The equivocal nature of special education intervention. *Early Child Development and Care, 86,* 23–37.

Kavale, K. A., & Forness, S. R. (1985). *The science of learning disabilities.* Boston: College Hill Press.

Kavale, K. A., & Forness, S. R. (1987). The far side of heterogeneity: Analysis of empirical subtyping in learning disabilities. *Journal of Learning Disabilities, 20,* 374–382.

Kavale, K. A., & Mattson, P. D. (1983). "One jumped off the balance beam": Meta-analysis of perceptual-motor training. *Journal of Learning Disabilities, 16,* 165–173.

Kawachi, I., Kennedy, B. P., & Wilkinson, R. G. (1999). The society and population health reader: Income inequality and health. *Review of the New England Journal of Medicine, 342,* 221.

Kawi, A. A., & Pasamanick, B. (1959). Prenatal and paranatal factors in the development of childhood reading disorders. *Monographs of the Society for Research in Child Development, 24*(4, Serial No. 73).

Keefe, B., & Swinney, D. (1979). On the relationship of hemispheric specialization and developmental dyslexia. *Cortex, 12,* 471–481.

Keller, R. W., Jr., & Snyder-Keller, A. (2000). Prenatal cocaine exposure. *Annals of the New York Academy of Sciences, 909,* 217–232.

Keogh, B. K. (1988). Improving services for problem learners: Rethinking and restructuring. *Journal of Learning Disabilities, 21,* 19.

Keogh, B. K. (1994). A matrix of decision points in the measurement of learning disabilities. In G. R. Lyon (Ed.), *Frames of reference for the assessment of learning disabilities: New views on measurement issues* (pp. 15–26). Baltimore: Brookes.

Kephart, N. C. (1960). *The slow learner in the classroom.* Columbus, OH: Merrill.

Kerbeshian, J., Burd, L., & Klug, M. G. (1995). Comorbid Tourette's disorder and bipolar disorder: An etiologic perspective. *American Journal of Psychiatry, 152,* 1646–1651.

Kercher, M. B., & Bauman-Waengles, J. A. (1992). *Performances of Black English speaking children on standardized language tests.* Paper presented at the American Speech-Language-Hearing Association annual convention, San Antonio, TX.

Kern, R. S., Green, M. F., Marshall, B. D., Jr., Wirshing, W. C., Wirshing, D., McGurk, S. R., Marder, Sr., & Mintz, J. (1999). Risperidone versus haloperidol on secondary memory: Can newer medications aid learning? *Schizophrenia Bulletin, 25,* 223–232.

Kerr, J. R. (1897). School hygiene in its mental, moral and physical aspects: Howard Medal prize essay. *Journal of Royal Statistical Society, 60,* 613–680.

Kershner, J. R. (1979). Rotation of mental images and asymetries in word recognition in disabled readers. *Canadian Journal of Psychology, 33,* 39–50.

Kestenbaum, C. J., & Williams, D. T. (1988). *Handbook of critical assessment of children and adolescents.* New York: New York University Press.

Kety, S. S. (1976). Biological concomitants of affective states and their possible roles in memory processes. In M. R. Rosenzweig & E. L. Bennett (Eds.), *Neural mechanisms of learning and memory* (pp. 321–326). Cambridge, MA: MIT Press.

Kidd, K. K., & Pauls, D. L. (1982). Genetic hypotheses of Tourette's syndrome. In A. J. Friedhoff & T. N. Chase (Eds.), *Advances in neurology: Gilles de la Tourette's syndrome* (Vol. 35, pp. 243–250). New York: Raven Press.

Kiessling, L. S., Marcotte, A. C., & Culpepper, L. (1993). Antineuronal antibodies in movement disorders. *Pediatrics, 92,* 39–43.

Kilby, G. A. (1983). An ex post facto evaluation of the junior first grade in Sioux Fall, South Dakota. *Dissertation Abstracts International, 43,* 3271A.

Kimball, J. G. (1990). Using the sensory integration and praxis tests to measure change: A pilot study. *American Journal of Occupational Therapy, 44,* 603–608.

Kimura, D. (1961). Cerebral dominance and the perception of verbal stimuli. *Canadian Journal of Psychology, 15,* 166–171.

Kimura, D. (1963). Speech lateralization in young children as determined by an auditory test. *Journal of Comparative and Physiological Psychology, 56,* 899–902.

Kimura, D. (1969). Spatial localization in left and right visual fields. *Canadian Journal of Psychology, 23,* 445–448.

Kimura, D. (1973). The asymmetry of the human brain. *Scientific American, 228,* 70–80.

Kinnier-Wilson, S. A. (1936). Central disturbances of movement. *Abhandlungen aus der Neurologie, Psychiatrie, Psychologie und Ihren Grenzgebieten, 75.*

Kinsbourne, M. (1984). Hyperactivity management: The impact of special diets. In M. Levine & P. Satz (Eds.), *Middle childhood: Development and dysfunction* (pp. 487–500). Baltimore: University Park Press.

Kinsbourne, M., & Caplan, P. J. (1979). *Children's learning and attention problems.* Boston: Little, Brown.

Kinsbourne, M., & Warrington, E. K. (1962). A study of fingeragnosia. *Brain, 85,* 47–66.

Kinsbourne, M., & Warrington, E. K. (1963). The development of finger differentiation. *Quarterly Journal of Experimental Psychology, 15,* 132–137.

Kirk, S. A. (1962). *Educating exceptional children.* Boston: Houghton Mifflin.

Kirk, S. A., McCarthy, J. J., & Kirk, W. D. (1968). *Illinois test of psycholinguistic abilities.* Urbana: University of Illinois Press.

Klesius, J. P., & Homan, S. P. (1985). A validity and reliability update on the informal reading inventory with suggestions for improvement. *Journal of Learning Disabilities, 18,* 71–76.

Klingner, J. K., Vaughn, S., Hughes, M. T., Schumm, J. S., & Elbaum, B. E. (1998). Academic outcomes for students with and without learning disabilities in inclusive classrooms. *Learning Disabilities Research and Practice, 13,* 153–161.

Knobloch, H., & Pasamanick, B. (1966). Prospective studies on the epidemiology of reproductive casualty: Methods, findings and some implications. *Merrill-Palmer Quarterly, 12,* 27–43.

Konecky, J., & Wolinsky, S. (2000). Through the legal maze: Legal issues and disability rights. *Learning Disabilities: A Multidisciplinary Journal, 10,* 73–84.

Konkol, R., Chapman, L., Breese, G., Coller, A., Kits, C., Finley, C., Vogel, R., Mailman, R., & Bendrich, E. (1987). Hemophilus meningitis in the rat: Behavioral, electrophysiological and biochemical consequences. *Annals of Neurology, 21,* 253–260.

Koorland, M. A. (1986). Applied behavior analysis and the correction of learning disabilities. In J. K. Torgeson & B. Y. L. Wong (Eds.), *Psychological and educational perspectives on learning disabilities.* New York: Academic Press.

Koppitz, E. M. (1975). *The Bender-Gestalt Test for young children: Research and application 1963–1973*. New York: Grune & Stratton.

Korhonen, T. T. (1991). Neuropsychological stability and prognosis of subgroups of children with learning disabilities. *Journal of Learning Disabilities, 24,* 48–57.

Kornhuber, H., Bechinger, D., Jung, H., & Sauer, E. (1985). A quantitative relationship between extent of localized cerebral lesions and intellectual and behavioral deficiency in children. *European Archives of Psychiatric and Neurological Science, 235,* 129–133.

Krageloh-Mann, I., Toft, P., Lunding, J., Andresen, J., Pryds, O., & Lou, H. C. (1999). Brain lesions in preterms: Origin, consequences and compensation. *Acta Paediatrica, 88,* 897–908.

Krashen, S. (2000). *Has whole language failed* [Online]. Available: www.usc.edu/dept /education/cmmr/text/krashen_wholelang.html

Krasuski, J., Horwitz, B., & Rumsey, J. M. (1996). Neuroimaging. In R. Lyon & J. M. Rumsey (Eds.), *A survey of functional and anatomical neuroimaging techniques* (pp. 25–52). Baltimore: Brookes.

Krech, D., Rosenzweig, M. R., & Bennett, E. L. (1960). Effects of environment complexity and training on brain chemistry. *Journal of Comparative and Psychology, 52,* 509–519.

Krech, D., Rosenzweig, M. R., & Krueckel, B. (1954). Enzymes concentrations in the brain and adjustive behavior patterns. *Science, 120,* 994–996.

Krober, H. L., Scheurer, W. E., & Sass, H. (1994). Cerebral dysfunction, neurologic symptoms and persistent delinquency: II. Results of the Heidelberg Delinquency Project. *Fortschrifte der Neurologic Psychiatry, 62,* 223–232.

Kurlan, R. (1998). Tourette's syndrome and "PANDAS": Will the relation bear out? Pediatric autoimmune neuropsychiatric disorders associated with streptococcal infection. *Neurology, 50,* 1530–1534.

Kurlan, R., Majumdar, L., Deeley, C., Mudholkar, G. S., Plumb, S., & Como, P. G. (1991). A controlled trial of propoxyphene and naltrexone in patients with Tourette's syndrome. *Annals of Neurology, 30,* 19–23.

Kurlan, R., Whitemore, D., Irvine, C., McDermott, P. M., & Como, P. G. (1994). Tourette's syndrome in a special education population: A pilot study involving a simple school district. *Neurology, 44,* 699–702.

Kushch, A., Gross-Glenn, K., Jallad, B., Lubs, H., Rapin, M., Feldman, E., & Durar, R. (1993). Temporal lobe surface area measurements on MRI in normal and dyslexic readers. *Neuropsychologia, 31,* 811–821.

Kutas, M., & Hillyard, S. A. (1980). Reading senseless sentences: Brain potentials reflect semantic incongruities. *Science, 207,* 203–205.

Labov, W. (1969). Some sources of reading problems for Negro speakers of non-standard English. In J. C. Baratz & R. W. Shuy (Eds.), *Teaching Black children to read* (pp. 29–67). Washington, DC: Center for Applied Linguistics.

Lahey, B. B., Applegate, B., McBurnett, K., Biederman, J., Greenhill, L., Hynd, G. W., Barkley, R. A., Newcorn, J., Jensen, P., Richters, J., Garfinkel, B., Kerdyk, L., Frick, P. J., Ollendick, T., Perez, D., Hart, E. L., Waldman, I., & Shaffer, D. (1994). *DSM-IV* field trials for attention deficit hyperactivity disorder in children and adolescents. *American Journal of Psychiatry, 151,* 1673–1685.

Lahey, B. B., Schaughency, E. A., & Hynd, G. W. (1988). Dimensions and types of attention deficit disorder. *Journal of American Academy of Child and Adolescent Psychiatry, 26,* 613–616.

Lahey, B. B., Schaughency, E. A., Strauss, C. C., & Frame, C. L. (1984). Are attention deficit disorders with and without hyperactivity similar or dissimilar disorders? *Journal of the American Academy of Child Psychiatry, 23,* 302–309.

Lambert, N. M., & Sandoval, J. (1980). The prevalence of learning disabilities in a sample of children considered hyperactive. *Journal of Abnormal Child Psychology, 8,* 33–50.

Langhorne, J. E., Loney, J., Paternite, C. E., & Bechtoldt, H. P. (1976). Childhood hyperkinesis: A return to the source. *Journal of Abnormal Psychology, 85,* 201–209.

Larry P. v. Riles, U.S. Federal District Court California. (1979).

Larsen, J. P., Hoien, T., & Odegaard, H. (1992). Magnetic resonance imaging of the corpus callosum in developmental dyslexia. *Cognitive Neuropsychology, 9,*123–134.

Lau v. Nichols. (1974). 414 U.S. Sec. 563. Decision upholding the office of Civil Rights requirement for school district to provide equal educational opportunity to limited English proficient students.

Laufer, M. W., & Denhoff, E. (1957). Hyperkinetic behavior syndrome in children. *Journal of Pediatrics, 50,* 463–474.

Laufer, M. W., & Scott, G. B. (2000). Medical management of HIV disease in children. *Pediatrics Clinics of North America, 47,* 127–153.

Law, S. F., & Schachar, R. J. (1999). Do typical clinical doses of methylphenidate cause tics in children treated for attention-deficit hyperactivity disorder. *Journal of the American Academy of Child and Adolescent Psychiatry, 38,* 944–951.

Learning Disabilities Association of America. (2000). *Learning disabilities and low income populations: Fact sheet.*

Leckman, J. F., & Cohen, D. J. (Eds.). (1999). *Tourette's syndrome–tics, obsessions, compulsions: Developmental psychopathology and clinical care.* New York: Wiley.

Leckman, J. F., Deltor, J., Hercherik, D. F., Young, J. G., Anderson, J. M., Shaywitz, B. A., et al. (1983). Acute and chronic clonidine treatment in Tourette's syndrome: A preliminary report on clinical response and effect on plasma and urinary catecholamine metabolities, growth hormone and blood pressure. *Journal of the American Academy of Child and Adolescent Psychiatry, 2,* 433–440.

Leckman, J. F., Goodman, W. K., Anderson, G. M., Riddle, M. A., Chappell, P. B., McSwiggan-Hardin, M. T., Walker, D. E., Scahill, L. D., Ort, S. I., Pauls, D. L., Cohen, D. J., & Price, L. H. (1995). CSF biogenic amines in obsessive compulsive disorder and Tourette's syndrome. *Neuropsychopharmacology, 12,* 73–86.

Leckman, J. F., Goodman, W. K., North, W. G., Chappell, P. B., Price, L. H., Pauls, D. L., Anderson, G. M., Riddle, M. A., McSwiggan-Hardin, M. T., McDougle, C. J., Barr, L. C., & Cohen, D. J. (1994a). Elevated levels of cerebrospinal fluid levels oxytocin in obsessive compulsive disorder: Comparison with Tourette's syndrome and healthy controls. *Archives of General Psychiatry, 51,* 782–792.

Leckman, J. F., Goodman, W. K., North, W. G., Chappell, P. B., Price, L. H., Pauls, D. L., Anderson, G. M., Riddle, M. A., McSwiggan-Hardin, M. T., McDougle, C. J., Barr, L. C., & Cohen, D. J. (1994b). The role of central oxytocin in obsessive compulsive disorder and related normal behavior. *Psychoneuroendocrinology, 19,* 723–749.

Leckman, J. F., King, R. A., & Cohen, D. J. (1999). Tics and tic disorders. In J. F. Leckman & D. J. Cohen (Eds.), *Tourette's syndrome—tics, obsessions, compulsions: Developmental psychopathology and clinical care* (pp. 23–42). New York: Wiley.

Leckman, J. F., Peterson, B. S., Anderson, G. M., Arnsten, A. F., Pauls, D. L., & Cohen, D. J. (1997). Pathogenesis of Tourette's syndrome. *Journal of Child Psychology and Psychiatry, 38,* 119–142.

Leckman, J. F., Riddle, M. A., Berrettini, W. H., Anderson, G. M., Hardin, M. T., Chappell, P. B., Bissette, G., Nemeroff, C. B., Goodman, W. K., & Cohen, D. J. (1988). Elevated CFS levels of dynorphin A[1–8] in Tourette's syndrome. *Life Sciences, 43,* 2015–2023.

Leckman, J. F., Sholomskas, D., Thompson, W. D., Belanger, A., & Weissman, M. M. (1982). Best estimate of lifetime psychiatric diagnosis. *Archives of General Psychiatry, 39,* 879–883.

Leckman, J. F., Walker, D. E., Goodman, W. K., Pauls, D. L., & Cohen, D. J. (1994). "Just right" perceptions associated with compulsive behaviors in Tourette's syndrome. *American Journal of Psychiatry, 151,* 675–680.

Leckman, J. F., Walkup, J. T., & Cohen, D. J. (1988). Clonidine treatment of Tourette's syndrome. In D. J. Cohen, R. D. Bruun, & J. F. Leckman (Eds.), *Tourette's syndrome and tic disorder: Clinical understanding and treatment* (pp. 292–301). New York: Wiley.

Leckman, J. F., Zhang, H., Vitale, A., Lahnin, F., Lynch, K., Bondi, C., Kim, Y. S., & Peterson, B. S. (1998). Trajectories of tic severity in Tourette's syndrome: The first two decades. *Pediatrics, 102,* 14–19.

Lee, L. (1971). *Northwestern Syntax Screening Test.* Evanston, IL: Northwestern University Press.

Lemann, N. (1997). The reading wars. *Atlantic Monthly, 280,* 128–134.

Lena, C., & Changeux, J. P. (1997). Pathological mutations of nicotinic receptors and nicotine-based therapies for brain disorders. *Current Opinion in Neurobiology, 7,* 674–682.

Lenneberg, E. H. (1967). *Biological foundations of language.* New York: Wiley.

Lerer, R. J. (1987). Motor tics, Tourette's syndrome and learning disabilities. *Journal of Learning Disabilities, 20,* 266–267.

Lerner, J. W. (1988). *Learning disabilities: Theories, diagnosis, and teaching strategies.* Boston: Houghton Mifflin.

Lesser, G. S., Fifer, G., & Clark, D. H. (1965). Mental abilities of children in different social class and cultural groups. *Monographs of the society for research in child development, 20*(Serial No. 102).

Lester, J., & Kelman, M. (1997). State disparities in the diagnosis and placement of pupils with learning disabilities. *Journal of Learning Disabilities, 30,* 599–607.

Li, A. K. F., Sauve, R. S., & Creighton, D. E. (1990). Early indicators of learning problems in high-risk children. *Journal of Developmental and Behavior Pediatrics, 11,* 1–6.

Liberman, A. M., Mattingly, I. G., & Turvey, M. (1972). Language codes and memory codes. In A. W. Melton & E. Martin (Eds.), *Coding processes and human memory* (pp. 307–334). Washington, DC: Winston and Sons.

Liberman, I. Y. (1973). Segmentation of the spoken word and reading acquisition. *Bulletin of the Orton Society, 23,* 65–77.

Liberman, I. Y., Cooper, F. S., Shankweiler, D., & Studdert-Kennedy, M. (1967). Perception of the speech code. *Psychological Review, 74,* 431–461.

Liberman, I. Y., Rubin, H., Duques, S., & Carlisle, J. (1985). Linguistic abilities and spelling proficiency in kindergarteners and adult poor spellers. In D. Gray & J. F. Kavanaugh (Eds.), *Behavioral measures of dyslexia* (pp. 163–176). Parkton, MD: York Press.

Liberman, I. Y., Shankweiler, D., & Liberman, A. M. (1989). The alphabetic principle and learning to read. In S. Shankweiler & I. Y. Liberman (Eds.), *Phonology and reading disability: Solving the reading puzzle. International academy for research in learning disabilities monograph series* (pp. 1–33). Ann Arbor: University of Michigan Press.

Liepmann, H. (1920). Apraxia. *Ergebness der Medicine (von Brugsch), 1,* 516.

Light, J. G., Pennington, B. F., Gilger, J. W., & DeFries, J. C. (1995). Reading disability and hyperactivity disorder: Evidence for a common genetic etiology. *Developmental Neuropsychology, 11,* 323–335.

Liljequist, R. S., Linnoila, M., & Mattila, M. J. (1974). Effect of two weeks treatment with chlorimipramine and nortriptyline alone or in combination with alcohol on learning and memory. *Psychopharmacology, 37,* 181–186.

Lindamood, C., & Lindamood, P. C. (1984). *Auditory discrimination in depth.* Austin, TX: ProEd.

Lindamood, P. C. (1994). Issues in researching the link between phonological awareness, learning disabilities and spelling. In G. R. Lyon (Ed.), *Frames of reference for the assessment of learning disabilities* (pp. 351–373). Baltimore: Brookes.

Lindamood, P. C., Bell, N., & Lindamood, P. (1992). Issues in phonological awareness assessment. *Annals of Dyslexia, 42,* 242–259.

Lindamood, P. C., & Bell, P. (2000). *Learning processing.* Austin, TX: ProEd.

Lindamood, P. C., & Lindamood, P. (2000). *Phoneme processing.* Austin, TX: ProEd.

Lindgren, S. D., & Benton, A. L. (1980). Developmental patterns of visuospatial judgment. *Journal of Pediatric Psychology, 5,* 217–225.

Lindsay, J. (1954). The Bender-Gestalt Test and psychoneurotics. *Journal of Mental Science, 100,* 980–982.

Lindsay, J., Ounstead, C., & Richards, P. (1979). Long-term outcome in children with temporal lobe seizure: III. Psychiatric aspects in childhood and adult life. *Developmental Medicine and Child Neurology, 21,* 630–636.

Lipkin, P. H., Goldstein, I. J., & Adesman, A. R. (1994). Tics and dyskinesias associated with stimulants treatment in attention-deficit hyperactivity disorder. *Archives of Pediatric and Adolescent Medicine, 148,* 859–861.

Littman, B. (1979). The relationship of medical events to infant development. In T. Fields (Ed.), *Infants born at risk: Behavior and development* (pp. 53–65). New York: Spectrum.

Livingstone, M. S. (1999). Reading and attention disorders. In D. D. Duane (Ed.), *The magnocellular/parietal system and visual symptoms in dyslexia* (pp. 81–92). Baltimore: York Press.

Livingstone, M. S., Rosen, G. D., Drislane, F. W., & Galaburda, A. M. (1991). Physiological and anatomical evidence for a magnocellular defect in developmental dyslexia. *Proceedings of the National Academy of Sciences, USA, 88,* 7943–7947.

Llinas, R. (1993). Is dyslexia a dyschronia? In P. Tallal & A. M. Galaburda (Eds.), *Temporal information processing in the nervous system: Special reference to dyslexia and dysphasia* (Vol. 682, pp. 48–56). New York: Annals of the New York Academy of Sciences.

Lobovits, A. (1982). Vision screening. In L. Barness (Ed.), *Advances in pediatrics* (Vol. 29, pp. 425–433). New York: Mosby.

Loge, D. V., Staton, D., & Beatty, W. W. (1990). Performance of children with ADHD on tests sensitive to frontal lobe dysfunction. *Journal of the American Academy of Child and Adolescent Psychiatry, 29,* 540–545.

Looker, A., & Conners, C. K. (1970). Diphenylhydation in children with severe temper tantrums. *Archives of General Psychiatry, 23,* 80–89.

Lorente, de No, R. (1947). Action potentials of the motoneurons of the hypoglossel nucleus. *Journal Cellular and Comperative Physiology, 29,* 207–287.

Lotas, M., Penticuff, J., Medoff-Cooper, B., Brooten, D., & Brown, L. (1992). The HOME scale: The influence of socioeconomic status on the evaluation of the home environment. *Nursing Research, 41,* 338–341.

Lowe, T. L., Cohen, D. J., Detlor, J., Kremenitzer, M. W., & Shaywitz, B. A. (1982). Stimulant medications precipitate Tourette's syndrome. *Journal of the American Medical Association, 247,* 1729–1731.

Lubs, H. A., Duara, R., Levin, B., Jallad, B., Lubs, M. L., Rabin, M., Kushch, A., & Gross-Glenn, K. (1991). Dyslexia subtypes. In D. D. Duane & D. B. Gray (Eds.), *The reading brain: The biological basis of dyslexia* (pp. 89–117). Parkton, MD: York Press.

Lubs, H. A., Rabin, M., Carland-Saucier, K., Wen, X. L., Gross-Glenn, K., Duara, R., Levin, B., & Lubs, M. L. (1990). Genetic bases of developmental dyslexia: Molecular studies. In J. Obrzut & G. Hynd (Eds.), *Neuropsychological foundations of learning disabilities: A handbook of issues, methods and practice.* Orlando, FL: Academic Press.

Lucas, A. R., Beard, C. M., Raiput, A. H., & Kurland, L. T. (1982). Tourette's syndrome in Rochester, Minnesota, 1968–1979. In A. J. Friedhoff & T. N. Chase (Eds.), *Advances in neurology: Gilles de la Tourette's syndrome* (Vol. 35, pp. 267–269). New York: Raven Press.

Lucas, A. R., Kauffman, P. E., & Morris, E. M. (1967). Gilles de la Tourette's disease: A clinical study of fifteen cases. *Journal of the American Academy of Child and Adolescent Psychiatry, 6,* 700–722.

Lucas, R. J., Ke, L., Bencherif, M., & Eisenhocer. (1996). Regulation of nicotine by its own receptors. *Drug Development Research, 38,* 136–148.

Luk, S-L. (1985). Direct observation studies of hyperactive behaviors. *Journal of the American Academy of Child Psychiatry, 24,* 338–344.

Luria, R. A. (1966). *Higher cortical functions in man.* New York: Basic Books.

Luster, T., & McAdoo, H. P. (1994). Factors related to the achievement and adjustment of young African American children. *Child Development, 65,* 1080–1094.

Lutz, E. G., & Feldman, J. (1977). Alternative drug treatments in Gilles de la Tourette's syndrome [Letter]. *American Journal of Psychiatry, 134,* 98–99.

Lykken, D. (1957). A study of anxiety in the sociopathic personality. *Journal of Abnormal and Social Psychology, 55,* 6–10.

Lyon, G. R. (Ed.). (1994). *Frames of reference for the assessment of learning disabilities: New views on measurement issues.* Baltimore: Brookes.

Lyon, G. R. (1995). Toward a definition of dyslexia. *Annals of Dyslexia, 45,* 3–27.

Lyon, G. R. (1996). Learning disabilities. *Future of Children, 6,* 54–76.

Lyon, G. R., & Krasnegor, N. A. (Eds.). (1994). *Attention, memory and executive functions* (p. 434). Baltimore: Brookes.

Lyon, G. R., & Moats, L. C. (1988). Critical issues in the instruction of the learning disabled. *Journal of Consulting and Clinical Psychology, 56,* 830–835.

Lyon, G. R., & Rumsey, J. M. (Eds.). (1996). *Neuroimaging: Future directions and clinical applications in the use of neuroimaging with children* (pp. 227–236). Baltimore: Brookes.

MacMillan, D. L., & Reschley, D. J. (1998). Overrepresentation of minority students: The case for greater specificity or reconsideration of the variables examined. *Journal of Special Education, 32,* 15–24.

Mahler, M. S. (1949). A Psychoanalytic evaluation of tic in psychopathology of children. In A. Freud, H. H. Hartmann, & E. Kris (Eds.), *Psychoanalytic study of the child* (Vols. 3, 4, pp. 279–210). New York: International Universities Press.

Mahler, M. S., & Luke, J. A. (1946). Outcome of the tic syndrome. *Journal of Nervous and Mental Diseases, 103,* 433–445.

Mak, F. L., Chung, S. Y., Lee, P. P., & Chen, S. (1992). Tourette's syndrome in the Chinese: A follow-up of 15 cases. In A. J. Friedhoff & T. N. Chase (Eds.), *Advances in neurology* (Vol. 35, pp. 281–283). New York: Raven Press.

Malison, R. T., McDougle, C. J., van Dyck, C. H., Scahill, L. D., Balwin, R. M., Seibyl, J. P., Price, L. H., Leckman, J. F., & Innis, L. B. (1995). [123 I] Beta-CIT SPECT imaging demonstrates increased striatal dopamine transporter binding in Tourette's syndrome. *American Journal of Psychiatry, 152,* 1359–1361.

Mamlin, N. (1999). Despite best intentions: When inclusion fails. *Journal of Special Education, 33,* 36–49.

Manis, F. R., Seidenberg, M. S., Doi, L. M., McBride-Chang, C., & Petersen, A. (1996). On the bases of two subtypes of developmental [corrected] dyslexia. *Cognition, 3,* 157–195.

Mannuzza, S., Klein, R. G., Bessler, A., Malloy, P., & LaPadula, M. (1993). Adult outcome of hyperactive boys: Educational achievement, occupational rank, and psychiatric status. *Archives of General Psychiatry, 50,* 565–576.

Manset, G., & Washburn, S. T. (2000). Equity through accountability? Mandatory minimum competency exit examination for secondary students with learning disabilities. *Learning Disabilities: Research and Practice, 15,* 160–167.

Marcel, T., & Rajan, P. (1975). Lateral specialization for recognition of words and faces in good and poor readers. *Neuropsychologia, 13,* 489–497.

Markowitsch, H. J. (2000). Memory and amnesia. In M. M. Mesulam (Ed.), *Principles of behavioral and cognitive neurology* (pp. 257–293). New York: Oxford University Press.

Marks, S. B. (1997). Reducing prejudice against children with disabilities in inclusive setting. *International Journal of Disability, Development and Education, 44,* 117–131.

Marsden, C. D. (1982). The mysterious motor function of the basal ganglia: The Robert Wartengerg lecture. *Neurology, 32,* 514–539.

Martin, F., & Lovegrove, W. (1998). Uniform-field flicker masking in control of specifically-disabled readers. *Perception, 17,* 203–214.

Martin, R. C. (1995). Heterogeneity of deficits in developmental dyslexia and implications for methodology. *Psychonomic Bulletin and Review, 2,* 494–500.

Marx, J. (1996). Searching for drugs that combat Alzheimer's. *Science, 273,* 50–53.

Masand, P. S., & Gupta, S. (1999). Selective serotonin-reuptake inhibitors: An update. *Harvard Review of Psychiatry, 7,* 69–84.

Mash, E. J., & Terdal, L. G. (Eds.). (1997). *Assessment of childhood disorders.* New York: Guilford Press.

Massey, A. (1996). Communication development and disorders in African American children. In A. G. Kamhi, K. E. Pollock, & J. L. Harris (Eds.), *Cultural influences on language: Implications for assessing African American children* (pp. 285–306). Baltimore: Brookes.

Masutto, C. (1994). Neurolinguistic differentiation of children with subtypes of dyslexic. *Journal of Learning Disabilities.*

Matejcek, Z. (1994). Emotional problems of children with learning disabilities. *Thalamus,* Special Edition, IARLD Conference for the Cruickshank Memorial Library, Toronto, August 1994.

Mather, N., & Roberts, R. (1995). Sold out? A response to McLeskey and Pugach. *Learning Disabilities Research and Practice, 18,* 239–249.

Matousek, M., & Petersen, I. (1973). Frequency analysis of the EEG in normal children and adolescents. In P. Kellaway & I. Petersen (Eds.), *Automation of clinical electroencephalography* (pp. 75–102). New York: Raven Press.

Mattes, J. A., & Gittelman, R. (1983). Growth of hyperactive children on maintenance regimen of methylphenidate. *Archives of General Psychiatry, 40,* 317–321.

Mattila, M. J., Liljequist, R. S., & Seppela, T. (1978). Effects of amitryptyline and mianserin on psychomotor skills and memory in men. *British Journal of Clinical Pharmacology, 5,* 538–558.

Mattis, S. (1978). Dyslexia syndromes: A working hypothesis that works. In A. L. Benton & D. Pearl (Eds.), *Dyslexia: An appraisal of current knowledge* (pp. 43–58). New York: Oxford University Press.

Mattis, S., French, J. H., & Rapin, I. (1975). Dyslexia in children and young adults: Three independent neuropsychological syndromes. *Developmental Medicine and Child Neurology, 17,* 150–163.

Mattson, R. H., Cramer, J. A., Collins, J. F., Smith, D. B., Delgado-Escueta, A. V., Browne, T. R., Williamson, P. D., Treitman, D. M., McNamara, J. O., McCutchen, C. B., et al. (1985). Comparison of carbamazepine, phenobarbital, phenytoin, and primidone in partial and secondarily generalized tonic-clonic seizures. *New England Journal of Medicine, 31,* 145–151.

May, D. C., & Welch, E. (1984). Developmental placement: Does it prevent learning problems? *Journal of Learning Disabilities, 17,* 338–341.

Mayes, L. C., Granger, R. H., Frank, M. A., Schottenfeld, R., & Bornstein, M. H. (1993). Neurobehavioral profiles or neonates exposed to cocaine prenatally. *Pediatrics, 91,* 778–783.

Mayes, L. C., Grillon, C., Granger, R. H., & Schottenfeld, R. (1998). Regulation of arousal and attention in preschool children exposed to cocaine prenatally. *Annals of the New York Academy of Sciences, 21,* 126–143.

Mayes, S. D., Handford, H. A., & Schaefer, J. H., et al. (1996). The relationship of HIV status, type of coagulation disorder, and school absenteeism to cognition, educational performance, mood, and behavior of boys with hemophilia. *Journal of Genetic Psychology, 157,* 137–151.

Mayeux, R., & Sano, M. (1999). Treatment of Alzheimer's disease. *New England Journal of Medicine, 341,* 1670–1679.

McCall, R. B. (1977). Childhood IQ as a predictor of adult educational and occupational status. *Science, 197,* 482–483.

McCally, M. (2000). Environment and health: An overview. *Canadian Medical Association Journal.*

McClearn, G. E. (1978). Review of "dyslexia-genetic aspects." In A. Benton & D. Pearl (Eds.), *Dyslexia: An appraisal of current knowledge* (pp. 285–298). New York: Oxford University Press.

McClowry, D. P. (2000). Development and assessment of school-age and adolescent children with human immunodeficiency virus. *Seminars in Speech and Language, 21,* 49–62.

McConnel, J. V. (1966). Learning in invertebrates. *Annual Review of Physiology, 28,* 107–136.

McConville, B. J., Fogelson, H. M., Norman, A. B., Klykylo, W. M., Maderscheid, P. Z., Parker, K. W., & Sandberg, P. R. (1991). Nicotine potentiation of haloperidol in reducing tic frequency in Tourette's disorder. *American Journal of Psychiatry, 148,* 793–794.

McCracken, J. T. (1991). A two-part model of stimulant action on attention-deficit hyperactivity disorder in children. *Journal of Neuropsychiatry and Clinical Neuroscience, 3,* 201–209.

McCracken, J. T. (1998). Attention deficit/hyperactivity disorder: II. Neuropsychiatric aspects. In E. C. Coffey & R. A. Brumbeck (Eds.), *Textbook of pediatric neuropsychiatry* (pp. 483–501). Washington, DC: American Psychiatric Press.

McEntee, W. F., & Nair, R. G. (1980). Memory enhancement in Korsakoff's psychosis by clonidine: Further evidence for a noradrenergic deficit. *Annals of Neurology, 7,* 466–470.

McGaugh, J. L., Introini-Collison, I., & Nagahara, A. H. (1988). Memory-enhancing effects of post-training naloxone: Involvement of β-noradrenergic influences in the amygdaloid complex. *Brain Research, 446,* 37–49.

McGee, R., Williams, S., Moffitt, T., & Anderson, J. (1989). A comparison of 13-year-old boys with attention deficit and/or reading disorder on neuropsychological measures. *Journal of Abnormal Child Psychology, 17*, 37–53.

McHugh, P. R. (1999). How psychiatry lost its way. *Commentary, 108*, 32–38.

McKeever, W. F. (1974). Does post-exposure directional scanning offer a sufficient explanation for lateral differences in tachistoscopic recognition? *Perceptual and Motor Skills, 38*, 43–50.

McKeever, W. F., & Huling, M. D. (1970). Lateral dominance in tachistoscopic recognition of children at two levels of ability. *Quarterly Journal of Experimental Psychology, 22*, 600–604.

McKinney, J. D., & Hocutt, A. M. (1988). Policy issues in the evaluation on the regular education initiative. *Learning Disability Focus, 4*, 15–23.

McKinney, J. D., Osborne, S. S., & Schulte, A. C. (1993). Academic consequences of learning disabilities: Longitudinal prediction of outcomes at 11 years of age [Special issue: Risk and resilience in individuals with learning disabilities: An international focus]. *Learning Disabilities Research and Practice, 8*, 19–27.

McLaughlin, M. J., & Henderson, K. (1998). Charter schools in Colorado and their response to the education of students with disabilities. *Journal of Special Education, 32*, 99–102.

McLoyd, V. C. (1998). Socioeconomic disadvantage and child development. *American Psychologist, 53*, 185–204.

McMonnies, C. W. (1992). Visuo-spatial discrimination and mirror image letter reversals in reading. *Journal of the American Optometric Association, 63*, 698–704.

Meadows, A. T., Gordon, J., Massari, D. J., Littman, P., Ferguson, J., & Moss, K. (1981). Declines in IQ scores and cognitive dysfunctions in children with acute lymphocytic leukemia treated with cranial irradiation. *Lancet, 2*, 1015–1018.

Meadows, A. T., & Silber, J. (1985). Delayed consequences of therapy for childhood cancer. *CA–A Cancer Journal for Clinicians, 35*, 271–286.

Mecham, M. J., Jex, J. L., & Jones, J. D. (1967). *Utah Test of Language Development.* Salt Lake City, UT: Communication Research Associates.

Meehl, P. E., & Rosen, A. (1955). Antecedent probability and the efficiency of psychometric signs, patterns or cutting scores. *Psychological Bulletin, 52*, 192–216.

Meier, J. H. (1987). *Screening and assessments of young children at developmental risk* (Publication No. OS-73-90). Washington, DC: Department of Health, Education, and Welfare.

Meige, H., & Feindel, F. (1907). *Tics and their treatment.* London: Sidney Appleton.

Meltzer, L., Roditi, B., Houser, R. F., Jr., & Perlman, M. (1998). Perceptions of academic strategies and competence in students with learning disabilities. *Journal of Learning Disabilities, 31*, 437–451.

Menkes, M. M., Rowe, J. S., & Menkes, J. H. (1967). A twenty-five year follow-up study on the hyperkinetic child with minimal brain dysfunction. *Pediatrics, 39*, 393–399.

Mercer, C. D., Forgnone, C., & Wolking, W. D. (1976). Definitions of learning disabilities used in the United States. *Journal of Learning Disabilities, 9*, 376–386.

Mercer, C. D., Jordan, L., Allsop, D. H., & Mercer, A. R. (1996). Learning disabilities definitions and criteria used by state education departments. *Learning Disability Quarterly, 19*, 217–232.

Mesulam, M. M. (2000). Memory and amnesia. In M. M. Mesulam (Ed.), *Principles of behavioral and cognitive neurology* (pp. 257–293). Oxford, England: Oxford University Press.

Meuldijk, R., & Colon, E. J. (1992). Methadone treatment of Tourette's disorder. *American Journal of Psychiatry, 149*, 139–140.

Meyer, M. S., & Felton, R. H. (1999). Repeated reading to enhance fluencing: Old approaches and new directions. *Annals of Dyslexia, 49,* 283–306.

Meyer, M. S., Wood, F. B., Hart, L. A., & Felton, R. H. (1998). The selective predictive values in rapid automatized naming within poor readers. *Journal of Learning Disabilities, 31,* 106–117.

Milner, B. (1971). Interhemispheric differences in the localization of psychological processes in man. *British Medical Bulletin, 27,* 272–277.

Minde, K., Weiss, G., & Mendelson, N. (1972). A five-year follow-up study of 91 hyperactive school children. *Journal of the American Academy of Psychiatry, 11,* 595–610.

Minshew, N. J. (1996). Autism. In R. D. Adams & M. Victor (Eds.), *Principles of child neurology* (pp. 1713–1730). New York: McGraw-Hill.

Minshew, N. J., & Pettegrew, J. W. (1996a). Developmental neuroimaging: Mapping the development of brain and behavior. In R. W. Thatcher, G. R. Lyon, J. Rumsey, & N. Krasnegor (Eds.), *Nuclear magnetic resonance spectroscopic studies of cortical development* (pp. 123–125). New York: Academic Press.

Minshew, N. J., & Pettegrew, J. W. (1996b). Nuclear magnetic resonance spectroscopic studies of cortical development. In R. W. Thatcher, G. R. Lyon, J. Rumsey, & N. Krasnegor (Eds.), *Developmental neuroimaging* (pp. 107–124). New York: Academic Press.

Mintz, M. (1998). Clinical features of HIV infection in children. In H. E. Gendelman, S. A. Lipton, L. Epstein, & S. Swindells (Eds.), *The neurology of AIDS* (pp. 385–407). New York: Chapman & Hall.

Minuchin, S., Rosman, B. L., & Baker, L. (1978). *Psychosomatic families.* Cambridge, MA: Harvard University Press.

Mirsky, A. F. (1987). Behavioral and psychophysiological markers of disordered attention. *Environmental Health Perspectives, 74,* 191–199.

Mirsky, A. F. (1996). Disorders of attention: A neuropsychological perspective. In G. R. Lyon & N. A. Krasnegor (Eds.), *Attention, memory, and executive function* (pp. 71–95). Baltimore: Brookes.

Mirsky, A. F., Anthony, B. J., & Duncan, C. C. (1991). Analysis of the elements of attention: A neuropsychological approach. *Neuropsychological Review, 2,* 109–145.

Mishkin, M. (1982). A memory system in the monkey. *Philosophical Royal Society London: (Biology), 298,* 326–334.

Mishkin, M., & Aggleton, J. (1981). Multiple functional contribution of the amygdaloid in the monkey. In Y. Ben-Ari (Ed.), *The Amygdaloid complex* (pp. 409–420). Amsterdam: Elsevier.

Mitchell, E., & Matthews, K. L. (1980). Gilles de la Tourette's disorder associated with pemoline. *American Journal of Psychiatry, 137,* 1618–1619.

Moats, L. C., & Lyon, G. R. (1993). Learning disabilities in the United States: Advocacy, science, and the future of the field. *Journal of Learning Disabilities, 26,* 282–294.

Molfenson, L., & Wilfert, C. (1998). Pathogenesis and interruption of vertical transmission. In P. A. Pizzo & C. Wilfert (Eds.), *Pediatric AIDS: The challenge of HIV infection in infants, children, and adolescents* (3rd ed., pp. 487–513). Baltimore: Williams & Wilkins.

Molfese, D. L., & Burger-Judisch, L. M. (1991). Dynamic temporal-spatial allocation of resources in the human brain: An alternative to the static view of hemisphere differences. In F. L. Kitterle (Ed.), *Cerebral laterality: Theory and research: The Toledo symposium* (pp. 71–102). Hillsdale, NJ: Erlbaum.

Molfese, D. L., & Molfese, V. J. (2000). Advancing brain-language models in the next millennium. *Brain and Language, 71,* 164–166.

Molfese, D. L., & Segalowitz, S. J. (1988). *Brain lateralization in children: Developmental implications.* New York: Guilford Press.

Mondrup, K., Dupont, E., & Braingerd, H. (1985). Progabide in the treatment of hyperkenitic extra pyramidal movement disorders. *Acta Neurologica Scandinavica, 72,* 341–342.

Monroe, M. (1932). *Children who cannot read.* Chicago: University of Chicago Press.

Monroe, M. (1935). *Monroe's Reading Aptitude Tests.* New York: Houghton Mifflin.

Morgan, W. P. (1896). A case of congenital word blindness. *British Medical Journal, 2,* 1378.

Morris, R., Blashfield, R. K., & Satz, P. (1981). Neuropsychology and cluster analysis: Potentials and problems. *Journal of Clinical Neuropsychology, 3,* 79–99.

Morris, R., Blashfield, R. K., & Satz, P. (1986). Developmental classification of reading-disabled children. *Journal of Clinical and Experimental Neuropsychology, 8,* 371–392.

Morris, R., Stuebing, K., Fletcher, J., Shaywitz, S., Lyon, R., Shankweiler, D., Katz, L., Francis, D., & Shaywitz, B. (1998). Subtypes of reading disability: A variability around a phonological core. *Journal of Educational Psychology, 90,* 347–373.

Morris, R. D., & Fletcher, J. M. (1988). Classification in neuropsychology: A theoretical framework and research paradigm. *Journal of Clinical Experimental Neuropsychology, 10,* 640–658.

Mortimore, P., & Sammons, P. (1987). New evidence on effective elementary schools. *Education Leadership, 45,* 4–8.

Morton, J. (1969). The interaction of information in word recognition. *Psychological Review, 76,* 165–178.

Morton, J., & Frith, U. (1995). Causal modeling: A structural approach to developmental psychopathology. In D. Cicchetti & D. J. Cohen. (Eds.), *Theory and methods: Wiley series on personality processes* (pp. 357–390). New York: Wiley.

Moss, D. E., Manderscheid, P. Z., Montgomery, S. P., & Norman, A. B. (1989). Nicotine and cannabinoids as adjuncts to neuroleptics in the treatment of Tourette's syndrome and other motor disorders. *Life Sciences, 44,* 1521–1525.

Moss, H. A., Brouwers, P., Wolters, P. L., Wiener, L., Hersh, S., & Pizzo, P. A. (1994). The development of a Q-sort behavioral rating procedure for pediatric HIV patients. *Journal of Pediatric Psychology, 19,* 27–46.

Mostofsky, S. H. (1999). Corpus callosum measurements in girls with Tourette's syndrome. *Neurology, 53,* 1345–1347.

Mostofsky, S. H., Mazzocco, M. M., Aakalu, G., Warsofsky, I. S., Denckla, M. B., & Reiss, A. L. (1998). Decreased cerebellar posterior vermis size in Fragile X syndrome: Correlation with neurocognitive performance. *Neurology, 50,* 121–130.

Moyer, S. B. (1982). Repeated reading. *Journal of Learning Disabilities, 15,* 619–623.

Murphy, C. C., Trevathan, E., & Yeargin-Allsopp, M. (1995). Prevalence of epilepsy and epileptic seizures in 10-year-old children: Results from the Metropolitan Atlanta Developmental Disabilities Study. *Epilepsia, 36,* 866–872.

Murphy, L. B., & Moriarty, A. E. (1976). *Vulnerability, coping and growth.* New Haven, CT: Yale University Press.

Murphy, T. K., Goodman, W. K., Fudge, M. W., Williams, R. C., Jr., Ayoub, E. M., Dalal, M., Lewis, M. H., & Zabriskie, J. B. (1997). B lymphocyte antigen D8/17: A peripheral marker for childhood-onset obsessive-compulsive disorder and Tourette's syndrome? *American Journal of Psychiatry, 154,* 402–407.

Murray, E. A., Cermak, S. A., & O'Brien, V. (1990). The relationship between form and space perception, constructional abilities, and clumsiness in children. *American Journal of Occupational Therapy, 44,* 623–627.

Myklebust, H. R. (1968). Learning disabilities: Definition and overview. In H. R. Myklebust (Ed.), *Progress in learning disabilities* (Vol. 1, pp. 1–15). New York: Grune & Stratton.

Myklebust, H. R., & Boshes, B. (1969). *Final report: Minimal brain damage in children.* Washington, DC: Department of Health, Education, and Welfare.

Naglieri, J. A., LeBuffe, P. A., & Pfeiffer, S. I. (1994). *Devereux scales of mental disorders* [manual]. San Antonio, TX: Harcourt Brace.

Nassogne, M. C., Evrard, P., & Courtoy, P. J. (1998). Selective direct toxicity of cocaine on fetal mouse neurons. *Annals of the New York Academy of Sciences, 21,* 51–68.

National Advisory Committee on Handicapped Children 1967 and U.S. Office of Education (USOE). 42 Fed. Reg., 250, 1977.

National Association of State Boards of Education. (2000). The continuing role of schools in HIV prevention and education. *Policy Information Clearinghouse, 8,* 1–2.

National Center for Children in Poverty. (2000). *Child poverty in the United States.* New York: Columbia University, The Joseph L. Mailman School of Public Health.

National Center for Education Statistics. (1999). *Dropout rates in the United States.* Retrieved from http://necs.ed.gov/pubs2001/dropout/index.asp

National Council for Teachers of Mathematics. (1980). *Priorities in school mathematics.* Reston, VA: National Council for Teachers of Mathematics.

National Education Association. (1999, October 4). *Bilingual education: An overview.* In C. Sund (Ed.), NEA Website. Washington, DC.

National Education Association. (2000, March 2). *Charter schools overvies.* In C. Sund (Ed.), NEA Website. Washington, DC.

National Institute of Mental Health. (1987). Physical and neurological examination for soft signs: Appendix A. In D. Tupper (Ed.), *Soft neurological signs.* Orlando, FL: Grune & Stratton.

National Institute of Mental Health. (1998). *Comprehensive community mental health services report.* Washington, DC: U.S. Department of Health and Human Services, Child, Adolescent, and Family Branch Center for Mental Health Services.

National Joint Committee for Learning Disabilities. (1981). *Learning disabilities: Issues in definition.* Unpublished manuscript. (Available from Drake Duane, c/o The Orton Society, 724 York Road, Baltimore, MD 21204)

National Joint Committee for Learning Disabilities. (1985). *Learning disability and the preschool child.* (ERIC Document Reproduction Service No. ED 206 544)

National Reading Panel. (2000). *Final report.* Washington, DC: National Institute of Child Health and Human Development.

Neal, J. (1942). *Encephalitis: A clinical study.* New York: Grune & Stratton.

Neha, A., Mullick, F., Ishak, K. G., & Zimmerman, H. (1990). Pemoline associated hepatic injury. *Gastroenterology, 99,* 1517–1519.

Neil, M. (1999, September 7). High stakes testing flunks. *USA Today,* p. 1.

Nelson, N. W., & Hyter, Y. D. (1990). *How to use Black English Sentence Scoring (BESS) as a tool of non-biased assessment.* Short course presented at the American Speech-Language-Hearing Association annual convention, Seattle, WA.

Newcomer, P., & Hammill, D. (1977). *The test of language development.* Austin, TX: ProEd.

Newman, M. B., Shytle, R. D., & Sanberg, P. R. (1999). Locomotor behavioral effects of prenatal and postnatal nicotine exposure in rat offspring. *Behavioural Pharmacology, 10,* 699–706.

Nichols, P. L., & Chen, T-C. (1981). *Minimal brain dysfunction: A prospective study.* Hillsdale, NJ: Erlbaum.

Nichols, S., Mahone, E. M., Sirois, P. A., Bordeaux, J. D., Stehbens, J. A., Loveland, K. A., & Amodei, N. (2000). HIV-associated changes in adaptive, emotional, and behavioral functioning in children and adolescents with hemophilia: Results from the hemophilia growth and development study. *Journal of Pediatric Psychology, 25,* 545–556.

Niemark, F. D., & Lewis, N. (1967). The development of logical problem solving strategies. *Child Development, 38,* 107–117.

Nijiokiktjien, C., de Sonneville, L., & Vaal, J. (1994). Callosal size in children with learning disabilities. *Behavioral Brain Research, 64,* 213–218.

Noffsinger, D. (1985). Dichotic-listening techniques in the study of hemisphere asymmetries. In D. F. Benson & E. Zaidel (Eds.), *The dual brain* (pp. 127–141). New York: Guilford Press.

Nomura, Y., & Segawa, M. (1979). Gilles de la Tourette's syndrome in Oriental children. *Brain and Development, 1,* 103–111.

Noshpitz, J. D. (Ed.). (1979). *Basic handbook of child psychiatry* (Vol. 1). New York: Basic Books.

Noshpitz, J. D., Harrison, S. I., & Spencer, F. C. (Eds.). (1998). *Basic handbook of child psychiatry* (Vol. 5). New York: Basic Books.

Nuress, J. R., & McGauvran, M. E. (1965). *Metropolitan Readiness Tests.* New York: Psychological Corporation.

Nuwer, M. (1997). Assessment of digital EEG, quantitative EEG, and EEG brain mapping: Report of the American Academy of Neurology and the American Clinical Neurophysiology Society [Review]. *Neurology, 49,* 277–292.

Obregon, M. (1994). *Exploring naming timing patterns by dyslexic and normal readers on the serial RAN task.* Unpublished master's thesis, Tufts University, Boston.

Occupational Safety and Health Administration. (1991). Occupational exposure to bloodborne pathogens. *Federal Register, 56,* 64175–64182.

O'Donnell, D. J. (1985). Conduct disorders. In J. M. Wiener (Ed.), *Diagnosis of childhood and adolescent disorders* (pp. 250–287). New York: Wiley.

O'Dougherty, M., Nuechterlein, K. H., & Drew, B. (1984). Hyperactive and hypoxic children: Signal detection, sustained attention and behavior. *Journal of Abnormal Psychology, 93,* 178–191.

Ogawa, S., Lee, T. M., Kay, A. R., & Tank, D. W. (1990). Brain magnetic resonance imaging with contrast dependent on blood oxygenation. *Proceedings of the National Academy of Sciences, USA, 87,* 9868–9872.

Olson, R. K., Forsberg, H., Wise, B., & Rack, J. P. (1994). Measurement of word recognition, orthographic, and phonological skills. In G. R. Lyon (Ed.), *Frames of reference for the assessment of learning disabilities* (pp. 243–268). Baltimore: Brookes.

Olson, R. K., Rack, J. P., Conners, F. A., DeFries, J. C., & Fulker, D. W. (1991). Genetic etiology of individual differences in reading disability. In L. V. Feagans, E. J. Short, & L. J. Meltzer (Eds.), *In subtypes of learning disabilities: Theoretical perspectives and research* (pp. 113–135). Hillsdale, NJ: Erlbaum.

Orton, S. T. (1928). Specific reading disability: Strephosymbolia. *Journal of the American Medical Association, 90,* 1095–1099.

Orton, S. T. (1937). *Reading, writing and speech problems in children.* Austin, TX: ProEd.

Orvaschel, H. (1985). Psychiatric interviews suitable for use in research with children and adolescents. *Psychopharmacology Bulletin, 21,* 737–745.

Orvaschel, H., Sholomska, D., & Weissman, M. (1980). *The assessment of psychopathology and behavior problems in children* [Mental health service system reports]. Rockville, MD: U.S. Department of Health and Human Services, NIMH, Division of Biometry and Epidemology.

Ostrom, N. N., & Jenson, W. R. (1988). Assessment of attention deficits in children. *Professional School Psychology, 3,* 254–269.

Otake, M., & Schull, W. J. (1984). In utero exposure to A-bomb radiation and mental retardation: A reassessment. *British Journal of Radiology, 57,* 409–414.

Ounstead, C. (1955). The hyperkinetic syndrome in epileptic children. *Professional School Psychology, 3,* 254–269.

Owen, F. W. (1978). Dyslexia-genetic aspects. In A. L. Benton & D. Pearl (Eds.), *Dyslexia: An appraisal of current knowledge* (pp. 265–285). New York: Oxford University Press.

Page, E. (1985). Review of the Kaufman Assessment Battery for Children. In J. V. Mitchell (Ed.), *The ninth mental measurements yearbook* (pp. 773–777). Lincoln: University of Nebraska Press.

Paine, R. S. (1964). Evolution of infantile postural reflexes in the presence of chronic brain syndrome. *Developmental Medicine and Child Neurology, 6,* 345–361.

Paine, R. S. (1965). The contribution of developmental neurology to child psychiatry. *Journal of the American Academy of Child Psychiatry, 4,* 353–386.

Palinskar, A. S., & Brown, D. A. (1987). Enhancing instructional time through attention to metacognition. *Journal of Learning Disabilities, 20,* 66–75.

Park, S., Como, P. G., Cui, L., & Kurlan, R. (1993). The early course of the Tourette's syndrome clinical spectrum. *Neurology, 43,* 1712–1715.

Pasamanick, B., Rogers, M. E., & Liliendfeld, A. M. (1956). Pregnancy experience and the development of behavior disorder in children. *American Journal of Psychiatry, 112,* 613–618.

P.A.S.E. v. Joseph P. Hannon, U.S. District Court, Northern District of Illinois, Eastern Division, No. 74 (3586), July 1980.

Pauls, D. L., Alsobrook, J. P., Gelernter, J., & Leckman, J. F. (1999). Genetic vulnerability. In J. F. Leckman & D. J. Cohen (Eds.), *Tourette's syndrome–tics, obsessions, compulsions: Developmental psychology and clinical care* (pp. 194–212). New York: Wiley.

Pauls, D. L., Hurst, C. R., Kruger, S. D., Leckman, J. F., Kidd, K. K., & Cohen, D. J. (1986). Evidence against a genetic relationship between Tourette's syndrome and attention deficit disorder. *Archives of General Psychiatry, 43,* 1177–1179.

Pauls, D. L., Leckman, J. F., & Cohen D. J. (1993). Familial relationship between Gilles de la Tourette's syndrome, attention deficit disorder, learning disabilities, speech disorders, and stuttering. *Journal of the American Academy of Child and Adolescent Psychiatry, 32,* 1044–1050.

Pauls, D. L., Raymond, C. L., Stevenson, J. M., & Leckman, J. F. (1991). A family study of Gilles de la Tourette's syndrome. *American Journal of Human Genetics, 48,* 154–163.

Peake, N. (1940). Relationships between spelling ability and reading ability. *Journal of Experimental Education, 9,* 192–193.

Pelham, W. E. (1985). The effects of stimulant drugs on learning and achievement in hyperactive and learning disabled children. In J. K. Torgeson & B. Wong, (Eds.), *Psychological and educational perspectives on learning disabilities* (pp. 259–295). New York: Academic Press.

Pelham, W. E., Bender, M. E., Coddell, J., Booth, S., & Moorer, S. H. (1985). Methylphenidate and children with attention deficit disorder: Dose effects on classroom, academic and social behavior. *Archives of General Psychiatry, 42,* 948–952.

Pelham, W. E., & Murphy, A. A. (1985). Behavioral and pharmacological Rx of attention deficit disorders and conduct disorders. In M. Hersen (Ed.), *Pharmacological and behavioral Rx: An integrative approach.* New York: Wiley.

Penfield, W., & Roberts, L. (1959). *Speech and brain mechanisms.* Princeton, NJ: Princeton University Press.

Pennington, B. F. (1991). *Diagnosing learning disorders: A neuropsychological framework.* New York: Guilford Press.

Pennington, B. F., Filipek, P. A., Churchwell, J., Kennedy, D. N., Lefly, D., Simon, J. H., Filley, C. M., Galaburda, A. M., & DeFries, J. C. (1999). Brain morphometry in reading-disabled twins. *Neurology, 53,* 723–729.

Pennington, B. F., Grossier, D., & Welsh, M. C. (1993). Contrasting cognitive deficits in attention deficit hyperactivity disorder versus reading disability. *Developmental Psychology, 29,* 511–523.

Pennington, B. F., Van Orden, G. C., Smith, S. D., Green, P. A., & Haith, M. M. (1990). Phonological processing skills and deficits in adult dyslexics. *Child Development, 61,* 1753–1778.

Perfetti, C. A., & Hogaboam, T. (1975). Relationship between single word decoding and reading comprehension skill. *Journal of Educational Psychology, 69,* 461–469.

Perlmutter, S. J., Leitman, S. F., Garvey, M. A., Hamburger, S., Feldman, E., Leonard, H. L., & Swedo, S. E. (1999). Therapeutic plasma exchange and intravenous immunoglobulin for obsessive-compulsive disorder and tic disorders in childhood. *Lancet, 9185,* 1153–1158.

Peters, J. E. (Ed.). (1987). A special or soft neurological examination for school age children: Appendix B. In D. E. Tupper (Ed.), *Soft neurological signs.* Orlando, FL: Grune & Stratton.

Petersen, S. E., Fox, P. T., Posner, M. I., Mintun, M., & Raichle, M. E. (1988). Positron emission tomographic studies of the cortical anatomy of single-word processing. *Nature, 331,* 585–589.

Peterson, B. S., Leckman, J. F., Arnsten, A. F., Anderson, G. M., Staib, L. H., Gore, J. C., Bronen, R. A., Malison, R., Scahill, L. D., & Cohen, D. J. (1999). Neuroanatomical circuitry. In J. F. Leckman & D. J. Cohen (Eds.), *Tourette's syndrome–tics, obsessions, compulsions: Developmental psychopathology and clinical care* (pp. 230–260). New York: Wiley.

Peterson, B. S., Riddle, M. A., Cohen, D. J., Katz, L. D., Smith, J. C., Hardin, M. T., & Leckman, J. F. (1993). Reduced basal ganglia volumes in Tourette's syndrome using three-dimensional reconstruction techniques from magnetic resonance images. *Neurology, 43,* 941–949.

Peterson, B. S., Skidlarski, P., Anderson, A. W., Zhang, H., Gatenby, J. C., Lacadie, C. M., Leckman, J. F., & Gore, J. C. (1998). Tourette's syndrome: A failure of subcortical inhibition. *Archives of General Psychiatry, 55,* 326–333.

Pettegrew, J. W., Panchalingam, K., Klunk, W. E., McClure, R. J., & Muenz, L. R. (1994). Alterations of cerebral metabolism in probable Alzheimer's disease: A preliminary study. *Neurobiology of Aging, 15,* 117–132.

Pettegrew, J. W., Panchalingam, K., Withers, G., McKeag, D., & Strychor, S. (1990). Changes in brain energy and phospholipid metabolism during development and aging in the Fischer 344 rat. *Journal of Neuropathology and Experimental Neurology, 49,* 237–249.

Petter, T., Richter, M. A., & Sandor, P. (1998). Clinical features distinguishing patients with Tourette's syndrome and obsessive-compulsive disorder from patients with obsessive-compulsive disorder without tics. *Journal of Clinical Psychiatry, 59,* 456–459.

Piaget, J. (1954). *The construction of reality in the child.* New York: Basic Books.

Piaget, J., & Inhelder, B. (1958). *The growth of logical thinking from childhood to adolescence.* New York: Basic Books.

Pick, A. (1908). Uber Storungen der Orientierung am eigenen Korper. *Arbeiten aus der Deutschen Psychiatrischen.* Berlin, Germany: Praeger.

Pierson, D. E., Walker, D. K., & Tivnan, T. (1984). A school-based program from infancy to kindergarten for children and their parents. *Personal Guidance, 62,* 448–455.

Pilotin, M. (2001). Where the stakes are high for students. *NEA Today, 19*(4), 10.

Pine, D., Shaffer, D., & Schonfeld, I. S. (1993). Persistent emotional disorder in children with neurological soft signs. *Journal of the American Academy of Child Adolescence Psychiatry, 32,* 1229–1236.

Pinnell, G. S. (1985). Helping teachers help children at risk: Insights from the reading recovery program. *Peabody Journal of Education, 62,* 70–85.

Pirozzolo, F. J., & Rayner, K. (1979). Cerebral organization and reading disability. *Neuropsychologia, 17,* 485–491.

Plenger, P. M., Dixon, C. E., Castillo, R. M., Frankowski, R. F., Yablon, S. A., & Levin, H. S. (1996). Subacute methylphenidate treatment for moderate to moderately severe traumatic brain injury: A preliminary double-blind placebo-controlled study. *Archives of Physical Medicine and Rehabilitation, 77,* 536–540.

Pliszka, S. R. (1989). Effect of anxiety on cognition, behavior, and stimulant response in ADHD. *Journal of the American Academy of Child and Adolescent Psychiatry, 28,* 882–887.

Pliszka, S. R., Greenhill, L. L., Crismon, M. L., Sedillo, A., Carlson, C., Conners, C. K., McCracken, J. T., Swanson, J. M., Hughes, C. W., Llana, M. E., Lopez, M., & Toprac, M. G. (2000a). The Texas children's medication algorithm project: Report of the Texas consensus conference panel on medication treatment of childhood attention-deficit/hyperactivity disorder: Part I. *Journal of the American Academy of Child Adolescent Psychiatry, 39,* 908–919.

Pliszka, S. R., Greenhill, L. L., Crismon, M. L., Sedillo, A., Carlson, C., Conners, C. K., McCracken, J. T., Swanson, J. M., Hughes, C. W., Llana, M. E., Lopez, M., & Toprac, M. G. (2000b). The Texas children's medication algorithm project: Report of the Texas consensus conference panel on medication treatment of childhood attention-deficit/hyperactivity disorder: Part II. *Journal of the American Academy of Child Adolescent Psychiatry, 39,* 920–927.

Pliszka, S. R., McCracken, J. T., & Mass, J. W. (1996). Catecholamines in attention-deficit hyperactivity disorder: Current perspectives. *Journal of the American Academy of Child and Adolescent Psychiatry, 35,* 264–272.

Plomin, R., & DeFries, J. C. (1983). The Colorado adoption project. *Child Development, 54,* 276–289.

Plomin, R., & DeFries, J. C. (1998). The genetics of cognitive abilities and disabilities. *Scientific American, 278,* 62–69.

Polakoff, S. A., Sorgi, P. S., & Ratey, J. J. (1986). The treatment of impulsive, aggressive behavior with nadolol. *Journal of Clinical Psychopharmacology, 6,* 125–126.

Pollack, M. A., Cohen, N. L., & Friedhoff, A. J. (1977). Gilles de la Tourette's syndrome: Familial occurrence and precipitation by methylphenidate therapy. *Archives of Neurology, 34,* 630–632.

Pontius, A. A. (1983). Finger misrepresentation and dyscalculia in an ecological context: Toward an ecological (cultural) evolutionary neuro-psychiatry. *Perceptual Motor Skills, 57,* 191–208.

Porges, S. W., & Smith, K. M. (1980). Defining hyperactivity: Physiological and behavioral strategies. In C. K. Whalen & B. Henker (Eds.), *Hyperactive children: The social ecology of identification and treatment* (pp. 75–104). New York: Academy Press.

Posner, M. I. (1988). Structures and functions of selective attention. In T. Boll & B. K. Bryant (Eds.), *Clinical neuropsychology and brain function: Research, measurement, and practice* (pp. 173–202). Washington, DC: American Psychological Association.

Posner, M. I., & Petersen, S. E. (1990). The attention system of the human brain. *Annual Review of Neuroscience, 13,* 25–42.

Posner, M. I., & Raichle, M. E. (1994). *Images to the mind.* New York: Freeman.

Posner, M. I., Walker, J. A., Friedrick, F. J., & Rafal, R. D. (1984). Effects of parietal lobe injury on covert orienting of attention. *Journal of Neuroscience, 4,* 1863–1874.

Practice parameters, attention deficit/hyperactivity disorders. (1997). *Journal of the Academy of Child and Adolescent Psychiatry, 36*(Suppl.), 85S–121S.

Prechtl, H. F. R., & Beintema, D. (1964). *The neurological examination of the full-term newborn infant.* London: Heinemann Medical Books.

Prechtl, H. F. R., & Stemmer, C. J. (1962). The choreoform syndrome in children. *Developmental Medicine and Child Neurology, 4,* 119–127.

Pribram, K., & McGuinness, D. (1992). Attention and para-attentional processing. Event-related brain potentials as tests of a model. *Annals of the New York Academy of Sciences, 658,* 65–92.

Price, R. A., Kidd, K. K., Cohen, D. J., Pauls, D. L., & Leckman, J. F. (1985). A twin study of Tourette's syndrome. *Archives of General Psychiatry, 42,* 815–820.

Price, R. A., Leckman, J. F., Pauls, D. L., Cohen, D. J., & Kidd, K. K. (1986). Gilles de la Tourette's syndrome: Tics and central nervous stimulants in twins and non-twins. *Neurology, 36,* 232–237.

Pryse-Phillips, W. (1999). Do we have drugs for dementia? No. *Archives of Neurology, 56,* 735–737.

Pugh, K. R., Shaywitz, B. A., Shaywitz, S. E., Constable, R. T., Skudlarski, P., Fulbright, R. K., Bronen, R. A., Shankweiler, D. P., Katz, L., Fletcher, J. M., & Gore, J. C. (1996). Cerebral organization of component processes in reading. *Brain, 119,* 1221–1238.

Quadfasel, F. A., & Goodglass, H. (1968). Specific reading disability and other specific disabilities. *Journal of Learning Disabilities, 1,* 590–600.

Quesney, L. F., Constain, M., Rasmussen, T., Olivier, A., & Palmini, A. (1992). Presurgical EEG investigation in frontal lobe epilepsy. *Epilepsy Research*(Suppl. 5), 55–69.

Quinn, P., & Rapoport, J. L. (1975). One year follow-up of hyperactive boys treated with imipramine or methylphenidate. *American Journal of Psychiatry, 132,* 241–245.

Rabin, M., Wex, X. L., Hepburn, M., Lubs, H. A., Feldman, E., & Duara, R. (1993). Suggestive linkage of developmental dyslexia to chromosome 1p340p36 [Letter]. *Lancet, 342,* 178.

Rabinovitch, R. D. (1968). Reading problems in children: Definitions and classification. In A. Keeney & V. Kenney (Eds.), *Dyslexia: Diagnosis and treatment of reading disorders* (pp. 1–10). St. Louis, MO: Mosby.

Rachelefsky, G. S., Wo, J., Adelson, J., Mickey, W. R., Spector, S. L., Katz, R. M., Siegel, S. C., & Rohe, A. S. (1986). Behavior abnormalities and poor school performance due to oral theophylline use. *Pediatrics, 78,* 1133–1138.

Rack, J. P., Snowling, M. J., & Olson, R. K. (1992). The nonword reading deficit in developmental dyslexia: A review. *Reading Research Quarterly, 27,* 28–53.

Ramey, C. T., & Campbell, F. A. (1994). Poverty, early childhood education, and academic competence: The Abecedarian experiment. In A. C. Houston (Ed.), *Children in poverty: Child development and public policy.* New York: Cambridge University Press.

Ramey, C. T., & Landesman-Ramey, S. (1998). Prevention of intellectual disabilities: Early interventions to improve cognitive development. *Preventive Medicine: An International Journal Devoted to Practice and Theory, 27,* 224–232.

Ramey, C. T., Yeates, K. O., & MacPhee, D. (1984). Risk for retarded development among disadvantaged families: A systems theory approach to preventive intervention. *Advances in Special Education, 4,* 249–272.

Rapin, A. G., Pollock, K. E., & Harris, J. L. (Eds.). (1996). *Communication development and disorders in African American children.* Baltimore: Brookes.

Rapoport, J. (1965). Childhood behavior and learning problems treated with imipramine. *International Journal of Neuropsychiatry, 1,* 635–642.

Rapoport, J., Buchsbaum, M., Weinberger, H., Zahn, T., Ludlow, C., Bartko, J., Mikkelson, E., Langer, D., & Banney, W. (1980). Dextroamphetamine: Cognitive and behavioral effects in normal and hyperactive boys and normal adult males. *Archives of General Psychiatry, 37,* 933–946.

Rapoport, J., Buchsbaum, M., Weingartner, H., Zahn, T., Ludlow, C., & Mikkelson, E. (1978). Dextroamphetamine: Behavioral and cognitive effects in normal prepubertal boys. *Science, 199,* 560–563.

Rapoport, J., Coffman, H., Guare, R., Fenton, T., Degraw, C., & Twarog, F. (1989). Effects of theophylline on behavior and learning in children with asthma. *American Journal of Disease of Children, 143,* 368–372.

Rapoport, J., Mikkelson, E. J., Ebert, M. H., Brown, G. L., Weise, V. L., & Kapin, I. J. (1978). Urinary catacholamine and amphetamine excretion in hyperactive and normal boys. *Journal of Nervous and Mental Disease, 66,* 731–732.

Rapoport, J., Zametkin, A., Donnelly, M., & Ismond, D. (1985). New drug trial on attention deficit disorder. *Psychopharmacology Bulletin, 21,* 232–236.

Rasmusson, A. M., Anderson, G. M., Lynch, K. A., McSwiggan-Hardin, M., Scahill, L. D., Mazune, C. M., Goodman, W. R., Price, L. H., Cohen, D. J., & Leckman, J. F. (1997). A preliminary study of tryptophan depletion on tics, obsessive compulsive symptoms, and mood in Tourette's syndrome. *Biologic Psychiatry, 41,* 117–121.

Ravitch, D. (2000). *Left back.* New York: Simon & Schuster.

Rawson, M. B. (1968). *Developmental language disability.* Baltimore: Johns Hopkins University Press.

Rayner, K., Pollatsek, A., & Bilsky, A. B. (1995). Can a temporal processing deficit account for dyslexia? *Psychonomic Bulletin and Review, 2,* 501–507.

Reid, A., Naylor, G., & Kay, D. (1981). A double-blind, placebo controlled crossover trial of carbamazepine in overactive, severely mentally handicapped patients. *Psychological Medicine, 11,* 109–113.

Reiss, A. L., Abrams, M. T., Greenlaw, R., Freund, L., & Denckla, M. B. (1995). Neurodevelopmental effects of the fMRI full mutation in humans. *Nature Medicine, 1,* 159–167.

Reiss, A. L., Freund, L. S., Baumgardner, T. L., Abrams, M. T., & Denckla, M. B. (1995). Contribution of the fMRI gene mutation to human intellectual dysfunction. *Nature Genetics, 11,* 331–334.

Reiton, R. M., & Wolfson, D. (1992). *The Halstead-Reiton Neuropsychological Test Battery* (2nd ed.). Tucson, AZ: Neuropsychology Press.

Remschmidt, H. (1975). The psychotropic effect of carbamazepine in non-epileptic patients with particular reference to problems posed by clinical studies in children with behavior disorders. In W. Birkmayer (Ed.), *Epileptic seizures, behavior, pain* (pp. 253–258). Bern, Switzerland: Huber.

Resnick, M. B., Gueroguieva, R. V., Carter, R. L., Ariet, M., Sun, Y., Roth, J., Bucciarelli, R. L., Curran, J. S., & Mahan, C. S. (1999). The impact of low birth weight, perinatal conditions, and sociodemographic factors on educational outcome in kindergarten. *Pediatrics, 104,* 1379.

Reynolds, A. J. (1992). Mediated effects of preschool intervention. *Early Education Development, 3,* 139–165.

Reynolds, A. J., & Wolfe, B. (1996). Special education and school achievement: An exploratory analysis with a central-city sample. *Educational Evaluation, 21,* 249–269.

Reynolds, C. R. (1984). Critical issues in learning disabilities. *Journal of Special Education, 18,* 451–476.

Reynolds, E. (1982). Pharmacological management of epilepsy associated with psychological disorders. *British Journal of Psychiatry, 141,* 549–557.

Reynolds, E., & Trimble, M. (1981). *Epilepsy and psychiatry.* Edinburgh, Scotland: Churchill Livingstone.

Riccardi, R., Brouwers, P., Dichiro, G., & Poplack, D. G. (1985). Abnormal computed tomography brain scans in children with acute lymphoblastic leukemia: Serial long term follow-up. *Journal of Clinical Oncology, 3,* 12–18.

Richardson, E. P. (1982). Neuropathological studies of Tourette's syndrome. In A. J. Friedhoff & T. N. Chase (Eds.), *Advances in neurology* (Vol. 35, pp. 83–87). New York: Raven Press.

Richters, J. E., Arnold, L. E., & Jensen P. S. (1995). NIMH collaborative multisite multimodal treatment study of children with ADHD: I. Background and rationale. *Journal of American Academy for Adolescence Psychiatry, 34,* 987–1000.

Rickler, K. C. (1982). Episodic dyscontrol. In D. F. Benson & D. Blumer (Eds.), *Psychiatric aspects of neurology disease* (pp. 49–73). New York: Grune & Stratton.

Riddle, K. D., & Rapoport, J. L. (1976). A 2 year follow-up of 72 hyperactive boys. *Journal of Neurology and Mental Disorders, 762,* 126–134.

Riddle, M. A., Bernstein, G. A., Cook, E. H., Leonard, H. L., March, J. S., & Swanson, J. M. (1999). Anxiolytics, adrenergic agents, and naltrexone. *Journal of the American Academy of Child and Adolescent Psychiatry, 38,* 546–556.

Riddle, M. A., Jatlow, P. I., Anderson, G. M., Cho, S. C., Hardin, M. T., Cohen, D. J., & Leckman, J. F. (1989). Plasma debrisoquin levels in the assessment of plasma homovanillic acid: The debrisoquin method. *Neuropsychopharmacology, 2,* 123–129.

Riddle, M. A., Rasmusson, A. M., Woods, S. W., & Hoffer, P. B. (1992). SPECT imaging of cerebral blood flow in Tourette's syndrome. In T. N. Chase, A. J. Friedhoff & D. J. Cohen (Eds.), *Advances in neurology. Tourette's syndrome: Genetics, neurobiology and treatment* (Vol. 58, pp. 207–211). New York: Raven Press.

Rie, H. E., Rie, E. D., Stewart, S., & Ambuel, J. (1976a). Effects of methylphenidate on underachieving children. *Journal of Counseling and Clinical Psychology, 44,* 250–260.

Rie, H. E., Rie, E. D., Stewart, S., & Ambuel, J. (1976b). Effects of methylphenidate on underachieving children: A replication. *American Journal of Orthopsychiatry, 46,* 313–322.

Riesen, A. H. (1970). Effects of visual environment on the retina. In D. B. Lindsley & F. A. Young (Eds.), *Early experience and visual information in perceptual and reading disorders* (pp. 249–260). Washington, DC: National Academy of Sciences.

Rinsland, H. (1945). *A basic vocabulary of elementary school children.* New York: Macmillan.

Rispens, J., van Yperen, T. A., & van Duijn, G. A. (1991). The irrelevance of IQ to the definition of learning disabilities: Some empirical evidence. *Journal of Learning Disabilities, 24,* 434–438.

Robertson, M. M. (2000). Tourette's syndrome, associated conditions and the complexities of treatment. *Brain, 123,* 425–462.

Robertson, M. M., & Reinstein, D. Z. (1991). Convulsive tic disorder: Georges Gilles de la Tourette, Guinon and Grasset on the phenomenology and psychopathology of the Gilles de la Tourette's syndrome. *Behavioral Neurology, 4,* 29–56.

Robertson, M. M., Scull, D. A., Eapen, V., & Trimble, M. R. (1996). Risperidone in the treatment of Tourette's syndrome: A retrospective case note study. *Journal of Psychopharmacology, 10,* 317–320.

Robinson, D., Wu, H., Munne, R. A., Ashtari, M., Alvir, J. M., Lerner, G., Koree, A., Cole, K., & Bogerts, B. (1995). Reduced caudate nucleus volume in obsessive-compulsive disorder. *Archives of General Psychiatry, 52,* 393–398.

Roche, A., Lipman, R., Overall, J., & Hung, W. (1979). The effects of stimulant medication on the growth of hyperkinetic children. *Pediatrics, 63,* 647–650.

Rodning, C., Beckwith, L., & Howard, J. (1989). Prenatal exposure to drugs: Behavioral distortions reflecting CNS impairment? *Neurotoxicology, 10,* 629–634.

Roeltgen, D. (1985). Agraphia. In K. M. Heilman & E. Valenstein (Eds.), *Clinical neuropsychology* (pp. 75–96). New York: Oxford University Press.

Rogawski, M. A., & Aghajanian, C. K. (1980). Modulation of lateral geneculate neuron excitability by noradrenaline microiontophoresis or locus coeruleus stimulation. *Nature, 287,* 731–734.

Rogeness, G. A., Javors, M. A., & Pliszka, S. R. (1992). Neurochemistry and child and adolescent psychiatry. *Journal of the American Academy of Child and Adolescent Psychiatry, 31,* 765–781.

Rogers, M. F., Lindegren, M. L., Simonds, R. J., Gwinn, M., & Bertolli, J. (1998). Pediatric HIV infection in the United States. In P. A. Pizzo & C. M. Wilfert (Eds.), *Pediatric AIDS: The challenge of HIV infection in infants, children, and adolescents* (pp. 3–11). Baltimore: Williams & Wilkins.

Rosenberg, L. A., & Rosenberg, A. M. (1965). The effect of tachistoscopic presentation on the Hutt-Briskin Bender-Gestalt scoring system. *Journal of Clinical Psychology, 21,* 314–316.

Rosenzweig, M. R., & Bennett, E. L. (1984). Basic processes and modulating influences in the stages of memory formation. In G. Lynch, J. L. McGaugh, & N. M. Weinberger (Eds.), *Neurobiology of learning and memory* (pp. 263–288). New York: Guilford Press.

Ross, M. S., & Modolfsky, H. (1978). A comparison of pimozide and haloperidol in the treatment of Gilles de la Tourette's syndrome. *American Journal of Psychiatry, 135,* 585–587.

Rosvold, H. E., Mirsky, A. F., Sarason, J., Bransome, E. D., & Beck, L. H. (1956). A continuous performance test of brain damage. *Journal of Consulting Psychology, 20,* 343–352.

Rourke, B. P. (1989). *Nonverbal learning disabilities: The syndrome and the model.* New York: Guilford Press.

Rourke, B. P. (1991). *Neuropsychological validation of learning disability subtypes.* New York: Guilford Press.

Rourke, B. P. (1994). Neuropsychological assessment of children with learning disabilities. In G. R. Lyon (Ed.), *Frames of reference for the assessment of learning disabilities* (pp. 475–509). Baltimore: Brookes.

Rowe, K. J., & Rowe, K. S. (1992). The relationship between inattentiveness in the classroom and reading achievement (Part B): An explanatory study. *Journal of the American Academy of Child and Adolescent Psychiatry, 31,* 357–368.

Rowland, J. H., Glidwell, O. J., Sibley, R. F., Holland, J. C., Trull, R., Berman, A., et al. (1984). Effect of different forms of central nervous system prophylaxis on neuropsychological function in childhood leukemia. *Journal of Clinical Oncology, 2,* 127–135.

Rozin, P. (1976). The psychological approach to human memory. In M. Rosenzweig & E. R. Bennet (Eds.), *Neural mechanisms of learning memory* (pp. 3–48). Cambridge, MA: MIT Press.

Ruedrich, S. L. (1996). Beta adrenergic blocking medications for treatment of rage outbursts in mentally retarded persons. *Seminars in Clinical Neuropsychiatry, 1,* 115–121.

Rumsey, J. M. (1996). Neuroimaging. In G. R. Lyon & J. M. Rumsey (Eds.), *Neuroimaging in developmental dyslexia: A review and conceptualization* (pp. 57–77). Baltimore: Brookes.

Rumsey, J. M., Andreason, P., Zametkin, A. J., Aquino, T., King, A. C., Hamburger, S. D., Pikus, A., Rapoport, J. L., & Cohen, R. M. (1992). Failure to activate the left temporoparietal cortex in dyslexia: An oxygen 15 positron emission tomographic study. *Archives of Neurology, 49,* 527–534.

Rumsey, J. M., Berman, K. F., Denckla, M. B., Hamburger, S. D., Kruesi, M. J., & Weinberger, D. R. (1987). Regional cerebral blood flow in severe developmental dyslexia. *Archives of Neurology, 44,* 1144–1150.

Rumsey, J. M., Casanova, M., Mannheim, G. B., Patronas, N., De Vaughn, N., Hamburger, S. D., & Aquino, T. (1996). Corpus callosum morphology, as measured with MRI, in dyslexic men. *Biological Psychiatry, 39,* 769–775.

Rumsey, J. M., Donohue, B. C., Brady, D. R., Nace, K., Giedd, J. N., & Andreason, P. (1997). A magnetic resonance imaging study of planum temporale asymmetry in men with developmental dyslexia. *Archives of Neurology, 54,* 1481–1489.

Rumsey, J. M., & Eden, G. (1998). Functional neuroimaging of developmental dyslexia: Regional cerebral blood flow in dyslexic men. In B. K. Shapiro, P. J. Accardo, & A. J. Capute (Eds.), *Specific reading disability: A view of the spectrum* (pp. 35–62). Timonium, MD: York Press.

Rumsey, J. M., Nace, K., & Andreason, P. (1995). Phonologic and orthographic components of reading imaged with PET. *Journal of the International Neuropsychological Society, 1,* 180.

Rumsey, J. M., Zametkin, A. J., Andreason, P., Hanahan, A. P., Hamburger, S. D., Aquino, T., King, A. C., Pikus, A., & Cohen, R. M. (1994). Normal activation of frontotemporal language cortex in dyslexia, as measured with oxygen 15 position emission tomography. *Archives of Neurology, 51,* 27–38.

Rutter, M. (1978). Prevalence and types of dyslexia. In A. L. Benton & D. Pearl (Eds.), *Dyslexia.* New York: Oxford University Press.

Rutter, M. (Ed.). (1983). *Developmental neuropsychiatry.* New York: Guilford Press.

Rutter, M., Chadwick, O., & Shaffer, D. (1983). Head injury. In M. Rutter (Ed.), *Developmental neuropsychiatry* (pp. 83–111). New York: Guilford Press.

Rutter, M., & Graham, P. (1968). The reliability and validity of the psychiatric assessment of the child: Interview with the child. *British Journal of Psychiatry, 114,* 563–579.

Rutter, M., Graham, P., & Yule, W. (1970). *A Neuropsychiatric study in childhood.* London: Spastics International Medical Publications.

Rutter, M., Tizard, J., & Whitemore, K. (1970). *Education, health and behavior.* London: Longman.

Rutter, M., Tizard, J., Yule, W., Graham, P., & Whitmore, K. (1976). Isle of Wight studies 1964–1974. *Psychological Medicine, 6,* 313–332.

Ryan, N. D. (1992). The pharmacological treatment of child and adolescent depression. *Psychiatric Clinic of North America, 15,* 29–40.

Ryan, S. G. (1998). Genetic susceptibility to neurodevelopmental disorders. *Journal of Child Neurology, 14,* 187–195.

Safer, D., Allen, R., & Barr, E. (1972). Depression of growth in hyperactive children on stimulant drugs. *New England Journal of Medicine, 257,* 217–221.

Safer, D., & Krager, J. M. (1988). A survey of medication treatment for hyperactive/inattentive students. *Journal of the American Medical Association, 260,* 2256–2258.

Safer, D. J., Zito, J. M., & Fine, E. M. (1996). Increased methylphenidate usage for attention deficit disorder in the 1990s. *Pediatrics, 98,* 1084–1088.

Salanova, V., Morris, H. H., Van Ness, P., Kotagal, P., Wyllie, E., & Luders, H. (1995). Frontal lobe seizures: Electroclinical syndromes. *Epilepsia, 36,* 16–24.

Sallee, F., Stiller, R., & Perel, J. (1992). Pharmacodynamics of pemoline in attention deficit disorder with hyperactivity. *Journal of the American Academy of Child and Adolescent Psychiatry, 31,* 244–251.

Sallee, F., Stiller, R., Perel, J., & Bates, T. (1985). Oral pemoline kinetics in hyperactive children. *Clinical Pharmacological Therapy, 37,* 606–609.

Sameroff, A. J. (1998). Environmental risk factors in infancy. *Pediatrics, 102,* 1287–1292.

Sanberg, P. R., McConville, B. J., Fogelson, H. M., Manderscheid, P. Z., Parker, K. W., Blythe, M. M., Klykylo, W. M., & Norman, A. B. (1989). Nicotine potentiates the effect of haloperidol in animals and in patients with Tourette's syndrome. *Biomedical Pharmacotherapy, 43,* 19–23.

Sanberg, P. R., Shytle, R. D., & Silver, A. A. (1998). Treatment of Tourette's syndrome with mecamylamine. *Lancet, 352,* 705.

Sanberg, P. R., Silver, A. A., Shytle, R. D., Phillip, M. K., Kahill, D., Fogelson, H. M., & McConville, B. J. (1997). Nicotine for the treatment of Tourette's syndrome. *Pharmacology and Therapeutics, 74,* 21–25.

Sandberg, S. T., Rutter, M., & Taylor, E. (1978). Hyperkinetic disorder in psychiatric clinic attenders. *Developmental Medicine and Child Neurology, 20,* 279–299.

Sandler, A. D., Watson, T. E., Footo, M., Levine, M. D., Coleman, W. L., & Hooper, S. R. (1992). Neurodevelopmental study of writing disorders in middle childhood. *Developmental and Behavioral Pediatrics, 13,* 17–23.

Santelli, J. S., Birn, A. E., & Linde, J. (1992). School placement for human immunodeficiency virus-infected children: The Baltimore experience. *Pediatrics, 89,* 843–848.

Sarnoff, A., Mednick, B., & Baert, A. (Eds.). (1981). *Prospective longitudinal research: An empirical basis for the primary prevention of psychosocial Disorders.* Geneva, Switzerland: World Health Organization.

Sarter, M., Bruno, J. P., Givens, B., Moore, H., McGaugh, J., & McMahon, K. (1996). Neuronal mechanisms mediating drug-induced cognition enhancement: Cognitive activity as a necessary intervening variable. *Cognitive Brain Research, 3,* 329–343.

Sattler, J. (1988). *Assessment of children* (3rd ed.). San Diego, CA: Author.

Satz, P. (1976). Cerebral dominance and reading disability: An old problem revisited. In D. S. Baker & R. M. Knights (Eds.), *Neuropsychology of learning disorders: Therapeutic approaches* (pp. 273–294). Baltimore: University Park Press.

Satz, P., Alfano, M. S., Light, R., Morgenstern, H., Zaucha, K., Asarnow, R. F., & Newton, S. (1999). Persistent post-concussive syndrome: A proposed methodology and literature review to determine the effects, if any, of mild head and other bodily injury. *Journal of Clinical and Experimental Neuropsychology, 21,* 620–628.

Satz, P., Buka, S., Lipsitt, L., & Seidman, L. (1998). The long-term prognosis of learning disabled children: A review of studies 1954–1993. In B. K. Shapiro, P. J. Accardo, & A. J. Capute (Eds.), *Specific reading disability: A view of the spectrum* (pp. 223–250). Timonium, MD: York Press.

Satz, P., & Fletcher, J. M. (1982). *The Florida Kindergarten Screening Battery.* Odessa, FL: Psychological Assessment Resources.

Satz, P., & Friel, J. (1973). Some predictive antecedents of specific reading disability: A preliminary one-year follow-up, 1977–1978. In P. Satz & J. J. Ross (Eds.), *The disabled learner: Early detection and intervention* (pp. 79–98). Rotterdam, The Netherlands: Rotterdam University Press.

Satz, P., & Morris, R. (1981). Learning disability subtypes: A review. In F. J. Pirozzolo & M. C. Wittrock (Eds.), *Neuropsychological and cognitive processes in reading* (pp. 109–141). New York: Academic Press.

Satz, P., & Sparrow, S. (1970). Specific developmental dyslexia: A theoretical formulation. In D. J. Baker & P. Satz (Eds.), *Specific reading disability: Advances in theory and methods* (pp. 17–39). Amsterdam, The Netherlands: Rotterdam University Press.

Satz, P., Taylor, H. G., Friel, J., & Fletcher, J. M. (1978). Some developmental precursors of reading disabilities: A 6 year follow-up. In A. E. Benton & D. Pearl (Eds.), *Dyslexia: An appraisal of current knowledge* (pp. 315–347). New York: Oxford University Press.

Saul, R. C. (1985). Nortriptyline in attention deficit disorder. *Clinic of Neuropharmacology, 8*, 382–384.

Saunders, R. E. (1973). *Links to writing, reading and spelling.* Cambridge, MA: Educators Publishing Service.

Sawaguchi, T., Matsumura, M., & Kuboto, K. (1988). Dopamine enhances the neuronal activity of spatial short-term memory task in the primate pre-frontal cortex. *Neuroscience Research, 5*, 465–473.

Scarborough, H. S. (1998). Early identification of children at risk for reading disabilities: Phonological awareness and some other promising predictors. In B. K. Shapiro, P. J. Accardo, & A. J. Capute (Eds.), *Specific reading disability: A view of the spectrum* (pp. 75–107). Timonium, MD: York Press.

Scarborough, H. S., & Dobrich, W. (1990). Development of children with early language delay. *Journal of Speech and Hearing Research, 33*, 70–83.

Schachar, R. J., Tannock, R., & Logan, G. (1993). Inhibitory control, impulsiveness, and attention deficit hyperactivity disorder. *Clinical Psychology Review, 13*, 721–739.

Scheibel, A., Conrad, T., Perdue, S., Tomiyasu, U., & Wechsler, A. (1990). A quantitative study of dendrite complexity in selected areas of human cerebral cortex. *Brain and Cognition, 12*, 85–101.

Schilder, P. (1931). Finger agnosia, finger apraxia, finger aphasia. *Nervenarzt, 4*, 625–629.

Schilder, P. (1935). *Image and appearance of the human body.* London: Kegan Paul, Trench, Trubner.

Schilder, P. (1938a). Organic background of obsessions and compulsions. *American Journal of Psychiatry, 94*, 1397–1413.

Schilder, P. (1938b). Psychological implications of motor development in children. *Institute on the Exceptional Child, Child Research Clinic, Woods School, 4*, 38–59.

Schneider, J. W., Griffith, D. R., & Chasnoff, I. J. (1989). Infants exposed to cocaine in utero: Implications for developmental assessment and intervention. *Infants and Young Children, 2*, 25–36.

Schroeder, J., Richter, P., Geiger, F. J., & Niethammer, R. (1993). Diskrete motorische und sensorische Stoerungen (neurologische soft signs) im Akutverlauf endogener Psychosen. *Zeitschrift fuer Klinische Psychologie, Psychiatrie und Psychotherapie, 41*, 190–206.

Schuerholz, L. J. (1997). Neuromotor functioning in children with Tourette's syndrome with and without attention deficit hyperactivity disorder. *Journal of Child Neurology, 12*, 438–442.

Schuerholz, L. J., Singer, H. S., & Denckla, M. B. (1998). Gender study of neuropsychological and neuromotor function in children with Tourette's syndrome with and without attention-deficit hyperactivity disorder. *Journal of Child and Neurology, 13*, 277–282.

Schull, W. J., & Otake, M. (1991). A review of forty-five years study of Hiroshima and Nagasaki atomic bomb survivors. Future studies of the prenatally exposed survivors. *Journal of Radiation Research, 32*(Suppl.), 385–393.

Schulte, A. C., Conners, C. K., & Osborne, S. S. (1999). Linkages between attention deficit disorders and reading disability. In D. Duane (Ed.), *Reading and attention disorders* (pp. 161–184). Baltimore: York Press.

Schulte, F. J. (1988). Pathophysiological mechanisms leading to permanent brain damage in surviving children. In F. Kubli, N. Patel, W. Schimidt, & O. Lindercamp (Eds.), *Perinatal events and brain damage in surviving children* (pp. 59–63). New York: Springer-Verlag.

Schultz, R. T., Carter, A. S., Gladstone, M., Scahill, L. D., Leckman, J. F., Peterson, B. S., Zhang, H., Cohen, D. J., & Pauls, D. L. (1998). Visual-motor, visuoperceptual and fine motor functioning in children with Tourette's syndrome. *Neuropsychology, 12*, 134–145.

Schultz, R. T., Cho, N. K., Staib, L. H., Kier, L. E., Fletcher, J. M., Shaywitz, S. E., Shankweiler, D. P., Katz, L., Gore, J. C., Duncan, J. S., & Shaywitz, B. A. (1994). Brain morphology in normal and dyslexic children: The influence of sex and age. *Annals of Neurology, 35,* 732–742.

Schumaker, J. B., & Deshler, D. C. (1988). Implementing the regular education initiative in secondary schools: A different ballgame. *Journal of Learning Disabilities, 21,* 36–42.

Scoville, W. B., & Milner, B. (1957). Loss memory after bilateral hippocampal lesions. *Journal of Neurology, Neurosurgery and Psychiatry, 20,* 11–21.

Seidman, L. J., Biederman, J., Weber, W., Hatch, M., & Faraone, S. V. (1998). Neuropsychological function in adults with attention-deficit hyperactivity disorder. *Biological Psychiatry, 44,* 260–268.

Seignot, M. J. N. (1961). Un Case de la Maladie des Tics de Gilles de la Tourette Gueri par le R-1625. *Annals Medicine Psycholgie, 119,* 578–579.

Seligman, M., & Groves, D. (1970). Non-transient learned helplessness. *Psychonomic Science, 19,* 191–192.

Sell, S., Merrill, R., Doyne, E., & Zimsky, E., Jr. (1972). Long term sequelae of Hemophilus Influenzae Meningitis. *Pediatrics, 49,* 206–211.

Selye, H. (1956). *The stress of life.* New York: McGraw-Hill.

Semrud-Clikeman, M. (1997). Evidence from imaging on the relationship between brain structure and developmental language disorders. *Seminars in Pediatric Neurology, 4,* 117–124.

Semrud-Clikeman, M., Biederman, J., Sprich-Buchminster, S., Lehman, B. K., Faraone, S. V., & Norman, D. (1992). Comorbidity between ADDH and learning disability: A review and report in a clinically referred sample. *Journal of the American Academy of Child and Adolescent Psychiatry, 31,* 439–448.

Sergeant, J. (1996). A theory of attention: An information processing perspective. In G. R. Lyon & N. A. Krasnegor (Eds.), *Attention, memory, and executive function* (pp. 57–69). Baltimore: Brookes.

Shaffer, D., Fisher, P., Dulcan, M. K., Davies, M., Piacentini, J., Schwab-Stone, M. E., Lahey, B. B., Bourdon, K., Jensen, P. S., Bird, H. R., Canino, G., & Gegier, D. A. (1996). The NIMH Diagnostic Interview Schedule for Children Version 2.3 (DISC-2.3): Description, acceptability, prevalence rates, and performance in the MECA Study. Methods for the epidemiology of child and adolescent mental disorders study. *Journal of the American Academy of Child and Adolescent Psychiatry, 35,* 865–877.

Shaffer, D., O'Connor, P., Shafer, S., & Purpis, S. (1983). Neurological soft signs: Their origins and significance for behavior. In M. Rutter (Ed.), *Developmental neuropsychiatry* (pp. 144–164). New York: Guilford Press.

Shaffer, D., Schwab-Stone, M., Fisher, P., Piacentini, J., Davies, M., Conners, C. K., & Regier, D. (1993). The diagnostic interview schedule for children-revised version (DISC-R): 1.

Shaffer, S. Q., Stokman, C. J., Shaffer, D., Ng, S., O'Connor, P., & Schonfeld, I. S. (1986). Ten-year consistency of neurological tests performance of children without focal neurological deficit. *Developmental Medicine and Child Neurology, 28,* 417–427.

Shankweiler, D., Liberman, I. Y., Mark, L. S., Fowler, C. A., & Fischer, F. W. (1979). The speech code and learning to read. *Journal of Experimental Psychology: Human Learning and Memory, 5,* 531–545.

Shapiro, A., & Shapiro, E. (1988). Treatment of tic disorders with haloperidol. In D. J. Cohen, R. D. Bruun, & J. F. Leckman (Eds.), *Tourette's syndrome and tic disorder: Clinical understanding and treatment* (pp. 268–280). New York: Wiley.

Shapiro, B. K., Accardo, P. J., & Capute, A. J. (Eds.). (1998). *Specific reading disability: A view of the spectrum.* Timonium, MD: York Press.

Shapiro, E. R. (1978). The psychodynamics and developmental psychology of the borderline patient: A review of the literature. *American Journal of Psychiatry, 135,* 1305–1315.

Shapiro, T., Burkes, L., Petti, T. A., & Ranz, J. (1978). Consistency of nonfocal neurological signs. *Journal of the American Academy of Child Psychiatry, 17,* 70–79.

Shashoua, V. E. (1968). RNA changes in goldfish brain during learning. *Nature, 217,* 238–240.

Shaw, G. A., & Giambra, L. (1993). Task-unrelated thoughts of college students diagnosed as hyperactive in childhood. *Developmental Neuropsychology, 9,* 17–30.

Shaywitz, B. A., Cohen, D., & Bowers, M. (1977). CSF monoamine metabolism in children with minimal brain dysfunction: Evidence for alteration of brain dopamine. *Journal of Pediatrics, 90,* 67–71.

Shaywitz, B. A., Fletcher, J. M., Holahan, J. M., & Shaywitz, S. E. (1992). Discrepancy compared to low achievement definitions of reading disability: Results from the Connecticut Longitudinal Study. *Journal of Learning Disabilities, 25,* 639–648.

Shaywitz, B. A., Fletcher, J. M., & Shaywitz, S. E. (1994). Interrelationships between reading disability and attention deficit-hyperactivity disorder. In A. J. Capute, P. J. Accardo, & B. K. Shapiro. (Eds.), *Learning disabilities spectrum: ADD, ADHD, & LD.* Timonium, MD: York Press.

Shaywitz, B. A., Holford, T. R., Holahan, J. M., Fletcher, J. M., Stuebing, K. K., Francis, D. J., & Shaywitz, S. E. (1995). A Matthew effect for IQ but not for reading: Results from a longitudinal study. *Reading Research Quarterly, 30,* 894–906.

Shaywitz, B. A., & Shaywitz, S. E. (1994). Measuring and analyzing change. In G. R. Lyon (Ed.), *Frames of reference for the assessment of learning disabilities* (pp. 59–68). Baltimore: Brookes.

Shaywitz, B. A., Shaywitz, S. E., Byrne, T., Cohen, D. J., & Rothman, S. (1983). Attention deficit disorder: Quantitative analysis of CT. *Neurology, 33,* 1500–1503.

Shaywitz, B. A., Shaywitz, S. E., & Fletcher, J. M. (1992). The Yale Center for the Study of Learning and Attention Disorder. *Learning Disabilities: A Multidisciplinary Journal, 3,* 1–12.

Shaywitz, B. A., Shaywitz, S. E., Liberman, I. Y., Fletcher, J. M., Shankweiler, D. P., Duncan, J. S., Katz, L., Liberman, A. M., & Francis, D. J. (1991). Neurolinguistic and biologic mechanisms in dyslexia. In D. D. Duane & D. B. Gray (Eds.), *The reading brain: The biological basis of dyslexia* (pp. 27–52). Parkton, MD: York Press.

Shaywitz, B. A., Shaywitz, S. E., Pugh, K. R., Skudlarski, P., Fulbright, R. K., Constable, R. T., Bronen, R. A., Fletcher, J. M., Liberman, A. M., Shankweiler, D. P., Katz, L., Lacadie, C., Marchione, K. E., & Gore, J. C. (1996). Functional magnetic resonance imaging as a tool to understand reading and reading disability. In R. W. Thatcher, G. R. Lyon, J. Rumsey, & N. Krasnegor (Eds.), *Developmental neuroimaging: Mapping the development of brain and behavior* (pp. 157–167). New York: Academic Press.

Shaywitz, S. E., Escobar, M. D., Shaywitz, B. A., Fletcher, J. M., & Makuch, R. W. (1992). Evidence that dyslexia may represent the lower tail of a normal distribution of reading ability. *New England Journal of Medicine, 326,* 145–150.

Shaywitz, S. E., Fletcher, J. M., Holahan, J. M., Shneider, A. E., Marchione, K. E., Stuebing, K. K., Francis, D. J., Pugh, K. R., & Shaywitz, B. A. (1999). Persistence of dyslexia: The Connecticut Longitudinal Study at adolescence. *Pediatrics, 104,* 1351–1359.

Shaywitz, S. E., Fletcher, J. M., & Shaywitz, B. A. (1994a). Issues in the definition and classification of attention deficit disorder. *Topics in Language Disorders, 14,* 1–25.

Shaywitz, S. E., Fletcher, J. M., & Shaywitz, B. A. (1994b). A new conceptual model for dyslexia. In A. J. Capute, P. J. Accardo, & B. K. Shapiro (Eds.), *Learning disabilities spectrum: ADD, ADHD, & LD.* Timonium, MD: York Press.

Shaywitz, S. E., & Shaywitz, B. A. (1988). Attention deficit disorder: Current perspectives. In J. F. Kavanaugh & T. J. Truss (Eds.), *Learning Disabilities: Proceedings of the national conference*. Parkton, MD: York Press.

Shaywitz, S. E., & Shaywitz, B. A. (1999). Dyslexia: From epidemiology to neurobiology. In D. D. Duane (Ed.), *Reading and attention disorders* (pp. 123–128). Baltimore: York Press.

Shaywitz, S. E., Shaywitz, B. A., Cohen, D., & Young, J. G. (1983). Monoaminergic mechanisms in hyperactivity. In M. Rutter (Ed.), *Developmental neuropsychiatry* (pp. 330–347). New York: Guilford Press.

Shaywitz, S. E., Shaywitz, B. A., Fletcher, J. M., & Escobar, M. D. (1990). Prevalence of reading disability in boys and girls: Results of the Connecticut Longitudinal Study. *Journal of the American Medical Association, 264,* 998–1002.

Shaywitz, S. E., Shaywitz, B. A., Pugh, K. R., Fulbright, R. K., Constable, R. T., Mencl, W. W., Shankweiler, D. P., Liberman, A. M., Skudlarski, P., Fletcher, J. M., Katz, L., Marchione, K. E., Lacadie, C., Gatenby, C., & Gore, J. C. (1998). Functional disruption in the organization of the brain for reading in dyslexia. *Proceedings of the National Academy of Sciences, USA, 95,* 2636–2641.

Sheard, M., Marini, J., Bridges, C., & Wagner, E. (1976). The effect of lithium on impulsive, aggressive behavior in man. *American Journal of Psychiatry, 133,* 1409–1413.

Sheffield, B. (1996). Handwriting: A neglected cornerstone of literacy. *Annals of Dyslexia, 46,* 21–35.

Shekim, W. O., Davis, L. C., Bylund, D. B., Brunnagraber, E., Fikes, L., & Lanham, J. (1982). Platelet MAO in children with attention deficit disorder and hyperactivity: A pilot study. *American Journal of Psychiatry, 139,* 936–938.

Shekim, W. O., DeKirmenjian, H., Chapel, J. L., Javid, J., & Davis, J. M. (1979). Norepinephrine metabolism and clinical response to dextroamphetamine in hyperactive boys. *Journal of Pediatrics, 95,* 389–394.

Shekim, W. O., Javid, J., Davis, J. M., & Bylund, D. B. (1983). Urinary MHPG and HVA excretion in boys with attention deficit disorder and hyperactivity treated with D-amphetamine. *Biological Psychiatry, 18,* 707–714.

Shirley, M. (1939). A behavior syndrome characterizing prematurely born children. *Child Development, 10,* 115–128.

Shokraii, N., & Youself, S. (1998). How congress can help limited English proficient students to learn English. *Heritage Foundation Backgrounder, 1206,* 1–12.

Shucard, D. W., Cummins, K., Gray, E., Larismith, J., & Welanka, P. (1985). Electrophysiological studies of reading-disabled children: In search of subtypes. In D. B. Gray & J. F. Kavanaugh (Eds.), *Behavioral measures of dyslexia* (pp. 87–106). Parkton, MD: York Press.

Shytle, R. D., Silver, A. A., Sheehan, K. H., Wilkinson, B. J., Newman, M., Sanberg, P. R., & Sheehan, D. (2000). *The Tourette's disorder scale (TODS): Development, reliability, and validity.* Manuscript submitted for publication.

Siegel, D. F., & Hanson, R. A. (1991). Kindergarten educator policies: Separating myth from reality. *Early Educational Development, 2,* 5–31.

Siegel, L. S. (1982). Perinatal and environmental factors as predictors of the cognitive and language development of preterm and full term infants. *Child Development, 53,* 963–973.

Siegel, L. S. (1983). The prediction of possible learning disabilities in pre-term and full-term children. In T. Field & A. Sostek (Eds.), *Infants born at risk: Physiological perceptual and cognitive processes* (pp. 295–315). New York: Grune & Stratton.

Silva-Araujo, A., Tavares, M. A., Patacao, M. H., & Coroliono, R. M. (1996). Retinal hemorrhages associated with in utero exposure to cocaine: Experimental and clinical findings. *Retina, 16,* 411–418.

Silva, P. A., McGee, R., & Williams, S. M. (1985). Some characteristics of 9-year-old boys with general reading backwardness or specific reading retardation. *Journal of Child Psychology and Psychiatry and Allied Disciplines, 26,* 407–421.

Silver, A. A. (1952). Postural and righting responses in children. *Journal of Pediatrics, 41,* 493–498.

Silver, A. A. (1984). Children in classes for the severely emotionally disturbed. *Journal of Developmental and Behavioral Pediatrics, 5,* 49–54.

Silver, A. A. (1988). Intrapsychic processes and adjustment in Tourette's syndrome. In D. J. Cohen, R. D. Bruun, & J. F. Leckman (Eds.), *Tourette's syndrome and tic disorder: Clinical understanding and treatment* (pp. 197–206). New York: Wiley.

Silver, A. A., & Hagin, R. A. (1964). Specific reading disability: Follow-up studies. *American Journal of Orthopsychiatry, 34,* 95–102.

Silver, A. A., & Hagin, R. A. (1972). Profile of a first grade: A basis for preventive psychiatry. *Journal of the American Academy of Child Psychiatry, 11,* 645–674.

Silver, A. A., & Hagin, R. A. (1981). *SEARCH: A scanning instrument for the prevention of learning disability* (2nd ed.). Cranford, NJ: Shoestring Press.

Silver, A. A., & Hagin, R. A. (1985). Outcomes of learning disabilities in adolescence. In S. Feinstein (Ed.), *Adolescent psychiatry* (pp. 197–213). Chicago: University of Chicago Press.

Silver, A. A., & Hagin R. A. (1990). *Disorders of learning in childhood.* Wiley, New York.

Silver, A. A., Hagin, R. A., & Beecher, R. (1981). A program for secondary prevention of learning disabilities: Results in academic achievement and in emotional adjustment. *Journal of Prevention in Psychiatry, 1,* 77–87.

Silver, A. A., & Sanberg, P. (1993). Transdermal nicotine patch potentiates the therapeutic action of haloperidol in Tourette's syndrome. *Lancet, 342,* 182.

Silver, A. A., Shytle, R. D., Phillip, M. K., & Sanberg, P. R. (1996). Case study: Long-term potentiation of neuroleptics with transdermal nicotine in Tourette's syndrome. *Journal of the American Academy of Child and Adolescent Psychiatry, 35,* 1631–1636.

Silver, A. A., Shytle, R. D., Sheehan, K. H., Sheehan, D. V., Ramos, A. E., & Sanberg, P. R. (2001). Multi-center double blind placebo controlled study of mecamylamine monotherapy for Tourette's disorder. *Journal of the American Academy of Child and Adolescent Psychiatry, 40,* 1103–1110.

Silver, J. M., Yudofsky, S. C., Slater, J. A., Gold, R. K., Stryer, B. L., Williams, D. T., Wolland, H., & Endicott, J. (1996). Propranolol treatment of chronically hospitalized aggressive patients. *Journal of Neuropsychiatry and Clinical Neurosciences, 11,* 328–335.

Silver, L. B. (1981). The relationship between learning disabilities, hyperactivity, distractibility, and behavioral problems. *Journal of the American Academy of Child Psychiatry, 20,* 385–397.

Silver, L. B. (1989). Psychological and family problems associated with learning disabilities: Assessment and intervention. *Journal of the American Academy of Child and Adolescent Psychiatry, 28,* 319–325.

Silverstein, F., Smith, C. B., & Johnstone, M. V. (1985). Effect of clonidine on platelet alpha 2-adrenoreceptors and plasma norepinephrine of children with Tourette's syndrome. *Developmental Medicine and Child Neurology, 27,* 793–799.

Simmons, J. E. (1987). *Psychiatric examination of children* (4th ed.). Philadelphia: Lea & Febiger.

Simon, H., Taghzouti, K., & LeMoal, M. (1986). Defects in spatial-memory tasks following lesions of septal dopaminergic terminals in the rat. *Behavioral Brain Research, 19,* 7–16.

Simonds, R. S. (1999). Epidemiology of HIV infection. In S. L. Zeichner & J. S. Read (Eds.), *Handbook of pediatric HIV care* (pp. 96–104). Philadelphia: Lippincott, Williams, & Wilkins.

Singer, H. S., Giuliano, J. D., Hansen, B. H., Hallett, J. J., Laurino, J. P., Benson, M., & Kiessling, L. S. (1998). Antibodies against human putamen in children with Tourette's syndrome. *Neurology, 50,* 1618–1624.

Singer, H. S., Reiss, A. L., Brown, R. N., Aylward, E. H., Shih, B. A., Chee, E., Harris, E. L., Reader, M. J., Chase, G. A., Bryan, R. N., & Denckla, M. B. (1993). Volumetric MRI changes in basal ganglia of children with Tourette's syndrome. *Neurology, 43,* 950–956.

Singer, L. T., Garber, R., & Kleigman, R. (1991). Neurobehavioral sequelae of fetal cocaine exposure. *Journal of Pediatrics, 119,* 667–672.

Skarda, D. (1974). *Preacademic program for children delayed in oral communication skills.* (ERIC Document Reproduction Service No. ED 096 776)

Skov, J., Lou, H., & Pederson, H. (1984). Perinatal brain ischemina: Impact at 4 years of age. *Developmental Medicine and child Neurology, 26,* 353–357.

Skuy, M., Taylor, M., O'Carroll, S., Fridjhon, P., & Rosenthal, L. (2000). Performance of Black and White South African children on the Wechsler Intelligence Scale for Children-Revised and the Kaufman Assessment Battery. *Psychological Reports, 86,* 727–737.

Slingerland, B. H. (1971). *Multisensory approach to language arts for specific learning disability children.* Cambridge, MA: Educators Publishing Services.

Small, L. (1980). *Neuropsychodiagnosis in psychotherapy.* New York: Brunner/Mazel.

Smalley, S. L., Bailey, J. N., Palmer, C. G., Cantwell, D. P., McGough, J. J., Del'Homme, M. A., Asarnow, J. R., Woodward, J. A., Ramsey, C., & Nelson, S. F. (1998). Evidence that the dopamine D4 receptor is a susceptibility gene in attention deficit hyperactivity disorder. *Molecular Psychiatry, 3,* 427–430.

Smith, J. B. (1971). Eye testing in children. *Pediatric Clinics of North America, 18,* 333–342.

Smith, M. S., & Bissell, J. (1970). Report analysis: The impact of Head Start. *Harvard Educational Review, 40,* 51–104.

Smith, N. B. (1928). Matching ability as a factor in first grade reading. *Journal of Educational Sociology, 19,* 500–571.

Smith, S. D., Brower, A. M., Cardon, L. R., & DeFries, J. C. (1998). Genetics of reading disability: Further evidence for a gene on chromosome 6. In B. K. Shapiro, P. J. Accardo, & A. J. Capute (Eds.), *Specific reading disability: A view of the spectrum* (pp. 63–74). Timonium, MD: York Press.

Smith, S. D., Kimberling, W. J., & Pennington, B. F. (1991). Screening for multiple genes influencing dyslexia. *Reading and Writing, 3,* 285–298.

Smith, S. D., Kimberling, W. J., Pennington, B. F., & Lubs, H. A. (1983). Specific reading disability: Identification of an inherited form through linkage analysis. *Science, 219,* 1345–1347.

Smith, S. D., Pennington, B. F., Kimberling, W. J., & Ing, P. S. (1990). Familial dyslexia: Use of genetic linkage data to define subtypes. *Journal of the American Academy of Child and Adolescent Psychiatry, 29,* 204–213.

Snow, C. E. (1986). Innovative second language education: Bilingual immersion program. *Center for Language Education and Research.*

Snow, C. E., Burns, M. S., & Griffin, P. (Eds.). (1999). *Report of the committee on the prevention of reading difficulties in young children* [National Research Council]. Washington, DC: National Academy Press.

Snow, C. E., & Hoefnagel-Hohle, M. (1977). Age differences in the pronunciation of foreign sounds. *Language and Speech, 20,* 357–365.

Snowling, M. J., Bishop, D. V., & Stothard, S. E. (2000). Is preschool language impairment a risk factor for dyslexia in adolescence? *Journal of Child Psychology and Psychiatry, 41,* 587–600.

Solanto, M. V. (1998). Neuropsychopharmacological mechanisms of stimulant drug action in attention-deficit hyperactivity disorder: A review and integration. *Behavioural Brain Research, 94,* 127–152.

Solomon, S., Hotchkiss, E., Saravay, S. M., Bayer, C., Ramsey, P., & Blum, R. S. (1983). Impairment of memory function by antihypertensive medication. *Archives of General Psychiatry, 40,* 1109–1112.

Sorkin, E. M., & Heel, R. C. (1986). Guanfacine: A review of its pharmacodynamic and pharmacokinetic properties, and therapeutic efficacy in the treatment of hypertension. *Drugs, 31,* 301–336.

Sparrow, S. S., & Satz, P. (1970). Dyslexia, laterality and neuropsychological development. In D. Bakker & P. Satz (Eds.), *Specific reading disabilities: Advances in theory and method* (pp. 41–60). Amsterdam: Rotterdam University Press.

Spearman, C. (1923). Further note on the "Theory of Two Factors." *British Journal of Psychology, 13,* 266–270.

Speech, T. J., Rao, S. M., Osmon, D. C., & Sperry, L. T. (1993). A double-blind controlled study of methyphenidate treatment in closed head injury. *Brain Injury, 7,* 333–338.

Spencer, T., Biederman, J., Harding, M., O'Donnell, D., Wilens, T., Coffey, B., & Geller, D. (1998). Disentangling the overlap between Tourette's disorder and ADHD. *Journal of Child Psychology and Psychiatry, and Allied Disciplines, 39,* 1037–1044.

Sperling, R. S., Shapiro, D. E., Coombs, R. W., Todd, J. A., Herman, S. A., McSherry, G. D., et al. (1996). Maternal viral load, zidovudine treatment, and the risk of transmission of human immunodeficiency virus type 1 from mother to infant. *New England Journal of Medicine, 335,* 1621–1629.

Sperry, R. W. (1985). Consciousness, personal, identity, and the divided brain. In D. F. Benson & E. Zaidel (Eds.), *The dual brain: Hemispheric specialization in humans: UCLA forum in medical sciences* (pp. 11–26). New York: Guilford Press.

Sprague, R. L. (1978). Principles of clinical trials and social ethical and legal issues of drug use in children. In J. S. Werry (Ed.), *Pediatric psychopharmacology* (pp. 109–135). New York: Brunner/Mazel.

Sprague, R. L., & Sleator, E. K. (1977). Methylphenidate in hyperactive children: Differences in dose effects on learning and social behavior. *Science, 198,* 1274–1276.

Spraings, V. (1966). *The Spraings Multiple Choice Bender-Gestalt Test.* Olympia, WA: Sherwood Press.

Spreen, O. (1987). *Learning disabled children growing up: A follow-up into adulthood.* In D. J. Bakker & O. Spreen (Eds.), Lisse, The Netherlands: Swets & Zeitlinger.

Spreen, O. (1989). Learning disability, neurology, and long-term outcome: Some implications for the individual and for society. *Journal of Clinical and Experimental Neuropsychology, 11,* 389–408.

Spreen, O., & Benton, A. L. (1969). *Spreen-Benton language examination profile.* Iowa City: University of Iowa.

Spreen, O., & Haaf, R. G. (1986). Empirically derived learning disability subtypes: A replication attempt and longitudinal patterns over 15 years. *Journal of Learning Disabilities, 19,* 170–180.

Sproles, E., Azerrad, J., Williamson, C., & Merrill, R. (1969). Meningitis due to hemophilus influenzae: Long term sequelae. *Journal of Pediatrics, 75,* 782–798.

Squire, L. R., & Barondes, S. H. (1973). Memory impairment during prolonged training in mice given inhibitors of cerebral protein synthesis. *Brain Research, 56,* 215–225.

Squire, L. R., & Becker, C. K. (1975). Inhibitors of cerebral protein synthesis impairs long term habituation. *Brain Research, 57,* 367–372.

Squire, L. R., Knowlton, B., & Musen, G. (1993). The structure and organization of memory. *Annual Review of Psychology, 44,* 453–495.

Stahl, S. A. (1999). Why innovations come and go (and mostly go): The case of whole language. *Educational Researches, 28,* 13–22.

Stahl, S. M., & Berger, P. A. (1981). Physostigmine in Tourette's syndrome: Evidence for cholinergic underactivity. *American Journal of Psychiatry, 138,* 240–242.

Stanovich, K. E. (1982). Individual differences in the cognitive processes of reading: I word decoding. *Journal of Learning Disabilities, 15,* 485–493.

Stanovich, K. E. (1986a). Cognitive processes and the reading problems of learning disabled children: Evaluating the assumption of specificity. In J. K. Torgeson & B. Y. L. Wong (Eds.), *Psychological and educational perspectives on learning disabilities* (pp. 87–131). New York: Academic Press.

Stanovich, K. E. (1986b). Matthew effects in reading: Some consequences of individual differences in the acquisition of literacy. *Reading Research Quarterly, 21,* 360–407.

Stanovich, K. E. (1988). Explaining the differences between the dyslexic and the garden-variety poor reader: The phonological-core variable-difference model. *Journal of Learning Disabilities, 21,* 590–604.

Stanovich, K. E., & Siegel, L. S. (1994). Phenotypic performance profile of children with reading disabilities: A regression based test of the phonological-core variable-difference model. *Journal of Educational Psychology, 86,* 24–53.

Stark, R., & Tallal, P. (1979). Analysis of stop consonant production errors in developmentally dysphasia children. *Journal of Acoustical Society of America, 66,* 1703–1712.

Stein, H. H., & Yellin, T. O. (1967). Pemoline and magnesium hydroxide: Lack of effect on RNA and protein synthesis. *Science, 151,* 96–97.

Stein, J. (1993). Dyslexia: Impaired temporal information processing? In P. Tallal & A. M. Galaburda (Eds.), *Temporal information processing in the nervous system: Special reference to dyslexia and dysphasia* (Vol. 682, pp. 83–86). New York: Annals of the New York Academy of Sciences.

Stein, J., & Walsh, V. (1997). To see but not to read: The magnocellular theory of dyslexia. *Trends in Neurosciences, 20,* 147–152.

Steinmetz, H., Volkmann, J., Jancke, L., & Freund, H. J. (1991). Anatomical left-right asymmetry of language-related temporal cortex is different in left- and right-handers. *Annals of Neurology, 29,* 315–318.

Stelmack, R. M., Saxe, B. J., Noldy-Cullum, N., Campbell, K. B., & Armitage, R. (1988). Recognition of memory for words and event-related potentials: A comparison of normal and disabled readers. *Journal of Clinical and Experimental Neuropsychology, 10,* 185–200.

Stephens, R. J., & Sandor, P. (1999). Aggressive behaviour in children with Tourette's syndrome and comorbid attention-deficit hyperactivity disorder and obsessive-compulsive disorder. *Canadian Journal of Psychiatry, 44,* 1036–1042.

Stewart, M. A. (1980). Genetic, perinatal and constitutional factors in minimal brain dysfunctions. In H. E. Rie & E. D. Rie (Eds.), *Handbook of minimal brain dysfunctions: A critical view* (pp. 155–168). New York: Wiley.

Stewart, M. A. (1983). *Severe perinatal hazards.* In M. Rutter (Ed.), *Developmental neuropsychiatry* (pp. 15–31). New York: Guilford Press.

Stockman, I. J. (1996a). Communication development and disorders in African American children. In A. G. Kamhi, K. E. Pollock, & J. L. Harris (Eds.), *Phonological development and disorders in African American children* (pp. 117–153). Baltimore: Brookes.

Stockman, I. J. (1996b). The promises and pitfalls of language sample analysis as an assessment tool for linguistic minority children. *Language, Speech, and Hearing Services in Schools, 27,* 355–365.

Stodolsky, S. S., & Lesser, G. S. (1967). Learning patterns in the disadvantaged. *Harvard Education Review, 37,* 546–593.

Stone, P. A. (1998). Effects of collaborative strategies by regular and special education teachers on middle school education students' success within inclusion. *Dissertation Abstracts International, 59,* 1860.

Stores, G. (1978). School-children with epilepsy at risk for learning and behaviour problems. *Developmental Medicine and Child Neurology, 20,* 502–508.

Stores, G., Zaiwalla, Z., & Berger, N. (1991). Frontal lobe complex partial seizures in children: A form of epilepsy at particular risk of misdiagnosis. *Developmental Medicine and Child Neurology, 33,* 998–1009.

Stothard, S. E., Snowling, M. J., Bishop, D. V. M., Chipchase, B. B., Kaplan, C. A. (1998). Language-impaired preschoolers: A follow-up into adolescence. *Journal of Speech Language and Hearing Research, 41,* 407–418.

Strang, J. D., & Rourke, B. P. (1985). Arithmetic disability subtypes: The neuropsychological significance of specific arithmetical impairment in childhood. In B. P. Rourke (Ed.), *Neuropsychology of learning disabilities: Essential of subtype analysis* (pp. 167–183). New York: Guilford Press.

Strauss, A. A., & Kephart, N. C. (1955). *The psychopathology and education of the brain-injured child: Progress in theory and clinic* (Vol. 2). New York: Grune & Stratton.

Strauss, A. A., & Lehtinen, L. E. (1947). *The psychopathology and education of the brain-injured child* (Vol. 1). New York: Grune & Stratton.

Strauss, A. A., & Werner, H. (1943). Impairment in thought processes of brain-injured children. *American Journal of Mental Development, 47,* 291–295.

Strayhorn, J. M. (1995). The case of the uncertain prescriber. *Journal of the American Academy of Child Adolescent Psychiatry, 34,* 253–254.

Streissguth, A. P., Aase, J. M., Clarren, S. K., Randels, S. P., Ladue, R. A., & Smith, D. F. (1991). Fetal alcohol syndrome in adolescents and adults. *Journal of the American Medical Association, 265,* 1961–1967.

Studdert-Kennedy, M., & Mody, M. (1995). Auditory temporal perception deficits in the reading-impaired: A critical review of the evidence. *Psychonomic Bulletin and Review, 2,* 508–514.

Stunkard, H. W. (1932). *Lectures in biology.* Unpublished manuscript, New York University College of Arts and Science.

Summers, W. K., Majovski, L. V., Marsh, G. M., Tachiki, K., & Kling, A. (1986). Oral tetrahydroaminoacridine in long term treatment of senile dementia, Alzheimer type. *New England Journal of Medicine, 315,* 1241–1245.

Suzanne, T. E., Sundheim, P. V., Ryan, R. M., & Voeller, K. S. (1998). Mental retardation. In C. E. Coffey & R. A. Brumbeck (Eds.), *Textbook of Pediatric Neuropsychiatry* (pp. 649–690). Washington, DC: American Psychiatric Press.

Swanson, J. M., & Kinsbourne, M. (1976). Stimulant related state-dependent learning in hyperactive children. *Science, 192,* 1354–1357.

Swanson, J. M., Kinsbourne, M., Roberts, W., & Zucker, K. (1978). Time response analysis of the effect of stimulant medication on learning ability of children referred for hyperactivity. *Pediatrics, 61,* 21–29.

Swartz, B. E., Halgren, E., Delgado-Escueta, A. V., Feldstein, P., Maldonado, H., & Walsh, G. O. (1990). Multidisciplinary analysis of patients with extratemporal complex partial seizures: II. Predictive value of semiology. *Epilepsy Research, 5,* 146–154.

Swedo, S. E., Leonard, H. L., Garvey, M., Mettelman, B. B., Allen, A. J., Perlmutter, L., Lougee, L., Dow, S. P., Zamkoff, J., & Dubbert, B. K. (1998). Pediatric autoimmune neuropsychiatric disorders associated with streptococcal infections: Clinical description of the first 50 cases. *American Journal of Psychiatry, 155,* 264–271.

Swedo, S. E., Leonard, H. L., Mettelman, B. B., Allen, A. J., Rapoport, J. L., Dow, S. P., Kanter, M. E., Chapman, F., & Zabriskie, J. B. (1997). Identification of children with pediatric autoimmune neuropsychiatric disorders associated with streptococcal infections by a marker associated with rheumatic fever. *American Journal of Psychiatry, 154,* 110–112.

Swedo, S. E., Rapoport, J. L., Cheslow, D., Leonard, H. L., Ayoub, E. M., Hoiser, D. M., & Wald, E. R. (1989). High prevalence of obsessive-compulsive symptoms in patients with Sydenham's chorea. *American Journal of Psychiatry, 146,* 246–249.

Szatmari, P., Offord, D. R., & Boyle, M. H. (1989). Ontario child health study: Prevalence of attention deficit disorder with hyperactivity. *Journal of Child Psychology and Psychiatry and Allied Disciplines, 30,* 219–230.

Tableman, B., & Katzenmeyer, M. (1985). Infant mental health services: A newborn screener. In B. Tableman & R. Hess (Eds.), *Prevention: The Michigan experience* (Vol. 3, pp. 21–33). New York: Haworth Press.

Takano, K., & Ishguro, T. (1993). A study of clinical pictures and monoamine metabolism of Gilles de la Tourette's syndrome. *Seichin Shinkeigaku Zasshi-Psychiatria et Neurologia Japonica, 95,* 1–29.

Talairach, J., & Tournoux, P. (1988). *Co-planar stereotaxic atlas of the human brain: 3-dimensional proportional system: An approach to cerebral imaging.* New York: George Thieme Verlag Stuttgart.

Tallal, P., Merzenich, M., Jenkins, W. M., & Miller, S. L. (1994). Moving research from the laboratory to clinics and classrooms. In D. D. Duane (Ed.), *Reading and attention disorders* (pp. 93–112). Baltimore: York Press.

Tallal, P., Merzenich, M., Miller, S., & Jenkins, W. (1998). Language learning impairment: Integrating research and remediation. *Scandinavian Journal of Psychology, 39,* 197–199.

Tallal, P., Miller, S. L., Bedi, G., Byma, G., Wang, X., Nagarajan, S. S., Schreiner, C., Jenkins, W. M., & Merzenich, M. M. (1996). Language comprehension in language-learning impaired children improved with acoustically modified speech. *Science, 271,* 81–84.

Tallal, P., Miller, S., & Fitch, R. H. (1993). Neurobiological basis of the case for the preeminence of temporal processing. In P. Tallal, A. M. Galaburda, R. R. Llinas, & C. von Euler (Eds.), *Temporal information processing in the nervous system: Special reference to dyslexia and dysphasia* (pp. 27–47). New York: New York Academy of Sciences.

Tallal, P., & Piercy, M. (1973). Developmental aphasia: Impaired rate of non-verbal processing as a function of sensory modality. *Neuropsychologia, 11,* 389–398.

Tandon, A., Ramji, S., Kurmari, S., Goyal, A., Chandra, D., & Nigam, V. R. (1998). Cognitive abilities of asphyxiated survivors beyond 5 years of age. *Indian Pediatrics, 35,* 605–612.

Tanner, C. M., Goetz, C. G., & Klawans, H. L. (1982). Cholinergic mechanisms in Tourette's syndrome. *Neurology, 32,* 1315–1317.

Tannock, R., & Girolametto, L. (1992). Language intervention with children who have developmental delays: Effects of an interactive approach. *American Journal of Mental Retardation, 97,* 145–160.

Tannock, R., Ickowicz, A., & Schachar, R. (1995). Differential effects of methylphenidate on working memory in ADHD children with and without comorbid anxiety. *Journal of the American Academy of Child and Adolescent Psychiatry, 34,* 886–896.

Tardieu, M., Mayaux, M., Seibel, N., et al. (1995). Cognitive assessment of school-age children with maternally transmitted human immunodeficiency virus type 1. *Journal of Pediatrics, 126,* 375–379.

Tarnowski, K. J., Prinz, R. J., & Nay, S. M. (1986). Sustained attention in hyperactive children. *Journal of Child Psychology and Psychiatry an Allied Disciplines, 22,* 213–220.

Taylor, E. (1983). Drug response and diagnosis validation. In M. Rutter (Ed.), *Developmental neuropsychiatry* (pp. 348–368). New York: Guilford Press.

Taylor, H. G. (1987). Childhood sequelae of early neurological disorders: A contemporary perspective. *Developmental Neuropsychology, 3,* 153–164.

Taylor, H. G., Michaels, R., Mazur, R., Baver, R., & Linden, C. (1984). Intellectual neuropsychological and achievement outcomes six to eight years after recovery from hemophilus influenzae meningitis. *Pediatrics, 74,* 198–205.

Teicher, M. H., Andersen, S. L., & Hostetter, J. C., Jr. (1995). Evidence for dopamine receptor pruning between adolescence and adulthood in striatum but not nucleus accumbens. *Developmental Brain Research, 89,* 167–172.

Teicher, M. H., Ito, Y., Glod, C. A., & Barber, N. I. (1996). Objective measurement of hyperactivity and attention problems in ADHD. *Journal of the American Academy of Child and Adolescent Psychiatry, 35,* 334–342.

Tejani, A., Dobias, B., & Samburskey, J. (1982). Long term prognosis after hemophilus influenzae meningitis: Prospective evaluation. *Developmental Medicine and Child Neurology, 24,* 338–343.

Telzrow, C. F. (1991). Pre-kindergarten children with special needs. *Elementary School Guidance and Counselors, 26,* 22–32.

Terman, L. (1916). *The measurement of intelligence.* Boston: Houghton Mifflin.

Terrell, F., & Terrell, S. L. (1996). An inventory for assessing cultural mistrust in Black children. In R. L. Jones (Ed.), *Handbook of tests and measurements for Black populations* (Vol. 1, pp. 245–248). Hampton, VA: Cobb & Henry.

Terrell, S. L., & Terrell, F. (1996). The importance of psychological and sociocultural factors for providing clinical services to African American children. In A. G. Kamhi, K. E. Pollock, & J. L. Harris (Eds.), *Communication development and disorders in African American children* (pp. 55–68). Baltimore: Brookes.

Terry, A. V., Buccafusco, J. J., & Pendergast, M. A. (1999). Dose-specific improvements in memory-related performance by rats and aged monkeys administered the nicotinic-cholinergic antagonist mecamylamine. *Drug Development Research, 47,* 127–136.

Thatcher, R. W. (1991). Maturation of human frontal lobes: Physiological evidence for staging. *Developmental Neuropsychology, 7,* 397–419.

Thatcher, R. W. (1994). Cyclic cortical reorganization: Origins of human cognitive development. In G. Dawson & K. W. Fischer (Eds.), *Human behavior and the developing brain* (pp. 232–266). New York: Guilford Press.

Thatcher, R. W. (1996). Multimodal assessments of developing neural networks: Integrating fMRI, PET, MRI, and EEG/MEG. In R. W. Thatcher, G. R. Lyon, J. Rumsey, & N. Krasnegor (Eds.), *Developmental neuroimaging: Mapping the development of brain and behavior* (pp. 127–139). New York: Academic Press.

Thatcher, R. W., Lyon, G. R., Rumsey, J., & Krasnegor, N. (Eds.). (1996). *Developmental neuroimaging: Mapping the development of brain and behavior.* New York: Academic Press.

ThinKids Project. (1998). Children's Board, Hillsborough County, Florida, unpublished.

Thomas, A., & Chess, S. (1980). *The dynamics of psychological development.* New York: Brunner/Mazel.

Thomas, C. J. (1905). Congenital word-blindness and its treatment. *Ophthalmoscope, 3,* 380–385.

Thompson, R. J., O'Quinn, A. N., & Logue, P. E. (1979). Gilles de la Tourette's syndrome: A review and neuropsychological aspects of four cases. *Journal of Pediatric Psychology, 4,* 371–387.

Thorndike, E. L. (1927). *The measurement of intelligence.* New York: Columbia University, Teachers College.

Thorndike, R. L., Hagen, E. P., & Sattler, J. M. (1986). *The Stanford-Binet Scale* (4th ed.). Chicago: Riverside.

Thorne, C., & Newell, M. L. (2000). Epidemiology of HIV infection in the newborn. *Early Human Development, 58,* 1–16.

Thurstone, L. L. (1938). Primary mental abilities. *Psychometric Monographs, 1.* Chicago: University of Chicago Press.

Tindal, G. (1985). Investigating the effectiveness of special education: An analysis of methodology. *Journal of Leaning Disabilities, 18,* 101–112.

Tindal, G., & Parker, R. (1991). Identifying measures for evaluating written expression. *Learning Disabilities Research and Practice, 6,* 211–218.

Tizard, B., Hughes, M., Carmichael, H., & Pikerton, G. (1983). Language and social class: Is verbal deprivation a myth? *Journal of Child Psychology and Psychiatry, 24,* 533–542.

Tjossen, T. D. (Ed.). (1976). *Intervention strategies for high risk infants and young children.* Baltimore: University Park Press.

Tolor, A., & Brannigan, G. G. (1980). *Research and clinical applications of the Bender-Gestalt Test.* Springfield, IL: Thomas.

Torgeson, J. K. (1998). Instructional interventions for children with learning disabilities. In B. K. Shapiro, P. J. Accardo, & A. J. Capute (Eds.), *Specific reading disability: A view of the spectrum.* Timonium, MD: York Press.

Torgeson, J. K., Wagner, R. K., Rashotte, C. A., Burgess, S., & Hecht, S. (1997). Contributions of phonological awareness and rapid automatic naming ability to the growth of word-reading skills in second- to fifth-grade children. *Scientific Studies of Reading, 1,* 161–185.

Towbin, A. (1980). Neuropathological factors in minimal brain dysfunction. In H. E. Rie & E. D. Rie (Eds.), *Handbook of minimal brain dysfunctions: A critical view* (pp. 185–209). New York: Wiley.

Tralli, R., Columbo, B., & Deshler, D. D. (1996). The strategies intervention model: A model for supported inclusion at the secondary level. *Remedial and Special Education, 17,* 204–216.

Traub, N. (1972). *Recipe for reading.* Cambridge, MA: Educators Publishing Service.

Tsukahara, M., Eguchi, T., & Kajii, T. (1986). Fetal alcohol syndrome: Analysis of five families (School of Health Sciences University of Tokoyo). *Japanese Journal of Human Genetics, 31,* 170–171.

Tuakli-Williams, J., & Carrillo, J. (1995). The impact of psychosocial stressors on African-American and Latino preschoolers. *Journal of National Medical Association, 87,* 473–478.

Tupper, D. E. (Ed.). (1987). *Soft neurological signs.* New York: Grune & Stratton.

Turner, A. M., & Greenough, W. T. (1985). Differential rearing on rat visual cortex synapses: I. Synaptic and neuronal density and synapses per neuron. *Brain Research, 329,* 195–203.

Ungar, G. (1970). Molecular mechanisms in information processing. *International Review of Neurobiology, 13,* 223–250.

Ungar, G. (1971). Bioessays for the chemical correlates of acquired information. In E. J. Fjerdingstad (Ed.), *Chemical transfer of learned information* (pp. 31–49). New York: Elsevier.

Ungar, G., Desiderio, D. M., & Parr, W. (1972). Isolation, identification and synthesis of a specific-behavior-inducing brain peptide. *Nature, 238,* 198–202.

U.S. Department of Education. (1998). *To assure the free public education of all children with disabilities* (Twentieth annual report to Congress on the implementation of the Individuals with Disabilities Act). Washington, DC: U.S. Department of Education.

U.S. Department of Education. (2000). A guide to the individual education program (OSERS).

Valles, E. C. (1998). The disproportionate representation of minority students in special education: Responding to the problem. *Journal of Special Education, 32,* 52–54.

Valverde, F., & Ruiz-Marcos, A. (1970). Effect on sensory deprivation in dendritic spines in the visual cortex of the mouse: A mathematical model of spine distribution. In F. A. Young & D. B. Lindsley (Eds.), *Early experience and visual information processing in perceptual and reading disorders* (pp. 261–290). Washington, DC: National Academy of Sciences.

Van der Linden, C., Bruggerman, R., & van Woerkom, T. C. A. (1994). Serotonin dopamine antagonist and Gilles de la Tourette's syndrome: An open pilot dose-titration study with risperidone [Letter]. *Movement Disorders, 9,* 687–688.

Van Dyck, C. H., McMahon, T. J., Rosen, M. I., O'Malley, S. S., O'Connor, P. G., Lin, C. H., Pearsall, H. R., Woods, S. W., & Kosten, T. R. (1997). Sustained-release methylphenidate for cognitive impairment in HIV-1 infected drug abusers: A pilot study. *Journal of Neuropsychiatry in Clinical Neuroscience, 9,* 29–36.

Van Strien, J. W., Stolk, B. D., & Zuiker, S. (1995). Hemisphere specific treatment of dyslexia subtypes: Better reading with anxiety-laden words? *Journal of Learning Disabilities, 28,* 30–34.

Van Woert, M., Rosenbaum, D., & Elma, S. J. (1982). Overview of pharmacological approaches to therapy for Tourette's syndrome. In A. J. Friedhoff & T. N. Chase (Eds.), *Advances in neurology* (Vol. 35, pp. 369–375). New York: Raven Press.

Vaughn, S., Elbaum, B. E., Schumm, J. S., & Hughes, M. T. (1998). Social outcome for students with and without learning disabilities in inclusive classrooms. *Journal of Learning Disabilities, 31,* 428–436.

Vellutino, F. R. (1978). Toward an understanding of dyslexia: Psychological factors in specific reading disability. In A. L. Benton & D. Pearl (Eds.), *Dyslexia: An appraisal of current knowledge* (pp. 61–111). New York: Oxford University Press.

Vellutino, F. R., & Scanlon, D. (1985). Verbal memory in poor and normal readers: Developmental differences in use of linguistic codes. In D. Gray & J. F. Kavanaugh (Eds.), *Behavioral measures of dyslexia* (pp. 177–214). Parkton, MD: York Press.

Vellutino, F. R., Scanlon, D. M., & Tanzman, M. S. (1994). Components of reading ability: Issues and problems in operationalizing word identification, phonological coding, and orthographic coding. In G. R. Lyon (Ed.), *Frames of reference for the assessment of learning disabilities* (pp. 229–241). Baltimore: Brookes.

Vernon, P. F. (1979). *Intelligence: Heredity and environment.* San Francisco: Freeman.

Voeller, K. K. S. (1998). Attention-deficit/hyperactivity disorder: I. Neurobiological and clinical aspects of attention and disorders of attention. In E. C. Coffey & R. A. Brumback (Eds.), *Textbook of pediatric neuropsychiatry.* Washington, DC: American Psychiatric Press.

Wada, J., & Rasmussen, T. (1960). Intracarotid injection of sodium amytal for the lateralization of cerebral speech dominance. *Journal of Neurosurgery, 17,* 262–282.

Wagner, M. (1991). *Quoted in fact sheet: Learning disabilities and low income populations.* Presented to the Adult Committee on Special Populations, sub-committee, Learning Disabilities Association of America, Pittsburgh, PA, August 2000.

Wagner, M., D'Amico, R., Mardu, C., Newman, L., & Blackorby, J. (1992). *What happens next? Trends in post school outcomes of youth with disabilities?* Menlo Park, CA: SRI International.

Wagner, R. K. (1986). Phonological processing abilities and reading implications for disable readers. *Journal of Learning Disabilities, 19,* 623–630.

Waizer, J., Hoffman, S. P., Polizos, P., & Englehardt, D. M. (1974). Outpatient treatment of hyperactive children with imipramine. *American Journal of Psychiatry, 131,* 587–591.

Waldman, I. D., Rowe, D. C., Abramowitz, A., Kozel, S. T., Mohr, J. H., Sherman, S. L., Cleveland, H. H., Sanders, M. L., Gard, J. M., & Stever, C. (1998). Association and linkage of the dopamine transporter gene and attention-deficit hyperactivity disorder in children: Heterogeneity owing to diagnostic subtype and severity. *American Journal of Human Genetics, 63,* 1767–1776.

Waldron, N. L., & McCleskey, J. (1998). The effects of an inclusive school program or students with mild and severe learning disabilities. *Exceptional Children, 64,* 395–405.

Walker, D. K., Singer, J. D., Palfrey, J. S., & Orza, M. (1988). Who leaves and who stays in special education: A 2-year follow-up study. *Exceptional Children, 54,* 393–402.

Walkup, J. T. (2000). The genetics of TS [Letter]. *Tourette's syndrome Association, 1,* 2.

Walkup, J. T., Khan, S., Schuerholz, L., Paik, Y., Leckman, J. F., & Schultz, R. T. (1999). Phenomenology and natural history of tic-related ADHD and learning disabilities. In J. F. Leckman & D. J. Cohen (Eds.), *Tourette's syndrome–tics, obsessions, compulsions: Developmental psychopathology and clinical care* (pp. 63–79). New York: Wiley.

Walkup, J. T., LaBurda, M. C., Singer, H. S., Brown, J., Riddle, M. A., & Hurko, O. (1996). Family study and segregation analysis of Tourette's syndrome: Evidence for a mixed model of inheritance. *American Journal of Human Genetics, 59,* 684–693.

Wand, R. R., Matazow, G. S., Shady, G. A., & Furer, P. (1993). Tourette's syndrome: Associated symptoms and most disabling features. *Neuroscience and Biobehavioral Reviews, 17,* 271–275.

Wanderman, R. (2000, Spring). How computers change the writing process for people with learning disabilities. *News from LDA of Maine,* 3–6.

Wang, M. C., Reynold, M. C., & Walberg, H. J. (1986). Rethinking special education. *Educational Leadership, 44,* 26–31.

Warren, K. R., & Bast, R. J. (1988). Alcohol-related birth defects: An update. *Public Health Reports, 103,* 638–642.

Washington, J. (1996). Issues in assessing the language abilities of African American children. In A. G. Kamhi, K. E. Pollock, & J. L. Harris (Eds.), *Communication development and disorders in African American children* (pp. 35–54). Baltimore: Brookes.

Washington, J. A., & Craig, H. K. (1992). Performances of low-income, African-American preschool and kindergarten children on the Peabody Picture Vocabulary Test-Revised. *Language, Speech, and Hearing Services in Schools, 23,* 329–333.

Washington, J. A., & Craig, H. K. (1994). Dialectal forms during discourse of poor, urban, African-American preschoolers. *Journal of Speech, and Hearing Research, 37,* 816–823.

Washington, J. A., & Craig, H. K. (1998). Socioeconomic status and gender influences on children's dialectal variations. *Journal of Speech, Language and Hearing Research, 41,* 618–626.

Washington, J. A., Craig, H. K., & Kushman, A. J. (1998). Variable use of African American English across two language sampling context. *Journal of Speech, Language and Hearing Research, 41,* 1115–1124.

Wasik, B. A., & Slaving, R. E. (1990). *Preventing early reading failure with one-to-one tutoring: A best evidence synthesis.* Baltimore: Center for Research on Effective Schooling for Disadvantaged Students.

Waterhouse, B. D., Moises, H. C., & Woodward, D. J. (1980). Noradrenergic modulation of somato-sensory cortical neuronal responses to iontophoretically applied putative neurotransmitters. *Experimental Neurology, 69,* 30–49.

Watkins, R. V., & Rice, M. L. (1991). Verb particle and preposition acquisition in language-impaired preschoolers. *Journal of Speech, Language and Hearing Research, 34,* 1130–1141.

Watson, C., & Willows, D. M. (1995). Information-processing pattern in specific reading disability. *Journal of Learning Disabilities, 28,* 216–231.

Weaver, C. (1994). *Reading process and practice.* Portsmouth, NH: Heinemann.

Wechsler, D. (1944). *The measurement of adult intelligence.* Baltimore: Williams & Wilkins.

Wechsler, D. (1974). *Wechsler Intelligence Scale for Children–Revised.* New York: Psychological Corporation.

Wechsler, D. (1975). Intelligence defined and undefined: A realistic appraisal. *American Psychologist, 30,* 135–151.

Wechsler, D. (1991). *Wechsler Intelligence Scale for Children* (3rd ed.). San Antonio, TX: Psychological Corporation.

Weikart, D. P. (1998). Changing early childhood development through educational intervention. *Preventive Medicine: An International Devoted to Practice and Theory, 27,* 233–237.

Weil-Malharde, H. (1936). Carbohydrate metabolism. *Nature, 138,* 581.

Weinberg, R. A. (1989). Intelligence and IQ: Landmark issues and great debates. *American Psychologist, 44,* 98–104.

Weiner, J. M. (Ed.). (1991). *Textbook of child adolescent psychiatry.* Washington, DC: American Psychiatric Press.

Weiner, W. J., & Lang, A. E. (1989). *Movement disorders: A comprehensive survey* (pp. 735). Mount Kisco, NY: Future Publishing.

Weiss, G. (1980). Critical diagnostic issues. In H. E. Rie & E. D. Rie (Eds.), *Handbook of minimal brain dysfunction: A critical view* (pp. 347–361). New York: Wiley.

Weiss, G. (1983). Long-term outcomes: Findings, concepts and practical implications. In M. Rutter (Ed.), *Developmental neuropsychiatry* (pp. 422–436). New York: Guilford Press.

Weiss, G., & Hechtman, L. T. (1993). *Hyperactive children grown up* (2nd ed.). New York: Guilford Press.

Weiss, G., Kruger, E., Danielson, W., & Elman, M. (1975). Effects of long term treatment of hyperactive children with methylphenidate. *Canadian Medical Association Journal, 112,* 159–165.

Weiss, G., Minde, K., Werry, J. S., Douglas, V., & Nemeth, E. (1971). Studies of hyperactive child: VIII. Five year follow-up. *Archives of General Psychiatry, 24,* 409–414.

Weiss, R. S. (1980). *Efficacy of INREAL intervention for preschool and kindergarten language handicapped and Bilingual (Spanish) children.* (ERIC Document Reproduction Service No. ED 204 071)

Weissman, C. S. (1985). *The impact of early intervention, PL 94–142, and other factors on mainstreaming.* (ERIC Document Reproduction Service No. ED 245 911)

Weistuch, L., Lewis, M., & Sullivan, M. W. (1991). Use of language interaction intervention in the preschools. *Journal of Early Intervention, 15,* 278–287.

Wender, P. H. (1971). *Minimal brain dysfunctions in children.* New York: Wiley-Interscience.

Wender, P. H. (1973). Some speculation concerning a possible chemical basis of minimal brain dysfunction. In F. de la Cruz, B. Fox, & R. Roberts (Eds.), *Annals of the New York Academy of Sciences* (Vol. 205, pp. 18–29).

Werry, J. S., Aman, M. G., & Diamond, E. (1980). Imipramine and methylphenidate in hyperactive children. *Journal of Child Psychology and Psychiatry, 21,* 27–35.

Werry, J. S., Aman, M. G., & Lampen, E. (1975). Haloperidol and methylphenidate in hyperactive children. *Acta Paedopsychiatrica, 42,* 26–40.

Wertheimer, M. (1923). Studies in the theory of Gestalt psychology. *Psychologische Forschung, 4,* 1–300.

Whitehouse, P. J., Price, D. L., Struble, L. G., Clark, A. W., Coyle, J. T., & DeLong, M. R. (1982). Alzheimer's disease and senile dementia: Loss of neurons in the basal forebrain. *Science, 215,* 1237–1239.

Whitt, J. K., Hooper, S. R., Tennison, M. B., Robertson, W. T., Gold, S. H., Burchinal, M., Wells, R., McMillan, C., Whaley, R. A., Combest, J., et al. (1993). Neuropsychologic functioning of human immunodeficiency virus-infected children with hemophilia. *Journal of Pediatrics, 122,* 52–59.

Wiener, F. D., Lewnau, L. E., & Erway, E. (1983). Measuring language competency in speakers of Black American English. *Journal of Speech and Hearing Disorders, 48,* 76–84.

Wiener, J. M. (Ed.). (1991). *Textbook of child and adolescent psychiatry.* Washington, DC: American Psychiatric Press.

Wilcox, L. D., & Anderson, R. T. (1998). Distinguishing between phonological difference and disorder in children who speak African-American Vernacular English: An experimental testing instrument. *Journal Communication Disorders, 31,* 315–333.

Wilens, T. E., & Biederman, J. (1992). The stimulants. *Psychiatric Clinics of North America, 15,* 191–222.

Wilens, T. E., Biederman, S., Baldessarini, R. J., Geller, B., Schleifer, D., Spencer, T. J., Birmaher, B., & Goldblatt, A. (1996). Cardiovascular effects of therapeutic doses of tricyclic antidepressants in children and adolescents. *Journal of the American Academy of Child and Adolescent Psychiatry, 35,* 1491–1501.

Wilens, T. E., Biederman, J., Mick, E., Geist, D. E., Steingard, R., & Spencer, T. J. (1993). Nortriptyline in the treatment of ADHD: A chart review of 58 cases. *Journal of American Academy of Child and Adolescent Psychiatry, 32,* 343–349.

Will, M. C. (1986). Educating children with learning problems: A shared responsibility. *Exceptional Children, 52,* 411–416.

Williams, D. T., Mehl, K., Yudofsky, S., Adams, D., & Roseman, B. (1982). The effect of propranolol on controlled rage outbursts in children and adolescents with organic brain dysfunction. *Journal of the American Academy of Child Psychiatry, 21,* 129–135.

Williams, J. P. (1984). Phonemic analysis and how it relates to reading. *Journal of Learning Disabilities, 17,* 240–245.

Williams, S. E., Ris, M. D., Ayyangar, R., Shefft, B. K., & Berch, D. (1998). Recovery in pediatric brain injury: Is psychostimulant medication beneficial? *Journal of Head Trauma Rehabilitation, 13,* 73–81.

Williamson, A., Spencer, S. S., & Spencer, D. D. (1995). Depth electrode studies and intracellular dentate granule cell recordings in temporal lobe epilepsy. *Annals of Neurology, 38,* 778–787.

Williamson, P. D. (1995). Frontal lobe epilepsy: Some clinical characteristics. *Advances in Neurology, 66,* 127–150.

Willig, A. C. (1985). A meta-analysis of selected studies on the effectiveness of bilingual education. *Review of Educational Research, 55,* 269–317.

Wilsher, C. R. (1987). Treatment of specific reading difficulties (Dyslexia). In D. Bakker, C. Wilsher, H. Debruyne, & N. Bertin (Eds.), *Developmental dyslexia and learning disorders* (pp. 95–109). Basel, Switzerland: Karger.

Wilson, S. A. K. (1925). The Croonian lectures on some disorders of motility and muscle tone with special reference to the corpus striatum. *Lancet, 11,* 1–10, 53–62, 169–178, 215–219, 268–279.

Witelson, S. F. (1976). Abnormal right hemisphere specialization in developmental dyslexia. In R. M. Knights & D. S. Bakker (Eds.), *Neuropsychology of learning disorders: Therapeutic approaches* (pp. 233–255). Baltimore: University Park Press.

Witelson, S. F. (1985). The brain connection: The corpus callosum is larger in left-handers. *Science, 229,* 665–668.

Witelson, S. F., & Kigar, D. L. (1988). Anatomical development of the corpus callosum in humans: A review with reference to sex and cognition. In D. L. Molfese & S. J. Sagalowitz (Eds.), *Brain lateralization in children* (pp. 35–57). New York: Guilford Press.

Witelson, S. F., & Pallie, W. (1973). Left hemisphere specialization for language in the newborn: Neuroanatomical evidence of asymmetry. *Brain, 96,* 641–646.

Wolf, M. (1999). What time may tell: Towards a new conceptualization of developmental dyslexia. *Annals of Dyslexia, 49,* 3–28.

Wolf, M., & Bowers, P. G. (1999a). The double-deficit hypothesis for the developmental dyslexias. *Journal of Educational Psychology, 91,* 415–438.

Wolf, M., & Bowers, L. (1999b). Retrieval rate, accuracy, and vocabulary elaboration (RAVE) in reading impaired children: A pilot intervention program. *Dyslexia: An International Journal of Theory and Practice, 5,* 1–29.

Wolf, M. H., Bally, R. E., & Morris, R. (1986). Automaticity, retrieval processes, and reading: A longitudinal study in average and impaired readers. *Child Development, 57,* 988–1000.

Wolf, P. H. (1959). Observations in newborn infants. *Psychosomatic Medicine, 21,* 110–118.

Wolff, P. H. (1993). Impaired temporal resolution in developmental dyslexia. *Annals New York Academy of Sciences, 682,* 87–103.

Wolraich, M., Hannah, J., Pinnock, T. Y., Baumgaertel, A., & Brown, J. (1996). Comparison of diagnostic criteria for attention-deficit hyperactivity disorder in a country-wide sample. *Journal of the American Child and Adolescent Psychiatry, 35,* 319–324.

Wolters, P. L., & Brouwers, P. (1998). Evaluation of neurodevelopmental deficits in children with HIV infection. In H. E. Gendelman, S. A. Lipton, L. Epstein, & S. Swindells (Eds.), *The neurology of AIDS* (pp. 425–442). New York: Chapman & Hall.

Wolters, P. L., Brouwers, P., Moss, H. A., & Pizzo, P. A. (1995). Differential receptive and expressive language functioning of children with symptomatic HIV disease and relation to CT scan brain abnormalities. *Pediatrics, 95,* 112–119.

Wolters, P. L., Brouwers, P., & Perez, L. (1999). Pediatric HIV infection. In R. T. Brown (Ed.), *Cognitive aspects of chronic illness in children* (pp. 105–141). New York: Guilford Press.

Wong, G. H., & Cook, R. J. (1971). Long term effects of haloperidol on severely emotionally disturbed children. *Australian and New Zealand Journal of Psychiatry, 5,* 296–300.

Wood, C., Powell, S., & Knight, R. C. (1984). Predicting school readiness: The validity of the development age. *Journal of Learning Disabilities, 17,* 8–11.

Wood, F., Felton, R., Flowers, L., & Naylor, C. (1991). Neurobehavioral definition of dyslexia. In D. D. Duane & D. B. Gray (Eds.), *The reading brain: The biological basis of dyslexia* (pp. 1–25). Parkton, MD: York Press.

Wood, F. B. (1990). Functional neuroimaging in neurobehavioral research. In A. A. Boulton, G. B. Baker, & M. Hiscock (Eds.), *Neuromethods* (Vol. 17, pp. 107–125). Clifton, NJ: Human.

Wood, F. B., & Flowers, L. (1999). Reading and attention disorders. In D. D. Duane (Ed.), *Functional neuroanatomy of dyslexic subtypes* (pp. 129–159). Baltimore: York Press.

Wood, F. B., Garrett, A. A., Hart, L. A., Flowers, D. L., & Absher, J. R. (1996). Event related potential correlates of glucose metabolism in normal adults during a cognitive activation task. In R. W. Thatcher, G. R. Lyon, J. Rumsey, & N. Krasnegor (Eds.), *Developmental neuroimaging: Mapping the development of brain and behavior* (pp. 197–206). New York: Academic Press.

Woodcock, R. B. (1987). *Woodcock Reading Mastery Test-Revised.* Circle Pines, MN: American Guidance Service.

Woodcock, R. B., & Johnson, M. B. (1977). *Woodcock–Johnson Psycho-Educational Battery.* Allen, TX: Developmental Learning Materials.

Worcester-Drought, C., & Allen, I. M. (1929). Congenital auditory imperception (congenital word-deafness): With report of a case. *Journal of Neurology and Psychopathology, 9,* 193–208.

Wright, P. W. D., & Wright, (1999). *Special Education Law.* Hartsfield, VA: Harbor House Law Press.

Yarrow, L., Rubenstein, J., Peterson, F., & Jankowski, J. (1973). Dimensions of early stimulation and their differential effects on infant development. *Merrill-Palmer Quarterly, 19,* 205–219.

Yatvin, J. (2000). Minority view. *Final report of the National Reading Panel.* Washington, DC: National Institute of Child Health and Human Development, Appendix C 1–6.

Yeni-Komshian, G. H., Isenberg, D., & Goldberg, H. (1975). Cerebral dominance and reading disability: Left visual field deficit in poor readers. *Neuropsychologia, 13,* 83–94.

Yingling, C. D., Galin, D., Fein, G., Peltzman, D., & Davenport, L. (1986). Neurometrics does not detect dyslexics. *Electroencephalography Clinical Neurophysiology, 63,* 426–430.

Yoshikawa, H. (1999). Welfare dynamics, support services, mothers' earnings, and child cognitive development: Implications for contemporary welfare reform. *Child Development, 70,* 779–801.

Young, W. W. (1936). The relation of reading comprehension to hearing comprehension and retention. *Journal of Experimental Education, 5,* 30–39.

Ysseldyke, J.E (1983). Current practices in making psychoeducational decisions about learning disabled students. *Journal of Learning Disabilities, 16,* 226–233.

Yudofsky, S., Williams, D., & Gorman, S. (1981). Propranolol in the treatment of rage and violent behavior in patients with chronic brain syndrome. *American Journal of Psychiatry, 138,* 218–220.

Zaidel, D. W. (1985). Hemifield tachistoscopic presentations and hemispheric specialization in normal subjects. In D. F. Benson & E. Zaidel (Eds.), *The dual brain* (pp. 143–155). New York: Guilford Press.

Zaidel, E. (1985). Introduction. In D. F. Benson & E. Zaidel (Eds.), *The dual brain* (pp. 47–63). New York: Guilford Press.

Zametkin, A. J., Liebernauer, L. L., Fitzgerald, G. A., King, A. C., Minkunas, D. V., Herscovitch, P., Yamada, E. M., & Cohen, R. M. (1993). Brain metabolism in teenagers with attention-deficit hyperactivity disorder. *Archives of General Psychiatry, 50,* 333–340.

Zametkin, A. J., Linnoila, M., Karoum, F., & Sallee, R. (1986). Pemoline and urinary excretion of catecholamines and indolamines in children with attention deficit disorder. *American Journal of Psychiatry, 143,* 359–362.

Zametkin, A. J., Nordahl, T. E., Gross, M., King, A. C., Semple, W. E., Rumsey, J., Hamburger, S., & Cohen, R. M. (1990). Cerebral glucose metabolism in adults with hyperactivity of childhood. *New England Journal of Medicine, 323,* 1361–1366.

Zametkin, A. J., & Rapoport, J. L. (1987). Neurobiology of attention deficit disorder with hyperactivity: Where have we come in 50 years? *Journal of the American Academy of Child and Adolescent Psychiatry, 26,* 676–686.

Zangwill, O. L. (1960). *Cerebral dominance and it relation to psychological function.* Edinburgh, Scotland: Oliver & Boyd.

Zeichner, S. L., & Read, J. S. (Eds.). (1999). *Handbook of pediatric HIV care.* Baltimore: Lippincott Williams & Wilkins.

Zemp, J. W., Wilson, J. E., Schlesinger, K., Boggan, W. O., & Glassman, E. (1966). Brain function and macromolecules: I. Incorporation of uridine into RNA of mouse brain during short-term training experience. *Proceedings of the National Academy of Sciences, USA, 55,* 1423–1431.

Zenski, J. P. (1987). *A study of the effects of a prefirst grade transition class as compared with first grade retention on reading achievement.* (ERIC Document Reproduction Service No. ED 248 459)

Zhurova, L. E. (1963). The development of analysis of words into their sounds by preschool children. *Soviet Psychology and Psychiatry, 2,* 17–27.

Zigmond, N., & Thornton, H. (1985). Follow up of post secondary age learning disabled graduates and drop-outs. *Learning Disabilities Research, 1,* 50–55.

Zimmerman, B. J. (1990). Social cognitive theory and self-regulated learning. In B. J. Zimmerman & D. H. Schunk (Eds.), *Self-regulated learning and academic achievement: Theory, research, and practice* (pp. 1–25). New York: Springer-Verlag.

Zimmerman, F. T., Burgemeinster, B. B., & Putman, T. S. (1947). A group study of the effect of glutamic acid upon mental functioning in children and adolescents. *Psychosomatic Medicine, 9,* 175–183.

Zimmerman, F. T., & Ross, S. (1944). Effect of glutamic acid and other amino acids on maze learning in the white rat. *Archives of Neurology and Psychiatry, 51,* 446–451.

Zohar, A. H., Pauls, D. L., Ratzoni, G., Apter, A., Dycian, A., Binder, M., et al. (1997). Obsessive-compulsive disorder with and without tics in an epidemiological sample of adolescents. *American Journal of Psychiatry, 154,* 274–276.

Zubin, J. (1975). Vulnerability: A new view of schizophrenia. *Clinical Psychologist, 29,* 16–18.

Zurif, E. B., & Carson, G. (1970). Dyslexia in relation to cerebral dominance and temporal analysis. *Neuropsychologia, 8,* 351–361.

Author Index

Subject Index